Foods

A Scientific Approach

Foods
A Scientific Approach

HELEN CHARLEY
Professor Emeritus of Foods and Nutrition, Oregon State University

CONNIE WEAVER
Professor and Head of Foods and Nutrition, Purdue University

THIRD EDITION

Merrill
Prentice Hall

Library of Congress Cataloging-in-Publication Data

Charley, Helen.
    Foods : a scientific approach / Helen Charley, Connie Weaver.
        p.   cm.
    Includes bibliographical references (p.   ) and index.
    ISBN 0–02–321951–3
    1. Food.   2. Nutrition.   3. Cookery.   I. Weaver, Connie. 1950–
. II. Title
TX354.C4723   1998
664—dc21

97–22861
CIP
AC

Cover photo: Alfred Pasieka/Science Photo Library
Editor: Kevin M. Davis
Developmental Editor: Carol S. Sykes
Production Editor: Sheryl Glicker Langner
Editorial/Production Supervision: Betsy Keefer
Design Coordinator: Karrie M. Converse
Text Designer: Gary Gore
Cover Designer: Russ Maselli
Production Manager: Pamela D. Bennett
Electronic Text Management: Karen L. Bretz
Director of Marketing: Kevin Flanagan
Marketing Manager: Suzanne Stanton
Advertising/Marketing Coordinator: Julie Shough

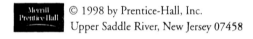

© 1998 by Prentice-Hall, Inc.
Upper Saddle River, New Jersey 07458

Earlier editions, entitled *Food Science,* © 1982 by John Wiley & Sons, Inc., and © 1971 by The Ronald Press Company.

Printed in the United States of America

10 9 8 7 6 5

ISBN: 0-02-321951-3

Prentice-Hall International (UK) Limited, *London*
Prentice-Hall of Australia Pty. Limited, *Sydney*
Prentice-Hall Canada Inc., *Toronto*
Prentice-Hall Hispanoamericana, S.A., *Mexico*
Prentice-Hall of India Private Limited, *New Delhi*
Prentice-Hall of Japan, Inc., *Tokyo*
Prentice-Hall Asia Pte. Ltd., *Singapore*
Editora Prentice-Hall do Brasil, Ltda., *Rio de Janerio*

Preface

Foods: A Scientific Approach continues the emphasis of previous editions of *Food Science* on the scientific aspects of the study of foods, drawing on the basic sciences of chemistry, physics, microbiology, and physiology. The objective in writing the text is to give the student an understanding of the complex nature of and the changes that can occur in foods as they are prepared, processed, and stored, whether at home, in the industrial kitchen, or in industry. The authors have attempted to glean from the literature, accumulated since the previous edition, facts and concepts that further this objective.

Special coverage is given to topics that are of current interest or the focus of recent scientific activity. Topics that are given special emphasis include the following: foods as carriers of pathogens and elementary precautions in preventing foodborne illnesses; the neurophysiological basis for the ability to sense qualities in foods; sensory and instrumental methods of measuring food quality; carbohydrate- and protein-rich foods as glassy/rubbery polymers whose structure, texture, and keeping qualities depend on temperature and the plasticizing effect of water; sugar and fat substitutes and adjustments when these are used in products; vegetable gums, their functions and uses in foods; and biotechnology-derived products (e.g., FLAVR SAVR tomato and microbial-derived chymosin). The annotated references for each chapter will aid the ambitious student and the time-pressed instructor in choosing supplemental reading selectively.

Foods: A Scientific Approach is written for a first course in foods for students who have had general chemistry and are at least enrolled in organic chemistry. A knowledge of elementary nutrition is assumed. This book can serve as a supplementary text for advanced students whose previous course in foods emphasized application and minimized theory. The authors have attempted to maintain the "scientific depth and completeness of coverage" as observed by a reviewer in the previous edition.

The authors appreciate the constructive suggestions from reviewers of portions of the manuscript: Suzanne R. Curtis, University of Maryland; Ronald R. Eitenmiller, University of Georgia; Mary K. Head, West Virginia University; ZoeAnn Holmes, Oregon State University; Manfred Kroger, Pennsylvania State University; Jane Love, Iowa State University; Marilyn Mook, Michigan State University; Carole S. Setser, Kansas State University; and Martha B. Stone, Colorado State University. We are indebted to Pauline Douglas for transportation to and from libraries, who toted a ton of bound volumes, and who acted as arbiter for intractable sentences. Dr. Mark Hines' perspective on instruments currently used in food research and in food quality assessment in industry was helpful in preparing Chapter 1.

Helen Charley
Connie Weaver

Brief Contents

PART I
FOOD QUALITY

Chapter 1 Evaluation of Food 3
Chapter 2 Sensory Perception of Foods 21
Chapter 3 Measures and Weights 24
Chapter 4 Heating and Cooling Foods and Food Safety 51

PART II
LIQUIDS AND
CRYSTALS

Chapter 5 Water 71
Chapter 6 Coffee, Tea, and Cocoa Beverage 90
Chapter 7 Ice Crystals and Frozen Desserts 107
Chapter 8 Sugars, Alternative Sweeteners, and Confections 118

PART III
STARCHES AND
STARCHY FOODS

Chapter 9 Starches and Vegetable Gums 130
Chapter 10 Cereals 162
Chapter 11 Flour and Dough Formation 174

PART IV
LEAVENING AGENTS
AND BREADS

Chapter 12 Leavening Agents 195
Chapter 13 Quick Breads 207
Chapter 14 Yeast Breads 221

PART V
FATS AND FAT-RICH
FOODS

Chapter 15 Fats and Oils 243
Chapter 16 Emulsions 268
Chapter 17 Pastry 280

PART VI   *Chapter 18* Introduction to Proteins   295
PROTEINS AND   *Chapter 19* Milk   308
PROTEIN-RICH   *Chapter 20* Cheese   325
FOODS   *Chapter 21* Eggs   341
                   Chapter 22 Meat   368
                   Chapter 23 Poultry   415
                   Chapter 24 Seafood   426

PART VII   *Chapter 25* Shortened Cakes   438
CAKES   *Chapter 26* Sponge, Angel Food, and Chiffon Cakes   457

PART VIII   *Chapter 27* Fruits   469
PLANT FOODS   *Chapter 28* Vegetables   498
                   Chapter 29 Legumes   534

PART IX   *Chapter 30* Geletin Gels   551
GELS   *Chapter 31* Fruit Pectin Gels   556

Contents

PART I   FOOD QUALITY   **1**

Chapter 1   **Evaluation of Food**   **3**

SENSORY EVALUATION OF FOOD QUALITY   3
Vocabulary of Sensory Analysis   3
Sensory Testing of Foods   5
INSTRUMENTAL MEASUREMENT OF FOOD QUALITY   12
Appearance   14
Flavor   15
Texture   16

Chapter 2   **Sensory Perception of Foods**   **21**

APPEARANCE OF FOOD   21
Visual Perception   21
Color of Foods   23
CHEMOSENSORY PROPERTIES   23
Odor   24
Taste   29
Mouthfeel   38
TEXTURE OF FOODS   39
Tactile Properties   39
Influence of Textures on Flavor   40

Chapter 3   **Measures and Weights**   **44**

TRADITIONAL AND METRIC MEASURING SYSTEMS   44
MEASURING UTENSILS   45
Capacities   45
Tolerances   46
Accuracy   47

MEASURING TECHNIQUES   47
  Liquids   47
  Fats   48
  Sugar   48
  Flour   48

Chapter 4   **Heating and Cooling Foods and Food Safety**   **51**

HEATING FOODS   51
  Intensity of Heat   51
  Quantitative Aspects   52
  Energy Transfer   53
  Heating Foods with a Conventional Range   54
HEATING FOODS IN A MICROWAVE OVEN   57
  The Oven and How It Functions   57
  Interaction of Food with Microwaves   58
  Advantages and Disadvantages   59
TESTS FOR DONENESS OF COOKED FOODS   60
COOLING AND REFRIGERATION OF FOODS   60
TEMPERATURE AND CONTROL OF PATHOGENS IN FOOD   61
  Effects of Heat   61
  Effects of Cold   62
PATHOGENS AND THEIR RESPONSE TO HEAT AND COLD   64

PART II   LIQUIDS AND CRYSTALS   **69**

Chapter 5   **Water**   **71**

NATURE OF WATER   72
  The Molecule   72
  Hydrogen Bonding and the States of Water   73
  Boiling of Water   74
FUNCTIONS OF WATER IN FOOD PREPARATION   79
  A Medium for the Transfer of Heat   79
  A Dispersing Medium   79
WATER RELATIONS IN FOODS   82
  Water—Bound or Free?   82
  Water Activity   83
  Water as a Plasticizer   84
CHARACTERISTICS OF WATER THAT AFFECT ITS USE   86
  Hardness of Water   86
  pH of Water   88
WATER AS A CLEANSING AGENT   88

Chapter *6* Coffee, Tea, and Chocolate Cocoa   **90**

COFFEE   90
  Characteristics of the Beverage   90
  Constituents in the Coffee Bean (Grounds)   90
  Market Forms of Coffee   93
  Preparing the Brew   94
  Methods for Making Coffee   95
  Staling of Coffee   98
TEA   99
  Kinds of Tea   99
  Quality of the Beverage   99
  Constituents in Tea   99
  Market Forms of Tea   102
  Preparing Tea Beverage   102
  Storage of Tea   103
CHOCOLATE AND COCOA BEVERAGE   103
  Conversion of Cacoa Bean to Chocolate   103
  Methylxanthines in Chocolate Products   104
  Preparing Cocoa or Chocolate Beverage   104

Chapter *7* Ice Crystals and Frozen Desserts   **107**

FACTORS AFFECTING ICE CRYSTAL FORMATION   107
  Components of the Mix   107
  The Freezing Process   111
HARDENING OF FROZEN DESSERTS   114
STILL-FROZEN DESSERTS   115
  The Mix   115
  Freezing the Mix   115
QUALITY CHARACTERISTICS OF FROZEN DESSERTS   115

Chapter *8* Sugars, Alternative Sweeteners, and Confections   **118**

SUGARS AND OTHER SWEETENERS   118
CONSUMPTION OF SWEETENERS   119
ALTERNATIVES TO SUGAR   119
SUCROSE   121
  Source   121
  Chemistry   122
  Solubility   124
  Effect of Sucrose on the Boiling Point of Water   124
  Melting and Caramelization   125

CANDIES   126
  Determining Doneness of Candies   126
  Interfering Agents and Sucrose Crystal Formation   128
  Agitation and Sucrose Crystal Formation   131
  Amorphous Candies   134
  Comparison of Candies and Frozen Desserts   134

PART III   STARCHES AND STARCHY FOODS   137

Chapter 9   **Starches and Vegetable Gums**   139

STARCHES   139
  Starch Chemistry   139
  Starch Granules   143
  Starch as a Thickening Agent   148
  Setting or Gelation of a Cooked Starch Paste   152
  Factors Affecting Starch-Thickened Products   152
VEGETABLE GUMS   155
  Seaweed Extracts   156
  Exudates   157
  Gums from the Endosperm of Seed   157
  Biosynthetic Gums   158
  Chemically Modified Carbohydrates   158

Chapter 10   **Cereals**   162

UTILIZATION OF CEREAL GRAINS   162
STRUCTURE OF CEREAL GRAINS   163
  The Cell   163
  Parts of a Cereal Grain   163
COMPOSITION AND NUTRITIVE VALUE OF CEREALS   164
ENRICHMENT AND FORTIFICATION OF CEREALS   167
MARKET FORMS OF CEREALS   167
CEREAL PRODUCTS THAT REQUIRE COOKING   167
READY-TO EAT CEREALS   168
COOKING CEREALS   169
  Purpose   169
  Precautions   169
  Proportions of Liquid   170
  Amount of Salt   170
  Cooking Time   170
  Effect of Alkaline Cooking Water   171
  Characteristics of Cooked Cereal   171
POPCORN   171

Chapter 11 **Flour and Dough Formation**   **174**

TYPES OF FLOUR   174
  Kinds of Wheat   174
  Effects of Milling   176
  Classed by Use   178
FORMATION OF DOUGH   179
  Components of Flour   180
  Role of Water   183
  Manipulation   184
  Effects of Sugar and Fat on Gluten   186
FLOUR IMPROVERS (DOUGH CONDITIONERS)   186
ENRICHMENT OF FLOUR   189
PASTA   189

PART IV   LEAVENING AGENTS AND BREADS   193

Chapter 12   **Leavening Agents**   **195**

STEAM AS A LEAVENING AGENT   195
  Proportions of Water to Flour   195
  Gas-Holding Properties of Batters and Doughs   195
AIR AS A LEAVENING AGENT   196
CARBON DIOXIDE AS A LEAVENING AGENT   196
  Release of Carbon Dioxide from Sodium Bicarbonate by Acid   197
BAKING POWDER   198
  Yield of Carbon Dioxide   198
  Acids Used in Baking Powders   198
BAKING SODA AND SOUR MILK   202
YEAST AS A SOURCE OF CARBON DIOXIDE   202
  Market Forms of Yeast   202
  Production of Carbon Dioxide   204
  In Sour Dough Bread   205

Chapter 13   **Quick Breads**   **207**

INGREDIENTS IN QUICK BREADS AND THEIR FUNCTIONS   207
  Flour   207
  Liquid   207
  Salt   207
  Leavening Agent   208
  Fat   208
  Sugar   208
  Eggs   208

BALANCING INGREDIENTS IN QUICK BREADS   209
MANIPULATION OF INGREDIENTS IN QUICK BREADS   209
Techniques   210
Utensils   210
Purposes   212

BAKING QUICK BREADS   212
Baking Time and Temperature   213
Changes Effected in Batters and Doughs   213

INDIVIDUAL QUICK BREADS   213
Formulas   213
Popovers   213
Cream Puffs   214
Muffins   216
Biscuits   219
Griddle Cakes and Waffles   220

Chapter 14   **Yeast Breads**   **223**

INGREDIENTS AND THEIR FUNCTIONS   223
Yeast   223
Flour   223
Liquid   224
Salt   224
Sugar   225
Fat   225
Yeast   225
Eggs   226

PROPORTIONS OF INGREDIENTS   226
Flour to Liquid   226
Salt and Sugar   226

MANIPULATION OF YEAST DOUGH   227
Basic Methods   227
Scalding the Milk   227
Dispersing the Yeast   228
Combining Flour and Liquid   228
Dough Development   228

FERMENTATION OF YEAST DOUGH   231
Temperature   231
Inflating the Dough   231
Punching the Dough   232

PROOFING   232
BAKING   233
Temperature   233
Changes Effected   233
Doneness   234
The Baking Pan   235

QUALITY OF BREAD   235
  Aroma   235
  Other Characteristics   235
STALING OF BREAD   235

PART V   FATS AND FAT-RICH FOODS   241

Chapter 15   **Fats and Oils**   243

CHEMISTRY OF FATS   243
  Fatty Acids   244
  Glycerides   246
CRYSTALS OF FAT   248
  Polymorphism   248
  Melting Points   249
CONSISTENCY OF FATS   252
COMPOSITION OF FOOD FATS   253
MODIFICATION OF NATURAL FATS   253
  Hydrogenization   253
  Interesterification   256
  Acetylation   256
FUNCTIONS IN FOODS   258
FAT SUBSTITUTES   258
DETERIORATION OF FATS   260
  Absorption of Odors   260
  Rancidity   260
  Antioxidants   262
FATS AS A MEDIUM FOR THE TRANSFER OF HEAT   264
  The Frying Process   264
  Absorption of Fat   265
  Hazards in Using Fats   266

Chapter 16   **Emulsions**   269

NATURE OF AN EMULSION   269
  Phases   269
  Functions of an Emulsion   269
EMULSIFYING AGENTS   271
  Manufactured   271
  Naturally Occurring   272
COMMON EMULSIONS   275
  French Dressing   275
  Mayonnaise   275
  Cooked Dressing   277
  Other Emulsions   277

STABILITY OF EMULSIONS   278
VINEGAR   278

Chapter 17   **Pastry**   **280**

INGREDIENTS AND THEIR FUNCTIONS   280
  Flour   280
  Salt   281
  Fat   281
  Liquid   281
PROPORTIONS OF INGREDIENTS   282
  Salt   282
  Fat   282
  Liquid   282
MANIPULATION OF INGREDIENTS   282
  Cutting Fat Into the Flour   283
  Stirring the Dough   283
INTERRELATIONS BETWEEN INGREDIENTS AND MANIPULATION   283
  Effects of Kind of Fat and Type of Flour   283
  Effects of Proportions of Fat and Water   284
  Effects of the Extent to Which Fat Is Cut into Flour   285
ROLLING AND SHAPING PASTRY   285
BAKING PASTRY   286
CHARACTERISTICS OF PASTRY   287
  Tenderness versus Toughness   287
  Flakiness   287
  Crispness   287
PUFF PASTRY   289

PART VI   PROTEINS AND PROTEIN-RICH FOODS   **293**

Chapter 18   **Introduction to Proteins**   **295**

AMINO ACIDS   295
  Structure   295
  R Groups   296
STRUCTURE OF PROTEINS   299
  Primary Structure   299
  Secondary Structure   300
  Tertiary Structure   300
  Quaternary Structure   302
  Conjugated Proteins   302
PROPERTIES   302

FUNCTIONS   303
  As Enzymes   303
  Nonenzymatic Browning   304
  Modifiers of Texture   304

Chapter 19   **Milk**   **308**

COMPOSITION   308
DISPOSITION OF CONSTITUENTS IN MILK   310
  Solution   310
  Colloidal Dispersion   310
  Emulsion   311
  Homogenization   313

PASTEURIZATION OF MILK   313
TYPES OF DAIRY PRODUCTS   314
  Fluid Milk   314
  Cream   315
  Evaporated Milk   315
  Condensed Milk   315
  Dried Milk Solids   315
  Butter   316
  Cultured Buttermilk   316
  Yogurt   316
  Sour Cream   317
  Caseins, Caseinates, and Whey Proteins   317
  Filled and Imitation Dairy Products   317

MILK FOAMS   317
  Foam Formation   317
  Evaporated Milk Foams   318
  Dried Milk Foams   318
  Whipped Cream   318

MILK PROTEINS AS EMULSIFIERS   320
EFFECTS OF HEAT ON MILK   321
  Effects on Casein Micelles   321
  Effects on Skin Formation   321
  Effects on Serum Proteins   321

HANDLING MILK AND FOODS MADE WITH MILK   322
  Holding Temperature and Safety   322
  Exposure to Light   322

Chapter 20   **Cheese**   **325**

TYPES OF NATURAL CHEESE   325
  Unripened Cheese   326
  Soft Ripened Cheese   327
  Semisoft Ripened Cheese   327
  Firm and Hard Ripened Cheese   327

FORMATION OF COTTAGE CHEESE   327
PRODUCTION OF CHEDDAR CHEESE   334
   Curd Formation   334
   Ripening   335

PASTEURIZED PROCESS CHEESE   336
COMPOSITION OF CHEESES   337
USES OF CHEESE   337
CHEESE IN COOKING   337
   Melting Cheese   337
   Blending Cheese with Liquid   339

Chapter 21   Eggs   341

STRUCTURE   341
   Shell   341
   Shell Membranes   341
   Albumen   341
   Yolk   342

COMPOSITION   343
   Egg White   343
   Egg Yolk   343

QUALITY OF EGGS   345
   Deteriorative Changes   345
   Handling Eggs to Maintain Quality   346
   Candling Eggs to Determine Quality   347
   Uses of Eggs of Different Quality Grades   347
   Resistance of Eggs to Spoilage   347
   Preserving Eggs by Freezing and Drying   350

SIZE OF EGGS   350
EGGS AS EMULSIFIERS   351
EGGS AS BINDING, THICKENING, AND GELLING AGENTS   351
   Effects of Heat on Egg Proteins   351

METHODS OF COOKING EGGS   352
   Cooked in the Shell   352
   Poached Egg   353
   Fried Egg   353
   Scrambled Egg   354
   Custards   354
   Soft Pie Filling   356

EGG FOAMS   356
   Foam-Forming Properties of Egg White Proteins   356
   Stages to Which Egg Whites are Beaten   357
   Factors Affecting Egg White Foams   360
   Egg Yolk Foams   361
   Meringues   361
   Puffy Omelet   362
   Soufflé and Fondue   363

EGG SUBSTITUTES   363

Chapter *22* **Meat** 368

CONSUMPTION OF MEAT   368
COMPOSITION   368
STRUCTURE OF MEAT   370
  Muscle Fibers   370
  Connective Tissue   374
  Fat   376

IDENTIFICATION OF MEAT   376
  Types of Meat   376
  Cuts of Meat   377

TENDERNESS OF MEAT   381
  Basis of Toughness   383
  Conditioning (Aging) of Meat   386
  Meat Tenderizers   386

INSPECTION   386
GRADES OF MEAT   387
  Quality Grades   387
  Yield Grades   387

COLOR OF MEAT   388
  Fresh Meat   388
  Cured Meat Pigments   390

STORING MEAT   391
COOKING MEAT   391
  Effects on Meat Pigment and Color   391
  Effects on Meat Proteins and Tenderness   393
  Effects on the Fine Structure of Muscle   396
  Effects on Flavor   398
  Effects of Initial Fat Content   400
  Effects on Nutritive Value   401
  Methods   401
  Storage of Cooked Meat   406

Chapter *23* **Poultry** 415

MARKET CLASSES OF POULTRY   415
PREPARING POULTRY FOR MARKET   415
INSPECTION AND GRADING   416
HANDLING RAW POULTRY   417
COMPOSITION AND STRUCTURE   417
COOKING POULTRY   419
  Methods   419
  Doneness of Poultry   421
  Cooking Losses   422
  Frozen Poultry   422
  Flavor of Cooked Poultry   422

YIELD   422
LEFTOVER COOKED POULTRY   422

Chapter 24 Seafood

TYPES OF FISH   426
COMPOSITION AND NUTRITIVE VALUE   427
PURCHASING FISH   427
  Market Forms   427
  Freshness in Fish   427

ISSUES OF SAFETY IN SEAFOOD CONSUMPTION   429
  Marine Toxins   429
  Bacterial and Viral Hazards   430
  Fishborne Parasites   430

STRUCTURE OF FIN FISH MUSCLE   431
INSTABILITY OF FISH MUSCLE TO FROZEN STORAGE   431
COOKING FISH   432
  Methods   433
  Assessing Doneness   434

PART VII   CAKES

Chapter 25 Shortened Cakes

INGREDIENTS AND THEIR FUNCTIONS   439
  Fat   439
  Emulsifier   442
  Sugar   443
  Eggs   445
  Flour   445
  Leavening Agent   446
  Liquid   447
  Salt   447

PROPORTIONS OF INGREDIENTS   447
  Balancing Ingredients in a Conventional Cake   447
  Single-Stage or Quick-Mix Formula   448
  Low Fat and Low-Sugar Formulas   449
  Adjustment for Altitude   449

COMBINING INGREDIENTS FOR SHORTENED CAKE   449
  Objectives   449
  Methods   450

BAKING   452
  Changes Effected by Baking   452
  Heat Penetration During Baking   453

Chapter 26 Sponge, Angel Food, and Chiffon Cakes

DESIRABLE CHARACTERISTICS   457

INGREDIENTS AND THEIR FUNCTIONS   457
  Eggs   457
  Sugar   459
  Acid   459
  Flour   459
  Angel Food Cake Packaged Mix   459
MANIPULATION OF ANGEL FOOD CAKE BATTER   459
  Making the Meringue   459
  Incorporation of Flour   461
MANIPULATION OF SPONGE CAKE BATTER   462
MANIPULATION OF CHIFFON CAKE BATTER   463
BAKING   463
  Baking Pan   463
  Baking Time and Temperature   463

PART VIII   PLANT FOODS   467

Chapter 27   Fruits   469

STRUCTURE OF PLANT TISSUE   469
  The Cell Wall   472
  Cytoplasm   475
  Vacuole   475
  Intercellular Spaces   476
COMPOSITION OF FRUITS   476
  Water   476
  Carbohydrates   478
  Protein, Fat, and Minerals   478
  Vitamins   478
  Organic Acids   478
RIPENING OF FRUIT   478
  Slowing Ripening and Postponing Senescence   480
PIGMENTS IN FRUITS AND VEGETABLES   481
  Chlorophyll and Carotenoids   481
  Flavonoid Pigments   481
POST HARVEST FACTORS THAT INFLUENCE QUALITY   489
  Moisture Content and Texture   489
  Discoloration and Its Prevention   490
PREPARATION OF FRUIT FOR SERVING   492
  Raw   492
  Cooked   492
CHANGES IN FRUIT CAUSED BY COOKING   493
  Crispness   493
  Tenderness   493
DRIED FRUIT   494
  Cooking   494
  Storing   494

Chapter 28 **Vegetables**   498

COMPOSITION   498
  Carbohydrates   498
  Minerals and Vitamins   500
  Organic Acids   500
TEXTURE OF VEGETABLES   501
QUALITY CHARACTERISTICS OF RAW VEGETABLES   502
  Storage to Maintain Quality   502
PREPARATION FOR COOKING   504
  Washing   504
  Waste in Preparation   504
COOKING METHODS   505
  Baking   505
  Boiling in the Skin   506
  Boiling Prepared Vegetables   506
  Steaming   506
  Panning or Stir-Frying   507
EFFECTS OF COOKING ON TEXTURE OF VEGETABLES   507
  Crispness   507
  Tenderness   507
  Texture of Cooked Potatoes   511
FLAVOR OF VEGETABLES AND THE EFFECTS OF COOKING   512
  Mild Vegetables   514
  Sulfur Compounds in Vegetables   515
PIGMENTS IN VEGETABLES AND THE EFFECTS OF COOKING   519
  Chlorophyll   519
  Carotenoids   522
  Anthocyanins   524
  Betalains   525
  Anthoxanthins   525
  Discoloration of Potatoes   526
NUTRITIVE VALUE AND PALATABILITY OF COOKED VEGETABLES   527

Chapter 29 **Legumes**   534

VARIETIES OF LEGUMES USED FOR FOOD   534
COMPOSITION AND NUTRITIVE VALUE   534
COOKING LEGUMES   540
  Soaking   540
  Cooking Time and Doneness   542
  Storage   543
  Seasoning   543
  Yields of Cooked Legumes   543
  Canning   544
FLATUS AFTER INGESTING LEGUMES   544

PART IX   GELS   547

Chapter 30   **Gelatin Gels**   551

MANUFACTURE OF GELATIN   551
GELATIN GEL FORMATION   551
  Dispersing Dried Gelatin   552
  Gelation of a Gelatin Sol   552

USE OF GELATIN IN FOODS   553
  Proportions of Gelatin   553
  Fruit and Vegetable Jellies   554
  Whips, Sponges, and Creams   554
  Unmolding Gelatin Gels   554

Chapter 31   **Fruit Pectin Gels**   556

PECTIN CHEMISTRY   556
SOURCES OF PECTIN   557
COMPONENTS OF PECTIN GELS   558
  Water   558
  Acid   558
  Pectin   558
  Calcium Ions   558
  Sucrose   559

CONTROLLING THE VARIABLES IN A PECTIN GEL   560
  Hydrogen Ion Concentration   561
  Sucrose Concentration   561
  Pectin Concentration   561

SETTING TIME AND TEMPERATURE   563
JELLY MADE WITH PECTIN CONCENTRATE OR POWDER   563
JELLY MADE WITH FRUIT PECTIN EXTRACT   564
  Extraction of Pectin   564
  Clarification   564
  Testing for Pectin   564
  Boiling the Jelly   564
  Assessing Doneness   565

KEEPING QUALITY OF PECTIN JELLY   565
  Crystals in Jelly   566

Index   569

PART I

Food Quality

Evaluation of Food

1

Quality of food can be evaluated both with human senses and with instruments. Human senses are used to perceive the sensory properties of foods and instruments are used to quantify physical properties contributing to the sensory and nonsensory characteristics of food quality.

Every time food is eaten a judgement is made. Consciously or otherwise the consumer decides that the food in question is or is not of acceptable quality, that it shall or shall not pass. Additionally, food is tested for research purposes or for quality assurance.

Testing of food quality is discussed in this chapter and the physiology of human sensory perception of foods is discussed in Chapter 2.

SENSORY EVALUATION OF FOOD QUALITY

Vocabulary of Sensory Analysis

Before describing sensory testing of foods, it is necessary to discuss classification systems of our sensory responses. Our vocabulary to describe colors and tastes is well developed. However, our vocabulary to describe odor and texture is woefully inadequate.

Classification of Odor

When olfactory receptors are isolated and characterized and their substrates specified, it may be possible to determine a natural classification scheme for odors. Current thinking holds that there are no odor primaries—a limited set of elements that can be combined in varying proportions to yield the spectrum of olfactory sensations. In this regard, olfaction is more like audition than vision. Given the lack of understanding of basic olfactory mechanisms, classification of odors is more of an art than a science and little agreement exists. Analogy is often employed in an attempt to verbalize differences in odors. For example, odors may be characterized as nut-like, fruity, oily, or minty.

Classification of Texture

There is no widespread agreement on terminology for the textural attributes of foods. Consequently, analogy is often used to describe texture. Thus the word creamy is used to indicate the texture of fudge or the consistency of cream sauce, neither of which is commonly made with cream. Velvety is another such word used to characterize the mouthfeel of ice creams and some cakes. Rubbery is used to describe some gels and the white of an egg that has been boiled rather than hard cooked.

A texture classification system (Tables 1-1 and 1-2) was developed by Szczesniak in 1963 for solid and semisolid foods (16) and later expanded to include liquid foods (14). This sensory texture profile is still the foundation of texture evaluation, but new reference foods have been suggested (8). In this scheme, textural characteristics are categorized as mechanical, geometric, or other. Primary mechanical characteristics include hardness, cohesiveness, viscosity, and elasticity, all of which are influenced by the attraction between constituents that make up a food. Adhesiveness, the fifth characteristic, applies to the attraction between surfaces. Secondary characteristics of mechanical food texture include brittleness, chewiness, and gumminess. Geometrical characteristics relate to particle size and shape, and other characteristics include wetness and oiliness. Juiciness not only relates to water content, but the force with which water squirts out of cells upon chewing (15). A second approach termed the Spectrum Method (5) considers the natural time course of sensations. Evaluations are made at each stage of food ingestion from the time a sample passes the lips to the afterfeel once the sample is swallowed.

Relatively little research has been done on texture perception, partly because of the complexity of sensations involved and partly because of the difficulty in preparing a range of test substances that vary in only one component of texture. Some attempts to develop

TABLE 1-1
Relations between Textural Properties and Popular Nomenclature

MECHANICAL CHARACTERISTICS		
Primary Parameters	Secondary Parameters	Popular Terms
Hardness		Soft → firm → hard
Cohesiveness	Brittleness	Crumbly → crunchy → brittle
	Chewiness	Tender → chewy → tough
	Gumminess	Short → mealy → pasty → gummy
		Thin → viscous
		Plastic → elastic
		Sticky → tacky → gooey

GEOMETRICAL CHARACTERISTICS	
Class	Examples
Particle size and shape	Gritty, grainy, coarse, etc.
Particle shape and orientation	Fibrous, cellular, crystalline, etc.

OTHER CHARACTERISTICS		
Primary Parameters	Secondary Parameters	Popular Terms
Moisture content		Dry → moist → wet → watery
Fat content	Oiliness	Oily
	Greasiness	Greasy

From Szczesniak, A. S., M. A. Branst, H. H. Friedman. 1963. "Development of standard rating scales for mechanical parameters of texture and correlation between the objective and the sensory methods of texture evaluation." *Journal of Food Science* 28:397–403.

TABLE 1-2

5

CHAPTER 1
EVALUATION
OF FOOD

Classification of Sensory Mouthfeel Terms for Liquids

Category	Typical Words
Viscosity-related terms	Thin, thick, viscous
Feel on soft tissue surfaces	Smooth, pulpy, creamy
Carbonation-related terms	Bubbly, tingly, foamy
Body-related terms	Heavy, watery, light
Chemical effect	Astringent, burning, sharp
Coating or oral cavity	Mouthcoating, clinging, fatty, oily
Resistance to tongue movement	Slimy, syrupy, pasty, sticky
Afterfeel—mouth	Clean, drying, lingering, cleansing
Afterfeel—physiological	Refreshing, warming, thirst quenching, filing
Temperature-related terms	Cold, hot
Wetness-related terms	Wet, dry

From Szczesniak, A. S. 1979. "Classification of mouthfeel characteristics of beverages." In P. Sherman, ed., *Food Texture and Rheology*. New York: Academia Press, 1–20. Classification system for beverages and semisolid foods.

physiochemical models for a particular component of texture have been successful. For example, the inverse of the frictional force of the food between the tongue and the roof of the mouth is a good predictor of smoothness (3).

Sensory Testing of Foods

Sensory evaluation has been defined (6) as a "scientific discipline used to evoke, measure, analyze and interpret those responses to products (foods and materials) that are perceived by the senses of sight, smell, taste, touch, and hearing." Sensory methods are useful for product development or reformulation, quality control, quality assurance, product sensory specification, raw materials sensory specification, product optimization, and support for advertising claims. Objectives of sensory testing fall into two general categories: affective and analytical. The experimenter may wish to learn whether the panelists prefer a product or to learn of its potential for acceptability by the consuming public. This affective testing is often called acceptance or consumer testing. On the other hand, the experimenter may wish to know whether there is a detectable difference between or among samples (difference or discrimination testing) or to learn the nature of any such differences (descriptive testing). Panels appropriate for performing the various types of sensory testing differ in terms of the number of judges that constitute a panel, in the qualifications of its members, and in what the panelists are asked to do.

Analytical Testing

Difference or Discrimination Testing. For this type of analytical testing, a group of panelists is used as an instrument to assess differences in color, odor, taste, texture, and other aspects of food quality. A small group of panelists is used for difference testing. Actually one extremely discriminating, painstaking, and unbiased individual would suffice. But the human instrument is frequently inconsistent in its ability to discriminate different aspects of food quality, and daily variations in physical condition may cause variations in operating efficiency. A cold, for example, may render a panelist useless for days. Psychological factors such as preoccupation, worry, and other stresses may prevent a judge from operating effectively, as may environmental factors such as distracting noises, extraneous odors, and uncomfortable temperature. Furthermore, it is not always easy for the experimenter to know when a judge is not in optimum adjustment for the job of food-difference testing. For these reasons, and because of differences in opinion of optimal quality, a panel of judges is used and the data are analyzed statistically. Sample size is determined by the type of product being evaluated, magnitude of the property under question, available resources, time constraints, and level of risk judged acceptable for an erroneous conclusion. Often, valid decisions can be made using 12 to 20 qualified judges with two replications.

Judges may be asked to indicate differences among foods in a variety of ways. In the *paired comparison* test, judges are given two coded samples. They may be asked to indicate whether the samples are alike or different (simple difference testing) or which sample has more or less of the attribute under consideration (directional difference testing). Three samples, two exactly alike are presented to the judge in the *duo-trio* test. One of the identical samples is labeled as the standard and the judge is asked to identify which of the other two coded samples is identical to the standard. The *triangle* test also uses two identical samples and one different sample, but all three samples receive different code numbers. In this test, the judge is asked to indicate the different or odd sample. The chance of guessing the correct answer is ⅓ compared to ½ for each of the previous tests. Judges may be asked to *rank* in order two or more coded samples for specified characteristics. Alternatively, they may be asked to rate each coded sample compared to a labeled control in the *rating difference* test. Statistical analysis of the data determines whether or not differences from the control are significant.

Examples of sensory score sheets for analytical and affective testing appear in Table 1-3. Whichever test is selected, samples should be coded with a random three-digit number to prevent biases associated with perceived good or bad numbers or letters such as A versus F. The way samples are positioned or ordered may also affect a judge's decision. For example, panelists showed a strong bias in favor of the second sample of sponge cakes presented when retasting was not allowed (7). Making the order of sample presentation random minimizes positional error. An example of sample presentation and a taste-testing booth is shown in Figure 1-1.

Discrimination tests are often used in industry for selection and training of panelists, for reduction of costs associated with an ingredient or processing change, for testing product stability (stale vs. fresh, development of off flavors), and for quality control. Difference testing frequently compares a product to a standard.

Descriptive Testing. Descriptive tests are designed to describe sensory properties and their intensity. They may be used to support or interpret instrumental methods, to support or interpret other sensory tests, as a research guidance tool, and as a quality control/quality assurance method. Typically, 6 to 12 trained panelists are required.

Descriptive tests fall into two categories: attribute rating and descriptive analysis. Sample score sheets of the several types of tests are given in Table 1-3. In attribute rating, there are two types of rating tests—*category scaling* and *ratio scaling*. The assignment may be to check the coded samples against a scale or against descriptive terms such as none, slight, moderate, strong, and extreme, which could apply to a number of attributes for foods, or against such terms as smooth, slightly lumpy, moderately lumpy, and very lumpy for sauce; or such terms as not present, just recognizable, slight, moderate, and strong for vanilla flavor in ice cream. These are examples of structured word *category scales.*

TABLE 1-3
Examples of Sensory Scorecards Evaluating Sweetness

Differences Tests

Paired comparison: Simple difference

Are samples 374 and 902 of equal sweetness or different? _____

Paired comparison: Directional difference

Which sample is sweeter?   374 _____   902 _____

Duo-trio comparison

Which sample is identical to the standard?   374 _____   902 _____

Triangle test

Which sample is the odd sample?   374 _____   902 _____   612 _____

Rank

Rank in descending order of sweetness samples 374, 902, and 612. Do not give the same rank to two samples.

CODE   RANK ASSIGNED

_____   _____

_____   _____

_____   _____

Rating difference

Rate samples 374, 902, and 612 as compared to the control sample.

No difference from control	Slight difference from control	Moderate difference from control	Large difference from control	Very large difference from control

Descriptive Tests

Category scaling: Structured

Rate samples (374, 902, 612) for intensity of sweetness.

Not sweet	Slightly sweet	Moderately sweet	Strongly sweet	Extremely sweet

Category scaling: Unstructured

Rate samples 374 and 902 for intensity of sweetness by drawing a vertical mark for each sample through the line and labeling it.

Not sweet   Extremely sweet

(continued)

Ratio scaling or magnitude estimation

Taste samples, one at a time, and assign a number for the sweetness relative to the reference which has a value of 10.

CODE   INTENSITY OF SWEETNESS

374   _____

902   _____

612   _____

Affective Tests

Paired preference

Which sample do you prefer?   374 ___   902 ___

Ranking

List the samples 374, 902, and 612 in the order of which you like the most to the least.

Code

_____ most liked

_____

_____ least liked

Hedonic rating scale

Rate sample 374 by checking the appropriate box.

VERBAL

☐ Dislike extremely   ☐ Dislike moderately   ☐ Dislike slightly   ☐ Neither like nor dislike
☐ Like slightly   ☐ Like moderately   ☐ Like extremely

FACIAL

☐   ☐   ☐   ☐   ☐

Figure 1-1. Panelist receives coded food samples through a bread-box opening in a taste-testing booth. (Reprinted by permission of the Institute of Food Technologists from Rutledge, K. P. and J. M. Hudson. 1990. "Sensory evaluation: Method for establishing and training description flavor analysis panel." *Food Technology* 44(12):82.)

Alternatively, judges may be asked to mark an unstructured line with verbal anchors at each end that describe the limits of the attribute. For analysis, the line is digitized so each point can have a numerical assignment.

A recent variation of attribute rating is the time-intensity approach in which intensity is continuously recorded over time. Resulting curves show maximum intensity and the time to reach it, the rate of sensation decay, and the total duration of the taste (Fig. 1-2). Time-intensity curves are used to evaluate artificial sweeteners (9) and they may also be used to determine the affinity of binding of a sweetener for its receptor (13). Responses may be entered directly into the computer with a joystick or mouse, and the data processed subsequently.

In *ratio scaling* or *magnitude estimation* tests, judges are asked to assess specific attributes between products or levels of a product constituent using a rating scale of his or her own choice. Samples are presented sequentially and if a reference is used, it is presented first. When numeric responses are requested of panelists, the assigned numbers (estimates) are evaluated statistically and the ratios between numbers indicate the relative intensity of the attribute. This type of testing can be used by a manufacturer of sweet drinks, for example, to learn the magnitude of a sensory response to each increment of sweetener. The minimum amount of sweetener necessary to achieve satisfaction allows judgement about the costs/sensory benefit ratio of the sweetener.

Descriptive analysis tests include *flavor profile analysis, texture profile analysis,* and *quantitative descriptive analysis.* In flavor profile analysis, the judge is asked to record aromas, flavors, and aftertastes in the order perceived and their intensities using a constant

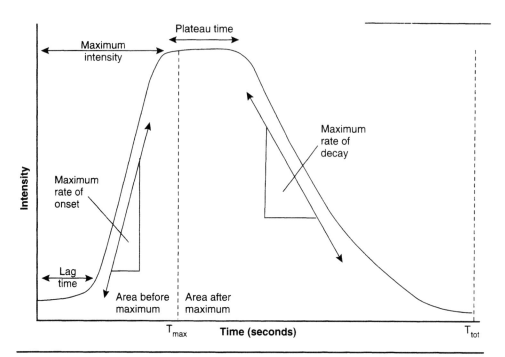

Figure 1-2. Typical time–intensity curve illustrating maximum intensity, time to maximum (T_{max}), total duration (T_{tot}), maximum rates of onset and decay, lag time, plateau time, and areas before and after maximum intensity. (Reprinted by permission of the Institute of Food Technologists from Noble, A. C., N. L. Matysiak, and S. Bonnans. 1991. "Factors affecting the time-intensity parameters of sweeteners." *Food Technology* 45(11):121.)

rating scale (usually threshold, 1, 2, and 3). Then the four- to five-member panel has an open discussion under the direction of a panel leader (Fig. 1-3). *Texture profile analysis* is similar except that panelists record the order and intensity of textural attributes from first bite through masticatory and residual phases. Then a panel leader leads a group discussion of the six- to nine-member panel. *Quantitative description analysis* employs statistical analysis of intensity scores for each attribute. Training of a panel to measure flavor in a statistically reliable manner can take as little as 20 hours if they will be limited to assessment of a single product, and as long as a year if they will work with an array of products (11).

Training of Judges. Training for either difference or descriptive testing involves repeated testing of the sensory property to be studied until the response of the judges satisfies preestablished criteria. The intent is to have judges behave as a calibrated instrument. Appropriate criteria for detecting sweeteners in a product might relate to the minimum concentration (*threshold*) required to be able to distinguish its presence or to the minimal detectable differences in concentration. There are standardized procedures for determining threshold concentration for odor or taste (1). Alternative criteria for a panelist to be considered trained might relate to accuracy of responses. Use of relevant reference standards can facilitate training by helping panelists develop appropriate terminology and to establish ranges of intensity. An ideal reference standard is simple and is used to charac-

Figure 1-3. Descriptive flavor analysis panel at work in a training session to become familiar with the flavors found in the food being tested. (Reprinted with permission of the Institute of Food Technologists from Rutledge, K. P. and J. M. Hudson. 1990. "Sensory evaluation: Method for establishing and training description flavor analysis panel." *Food Technology* 44(12):78.)

terize only one term. Incorporation of a reference into odor threshold testing improves comparability among studies (10). If standard references are not specified, a working set of attribute scales can be developed for a specific panel. For example, if a panel is asked to judge staleness of bread, training might involve studying the firmness, moistness, and cell structure of an interior slice of bread, and separately, the firmness, moistness, and toughness of the crust.

Acceptance or Consumer Testing

A fairly large number of individuals (75 or more), representative of the public or a large market segment of it, is essential for acceptance testing if results are to be valid. Panelists require little, if any, preliminary training. Three common types of affective tests are: *paired comparison, ranking,* and *rating.* In the consumer application of a paired comparison test, judges are asked which of two samples they prefer. When three or more coded samples are to be evaluated, a consumer may be asked to *rank* the samples in order of preference. The degree of liking requires rating tests. A popular example is the hedonic rating scale in which consumers are asked to record their reactions on a seven-point or nine-point scale that ranges from like extremely to dislike extremely. The verbal scale may be replaced with other response formats including a facial hedonic scale or an unstructured line scale. Ratings are converted to numerical scores that can be evaluated statistically. Consumers may also be asked to indicate the extent to which or the frequency with which they anticipate using the product. Industry uses internal food testing panels initially as they develop a new product. Then they may test 150 or more consumers to learn how the public might react to the product before the company attempts to put it on the market.

INSTRUMENTAL MEASUREMENT OF FOOD QUALITY

Instrumental tests for food quality include all those that do not rely mainly on human senses, although some methods use a combination of sensory and instrumental evaluation. Instead of assessing the color of cooked carrots or cooked green beans by eye, the carotene content of the former and the chlorophyll content of the latter can be determined by chemical means or by an instrument that measures color in just noticeable differences. Instead of using taste to compare three samples of lemon juice for tartness, one can measure their hydrogen-ion concentrations with a pH meter. Controlling pH is crucial to the thermal processing requirement and microbial safety of many foods. Water content can be measured by weighing a sample before and after drying in an oven. Alternatively, a moisture analyzer (Fig. 1-4) can give a reading within five minutes. The concentration of sugar in a syrup can be measured by a refractometer (Fig. 1-5). Specific gravity—density of a substance relative to the density of water—can be determined by weighing a given volume of a sample and dividing that by the weight of the same volume of water at a specified temperature. Specific gravity of a liquid can be determined with a hydrometer. Study of the structure of the cells of plants and of the fibers of the lean of meat, as well as of the distribution of ingredients in cake batter, requires the aid of a microscope. Size of a loaf of bread or a cake can be measured by how much seed it displaces in an apparatus (Fig. 1-6) of known volume. Alternatively, the area of a trac-

Figure 1-4. A moisture analyzer. (Courtesy of CEM Corporation.)

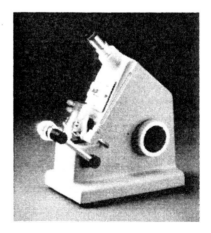

Figure 1-5. A refractometer measures the refractive index of liquids and percent soluble solids of solutions. (Courtesy of Milton Roy Company, Rochester, NY, a subsidiary of Sundstrand Corporation.)

ing or ink print of a cross-section of the baked product can be measured with a planimeter. Particle size can be determined under a microscope or by laser diffraction.

A large number of methods and instruments have been devised to assess the three physical attributes of quality: appearance, flavor components, and texture of foods (4). Many of these methods and instruments are unique to a specific food or application and others may have more general application. The choice of test depends on its purpose. Generally, measurements for research purposes should be sensitive and accurate. Quality assurance tests usually are quicker, are simple to operate, and produce relatively simple results. For example, a sensitive and sophisticated oscillation rheometer (Fig. 1-7) for analysis of food texture may be used in a research laboratory, but a very simple Bostwick consistometer (Fig. 1-8) may be used on the manufacturing plant floor for a quick and simple test of tomato puree consistency.

Several professional societies have developed standardized procedures for testing raw materials and finished food products. The American Association of Cereal

Figure 1-6. Apparatus for measuring volume of baked foods by seed displacement. (Courtesy of National Manufacturing Company, Lincoln, NE.)

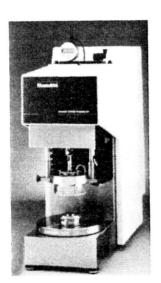

Figure 1-7. A rheometer can apply an oscillatory strain to a sample and the resulting stress that develops measures both elasticity and viscosity. (Courtesy of Rheometrics, Inc., Pisataway, NJ.)

Figure 1-8. A consistometer can measure the flow properties of products such as preserves or tomato sauce by measuring the distance a constant volume of product flows during a specified time. (Courtesy of CSC Scientific Co., Inc., Fairfax, VA.)

Chemists (AACC), the Association of Official Analytical Chemists (AOAC), and the American Oil Chemists Society (AOCS) all oversee and publish official methods for testing food and agricultural products. A partial list of suppliers of instruments that measure physical properties of foods is given by Giese (4). The pages that follow will highlight some of the common instrumental methods used to evaluate physical properties of food.

Appearance

Color is the most readily measured attribute of appearance. Several instruments exist for color measurement, the most common being the Hunter colorimeter system. The Hunter colorimeter system (Fig. 1-9) measures color and luminescence on three scales: *L*, *a*, and *b*. These parameters are described numerically and are visually represented in Figure 1-10. The *L* scale is a black-to-white scale ranging from 0 to 100. The *a* and *b* scales can be either positive or negative. A positive Hunter *a* value represents redness, a negative Hunter *a* represents greenness. A positive Hunter *b* represents yellowness and a negative Hunter *b* represents blueness. Sometimes a ratio of Hunter values most accurately represents the targeted color. The ratio of Hunter *a* to *b* (red to yellow) is often used for tomato products. Other color meters (Fig. 1-11, p. 16) use the tristimulus or three-dimensional coordinate system (*X*, *Y*, and *Z* coordinates) to define color. Chromaticity coordinates are obtained from reflectance readings taken with specific colored filters and plotted on a diagram. The instruments enable people to describe the redness of a strawberry for comparisons not possible with the human eye. Strawberry varieties can be compared for color across years or in processing plants in separate locations. Limitations of these instruments relate most frequently to sample preparation. Contours in the sample can alter reflection of the light independent of inherent color.

Other instruments measure the light reflected at specific wave lengths. Such instruments are useful for measuring differences in lightness and darkness and may be used in industry to monitor browning of fried or baked products.

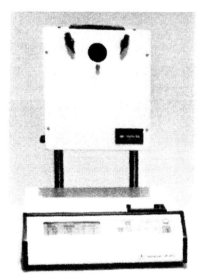

Figure 1-9. A colorimeter can be used to determine hue and lightness or darkness of samples. (Courtesy of Hunter Lab, Rosten, VA.)

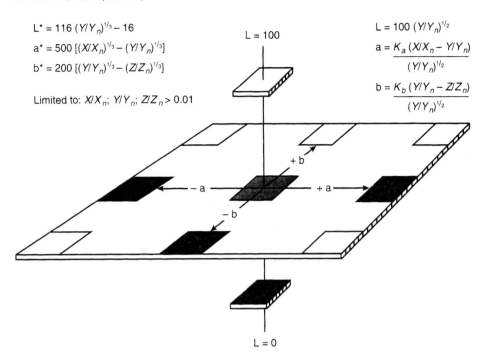

$$L^* = 116\,(Y/Y_n)^{1/3} - 16$$

$$a^* = 500\,[(X/X_n)^{1/3} - (Y/Y_n)^{1/3}]$$

$$b^* = 200\,[(Y/Y_n)^{1/3} - (Z/Z_n)^{1/3}]$$

Limited to: X/X_n; Y/Y_n; $Z/Z_n > 0.01$

$$L = 100\,(Y/Y_n)^{1/2}$$

$$a = \frac{K_a\,(X/X_n - Y/Y_n)}{(Y/Y_n)^{1/2}}$$

$$b = \frac{K_b\,(Y/Y_n - Z/Z_n)}{(Y/Y_n)^{1/2}}$$

L = 100

+ b

− a   + a

− b

L = 0

Where: 1. X, Y, Z are tristimulus values.
2. X_n, Y_n, Z_n are tristimulus values for perfect diffuser for illuminant used.
3. K_a, K_b are chromaticity coefficients for illuminant used.

Illuminant	X_n	Y_n	Z_n	K_a	K_b
A	109.828	100.000	35.547	185	38
C	98.041	100.000	118.103	175	70
D$_{65}$	95.018	100.000	108.845	172	67

Figure 1-10. The L, a, b, color solid used with the HunterLab colorimeter system to determine values for L, light-dark; a, red-green; and b, yellow-blue. (Courtesy of HunterLab, Reston, VA.)

Flavor

Flavor parameters are complex, and their analysis is usually restricted to sensory analysis for many purposes. However, flavor researchers and flavor industries use sophisticated instruments to identify and quantitate components of flavor. Components of flavor can be separated by gas or high-pressure liquid chromatography methods, and either detected by a person who sniffs the column outlet as the various odors come off the column or detected and quantitated instrumentally by mass spectroscopy or other means.

Figure 1-11. A tristimulus colorimeter used to measure color of food and beverages. (Courtesy of Minolta Corporation, Ramsey, NJ.)

Attempts have been made to measure human responses to odorants. An automated system that delivers odor stimuli via face masks was described (17). The response of the eyes by video camera and respiratory changes by a pneumotachograph are recorded.

Texture

A number of instruments are available for measuring the textural properties of foods (6). Some are designed for use with foods that are fluid and so exhibit viscous flow. For such foods, instruments are used to measure viscosity or the resistance of the material to flow. Other instruments are appropriate for use with solid and semisolid foods. These instruments measure deformation or disintegration of food under force. Textural properties are measured in units of time, mass, or distance.

Foods That Exhibit Viscous Flow

Viscometers work on two general principles. Capillary viscometers, of which the Ostwald is a well known example, measure the resistance of a liquid to flow in terms of the time required for a unit volume of the liquid to flow through a capillary tube. Gravity is the driving force that causes the liquid to flow. The greater the time, the more viscous the liquid. The jelmeter (Fig. 31-3) is a modification of a capillary viscometer, adapted to measure the viscosity of a fruit pectin sol used to make jelly. To make the test, the liquid in the holding tube of the jelmeter is allowed to flow through the attached capillary tube for one minute. The less liquid that flows through the tube, the more viscous the pectin sol. Details of how the jelmeter performs its function and how it is calibrated are given in Chapter 31.

A simple device to measure the viscosity of nonopaque liquids such as oil or sugar solutions requires a graduated cylinder to hold the liquid and a stainless steel ball calibrated by diameter to indicate viscosity. The time the steel ball requires to fall a specified distance in the liquid is an index to the viscosity of the liquid. The longer the time required, the more viscous the liquid. An orifice-type viscometer such as a Zahn cup can be used to

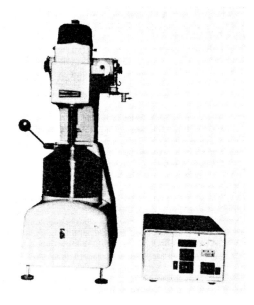

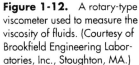

Figure 1-12. A rotary-type viscometer used to measure the viscosity of fluids. (Courtesy of Brookfield Engineering Laboratories, Inc., Stoughton, MA.)

Figure 1-13. A visograph measures the viscosity of starch or flour suspensions during controlled heating and cooling phases. (Courtesy of C. W. Brabender Instruments, Inc., South Hackensack, NJ.)

check the thickness of a batter used to coat food for deep fat frying or to monitor the change in thickness of pancake batter over time. The Zahn cup has an orifice in the bottom through which the contents of the cup flows. The time required for this can indicate how much the batter will spread on a griddle.

The consistometer (Fig. 1-8) is a crude but useful instrument to measure the flow of very thick foods such as catsup, apple sauce, tomato paste, and starch-thickened sauces. For the test, a specific volume of the food being tested is allowed to flow down an inclined plane under force of gravity. The distance the product flows in a specified time is an index to its viscosity.

Rotary viscometers are based on the principle that the thicker the liquid, the more force required to rotate an object in it. A rotary viscometer (Fig. 1-12) measures viscosity in terms of the force required to overcome the drag on a rotating spindle, paddle, or cylinder submerged in the liquid.

A visco amylograph (Fig. 1-13) is a specialized type of rotary viscometer designed to measure, under programmed heating, the thickening or increase in viscosity of a suspension of starch or flour in water and the change in viscosity under programmed cooling that follows. The viscosity of hot starch pastes is of interest for starches to be used to make soups or gravies. The viscosity of cooled starch pastes is applicable to puddings and pie fillings.

Solid and Semisolid Foods

Instruments designed to measure the physical properties of solid and semisolid foods are usually designed with either a probe-type attachment that can penetrate or compress a food or knife- or bar-attachment that can break or shear the food tested. Force is applied to make the test with these instruments. An early device of the probe-type that measures the force required to penetrate the surface of fruit such as pears is the Magness-Taylor fruit tester. The pressure required indicates whether the pears are mature enough for harvest so that they can go into temporary cold storage.

A penetrometer comes with either needle-shaped or cone-shaped probes (Fig. 1-14) that can be attached to the lower end of a driving rod. Weights are added to the top of the rod. When the rod is released, the attached weight is the driving force that causes the probe to penetrate the test item. The more the item resists penetration, the less the reading (distance) recorded on the dial. The penetrometer with the cone attachment can be used to measure firmness or rigidity of a gelatin gel, fruit pectin jelly, or starch-thickened pudding or pie fillings. The needle probe can be used to measure firmness of cheese, fruits, or vegetables.

A shear press is used to determine the tenderness of cooked or canned vegetables. The part of a shear press that does the shearing consists of parallel steel plated bars that pass through parallel slots in the top of a box that holds the test samples. As the assembly of bars are forced through the sample and into the slits, they shear off layers of the test material, which exits in identical slits in the bottom of the sample box. The force required to shear the fibrous tissue of a food is an index to the range between tenderness and toughness. A device that measures tenderness of meat by the force to shear the tissues is the Warner-Bratzler meat shear apparatus.

A shortometer (Fig. 17-3) is used to measure the force required to break a crisp baked product such as pastry or cookies. The item to be tested is placed across parallel bars. As

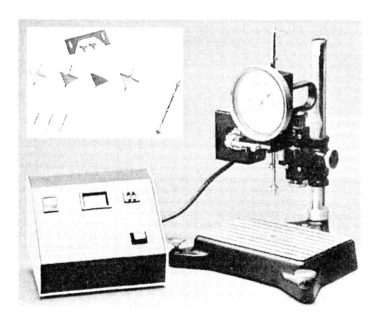

Figure 1-14. A penetrometer assesses tenderness by measuring the distance a cone- or needle-shaped attachment penetrates a food under a constant load. (Courtesy of Precision Scientific, Bellwood, IL.)

the breaker bar is lowered against the test item, the resistance of the test piece to breakage is registered.

A texture analyzer (Fig. 1-15) with its multiple attachments is a versatile instrument for assessing the texture of foods. It has a drive mechanism that applies force toward the food during a compression or away from the food during a tension, and a means of recording the effects of the applied force as the test is being made. From the results, several aspects of texture including hardness, cohesiveness, stretchiness, fracturability, chewiness, and gumminess can be attained.

Assessing physical properties of foods is important to determine how foods will handle during processing, to indicate product quality, and to understand consumer preference (5). Many quality parameters such as freshness or expected shelf life cannot be determined by a single analytical test. A series of laboratory measurements used together sometimes produce a pattern that correlates with an aspect of food quality. This approach is called chemometrus (2). Future directions of measures of physical properties of food will include techniques that can be used to study foods at the molecular level. For example, magnetic resonance imaging (MRI), currently used to scan patients in hospitals, and nuclear magnetic resonance (NMR), now used to study water/starch relationships, will be used to determine composition and structure of foods during processing (12). On-line sensing will be used to determine the moisture content of individual fruits, the fat content of meat patties, and the changes in starch molecules as bread cools or as foods move along conveyor belts during processing.

Figure 1-15. A texture analyzer pictured with a probe attachment. (Courtesy of Texture Technologies Corporation, Scarsdale, NY.)

REFERENCES

1. ASTM 1988. "Standard practice for determination of odor and taste thresholds by a forced-choice ascending concentration series method of difference." *Comm. E-18.* American Society for Testing and Materials, Philadelphia, PA. Pp. 34–39. Standard procedures for threshold testing.

2. Bailey, P. J. and B. G. Rohrback. 1994. "Applications of chemometrus in the food industry." *Food Technology* 48:69–72. Correlation of instrumental data patterns with product quality.

3. Cussler, E. L., J. Kokini, R. L. Weinheimer, and H. R. Moskowitz. 1979. "Food texture in the mouth." *Food Technology* 33(10):89–92. Physiochemical models for food texture.

4. Giese, J. 1995. "Measuring physical properties of foods." *Food Technology* 49(2):54–63. An overview of analysis of physical properties of food.

5. Hegenbart, S. 1992. "Putting mouthfeel into words." *Food Product Design* 2:20–41. Description of Spectrum Method.

6. Institute of Food Technologists, Sensory Evaluation Division. 1981. "Sensory evaluation guide for testing food and beverage products." *Food Technology* 35(11):5059. Definition of sensory evaluation.

7. Kim, K. and C. S. Setser. 1980. "Presentation order bias in consumer preference studies on sponge cakes." *Journal of Food Science* 45:1073–74. Positional bias in sensory testing.

8. Muñoz, A. M. 1986. "Development and application of texture reference scales." *Journal of Sensory Studies* 1:55–83. New reference foods for sensory texture rating scales.

9. Noble, A. C., N. L. Matysiak, and S. Bonnans. 1991. "Factors affecting the time-intensity parameters of sweeteners." *Food Technology* 45(11):121–26. Time-intensity sensory evaluation.

10. Rabin, M. D. and W. S. Cain. 1986. "Determinants of measured olfactory sensitivity." *Perception and Psychophysics* 39(4): 281–86. Value of references in threshold odor testing.

11. Rutledge, K. P. and J. M. Hudson. 1990. "Sensory evaluation: Method for establishing and training description flavor analysis panel." *Food Technology* 44(12):78–84. Training panel for the Spectrum™ method of descriptive flavor analysis.

12. Schrader, G. W., J. B. Litchfield, and S. J. Schmidt. 1992. "Magnetic resonance imaging application in the food industry." *Food Technology* 46(12):77–83. MRI application to study food molecules.

13. Shamil, S., G. G. Birch, A. A. S. F. Jackson, and S. Meck. 1988. "Use of intensity-time studies as an aid to interpreting sweet taste chemoreception." *Chemical Senses* 13(4): 597–605. Use of time-intensity sensory evaluation to determine binding affinities of receptors to sweetness.

14. Szczesniak, A. S. 1979. "Classification of mouthfeel characteristics of beverages." In P. Sherman, ed., *Food Texture and Rheology.* New York: Academia Press, Pp. 1–20. Classification system for beverages and semisolid foods.

15. Szczesniak, A. S. and R. Ilker. 1988. "The meaning of textural characteristics—juiciness in plant foodstuffs." *Journal of Texture Studies* 19:61–78. Elements of sensory qualities of juiciness.

16. Szczesniak, A. S., M. A. Branst, and H. H. Friedman. 1963. "Development of standard rating scales for mechanical parameters of texture and correlation between the objective and the sensory methods of texture evaluation." *Journal of Food Science* 28:397–403. Lists of foods illustrating gradations in textural characteristics.

17. Walker, J. C., D. B. Kurtz, F. M. Stone, M. W. Ogden, and J. H. Reynolds IV. 1990. "Apparatus for the automated measurement of the responses in humans to odorants." *Chemical Senses* 15:165–76. Objective testing of odor responses.

Sensory Perception of Foods

2

Quality is an important determinant of whether or not a food is eaten or purchased, a product is successful on the market, or a customer returns to a restaurant. For a food to nourish the body, it must pass the palate.

One objective in the study of foods is to develop the ability to prepare and provide palatable products. Quality of food is often assessed in terms of appearance, odor, taste, and texture and sometimes by sound.

APPEARANCE OF FOOD

Visual Perception

Perception of the size and shape of pieces of food, of the brownness of the crusts of breads and pies, of the brightness and trueness of the color of fruits and vegetables, and of characteristics such as transparency, opaqueness, turbidity, dullness, and gloss are mediated by the eye (1). We see an object when radiant energy from it impinges upon the retina of the eye. The retina contains two types of receptor cells, categorized by their shapes as rods (long and slender) and as cones (tapering). An estimated 110 to 130 million rods and 6 to 7 million cones are found in the human retina. Radiant energy absorbed by pigments in these receptors triggers nerve impulses that are transmitted to the brain by way of the optic nerve. The visual sensation that results is light, upon which perception of the form and the color of objects depends. What is perceived is a conscious response to stimulation of the visual apparatus.

The rods and cones are sensitive to those rays that vary in wave length from approximately 400 to 700 millimicrons (1 millimicron, abbreviated mμ, equals 0.000001 or 10^{-6} millimeter), a very narrow segment of the entire electromagnetic spectrum (Fig. 2-1). The rods, which are more sensitive to light than the cones, are responsible for black and white vision. Nerve impulses in the rods are initiated when light bleaches the pigment, rhodopsin, for the generation of which vitamin A is essential. The cones require a stronger stimulus to initiate nerve impulses. They are responsible for color vision.

Several hundred hues are distinguished by three different classes of cones (blue, red, and green) that have different, but overlapping absorption spectra (25) (Fig. 2-2). The discovery of at least nine genes for cones plus two red cone subtypes suggest that color vision is complex.

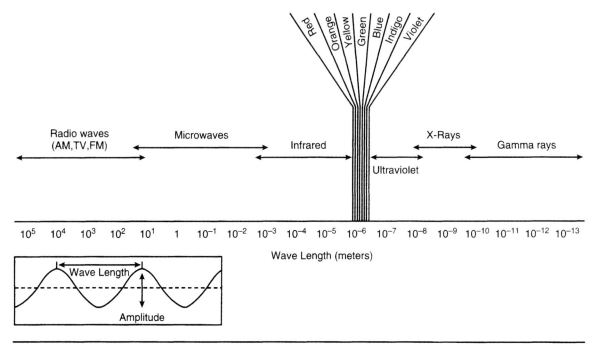

Figure 2-1. Electromagnetic spectrum. (By permission of Felix Cooper.)

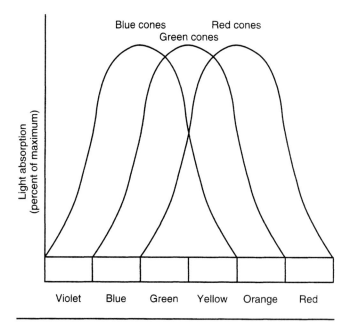

Figure 2-2. The three classes of cones overlap in their sensitivity to color, thus enabling us to see several hundred different hues. For example, red light stimulates only red cones, but green light stimulates all three classes of cones, but to a varying degree.

Color of Foods

The individual waves that make up white light can be separated into all the colors of the rainbow by passing the light through a prism (28). An object that reflects all these rays appears white; one that absorbs all the components of white light appears black. The eye (together with the brain) is able to distinguish among the waves that constitute white light. Those rays with the shortest wave lengths (near one end of the visible spectrum) elicit the response called violet, and the longest waves at the other end the response called red. Objects appear colored because the light from them that reaches the eye contains only a part of the waves from the visible portion of the spectrum. Spinach is green because it absorbs part of the radiation that makes up white light but reflects those rays that elicit the response to which the term green is given.

The color of foods contributes immeasurably to one's aesthetic appreciation of them. For example, visualize broccoli that has been properly prepared that is bright green in color versus overcooked broccoli that has turned to olive green. Or, visualize freshly sliced apples versus apple slices that have turned brown.

In addition to giving pleasure, the color of foods is associated with other attributes. For example, the ripeness of fruits such as bananas and strawberries is judged by color. Color is used as an index to the quality of a number of foods. The strength of coffee and tea is judged in part by the color of the beverages. The color of roast beef is used as an index to doneness. Toast that is too brown is likely to be rejected in anticipation of a somewhat scorched, bitter taste. Fruits that are clear and bright in color have more sales appeal than do those that are dark and dull in part because of the superior flavor expected in the former. Artificially colored foods such as fruit drinks, Popsicles, and jellies sell better if they are appropriately colored to resemble the natural fruit color.

CHEMOSENSORY PROPERTIES

Once food passes the sight test, sensory systems sensitive to the chemical constituents of foods in the nose and mouth are utilized to obtain additional information about the quality of a food. Taste, odor, and chemically mediated thermal, tactile, and pressure sensations (referred to as chemesthesis) all contribute to the flavor of foods. Flavor is an amalgam of all sensory properties of a food. Psychological factors also contribute to the acceptability of a food. Pleasant associations increase the likelihood that a food will be liked, unpleasant associations that it will be rejected. One's reaction to a particular food or to the way a food has been prepared is conditioned by association. Cinnamon flavor in mint candy wafers tinted green comes as a surprise, as does vanilla flavor in strawberry pink ice cream. Many such subtle factors contribute to one's assessment of the appeal of foods. Although food scientists and technologists are interested in sensory evaluation of the flavor of foods, physiologists and psychologists in the main have been the ones who have attempted to ascertain how flavor sensations are perceived.

Knowledge about the senses derives from multiple sources including the neurosciences, psychology, nutrition, food chemistry, and genetics. In the following sections, the basic mechanisms by which substances are smelled or tasted will be discussed. First, a stimulus reaches the mouth or nose, where it interacts with a receptor or membrane channel. This initiates a series of poorly understood intracellular reactions leading to depolarization of the receptor cell and generation of an action potential that is transmitted to the brain where it is interpreted. Such mechanisms are used by all cells in response to changes in their chemical environment. Thus, cells responsible for taste and smell are examples of chemoreceptors. The brain decodes taste and odor information and integrates it with other physiological and emotional information collected during ingestion and digestion of food. We have much to learn about this process. One recent suggestion is that pleasure associated with taste (i.e., sweet) and smell is enhanced by stimulation of the opiate system in the brain (4).

Odor

The odor of a food contributes immeasurably to the pleasure of eating. Odor, like appearance, may be a valuable index to the quality of a food and even to its wholesomeness and edibility. Rather than say a food tastes good, in most instances one probably should say it smells good. Although a person with a cold complains that food has no taste, the sensitivity of the olfactory organ—not of the taste buds—is impaired. It is the ability to detect odors that is missing and missed. The pleasant sensations in eating come more from odor than from taste.

Sensing an Odor

Information regarding the odor of food is obtained through the olfactory epithelium, a yellow pigmented area about the size of a postage stamp, located in the upper part of the nasal cavity and above the turbinate bones (Fig. 2-3a). Olfactory neurons through which odors are detected are located in this area. They number from 10 to 20 million in humans compared to 100 million in the rabbit, an animal with a keen sense of smell. Each olfactory cell terminates in 5 to 20 hairlike projections or extensions of the cell wall, called cilia, which extend into the mucous lining of the olfactory epithelium. Single neurons comprising the first cranial nerve (also called the olfactory nerve) make contact with the external environment through the olfactory epithelium and the olfactory bulb, which is just above the odor-detecting area and separated from it by the perforated cribriform plate. Olfactory information is transmitted from the olfactory bulb to the limbic system, which also serves as the emotional center of the brain. The nose is also innervated with fibers from the fifth cranial (or trigeminal) nerve, which senses pain and irritation, a fact that accounts for the sensitivity of the nose to pepper. The simplified drawing of the microscopic appearance of a section of the olfactory epithelium in Figure 2-3b shows olfactory cells with their terminal hairs and the nerve fibers that serve the area. Olfactory cells turnover on average every 15 days.

Normally, most of the inhaled air flows past the olfactory area but does not impinge directly upon it. However, in the act of swallowing a slight vacuum is formed in the nasal

Figure 2-3. (a) Nasal cavity, showing location of the olfactory area above the turbinate bones, with the olfactory bulb above and the olfactory epithelium below the cribriform plate. (b) Simplified drawing of a section of the olfactory epithelium showing olfactory cells with nerves leading to the olfactory bulb and with terminal hairs projecting into the mucous lining of the epithelium. Also shown are supporting cells and trigeminal nerve. (c) According to the stereochemical theory, the odor of a molecule depends on its size and shape or its charge, which in turn determines on which slots or pits of the olfactory nerve endings it will fit. A molecule that fits the pepperminty cavity is shown. (From "The Stereochemical Theory of Odor" by J. E. Amoore, J. W. Johnston, Jr., and M. Rubin. Copyright © 1964 by Scientific American, Inc. All rights reserved.)

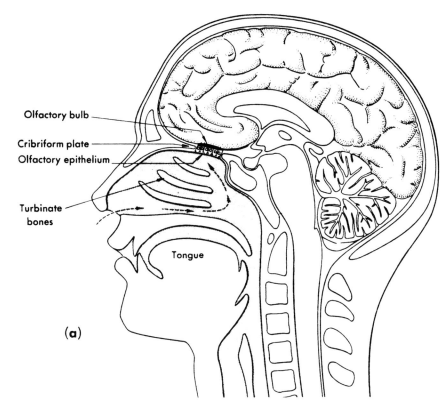

Olfactory bulb

Cribriform plate

Olfactory epithelium

Turbinate bones

Tongue

(a)

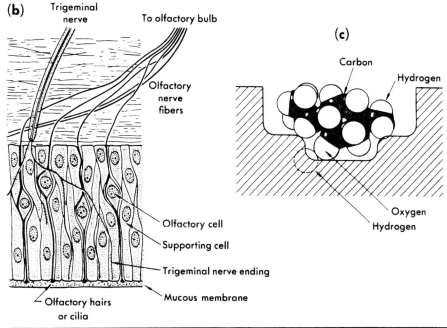

(b)

Trigeminal nerve

To olfactory bulb

Olfactory nerve fibers

Olfactory cell

Supporting cell

Trigeminal nerve ending

Mucous membrane

Olfactory hairs or cilia

(c)

Carbon

Hydrogen

Oxygen
Hydrogen

cavity and as food starts down the esophagus a small gust of odor-laden air from the food is drawn up into the olfactory area. This retronasal flow of odors accounts for much of the flavor of foods. Sniffing to better sense an odor also draws air up to this organ.

Odor Detection

For a substance to produce an odor it must be volatile, and the molecules of the substance must make contact with receptors or channels on cilia in the olfactory epithelium (24). A multigene family thought to encode odorant receptors has been discovered (9). When an odorant activates an olfactory receptor, second messenger systems are stimulated leading to changes in membrane conductance and ultimately depolarization. The resulting action potential is transmitted as an electrical impulse by nerves to the brain where the message is decoded. Activation of membrane channels can have the same effect. Meanwhile, the odorant also activates phosphorylation—a chemical message created by adding a phosphate group that alters the shape of the molecule—of proteins in olfactory cilia (7) that stops the odor signal. Rapid dephosphorylation of the proteins ready the receptor to respond again.

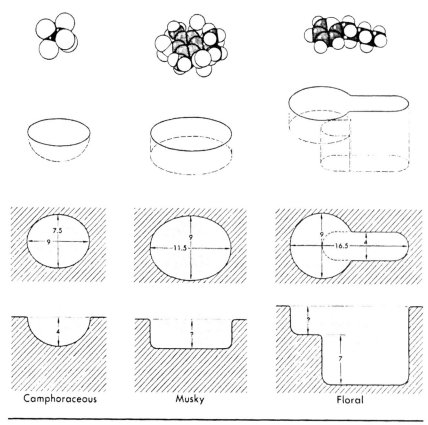

Camphoraceous   Musky   Floral

Figure 2-4. The geometry of the primary odors and their receptor sites. The shapes of the first five sites are shown in perspective and (with the molecules silhouetted in them) from above and the side; dimensions are in angstrom units. Molecules that are pungent or putrid are so

Odor Stimuli

Just why a molecule provokes a certain odor sensation has interested a number of investigators. Attempts have been made to single out the group or groups of atoms that confer on a molecule its characteristic odor. Compounds that differ markedly in structure may have similar odors; conversely, small differences in structure may give molecules markedly different odors. So far, no odorant receptor molecule has been specifically linked to a single odorant. An initial attempt to classify odors related the contour of the molecule to the particular odor sensation it provokes (2). According to this theory, the geometry of the molecule is of primary importance as far as odor is concerned as illustrated in Figure 2-4. Later, the concept that the odor of a compound depends not only on the proportions of the molecule, but also on the ease with which the molecule can pass from the air to the moisture on the surface of the olfactory receptors and from there to the lipid layer underneath was incorporated into odor theory. Instead of a few primary odors, a spectrum of odors was envisioned, as shown in Figure 2-5. Chemical functional groups of odorants such as oxygen-containing carbonyl groups and chain length influence odor responses (34).

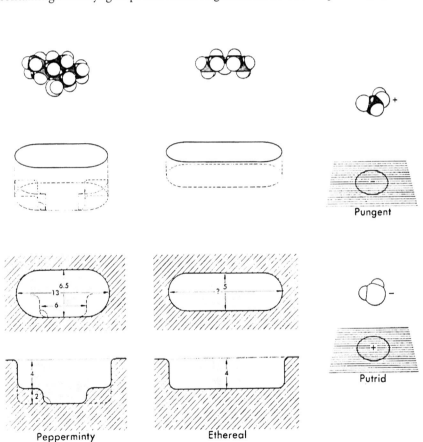

Figure 2-4. *(Continued)* because of charge, not shape, according to this theory. (From "The Stereochemical Theory of Odor" by J. E. Amoore, J. W. Johnston, Jr., and M. Rubin. Copyright © 1964 by Scientific American, Inc. All rights reserved.)

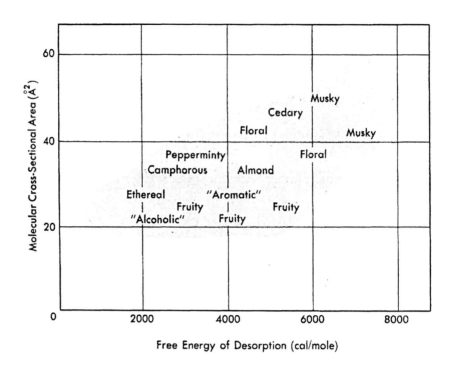

Figure 2-5. The odor spectrum lends support to the theory that the odor of a molecule depends on its cross-sectional area and the ease with which it can pass from air to water to lipid. (From J. T. Davies, *Journal of Theoretical Biology* 8:6, 1965. Copyright © by Academic Press, Inc., New York.)

Current evidence (9) suggests that olfactory perception requires a large number of receptors to distinguish the full spectrum of odors in contrast to color vision that requires only red, blue, and green photoreceptors. The code for olfactory perception is not well understood. A popular view holds that quality is based on a spatiotemporal and selected sensitivity mechanism (34). Because of the physical and chemical properties of odorants (e.g., solubility in air, water, lipid), their passage through air, water, and mucus phases will result in a spatial and temporal distribution across the olfactory epithelium. The pattern of stimulation, possibly coupled with some receptor specificity, may hold the key to understanding odor quality.

Odor Sensitivity

The concentrations at which substances can be detected in air are incredibly low. One odorous substance, vanillin, can be sensed when the concentration is only 2×10^{-10} (0.0000000002) milligram per liter of air, a low concentration indeed. Methyl mercaptan added to the gas supplied to a kitchen range to give it a noticeable odor is said to be detected with only 1 milligram in 25 million liters of gas; what is more, only about $\frac{1}{10}$ liter of air is inhaled at each breath and not more than two percent of this contacts the olfactory organ.

It is estimated that the olfactory sense of humans has the capacity to distinguish 16 million odors. Thus, the olfactory system is an elaborate chemical recognition system.

Taste

Important as odor is in the sensory evaluation of foods, few people would be content just to smell food before swallowing it. We value food for its taste, in the restricted sense of the word.

Sensing Taste

Taste is sensed by receptor cells in the taste buds, which are located in the papillae (bright-pink spots) on the tongue, the soft palate, the pharynx, the epiglottis, the larynx, and the upper third of the esophagus. The location of papillae on the tongue can be seen in Figure 2-6. Nerves to the back part of the tongue, exposed by dissection, are also shown.

Taste buds are located on areas of the oral cavity that food contacts most during chewing and swallowing. Fungiform papillae and the taste buds they contain are found on the dorsal surface and toward the front of the tongue, as are the filiform papillae. The latter contain no taste buds, but are sensitive to touch. Foliate papillae are found on the back sides of the tongue and the few (7 to 10) circumvallate papillae across the back, arranged in a V-shape. The central surface of the tongue contains no taste buds.

Some papillae contain more taste buds than do others. The diagram in Figure 2-7 shows papillae (much enlarged) of the tongue and taste buds located in one circumvallate papilla. A taste bud is made up of 50 to 150 cells grouped in a knoblike cluster. A

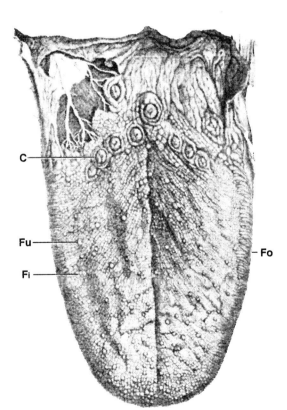

Figure 2-6. Tongue, showing papillae. Taste buds are found in the circumvallate (C), the fungiform (Fu), and the foliate (Fo), but not in the filiform (Fi) papillae (from Wenzel). (From H. C. Warren and L. Carmichael, *Elements of Human Psychology.* Copyright © 1930 by Houghton Mifflin Company, Boston. Reprinted by permission.)

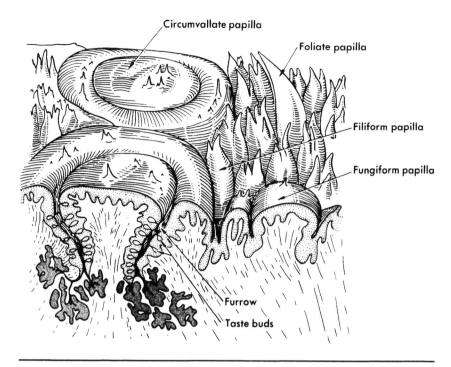

Figure 2-7. Mucous membrane covering the tongue much enlarged to show the papillae and the taste buds in one circumvallate papilla. (Reprinted by permission of Macmillan Publishing Co., Inc., from *The Human Body: Its Structure and Physiology,* 4th edition, by Sigmund Grollman. Copyright © 1978. Sigmund Grollman.)

simplified diagram of a taste bud is shown in Figure 2-8. Cells that make up a bud are of several types including supporting cells and taste receptor cells. Receptor cells terminate in a microvillus, a hairlike projection into a pore at the top center of the taste bud.

Taste Detection

To be tasted, a substance must be dissolved in a fluid and make contact with the microvilli. When a stimulus interacts with the taste receptor cell, a series of reactions occur resulting in cell depolarization and release of neurotransmitters that convey taste information between neurons to the brain. Nerve fibers that make contact with the taste cells are from the seventh (chorda tympani) and ninth (glossopharyngeal) cranial nerves, and from a branch of the tenth (vagus), as shown in Figure 2-9. In the brain stem, gustatory, and visceral sensory information about digestive activity converge. Taste information from the brain stem is further relayed to the thalamus and cortex and integrated with information on appetite and emotions.

The number of taste buds in humans is estimated at 4,500, much fewer than the number reported in some animals such as the antelope. Taste receptor cells degenerate and are replaced on an average of every 10½ days. As an individual ages the number of taste buds declines. Atrophy of the papillae begins when one is about 45. Such anatomical changes do not correlate well with taste function, which is well preserved through the seventh decade of life.

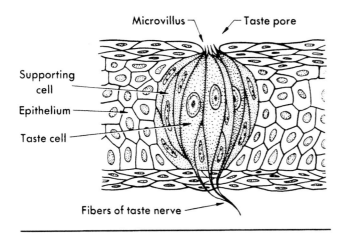

Microvillus — Taste pore

Supporting cell
Epithelium
Taste cell

Fibers of taste nerve

Figure 2-8. Diagram of a taste bud. Taste cells with their nerve fibers and with their microvilli projecting into the taste pore are shown, as are supporting cells. (Adapted from Fred D'Amour. *Basic Physiology*, University of Chicago Press, Chicago, 1961, p. 623.)

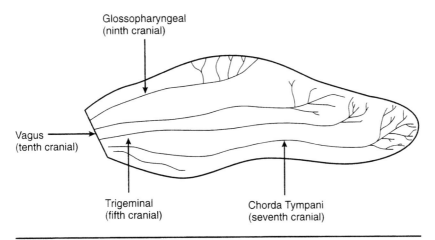

Glossopharyngeal
(ninth cranial)

Vagus
(tenth cranial)

Trigeminal
(fifth cranial)

Chorda Tympani
(seventh cranial)

Figure 2-9. Vertical section of the tongue showing the location of the important sensory nerves associated with taste sensation. (Redrawn with permission from the Institute of Food Technologists from *Food Technology* 48(4):79, 1994.)

Taste Stimuli

Taste sensations that the taste buds register are categorized as sweet, salt, sour, bitter, and possibly umami, the savory taste. Teleologically, it has been argued that sweet signals the presence of calories; salty signals electrolytes; sour signals the presence of acids; bitter may serve as a signal for poison; and umami may signal amino acids and protein. Although taste buds in the different areas of the tongue may not be equally sensitive to all taste stimuli, many taste cells respond to more than one stimulus (13) and all qualities can be perceived in all regions of the oral cavity. The question of whether all tastes derive from combinations of four to five primaries or spatiotemporal patterning has not been resolved (32). Great advances are currently being made in elucidating the basic taste transduction mechanisms.

Sour. The sensation known as *sour* is associated with hydrogen ions supplied by acids such as vinegar or those found in fruits and vegetables, and by acid salts such as cream of tartar.

Hydrogen ions are thought to enter the taste cell through sodium ion channels that depolarize the cell and lead to neurotransmitter release in mammalians (23). The intensity of the sour sensation produced by an acid depends more upon the hydrogen ion concentration than upon the total acidity; however, sourness and hydrogen ion concentration do not run exactly parallel. It is more related to potential than actual hydrogen ion concentration in a food.

Salt. *Salt* taste is due to ions of salts. Those of sodium chloride (table salt) are the most common source of the salt sensation. Until recently, it was believed that sodium ions initiated the salty taste following passage through amiloride sensitive sodium channels in receptor cells (3). However, new data raises questions about such channels in humans (36). The anion used to make the salt also influences taste. The chloride anion adds no additional taste, whereas, citrates and phosphates add additional chemical flavors that diminish perceived saltiness. The pleasantness of the salty taste is influenced by one's usual salt intake (21).

Sweet. Substances which elicit the sweet sensation are primarily organic compounds. Alcohols, certain amino acids, and aldehydes such as cinnamic aldehyde (found in cinnamon) taste sweet. Glycerol (glycerine) tastes mildly sweet. Sugars, however, are the main source of sweetness in foods.

According to one popular concept, molecules that taste sweet have functional groups that form a spacial shape characteristic of an AH, B, X triangle with approximate dimensions of 3:4:5. The AH, a proton donor ($=NH$ or $-OH$) and the B, a proton acceptor must be positioned in such a way that they can hydrogen bond to a similar system AH-B at a receptor site on a taste bud (35), shown schematically in Figure 2-10. In sugars, $-OH$ groups are thought to be the AH and B groups (35). The X is a hydrophobic group that also interacts with the receptor (17). When a sweet compound interacts with the receptor, the membrane of the taste receptor is depolarized, initiating a nerve impulse that results in

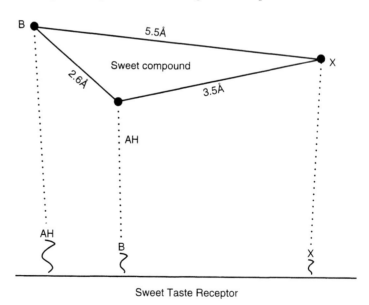

Figure 2-10.
Binding of a sweet compound with AH-B-X triangle to sweet receptor.

the sensation of sweetness as shown in Figure 2-11. The better the fit between the sweetener and the receptor, the sweeter the compound. Size is also important; sweet compounds usually are between 0.52 and 0.72 cm^3/g (6).

The AH, B, X theory cannot predict the intensity of sweetness of compounds, however. One attempt to quantitatively correlate the structure of a compound with its sweetness is by the concept of molecular connectivity (11). This concept quantitatively predicts sweetness by taking into account the whole molecule and determining a structural parameter, $^3\chi_m$ (pronounced three Chi M), which is calculated from each atom and its position in the molecule. The higher the $^3\chi_m$ in value, the sweeter the molecule. The $^3\chi_m$ value can predict relative sweetness for sugars, but is not as useful for noncarbohydrate sweet compounds. An understanding of sweetness intensity comes from a recent model of a sweet receptor, which has up to eight optional interaction sites with sweeteners designated as AH, B, G, D, Y, XH, E_1, and E_2 (Fig. 2-12). Simultaneous binding of a compound with any two sites generates a sweet taste, but interactions with four or more are necessary for intensely sweet tastes.

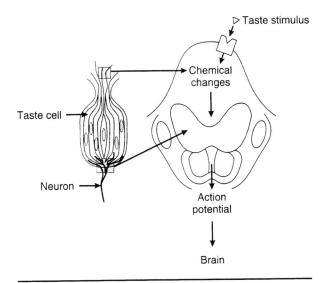

Figure 2-11. Proposed mechanism of sweet taste detection. A sweet substance interacts with a receptor that leads to calcium ion mediated chemical changes resulting in an action potential which transmits electrical signals to the brain.

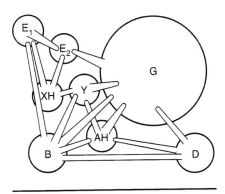

Figure 2-12. Spatial arrangement of the eight potential interaction sites of sweetening agents. Where B = an anionic group (CO_2^-, SO_3^- or CN_4^-), AH = a hydrogen-bond donor group (NH, OH), G = a hydrophobic group (hydrocarbon group), D = a hydrogen bond acceptor group (CN, NO_2, Cl), Y, E_1, E_2 = hydrogen bond acceptor ligands (CO, halogen atoms), and XH a hydrogen bond donor group (NH, OH). (From J.-M. Tinti and C. Notre. "Sweetness Discovery, Molecular Design and Chemoreception," D. E. Walters et al., eds. *ACS Symposium Series 450*, 209. Copyright 1991 American Chemical Society.)

TABLE 2-1
Relative Sweetness of Sugars

Sugar	Rank
Fructose	1.15–1.32
Sucrose	1.00
Glucose	0.56–0.83
Galactose	0.59
Mannose	0.59
Maltose	0.46
Lactose	0.30
Xylose	0.57–0.87
Sorbitol	0.50–0.82
Xylitol	0.96–1.18
Mannitol	0.51–0.62

From Schultz, H. G. and F. J. Pilgrim. 1957. "Sweetness of various compounds and its measurements." *Food Research* 22:206–13; and Yamaguchi, S., T. Yoshikawa, S. Ikeda, and T. Ninomiya. 1970. "Studies on the taste of some sweet substances: Measurement of the relative sweetness." *Agr. Biol. Chem.* 34:181–86.

Sugars. Sugars have been ranked in descending order of sweetness as shown in Table 2-1 (33) based on concentrations judged as equisweet. In another study, three sugars were compared for relative sweetness to sugar alcohols (40). Aside from type of sugar, the relative sweetness also depends on concentration of sugar. For example, fructose dissolved in water at low concentrations was ranked 1½ times as sweet as sucrose, but at higher concentrations, the sweetening power of the two sugars was essentially the same. Relative sweetness may also depend on the age of the solution, the extent to which it has mutarotated (27), the temperature of the solution, and the presence of acids, salts, and other constituents. For example, in acidic beverages the sweetening power of fructose and sucrose was essentially the same as was also true in white cake, sugar cookies, and vanilla pudding (10, 16). The most rapidly growing sweetener segment of the food industry is high-fructose corn syrup (HFCS). This product is produced from corn starch and is less expensive than sucrose.

Sweeteners Other Than Sugars. Sweeteners other than sugars are available for those who wish to reduce calories or vulnerability to tooth decay through decreased plaque formation (15). Saccharin is a noncaloric substance that has been approved for use by the Food and Drug Administration (FDA), and was the only alternative sweetener for many years. As a sweetener, it is usually marketed as a sodium salt. Saccharin in this form is 300 times sweeter than sucrose. It should be noted that such ratings are based on concentration ranges for equisweet solutions, but from a sensory perspective, a difference of this magnitude would never be reported for any two concentrations. The ammonium salt of saccharin called sucramine is 700 times sweeter. Cyclamic acid and its calcium and sodium salts, known as cyclamates, are 30 times sweeter than sucrose, or ⅒ as sweet as saccharin. Cyclamates were withdrawn from the market because of the possible hazards to health in their unrestricted use, but their re-entry into the market place is pending reevaluation by the FDA. A widely used nonsugar sweetener currently is aspartame, a compound that combines the two amino acids aspartic acid and phenylalanine, marketed under several brand names including, NutraSweet or Equal. It is 180 to 200 times sweeter than sucrose, but is not stable to baking unless encapsulated. Individuals with an inborn error of metabolism, phenylketonuria, cannot tolerate phenylalanine. Another amino acid pair containing aspartic acid and alanine amide (common name alitame), which is pending approval by the FDA, holds promise because it is more than 2,000 times sweeter than sucrose and is heat stable. Alitame can be used in confectionery, heat pasteurized foods, and bakery products. A relatively new intense sweetener is Acesulfame K (K refers to the potassium salt). This compound is approximately 200 times sweeter than sucrose and is stable to heat. It has been approved by FDA as a table top sweetener and for use in chewing gum and dry beverage mixes and is marketed in the U.S. under the brand name Sunette.

Several intensely sweet compounds have not yet been approved for use in the U.S. Sucralose is chlorinated sucrose with a sweetness intensity of 600 times sucrose. It is heat stable and is under review by FDA for use in a wide variety of products including baked goods. Two high molecular weight proteins from east African plants, thaumatin and monellin, are several thousand times as sweet as sucrose. A compound known as sucrononic acid discovered in 1987 has a sweetness approximately 200,000 times that of sucrose (20).

Several reduced calorie, noncariogenic (does not promote dental carries) sweeteners are on the market. One such product is isomalt, which is produced from sucrose. Isomalt has ½ of the calories of sucrose. Synthetic sweeteners frequently leave a bitter aftertaste. As we better understand the relationships between structure of compounds and intensity of sweeteners, it should be possible to design intensely sweet compounds which have no bitter overtones.

Bitter. A number of different types of compounds taste *bitter.* Alkaloids such as caffeine and theobromine (formulas in Chapter 6), nicotine, quinine, and strychnine are bitter. Other bitter compounds include glycosides of phenolic compounds, such as naringin in grapefruit (0.75 percent of the peel), and a miscellaneous group of substances including bile salts and the salts of magnesium (magnesium sulfate is epsom salts), ammonium, and calcium. Receptors for bitter have less specific geometric requirements than do sweetener receptors. Only one polar group (AH or B) and a hydrophobic group is required. As hydrophobicity increases so does bitterness. Attempts to isolate receptor proteins for bitter (12) have failed.

Umami. Umami is the intrinsic taste of monosodium glutamate (MSG), 5′-guanylate (GMP), and 5′-inosinate (IMP), which is in addition to their function as flavor potentiators (discussed later in this chapter). It is a Japanese word meaning delicious or savory. MSG and salt stimulate different receptors (19); thus, the tastes are independent.

Taste Sensitivity

The concentration of a substance in saliva required to trigger the sensation of taste is generally much higher than the concentration of a substance in air required to provoke the sensation of odor. Tastes of different sapid (having taste) substances are not sensed with equal ease. Time and concentration influence taste sensitivity.

Time. It takes time to perceive a taste, time for maximum intensity to develop, and time for the taste to subside (Fig. 1-2). Salt on the tongue is sensed in a fraction of a second, whereas a bitter substance may require a full second after it makes contact with the tongue before it is sensed by the taste buds. Once perceived, bitter sensations tend to linger, however. Most bitter substances are only slightly soluble in water.

Time of exposure to a stimulus also influences perception of taste and odor. Constant exposure of a taste or odor receptor to a stimulus results in a decrease in frequency of nerve impulses sent to the brain. When this occurs, receptors are said to fatigue. Thus, a strong odor is not as unpleasant for one who works in such an environment as it is for a visitor. An individual can become accustomed to a taste or odor that seems too strong initially. Adaptation is a mechanism to protect the brain from redundant information (22). However, it is a disadvantage during sensory evaluation of a product. Adaptation can take several minutes, but ability of the receptors to recover and perceive the taste or odor again is even slower.

Concentration. The concentration needed to bring about a sensation varies with the substance in question. That concentration required for detection of a stimulus in a given medium is termed a detection threshold and for identification is known as a recognition threshold for that particular substance. Individuals differ in their sensitivity to sapid substances. The average detection threshold is 1 part in 200 by weight for sugar, and 1 part in 400 for salt, 1 part in 130,000 for hydrochloride acid (sour), and 1 part in 2,000,000 for quinine (bitter). The effect of temperature on taste sensation is discussed later in this chapter.

Taste Interactions

Because foods contain mixtures of substances that elicit all primary taste sensations, the possibility of their interacting has been investigated (14).

Subthreshold Taste Interactions. For some individuals at least, sodium chloride in subthreshold concentrations reduces the tartness of acid. The effect is greater with malic and tartaric than with acetic and citric acids. Subthreshold concentrations of salt also increase the apparent sweetness of sucrose and may reduce bitterness. These effects of salt may account for the preference of some individuals for a sprinkling of salt on grapefruit and for the fact that a small amount of salt improves the flavor of fruit pies. Conversely, acids in subthreshold concentration intensify the saltiness of sodium chloride, so it is easy to oversalt tart foods. Sugar in subthreshold concentration reduces the saltiness of sodium chloride, so a pinch of sugar may improve vegetable soup or chili that has been oversalted.

Suprathreshold Tastes Interactions. Generally mixtures of suprathreshold concentrations of sapid substances results in a suppression of the intensity of each component. At suprathreshold concentrations, sugar decreases the apparent sourness of acid, saltiness of salt, and bitterness of caffeine. A lemonade that is too tart or a potato salad that is too salty can be made acceptable by adding more sugar, and coffee with sugar is not so bitter as that without. Conversely, salt decreases the apparent sweetness of sucrose. However, acid increases the bitterness of caffeine. Acid has been reported to both increase and decrease the apparent sweetness of sucrose. These conflicting results may relate to the level of the test substance being studied above the threshold concentration (29).

Influence of Odor on Taste

There are mixed reports regarding an influence of odors on taste perception. However, effects on product acceptability are readily apparent. This may relate to expectations about the interplay of odor and taste.

Flavor Potentiators

Flavor potentiators are substances that add to or improve the flavor of foods, when present in subthreshold concentrations. They may achieve their effect by suppressing selected masking tastes (an action experimentally documented) or true enhancement of the taste intensity of another compound (still only theoretical). By either mechanism, examples of such effects are widely recognized. Table salt in subthreshold concentrations is a flavor potentiator. One potentiator that has been in use for some time is monosodium glutamate, the sodium salt of glutamic acid. It is odorless, but in dilute solutions it produces either a salty or a sweet sensation. Monosodium glutamate in a high protein food appears to balance and blend the taste complex and to produce a sensation described as mouth filling. The flavor appeal of mushrooms, alone or with other foods, may stem in part from their high glutamic acid content. The use of monosodium glutamate as a food additive has been approved by the FDA. The $5'$-nucleotides, disodium $5'$-inosinate and disodium $5'$-guanylate, are two flavor potentiators that were approved as food additives in 1962. They are more potent enhancers of meat flavor than monosodium glutamate. MSG and the sodium salt of $5'$-nucleotides act synergistically. Methyl xanthines including caffeine (coffee and colas), theophylline (tea), and theobromine (chocolate) potentiate acesulfame-K, salt, and quinine hydrochloride (31).

Differences in Ability to Smell and Taste

The ability of an individual to detect selected tastes and odors and the intensity of perception is in part genetically determined. For example, the ability to taste the compound, phenylthiocarbamide (PTC), and related compounds that contain the

$$\overset{\displaystyle N}{\underset{\displaystyle -N-C-}{\|}}$$

group, is an inherited Mendelian trait. Tasters experience an unpleasant, bitter sensation. Others are relatively insensitive to PTC. Approximately ¼ of the Caucasian U.S. population cannot taste PTC and are said to be taste blind. The difference between tasters and those who are taste blind may relate to a difference in lipid composition of taste receptor membranes. Bitter components absorb onto the lipid layer of membranes that causes changes in membrane potential (21).

Genetic control over the ability to smell has been studied less than taste. The ability to smell the steroid androstenone, a sexual stimulant in swine, is apparently genetically influenced (5). Approximately ⅓ of the population cannot smell the steroid, ⅓ do not describe it as unpleasant, and ⅓ find it strongly disagreeable. However, genetics interact with the environment in a complex manner because the ability to perceive this compound can be induced upon regular exposure. It is possible that ability to perceive other odors and tastes can improve with experience.

Taste and especially smell acuity are well maintained over the life cycle. Large population studies reveal measurable differences by age 60 but the practical significance of the changes has yet to be established. The average detection threshold for elderly persons was 5 times higher than for young people, ranging from 2.72 times higher for sweetness to 11.58 times higher for saltiness (30). Similarly, olfactory thresholds are 2 to 15 times higher in older individuals compared to young subjects. The elderly also lose their ability to discriminate among differences in intensity of a taste or smell. Differences often have to be twice as great to be detected in the elderly.

Mouthfeel

The way food feels in the mouth is termed mouthfeel. Even though color, odor, and taste are acceptable, a food may still be rejected on the basis of mouthfeel. When foods are acceptable, mouthfeel will play an important part in the sensory pleasure of eating. Nerve fibers from the trigeminal (fifth cranial) nerve (Fig. 2-9) are the means by which mouthfeel is sensed. Fibers from this nerve are sensitive to heat and cold, tactile sensations, and selected chemicals (e.g., capsaicin, piperine). These fibers mediate painful sensations as may result from excessive exposure to certain irritants.

Temperature

Hot and cold are sensations that contribute to the composite flavor of a food. Such expressions as hot chocolate, piping hot pizza, chilled salad, iced tea, ice cold watermelon, and frosted sherbet all attest to the importance of temperature in one's appreciation of food.

Temperature of food is an important aspect of quality. In addition, temperature influences the volatility of compounds that elicit odor and affects the ability of taste buds to pick up taste sensations. Flavor and juiciness of beef steaks were rated higher when served at 50°C (122°F) than at 22°C (room temperature) (26). Taste sensations are less intense as the temperature of a food is lowered below 20°C (68°F) and raised above 30°C (86°F). Variations within this temperature range apparently make little difference in the intensity of taste sensations. Thus really hot coffee is not so bitter as that which has cooled in the cup; iced coffee is not so bitter as that which is warm but not really hot. Melted ice cream tastes unpleasantly sweet, although in the frozen state it is acceptable. The diminished taste of cold foods may be due in part to the fact that molecules of substances that provoke sensations are more sluggish when cold, although no doubt very cold substances anesthetize the taste buds, too. Foods hot enough to burn the tongue diminish or destroy the sensitivity of the taste buds to taste stimuli. The cells in an injured taste bud are regenerated, but several days are required.

Tactile Sensations

Mouth, tongue, and jaws can assess the shape, form, and feel of a food, that is, its tactile character. This makes up a part of the sensory impressions associated with eating. One reason carbonated beverages are popular is that the bubbles of carbon dioxide are liberated from the liquid with enough force to stimulate the tactile nerve fibers in the mouth. A child's characterization of carbonated beverages as tickle water recognizes the tactile stimuli.

Astringency makes an important contribution to the tactile sensations of some foods. It is a dry, puckery sensation believed to be due to precipitation of proteins in the saliva and in the mucous membrane lining of the mouth, which deprives them of their lubricating character. Astringent substances may also constrict the ducts leading from the salivary glands to the mouth. The pleasure from drinking cider derives in part from its being mildly and pleasantly astringent. In contrast, unripe persimmons are excessively and unpleasantly astringent. In some instances the tactile properties of a food are part of a composite known as texture, to be discussed below.

Influence of Mouthfeel on Taste Sensations

The mouthfeel of a food influences its acceptability. In addition, it affects the taste of a food (16). The taste of a watery food is more pronounced than that of one that is thick or viscous. Flavorful tomato juice may seem less so when served molded as an aspic. Sweetness and tartness in an orange ice stand out more than they do in an orange sherbet made from the same mix, but with the addition of gelatin or egg white to the latter.

TEXTURE OF FOODS

The texture of a food as well as its color and flavor influences its acceptability, and in some cases, may be the deciding factor in a product's appeal. Structural components of foods confer on them a wide range of geometric and mechanical properties including appearance, feel, and resistance to flow, referred to collectively as texture. Which particular aspect of texture predominates varies from food to food.

The texture of foods can be experienced through our sense of touch. There are no unique physiological receptors for texture. Force may be required to deform a food, thus putting pressure on the teeth. Tactile sensations in the mouth make it possible to detect whether a food is grainy, brittle, soft, or chewy. Sight and sound also contribute to our perception of texture. We use sight to anticipate texture. Spaghetti sauce that is thick enough to stay on top of pasta rather than flow through it is judged to be of higher quality based solely on appearance. Sight plays a role in assessing the structure of foods like bread and cakes. The crunching sounds of snack foods are used to assess texture before and after they enter the mouth.

The perception of most aspects of texture requires the active manipulation and deformation of food as it is chewed, passed over the sensory receptors, and swallowed. Assessment of texture in mayonnaise begins with opening the jar and continues through inserting the knife into the jar, spreading the mayonnaise onto the bread, and eating the sandwich (8). Some foods are a combination of solids and fluids that can make texture characterization very complex. A macaroni and cheese entree consists of a solid component (macaroni) dispersed within a fluid matrix (cheese sauce). Both contribute to the overall texture.

Tactile Properties

Graininess is one aspect of texture. Texture in ice cream and fudge, which depends upon the size of the crystals and how they feel on the tongue, is characterized as coarse or smooth. Coarse-textured crystalline products are said to be grainy. In muffins, biscuits, yeast bread, and cake, texture depends upon the character of the crumb around the cells or holes. The latter are referred to as the grain of a baked product, assessed by sight as well as by mouthfeel. Lean meats are described as having fine or coarse texture, sometimes also called grain. In this instance the size of the structural units—muscle fibers—that make up the lean is involved.

The *brittleness* of food is another aspect of texture. Tissues in a raw vegetable or fruit are somewhat brittle or crunchy. The cells offer moderate resistance to fracturing by the pressure of the teeth. Brittleness of food is likely to involve receptors sensitive to the vibrations produced when cell walls are ruptured under pressure. The textural quality of a raw apple is generally more acceptable if the fruit is crisp, that is, is turgid with water. Raw celery and raw carrot sticks are valued for their crispness and crunchiness. An apple may be crisp but so may a cracker, the one because it has an abundance of water, the other because it has little. The crispness or crunchiness of toasted, flaked cereal, crisp cookies, and well-baked pie crust contributes to the pleasure derived from eating them. With all four, moisture reduces crunchiness. Crispness is judged to be primarily acoustic (39). However, it relates more to vibrations produced during chewing than to sound because the quality is also perceived when hearing is blocked.

With some foods *consistency* makes an important contribution to tactile sensations. Fondant, fudge, ices, and ice creams may be too hard, too soft, or desirably firm. Gravies, sauces, and syrups range in consistency from thick to thin. Temperature may affect markedly the consistency of foods. Cold syrup is thick, or viscous; hot syrup is much less viscous. Cheese, an elastic solid at room temperature, becomes liquid enough to flow or pour when heated. A food may be a slightly viscous fluid as is broth in which less tender meat or poultry has been cooked, or it may be an elastic solid as is the same broth after it has been refrigerated for some time. The consistency of a soft custard, besides being thick or thin, may be smooth or curdled; that of cream soups and gravies may be smooth or lumpy. Mashed potatoes may be mealy or pasty. Gels made with gelatin, with fruit pectin, or with eggs as in a baked custard may be rubbery or friable, weak or firm. Particles of cooked cereal should be separate and distinct but, improperly cooked, the cereal may be pasty. All of the characteristics enumerated above relate to consistency, some to texture.

Chewiness is one aspect of the mouthfeel of certain foods. A food that resists chewing stimulates receptors for pressure around the teeth. Muscles of the tongue and jaw are stimulated. Chewy foods may be tender, tough, or just moderately chewy. The tactile sensations derived from eating a raw apple harvested on a cool day in early fall contrast with those experienced when a cooked apple is eaten. Although the teeth must exert enough pressure to fracture cells in a raw apple, much less force is needed to cleave (separate) cells along the middle lamella (Chapter 27) in cooked tissue. Fruits, vegetables, and meats are cooked to make them tender. Tenderness in fruits and vegetables depends on how easily the cells separate; in meats ease of separation of the lean tissue is involved, but so is the elasticity of the separated constituents of the meat. Tenderness in pastry is another matter. It is assessed by the ease with which the crisp crust breaks and is termed friability or brittleness.

Influence of Texture on Flavor

The texture of food is also important because of its effect on flavor. Fudge candies made from two portions of the same syrup, one beaten while the syrup is still hot and the other after it has cooled, do not taste exactly alike because of differences in texture. Ice creams from the same mix, half of which is frozen so that the product is coarse and the other half fine, have different flavors.

An understanding of how color, odor, taste, and texture are perceived and what aspects of each determine acceptability of a food enables the food scientist to manipulate foods and ingredients for desired outcomes.

REFERENCES

1. Amerine, M. A., R. M. Pangborn, and E. B. Roessler. 1965. *Principles of the Sensory Evaluation of Food.* New York: Academic Press. Pp. 220–27. Vision and the appearance of foods.

2. Amoore, J. E., J. W. Johnston, Jr., and M. Rubin. 1964. "The stereochemical theory of odor." *Scientific American* 210(2):42–49. Size and shape of molecules as related to odor.

3. Avenet, P., and Lindemann, B. 1989. "Chemoreception of salt taste." In *Chemical Senses: Receptor Events and Transduction in Taste and Olfaction.* Vol. 1. Brand, J. G., J. H. Teeter, R. H. Cagan, and M. R. Kare, eds. New York: Marcel Dekker. Pp. 171–82. Mechanism of salt transduction.

4. Bartoshuk, L. M. 1991. "Sweetness: History, preference, and genetic variability." *Food Technology* 45(11):108–13. Pleasantness of sweetness involves endogenous opiates.

5. Beauchamp, G. K. 1990. "Research in chemosensation related to flavor and fragrance perception." *Food Technology* 44(1):98–100. Genetic differences and the neuroscience of taste and smell.

6. Birch, G. G. 1991. "Chemical and biochemical mechanisms of sweetness." *Food Technology* 45(11):114–20. Mechanism of sweet taste.

7. Boekhoff, I., S. Schleicher, J. Strotmann, and H. Breer. 1992. "Odor-induced phosphorylation of olfactory cilia proteins." *Proceedings of the National Academy of Science* USA 89:11983–987. Uncoupling of transduction cascade due to phosphorylation of olfactory cilia proteins ends odor signals.

8. Borwankar, R. P. 1992. "Food texture and rheology: A tutorial review." In *Rheology of Foods,* R. Borwankar and C. F. Shoemaker, eds. New York: Elsevier Applied Sciences. Pp. 1–16. Description of rheology vs. texture.

9. Buck, L., and R. Axel. 1991. "A novel multigene family may encode odorant receptors: A molecular basis for odor recognition." *Cell* 65:175–87. Describes research on genes which code for odor receptors.

10. Cardello, A. V., D. Hunt, and B. Mann. 1979. "Relative sweetness of fructose and sucrose in model solutions, lemon beverage and white cake." *Journal Food Science* 4:748–51. Effects of concentration and acidity.

11. Daniel, J. R., and R. L. Whistler. 1982. "Sweetness-structure correlation in carbohydrates." *Cereal Chemistry* 59:92–95. The theory of molecular connectivity for sweetness.

12. Dastoli, F. R., D. V. Lopiekes, and A. R. Doig. 1986. "Bitter-sensitive protein from porcine taste buds." *Nature* 218:884–85. Attempt to isolate bitter receptors.

13. Ennis, D. M. 1991. "Modeling the sweet taste of mixtures." *Food Technology* 45(11):140–45. Modeling sweet-receptor interactions.

14. Fabian, F. W., and H. B. Blum. 1943. "Relative taste potency of some basic food constituents and their competitive and compensatory action." *Food Research* 8:179–93. Effects of subthreshold concentrations of taste substances on discernment of others.

15. Gisse, J. H. 1993. "Alternative sweeteners and bulking agents." *Journal of Food Technology* 47:114–26. A Review.

16. Hardy, S. K., C. P. Brennand, and B. W. Wyse. 1979. "Fructose: Comparison with sucrose as sweetener in four products." *Journal of the American Dietetic Association* 74:41–46. Lemonade, sugar cookies, white cake, and vanilla pudding.

17. Kier, L. B. 1972. A molecular theory of sweet taste. *Journal of Pharmaceutical Science* 61:1394–397. Proposal for X site for intense sweetness.

18. Kumazawa, T., T. Nomura, and K. Kurihara. 1988. "Liposomes as a model for taste cells: Receptor sites for bitter substances including $N - C = S$ substances and mechanism of membranes potential changes." *Biochemistry* 27:1239–44. Explanation for genetic differences in ability to taste PTC.

19. Kurihara, K., M. Kashiwayanagi, T. Nomura, K. Yoshii, and T. Kumazawa. 1989. "Chemical stimulus dissemination by specific and nonspecific receptor mechanisms and their transduction sequences." Brandt, J. G., J. H. Teeter, R. H. Cagan, and M. R. Kare, eds. In *Chemical Senses: Receptor Events and Transduction in Taste and Olfaction.* Vol. 1. New York: Marcel Dekker. Pp. 57–59. A discussion of umami taste.

20. Lindley, M. G. 1991. "From basic research on sweetness to the development of sweetness." *Food Technology* 45(11):134–38. Development of intensely sweet compounds.

21. Lynch, N. M. 1987. "In search of the salty taste." *Food Technology* 41(11):82–86. Mechanisms of salt perception.

22. Mahoney, M. O. 1986. "Fatigue and adaptation effects." *Food Technology* 40(11):67. Presents biological role for adaptation.

23. McLaughlin, S., and K. F. Margolskee. 1994. "The sense of taste." *American Scientist* 82:538–45. A review.

24. Mori, K., and Yoshikara, Y. 1995. "Molecular recognition and olfactory processing in the mammalian olfactory system." *Progress in Neurobiology* 45:585–619. Review of odor sensing.

25. Nathans, J., D. Thomas, and D. S. Hogness. 1986. "Molecular genetics of human color vision: The genes encoding blue, green, and red pigments." *Science* 232:193–202. Three classes of cones.

26. Olson, D. G., F. Caporaso, and P. W. Mandigo. 1980. "Effects of serving temperature on sensory evaluation of beef steaks from different muscles and carcass maturities." *Journal of Food Science* 45:627–31. The effect of temperature on flavor of beef.

27. Pangborn, R. M., and S. C. Gee. 1961. "Relative sweetness of α- and β-forms of selected sugars." *Nature* 191:810–11. Effects of mutarotation.

28. "Photographic Essay: The Science of Color." *Life* 17(1):39–50. July 3, 1944. Vision and the nature of color, profusely illustrated.

29. Pilgrim, F. J. 1961. "Interaction of suprathreshold taste stimuli." In *Physiological and Behavioral Aspects of Taste.* Morley R. Kare and B. P. Halpern, eds. Chicago: University of Chicago Press. Pp. 66–78. Effects of the level of taste stimuli on the perception of others.

30. Schiffman, S. S. 1991. "Taste and smell losses with age." *Contemporary Nutrition* 16 No. 2. The influence of age on ability to taste and smell.

31. Schiffman, S. S., 1987. "Recent developments in taste enhancement." *Food Technology* 41(6):72–73, 124. Flavor enhancers.

32. Schiffman, S. S., and R. P. Erickson. 1980. "The issue of primary tastes versus a taste continuum." *Neuroscience and Biobehavioral Reviews* 4:109–17. An argument for a taste continuum rather than four primary tastes.

33. Schutz, H. G., and F. J. Pilgrim. 1957. "Sweetness of various compounds and its measurements." *Food Research* 22:206–13. Sugars compared.

34. Scott, J. W., L. M. Davis, D. Shannon, and C. Kaplain. 1996. "Relation of chemical structure to spatial distribution of sensory responses in rat olfactory epithelium." *Journal of Neurophysiology* 75:2036–49. Spatial Nature of Odor Theory.

35. Shallenberger, R. S. 1996. "The AH, B glucophore and general taste chemistry." *Food Chemistry* 56:209–14. Electrostatic mechanisms for tastes.

36. Smith, C. V., and C. A. Ossebaard. "The perception of saltiness is eliminated by adaptation to NaCl but not by alimoride treatment." Association of Chemoreception Sciences, 18th Annual Meeting. 4/17–21/96. Sarasota, FL.

37. Tateba, H., and S. Mihara. 1990. Structure-odor relationships in monoterpenelactones. *Agricultural and Biological Chemistry* 54:2271–76. AH, B, X theory for detecting caramel odors.

38. Tinti, J. -M., and C. Nofre. 1991. "Why does a sweetener taste sweet?" In *Sweetness Discovery, Molecular Design, and Chemoreception.* Walters, D. E., F. T. Orthoefer,

and G. E. DuBois, eds. ACS Symposium Series 450. American Chemical Society. Washington, D.C. Pp. 206–13. New model for sweet taste with eight recognition sites.

39. Vickers, Z. 1991. "Sound perception and food quality." *Journal of Food Quality* 14:87–96. A review of crispiness.

40. Yamaguchi, S., T. Yoshikawa, S. Ikeda, and T. Ninomiya. 1970. "Studies on the taste of some sweet substances: Measurement of the relative sweetness." *Agr. Biol. Chem.* 34:181–86. Three simple sugars, three sugar alcohols, and sucrose compared.

Measures and Weights

3

Food quality and its importance are emphasized in Chapters 1 and 2. Many factors contribute to the quality of foods. Whether the object is quality control on a commercial scale or duplication of a single product from a cherished recipe, the use of exact quantities of ingredients is critical. This chapter is concerned with the quantitative aspects of quality control. Exact quantities can be obtained on the basis of either weight or volume. Most ingredients are weighed in scientific work and in the formulation of commercial products. Volume is used as a measure of quantity in household procedures.

TRADITIONAL AND METRIC MEASURING SYSTEMS

The system of weights and measures traditionally used in the United States was borrowed from the British. The metric system prevails worldwide; and the United States is gradually converting to the metric system. Many foods continue to be marketed in the traditional way, with the metric equivalent indicated on the label.

Any system used to denote quantity requires standardized units. In the traditional (American) system, basic units to measure volume, weight (mass), and distance are the gallon, pound, and yard, respectively. Corresponding units in the metric system are the liter, kilogram, and meter. Other metric units derived from these basic ones differ from each other by factor(s) of 10 (Table 3-1). An Angström (Å), not shown, is 0.1 nanometer or 10^{-10} meter. A prefix with the name of a basic unit eliminates the need to use all the zeroes, and a symbol instead of the prefix makes recording quantities simpler still. The relationship between different measures in the metric system is straight forward. For example, one liter (1) is $10 \times 10 \times 10$ milliliters (ml) and one milliliter is $10 \times 10 \times 10$ microliters (μl). Measurements for volume in the traditional system are the gallon and its fractions (the quart, pint, and fluid ounce), peck, and bushel. Few could say offhand the relationship between a gallon and a bushel (231 cubic inches versus 2,150.4 cubic inches).

Because the two systems are used concurrently, knowledge of their numeric equivalents is desirable. Quantities frequently used are listed in Table 3-2.

An individual who works with foods should be familiar with both metric and traditional units of measurement. Metric measurements are used in experimental work, so knowledge of this system is essential for reading and comprehending scientific literature. Ingredients for a product such as a cake mix are combined on the basis of weight, standard practice in the food industry, but the packages of such products for the consumer give information in household units of volume. Household units are used by dietitians when they

TABLE 3-1
Metric Measures

Quantity		Prefix	Symbol
0.000,000,001	10^{-9}	nano	n
0.000,001	10^{-6}	micro	μ
0.001	10^{-3}	milli	m
0.01	10^{-2}	centi	c
0.1	10^{-1}	deci	d
1.0			
10	10^{1}	deka	da
100	10^{2}	hecto	h
1,000	10^{3}	kilo	k
1,000,000	10^{6}	mega	M
1,000,000,000	10^{9}	giga	G

AHEA *Handbook for Metric Usage*. Washington, D.C.: American Home Economics Association.

TABLE 3-2
Traditional Measurements and Metric Equivalents

2.2 lb = 1 kg	1 c = 236.6 ml
1 lb = 454 g	1 fl oz = 29.6 ml
1 oz = 28.35 g	1 Tbsp = 14.8 ml
1 gal = 3.79 l	1 tsp = 4.9 ml
1 qt = 946 ml	

AHEA 1993. *Handbook of Food Preparation*. Washington, D.C.: American Home Economics Association. Pp. 46–47.

counsel patients and are still used in institutional food service. This dual system will continue until conversion to the metric system is complete.

Weighing ingredients has advantages over measuring them, provided that balance or scale is accurate and sufficiently sensitive for the quantity being weighed (6). Weighing is the only practical way to handle large quantities of dry ingredients. Even for small amounts of an ingredient such as flour, weighing is more precise and it eliminates having to sift the flour. In many instances, weighing is faster than measuring. However, practically all recipes give measures rather than weights, so ingredients are combined on the basis of the volume of household measuring utensils. Duplicate volumes of the same ingredient do not always weigh the same. To obtain the specified amount of an ingredient by measuring it, two conditions are essential—accurate measuring utensils and correct use of them.

MEASURING UTENSILS

Capacities

Traditional

One set of household measuring utensils that has been in use for many years is based on the standard quart measure (3). In this system a standard one cup measure holds ¼ of a quart, or 236.6 milliliters. The volume is 8 fluid ounces, English measure. Each tablespoon holds ⅟₁₆ of a cup, so one fluid ounce equals two tablespoons. Most measuring cups are subdivided into the following fractions of a cup: ¾, ⅔, ½, ⅓, ¼. In addition to the cup measure with its subdivisions, metal and plastic fractional measures with capacities of 1, ½, ⅓, and ¼ cup are available in sets. For quantities less than ¼ cup, measuring spoons should be used. One tablespoon, one teaspoon, with a capacity ⅓ that of the tablespoon, and two fractional teaspoons, ½, and ¼, comprise a set of measuring spoons.

Metric

Measurements based on the metric, also called the SI, system are available. Volumes of the measuring utensils in this system are 1,000, 500, 250, 125, 50, 25, 5, 2, and 1 milliliters (2). The 250-milliliter and the 125-milliliter metric measures have capacities approximately equal to the 1 cup and the ½ cup measures, respectively; and the 15-milliliter and the 5-milliliter measures the volumes of the tablespoon and teaspoon, respectively. Utensils for measuring liquids are divided in 25 ml increments. Figure 3-1 shows common measuring devices.

Tolerances

Some years ago the American Home Economics Association (AHEA), in cooperation with the American Standards Association, formulated a set of standards and proposed tolerances for household measuring utensils (3). The capacity of a standard measuring cup is 8 fluid ounces or 236.6 milliliters. A deviation of five percent from this precise volume is considered an allowable, or tolerable, amount. For the 1-cup measure, this tolerance amounts to 11.8 milliliters. The capacity of a standard tablespoon is 14.8 milliliters and of a standard teaspoon 4.9 milliliters, with tolerances of ¾ and ¼ of a milliliter, respectively. With a five percent tolerance, the 250 milliliter metric measure could range in volume from 237.5 to 262.5 milliliter. Insisting on greater precision would add to the cost of manufacture of the measuring utensils, whereas a deviation greater than five percent could make an appreciable difference in the proportion of ingredients and in the quality of the finished product.

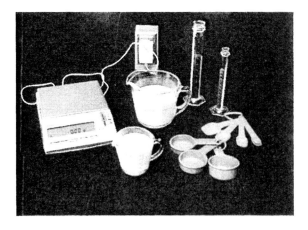

Figure 3-1. Household devices for measuring volume and more precise graduated cylinders and electronic balance of the laboratory. (Photo by John Underwood.)

Accuracy

Unfortunately, not all measuring utensils on the market meet this minimum tolerance. Two items—tap water and a graduated cylinder—suffice to test the accuracy of a measuring utensil. The capacity of the graduated cylinder should be equal to or slightly greater than the capacity of the measuring utensil being tested. To check the accuracy of a measuring utensil, it is filled with water to the mark which indicates the fraction of the cup measure being tested. This water is then transferred, without spilling, to a graduated cylinder and the volume read in milliliters. Two precautions should be observed. Both the measuring utensil and the graduated cylinder should be on a level surface, and the eye should be level with the water level at the bottom of the meniscus (the lowest level of the surface of the liquid). An alternate way to test the accuracy of a measuring utensil is illustrated as follows: to check a ¼-cup measure, for example, it is filled level-full four times and the liquid is transferred to the 1-cup measure or filled twice to see if the water level comes to the ½-cup mark. If it does not, then one of the measures is inaccurate, assuming of course, that the ¼-cup measure was filled level-full and no water was spilled in the transfer.

A word of caution. Suppose on three successive tries a metric measure that holds exactly 250 milliliter was filled with liquid. On all three occasions the volume of the liquid remeasured in a graduated cylinder was 230 milliliter. The precision of the activity would be remarkable, to say the least, but the accuracy leaves something to be desired. Filling a teaspoon three times instead of a tablespoon once or a 5 milliliter measure three times instead of a 15 milliliter once gives three times the chance for error in measuring technique.

MEASURING TECHNIQUES

Accurate measuring utensils are essential for obtaining exact quantities of ingredients, but the method used to measure an ingredient is as important as the accuracy of the measuring utensils (4). Method of measuring involves two considerations: choosing the right utensil for the particular ingredient, and using the correct technique for handling each.

Liquids

Liquid ingredients are the easiest to measure. Causes of inaccurate measurement are over- or underfilling or insufficient drainage of the measuring utensil. A measure with subdivisions and with headspace above the top mark is recommended for liquids that flow readily. The smallest measuring utensil that will hold the volume desired should be used. For example, a ½-cup of liquid should be measured in a cup measure—not a pint—with subdivisions.

With a glass measure it is possible to read the level of the liquid at the bottom of the meniscus. A measure with a pouring spout minimizes the chances of spilling liquid when it is transferred to the mixing or cooking utensil. Fractional measures are satisfactory for measuring liquids that are sufficiently viscous, such as molasses and honey. Surplus liquid can be removed from the top of the measure by rapidly moving a spatula with a straight edge across the top of the utensil. A rubber scraper should be used to remove thick liquids from the measuring utensil.

Fats

Fats are more accurately weighed than measured. When measured, a fractional measuring utensil should be used. It is practically impossible to level ½ cup of fat in a 1-cup measure. Fat at room temperature is easier to measure than fat that is cold and hard. There is less chance of trapping air when it is packed in the utensil, and it is easier to level the fat in the measure when it is soft. A flexible rubber scraper may be used to transfer the fat from the measuring utensil. Butter or margarine marketed in ¼-pound units need not be measured. One pound measures two cups. If a recipe calls for ½-cup of butter, a ¼-pound stick may be used without measuring. A cup of whipped butter or margarine weighs only ⅔ of the regular form (1).

Sugar

Granulated sugar and certain other dry ingredients that do not pack appreciably may be measured in fractional measures or in a 1-cup measure with subdivisions. No special precautions need be taken in measuring granulated sugar. Coarser crystals do not pack as well as fine ones, so the weight of a cup filled with coarse sugar may be less than standard weight.

Unlike granulated sugar, crystals of brown sugar have a film of syrup on the surface that prevents them from sliding past each other freely. Brown sugar should be packed into the measure firmly enough to hold the shape of the utensil when it is turned out. Special free-flowing brown sugar is measured like granulated sugar. A cup of this special sugar weighs ¼ less than a cup of regular brown sugar (1). Much of the syrup found on the surface of particles of conventional brown sugar is held within the spongelike pores of free-flowing brown sugar. This reduces stickiness of the surface. Confectioner's sugar has a tendency both to lump and to pack. Lumps should be rolled or mashed and the sugar sifted and measured as for flour.

Flour

Measuring flour presents more problems than measuring liquids or fats. Particles of flour vary widely in shape and particularly in size (see Fig. 11-4). As a result, flour shows a marked tendency to pack (5). For this reason, there is no absolute value for the weight of a cup of flour. However, most recipes assume a certain weight. The object in measuring flour is to manipulate it so the filled measure holds the standard weight, and the technique should be such that variation in weight with subsequent measurings is minimal. The former is a matter of accuracy and the latter of precision.

Flour is best measured in a fractional measure. There are two commonly accepted techniques for measuring flour. In one, small portions of flour (not more than two or three cups) are sifted. Then this loosened, aerated flour is transferred to the measuring utensil that is filled to overflowing without packing the flour. The surplus is removed from the measure with the straight edge of a spatula.

A second technique calls for sifting the flour directly into the measure until the flour overflows slightly. Then the excess flour is removed with the straight edge of a spatula. Sifting the flour directly into the measure has the advantage of taking less time and fewer operations and so is more efficient. The weight of a cup of flour so filled varies little with repeated fillings. However, it may average one teaspoon less than a cup of flour measured by sifting the flour and then transferring it to the measure.

For certain recipes where an exact amount of flour is unnecessary, stirring the flour in the container before measuring may be sufficient (4, 5). Instantized flour has fairly large particles of uniform size (see Chapter 11). Because this flour does not pack, measuring it presents no special problem, and sifting it before it is measured is unnecessary.

Whole wheat flour and cornmeal should be stirred before being spooned into the measuring utensil. Flours differ in density: a cup of sifted cake flour weighs 96 grams, and the value for pastry flour is 99 grams per cup (1). The value of 116 grams per cup of all-purpose flour reflects its greater density.

Miscellaneous Ingredients

Occasionally a product may require an ingredient such as salt, baking powder, or spice in an amount less than the capacity of any measuring utensil. To measure ⅛ teaspoon of a dry ingredient, the procedure is to fill the ¼-teaspoon measure level-full and then divide the ingredient in half, removing the unwanted portion. For ¹⁄₁₆ teaspoon the process is repeated on the ⅛ teaspoon remaining in the spoon. Baking powder, soda, and spices should be aerated by stirring before they are measured.

If precautions given above are observed, measuring ingredients by volume can give reasonably accurate results. However, weighing ingredients can be more precise, and it is the preferred technique where quality control is critical.

The average weight of one cup of a number of foods is given in the AHEA *Handbook of Food Preparation* (1). Equivalent quantities of frequently used ingredients are given in Table 3-3.

TABLE 3-3
Equivalent Quantities of Frequently Used Ingredients (based on one cup, unless otherwise specified)

Cereals		*Fats*	
Cornmeal, yellow	153 g	Butter	224 g
Oats, rolled	71 g	Hydrogenated fat	204 g
Rice, long grain white	181 g	Margarine, stick	227 g
		Lard	204 g
Dairy products		Salad oil	218 g
Cream, light	240 g	*Flour*	
Cream, whipping, heavy	236 g		
Cheese, grated cheddar	113 g	All purpose	
Half and half	242 g	Sifted	116 g
Milk, condensed	306 g	Stirred	125 g
Milk, evaporated	252 g	Cake	
Milk, fluid	242 g	Sifted	96 g
Milk, nonfat instant	75 g	Stirred	110 g
		Whole wheat, stirred	133 g
Eggs		*Gelatin*	
Whole, 1 large	45 ml		
White, 1 large	32 ml	Flavored, 1 Tbsp	12 g
Yolk, 1 large	16 ml	Granular, 1 Tbsp	7 g
Dried, sifted	89 g	Sugar-free, 1 Tbsp	5 g

(continued)

TABLE 3-3   *(Continued)*
Equivalent Quantities of Frequently Used Ingredients (based on one cup, unless otherwise specified)

Leavening agents			
Baking soda, 1 tsp	4.0 g		
Cream of tartar, 1 tsp	3.1 g		
Baking powder, 1 tsp	3.8 g		
Yeast			
Active dry, 1 tsp	2.3 g		
Compressed, 1 tsp	4.2 g		

Pasta	
Macaroni, 1-inch pieces	123 g
Spaghetti, 2-inch pieces	94 g

Sweeteners	
Corn syrup	329 g
Molasses	309 g
Sugar, brown packed	201 g

Sugar, confectioners, 1 Tbsp	8 g
Sifted	96 g
Stirred	122 g
Sugar, white granulated	201 g

Thickeners	
Cornstarch, 1 Tbsp	8 g
Flour, 1 Tbsp	8 g
Tapioca, 1 Tbsp	9.5 g

Miscellaneous	
Aspartame, 1 pkt	1 g
Chocolate, 1 oz	28 g
Cocoa, 1 Tbsp	6.4 g
Saccharine, 1 pkt	1 g
Salt, 1 tsp	6 g
Tea, 1 tsp	1.5 g

Source: AHEA 1993. *Handbook of Food Preparation.* Washington, D.C.: American Home Economics Association.
Pp. 175, 177, 180–83, 195–99.

REFERENCES

1. AHEA 1993. *Handbook of Food Preparation.* Washington, D.C.: American Home Economics Association. Pp. 46–47: Equivalent conventional and metric units of measure. 175, 177, 180–83, 195–99: equivalent conventional and metric measures of ingredients.

2. AHEA 1977. *Handbook for Metric Usage.* Washington, D.C.: American Home Economics Association. Pp. 10–11.

3. ASA 1963. *American Standard dimensions, tolerances, and terminology for home cooking and baking utensils.* ASA Z 61.1-1963. New York: American Standards Association, Inc.

4. Arlin, M. L., M. M. Nielson, and F. T. Hall. 1964. "The effect of different methods of flour measurement on the quality of plain two-egg cakes." *Journal of Home Economics* 56:399–401. Sifted *vs.* unsifted flour compared.

5. Matthews, R. H., and O. M. Batchelder. 1963. "Sifted *vs.* unsifted flour: Weight variations and results of some baking tests." *Journal of Home Economics* 55:123–24. Effects on muffins and cakes.

6. Miller, B. S., and H. B. Trimbo. 1972. "Use of metric measures in food preparation." *Journal of Home Economics* 64(2):20–25. Advantages of the metric system and of weighing over measuring.

Heating and Cooling Foods and Food Safety 4

Energy, either its application or its removal, is involved at many points in the preparation of foods. For example, heat is utilized to remove excess moisture from frostings and jellies, to alter the texture and flavor of potatoes, to decrease the bulk of a vegetable such as spinach, to inactivate microorganisms in or on the surface of foods, to alter consistency and form the texture of breads, to change the fluid mixture for a custard into a gel, and to improve the flavor and alter the consistency of cereals. In other instances, removal of heat rather than its application is desired. Many foods remain safe to eat and palatable for a longer time if they are kept cold. For example, refrigeration reduces the rate at which microorganisms present in milk or on the surface of meats multiply; it retards the rate at which butter, salad oil, nuts, and other fat-rich foods become rancid; it retards ripening of fruits and senescence of fresh vegetables; and it can convert a mixture for a gelatin salad or dessert into a gel. Cooled to still lower temperature and maintained in the frozen state, meats and fruits and vegetables can be preserved for periods varying from three months to a year.

Instances in which the input or removal of energy and the achievement or maintenance of a certain temperature are critical in the preparation of individual foods are given in the chapters in which the information is relevant. General principles of heating and cooling foods and the effects of heat and cold on the safety of foods are emphasized in this chapter.

HEATING FOODS

Energy is required to heat foods. When gas is used, this energy is obtained from combustion of the fuel. Resistance to the passage of an electric current by the coils of the heating element is the source of heat in an electric range. In either case the energy came orginally from the sun. Microwaves generate heat (molecular motion) in the food itself.

Intensity of Heat

Intensity of heat, that is, the extent to which energy has set molecules into motion, is measured in degrees by a thermometer. Two scales are in common use, the Celsius (or centigrade) and the Fahrenheit.

A third scale, the Kelvin (or absolute), is used for scientific purposes. The relations between °K and °C are:

°K	°C
0	−273
273	0
373	100

A listing of commonly used temperatures together with their descriptive designations follows:

TABLE 4-1
Commonly Used Temperatures and Their Descriptive Designations

TEMPERATURE		VERBAL DESIGNATION
°C	°F	
−18	0	Maximum temperature for holding frozen foods
0	32	Freezing point (pure water)
4	40	Refrigerator temperature
20–25±	68–77±	Room temperature
37	98.6	Lukewarm (body temperature)
65±	149±	Scalding (liquid)
85	185	Simmering (water)
100	212	Boiling (water)
116	240	Steam pressure 10 pounds per square inch (psi) or 69 Kilopascals (kPa)
121	250	Steam pressure 15 psi or 103 kPa

A table that gives conversions of temperatures from −29° to 309°C (−20° to 588°F) is available (1).

Room temperature specified in an experiment may vary from 20° to 25°C (68° to 77°F). The specific temperature should be and usually is given. Scalding temperature given is approximate only because scalding temperature varies with the material. Different temperatures are required for water to scald peaches or tomatoes to make the skins slip, to scald chickens and turkeys to loosen feathers, to scald dishes to inactivate microorganisms on the surface, and to scald milk to make custard with improved flavor, or to make yeast bread dough of better handling property and baked products of better quality.

Water boils at 100°C (212°F) at sea level and under standard atmospheric conditions. The boiling point decreases 1.1°C (1.9°F) for each 1,000 feet (305 meters) above sea level. Under steam pressure of 10 psi (69 kPa), water boils at 116°C (240°F). To maintain the same temperature at higher elevations requires an increase in steam pressure of 0.5 psi (3.4–3.5 kPa) for each 1,000 feet (305 meters).

Quantitative Aspects

When a substance is heated, the amount of energy involved depends not only upon how agitated the molecules of a substance are (the temperature), but also upon the number of molecules in motion. In two containers of boiling water, one containing one cup and the other one gallon, the intensity of heat is the same. However, the amount of energy needed to bring the gallon of water to a boil is greater. Two units have been used to express the amount of energy. One is the calorie, which is the amount of energy expended in raising the temperature of one gram of water 1° Celsius (from 14.5°C to 15.5°C) or the large calorie, which is the energy needed to raise the temperature of one kilogram of water 1° Celsius. This kilocalorie is the unit used to express the energy value of foods. The second unit is the British thermal unit, abbreviated Btu, which is the amount of energy required to raise the temperature of one pound of water from 63°F to 64°F. This unit is commonly used to specify the heating potential of fuels. Both the calorie and the British thermal unit are replaced in the SI system (International System of Units) by the joule, or more commonly the kilojoule, abbreviated kJ (2). One kilocalorie equals 4.185 kilojoules.

Energy Transfer

Foods are cooked on conventional ranges powered by gas or electricity or, in microwave ovens. In the latter, energy in the form of high-frequency radio waves (microwaves) is used to heat the food. A discussion of the way heating is accomplished and the factors that affect the transfer of energy is pertinent. Energy gets from the source to the food that is heated by radiation, conduction, or by convection currents (5). More than one method of transfer is involved in most instances.

Radiation

Units of energy, known as quanta, which travel as electromagnetic waves or rays, are one source of heat. These infrared rays are longer than those of visible light, but shorter than radio and sound waves (See Fig. 2-1). When energy is transmitted by radiation, it goes directly from the source to the object heated, unassisted by an intervening medium. In fact, an intervening surface only reduces the amount of energy transmitted by radiation. Energy that reaches the earth from the sun does so by radiation. Radiation is a rapid method of heating, for radiant energy travels with the speed of light (186,000 miles per second). Although the rays of energy travel in a straight line, they do fan out from the source. The farther an object from the source of radiant energy, the fewer rays it receives and the less it is heated. Sources of radiant energy used in cooking include the broiler on a range, the toaster, and the glowing coals of a campfire. Once coils on the surface of an electric range are hot enough to glow, they radiate energy as does a gas flame.

Conduction

When heat travels by conduction, kinetic energy or agitation is transmitted from molecule to molecule (5). A cold object is heated by conduction only when in direct contact with a source of heat. Heat is transmitted to a saucepan by conduction where the pan contacts the coils of an electric unit. Heat moves from the bowl of a spoon resting in boiling liquid to the end of the handle by conduction. Conduction is a comparatively slow method of transferring heat, although some materials are better conductors than others. Metals are good conductors. Water conducts heat more rapidly than air, which is a poor conductor (5, 27). Foods cook even more rapidly in hot fat because fat can be heated to temperatures far above that of boiling water.

A third method of energy transfer is by convection currents. The energy that does the heating arrives via air, water, or liquid fat. When a gas or a liquid is heated, it becomes less dense than its cold counterpart. Hot gases and liquids rise and cold ones flow downward to where the heat is applied. This sets up a flow from bottom to top and then from top to bottom. This circular flow of convection currents tends to keep the temperature somewhat uniform throughout the medium. Although currents of hot water, hot fat, and hot air can circulate rapidly to the object being heated, the energy must pass from the hot medium to the object by conduction. Where convection currents are involved, heating is accomplished more rapidly than by conduction alone, but much slower than by radiation. Convection currents are involved in cooking food in water, in deep fat frying, and in baking in an oven.

Heating Foods with a Conventional Range

The source of the energy, the utensil used, and the nature of the food influence the transfer of energy when a food is heated. In most instances the transfer of energy is complicated.

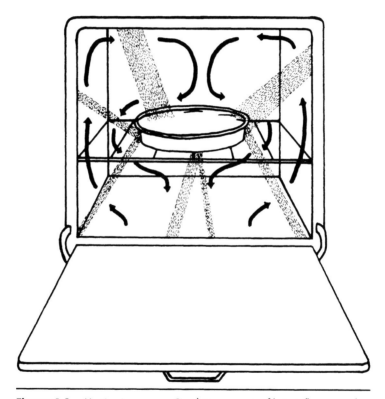

Figure 4-1. Heating in an oven. Circulating currents of hot air flow around the container of food. Energy that reaches the food in this way passes from the hot air through the utensil and into the food by conduction. Electromagnetic waves of radiant energy that pass the lining of the oven from the source (gas flame or glowing electric coils) go directly to the utensil or its contents. Part of this energy is deflected by the utensil; the remainder reaches the food and heats it. Utensils differ in their ability to transmit radiant energy.

In an Oven

The heating unit in an oven is placed at the bottom for a good reason. As the lower layer of air is heated, it becomes less dense and rises, whereas the colder, heavier air flows to the bottom of the oven where it, in turn, is heated (Fig. 4-1). This sets up circulating currents of air in the oven that tend to make the temperature uniform. Heating is more uniform in the center of an oven. Temperatures tend to be hotter at the top and bottom of an oven and at the back and sides. When more than one pan is placed in an oven, pans should be staggered so that the circulation of air and passage of radiant energy will not be impeded (Fig. 4-2).

A high proportion (⅔ to ¾) of the energy available in an oven is due to radiant energy, the remainder to currents of hot air. The material of a baking utensil affects how this energy is transmitted to food. Metal utensils transmit energy from currents of hot air by conduction, as do metal skewers in a baked potato or a roast. Radiant energy is a different matter. Metal utensils with dark or dull surface are emissive, that is, they absorb radiant energy and emit it to food by conduction. Utensils made of shiny metal reflect rather than absorb radiant energy. The emissivity of a utensil is more important than is its conductivity for efficient heating in an oven. A utensil that heats food too rapidly may allow food to brown excessively or unevenly. A dark or dull baking sheet may not be the best choice for thin, rich cookies or pastry. A glass utensil is emissive, absorbing most of the radiant energy that strikes it. Adjustment of the baking temperature can compensate in part for differences in the efficiency of baking utensils, as is done for glass, although there is still a residual pan effect.

A conventional electric oven with one high-output bottom heating element and a lining that absorbs radiant energy and the use of a reflective baking utensil so that food heats more uniformly is not an energy-efficient arrangement. An experimentally designed oven with two low-output heating elements, one at the top and the other at the bottom of the oven and a reflective lining used with an emissive utensil increased the heating efficiency 75 percent (20).

Figure 4-2. When a single baking utensil is used in an oven, the rack should be adjusted so that the utensil is centered in the oven. If more than one utensil is used, racks and utensils should be positioned to facilitate circulation of hot air and to provide for uniform exposure to radiant energy. (Courtesy of Robertshaw Controls, New Stanton Division, Youngwood, Pennsylvania.)

Forced convection ovens and forced convection–microwave oven combinations are available. Foods heat somewhat faster in a forced convection oven because convection currents that arise due to differences in density of air are forced to cycle faster. A reduction of baking time of a few minutes up to almost ⅓ of the total may be possible, depending on the size of the product. Lowering the setting on the thermostat 15°C (25°F) or more may prevent excessive browning of the surface and allow time for underheated centers to finish cooking. Forced convection ovens are most useful in institutional settings.

On a Surface Unit

Heat from a gas burner reaches a container by means of convection currents of hot air formed by radiation from the flame of the burning gas. A utensil used on a gas burner should be able not only to transmit by conduction the heat brought to it by the convection currents of hot air, but also to transmit radiant energy. On a surface electric unit where part of the heat is transmitted by conduction, a utensil with a flat bottom to make good contact with the coils or with the heated area on a smooth top range is desirable as is the ability of the material to conduct heat. A container made from highly emissive material will permit maximum transmission of radiation from glowing coils or from a gas flame.

When the liquid next to the bottom and sides of a container becomes hot, convection currents that tend to equalize the temperature throughout are established. Solid foods such as potatoes in boiling water or doughnuts in hot fat are heated by conduction from the hot liquid.

If the material from which a container is made transmits heat too efficiently, localized heating spots may cause the food to scorch even when there is ample water in the pan. Glass, ceramic ware, enameled iron, and stainless steel utensils are vulnerable to this defect. A copper bottom on a stainless steel container eliminates this disadvantage. A container too small for the unit wastes heat regardless of the method of heat transfer.

Liquid is a better conductor of heat than air in an oven. For this reason one can reach into a hot oven to remove food without getting burned by hot air but not into boiling water. For the same reason less time is required to cook a potato in boiling water (100°C or 212°F) than to bake one in a hot oven (204°C or 400°F), and it takes as long to bake biscuits in a hot oven (218°C or 425°F) as to cook the same dough as dumplings in boiling liquid (100°C or 212°F). Differences in conductivity account for the fact that removing a baking pan from a hot oven with a bare hand causes a blister but taking biscuits from the same pan does not; water at room temperature feels cooler than air at the same temperature.

Over Hot or Boiling Water

To heat foods in this way, two vessels are required, one that fits into the other, the inner one to hold the food and the outer one to hold water. Whether a double boiler or double jacketed equipment is used, the barriers to the transfer of heat are the same. Assume equipment is made of metal and electric coils are the source of heat. Much of the radiation from the glowing coils is deflected by the surface of the metal. Where the bottom of the outer vessel contacts the hot coils, heat passes through the metal by conduction and heats the adjacent layers of water. Convection currents set up in the water bring heat to the outer surface of the inner vessel. Heat from this hot water is transmitted through the metal wall of the inner vessel, again by conduction, heating the adjacent layer of food. This layer, being lighter, rises and colder liquid descends. In this way the contents of the inner vessel are

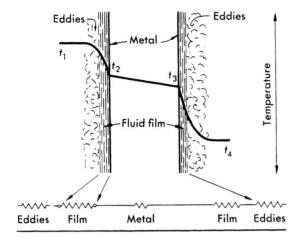

Figure 4-3. Thermal resistances encountered when heat is transferred from one fluid to another through metal (as in the top of a double boiler), shown schematically. (From James B. Austin. *The Flow of Heat in Metals.* Copyright © 1942 by the American Society for Metals, Metals Park, OH. Reprinted by permission.)

heated. Metal is a good conductor of heat, as shown by the small drop in temperature (t_2 to t_3) in the diagram in Figure 4-3. Heat transfer into the contents of the inner vessel would be more rapid were it not for the tightly adhering films of water on the surfaces of the utensil and the adjacent eddies of liquid. Stirring hastens equalization of the temperature.

The temperature of a food cooked in this way does not exceed the 100°C (212°F) of the boiling water that surrounds it. Water in the outer vessel cushions the product from the intense heat of a gas flame or an electric element. Sticking and scorching are eliminated. A product such as an egg-thickened custard may curdle if the temperature is only a few degrees above simmering, so it must be cooked surrounded by water maintained at a temperature no higher than simmering. Starch-thickened sauces, puddings, and soft pie fillings finish cooking over boiling water with only an occasional stirring. However, unless the product is brought to a boil on a hot unit first, the cooking time is excessively long.

HEATING FOODS IN A MICROWAVE OVEN

The invention of the microwave oven has been singled out as one of ten important innovations in the area of foods in the last 50 years (24). Its design is sound, and based on fundamental principles. It is a safe, convenient piece of equipment found in a high proportion of U.S. households. Microwavable foods, however, are formulated empirically, not on the basis of microwave fundamentals.

The Oven and How It Functions (3, 10, 11)

The microwave oven is a metal box that houses the magnetron. The magnetron is a device that converts electricity at a low frequency of 60 cycles or hertz (Hz) per second to electromagnetic radiation (14). A short guide directs these waves into the cavity of the oven. In the electromagnetic field that is generated in the oven, positive and negative charges change directions millions of times per second. Microwave ovens for household use operate at a frequency of 2,450 megahertz (MHz) per second, those for commercial use at 915 MHz. The microwaves generated in the oven are longer than infrared waves, found in a conventional oven, and are located in the region of short radio waves (see Fig. 2-1). The length of the waves, which depends on their frequency, is 12.2 centimeters at 2,450 MHz and 33 centimeters at 915 MHz. Electromagnetic waves travel at the speed of light and in a straight line. When a wave reaches a wall of the oven, it is reflected by the metal back into the oven, much as is radiant energy in a conventional oven. As these waves criss-cross the cavity of the oven, areas of varying temperature are formed. A metal stirrer in the oven scrambles the waves, which makes for more even heating, as does a rotating platform or carousel provided on some ovens. Cooking power available in a household microwave oven ranges from 400 to 1,000 watts, that in a commercial oven from 5 to 100 kilowatts (23). Directions for checking the wattage in a microwave oven are given in the AHEA *Handbook of Food Preparation* (1).

Controls on a microwave oven consist of a master switch, a button to start the cooking, and a timer. Cooking power can be varied on some ovens. A defrost setting cycles power on and off. Automatic features on some ovens, given the weight of the item, set cooking time and power level. Others determine doneness and either turn the power off or step it down. A glass tray or carousel in the oven elevates food so microwaves can contact the bottom of the food. Perforations in the metal door of the oven, which permit a view of the interior, are too small for the passage of microwaves, but dimensions of the door opening are large enough. Ovens are checked for leakage of microwaves before they leave the factory.

Body tissue that is exposed to microwaves can be damaged by the heat generated (21), so the oven door should fit securely to prevent leakage of the microwaves. Damage to the seal around the door should be avoided, and the seal should be kept free of spatters and spills and scrupulously clean. Staying at arm's length from the door of the oven when it is in operation minimizes the hazards should stray electromagnetic waves escape.

Utensils that transmit microwaves and are not themselves heated are used in microwave cooking. Satisfactory utensils are made from heat-resistant glass, paper, china without metallic trim, ceramics, and some plastics. Utensils made from metal reflect microwave energy should not be used in the oven. Should metal touch the sides of the oven, arching may result. The oven should not be in operation without food or liquid to absorb the microwaves.

Interaction of Food with Microwaves (10, 11, 14, 18)

Foods in a microwave oven are not exposed to heat. Instead, heat is generated in the food. A material exposed to microwaves either reflects (metal), transmits, (glass) or absorbs the waves. Absorption, when it occurs, is instantaneous, as is the heating that accompanies it. The heating that occurs is due to the motion of molecules responding to rapid change in polarity of the electric field generated in the oven. Dipolar molecules of water are one constituent that responds in this way, as are ions of dissociated salts. Air is transparent to microwaves, so the cavity of the oven stays cool. The frequency of radiation determines how deep microwaves can penetrate a food (limited to a few centimeters at 2,450 MHz), but the composition of a food influences the actual depth of absorption. Heat generated in the surface layers of a food must still move to the interior by conduction. The amount of heat generated in a food by microwaves depends upon (1) the ability of the food to store electrical energy (its dielectric constant), (2) its ability to convert electrical energy into heat (the loss factor), (3) its density, and (4) its specific heat. Although the response of molecules of water to microwaves is a major factor in heating, foods low in moisture are heated.

Microwaves penetrate deeper into such foods, and the low specific heat of the latter means that less energy is required to heat them. Oils heat readily because of their low specific heat, approximately half that of water.

Advantages and Disadvantages (3, 14, 23)

The major advantage of a microwave oven is that it heats food rapidly. The oven is valued especially for the speed by which it can bring refrigerated and frozen prepared foods to serving temperature. Cooking time is influenced by cooking power. The higher the wattage the more numerous are the microwaves generated. Composition of the food, its density, and its initial temperature are additional factors.

The microwave oven is advantageous when hot food must be available for serving over an extended period. A frozen entree heated to serving temperature by microwaves retained 93.5 percent of the thiamin of the freshly prepared product (15). This contrasts with retentions of 78, 74, and 67 percent when a freshly prepared entree was held at serving temperature for one, two, and three hours, respectively.

Energy efficiency is obvious when a single item can be heated in less time in a microwave oven than on a six-inch electrical unit on a range, both with the same input of electricity. One medium sized potato will cook in approximately four minutes in a microwave oven, compared to 45 minutes to one hour in a conventional one. However, cooking time increases with load size in a microwave oven; Four potatoes require 8 to 12 minutes. In one study, 13 food items were either baked, broiled, or roasted in both a microwave/forced convection and in a conventional oven (22). The cost of electricity to cook the 13 items, at eight cents per kilowatt hour, was 25 percent less when the microwave/forced convection oven was used. Total cooking time for the 13 items was 20 percent less with this oven.

The failure of most foods to brown in a microwave oven is a disadvantage. The air in the oven is cool and evaporation from the surface of a food has a cooling effect. A device that can be preheated in the oven may be used to brown the surface of a food prior to cooking or a broiler may be used to brown it afterwards. Failure to brown may be disguised by applying such items as chopped nuts, toasted seeds or bread crumbs, brown sugar, paprika, crushed potato chips, grated chocolate, grated cheese, or chopped bacon.

Uneven heating in a microwave oven is another drawback to its use. Sauce on a composite food may be hot enough to burn but the underlying pasta or pizza crust barely warm (14, 23). Uneven heating is likely when a frozen food is defrosted or a frozen entree is heated for serving. Ice and water do not respond in the same way to microwaves. Any thawed area in a frozen product may become steaming hot even though adjacent areas are still frozen (14, 23). Unheated spots in a food are of special concern because of the possible survival of two foodborne pathogens, *Trichinella spiralis* in pork and *Salmonella* in poultry. Both pathogens can be eliminated by adequate heating. Covering the food with plastic wrap that does not stretch, stick, or melt may result in more even heating (4). Uneven heating can be minimized by rotation of a food on a carousel, turning the food by hand, inverting the food, or stirring it frequently. Arrangement of pieces in a circle, thicker portions to the outside, makes for more even heating. Round utensils eliminate overheated portions in square corners. Large items divided into smaller pieces heat more evenly. Temperature in a cooked food will equalize if it is covered with foil and allowed to stand a few minutes with the power off.

The rapid conversion of water to steam may cause foods with a skin or membrane, such as apples, egg yolk, potatoes, poultry, and wieners to explode unless pierced with a fork. Heating may be too rapid to allow for changes that need to occur in a specific sequence in a product (14, 23). This may account for the fact that yeast dough and sponge cake batter are best cooked in a conventional oven. The rapid heating by microwaves loses much of its advantage in the case of less tender meat that requires extended cooking to be palatable.

Certain procedures should not be attempted in a microwave oven. Included are cooking and reheating eggs, deep-fat frying, processing jars of canned food, and melting paraffin. All are hazardous.

TESTS FOR DONENESS OF COOKED FOODS

There are a number of ways to tell when foods are done, few of which are precise end points. Most of them work reasonably well for the experienced. A thermometer can be used to determine more or less precisely the doneness of some foods. The boiling point of candy and jelly and the internal temperature of roast meat and broiled steaks can be used to assess doneness. Less precise and more subjective criteria for doneness include judging the doneness of stirred custard by the way it coats the spoon (see Fig. 21-6), of a poached or fried egg by the opaqueness of the white, of a baked product such as cake by its springiness when touched by a finger, and of fruits, vegetables, and meats by the ease with which they are pierced by a fork. The brownness of a baked product may be, but sometimes is not, a good index to doneness. A loaf of bread, for example, usually gets brown some time before the center of the loaf gets hot enough to set the crumb. Time tables are useful guides to approximate cooking times.

COOLING AND REFRIGERATING FOODS

Discussion to this point has centered on heating foods. In many instances a food needs to be cooled instead. How fast a food cools depends on the cooling medium, on the material of the container, and the nature of the food itself. Foods are cooled in air or in water. The low density of air makes it a poor conductor of heat. Spreading food to increase its surface area speeds cooling. Water is a good coolant; it is denser than air and it has a high specific heat. The temperature of a hot food will drop more rapidly if surrounded by water at 20°C (68°F) instead of by air at 4°C (40°F), the temperature in a refrigerated cabinet. Food cools faster in a container that is a good conductor of heat, such as one made of metal.

Solid foods cool more slowly than do liquid because much of the heat must pass from the interior to the surface by conduction, a slow process. Convection currents that form in cooling liquids speed the cooling by exposing more of the hot material to the cooler surface of the utensil. Stirring the hot liquid hastens cooling.

Convection currents operate in a refrigerated cabinet as in an oven, except that the cooling coils are at the top in a cabinet and the source of heat at the bottom in an oven. Heat from the warmed air that rises and flows past the cooling coils is absorbed by the refrigerant. The cooled, denser air flows toward the bottom of the cabinet. Overcrowding in the cabinet interferes with the circulation of air essential for maintaining a uniform temperature throughout. The temperature in the cabinet should be maintained above freezing but no higher than 4°C (40°F).

TEMPERATURE AND CONTROL OF PATHOGENS IN FOODS

Disease-producing microorganisms from soil, water, animal, and human carriers can contaminate foods. Illness may be caused by eating a food that contains a sufficient number of organisms or one that contains a toxin formed by the organism. Three microorganisms long recognized as hazardous if present in food are *Clostridium botulinum, Salmonella,* and *Staphylococcus aureus.* Others later recognized as pathogens carried by food, referred to as new or emerging bacteria (12), have been added to the list. Included are *Campylobacter jejuni, Clostridium perfringes,* a strain of *Escherichia coli* designated 0157:H[7], *Listeria monocytogenes, Vibrio parahaemolyticus,* and *Yersinia enterocolitica.*

Foodborne illness is preventable if certain precautions are taken as a food moves along the chain from grower-producer to consumer and by the consumer. A Hazard Analysis and Critical Control Point (HACCP) system is proposed to ensure that a food is microbiologically safe (7). Involved are identification of the hazard(s) for a given food and points from source to consumption where controls are essential to ensure that the food is safe to eat. Temperature can be an effective measure in the prevention of foodborne illness. Temperatures from −18° to 121°C (0° to 250°F) span the range that influences the spoilage of foods and their safety from a microbiological standpoint. Temperature can promote, control, or prevent growth of pathogens that could make food unsafe to eat as well as those organisms that make food unpalatable.

Effects of Heat

Heat at the high end of the temperature range can destroy microorganisms. How hot the food should be to accomplish this is influenced by the hydrogen ion concentration (pH) (Fig. 4-4). For processing food in jars or cans to preserve them for extended storage, a pH of 4.6 marks the division between those foods that are high in acid (fruits and pickled vegetables) and low-acid foods (other vegetables, meat, poultry, and fish). Acidic foods can be effectively sterilized at the temperature of boiling water (100°C or 212°F), but a higher temperature is needed to destroy heat-resistant spores in low-acid foods. Processing low-acid foods under steam pressure, as in canning, provides the needed high temperature (116°C or 240°F). A hermetic seal on containers prevents recontamination. The microorganism of concern in such foods is *Clostridium botulinum.* Should spores of this organism survive in inadequately processed low-acid foods, they could grow in the oxygen-free environment of the sealed container and form a potent toxin. Ingestion of the toxin-containing food could cause paralysis, manifested as double vision, difficulty in swallowing, and respiratory failure. The toxin can be destroyed by boiling the food for 10 minutes.

Cooking can make foods safe to eat, even low-acid ones in which spores could survive, provided the cooked food is served promptly or held for serving at a temperature high enough (60°C or 140°F) to prevent growth of microorganisms. Unused portions should be cooled promptly and then held at 4°C (40°F) or lower. It is hazardous to hold foods at temperatures that are neither hot nor cold, referred to as the danger zone (Fig. 4-5), with 2 to 3 hours maximum for holding food in this temperature range.

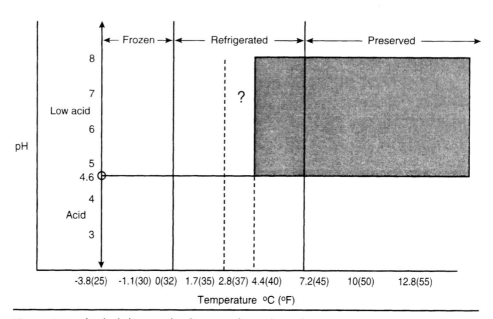

Figure 4-4. The shaded area in this diagram indicates that pathogens can grow at temperatures above 4°C (40°F) in low acid (pH 4.6 or above) conditions. The question mark in the area between 37°F and 40°F indicates that, should psychrophilic organisms such as *Listeria* or *Yersinia* be present, growth can occur below 40°F (4°C). (From D. A. Corlett, Jr. 1989. *Food Technology* 43(2):92. Reprinted by permission.)

Effects of Cold

At the low end of the temperature range (-18°C or 0°F), a high proportion of water in a food has been converted to ice crystals. At that temperature, the liquid that remains unfrozen exists as a viscous matrix (a glass), with constituents essentially immobile and so unable to support the growth of microorganisms.

Short term storage of refrigerated perishable foods has a good safety record. In many foods traditionally refrigerated, the presence of substances with preservative action allows some mishandling without serious consequences. Mayonnaise is an example. In theory, mayonnaise should spoil readily because of the egg yolk, but the acid ingredient in the product lowers the pH to 4.6 or below (Fig. 4-4). Organisms that might make the mayonnaise unfit to eat not only do not grow at the low pH but they actually die during refrigerated storage (25). The salt, too, has a preservative effect. Eggs keep as well as they do in the refrigerator because, in addition to the shell that acts as a physical barrier to organisms, the white contains antimicrobial agents (Chapter 21).

A temperature of 4°C (40°F) is the maximum recommended for holding perishables under refrigeration. The shaded area in Figure 4-4 indicates that it is hazardous to hold such foods at temperatures above 4°C (40°F) if the pH of the food is above 4.6. The safety of holding foods even at 4°C (40°F) is questioned because of the discovery that some foodborne pathogens can grow at that temperature or even lower. These psychrophilic (literally cold-loving, but more accurately cold-tolerating) organisms include *Yersinia enterocolitica*, *Listeria monocytogenes*, two types of *Clostridium botulinum* (Type E and nonproteolytic Type B) and pathogenic *Escherichia coli* (16, 19). Growth of these and other organisms on

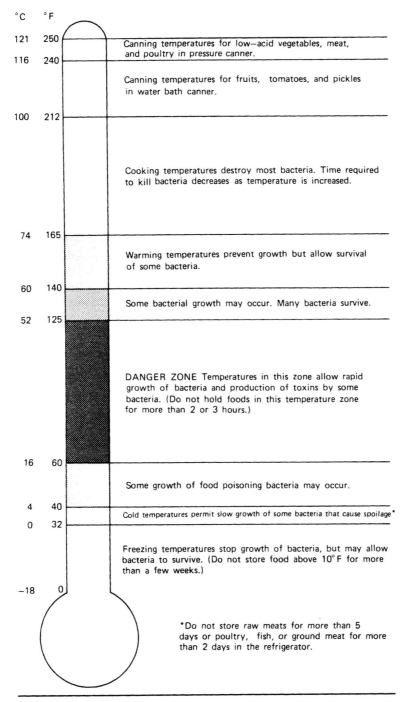

Figure 4-5. Temperature of foods for the control of bacteria. (From *Keeping Foods Safe to Eat.* Home and Garden Bulletin No. 162, sl. rev. 1978.)

foods can occur at temperatures a few degrees above 4°C (40°F). Adequate refrigeration is especially important for the array of packaged low acid (high pH) foods displayed in refrigerated cabinets at the food market. Items are formulated and/or processed just enough to give them an extended shelf life. They are not sterile or even safe unless they are held under adequate refrigeration.

Temperature is a major factor that controls the growth of microorganisms. Heating a food to a sufficiently high temperature or holding it at a sufficiently low temperature are effective ways to limit microbial growth. This includes organisms that cause foods to spoil and those pathogens that are responsible for foodborne illness.

PATHOGENS AND THEIR RESPONSE TO HEAT AND COLD

A brief account of microorganisms that might contaminate food and the response of these organisms to temperature follows (12, 13, 19, 26).

Clostridium botulinum, one of the old pathogens, was discussed earlier. This organism is found in the soil where it thrives in anaerobic (oxygen-free) conditions. The intimate contact of vegetables with soil means that they are likely to be contaminated, but any food may harbor the organism. In addition to toxins from the two types of *Clostridium botulinum* that can grow under anaerobic conditions even when refrigerated and toxins associated with underprocessed low-acid canned foods, cases of botulism have been traced to leftover baked foil-wrapped potatoes, cooked, chopped onions held for service, and chopped garlic in oil that a restaurant used to make garlic butter. In each case, the product was temperature-abused (12).

Salmonella species live in the intestinal tract of animals, so meat, poultry, and raw milk may be contaminated. Infected meat and poultry can contaminate other foods by way of knives, cutting boards, and hands. The organism is sensitive to pasteurization temperature and mandatory pasteurization of broken-out eggs used in the food industry has reduced eggs as a source of *Salmonella*. The organism is easily destroyed by cooking. *Salmonella* is a major cause of foodborne illness (6).

Staphylococcus aureus is present in the nose and throat and on the skin of a high proportion of individuals, so coughing, sneezing, or handling can contaminate food. Illness is caused by a heat-stable toxin formed by the organism. The organism thrives in protein-rich cooked food in which competetive organisms have been eliminated by heat. Foods likely to contain the toxin are temperature-abused poultry, meat, cream fillings in bakery products, and salads (chicken, meat, egg) that require much handling. The organism is salt tolerant. It can grow in cured meat in which the salt has inhibited other spoilage organisms that would otherwise warn that the meat was unsafe to eat. The organism can grow from 6.7° to 47.5°C (44° to 115°F), with optimum temperature of 35° to 37°C (95° to 98.6°F). Cooking destroys the organism but not the preformed, heat-stable toxin that causes the illness. Minimum handling of food to reduce contamination and prompt cooling and refrigeration to limit growth of the organism and toxin production are essential precautions.

Campylobacter jejuni is found in the intestines of poultry, cattle, swine, and humans. Raw meat, poultry, and milk may be contaminated, as may any food handled by an infected individual who practices poor hygiene. Unchlorinated water may be a source of the organism, too. The organism can grow between 30° and 47°C (86° and

117°F), with an optimum temperature for growth near 42°C (108°F). It does not grow below 30°C (86°F). Pasteurization at 71.7°C (161°F) destroys it, as does cooking. Although the organism grows over only a restricted range in temperatures that should be easy to avoid, it is estimated that *Campylobacter* is responsible for as many cases of illness as *Salmonella.*

Clostridium perfringes is found in the soil and in the intestines of warm blooded animals. A toxin either preformed in the food or formed in the intestine after contaminated food is ingested causes the illness. Slow cooling of such items as turkey and large cuts of meat cooked a day ahead of time (a not uncommon institutional practice) and keeping foods warm rather than hot for an extended serving period promote growth of these organisms. Such foods should be held at 60°C (140°F) or above or cooled promptly and then held at 4°C (40°F) or below. Leftovers should be heated sufficiently (75°C or 167°F) before they are eaten.

Yersinia enterocolitica is believed to contaminate foods from porcine waste, and swine are considered a reservoir for these organisms. Cases of yersiniosis have been traced to chocolate milk, raw and pasteurized milk, and tofu made with unchlorinated spring water. The organism grows best at 22° to 29°C (72° to 84°F). However, it can grow from 0°C to 45°C (32°F to 113°F). Refrigeration cannot be relied on to control growth of this organism. *Yersinia* was the first organism identified as psychrophilic. The organism is sensitive to a temperature of 50°C (122°F), so pasteurization destroys it, as does cooking.

Listeria monocytogenes is found in soil, water, and vegetation, as well as the intestines of animals, including man. Soft cheese, milk, and cole slaw made from cabbage grown in soil fertilized with waste from infected sheep have caused outbreaks of listeriosis. Mortality may be as high as 30 percent. *Listeria* can grow at 4°C (40°F), so refrigeration cannot be relied on to control growth, should these organisms be present in a food.

Escherichia coli are part of the flora of the intestinal tract. Most are harmless, but pathogenic strains do exist. One in particular, designated 0157:H7, can cause severe and even fatal illness (17). Animals, especially cattle are considered a reservoir for this strain. Should the surface of a steak or roast be contaminated, the heat of cooking will destroy the organism. Ground meat should be heated until all pink color has disappeared or to a temperature of 68°C (155°F).

Vibrio parahaemolyticus is a salt-tolerant organism associated with the marine environment. Raw fish and shellfish may carry the organism. Icing or refrigeration of fresh fish controls the growth of *Vibrio,* and adequate heating makes fish safe to eat.

Foodborne illness is largely preventable. An important first step to this end is the recognition that foods may contain pathogens. Sanitary handling of food minimizes avoidable contamination. Any surface that a food contacts (container to transport it, work surface, equipment, utensils, and hands) should be scrupulously clean. A knowledge of which foods are likely to be contaminated and the vulnerability of any pathogen(s) that might be present—a hazard analysis approach—provides a basis for choosing appropriate measures to make and keep foods safe to eat. Temperature control measures involve adequate heating and then holding foods for serving at 60°C (140°F) or above or cooling foods promptly and then holding them under adequate refrigeration at 4°C (40°F) or lower. Foods held at temperatures between 4°C (40°F) and 60°C (140°F), the danger zone, are unsafe to eat.

REFERENCES

1. AHEA 1993. *Handbook of Food Preparation.* Washington, D.C.: American Home Economics Association. Pp. 5, 18, 41. Oven temperatures, microwave oven wattage, temperature conversions.

2. AHEA 1977. *Handbook for Metric Usage.* Washington, D.C.: American Home Economics Association. Pp. 28 Conversion of calories to joules.

3. Annis, P. J. 1980. "Design and use of domestic microwave oven." *Journal of Food Protection* 43:1629–32. The oven and how it functions.

4. Armbruster, G., and C. Haefle. 1975. "Quality of foods after cooking in 915 MHz and 2450 MHz microwave appliances using plastic film cover." *Journal of Food Science* 40:721–23. Three wraps compared; advantages of a satisfactory wrap.

5. Austin, J. B. 1941. *The Flow of Heat in Metals.* Cleveland, OH: American Society for Metals. Pp. 3–17, 84. Nature of heat: explanation of the high heat conductivity of metals.

6. Bean, N. H., and P. M. Griffin. 1990. "Foodborne disease outbreaks in the United States, 1973–1987: Pathogens, vehicles, and trends." *Journal of Food Protection* 53:804–17. *Salmonella*—a leading cause.

7. Corlett, D. A., Jr. 1989. "Refrigerated foods and use of Hazard Analysis and Critical Control Point principles." *Food Technology* 43(2):91–94. Potential hazards of new generation refrigerated foods.

8. Cornehl, B., and V. N. W. Swartz. 1931. "Speed and efficiency of oven utensils." *Journal of Home Economics* 23:464–67. Aluminum, china, glass, cast iron, enameled iron, and stainless steel compared.

9. Cross, G. A., and D. Y. Fund. 1982. "Effect of microwaves on nutrient values of foods." *CRC Critical Reviews in Food Science and Nutrition* 16:355–81.

10. Curnutte, B. 1980. Principles of microwave radiation. *Journal of Food Protection* 43:618–24, 632. Generation of microwaves; utilization in heating foods.

11. Giese, J. 1992. "Advances in microwave food processing." *Food Technology* 46:118–23. Summary of some of the basics.

12. Institute of Food Technology. 1986. "New bacteria in the news—a special symposium. *Food Technology* 40(8):16–26. Seven pathogens.

13. Institute of Food Technology. 1988. "Scientific Status Summary. Bacteria associated with foodborne diseases." *Food Technology* 42(4):181–200. Extensive coverage of eleven pathogens.

14. Institute of Food Technology. 1989. "Scientific Status Summary. Microwave food processing." *Food Technology* 43(1):117–26. The oven, the process, its effects on food, and the outlook.

15. Kahn, L. N., and G. E. Livingston. 1970. "Effects of heating method on thiamine retention in fresh and frozen prepared foods." *Journal of Food Science* 35:349–51. Microwave, infrared, and hot-water thawing compared.

16. Lechowich, R. V. 1988. "Microbiological challenge of refrigerated foods." *Food Technology* 42(12):84–85, 89. Hazards of psychrophiles in low-acid, convenience foods.

17. Mermelstein, N. H. 1993. "Controlling *E. coli* 0157:H7 in meat." *Food Technology* 47(4):90–91. Account of one outbreak caused by the organism.

18. Mudgett, R. E. 1986. "Microwave properties and heating characteristics of foods. *Food Technology* 40(6):84–93, 98. Technical treatment.

19. Palumbo, S. A. 1986. "Is refrigeration enough to restrain foodborne pathogens?" *Journal of Food Protection* 49:1003–9. Answer—not always.

20. Peart, M. V., S. T. Kern, and D. P. DeWitt. 1980. "Optimizing oven radiant energy use." *Home Economics Research Journal* 8:242–51. Development of an oven system more efficient than those currently available.

21. Rosén, C.-G. 1972. Effect of microwaves on food and related materials. *Food Technology* 26(7):36–37, 39–40, 55. Technical evaluation of suspected adverse effects of microwaves.

22. Samuel, B. C., and R. Lovingood. 1986. "Microwave/conventional ovens: Trade-offs

in energy use time and food quality." *Journal of Microwave Power* 21:1–8. Thirteen foods baked, broiled, or roasted.

23. Schiffman, R. F. 1986. "Food product development for microwave processing." *Food Technology* 40(6):94–98. Response of foods to microwave.

24. Shukla, T. P. 1990. "Heating food in the microwave oven." *Cereal Foods World* 35: 761–62. Praise for the oven; reservations in regard to microwavable products available.

25. Smittle, R. B. 1977. "Microbiology of mayonnaise and salad dressing: A review." *Journal of Food Protection* 40:415–22. Preservative action of acetic acid.

26. Wolf, I. D., and R. V. Lechowich. 1989. "Current issues in microbiological food safety." *Cereal Foods World* 34:468–72. Pathogens, food carriers, and control.

27. Worthington, R. 1928. "Heat conductivity of metals as factors in heat transfer." *Chemical Metalic Engineering* 35:381–82. Effects of air and water films on heat conductivity of metals.

PART II

Liquids and Crystals

Water

5

Water is a ubiquitous substance with a number of unique properties often taken for granted. Water influences the appearance, texture, and flavor of foods and it performs a number of important functions in food preparation.

All living things, including foods of plant and animal origin, are made mainly of water. High moisture content gives raw fruits and vegetables their crisp, crunchy texture and meats their turgor. Even seemingly dry foods such as dried beans, dried fruits, cereal, and flour contain appreciable quantities of moisture, although much less than when these foods were immature. The moisture content of a food cannot be judged by appearance. Strawberries appear to have more moisture than cabbage, milk more than green beans, and dry flour seems devoid of moisture. (Table 5-1).

Not only is water an integral part of all foods, but many of the changes that take place when foods are combined or cooked do so only because of the presence of water. Water acts as a solvent or dispersing agent for ingredients. Water makes possible ionization of acids and bases that can then react, as when biscuits, muffins, and shortened cakes are leavened with baking powder. With acid present, water can hydrolyze sucrose to simpler sugars, a reaction desired in fondant, brown sugar fudge, fruit pectin jellies, and yeast bread dough. Water gives coherence to batters and doughs and makes possible the gelatinization of starch, which contributes to the structure of the baked products. The water-holding capacity of muscle influences the color and also the tenderness of the meat. Foods high in moisture are readily spoiled by microorganisms unless means are used to limit their access

TABLE 5-1
Moisture Content of Common Foods

Tomatoes	94%	Cream, coffee	72%
Watermelon	93	Round steak	67
Cabbage	92	White bread	36
Strawberries	90	Prunes, dried	28
Green beans	90	Butter	15
Broccoli	89	All-purpose flour	12
Peaches	89	Beans, dried	11
Whole milk	87	Rolled oats	8

Source: U.S. Dept. Agr. Handbook No. 456. *Nutritive Value of American Foods in Common Units.* Issued November 1975.

to the water. Water is useful in cooling as well as in heating foods. And not least, water is a good cleansing agent for both the foods themselves and for utensils and dishes used in the preparation and serving of food.

NATURE OF WATER

The Molecule

A brief discussion of the nature of water and its many unique properties precedes that of the role of water in food preparation. Chemically, water consists of one atom of oxygen united to two atoms of hydrogen. An atom of oxygen has a nucleus with eight protons, an inner electron shell that contains two electrons, and an outer shell that contains only six electrons (a deficiency of two). A hydrogen atom has a nucleus with one proton and an inner electron shell with only one electron. A stable molecule of water is formed when each of the two atoms of hydrogen shares its one electron with the oxygen atom and the oxygen shares two of its electrons, one with each of the two hydrogen atoms (8) (Fig. 5-1). Thus a molecule of water contains two pairs of electrons shared covalently. The two hydrogens are positioned relative to the oxygen to form an angle of approximately 105 degrees.

Overall, a molecule of water is electrically neutral. However, the distribution of charges in the molecule is asymmetric, with the slightly more negative oxygen balancing the slightly more positive hydrogens. A water molecule is envisioned as occupying the center of a tetrahedron, a solid with four faces, each of which is defined by an equilateral triangle, with the charges oriented as shown in Figure 5-2.

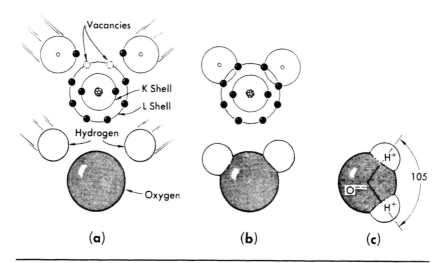

Figure 5-1. Formation of a water molecule. (*a*) Two atoms of hydrogen and one of oxygen, shown schematically, unite. (*b*) Each hydrogen atom shares with the oxygen a pair of electrons, shown in equilibrium position. (*c*) Unequal distribution of positive and negative charges makes the water molecule permanently dipolar. (Illustrations from *Water: The Mirror of Science* by K. S. Davis and J. A. Day. Copyright © 1961 by Educational Service, Inc. Used by permission of Doubleday, a division of Bantam Doubleday Dell Publishing Group, Inc.)

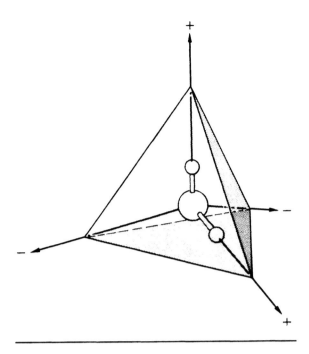

Figure 5-2. Orientation of charges around a molecule of water gives it the shape of a tetrahedron. (From O. Fennema and W. D. Powrie. *Advances in Food Research* 13:223. Copyright © 1964 by Academic Press, Inc., New York. Reprinted by permission.)

Hydrogen Bonding and the States of Water

A water molecule with its positive and negative poles is permanently dipolar. Unlike charges attract, so a water molecule is attracted to other substances that carry either a positive or a negative charge. This includes other water molecules (16). Attraction between a positive pole of one water molecule and a negative pole of another leads to association of water molecules through a type of secondary valence bond, known as a hydrogen bond, as shown:

$$H — O \text{----} H — O$$

The energy required to break a weak hydrogen bond is approximately $\frac{1}{20}$ of that required to break a covalent or shared bond that joins hydrogen to the oxygen within the molecule of water. Each water molecule has the potential for uniting by hydrogen bond with four adjacent water molecules, two by way of the oxygen and one each by way of the two hydrogens. The ability of water to form hydrogen bonds gives it many of its unique properties. Water can exist in three states depending on the extent to which the molecules are hydrogen bonded.

Water in the Liquid State

Water is a liquid at temperatures between 0° and 100°C (32° and 212°F) at normal atmospheric pressure. The flow properties are due to hydrogen bonds that link adjacent molecules of water. Otherwise, under these conditions water would be a gas because of the small mass of the molecule. In liquid form, molecules associate in small clusters that break up and reassociate continuously. These clusters move about freely and there is much hydrogen-bond interchange (5).

Water in the Crystalline State

When the temperature of water is lowered, the motion of the molecules in the liquid is slowed. The volume of the water shrinks slightly as it cools. Hydrogen bonding within the clusters persists longer as the temperature drops. By the time water is cooled to 4°C (39°F), the water molecules have begun to associate via hydrogen bonding in a precise arrangement. This continues and the volume of the water begins to expand as the temperature drops from 4°C to 0°C (39° to 32°F). If additional heat is withdrawn from water after it reaches 0°C (32°F), crystals appear, and as water changes to ice crystals expansion is abrupt. This ice water becomes crystalline and solid, that is, ice. The angle at which the bonding in the crystal lattice forms leaves unfilled spaces that are hexagonal in shape (Fig. 5-3). These spaces are so positioned as to give rise to innumerable channels that pervade ice. As a result, ice occupies $\frac{1}{11}$ more space than the water from which it was formed. Ice, less dense than water, floats to the surface.

When water molecules crystallize from the vapor state, single crystals are obtained as snowflakes with the typical hexagon shape. The reverse of the condensation of water vapor as snowflakes is the change from ice crystals to water vapor without the ice melting. This phenomenon is known as sublimation. Slow removal by sublimation of moisture from improperly packaged frozen food results in excessive drying, hardening, and discoloration of the surface, a condition known as freezer burn. Freeze drying, done under a vacuum, speeds the sublimation process, resulting in minimum damage to food. Freeze-dried foods rehydrate better than ordinary dried foods because structural components remain in place and excessive hydrogen bonding between components of the food is eliminated.

Water in the Gaseous State

In addition to existing as a liquid and as a solid, water may exist also in the gaseous state as either water vapor or steam. If a container of water is left uncovered and exposed to the air for some time, the level of water will gradually lower and the container will eventually become empty. For this evaporation to take place, individual molecules of water must have attained sufficient kinetic energy because of random motion (2) so they can escape into the atmosphere. This involves breaking hydrogen bonds that are essential to the liquid state. The rate of evaporation varies with temperature and humidity of the air. Had the container been covered instead of open, molecules of water vapor would have accumulated above the surface. As the number of molecules of water vapor increases so, too, do their chances of contacting the surface of the liquid and reuniting with it. After a time an equilibrium would be reached, with the number of molecules leaving the liquid as vapor balanced by the number returning to it. At equilibrium, the pressure exerted by the molecules of water vapor on the surface of the liquid below represents the *vapor pressure* of the water.

Boiling of Water

Changes Observed as Water Is Brought to a Boil

When cold tap water is heated, small bubbles can be observed in the water where it contacts the bottom and sides of the container. These bubbles form because air is less soluble in hot water than in cold. When water reaches simmering temperature, larger bubbles,

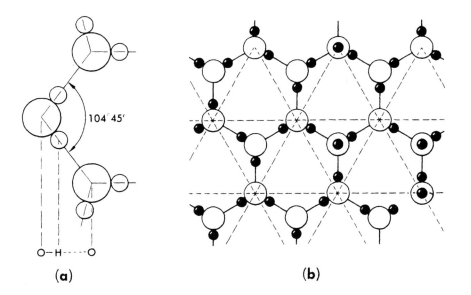

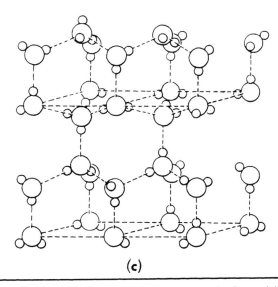

Figure 5-3. Lattice of crystallized water (ice). (a) Two water molecules, each hydrogen bonded to a third with a bond angle of approximately 105°. (b) Water molecules bonded to form crystals leave hexagon-shaped spaces in ice. (c) Three-dimensional model of crystallized water. (From A. Frey-Wyssling and K Mühlethaler, *Ultrastructural Plant Cytology.* Copyright © 1965, P. 23, by Elsevier Publishing Company, Amsterdam. Reprinted by permission of authors and publisher.)

which form mainly on the bottom of the container, float lazily to the surface of the water before they break. In this instance the bubbles are of water vapor. When water reaches the state of boiling, the bubbles not only form rapidly but also break before they reach the surface; and as they leave the water the surface is agitated. When water boils, the molecules leave the liquid as steam, not singly but in battalions. For water molecules to change to water vapor, in the phenomenon known as boiling, both the force of attraction between water molecules and the atmospheric pressure must be overcome. The latter is due to the weight of the air resting on the surface of the liquid. At sea level the standard value for the weight of the column of air is equal to 760 mm of mercury, or 15 pounds per square inch (103 kPa). At sea level and with standard barometric pressure, pure water boils at 100°C (212°F).

Specific Heat. Figure 5-4 shows the energy involved in the heating of 1 gram (1 ml) of water. As the graph shows, 100 calories are required to bring the temperature of 1 gram of water from 0°C to 100°C. This is 1 calorie for each 1-degree rise in temperature or a *specific heat* of 1 (derived from the ratio of the two). Water has a higher specific heat than most substances. This characteristic is utilized to cushion or protect certain foods against a too-rapid rise in temperature. Examples are heating a food over boiling water instead of in direct contact with a hot unit and surrounding the container with custard or soufflé with hot water when it is put into the oven to bake. The high specific heat of water accounts in part for the fact that it is a good coolant. Fats, also used to transmit heat in food preparation, have a much lower specific heat than water. Olive oil, for example, has a specific heat of

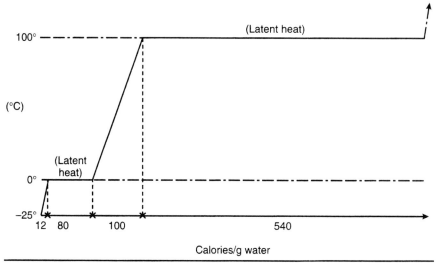

Figure 5-4. Specific and latent heats of water are plotted on this graph. Approximately 24 calories are required to heat 1 gram of ice at −25° to 0°C. An additional 80 calories are required to convert the 1 gram of ice at 0°C to water at the same temperature. The 80 calories represent latent heat of melting. To bring the temperature of 1 gram of water at 0°C to the boiling point (100°C) requires 100 calories, a specific heat of 1. To convert 1 gram of water at the boiling point to steam requires 540 calories. The 540 calories represent latent heat of vaporization. (After *Water: The Mirror of Science* by K. S. Davis and J. A. Day. Copyright © 1961 by Educational Services, Inc. Used by permission of Doubleday, a division of Bantam Doubleday Dell Publishing Group, Inc.)

0.471. Oil will heat to temperature more than twice as fast as an equal amount of water, the input of energy being the same. The specific heat of air of 0.3329 is less than that for fat. Lower still are the specific heats of two metals from which cooking utensils are made, 0.214 for aluminum and 0.119 for cast iron.

Latent Heat. Referring again to Figure 5-4, the graph shows that although it takes 12 calories to raise the temperature of one gram of water (ice) from $-25°$ to $0°C$, the temperature then remains at $0°C$ until 80 (approximately) additional calories have been absorbed. The 80 calories are called *latent heat* because the input of energy is not accompanied by a rise in temperature. These 80 calories are needed to melt the one gram of ice by disrupting the hydrogen bonds that maintain the orderly arrangement of molecules in the crystals of ice. The result at this point is one gram of ice water still at $0°C$. Only after the ice melts does the temperature again begin to rise and again one degree for each calorie absorbed.

Thus 100 calories will bring the temperature of one gram of ice water (at $0°C$ or $32°F$) to $100°C$ ($212°F$), but the water still remains in the liquid state. It is estimated that approximately 40 percent of the water molecules are still hydrogen bonded. To change one gram of water at the boiling point ($100°C$) to vapor requires an additional 540 calories. Again *latent heat* is involved, this time heat of vaporization. The 540 calories are a measure of the energy required for the water molecules to overcome the force of atmospheric pressure and the attraction of the hydrogen bonds that remain in water at the boiling point.

Latent heat of vaporization of water in addition to its high specific heat gives a factual basis for the observation that a watched pot never boils. A steam burn is so severe because of the 540 calories of latent heat of vaporization that are released when the steam condenses. Water may be used to keep foods cool because of latent heat of vaporization. Without refrigeration, foods may be kept reasonably cool by storing them in a cloth that is kept damp. Spraying fruits and vegetables on display in a produce department with a fine mist of water not only prevents wilting, but it also helps to keep the food cool as the water evaporates from the surface. Latent heat of fusion explains why ice is a good coolant. And the country practice of putting a tub of water in a cellar on a cold night to keep fruits and vegetables from freezing worked because each gram of water which was converted to ice released 80 calories.

Fast versus Slow Boiling

Once water in an open container is hot enough to boil, the temperature will go no higher no matter how hot the heating unit, but it will evaporate faster. Sometimes this is desired. Evaporation of water from the syrup is the chief object of cooking candies and fruit pectin jellies. A rapid boil may be used to eliminate residual cooking water around certain vegetables to conserve nutrients. But when the object is to heat foods, not to evaporate water, rapid boiling only wastes energy and does not speed cooking. Excessive evaporation when foods are cooked at a rapid boil may result in their being scorched. Foods high in starch are more likely to boil dry because starch absorbs water when it is gelatinized. Dried foods that absorb moisture as they cook may become dry and scorch. Meats, fruits, and most vegetables contribute water to that added to the utensil in which they are cooked.

If foods are to be cooked in a small amount of water, a heavy container with a tight-fitting lid is essential. A utensil with a small diameter reduces the rate at which water evaporates. A lid on the pan serves to condense steam and as this water returns to the pan the loss of water by evaporation is slowed. The intensity of heat must be controlled to limit evaporation when a small amount of water is used.

Factors Affecting the Boiling Point of Water

Altitude. Water does not always boil at 100°C (212°F) (1). The weight of the column of air that rests on the surface of water varies with altitude, and this affects the temperature at which water boils. For each 960-foot increase in altitude above sea level, the boiling point of water is lower by 1°C (1.8°F). As a consequence of this reduction, a longer time is required to cook foods to a given stage of doneness at higher altitudes. This effect of altitude was noted by Marco Polo as he, his father, and his uncle traveled the land route from their home in Venice to the land of the great Kublai Khan. He recorded this observation as they made their way along the top of the world:

> So great is the height of the mountains, that no birds are to be seen near their summits; and however extraordinary it may be thought, it was affirmed, that from the keenness of the air, fires when lighted do not give the same heat as in lower situations, nor produce the same effect in dressing victuals [i.e., cooking foods]!*

Foods not only may need to cook longer at higher elevations but the proportions of ingredients, especially water, may need to be altered because of the lower boiling point. Modifications of recipes and of cooking times have been developed for high altitude regions that occupy approximately ⅓ of the United States (15).

Barometric Pressure. Even at the same altitude atmospheric conditions change frequently, and this causes fluctuations in the temperature at which water boils. If barometric pressure is low, water boils below 100°C and evaporates faster.

When the weather is changing from clear to cloudy, barometric pressure is usually low (air is less dense) so the boiling point of water is lower. A change from cloudy conditions to bright is usually accompanied by high barometric pressure (more dense air) and an elevation in the boiling point. The boiling point of water should be determined and adjustment made prior to using a thermometer to assess the doneness of boiling syrup of candy and fruit pectin jellies.

Steam Pressure. The boiling point of water may be raised above 100°C in a pressure saucepan or a pressure canner. When water boils in either of these utensils once they are sealed, the steam that forms is confined within the container.

One volume of water can give rise to 1600 to 1800 volumes of steam (one teaspoon of water can yield approximately 2 gallons of steam). When this steam is confined within the space formerly occupied by the air, the pressure builds rapidly. As the pressure rises more heat must be applied to the water to give the molecules sufficient energy to escape as steam. As the steam pressure rises so does the boiling point; and it will continue to do so as more heat is applied, converting more water to steam. At 5 pounds steam pressure (34 kilopascals) water boils at 109°C (228°F); at 10 pounds (69 kilopascals) it boils at 115°C (240°F); and at 15 pounds (103 kilopascals) it boils at 121°C (250°F). The pressure in a pressure saucepan or pressure canner must be increased 1 pound (7 kilopascals) for each 2,000-foot increase in altitude to compensate for the effect of altitude on the boiling point of water.

---

* *The Travels of Marco Polo the Venetian*, by Marco Polo. Everyman's Library Text. Ernest Rhys, editor. Copyright © 1926 by E. P. Dutton & Co., Inc. Reprinted by permission of Elsevier-Dutton Publishing Co., Inc.

Because steam under pressure exerts much force, the pressure saucepan or canner and the closure must be built to withstand the pressure. When steam is confined in such utensils, it is dangerous to try to remove the lid without first cooling the utensil to reduce the steam pressure to zero. The petcock should be opened to make certain no steam is confined.

Unless the petcock is opened or the pressure gauge removed when the steam pressure reaches zero, a partial vacuum forms. Should this happen, the contents of the cooker or canner may begin to boil again even though the temperature has dropped below 100°C (212°F). This is one cause of loss of liquid from jars in canning. When a partial vacuum forms, less than the usual amount of pressure is exerted on the surface of the water and the boiling point is lowered. For instance, when sealed fruit jars are removed from a pressure canner, a partial vacuum may form in the jars that permits the liquid to boil after the jars are cool enough to be handled comfortably.

Solutes. Salt and sugar, two common ingredients in foods, elevate the boiling point of water (Chapter 8) and depress its freezing point (Chapter 7). Presence of either substance in water dilutes the water molecules and so lowers the vapor pressure of the water (2). To compensate for this reduced vapor pressure the water that contains sugar or salt must be heated above 100°C (212°F) at sea level before it can boil.

FUNCTIONS OF WATER IN FOOD PREPARATION

A Medium for the Transfer of Heat

One important function of water in preparing foods is that it serves as a medium for the transfer of energy from heating unit to food. If a container were placed over a lighted gas burner or on a hot electric unit (with food but no water), it would be hottest where it was contacted by the flame or where it rested on the hot coils. The food would scorch where it contacted the container before the remainder of the food had a chance to become warm. Water absorbs heat, and this sets up convection currents that equalize the temperature throughout. Water is a good conductor of heat; that is, it readily gives up heat to or absorbs it from food in contact with it. A more detailed discussion of the role of water in the transfer of heat is given in Chapter 4.

A Dispersing Medium

Water serves as a means of dispersing many constituents present in foods and used in food preparation. For some constituents it acts as a solvent. Others are dispersed colloidally or as suspended matter.

Solutions

Water dissolves such substances as salt, sugars, water-soluble vitamins, and minerals, and flavoring substances such as those extracted from tea leaves and coffee beans.

Solutions are of two types—ionic or molecular. In a crystalline material such as table salt the sodium ion has donated one electron in its outer shell to a chlorine atom that lacks one electron in its outer shell, as shown in Figure 5-5. Two oppositely charged ions, a positive sodium ion and a negative chloride ion, are the result. In a crystal of sodium chloride (Fig. 5-6) these two types of ions are bonded to each other by electrostatic forces. Water reduces the attractive force between oppositely charged sodium and chloride ions

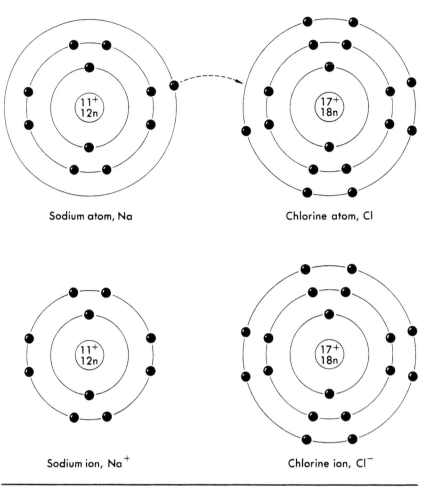

Figure 5-5. A positive sodium ion and a negative chloride ion result when a sodium atom donates an electron to a chlorine atom. (From Brownlee, Fuller, Hancock, Sohon, and Whisit. *Elements of Chemistry* revised by Paul J. Boylan. Copyright © 1962 by Allyn and Bacon, Inc. Reproduced by permission of Allyn and Bacon.)

to approximately one percent of what it was in the crystal of sodium chloride (5). The ions become hydrated (Fig. 5-7) and are removed from the surface of the crystal. In this way solution of the crystal is effected. Acids and bases, like salts, ionize in water. Because of this the acid and base in baking powder react and give off the gas that helps to leaven quick breads (Chapter 12). Molecules or ions in solution are known as the solute, and the liquid in which they are dissolved the solvent.

Molecules of many compounds in foods are associated through hydrogen bonds. Molecules of sucrose in a sugar crystal are an example. When a crystal of sugar comes in contact with water, water molecules unite by hydrogen bonds to polar groups on sucrose molecules on the surface of the crystal. Hydrated sucrose molecules are removed layer by layer from the surface of the crystal. Heating the water reduces the attraction of water molecules for each other and gives them enough energy to overcome the attraction of sugar

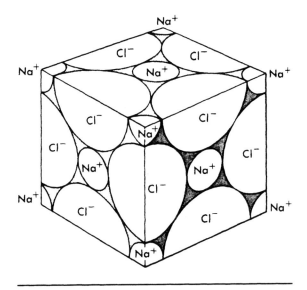

Figure 5-6. Sodium and chloride ions in the sodium chloride crystal lattice. (Reprinted by permission from *Chemical Systems* by Chemical Bond Approach Project. Copyright © 1964 by Earlham College Press, Inc. Published by Webster Division, McGraw-Hill Book Company.)

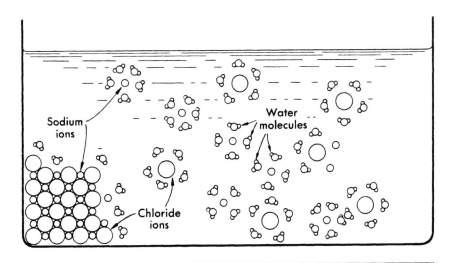

Figure 5-7. Polar water molecules weaken ionic bonds. A sodium chloride crystal dissolves as sodium and chloride ions become hydrated. (From H. C. Metcalfe et al. *Modern Chemistry.* Copyright © 1962 by Holt, Rinehart and Winston, Inc., New York. Reprinted by permission.)

molecules for each other. Solubility of substances such as sugar, where hydrogen-bond interchange is involved, increases with an increase in the temperature of the water. Thus sugars are more soluble in hot water than in cold.

Properties of a solution that depend upon the number of solute particles (ions or molecules) are known as colligative properties (2). Colligative properties of an aqueous solution include freezing point (Chapter 7), boiling point (Chapter 8), osmotic pressure (Chapter 28), and relative vapor pressure (section on a_W, this chapter). The dipolar character of water molecules and their propensity for hydrogen bonding affect the colligative properties of solutions. Their colligative properties differentiate solutions from colloidal dispersions and suspensions.

Colloidal Dispersions

A number of constituents are present in foods, not as true solutions, but as colloidal dispersions. Two distinguishing features of colloids are (1) their size, from 1 millimicron to 0.1 micron, and (2) their enormous surface area in relation to their mass. Substances of colloidal dimensions include pectin, vegetable gums, and proteins. Properties inherent in a colloidal system derive from the unique character of matter at the boundaries of a surface. Surface phenomena are involved in both stabilization and destabilization of colloidal dispersions. Two factors, the charged surfaces of a colloid and polar groups on the surface, are involved in colloidal dispersions. Charged surfaces provide the repulsion necessary to keep the particles dispersed. Hydrophobic (water hating) colloids rely mainly on the repulsion of charged surfaces for stability of a dispersion. The casein of milk is a hydrophobic colloid. Neutralization of charges, as when milk sours or cream is served with tart fruit, removes the stabilizing factor and formation of a clot or a gel is the result. Water molecules that hydrogen bond to polar groups on the surface of a hydrophilic (water loving) colloid act as a physical barrier to coalescence of colloidal particles. Maintenance of this water shield is essential for stability of the dispersion. Its removal by heat or by addition of salts destabilizes the dispersion. Thus the hydrophilic dispersion that is egg white is sensitive to and altered by heat. In addition to such colloids as vegetable gums and pectin, dispersions of the proteins of milk, eggs, meats, legumes, and cereals have important functions in many foods. Knowledge of how they react and skill in handling colloidal dispersions are required if quality products result.

Colloidal dispersions can exist as viscous but pourable sols or as gels. Gels are a two-phase system with molecules of the colloid confining the aqueous phase and also supported by it. Gels in some ways resemble solids, with ratios of elastic/plastic character that vary with the colloid. Casein in fluid milk is present as a sol; in cottage cheese it is in the form of a gel. Colloidal dispersions can be induced to foam, too. When the blades of a beater entrain sufficient air bubbles into a colloidal dispersion such as egg white, films of liquid are reduced eventually to a thinness of colloidal dimensions.

Suspensions

Still another type of dispersion is a suspension. Here the particles of the substance are so large or so complex that they can neither dissolve nor be colloidally dispersed in water. A common example of such a suspension is that of starch granules in cold water. When corn starch is used to make a thickened pudding or soft pie filling, the starch granules are suspended in cold liquid and the temporary suspension is stirred and heated until the starch granules are swollen sufficiently to remain permanently suspended throughout the pudding.

WATER RELATIONS IN FOODS

Water—Bound or Free?

Water makes up a major portion of many foods, constituting from near 70 percent to more than 90 percent of fruits, vegetables, and meats (Table 5-1). Part of this water is readily separated from other constituents present, as happens when fresh fruits and vegetables are sliced or shredded, especially if salt or sugar is added. However, part of the water is separated with difficulty. To remove more and more water, increasingly drastic measures are required. The level of moisture in a food has a marked effect on its texture. The crispness of a newly harvested apple contrasts with that of one stored for a few days in a warm, dry environment or with the rubbery texture of the fruit when dried. The apparent dryness of flour with 12 percent moisture and the limpness of a potato chip with a small increase in moisture above the 1.5 to 2 percent as it came from the fryer suggest that carbohydrate and protein constituents in foods associate with water in seemingly different ways.

To account for these and similar phenomena the concept of bound vs. free water was advanced (9). According to this convention, water molecules hydrogen bonded to polar groups in foods are restricted in motion; that is, they are bound. Successive layers of water molecules increasingly distant from the hydrophilic site are less and less restricted in motion until finally they are as free for hydrogen bond interchange as molecules in bulk water. A number of criteria, none entirely satisfactory, have been suggested to distinguish bound water from free. Among those are that bound water does not act as a solvent for such constituents as salts, sugars, and acids; it is unfreezable; it exhibits essentially no vapor pressure; and its density is greater than that of free water. The validity of the concept of bound water is now questioned (10, 20).

Water Activity

The ancient practice of preserving foods by drying, which concentrates the solutes, or adding salt represents an early recognition of the role of water in the spoilage of foods. Drying to control chemical, enzymatic, and microbiological deterioration of foods remains an important method of preserving food today.

The concept of water activity—not total water or how free or bound that water is—as the factor that influences keeping quality of food was introduced in the 1950's (18, 26). Water activity (a_W) is defined as the ratio of the vapor pressure of water in a solution (P_S) to the vapor pressure of pure water (P_W):

$$a_W = \frac{P_S}{P_W}$$

Solutes lower the vapor pressure of water and its a_W. This is attributed to a dilution effect on water (2) and to reduction of random motion of molecules and their ability to escape from the surface of the liquid as vapor. Salt lowers water activity more effectively than does sugar. A 10 percent solution of sodium chloride has an a_W of 0.93 (vs. 1.00 for pure water); a 10 percent solution of sucrose has an a_W 0.994 (13).

Water activity is high in fresh fruits and vegetables and in meats because of the high moisture and low concentration of solutes, so these foods are highly perishable (6). Some methods of food preservation are successful because they lower the a_W enough to prevent deterioration of food caused by the action of enzymes and microorganisms. Examples of such methods include decrease of moisture in tissues by dehydration or freezing, use of sugar in high concentration as in jams and jellies, and use of a concentrated solution of salt as in brining.

Whether a food exposed to the air dehydrates or takes on moisture depends on the relationship between the a_W of the water in the food and the relative humidity of the air. Relative humidity is the ratio of the vapor pressure of the moisture in the air to that of pure water at the same temperature. Because it is customarily expressed as percent, $RH = a_W \times 100$. A raw apple exposed to air in a warm place for several days will lose moisture, eventually becoming spongy and shriveled, but dried fruit (in which the sugar has been concentrated) left in an open container in the same place may absorb moisture from the air. A plot of the moisture content of a material in equilibrium with different water activities or relative humidities, at a constant temperature, yields a moisture vapor isotherm. If the moisture content is decreasing, as with a raw apple, the isotherm is one of desorption. If dried material is taking up moisture, an adsorption isotherm results (17) (Fig. 5-8).

The a_W of a food is used by the food industry as one criterion for assessing its stability (11). Bacteria require a higher a_W range for growth than do either yeasts or molds. Molds can tolerate a lower a_W range than can yeasts (Fig. 5-9). Enzymes are active at an a_W range too low to support growth of microorganisms. Extensive work has been done with individual microorganisms to determine the minimum a_W below which growth and production of toxin will not occur (7, 21, 23). Reservations have been expressed about reliance on the a_W of complex food systems for this purpose (12, 24). The a_W is valid only when temperature is controlled. The a_W of a food achieved by the addition of one solute such as sugar may limit the growth of a specific organism, while the same a_W achieved by adding salt or glycerol does not (21). In some instances the a_W of a food of known moisture content may differ, depending on whether it is read from a desorption or an adsorption isotherm. The validity of a_W is questioned unless the system is in a state of equilibrium (19) that seldom prevails in complex foods.

Water as a Plasticizer

The concept of water as a plasticizer of foods of low and intermediate moisture contents and how this affects the stability of foods was introduced in the 1980s (14). The plasticizing effect is ascribed to the separation of the large carbohydrate and protein constituents in foods by the small water molecules and the resultant increase in free volume around the

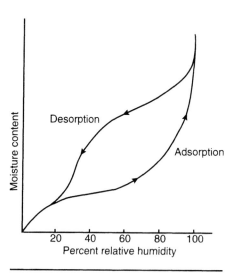

Figure 5-8. A generalized sorption isotherm. (From T. P. Labuza. *Food Technology* 22:264. 1968. Reprinted by permission.)

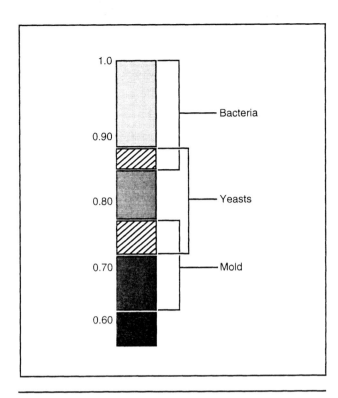

Figure 5-9. The approximate a_w ranges that support the growth of bacteria, yeasts and molds. (From J. A. Troller. *Food Technology* 34(5):80. 1980. Reprinted by permission.)

constituents that gives them elbow room. How flexible or mobile the molecules are is influenced by the proportions of plasticizing water molecules in the system.

Any material in a solid state can be amorphous, crystalline, or partially crystalline and partially amorphous. The latter is the condition that prevails in many foods. Amorphous material can exist either in a brittle, glasslike or a fluid, rubbery state. Material in the glassy state is so viscous that it cannot flow under its own weight, and molecules are for practical purposes immobile. Constituents in the rubbery state are mobile, diffusion is possible, and chemical reactions can take place. Heat can convert a glassy polymer into a fluid rubber. Conversely, cooling material in the rubbery state may make it glasslike. The transition from one state to the other occurs over a narrow range in temperatures designated the glass transition temperature (T_g) (14). The T_g is influenced by the amount of water present and its plasticizing effect. A polymeric component in a food devoid of plasticizing moisture undergoes transition from the glassy to the rubbery state only at a temperature of 200°C (392°F) (3). At a moisture level similar to that in living tissue the glass transition temperature would be below zero, ensuring the rubbery state at ambient temperature so metabolic processes can occur.

Food in the rubbery state is susceptible to enzymatic and microbiological deterioration unless measures such as lowering the temperature are taken. The diagram in Figure 5-10 shows the interrelations of the three states—liquid, rubbery, and glassy—of food systems as affected by both water content and temperature (4). With high moisture and a temperature above freezing the liquid state prevails. Above the glass transition temperature, the rubbery state exists; below this temperature the material is a glasslike solid.

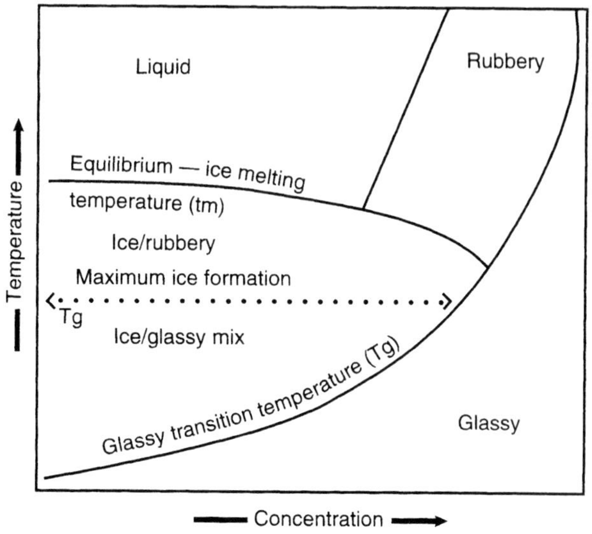

Figure 5-10. Interrelations of the liquid, rubbery, and glassy states of a food system as influenced by both content of water and temperature. (From Daniel Best. *Prepared Foods* 161(9):59. 1992. Reprinted by permission.)

That foods can exist in a precarious glassy/rubbery state, dependent on moisture and temperature, can explain such phenomena as the caking of dried milk and the graininess or stickiness that develops on the surface of hard candy upon exposure to moist air (27). A shift from a glass to a rubber is involved when starch is cooked. Bread staling is inhibited when it is held in a freezer because the temperature is below the glass transition temperature of the cooked starch.

The concept of water as a plasticizer as it influences the glassy/rubbery states of food polymers through its effect on the glass transition temperature has many ramifications. Proponents of the concept suggest that to the extent that water influences the structure, quality, and stability of foods, it does so through its plasticizing action (14, 20). Concepts such as bound water, which they categorize as a myth, moisture vapor isotherms and water activity are of little help in understanding water relations in foods. However, another view (25) is that both water activity and glass transition concepts can contribute to a better understanding of water relations in foods.

CHARACTERISTICS OF WATER THAT AFFECT ITS USE

Hardness of Water

The quality of water used in food preparation is important. When a community boasts of a pure water supply, it is referring to the absence of harmful bacteria, which have been filtered from the water or destroyed by chemicals. But water may contain dissolved substances that make it impure in a chemical sense. One such substance is air, which consists of nitrogen, oxygen, and carbon dioxide. When water is boiled, the dissolved air is removed and as a result boiled water tastes flat. As water filters through the soil, it removes microorganisms but it also may dissolve various substances, some of which affect the taste of water, others the ability of water to extract solubles from such things as tea and coffee, and still others that make the water hard.

Type and Degree of Hardness

Hardness of water is due to the presence of calcium or magnesium ions (5). These may make the water temporarily or permanently hard, depending on whether they are present in the form of soluble carbonates or sulfates, respectively. If calcium bicarbonate, $Ca(HCO_3)_2$, or magnesium bicarbonate, $Mg(HCO_3)_2$, is present, the water is said to be temporarily hard. Permanently hard water contains either calcium sulfate, $CaSO_4$, or magnesium sulfate, $MgSO_4$. Hardness of water is expressed in parts per million or in units called grains, with one grain equivalent to 0.064 gram of calcium carbonate. Based on the grains of carbonate per gallon, water is classified as follows:

Soft	1 to 4 grains per gallon
Medium	5 to 10 grains per gallon
Hard	11 to 20 grains per gallon

Softening Hard Water

One way to soften temporarily hard water, that is, eliminate the calcium and magnesium ions, is to boil it. Heat converts soluble bicarbonates into insoluble carbonates and so removes the unwanted calcium or magnesium ions from the water. A grayish-tan layer of sediment accumulates in a utensil in which temporarily hard water is boiled day after day, due to the deposition of these insoluble carbonates. Permanently hard water cannot be softened by boiling. Some type of chemical water softener must be used to eliminate the calcium or magnesium ions. Temporarily hard water may be softened by the addition of the same chemicals used to soften permanently hard water. Some water softeners react with calcium and magnesium ions in hard water to form insoluble salts. Sodium carbonate, Na_2CO_3, which is the alkaline salt formed by the reaction of strongly basic sodium hydroxide and weakly acidic carbonic acid, is one such chemical that may be used to precipitate the unwanted ions as insoluble calcium or magnesium carbonate. Polyphosphate salts soften water by binding calcium or magnesium ions.

Ion exchange is an alternate way of removing unwanted ions from hard water. In this method the water is allowed to percolate over a bed of insoluble, granular material that removes calcium or magnesium ions from the water in exchange for sodium or hydrogen ions. When zeolites (hydrous silicates) are used, sodium ions from the zeolite are exchanged for calcium or magnesium ions of the water. When the chemical can bind no more calcium ions, the complex is regenerated by flushing it with a solution of sodium chloride, which removes the calcium or magnesium ions and replaces them with sodium ions. When resins are used instead of zeolite, hydrogen ions rather than sodium ions replace the calcium and magnesium ions.

Hard Water in Cooking

Hardness of water is of concern when foods are cooked. Calcium or magnesium ions in water may interfere with the tenderizing of certain foods during cooking. For example, it is difficult to cook dried beans, peas, and lentils in extremely hard water. Hardness of water is a disadvantage in making beverages. To make iced tea, it is customary to brew tea extra strong to allow for dilution by melting ice. If the water used to make tea is hard, the beverage is more likely to become clouded. Sodium ions frequently present in softened water increase the time during which water remains in contact with coffee grounds when the beverage is made by the drip method (Chapter 6).

pH of Water

Aside from being soft or hard, water may be acidic, alkaline, or neutral. Water at a pH of 7 is neutral. Tap water may be neutral but is likely to be adjusted to be slightly alkaline (pH 7.5 to 8.5). Within this pH range both corrosion of water pipes and deposition of carbonates in the pipes are at a minimum. The boiling of water removes carbon dioxide that has dissolved in it from the air, making the water more alkaline.

WATER AS A CLEANSING AGENT

Water is a cleansing agent of importance in the preparation and serving of food. Water removes soil and some of the microorganisms that are present on the surface. It removes food particles and a good share of the microorganisms from cooking utensils and work surfaces with which food comes in contact during preparation. It does the same for dishes and silver used in the serving of foods. Soap or detergent increases the cleansing power of water.

When soap is used with unsoftened, hard water, it must first react with any calcium or magnesium ions present before it can perform its function of lowering the surface tension of water, that is, "making the water wetter." This not only wastes soap, but the curds so formed deposit as a film on dishes and glassware and interfere with the cleansing action of water.

Detergents lower the surface tension of water without having to react with any calcium or magnesium ions present; because of this advantage, they have largely replaced soap. Many dishwashing detergents are so formulated that their cleansing action is not impaired by the presence of either type of calcium or magnesium salt. Some detergents do not make water foam as soap does. Soap left in the waste water when it returns to the soil is decomposed by microorganisms. This was not true of early detergents, now replaced by biodegradable (decomposable by microorganisms) types.

REFERENCES

1. AHEA 1993. *Handbook of Food Preparation.* Pp. 14, 16. Altitude and boiling; altitude and steam pressure.
2. Andrews, F. C. 1976. "Colligative properties of simple solutions." *Science* 194:567–71. Vapor pressure of solutions, boiling point elevation, freezing point depression, and entropy; thermodynamic treatment.
3. Atkins, A. G. 1987. "Basic principles of mechanical failure in biological systems." In *Food Structure and Behaviour.* J. M. V. Blanshard and P. Lilliford, eds. New York: Academic Press. Pp. 160–61. Water content and T_g of biological material.
4. Best, D. 1992. "New perspectives on water's role in formulation." *Prepared Foods* 161(9):59–66. Readable discussion of the glassy/rubbery states of foods; water as a plasticizer.
5. Buswell, A. M., and W. H. Rodebush. 1956. "Water." *Scientific American* 194(4):6–89. Water as a solvent and the freezing of water.
6. Chirife, J., and C. Ferro Fontan. 1982. "Water activity of fresh foods." *Journal of Food Science* 47:661–63. Fruits (42), vegetables (39), and meats analyzed.
7. Christian, J. H. B. 1981. "Specific solute effect on microbial relations." In *Water Activity: Influence on Food Quality.* L. B. Rockland and G. F. Stewart, eds. New York: Academic Press. Pp. 825–54. Response of microorganisms to solute-effect as well as to a_w.
8. Davis, K. S., and J. A. Day. 1961. *Water: The Mirror of Science.* Anchor Books S 18. Garden City, NY: Doubleday. Pp. 24–36, 90–102. Simplified account of some of the unique properties of water.

9. Franks, F. 1983. "Bound water: fact or fiction." *CryoLetters* 4:73–74. An early questioning of the concept.

10. Franks, F. 1986. "Unfrozen water: yes; Unfreezable water: hardly; bound water: certainly not." *CryoLetters* 7:207. Additional questioning of the concept of bound water.

11. Franks, F. 1991. "Hydration phenomena: An update and implications for the food processing industry." In *Water Relationships in Foods–Advances in the 1980s and Trends for the 1990s.* H. Levine and L. Slade, eds. New York: Plenum Press. *Advances in Experimental Medicine and Biology.* Vol. 302:1–19.

12. Franks, F. 1982. "Water activity as a measure of biological viability and quality control." *Cereal Foods World* 27:403–7. Significance of the concept; usefulness and limitations.

13. Labuza, T. P. 1974. "Sorption phenomena in foods." In *Theory, Determination and Control of Physical Properties of Food Materials.* C. Rha, ed. Dordrecht, Holland: D. Reidel Pub. Co. Pp. 197–219.

14. Levine, H., and L. Slade. 1988. "Water as a plasticizer: Physico-chemical aspects of low-moisture polymeric systems." In *Water Science Reviews,* Vol. 3. F. Franks, ed. Cambridge, MA: Cambridge University Press. Pp. 79–185. Role of water in the metastable state of food polymers.

15. Lorenz, K. 1975. "High altitude food preparation and processing." CRC *Critical Reviews in Food Technology* 5:403–41. A review of many aspects including boiling of water.

16. Matz, S. A. 1965. *Water in Foods.* Westport, CT: Avi Publishing Co. Pp. 1–9. Technical treatment of the nature of water.

17. Rockland, L. B., and S. K. Nishi. 1980. "Influence of water activity on food product quality and stability." *Food Technology* 34(4):42–51, 59. Water activity more important than percent moisture; adsorption vs. desorption isotherms.

18. Scott, W. J. 1957. "Water relations of food spoilage microorganisms." *Advances in Food Research* 7:83–127. Water and the keeping quality of foods.

19. Simatos, D., and M. Karel. 1988. "Characterization of the condition of water in food—physicochemical aspects." In *Food Preservation by Moisture Control.* C. C. Seow, ed. Amsterdam: Elsevier. Pp. 1–41. A vote for the usefulness of a_W in nonequilibrium situations.

20. Slade, L., H. Levine, and J. W. Finley. 1988. "Protein-water interactions: Water as a plasticizer of gluten and other protein polymers." In *Protein Quality and the Effects of Processing.* D. Phillips and J. W. Finley, eds. New York: Marcel Dekker. Pp. 23–27. The myth of bound water; part of a long discourse.

21. Sperber, W. H. 1983. Influence of water activity on foodborne bacteria—a review. *Journal of Food Protection* 46:142–50. Interaction of solute and microbial growth.

22. Troller, J. A. 1980. "Influence of water activity on microorganisms in foods." *Food Technology* 34 (5):76–80, 82. Response of microorganisms to reduced a_W.

23. Troller, J. A., and J. V. Stinson. 1975. "Influence of water activity on growth and enterotoxin formation by *Staphylococcus aureus* in foods." *Journal of Food Science* 40:802–4. Two strains of the microorganism compared in two media.

24. van den Berg, C. 1986. "Water activity." In *Concentration and Drying of Foods.* D. MacCarthy, ed. London: Elsevier Applied Science. Pp. 11–36. Use and misuse of a_W; effect of solutes.

25. van den Berg, C. 1991. "Food—water relations: Progress and integration, comments, and thoughts." In *Water Relationship in Foods—Advances in the 1980s and Trends for the 1990s.* H. Levine and L. Slade, eds. *Advances in Experimental Biology and Medicine.* Vol. 302:21–28. A better understanding of the role of water in foods from water activity and glass transition concepts.

26. van den Berg, C., and S. Bruin. 1981. "Water activity and its estimation in food systems: Theoretical aspects." In *Water Activity: Influence on Food Quality.* L. B. Rockland and G. F. Stewart, eds. New York: Academic Press. Pp. 1–61. A cautionary word in regard to excessive reliance on a_W.

27. White, G. W., and S. H. Cokebread. 1966. "The glassy state in certain sugar-containing food products." *Food Technology* 1:73–82. Early application of the glassy state concept to foods.

Coffee, Tea, and Chocolate and Cocoa

6

Coffee and tea beverages are consumed for their appealing flavor and for their stimulating effect. Served hot, as coffee usually is, or iced, as tea frequently is, they provide desirable temperature contrasts with meals. More coffee than tea is consumed in the United States. Hot chocolate and cocoa beverages prepared with milk or milk solids contain nutrients supplied by the milk.

COFFEE

Coffee is the most popular hot beverage in this country. Brazil is the source of approximately half the world's coffee. Colombia, which is the second most important source, along with other Latin American countries, supplies one-fourth. African countries, including Ghana, Kenya, and Ethiopia, supply one-sixth of the world's coffee.

Characteristics of the Beverage

Quality coffee beverage is clear and has a high aroma. The color, which may range from deep amber to rich brown, depends on the strength of the brew and the degree of roast. Good coffee has a silky feel on the tongue. It has a mellow taste and is slightly astringent rather than either flat or excessively bitter.

The coffee used to make the beverage consists of ground, roasted beans (seeds) of the coffee tree, the main species of which are *arabica* and *robusta*. Climatic conditions in the country where the coffee is grown influence the character of the green coffee bean; the quality is modified by blending beans from different areas and by the roasting process.

Constituents in the Coffee Bean (Grounds)

Effects of Roasting on Constituents

Roasting brings about two kinds of changes in the green coffee bean. Structural changes are effected by tiny bubbles of steam that form as the green bean is heated. These make the roasted bean light and porous. This porosity makes possible greatly increased contact between water and ground coffee beans when the beverage is brewed. Even more important are the chemical changes. Some of these liberate or form compounds in the bean that influence the taste, the aroma, and the appearance of the brew. The color of the bean, which depends on the degree of roasting, varies from a light cinnamon to dark brown. The degree of roasting, of course, affects the color of the beverage. Caramelized carbohydrates contribute to the color of the brew.

Caffeine

The roasted coffee bean contains one to two percent caffeine, a bitter constituent that gives the brew its stimulating effect. It is also a diuretic. Caffeine has the formula:

ιeobromine)

As sho   ιffeine in that the former has
a hydr   ïeine content of coffee beverage va   : made in a percolator, automatic   r 5-ounce cup (150 ml). This
contra   appreciably more—142 and
151 m   ιp coffee makers, respectively
(2). Tl   fee (5 brands) was roughly ⅔
that of   ʾalues for decaffeinated coffee
were 1   ;rams per cup for brewed de-
caffein   ;ed from 32 to 65 milligrams
per 12

T   ues compiled from a number
of sou   l0 to 150 milligrams for drip,
40 to   decaffeinated coffee per five-
ounce

T   )f the coffee market. Solvents
used t   rbon dioxide (9). The latter,
when   id and a good solvent for caffeine.   prevent loss of flavor.

Carbo

Anoth   quality of the beverage is carbon dioxide. This gas, which collects in the spaces in the coffee bean formed by the pockets of steam, is responsible for ground coffee floating when it first comes in contact with water. Some of the zip in the taste of the brew comes from the carbon dioxide.

Organic Acids

Two of the acids found in roasted coffee are phenolic compounds. One of these is caffeic acid. The other, which contains caffeic acid, is chlorogenic acid, which has this formula:

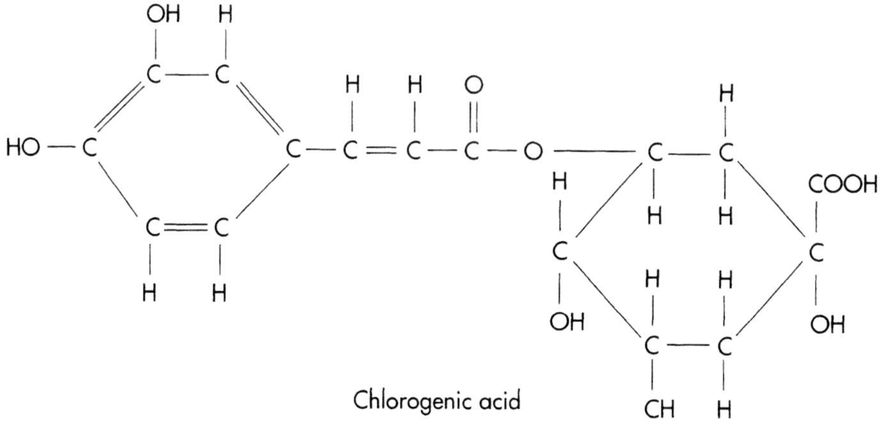

Chlorogenic acid

Chlorogenic acid is the main soluble constituent in coffee. It accounts for more than four percent of the weight of the roasted coffee bean and approximately ⅔ of all acid in coffee beverage. It is a somewhat sour and slightly bitter substance. Because of the quantity present it no doubt makes an appreciable contribution to the taste of the brew.

Other organic acids found in roasted coffee include citric, malic, tartaric, and somewhat smaller amounts of oxalic. These acids are readily extracted from roasted coffee, which explains why the taste of weak coffee is predominantly sour.

Trigonelline

Another constituent, which makes up approximately five percent of the water soluble material in roasted coffee, is trigonelline (the methylbetaine of nicotinic acid); its formula is:

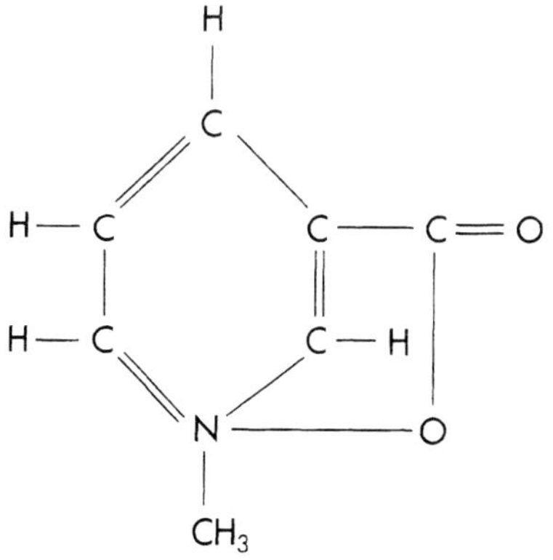

Trigonelline

Trigonelline is approximately ¼ as bitter as caffeine. During the roasting of coffee, part of the trigonelline is converted to nicotinic acid so coffee averages 0.5 milligram of niacin per cup.

A number of volatile constituents are formed during roasting, and these interact with each other and with the breakdown products of carbohydrates to yield substances that contribute to the aroma of coffee (25).

Coffee Aroma

The aroma of coffee has been more difficult to analyze than the taste. More than 100 compounds have been identified in the volatiles from coffee. Several volatile organic acids are present, acetic being the main one. A number of aldehydes and ketones, including diacetyl, acetylmethyl carbinol, and furfural, are present. Pyridine, apparently formed from trigonelline during roasting, is present, as are guaiacol and p-vinyl guaiacol. The last two, together with carbon dioxide, are decomposition products of chlorogenic acid. Guaiacol is a brown, oily substance with a burnt or tarlike odor. The unsaturated nature of these compounds is illustrated by the formulas given for two—furfural and guaiacol:

Furfural   Guaiacol

Furan and 2-methyl furan have been isolated from roasted coffee in appreciable amounts, as has dimethyl disulfide. None of these constituents predominates in the aroma of coffee, and the unique combination of substances essential for the characteristic aroma is still unknown. The presence of phenolic substances and of sulfur-containing compounds appear to distinguish the aroma of coffee from that of coffee substitutes.

Market Forms of Coffee

Coffee is available either as instant or as beans of various grinds. Both instant coffee and ground coffee beans are available decaffinated.

Instant

Instant coffee is dehydrated coffee beverage. When it is manufactured, constituents are extracted from the bean with hot water as in making beverage to serve fresh. The brew is concentrated and then dried. Drying is effected by exposing a fine spray of the concentrate to hot air or by freezing the concentrate and then exposing it to a vacuum that allows the ice to change to vapor without melting. Freeze dried coffee retains somewhat more aroma because it is not subjected to high temperature.

Grinds

Grinds of coffee on the market are designated by such terms as fine, drip, flaked, electric percolator, and regular. The range in size of particles within any one grind varies greatly. Terms used to designate the different grinds are confusing or inadequate. Fine refers to the size of the particles; flaked denotes shape; drip and electric percolator refer to methods for making coffee; regular has no obvious association. The grind for espresso coffee is extremely fine but short of pulverization. In general, the finer the grind, the smaller is the proportion of coffee to water needed to yield brews of comparable strength. The effect of the grind on the overall quality of the brew is an unsettled question, as is the issue of which grind is best for each type of coffee maker.

Preparing the Brew

Although instant coffee has gained wide acceptance because of speed, convenience, and cost, it has not replaced brewed coffee. This section deals with some of the fine points of brewing the beverage.

A number of factors influence the concentration in the beverage of the various constituents from the ground coffee bean. Proportion of ground coffee to water and the freshness of the roasted coffee used to make the brew determine the amounts of these constituents available. The grind, the method used to brew the coffee, the temperature of the water, and the length of time it is in contact with the grounds influence the percentage of available constituents actually extracted and in the brew. All these factors affect the strength of coffee.

Proportions of Coffee to Water

The proportion of ground coffee to water initially determines the potential strength of the beverage. When 1 tablespoon (15 milliliters) of coffee per cup (250 milliliters) of water is used, the brew is weak, with 2 tablespoons (30 milliliters) a brew of medium strength is obtained, and with 3 tablespoons (45 milliliters) per cup of water the coffee is strong. The preferred strength of brewed coffee differs from one part of the country to another as well as from individual to individual. To ascertain the number of servings from a given amount of water and grounds, two points need to be considered. Coffee grounds retain a part of the water added and a full measuring cup of brew makes 1½ servings of coffee.

Brewing Temperature and Time

Hot water is applied to coffee grounds to make the brew: The hotter the water, the more solubles extracted (6). Substances responsible for the aroma are readily extracted, as are carbon dioxide and caffeine. The temperature of the water when it is in contact with the grounds should be at least 85°C (185°F) to extract enough soluble solids to give desired body. At this temperature nearly ¾ of the caffeine is extracted. The maximum temperature recommended for the water when it is in contact with the grounds is 95°C (203°F). Water that is hotter than this extracts such a high proportion of soluble constituents as to make the beverage excessively bitter. Loss of carbon dioxide and of aroma from the beverage occurs, too. When the temperature of the water is at or near the maximum recommended and all of the hot water is in contact with the grounds at once, desirable proportions of the various constituents are extracted in two minutes' brewing time. Approximately 80 percent of the caffeine and of the trigonelline, nearly 70 percent of the chlorogenic acid, just under ¼ of the total soluble solids, and somewhat more than half the color are extracted under these conditions (12). When coffee is made in a percolator, only a small amount of the water comes in contact with the grounds at any one time so percolation time needs to be longer. When the flow rate on an automatic coffee maker was adjusted, a brewing time of seven to nine minutes gave a compromise between increasing the amounts of constituents extracted and avoiding loss of those already extracted (10). If contact time is too brief or if the water is not hot enough, the brew is flat, insipid, and predominantly sour. If brewing time is too long, the brew is likely to be unpalatably bitter and astringent.

The best beverages are those for which the brewing temperature and time are such as to extract 18 to 22 percent of the weight of the grounds. Overextraction (22 to 30 percent) gives a beverage that is excessively bitter. Connoisseurs of coffee have indicated a preference for coffee beverage that contains from 1.21 to 1.25 percent soluble solids. Substances dissolved in the brew affect the specific gravity, and measuring the specific gravity is an objective way to assess the strength of brewed coffee (23).

Effect of Water on Coffee Beverage

The water used to brew coffee influences the quality of the beverage. Naturally soft water is best. Water may be brought to the boiling point before it is applied to the grounds, but it should not continue to boil. Boiled water tastes flat because of loss of dissolved air. Coffee made with such water also tastes flat. Substances dissolved in water that affect its taste are likely to influence the taste of the brew, too. Carbonate or bicarbonate ions in the water prolong the time water remains in contact with grounds, as does the presence of sodium ions in water softened by ion exchange.

Material from Which the Coffee Maker Is Made

A coffee maker of nonmetal is preferable because metals affect the flavor adversely. Utensils of glass or pottery are good from this standpoint. The oily guaiacol, fats, oils, and waxes make it hard to keep a metal coffee pot clean. Utensils should be washed thoroughly with hot water containing soap or detergent to remove the oily film that collects. They should be rinsed just as thoroughly, because traces of soap or detergent spoil the taste of the brew.

Methods for Making Coffee

Steeped Coffee

There are four methods for brewing coffee. Steeping, popular for picnics and camping, is a simple method for which no special equipment is needed. The coffee grounds (regular grind usually recommended) are held in contact with hot water (above simmering but below boiling) for two to four minutes. The brew is then decanted into a preheated pot. Steeped coffee can be very good indeed, but this method can also produce a most unpalatable brew. It is difficult to control the temperature during both the steeping period and that required for convection currents to settle the fine particles in the brew. If the grounds are mixed with egg white before they are put in the hot water, the coagulating egg white traps and carries down the fine particles. Steeped coffee prepared in this way is clear and mild in flavor. For steeping large quantities, the grounds may be tied loosely in a bag of cheesecloth or other porous fabric. See Figure 6-1a.

Percolated Coffee

For coffee made in a percolator (Fig. 6-1b), water near the boiling point is applied in small jets to grounds (regular grind is usually recommended) in the perforated coffee basket. Steam, which exerts pressure on the surface of the water under the dome that is attached to the tube supporting the coffee basket, forces water up the tube and onto the coffee. Thus a percolator acts like a steam-jet pump. Once percolation begins, the heat should be adjusted so the jets of water hit the lid of the percolator gently and approximately every two seconds. Percolation time, which depends on the speed of percolation, varies from 8 to 15 minutes. A perforated cover on top of the coffee basket spreads the water. The pot should be at least ⅔ full when the brew is made. When percolation stops, the grounds should be removed because they absorb aroma.

With this method of making coffee the temperature of water when it contacts the grounds tends to be too high. All of the brew is at or near the boiling point for the entire period of percolation. For this reason much of the desirable aroma of the beverage is boiled away. In the case of a percolator with a valve, only that portion of the brew in the depression over which the valve fits boils before each jet of water. Some electric percolators are equipped with a valve.

Coffee in a Vacuum Coffee Maker

A third method of making coffee is in a vacuum coffee maker. Steam confined in the base of a vacuum coffee maker exerts pressure on the surface of the boiling water (Fig. 6-1c). This forces the water, against gravity, up the tube of the coffee maker and onto the coffee grounds (fine grind is usually recommended). If the coffee maker is assembled before the water boils, the water will rise to the grounds before it is hot enough to give good extraction. A layer of water remains in the base to maintain steam and to keep the base from cracking or warping. Steam is essential for the working of a vacuum coffee maker just as it is with a percolator. The heat should be lowered to give just enough steam to hold the water in contact with the grounds for from two to four minutes. The dry grounds will float. To ensure good contact with water the grounds should be stirred.

When the coffee maker is removed from the heat, the steam condenses. As a vacuum begins to form the beverage is drawn down into the lower part. If the seal between the upper and lower parts of a vacuum coffee maker is broken, a vacuum will not form; the beverage will remain in the funnel part with the grounds. Should this happen, the funnel should be adjusted so the seal forms and the coffee maker returned to the hot unit until the lower part again is filled with steam. When this condenses, a vacuum forms and the beverage will be pulled to the lower part. Coffee made this way usually has good flavor because the beverage never boils.

Coffee in a Drip Coffee Maker

The fourth method for brewing coffee is in a drip coffee maker (Fig. 6-1d). Freshly boiling water is poured into the water receptacle or the cold water is heated in it. From this the

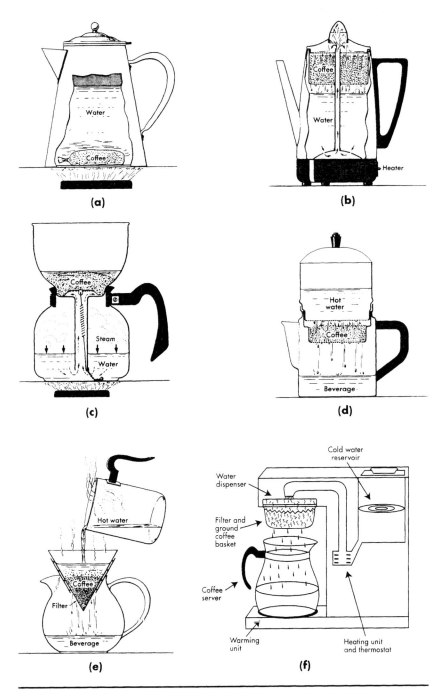

Figure 6-1. Types of coffee makers. (Figure 6-1a-e from *Coffee-Making Equipment* by P. B. Potter and A. H. Fuller. *Virginia Agricultural Experiment Station Bulletin* 367. 1945. Figure 6-1f reprinted with the permission of Simon & Schuster, Inc., from the Macmillan College text *Introductory Foods 9/E* by Marion Bennion. Used by permission of Prentice Hall.)

hot water drips or flows to the ground coffee in the basket below (drip grind is usually recommended). From the grounds the brew drips through the perforated bottom of the coffee basket and into the preheated pot below. A filter in the bottom of the coffee basket holds back fine particles and ensures a clear brew. The number and size of the holes in the water basket control the rate at which the water flows onto the grounds. The number and size of the holes in the coffee basket influence how fast the beverage leaves the grounds. Efficiency of extraction depends mainly on construction of the drip coffee maker and the fineness of the coffee used. In one variation of the drip coffee maker, hot water is poured directly onto grounds in a filter-lined funnel (Fig. 6-1e). Another type, an automatic drip coffee maker heats cold water in its reservoir and then forces jets of hot water onto grounds in the coffee basket below (Fig. 6-1f).

Unless grounds are sequestered from the brew, they should be removed from the coffee maker at the end of the extraction period. Otherwise, they absorb aroma from the beverage.

Effects of Holding on Brewed Coffee

Coffee is improved if it is held at serving temperature for three to five minutes before it is served. Individual constituents merge and blend and the brew becomes more mellow in flavor during this ripening period. If coffee beverage is held longer, some loss of flavor results (21). Interaction of constituents in the brew or loss of volatile substances may account for deterioration. If the beverage must be held for an hour, a holding temperature of 93°C (200°F) is preferred to lower temperatures. Color and clarity are not so good if the brew is held much longer than one hour.

Staling of Coffee

Changes Involved

Constituents in the green coffee bean are quite stable. When the bean is roasted, this is no longer true. Once it is ground and exposed to the air, the roasted bean has an even more limited storage life. The staling of coffee is accompanied by a loss of carbon dioxide. In addition, the guaiacol becomes oxidized, and changes in the unsaturated volatile compounds alter their odor and possibly make them less soluble in water. Coffee brewed from stale grounds tastes flat and lacks aroma.

Retarding Staling

Freshness of ground coffee is maintained commercially by limiting the moisture content and packaging the product under vacuum. The minimum shelf life of roasted, ground coffee is two years; of spray-dried instant, one and a half years; and of freeze-dried instant, one year (1).

Once a container of vacuum-packed coffee is opened, it should be handled to minimize staling. Storing the grounds in a cool place will delay the onset of staleness. A storage temperature of 4.4°C (40°F) is superior to 18°C (65°F) or higher (6). Even more detrimental to freshness than heat is moisture (15). Were it possible to keep moisture-laden air away from ground coffee, it would remain reasonably fresh up to six weeks. From a practical standpoint, this is not possible. Once a can of coffee is opened or beans are ground, contact with moist air should be kept to a minimum and the contents of the can kept cool.

TEA

99
■
CHAPTER 6
COFFEE,
TEA, AND
CHOCOLATE
AND COCOA

Tea is the most universally used beverage. It is prepared from the dried shoots of an ever-green shrub, *Thea sinensis,* a camellia. The main tea-producing areas are India, China, Sri Lanka (Ceylon), Japan, and Taiwan. In the United States, standards for purity, quality, and fitness for consumption of imported tea are maintained under the authority of the Tea Importation Act of 1897.

Kinds of Tea

High quality tea comes from the bud and the first two leaves of the growing shoot, although more mature leaves are used in some teas. The quality of tea beverage is influenced by the climate where the tea plant is grown. Teas also differ because of the way the leaves are treated before they are dried (18). For green tea, the fresh leaves are heated or steamed to inactivate enzymes before they are rolled and dried. For black tea, the leaves are allowed to wither before they are rolled. Then they are held a few hours before they are heated and dried. During this holding period enzymes in the green leaf catalyze the oxidation of constituents that results in changes in color, taste, and aroma. Such tea is described as fermented, although the changes are due mainly to oxidation. Oolong tea is only partly fermented; and a brew from Oolong tea has some of the characteristics of both green and black tea. Much of the tea consumed in the United States is black tea. Tea is dried to a moisture content of approximately three percent.

Quality of the Beverage

Tea beverage of high quality is clear and bright. A flavorful cup of tea has a quality known as briskness, and a distinct but subtle aroma. Some astringency is inherent in tea, but green tea is more astringent than black. The strength of the beverage determines whether the taste of the tea is mild or robust. Green tea is pale, greenish yellow, and the black tea is a deep amber color.

Constituents in Tea

Caffeine

Tea beverage, as with coffee, is valued for the stimulating effect of the caffeine it contains. Tea leaves contain more caffeine (2.7 to 4.6 percent of the dried green tea leaf) than roasted coffee, but the concentration in the beverage averages somewhat less in tea. Values found in the literature include 70 mg, per cup of beverage (type of tea and details of steeping unspecified) (14) and 28 mg, 44 mg, and 47 mg per cup for black tea in bags (three brands) steeped one, three, and five minutes, respectively (2). Comparable values given for loose black tea are 31 mg, 38 mg, and 40 mg per cup of beverage. Green and Oolong tea beverages, bagged or loose, contain less caffeine than black tea. Tea contains, in addition to caffeine, small amounts of two other methyl xanthines: theobromine and theophylline, dimethyl and monomethyl xanthine, respectively (18).

Phenolic Constituents in Green Tea

Tea leaves are extraordinarily rich sources of a group of compounds known as polyphenolic substances, which account for almost ⅓ of the weight of dried leaf (17). The color of the beverage and much of its taste, especially astringency, is attributed to these polyphenolic compounds, or to their oxidation products in black tea. Green tea contains a number of flavonols with the basic structure:

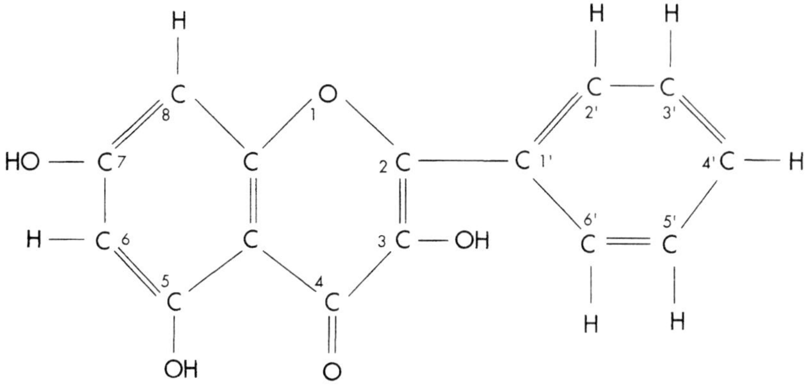

Basic structure of flavonols in tea

Specific flavonols found in tea include myricetin (hydroxyls at carbons 3′, 4′, and 5′), quercetin (hydroxyls at positions 3′ and 4′), and kaempferol (hydroxyl at position 4′), and their glycosides.

Other phenolic compounds found in tea in even greater concentration than the flavonols are the flavanols. This group constitutes 80 percent of the total polyphenols in tea. These include catechin and gallocatechin (hydroxyls at positions 5′ as well as at 3′ and 4′ as in catechin), their esters with gallic acid, catechin gallate, and gallocatechin gallate, and their epimers. The formulas for these phenolic compounds are:

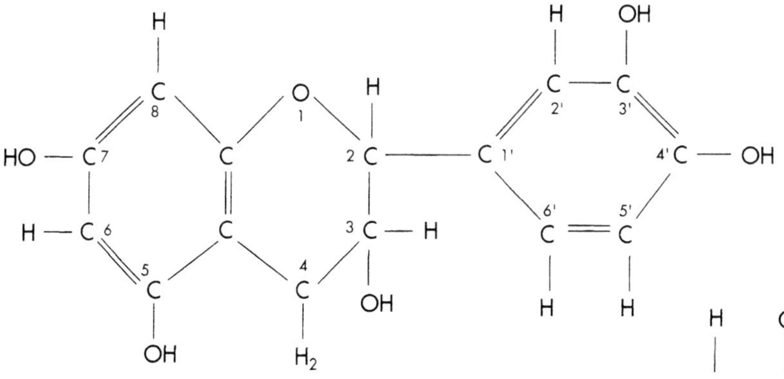

Catechin*

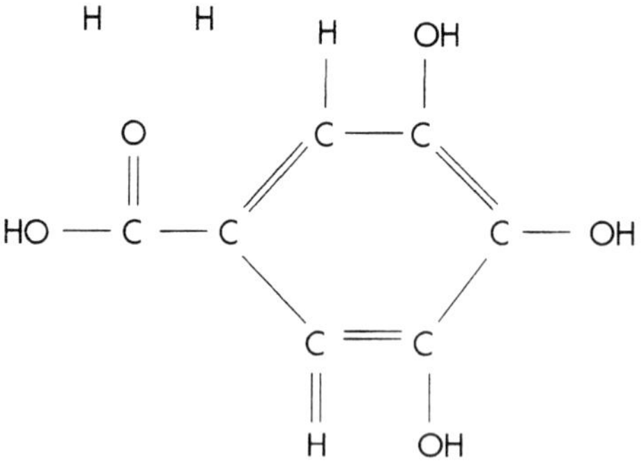

Gallic acid

*Gallocatechin has an −OH at carbon 5′.

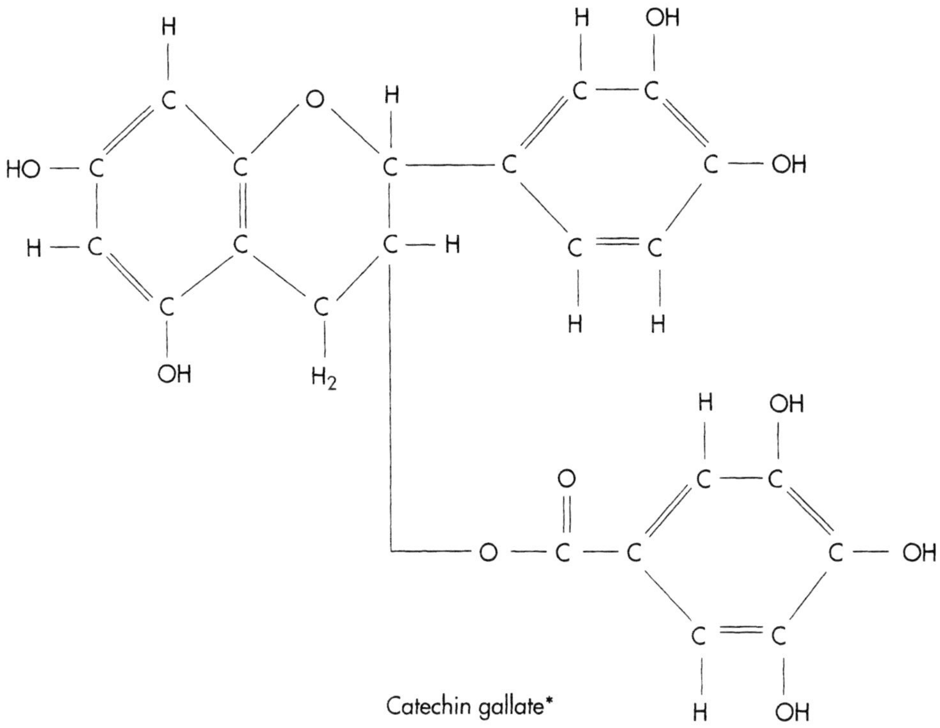

101

■

CHAPTER 6
COFFEE,
TEA, AND
CHOCOLATE
AND COCOA

Catechin gallate*

*Gallocatechin gallate has an − OH at carbon 5'.

*Epi*gallocatechin gallate is the main flavanol in dried green tea. The catechins are responsible for the slightly astringent, metallic taste of green tea beverage. They are involved also in browning and other types of discoloration in foods of plant origin. (See Chapters 27 and 28.) Another phenolic constituent in tea, theogallin, accounts for approximately one percent of the dry weight of the leaf. Chlorogenic acid, also a phenolic compound, is a minor constituent in tea.

Phenolic Constituents in Black Tea

More than ¾ of the polyphenolic constituents of tea may be extracted after the leaves are fermented. In addition to those compounds found in green tea, new ones appear in black tea (18). Rolling the leaves prior to fermentation permits the polyphenolase enzyme to come in contact with the phenolic substrates and catalyze their oxidation. Theaflavins formed when flavanols are oxidized make up approximately two percent of the weight of dried black tea. Alone, they are very astringent, and the amount of caffeine in tea should make it very bitter. It appears that theaflavins modify the bitterness of caffeine and caffeine the astringency of theaflavins, giving the beverage its characteristic briskness (13, 17).

A second group of substances that appear in fermented tea are the thearubigins, the structures of which are still questioned (18). These constitute from 7 to 20 percent of the weight of dried black tea. The bright orange theaflavins give sparkle to tea and the rusty brown thearubigins depth to the color. As fermentation proceeds the thearubigins increase and the theaflavins decrease.

The concentration of phenolic substances is greatest in the bud and the first leaf of the harvested tea shoot, progressively less in leaves one to three, and least in the stem. A high phenolic content gives a tea with a high color. Tea leaves are separated into classes according to size and so marketed. The terms orange pekoe, pekoe, and souchong denote progressively larger leaves of black tea. The term broken inserted before each term indicates that the leaves are not intact. Smaller pieces of tea leaves are known as fannings, and finer fragments are designated dust. These are used in tea bags.

Aroma

The aroma of tea contributes to its appeal. The volatile compounds responsible have been referred to as essential oils. Approximately 30 compounds have been identified in the aroma of green tea, the major ones being benzyl alcohol, phenylethyl alcohol, a hexenol, linalool, geraniol, and methyl salicylate (26). The aroma of black tea is more complex. More than 300 compounds are present, half of which have been identified and none of which alone gives a unique black tea aroma (20). The breakdown of amino acids that occurs as the flavanols are oxidized gives rise to aldehydes in black tea aroma (4). Theanine, the ethyl amide of glutamic acid, is the main amino acid in the fresh leaf (3), contributing one to two percent of the dried weight. *Trans*-2-hexenal formed from linolenic acid is a major component of the aroma (7). Other constituents such as linalool and theaspirone arise from the oxidation of beta-carotene of the leaf (19).

Market Forms of Tea

Consumers have a choice of green, Oolong, or black tea. Tea comes loose or in tea bags. Named blends, such as English Breakfast, are available. Instant tea, spray or freeze dried in much the same way as instant coffee, is advantageous for making iced tea. Adding dried fruit such as orange peel, berries, or rose hips, or spices such as cinnamon or cloves gives tea beverage of distinctive flavor.

Herbal teas are made from the tissues of a variety of plants. Dozens of plants are used for this purpose ranging from alfalfa to sage, from burdock to red clover. Every part of a plant is represented by one or more herb. Included are leaves (blackberry, catnip, dandelion, mullein, nettle), roots (chicory, dandelion, gentain, licorice, sarsaparilla), flowers (camomile, lavender, linden), berries (elder, juniper, hawthorne), fruit (rose hips), and seeds (anise, flax). Although the major active principle(s) in these plants may be known, information appears to be lacking in regard to constituents present in such tea beverages.

Preparing Tea Beverage

Steeping Temperature and Time

Desired soluble constituents, some of which are volatile, are extracted from tea leaves by steeping the leaves in hot water. The temperature of the water when it is in contact with the leaves is as important in making tea as it is in making coffee. Water that has just come to a rolling boil—not boiled water, which makes flat-tasting tea—should be added at once to tea leaves in a preheated pot. Unless the pot is very hot, the temperature of the water will drop too low during steeping for the best extraction. A lid on the pot as the tea steeps helps prevent loss of heat and escape of steam and aroma from the beverage.

A steeping period of five minutes with water at 88°C (190°F) is required to give tea of the same strength as that steeped three minutes at a temperature of 93°C (200°F) (16).

Minimum temperature of the water when it is in contact with tea leaves is simmering (85°C or 185°F). At this temperature—which should be maintained for the entire period of extraction—the time required to steep tea is six to seven minutes. Extracting caffeine from the tea leaves is not a problem because a high percentage of it is removed in two minutes by water at 85°C (185°F). Thearubigins are more readily extracted than theaflavins (22). If water boils when it is in contact with tea leaves, a high proportion of polyphenolic compounds are extracted. These make the hot beverage excessively astringent.

The tea pot should be made of a material other than metal. This is even more important for tea than for coffee because of the high proportion of polyphenolic substances in tea that react with metal.

Effect of Acid on Color of Black Tea

The color of black tea beverage is influenced by the hydrogen ion concentration of the water. Thearubigins in tea brew are weak acids that ionize. The anions are highly colored. If the water used to brew tea is alkaline, the color of the beverage is deeper, an effect due to greater ionization of thearubigins. If acid is added to tea, the hydrogen ions depress the ionization of thearubigins, which makes the beverage lighter. This accounts for the effect of lemon juice on the color of tea. Theaflavins are not involved in the change in color of tea associated with a change in acidity.

Cloudy Tea

Under certain conditions chilled tea beverage becomes cloudy or turbid. Formation of a complex between caffeine and theaflavins and thearubigins is believed to be responsible. The caffeine carries a positive charge and the thearubigin ions a negative charge. When the concentration of the two is high, a precipitate forms. The stronger the tea, the more likely is the complex to form. It is most likely to occur if the water is allowed to boil when it is in contact with the leaves. Iced tea is more likely to become cloudy than hot tea. This complex can be broken by adding hot water or acid to the beverage.

Storage of Tea

Staleness of tea is not as obvious as is staleness of coffee, but loss of flavor does occur as tea is stored (24). Oxidation of fatty acids and theaflavins and loss of theanine and volatile aldehydes occur. High moisture (6.5 to 7.5 percent) is particularly detrimental. Tea should be stored in a closed container at a temperature below 30°C.

CHOCOLATE AND COCOA

Chocolate and cocoa beverages are suspensions of the solid particles of the cacao bean, in contrast to coffee and tea, which are solutions. Milk used to make chocolate and cocoa beverages contributes nutrients to the diet.

Conversion of Cacao Bean to Chocolate

Beans (seeds) of the plant, *Theobroma cacao,* are made into chocolate by a process adapted from that used by the Aztec Indians (11). The harvested seed pods are opened to expose the seeds and the mucilagenous pulp around them. The pods are stacked and held for two

103

■

CHAPTER 6
COFFEE,
TEA, AND
CHOCOLATE
AND COCOA

to eight days, depending on ambient temperature, to allow fermentation. During this critical first step in the conversion of seeds to chocolate, changes take place in the raw bean that are essential for subsequent development of color and flavor of chocolate. Enzymes convert proteins to polypeptides and amino acids. Other enzymes hydrolyze sucrose to glucose and fructose. The fermented beans are dried, during which time desirable oxidative processes take place. Roasting of the dried beans is the next step. A high roasting temperature and a low moisture content cause the products of the hydrolysis of protein to react with the sugars. This begins a sequence of chemical events known as the Maillard reaction, which results in the characteristic aroma and typical brown color of chocolate.

Once the beans are roasted, the shells are removed and the nibs, as they are now called, are mechanically subdivided into particles so small they are barely detectable on the tongue. The process, called conching from the conch-shaped device once used when grinding was done by hand, may continue for up to 72 hours. The end product, known as chocolate liquor, contains the fat in which are suspended the solid particles of the conched nibs. At this point, the fat may be pressed from the chocolate liquor, leaving the solid particles as cocoa. Alkaline treatment, called dutching, of the nibs, the liquor or cocoa is optional, the purpose of which is to modify the flavor and deepen the color of the finished product.

Baking chocolate is solidified chocolate liquor. Sugar is added to the liquor to make semisweet chocolate, and both sugar and milk solids added to make milk chocolate. Both regular and dutch process cocoas are available. The fat from chocolate, known as cocoa butter, has unique melting properties. Solid at room temperature, it liquefies readily at body temperature, a property that is part of the appeal of confections made with chocolate.

Methylxanthines in Chocolate Products

Chocolate and cocoa beverages contain methylxanthines, as do coffee and tea, but theobromine predominates over caffeine in the former (27). The theobromine content of hot chocolate made from five cocoa mixes averaged 65 mg per five-ounce cup and the caffeine content 4 milligrams per cup. Values for chocolate milk (four different mixes) averaged 58 milligrams theobromine and 2 milligrams caffeine for an eight-ounce glass.

Unsweetened baking chocolate contains approximately 13 milligrams of theobromine per gram (5). Values for semisweet, dark sweet, and milk chocolate are approximately six, four, and two milligrams per gram, respectively. Carob bean chips and nuggets contain only about ½ milligram per gram. The chocolate products above contain roughly ⅒ as much caffeine as theobromine. Cocoa contains approximately 20 milligrams of theobromine per gram and ⅙ as much caffeine.

Preparing Cocoa or Chocolate Beverage

Powdery cocoa and fat-rich chocolate do not blend readily with liquid to make a beverage. Either is first combined with approximately an equal volume of sugar and approximately four volumes of water and cooked over low heat, stirring occasionally, until the blend is thick and glossy. This syrup then blends with cold or hot liquid. Solids in the beverage tend to settle to the bottom of the container. Settling is prevented in commercial chocolate milk by the addition of a vegetable gum that thickens the liquid and keeps the particles suspended.

REFERENCES

1. Adinolfi, J. 1981. "How long is coffee's shelf life?" *Food Technology* 35(6):42. Grounds and spray and freeze dried compared.

2. Bunker, M. L., and M. McWilliams. 1979. "Caffeine content of common beverages." *Journal of the American Dietetics Association* 74:28–32. Coffee, instant and brewed; tea, loose and in bags; cola beverages.

3. Cartwright, R. A., E. A. H. Roberts, and D. J. Wood. 1954. "Theanine, an amino acid N-ethyl amide present in tea." *Journal of the Science of Food and Agriculture* 5:597–99. The main amino acid, accounting for one to two percent of the dried leaf.

4. Co, H., and G. W. Sanderson. 1970. Biochemistry of tea fermentation: Conversion of amino acids to black tea aroma constituents. *Journal of Food Science* 35: 160–64. Source of part of tea aroma.

5. Craig, W. J., and T. T. Nguyen. 1984. "Caffeine and theobromine levels in cocoa and carob products." *Journal of Food Science* 49:302–3, 305. Data on the products and on foods that contain them.

6. Farber, I. 1959. "Volatile reducing substances and the evolution of the aroma of coffee." *Food Research* 24:72–78. Effect of storage temperature on loss of volatile constituents.

7. Gonzales, J. G., P. Coggon, and G. W. Sanderson. 1972. "Biochemistry of tea fermentation: Formation of *t*-2-hexenal from linolenic acid." *Journal of Food Science* 37:797–98. A major constituent in tea aroma.

8. IFT. 1987. "Evaluation of caffeine safety." *Food Technology* 41(6):105–11, 113. Compilation of data on the caffeine contents of coffee, tea, chocolate beverages, and soft drinks.

9. Katz, S. N. 1987. "Decaffeination of coffee." In *Coffee*. Vol. 2. *Technology*. J. R. Clarke and R. MacRae, eds. New York: Elsevier Applied Science. Pp. 59–71. The process; market shares of the product.

10. Lee, T. A., R. Kempthorne, and J. K. Hardy. 1992. "Compositional changes in brewed coffee as a function of brewing time." *Journal of Food Science* 57:1411–19.

Optimum brewing time for extraction and retention of constituents.

11. Martin, R. A., Jr. 1987. "Chocolate." *Advances in Food Research* 31:215–49. Production, composition; part of a long review of confections.

12. Merritt, M. C., and B. E. Proctor. 1959. "Extraction rates for selected components of coffee brew." *Food Research* 24:735–43. Effects of time and temperature on extraction of main constituents.

13. Millin, D. J., D. J. Crispin, and D. Swaine. 1969. "Non-volatile components of black tea and their contribution to the character of the beverage." *Journal of Agricultural and Food Chemistry* 17:717–21. Constituents that contribute to the taste of black tea.

14. Nagy, M. 1974. "Caffeine content of beverages and chocolate." *Journal of the American Medical Association.* 229:337. Brewed, instant, decaffeinated coffee, and cola drinks.

15. Prescott, S. C., R. L. Emerson, and L. V. Peakes, Jr. 1937. "The staling of coffee." *Food Research* 2:1–19. An attempt to analyze the staling of coffee; effect of humidity on staling.

16. Punnett, P. W. 1955. "The role of temperature in tea brewing." *Tea and Coffee Trade J.* 109:73–74. Effect of temperature on brewing time and on quality of tea beverage.

17. Roberts, E. A. H. 1958. "Chemistry of tea manufacture." *Journal of the Science of Food and Agriculture* 9:381–90. Phenolic constituents in both green and black tea.

18. Sanderson, G. W. 1972. "The chemistry of tea and tea manufacturing." In *Recent Advances in Phytochemistry.* V. C. Runeckles, ed. New York: Academic Press. Vol. V: 247–315. A review.

19. Sanderson, G. W., H. Co, and J. G. Gonzales. 1971. "Biochemistry of tea fermentation: the role of carotenes in black tea aroma formation." *Journal of Food Science* 36:231–36. Beta-carotene as a source of odorous compounds.

20. Sanderson, G. W., and H. N. Graham. 1973. "On the formation of black tea aroma." *Journal of the Science of Food and Agriculture* 21:576–85. A summary.

21. Segall, S., and B. E. Proctor. 1959. "The influence of high holding temperature upon the components of coffee brew." *Food Technology* 13:266–69. An attempt to pinpoint causes for deterioration of flavor in the brew. Technical.

22. Smith, R. F., and G. W. White. 1965. "Measurement of color in tea infusions." "Effects of methods of preparation on the color of tea infusions." *Journal of the Science of Food and Agriculture* 16:212–19. Effects of water quality and steeping time on extraction of theaflavins and thearubigins.

23. Sprague, E. 1925. "Studies of coffee making by precise methods." *Journal of Home Economics* 17:206–11. An early attempt to assess objectively the strength of coffee brew.

24. Stagg, G. V. 1974. "Chemical changes during the storage of black tea." *Journal of the Science of Food and Agriculture* 25:1015–34. Importance of low moisture.

25. Viani, R., and I. Horman. 1974. Thermal behavior of trigonelline. *Journal of Food Science* 39:1216–17. Products of pyrolysis.

26. Yamanishi, T., T. Kiribuchi, M. Sakai, N. Fugita, Y. Ikeda, and K. Sasa. 1963. "Studies on the flavor of green tea. Part V. Examination of the essential oil of the tea leaves by gas liquid chromatography." *Agricultural and Biological Chemistry* 27:193–98. Major components of the approximately 30 identified.

27. Zoumas, B. L., W. R. Kreiser, and R. A. Martin. 1980. "Theobromine and caffeine content of chocolate products." *Journal of Food Science* 45:314–16. Cocoa, chocolate, and chocolate beverages analyzed.

Frozen Desserts

7

Ice cream, sherbet, ices (sorbet), and yogurt are popular frozen items. Crystals of ice constitute the bulk of such frozen products and all contain sweetener. Additional ingredients differentiate one commercial frozen item from another (Table 7-1). Ice cream and sherbet are frozen, pasteurized mixes that contain one or more optional dairy ingredients. The two differ in the percentages of milk fat and nonfat milk solids specified in Federal standards. Ice cream has a 10 percent minimum of both milk fat and nonfat milk solids, except that each one percent decrease in milk solids can be balanced by a one percent increase in milk fat, so that the two ingredients total 20 percent. If egg yolk solids equal 1.4 percent, the appropriate name for the product is frozen custard or French ice cream. Sherbet contains not less than one percent nor more than two percent of milk fat and not less than one percent of nonfat milk solids. If sherbet contains a fruit ingredient, the titratable acidity is not less than 0.35 percent. Ices contain no milk-derived ingredient and no egg except the white.

Yogurt, a fermented milk product (Chapter 19), is popular as a frozen item. Sweetener, stabilizer, and fruit or fruit juice are added to cultured yogurt before it is frozen. Federal standards exist for cultured yogurt, but none have been established for the frozen product.

Mellorine—imitation ice cream—is made by freezing a pasteurized mix that contains a minimum of 6 percent fat, only a part of which may be milk fat. Mellorine contains a minimum of 2.7 percent protein, derived not exclusively from nonfat milk solids but of a quality not less than that of milk protein. Mellorine is fortified with vitamin A to give 40 International Units per gram of fat.

Small ice crystals are required in frozen products if they are to have the desired creamy texture. Considered in this chapter are the ingredients in the mix and their functions, as well as the freezing process and how it affects the quality of the frozen product. A discussion of how and why ice crystals form is given in Chapter 5.

FACTORS AFFECTING ICE CRYSTAL FORMATION

Components of the Mix

Water, alone or as supplied by milk, cream, or fruit juice, is the main constituent. Sugar (sucrose) is included in most products, so the mix for a frozen dessert is actually a sweetened liquid. As the mix freezes, air bubbles are incorporated in the liquid and the crystals of ice that form are suspended in it (1). A frozen dessert is a solution, a suspension, and a

TABLE 7-1
Requirements for Standardized Frozen Desserts[a]

Item	Fat	Solids	Weight/Gallon
Ice cream	10% milk fat, minimum	10% non-fat milk solids, minimum	4.5 lbs.
Frozen custard or French ice cream	Same as for ice cream, plus 1.4% egg yolk solids, minimum		4.5 lbs.
Ice cream, bulky flavors (Chocolate, Nuts, Fruit)	8% milk fat, minimum	8% non-fat milk solids, minimum	4.5 lbs.
Mellorine	6% animal or vegetable fat, only part milk fat, minimum (Vitamin A to ensure 40 IU per gram of fat)	2.7% non-fat milk solids, minimum	4.5 lbs.
Sherbet [a]	1–2% milk fat (0.35% minimum titratable acidity as lactic acid)	1% non-fat milk solids, minimum	6 lbs.
Water ice (Sorbet)	Same as for sherbets except no milk products and no egg except the white		6 lbs.

[a]Minimum percentage of fruit in sherbet: 2% citrus, 5% berry, and 10% other fruit.
Source: Code of Federal Regulations Title 21, Part 135. Food and Drug Administration, 1996.

foam. If the mix contains cream, an emulsion is involved too. Commercial frozen items contain stabilizers and, in the case of ice cream, emulsifiers. The structure of ice cream viewed with a light microscope is shown in Figure 7-1.

Sugar

Sugar in the unfrozen mix affects ice crystal formation in two ways. For one, it lowers the freezing point of water. When sugar molecules are present, the water molecules must be slowed down more, that is, must have more heat removed, before ice crystals begin to form. It is possible that orientation of water molecules around hydrated sugar molecules makes more difficult participation of these water molecules in the ice crystal lattice. Each gram-molecular weight of sugar (342 grams of sucrose, or 1¾ cups) per liter (approximately one quart) of water lowers the freezing point by 1.86 Celsius degrees. The freezing point of most frozen desserts ranges from −1.4° to −3.0°C (29.5° to 26.6°F), depending on the concentration of sugar. A typical commercial ice cream has a freezing point of −2.6°C (27.3°F); without sugar the freezing point would be −0.78°C (30.6°F). The proportion (24) of sugar in a mix influences the ratio of crystals to unfrozen mix at a given temperature: Too low and the frozen product is too hard; too high and it is too soft at −18°C (0°F), the temperature in a household freezer. The proportion of sugar is greater in ices and sherbets than in ice creams and ice milks to compensate for the acids

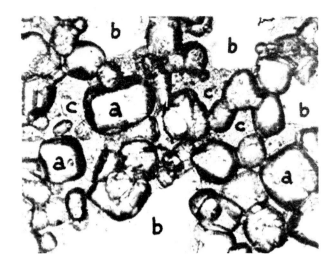

Figure 7-1. Structure of ice cream as viewed with a light microscope: (*a*) ice crystals, (*b*) air cells, and (*c*) unfrozen material. Magnification × 250. (From Wendell S. Arbuckle. *Missouri Agricultural Experiment Station Research Bulletin* 320. 1940. Reproduced by permission.)

in the first two. This means that for an ice to begin to freeze, the temperature must be lowered more than for ice cream.

A second effect of sugar in a mix for a frozen dessert is that the sugar helps keep the size of the crystals small. When milk and cream are used in a mix to be frozen, they contribute some sugar in the form of lactose. The amount of this disaccharide desirable in ice cream is limited because of its low solubility in cold water and its tendency to precipitate. Lactose crystals (called sandiness) are likely to form when a high proportion of dried milk solids is used in a frozen dessert. A frozen dessert contains more sugar than its sweetness suggests because of the effect of low temperature on taste buds.

Another function of sugar in a frozen dessert is to supply bulk. When sugar is replaced by the small quantity required of a high potency sweetener, such as aspartame, an ingredient that compensates for the lack of bulk is needed. Polydextrose and maltodextrin are two effective bulking agents (13). An alternative to inclusion of a bulking compound is to increase the nonfat milk solids and include the enzyme lactase, which converts the lactose to two simple sugars. Such a product is reported to be superior to a product made with a bulking agent (16).

Fat

A number of substances used in frozen desserts that have no effect on the freezing point of the mix help keep ice crystals small, too. Presumably, these substances do so because they act as mechanical barriers to the deposition of water molecules on ice crystals. Water molecules slowed down sufficiently by the removal of heat to unite to water molecules already immobilized in the crystalline state are unable to do so when a foreign molecule or particle intervenes. Instead of an ice crystal already started becoming larger by the addition of molecules of water to its surface, new crystals begin to form. Hence, more—but smaller—crystals form in the presence of interfering substances.

One such substance is fat supplied by milk or cream. Other factors being the same, an ice cream made from cream with 18 percent milk fat will have smaller crystals (finer texture) than a frozen product made from whole milk with a lower fat content. Homogenized milk or cream is even more effective in limiting the size of ice crystals because of the much greater number of fat globules formed as the result of homogenization. Frozen desserts made with evaporated milk have a finer texture than those made with fluid milk (12). In part, this effect arises because the fat has been homogenized. Fats influence the texture of ice cream in another way. In two frozen products with ice crystals of equal size, the one with the higher fat content will seem finer in texture. This phenomenon is attributed to the lubricating effect of the fat on the ice crystals (10).

Low calorie substitutes may replace much of the milk fat in dairy desserts. Polydextrose is such an ingredient (13). Besides contributing bulk, it mimics the texture and mouthfeel of fat. Another is Simplesse®, which consists of microparticles of milk and/or egg white proteins so small they simulate the feel of fat on the tongue. A frozen dairy dessert with no more than 40 calories per standard serving may be labeled low calorie. One that contains ½ the fat and ⅓ fewer calories may be labeled light or lite (22).

Nonfat Milk Solids

Milk solids limit the size of ice crystals more effectively than emulsified fat (10). The greater concentration of milk solids in undiluted evaporated milk is another reason it makes fine-textured ice creams. These solids increase the viscosity of the mix and favor the incorporation of air bubbles as the mix is agitated during freezing.

Because of the milk solids, milk sherbets are usually finer textured than those made with a water base. Also, the acid from the fruit juice brings about changes in the milk protein that cause the milk to thicken perceptibly. This thickening interferes with the development of large ice crystals. In addition, the viscous mix allows the incorporation of many air bubbles. Delay in freezing the mix for a milk sherbet may result in curdled milk, particularly if the fruit juice is decidedly tart. Thickening milk with eggs as for custard or setting the milk with chymosin before it is frozen favors the formation of smaller ice crystals. The gel structure may possibly interfere mechanically with the formation of large ice crystals.

Emulsifiers

Frozen dairy desserts made at home from cream and homogenized milk contain fat in emulsified form. For commercial ice cream, an emulsifier is usually added to the ice cream mix before it is homogenized. Emulsifiers and emulsions are discussed in Chapter 18. Mono- and diglycerides and polyoxyethylene derivatives of fatty acid esters are emulsifiers used in ice cream (4, 14). The added emulsifier supplements the milk proteins, chiefly casein, in the promotion of a finer dispersion of fat in the unfrozen mix. As a result, agitation of the mix as it freezes produces numerous, small ice crystals and incorporates many air bubbles. An equally important and seemingly contradictory function of an emulsifier in ice cream is that it brings about partial destabilization of the emulsified fat droplets as the mix freezes (14, 17, 20). As air bubbles are drawn into the mix, these droplets are oriented at the air/liquid interface (7) and they adhere. Thus fat stabilizes the foam and gives structure to ice cream (6, 9, 23), conferring stiffness, dryness, and melt-resistance. If destabilization is excessive, however, clumping of the fat and a buttery mouthfeel, as well as breakdown of the foam, and appearance of whey results. An emulsifier attracted more to the fat than to the aqueous phase of the mix is less likely to result in excessive de-emulsification (18, 20).

The extensive interfaces formed in ice cream (air/liquid, fat/liquid and ice/liquid) have a major effect on the consistency of the frozen product (6). The consistency of soft serve ice cream comes more from partial destabilization of the emulsion and less on the ice crystal/unfrozen mix ratio than does that of regular ice cream.

Stabilizers

Once small ice crystals form in a frozen dessert, the object is to keep them small. During frozen storage some of the smaller crystals melt; at the same time, water molecules unite with larger ice crystals. Growth of larger ice crystals at the expense of smaller ones during storage tends to make the frozen product coarse. The growth of ice crystals can be minimized by storing the frozen product at a low temperature that does not fluctuate.

Even under optimum conditions, frozen desserts that contain no stabilizer become coarse in texture when stored for an extended period. Inclusion in the mix of one or more ingredients which prevent ice crystals from growing larger is essential if the frozen dessert is to be stored for more than a few hours. Gelatin was the first stabilizer to be used in ice cream (4), and it is included in recipes for some desserts to be frozen at home. Stabilizers used commercially include a number of vegetable gums (acacia, agar, alginate, carrageenan, furcelleran, guar, karaya, locust bean, tragacanth, xanthan). The highly polymerized molecules that constitute vegetable gums (Chapter 9) have numerous hydrogen bonding sites. They function as stabilizers through their ability to make the mix viscous (21). Stabilizers enable frozen desserts to better withstand "heat shock" or fluctuations in temperature with alternate thawing and freezing. The effects of wide fluctuation in storage temperature on ice cream are shown in the photomicrograph in Figure 7-2. Stabilizers also aid in the formation of small ice crystals as freezing occurs. A sherbet that contains gelatin or egg white is finer in texture than an ice made from water, fruit juice, and sugar only. Stabilizers not to exceed 0.5 percent of the finished weight are permitted in commercial ice cream.

The Freezing Process

Removal of Heat

Conversion of water in a mix for a frozen dessert to ice crystals requires withdrawal of heat—80 calories for each gram of ice water changed to ice. This can be done by (a) surrounding a container of mix with brine made from ice and salt or by (b) exposing the mix to cooling coils that contain a refrigerant. When brine is used to absorb heat from a mix, the temperature attained in the brine varies with the proportion of salt to ice and with the size of the salt crystals and the pieces of ice. Although brine made from one part salt and three parts ice by weight can reach a theoretical $-6°F$ ($-21°C$), the actual temperature attained is not that low and it fluctuates with the melting of ice and the dissolving of salt (2). Commercially, heat is removed from a mix by exposing it to cooling coils that contain a refrigerant. The equipment for this works on the same principle as a refrigerator or a freezer. The refrigerant, a gas such as ammonia, is condensed under pressure to the liquid state. Under the lower pressure in the cooling coils, the liquid returns to the vapor state. As it does, heat is absorbed and the coils become extremely cold. The refrigerant provides a lower and more uniform temperature than does the freezing mixture of salt, ice, and brine (2), an advantage for commercial products for which quality control is essential. However, a satisfactory product can be obtained when a mixture of salt, ice, and brine is used to freeze it.

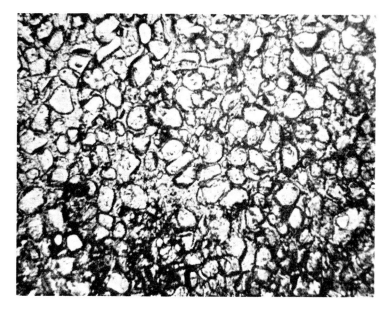

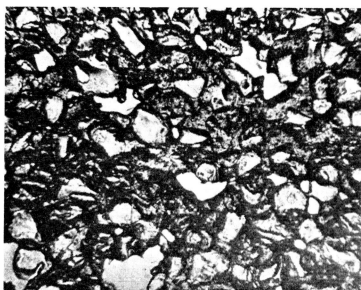

Figure 7-2.
Effects of storage temperature on size of crystals in ice cream. (*Top*) Stored at constant low temperature. (*Bottom*) Stored at fluctuating temperature for five days. Magnification × 100. (From W. C. Cole. *Journal of Dairy Science* 15: 432. 1932. Reproduced by permission.)

The Freezing Mixture

Salt, ice, and brine are in an unstable equilibrium in a freezing mixture. Ice alone cannot freeze water—owing to the latent heat involved (see Chapter 5)—much less the mix for a frozen dessert with its dissolved substances that lower the freezing point. In the freezing mixture, the salt added to the ice dissolves in the water on the surface of the melting ice and lowers its freezing point. This means that the resultant brine can give up more heat to the unmelted ice and get colder without freezing than can ice water alone.

Salt depresses the freezing point of water more effectively than sugar for two reasons. As a molecule of salt gives rise to both sodium and chloride ions, the freezing point of water is depressed twice 1.86 Celsius degrees for each gram-molecular weight of salt (58 grams, or 3⅓ tablespoons) per liter of water. This lowering of the freezing point, dependent on the number of solute particles, is a colligative property. Also, a gram-molecular weight of salt is less than a gram-molecular weight of sugar, so, gram for gram, salt makes it possible to get a colder brine than sugar. How cold it is possible for the brine to get depends on the concentration of salt, but how cold the brine actually becomes also depends upon the amount of ice that melts. The solubility of salt in water limits the lowest temperature attainable by a mixture of ice and salt to −21°C (−6°F), a minimum achieved by combining 29 parts salt with 71 parts ice.

The three parts of a freezing mixture work together as follows. The brine is colder than ice and is the part that actually withdraws heat from the mix through the walls of the metal container. Freezing does not begin until the brine forms and gets cold enough to lower the temperature of the mix to its freezing point. As the ice melts, it absorbs heat from the brine and so lowers its temperature. Salt, as it dissolves, maintains the concentration of the brine. The resultant depression of the freezing point of the water makes it possible for melting ice to absorb more heat from the brine. The freezing mixture is thus a dynamic combination of brine that is colder than ice and actually absorbs heat from the mix, ice that as it melts keeps the brine cold, and salt that, as it dissolves, keeps the brine concentrated.

To prepare the freezing mixture for ice creams, ¼ cup (50 milliliters) of rock salt for each quart (liter) of chipped ice (one part salt to eight parts ice by weight) will give a brine cold enough to effect the freezing in a reasonable time. A coarse salt is recommended because finer salt tends to cake. A higher proportion of salt to ice—⅓ cup (75 milliliters) per quart (liter) or one part to six by weight—is used for ices because of the higher proportion of sugar in the mix. Lower ratios of salt to ice increase the time needed to freeze a mix. Ratios of salt to ice that are too high waste salt and ice and drop the temperature of the mix so fast that it hardens before air is incorporated. Keeping the temperature of the brine low as freezing continues is dependent upon having ice to continue to melt, and to absorb 80 calories for each gram that does melt, and salt to continue to dissolve.

Agitation and Ice Crystal Formation

For most frozen desserts, agitation of the mix as it freezes is essential for the formation of a smooth textured product. Until the temperature of the mix is lowered to the freezing point, rapid agitation of the mix should be avoided; otherwise excessive de-emulsification of the fat and coalescence of fat droplets may occur (23). Once the temperature is lowered to the freezing point, vigorous agitation of the mix initiates the formation of many crystal nuclei. Agitation should be uninterrupted as the temperature drops through the zone of maximum deposition of water molecules in the crystalline state. As ice crystals form and water is removed from the syrup, the concentration of sugar in the syrup increases and the temperature at which the remaining water crystallizes becomes progressively lower. As the temperature is lowered the ratio of crystals to syrup increases, and the frozen product becomes thicker or stiffer.

As the mix freezes, it increases in volume. Part of the increase is due to the expansion of water as it crystallizes, but more is due to bubbles of air incorporated in the viscous mix as it is agitated. The increase in volume, termed overrun, may be 80 to 100 percent or more. Some overrun is desirable to keep the frozen product from being too compact. If excessive, the product tends to be frothy and to lack flavor.

Freezing in a Household Ice Cream Freezer

Essential parts of a freezer include (1) a metal can to hold the mix to be frozen because metal is a good conductor, (2) a dasher that fits into the can, preferably one that is constructed to give triple action, which does a more efficient job of agitating the mix as it freezes and which incorporates more air into the mix, and (3) a bucket, preferably wooden as it is a relatively poor conductor of heat, to hold both the metal can and the freezing mixture.

Bacterial contamination is a hazard in making ice cream (11). Any surfaces with which the mix makes contact should be scrupulously clean. In addition, contamination of the frozen dessert with the mixture used to freeze it should be avoided.

Preliminary chilling of the mix shortens the freezing time. With the mix to be frozen in the metal container and the freezing mixture of ice, salt, and brine around it, agitation of the mix should begin. The dasher should be rotated slowly at first (for approximately three minutes), until the temperature of the mix is lowered by the brine to the point at which the mix begins to freeze. Once crystallization begins, the dasher should be rotated rapidly (160 revolutions per minute) until the temperature of the mix drops through the zone of maximum ice crystal formation (approximately six minutes). This is essential if ice crystals are to be small. After that, agitation should continue but at a slower rate until the dasher is too hard to turn. This occurs when 60 percent or more of the water in the mix is frozen.

HARDENING OF FROZEN DESSERTS

A mix for ice cream will become too difficult to manipulate in a freezer before enough of the water has been converted to ice for the frozen product to have a desirable consistency for serving. For this reason, the partially frozen mix is held in contact with a coolant and allowed to continue to freeze and harden without agitation. How hard the frozen product becomes depends on how low the temperature goes and also on the proportion of sugar in the mix. The two factors are interrelated. Because of the higher proportion of sugar, ices and sherbets must be brought to a lower temperature than ice creams and ice milks before the ratio of ice crystals to unfrozen mix is high enough to give a desirable consistency for serving. Allowing a frozen dessert to stand for a short time after it is frozen will mellow and improve the flavor as well as harden it.

Commercial ice cream is discharged from the freezer at a temperature near −6°C (21°F) (5), with approximately half the water converted to ice crystals. Additional freezing and hardening at −35°C (−31°F) follows, with a high proportion of water now in the form of ice. As a result of hardening, the unfrozen portion of the ice cream becomes a concentrated sugar glass with a glass transition temperature near −23°C (−9°F) (8). Below this temperature water molecules are essentially immobile and ice crystals are stable. If the temperature of the ice cream rises above the glass transition temperature, mobility increases and ice crystals grow larger. The speed and extent of growth depend on how high the holding temperature is above the glass transition temperature. Although a low holding temperature is needed to keep ice crystals from growing, the frozen product may be too firm to serve if taken directly from the freezer. Most ices and ice creams have a desirable consistency at a temperature of −12° to −10°C (14° to 10°F). Frozen products are more flavorful at the higher temperature.

STILL-FROZEN DESSERTS

The Mix

In the absence of agitation to aid in the formation of small crystals in a frozen dessert, a higher proportion of interfering substances is needed in the mix (3). Mixes for still-frozen products rely heavily on a high proportion of fat droplets and the incorporation of innumerable small bubbles of air, before the mix is frozen, to keep the crystals small. Whipped gelatin, whipped cream, whipped evaporated milk, and beaten egg white are used to introduce air bubbles into still-frozen desserts. Faster freezing also aids in the formation of small crystals. For this reason a high proportion of sugar in a mix to be still-frozen is a disadvantage. Two products that may be satisfactorily still-frozen are mousses and parfaits.

Freezing the Mix

The mix should be chilled before it is put to freeze. Still-frozen desserts may be frozen by surrounding the mix with a freezing mixture of one part salt to three or four parts ice by measure. An alternative is the freezing compartment of a refrigerator. The thermostat should be set as low as possible a half hour or so before the mix is put to freeze. Good contact between the bottom of the freezing tray that contains the mix and the cooling surface of the refrigerator aids in rapid withdrawal of heat from the mix. A film of water between the two ensures good contact and eliminates air, which is a poor conductor. Rapid drop in temperature favors the formation of many ice crystal nuclei, which helps keep the crystals small.

QUALITY CHARACTERISTICS OF FROZEN DESSERTS

In addition to flavor, three main characteristics by which the quality of a frozen dessert may be assessed are texture, consistency, and body. Texture refers to the feel of the frozen dessert on the tongue. It may be coarse or fine, depending on the size of the ice crystals. When crystals are small (less than $35\mu m$), the ice cream is very smooth. Somewhat larger crystals, 35 to 55 μm in size, yield a smooth textured product. Frozen products with crystals larger than 55 μm are coarse textured (5). Crystals from mixes with a high proportion of fat seem finer than they actually are, presumably because fat lubricates the crystals.

Consistency refers to the hardness or softness of a frozen dessert. Frozen products should be firm enough to hold their shape. This characteristic is influenced mainly by temperature but also, to some extent, by the viscosity of the syrup that remains unfrozen. A typical mix extruded from the freezer near $-6°C$ has approximately ½ the water in the form of ice crystals; stored at $-11°C$ has ¾, and hardened at $-30°C$ has more than ⁹⁄₁₀ of the water is in crystalline form (6).

Aside from texture, which depends on the size of the ice crystals, and consistency, which depends upon the ratio of ice crystals to syrup, the way a frozen dessert behaves when it warms and begins to melt is a characteristic of consequence in determining quality. The body of a frozen dessert may be too viscous and spongy on the one hand or too watery and compact on the other. Body is influenced primarily by the characteristics of the liquid in which the crystals are suspended.

REFERENCES

1. Arbuckle, W. S. 1940. "A microscopic and statistical analysis of texture and structure in ice cream as affected by composition physical properties and processing method." *Missouri Agricultural Experiment Station Research Bulletin* 320:25–32. Effects of fat, sugar, serum solids, and gelatin on structure and texture; illustrated with photomicrographs.

2. Arbuckle, W. S. 1986. *Ice Cream.* Westport, CT: The Avi Publishing Company. Pp. 84–94, 343–51. Emulsifiers and stabilizers; freezing mechanically.

3. Bentley, L., and B. M. Watts. 1939. "Use of stabilizers in unagitated ice cream." *Food Research* 4:101–11. Effectiveness of agar, pectin, rennin, gelatin, starch, egg yolk, and dried skim milk in controlling crystal size.

4. Berger, K. G. 1990. "Ice cream." In *Food Emulsions.* K. Larsson and Stig Friberg, eds. New York: Marcel Dekker, Inc. Pp. 367–444. An overview of the subject.

5. Berger, K. G., B. K. Bullimore, G. W. White, and W. B. Wright. 1972. "The structure of ice cream—Part 1." *Dairy Industries* 37(8):419–25. Air cells, fat globules, and ice crystals.

6. Berger, K. G., B. K. Bullimore, G. W. White, and W. B. Wright. 1972. "The structure of ice cream—Part 2." *Dairy Industries* 37(9):493–97. Fat/mix, air/mix, and ice/mix interfaces in ice cream.

7. Berger, K. G. and G. W. White. 1971. "An electron microscopic investigation of fat destabilization in ice cream." *Journal of Food Technology* 6:285–94. The role of destabilization.

8. Blanshard, J. M. V., and F. Franks. 1987. "Ice crystallization and its control in frozen-food systems." In *Food Structure and Behavior.* J. M. V. Blanshard and P. Lilliford, eds. London: Academic Press, Ltd. Pp. 51–65. The glassy state in hardened ice cream.

9. Buchheim, W., and F. Dejmek. 1990. "Milk and dairy-type emulsions." In *Food Emulsions.* K. Larsson and S. Friberg, eds. Pp. 203–46. Stabilization of air cells in ice cream.

10. Cole, W. C., and J. H. Boulware. 1940. "Influence of some mix components upon the texture of ice cream." *Journal of Dairy Science* 23:149–57. Effectiveness of butterfat *vs.* milk solids.

11. Foltz, V. D., and W. H. Martin. 1941. "A study of homemade ice cream." *Food Research* 6:31–38. Bacterial contamination and possible sources.

12. Given, M. 1928. "Texture of ice cream as influenced by some constituents." *Industrial and Engineering Chemistry* 20:966–68. Effects of gelatin, egg (custard), and evaporated milk.

13. Goff, D. H., and W. K. Jordan. 1984. "Aspartame and polydestrose in calorie-reduced frozen dessert." *Journal of Food Science* 49:306–7. Formulation of a product with 30 to 40 percent fewer calories than ice milk.

14. Goff, D. H., and W. K. Jordan. 1989. "Action of emulsifiers in promoting fat destabilization during the manufacture of ice cream." *Journal of Dairy Science* 72: 18–29. Both whipping and ice crystallization involved in destabilization.

15. Govin, R., and J. G. Leeder. 1971. Action of emulsifiers in ice cream utilizing the HLB concept. *Journal of Food Science* 36: 718–22. The importance of controlled deemulsification.

16. Keller, S. E., J. Fellows, T. C. Nash, and W. H. Shazer. 1991. Formulation of aspartame-sweetened frozen dairy dessert without bulking agents. *Food Technology* 45(2): 102, 104, 106. Effectiveness of lactase-treated nonfat milk solids.

17. Kloser, J. J., and P. G. Keeney. 1959. "A study of some variables that affect fat stability and dryness in ice cream." *Ice Cream Review* 42(10):38–41, 56–60. An early attempt to elucidate the role of emulsifiers.

18. Knightly, W. H. 1963. "Surfactants in food manufacturing." 2. "Applications and mode of action." *Food Manufacture* 38:661–66. Functions of emulsifiers in frozen desserts.

19. Leeder, J. G. 1971. "A new concept about the function of emulsifiers in ice cream." *American Dairy Review* 33(10):28 B,D. Importance of the HLB of the emulsifier.

20. Lin, P., and J. G. Leeder. 1974. "Mechanism of emulsifier action in an ice

cream system." *Journal of Food Science* 39:108–11. An attempt to account for the destabilizing action.

21. Moore, L. J., and C. F. Shoemaker. 1981. "Sensory texural properties of stabilized ice cream. *Journal of Food Science* 46:399–402, 499. Action of stabilizers, a viscosity effect.

22. Shank, F. R., and R. L. Carson. 1990. "Light dairy products: regulatory issues." *Food Technology* 44(10):88–92. Labeling terminology.

23. Sherman, P. 1965. The texture of ice cream. *Journal of Food Science* 30:201–11. The effects of freezing on the fat globules of ice cream.

24. Tharp, B. W., and T. Gottemoller. 1990. "Light frozen dairy desserts: Effects of compositional changes in processing and sensory characteristics." *Food Technology* 44(10):86–87. Supplemental ingredients in low-calorie products.

Sugars, Alternative Sweeteners, and Confections

8

Sweets are almost universally liked, and sugars are valued for the sweet taste they impart to foods. The sweetness of common sugars relative to that of sucrose is given in Chapter 2. Compounds other than sugars elicit the sweet taste, too.

Sugars perform functions in foods in addition to modifying taste. They influence the properties of water (Chapter 5) and they are an important ingredient in frozen dairy desserts (Chapter 7). The functions of sugar in quickbreads, yeast breads, cakes, and fruit pectin jellies are discussed in chapters devoted to these topics. Sugars and alternative sweeteners are discussed in the first part of this chapter. Discussion of the function of sugars in candy making follows.

Confections are either crystalline, as in fondant, fudge, and panocha; or are noncrystalline as in caramels, brittles, glacés, and chewy taffies; or have a special texture, as in gum drops (a gel), marshmallows (combination of foam and gel), divinity, and seven-minute frosting (combination of foam and crystals). Crystalline candies are sugar crystals surrounded by and suspended in saturated sugar syrup.

Material on ice crystal formation in frozen desserts (Chapter 7) also applies to sucrose crystal formation in crystalline confections. A noncrystalline candy such as caramels is just a very thick syrup. Certain noncrystalline candies, such as brittles and lollipops, have a low moisture content (one to two percent) and are hard and glasslike.

A discussion of sweeteners precedes consideration of the details of using sugar in making candies.

SUGARS AND OTHER SWEETENERS

Sugars are synthesized by plants and are present in solution in the cell sap. Sugars contribute to the taste appeal of ripe fruits and many vegetables as well. Three sugars, glucose, fructose, and sucrose, are the main source of sweetness in fruits and vegetables. These sugars are present also in the nectar of flowers that bees collect to make honey. Much of the sucrose in nectar is changed by the enzyme invertase secreted by the bee to glucose and fructose. Honey is a concentrated solution of these two sugars (nearly 80 percent) (5), with less than two percent sucrose. The sugar, xylose, and the polyhydric alcohols, xylitol and sorbitol, present in small amounts in fruits and vegetables (14), contribute sweetness. The sucrose contents of sugar cane and sugar beets are high enough to make them economically profitable as raw material for commercial granulated sugar.

Corn syrups, now important sweeteners, are manufactured from cornstarch. The syrups contain varying proportions of glucose, maltose, and dextrins, all products of the hydrolysis of starch (Chapter 9). When corn syrup high in glucose is treated with an isomerase, part of the glucose is converted to the much sweeter fructose (2). A typical high fructose corn syrup contains 42 percent fructose, 50 percent glucose, and 8 percent maltose and higher saccharides. High fructose corn syrup is similar in composition to honey and invert sugar (discussed later in this chapter).

Sweeteners other than sugar are synthesized by plants, too (7). Glycyrrhizin is one such sweet substance. It is a triterpenoid saponin, obtained from the roots of the licorice plant. Glycyrrhizin, 50 to 100 times as sweet as sucrose, is used as a flavor and sweetener in confections. Thaumatins are high potency sweet proteins obtained from the fruit of a plant in Sudan. Because the sweet taste is a lingering one, thaumatins are used in chewing gum. Monellin comes from the fruit, known as the serendipity berry, of a West African vine. It is comparable in sweet potency to thaumatins. Monellin consists of two dissimilar polypeptides, neither alone sweet, suggesting that one supplies the AH group and the other the B group required to initiate the sweet sensation (Chapter 2). Leaves of an herb that grows near the Paraguay-Brazil border contain sweet substances of which stevioside is one. It is a glycoside or sugar derivative of an unsaturated hydrocarbon called steviol. Stevioside is now under study as a possible alternative sweetener (11).

The sweet taste of sugars is appealing, but sugars are cariogenic. In addition, a diet high in calories, especially calories from sugar, is believed to have an adverse effect on health. For these reasons, sugars are de-emphasized on the Food Pyramid, and a diet low in sugar is recommended.

CONSUMPTION OF SWEETENERS

The per-capita consumption of caloric sweeteners increased from 124 pounds in 1980 to 148 pounds in 1994 (from 56 kilograms to 67 kilograms) (as shown in Table 8-1)(16). This, despite the recommendation of nutritionists to use less sugar and the professed interest of consumers to do so! The per-capita consumption of cane and beet sugar, once the main sweetener, dropped from 84 pounds in 1980 to 65 pounds in 1994 (from 38 to 30 kilograms). This decrease in consumption was more than offset by more than a doubling in the per-capita consumption of corn sweeteners that increased from 38 pounds to 81 pounds (18 to 37 kilograms) over the same period. The 43-pound (19-kilogram) increase in consumption of corn sweeteners gave a net increase per-capita of 24 pounds (11 kilograms) of caloric sweeteners. Consumption of saccharin changed little. Aspartame was first approved as a tabletop sweetener and for use in dry mixes in 1981 and in carbonated beverages in 1983 (9). Two years later, in 1985, the per-capita consumption had the sweetness equivalence of 12 pounds (5.5 kilograms) of sucrose (16). The per-capita consumption of aspartame in 1991 was equivalent in sweetness to 17 pounds (8 kilograms) of sucrose.

ALTERNATIVES TO SUGAR

The use of alternative sweeteners, considered food additives, is regulated by the Food Additive Amendment to the Food, Drug, and Cosmetic Act. Substances in common usage prior to passage of the amendment in 1958 were listed as generally recognized as safe,

119

■

CHAPTER 8
SUGARS,
ALTERNATIVE
SWEETENERS,
AND
CONFECTIONS

TABLE 8-1
Per-Capita Consumption of Sweeteners

	1980	1994
Caloric sweeteners	124 pounds (56 kilograms)	148 pounds (67 kilograms)
Cane and beet sugars	84 pounds (38 kilograms)	65 pounds (30 kilograms)
Corn sweeteners (dry weight)	38 pounds (18 kilograms)	81 pounds (37 kilograms)

	1980	1985	1991
Non-sugar sweeteners (sucrose equivalent)			
Saccharin	7.7 pounds (3.5 kilograms)	—	7.3 pounds (2.3 kilograms)
Aspartame	—	12 pounds (5.5 kilograms)	17 pounds (8 kilograms)

the GRAS list. The amendment specified conditions under which a substance not on the original list could achieve GRAS status and so be approved for food use by the Food and Drug Administration. The search continues for low or non-caloric substances, manufactured or natural, to replace sugar. Interestingly, the sweetness of each of the three synthetics—saccharin, acesulfame K, and aspartame—approved for use in foods was discovered by accident (7).

A potent sweetener such as saccharin or aspartame can replace sugar in a beverage because the match of their taste profiles to that of sugar is the main concern. In most foods, however, sugar performs other important functions. When sugar is decreased in or omitted from such foods, a substitute that performs the functions of the missing sugar, including bulk, is required (7). Bulking agents include nonsweet and noncaloric derivatives of cellulose (Chapter 9). Maltodextrins are another. They are formed by limited hydrolysis of starch and supply the same number of calories but are not sweet. Polydextrose, made by the condensation of dextrose (glucose), is designed to function as a replacement for sugar. The energy value of polydextrose is one kilocalorie per gram, so substituting it for sugar can effect a reduction of calories as shown in the following example (7). A formula for a hard candy made with 59 percent sucrose (59 grams at 4 kilocalories per gram) and 18.6 percent corn syrup (18.6 grams at 2.8 kilocalories per gram) yields approximately 288 kilocalories. Substituting polydextrose for all of the corn syrup and 1/3 of the sucrose gives a formula with 38.8 percent sucrose (38.8 grams at 4 kilocalories per gram) and 38.8 percent polydextrose (38.8 grams at 1 kilocalorie per gram) for a total of 194 kilocalories. Replacing the remainder of the sugar with isomalt at two kilocalories per gram reduces the calories further to a total of 117. Other alternatives to sugar are the polyhydric alcohols, xylitol, sorbitol, mannitol, and maltitol. Commercial versions of these polyols are made by hydrogenation of the appropriate sugar, xylose, glucose, fructose, and maltose, respectively (7). These sweet alcohols are considered carbohydrates with an energy value of four kilocalories per gram (6). When crystals of xylitol and sorbitol dissolve in water, heat is absorbed. The cooling effect of xylitol is 37 calories (153 joules) per gram, that of sorbitol is 23 calories (96 joules) per gram. These compare with 14 calories (59 joules) per gram for glucose and 4.3 calories (18 joules) per gram for sucrose (10). Polyols are used in chewing gum for their cooling effect and because they do not promote dental caries. Xylitol, the sweetest of the polyhydric alcohols, can replace sugar in hard candies. In combination with another polyol or polydextrose, xylitol can be used to produce sugar-free confections (15).

121
■
CHAPTER 8
SUGARS,
ALTERNATIVE
SWEETENERS,
AND
CONFECTIONS

SUCROSE

Sugar (sucrose) is a crystalline ingredient (Figure 8-1) used in making candies and other confections. Although the consumption of sucrose has declined in the last decade, it is still a major ingredient in candies, accounting for 44 percent of the net weight of confections shipped in this country (12). Properties of sucrose related to candy making precedes the discussion of individual confections.

Source

Commercial granulated sugar (sucrose) is manufactured from two plants, sugar cane and sugar beets (1). Stalks of sugar cane from which the leaves have been removed are crushed between heavy rollers to express the juice; sugar beets are cut into thin strips and the tissue extracted with hot water. The thin juice contains 10 to 15 percent sucrose, together with nonsucrose constituents derived from the plant tissue. Treatment of the juice with lime and carbon dioxide precipitates the bulk of the impurities, from which the juice is separated by decantation. Other impurities, including coloring matter, are removed from the juice in a series of steps referred to as refining. This refined liquor is evaporated at a low

Figure 8-1. Scanning electron micrograph of raw sugar (sucrose) crystals. Original magnification, 100×. (Used by permission of California and Hawaiian Sugar Company.)

temperature under a vacuum to concentrate the sucrose sufficiently for crystallization to take place. Adhering syrup is removed from the crystals by centrifugation. Crystals of refined white sugar contain no more than 0.05 percent impurities. The size of the crystals (Figure 8-2) is controlled by the crystallization process and by sieving. The low moisture content eliminates caking of the crystals. Food grade molasses is syrup removed at intermediate stages in the refining of cane juice. Brown sugars are also made by crystallizing sucrose from syrups at different stages in the refining process.

Chemistry

Sugars belong to a class of compounds known as carbohydrates. Saccharide is a term that denotes sugar, or substances derived from sugar. Monosaccharides are simple or single sugars. Disaccharides are derived from monosaccharides, and when hydrolyzed, yield two molecules of simple sugar. Molecules containing several sugar residues such as starches and cellulose are known as polysaccharides.

Sucrose is a disaccharide formed by the union of one molecule of the monosaccharide glucose (dextrose) with one of the monosaccharide fructose (levulose) through carbons 1 and 2 and with the loss of one molecule of water:

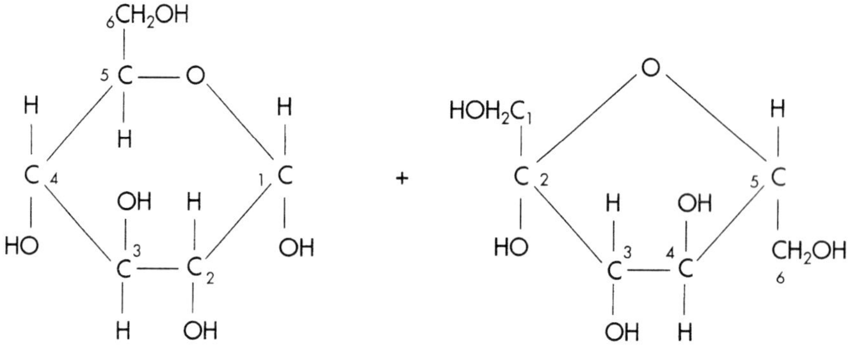

Glucose   Fructose

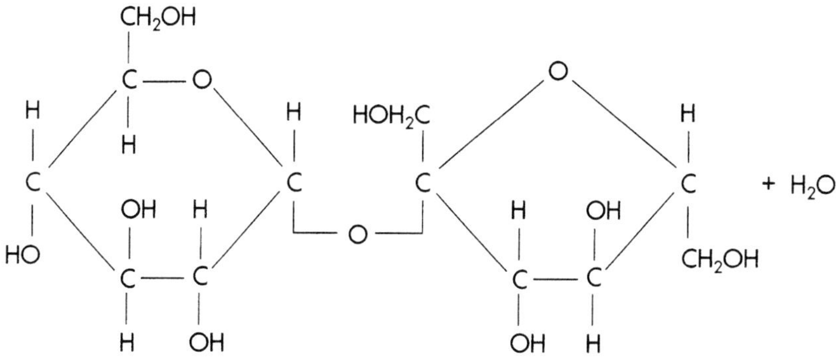

Sucrose   Water

Thus sucrose is made from and can give rise to one molecule of glucose and one of fructose.

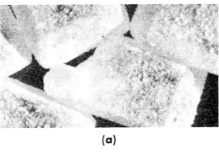

(a)

123

■

CHAPTER 8
SUGARS,
ALTERNATIVE
SWEETENERS,
AND
CONFECTIONS

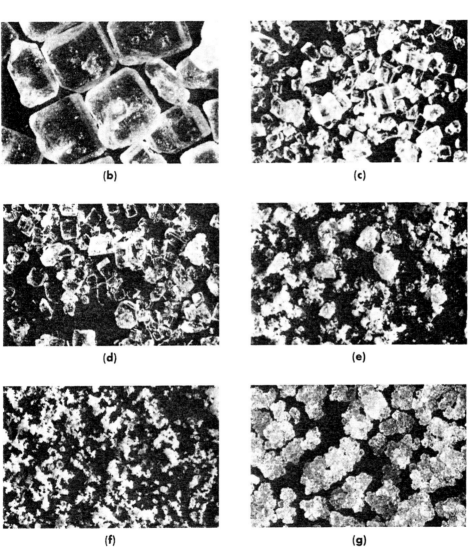

Figure 8-2. Relative sizes of sugar crystals commonly available: (*a*) topping sugar, (*b*) medium granulated, (*c*) extra-fine granulated, (*d*) fruit-fine granulated; powdered sugars made by grinding or pounding granulated sugar and usually containing 3 percent cornstarch added to prevent caking in (*e*) standard powdered, and (*f*) 6× powdered; (*g*) clusters of crystals of brown sugar. (From J. A. Dunn and J. R. White, *Cereal Chemistry* 14: 792, 794, 1937. Reproduced by permission.)

TABLE 8-2

Effect of Temperature on Solubility of Sucrose, Fructose, and Sodium Chloride (grams per 100 grams of water)

Temperature (°C)	Sucrose[a] (grams)	Fructose (grams)	Sodium Chloride (grams)
0	179.2		35.6
10	190.5		
20	203.9	375.0	36.0
30	219.5		
40	238.1	538.0	
50	260.4		
100	487.2		37.8
115	669		

[a]Source: C. A. Browne, A Handbook of Sugar Analysis, copyright © 1912 by John Wiley & Sons, Inc., New York, p. 649.

Solubility

The first step in making candies and frostings is to dissolve the dry, coarse crystals of granulated sugar in water. An excess of water is used to ensure complete solution. Sucrose is highly soluble in water, more so than glucose, but less so than fructose. Lactose is least soluble of the common sugars. The solubility of any sugar in water increases with an increase in temperature. Table 8-2 gives the solubility of sucrose in water at various temperatures. When the amount of sucrose specified in the table is dissolved in 100 grams of water at a given temperature, a saturated solution is developed. At 20°C (68°F) a 67 percent sucrose solution (203.9 grams of sucrose per 100 grams of water) is saturated; at 115°C (239°F) the concentration of sucrose in a saturated solution is 87 percent. Solubility of fructose at two temperatures and of sodium chloride at three temperatures is also given.

Hydroxyl groups on sugar molecules confer on them their solubility in water. Elevating the temperature makes little difference in the solubility of sodium chloride where ionic bonds are involved, but a marked difference in the solubility of sugar where hydrogen bonds are involved.

The high solubility of sucrose in water is an advantage in making candies and frostings but a disadvantage when the candy absorbs moisture from the atmosphere and becomes sticky or soft. Those candies with a high proportion of fructose are especially likely to take up moisture. A difference of one percent in relative humidity when a candy is made may affect the consistency of the finished confection.

Effect of Sucrose on the Boiling Point of Water

A substance like sugar that dissolves in water elevates the boiling point, a colligative property that depends on the number of solute particles. Each mole of sucrose (342 grams) dissolved in a liter of water elevates the boiling point 0.52°C. A mole of salt (58 grams) per liter of water elevates the boiling point twice this much or 1.04°C because each molecule of salt ionizes to give one sodium and one chloride ion. Table 8-3 gives the boiling points

125

CHAPTER 8
SUGARS,
ALTERNATIVE
SWEETENERS,
AND
CONFECTIONS

TABLE 8-3
Effect of Concentration of
Sucrose on Boiling Point
of Syrup

Sucrose (%)	Boiling Point (°C)
0	100 (water)
10	100.4
20	100.6
40	101.5
60	103.0
80	112
85[a]	114 (soft ball stage for candies)
90.8	130
100	160 (molten sugar)

[a]Approximate.

Source: C. A. Browne, *A Handbook of Sugar Analysis,* copyright © 1912 by John Wiley & Sons, Inc., New York, p. 651.

for sucrose solutions of different concentrations. Notice the steep rise in the boiling point after the concentration of the sucrose in the syrup reaches 80 percent.

The boiling point of a sucrose syrup is an index to its concentration. One can measure indirectly the concentration of sugar in a syrup by measuring the temperature at which the syrup boils. By this means it is possible to determine when a sugar syrup has reached the concentration desired. Allowance must be made for variations in barometric pressure, for the presence of other sugars, and for altitude.

Melting and Caramelization of Sucrose

As the water in a solution of sucrose evaporates and the concentration of the sucrose increases, the temperature of the syrup (the boiling point) rises and will continue to do so until all of the water has boiled away. When this happens, the liquid that remains is molten sugar. The melting point of sugar is 160°C (320°F). Sugar crystals can be melted by putting dry sugar in a heavy pan, placing the pan over low heat and shaking it so that sugar on the bottom does not overheat before the remainder has a chance to reach the melting point. Molten sugar, removed from the source of heat and left undisturbed, supercools. It then becomes a clear, glassy, noncrystalline, brittle solid.

If molten sugar is heated a few degrees above the melting point (to 170°C or 338°F), the sucrose begins to caramelize. Caramelized sugar is used to make burnt-sugar frostings. The decomposition of sucrose by heat gives rise to a complex mixture of aldehydes and ketones in which furfural and 5-hydroxymethyl furfural are prominent constituents. The products of the pyrolysis of sucrose include, in addition, a mixture of cresols, eight of which have been identified (13). When soda is added to caramelized sugar, the heat plus the acids present release carbon dioxide, bubbles of which inflate the molten mass. When cooled it is porous and brittle. When a syrup of sucrose and water is heated to the soft crack stage (named for the sound the hot syrup makes when a small amount of it is spooned into cold water), it takes on a pale amber tint. This is not due to caramelization, but is attributed to liberation of furfural from the sugar by the high temperature followed by the formation of polymers which tint the syrup.

CANDIES

Determining Doneness of Candies

Boiling Point of the Syrup

Once sucrose is in solution, the next step is to boil away the right amount of excess water that was added originally to ensure solution of the large sugar crystals. One of the problems in making any confection is to know how long to cook the syrup, that is, how much water to boil away to give a product of the desired consistency. The chief factor that determines consistency in the finished product is the concentration of sugar in the syrup. For this the temperature of the boiling syrup is an index. For either noncrystalline or crystalline products, a thermometer can be used to determine when the boiling syrup is done. A thermometer will not give a true reading unless the syrup is boiling, the bulb of the thermometer is submerged in the boiling syrup but not touching the pan, and the eye is level with the top of the column of mercury when the temperature is read.

For noncrystalline candies such as caramels, the object is to concentrate the syrup so it will be neither too thin nor too thick when it has cooled to room temperature. The syrup should be just viscous enough that the pieces when cut will hold their shape and can be handled. Almost all the water is evaporated from syrup for brittles, glacé, and toffee. The high proportion of interfering substances permits these supersaturated syrups to supercool and form candies that are vitreous.

For crystalline candies the object is to obtain in the finished product the correct ratio between sucrose crystals and remaining saturated syrup. The following example will explain how this is accomplished. When sucrose syrup boils at 115°C (239°F), each 100 grams of water in the syrup has dissolved in it 669 grams of sucrose. When this syrup is cooled to 40°C (104°F), each 100 grams of water at this temperature can dissolve only 238 grams of sucrose. The liquid thus holds more solute than it can dissolve at that temperature and is said to be *supersaturated*. The difference between the amount of solute that the 100 grams of water holds and the amount it can dissolve at 40°C (669 minus 238, or 431 grams) is a measure of how supersaturated the syrup is. This extra sucrose is held precariously in solution, and with a little encouragement, it will precipitate as crystals until the remaining syrup is just saturated. The higher the boiling point, the more supersaturated the syrup when it has cooled and the more sucrose precipitated. The more sucrose that crystallizes, the less the amount of syrup that remains, and the firmer the candy.

The boiling point is not a true index to the concentration of sucrose when other sugars are present with sucrose in a syrup, because they contribute to the elevation of the boiling point, too. When other sugars are present, the syrup must be cooked to a higher temperature to concentrate the sucrose sufficiently. A second point needs to be considered, too. Ingredients other than sugar may not affect the boiling point, yet their presence in the syrup makes it more viscous. With a more viscous syrup less sucrose needs to precipitate to give the candy the desired consistency. This means that when milk solids, cocoa, chocolate, fat, or dextrins are present, the sucrose in the syrup need not be so concentrated. Thus syrup for fudge reaches the soft ball stage at a slightly lower boiling point than fondant (see Table 8-4).

Formulas for different candies and the temperature to which each should be brought are given in Table 8-4.

TABLE 8-4
Formulas for Candies

CRYSTALLINE		AMORPHOUS OR NONCRYSTALLINE				SPECIAL TEXTURES	
Fondant	Fudge	Caramels	Taffy	Toffee	Lollipops	Divinity	Marshmallows
1 cup sugar	1 cup sugar	1 cup sugar	1 cup sugar	1 cup sugar	1 cup sugar	1 cup sugar	1 cup sugar
1 Tbsp corn syrup	1 Tbsp corn syrup	1 cup corn syrup	1/4 cup corn syrup	1 Tbsp corn syrup	1/3 cup corn syrup	2 Tbsp corn syrup	1 Tbsp corn syrup
or							
1/16 tsp cream of tartar							
	1 Tbsp butter	1/4 cup butter		3/4 cup butter		1 egg white	1 Tbsp gelatin
1/2 cup water	1/2 cup milk	1 cup cream or evaporated milk	1/3 cup water	1/4 cup water	1/2 cup water	1/4 cup water	1/4 cup water
*114°C (237°F) Soft ball	112°C (234°F) Soft ball	120°C (248°F) Firm ball	127°C (261°F) Hard ball or 135°C (275°F) Soft crack	149°C (300°F) Hard crack	154°C (310°F) Hard crack	122°C (252°F) Hard ball	120°C (248°F) Firm ball

*Boil syrup to 1°C less for each 900 feet (274 meters) elevation above sea level or to 1°F less for each 500 feet (152 meters) above sea level.

127

Consistency of the Syrup (Cold Water Test)

A second index to the doneness of a candy syrup that takes into account these factors, as well as the concentration of sucrose, is the consistency of the cooled syrup. This should be tested near the end of the cooking period. The syrup should be removed from the heat while the test is made. A small amount of the candy syrup is poured into *cold* water and its behavior noted.

For example, syrup that is at the soft ball stage can be collected from the bottom of the container of cold water, but it is so soft that it runs through the fingers. Syrup cooked to the soft ball stage is really soft. An end point that is so subjective is liable to errors in judgment. Syrups for both fudge and fondant are sometimes overcooked when this method of assessing doneness is used. Too often the syrup for fudge is cooked beyond this stage to the firm or even the hard ball stage. Table 8-5 gives the stages of doneness of a sugar syrup as assessed by its consistency in cold water.

Interfering Agents and Sucrose Crystal Formation

Functions of Interfering Substances

The proportion of interfering substances present in a candy syrup influences the amount of sugar, if any, that crystallizes from the syrup as well as the size of the sucrose crystals.

Under the appropriate conditions, sucrose molecules in a syrup can align themselves in a manner unique to the sugar molecule to form crystals. Forces holding the molecules together in the crystals are hydrogen bonds between hydroxyl groups on contiguous molecules. A molecule of any sugar other than sucrose has a different shape, is foreign, and will interfere with sucrose molecules in solution joining or adding to sucrose crystals already

TABLE 8-5
Consistency Tests for Doneness of Syrups

Test	Boiling Point at Sea Level*		Description of the Syrup
	°C	°F	
Thread	110–112	230–234	Forms a 5-cm (2-in) thread when poured from a spoon
Soft ball	112–115	234–240	Forms a ball in cold water so soft it loses its shape when removed
Firm ball	118–120	244–248	Forms a ball in cold water that maintains its shape when removed
Hard ball	121–130	250–266	Forms a ball in cold water that can barely be manipulated when removed
Soft crack	132–143	270–290	Separates upon contact with cold water into threads that crack under pressure of fingers
Hard crack	149–154	300–310	Separates upon contact with cold water into fine, brittle threads
Melted sugar	160	320	Clear, viscous liquid
Caramel	170–177	338–348	Brown viscous liquid

*Reduce temperature 1°C for each 900 feet (274 meters) above sea level or 1°F for each 500 feet (152 meters) above sea level.

started. This is true for molecules of glucose and fructose even though they are part of the sucrose molecule itself. When interfering sugars, such as glucose and fructose are present in a syrup, many sucrose crystals tend to form instead of only a few that grow exceedingly large. Thus foreign sugars favor the formation of more (and smaller) crystals in crystalline candies. Aside from foreign sugars, other substances may interfere with the formation of large sucrose crystals in crystalline candies. In fact, a high proposition of interfering substances in a candy syrup may prevent crystallization altogether that makes possible non-crystalline candies.

129

■

CHAPTER 8
SUGARS,
ALTERNATIVE
SWEETENERS,
AND
CONFECTIONS

Proportions of Interfering Substances

Two methods are employed to ensure the optimum concentration of interfering substances in candies. The interfering substances may be added to the syrup or they may be formed from sucrose as the candy cooks.

When interfering substances as such are added, the quantity should be measured with care. This is particularly true for crystalline candies. A common way to provide interfering sugars is to use corn syrup. Corn syrup is made from cornstarch. When molecules of starch are hydrolyzed, dextrins, maltose, and finally glucose are formed. Either acid and heat or enzymes catalyze the reaction:

$$\text{Starch} + \text{Water} \xrightarrow[\text{Acid plus Heat}]{\text{Enzymes or}} \text{Dextrins} + \text{Maltose} + \text{Glucose}$$

Enzyme-hydrolyzed corn syrup is marketed under the trade name of Sweetose. If starch has been converted to glucose completely, the syrup has a dextrose equivalent (DE) of 100 percent; syrups with lower DE have more dextrins and maltose and less glucose. For each cup (250 milliliters) of sugar used to make fondant and fudge, one tablespoon (15 milliliters) of corn syrup will provide enough interfering substances to control effectively the size of the crystals. Honey, which contains both glucose and fructose, may be used to provide interfering sugars in candies.

Interfering sugars, instead of being added in a definite quantity, may be formed from some of the sucrose molecules as the candy syrup is boiled. Sucrose molecules will react with water molecules when the syrup is heated in the presence of acid. For each molecule of sucrose hydrolyzed, one molecule each of glucose and fructose is obtained:

$$\underset{\text{Sucrose}}{C_{12}H_{22}O_{11}} + \underset{\text{Water}}{H_2O} \xrightarrow[\text{Sucrose}]{\text{Acid plus heat or}} \underset{\text{Glucose}}{C_6H_{12}O_6} + \underset{\text{Fructose}}{C_6H_{12}O_6}$$

$$\underset{\text{Invert sugar}}{\underline{\hspace{3cm}}}$$

This reaction (the reverse of that shown earlier in the section on chemistry) may be catalyzed by the enzyme sucrase also. The equimolar mixture of glucose and fructose that results is known as invert sugar.

When acid is added to candy syrup to help form invert sugar, the amount added is even more critical than in the case of corn syrup. The amount of sucrose converted to invert sugar depends upon the concentration of hydrogen ions (amount of acid) present when the candy syrup is boiled (18). The alkalinity of the water and its neutralizing value must be taken into consideration when acid is used to hydrolyze the sucrose (4). One way to control the amount of acid in fondant is to use a carefully measured amount of cream of tartar. This compound, $KHC_4H_4O_6$, is the acid salt of tartaric acid. Vinegar, used in some recipes for taffy, serves the same purpose, as does acid present in the syrup around the crystals of brown sugar used to make panocha, which is similar to fudge.

When acid is used in candy, the length of the cooking time is critical (3). A cooking time that is too short gives insufficient invert sugar and a candy that is likely to be coarse and grainy. Some invert sugar is desired in candy to keep crystals small or the texture fine, but prolonged cooking will yield too much invert sugar. In this case, too little sucrose crystallizes and the candy is too soft to handle. One reason for this is that invert sugar increases the solubility of sucrose. With six percent invert sugar the solubility of sucrose at room temperature is increased from 67 percent to 80 percent. At any given concentration of sucrose, fewer crystals would be expected to precipitate in the presence of invert sugar than in its absence. In addition, the two molecules that make up the invert sugar formed elevate the boiling point twice as much as does the sucrose from which it was derived. This means that the boiling point of the syrup in the presence of excess invert sugar is not a true index to the concentration of sucrose and hence to the doneness of the syrup. From 6 to 15 percent of invert sugar in fondant is sufficient to keep the crystals small (8); more than this (16–23%) gives a candy semifluid consistency.

A soft fondant has an advantage if it is to be melted and used to make mint wafers or as a coating for bonbons. A firmer fondant is needed for molding cream centers to be dipped in melted fondant or melted chocolate. Chocolate-covered bonbons that are semifluid in consistency are made by incorporating the enzyme sucrase in the fondant centers before they are dipped in chocolate. This enzyme converts enough of the sucrose to invert sugar during storage so that the sucrose crystals partially dissolve.

Effect of Interfering Substances on Consistency

Some interfering substances influence the consistency of a candy as well as the size of the sucrose crystals. Fat globules and the proteins from milk, as well as the solids from cocoa and chocolate, influence the viscosity of the syrup. When the syrup is more viscous because of the presence of these constituents, the crystal-to-syrup ratio need not be so high. It is for this reason that the boiling points for fondant and fudge differ. The final temperature for the syrup for the fondant recipe given in Table 8-4 is 114°C, while that for fudge is 112°C. Both syrups reach the soft ball stage and so have the same consistency or flow properties when tested in cold water, and the candies should have the same consistency. Fondant will have a higher ratio of sucrose crystals to saturated syrup; in fudge the milk solids, the butter, and the solids from the cocoa contribute enough thickness to the syrup to compensate for the lower ratio of crystals to syrup. Both fondant and fudge differ from the original sugar in that the sucrose crystals are smaller and are now suspended in syrup.

Prevention of Crystal Formation

A high proportion of interfering substances in a candy syrup may prevent crystallization of sucrose altogether. This is desired in amorphous or noncrystalline candies such as caramels, taffy, toffee, and brittles. Compared with fondant and fudge, taffy has a high proportion of corn syrup, toffee a high proportion of fat, and caramels a high proportion of both. Table 8-3 gives the proportions of ingredients in different candies. Noncrystalline candies are either very thick syrups or hard and glasslike. Their consistency depends chiefly on how much the syrup was concentrated before it was removed from the heat. Syrups for noncrystalline candies are sufficiently concentrated so they will not flow at room temperature. Syrup for toffee, a brittle candy, is heated to the hard crack stage, and that for taffy to the soft crack or the hard ball stage, depending on whether a brittle or a chewy product is desired. Syrup for caramels that have a chewy consistency is heated to the firm ball stage. The brown color and characteristic flavor of caramels and toffee are attributed to a reaction between protein and sugar brought about by the high temperature.

Aside from their use in candies, interfering sugars are useful in preventing crystallization of sucrose in syrups. Syrup for preserves is cooked until the sucrose concentration is near 65 percent. Slight overcooking gives a supersaturated syrup and the likelihood of large sucrose crystals forming eventually unless acid is present to invert some of the sucrose as the preserves cook. For this reason lemon juice is added to watermelon preserves. In most fruit pectin jellies the sucrose concentration must be at or close to 65 percent. Jellies made with pectin concentrate have such a short boiling period (usually one minute) that very little invert sugar is produced and sucrose crystals may form in the jelly during storage.

Agitation and Sucrose Crystal Formation

Fondant and Fudge

The texture of a crystalline candy or frosting is influenced not only by the proportion of interfering agents present but also by the number of crystal nuclei that form once crystallization begins. If syrup for fondant or fudge is beaten while still hot, too few crystals are initiated and grow larger as the syrup cools, the result being coarse, grainy candy. On the other hand, when fondant syrup is allowed to stand undisturbed, eventually a few crystals begin to form, initiated by dust or lint, or possibly seeded by sucrose crystals from syrup splashed on the sides of the pan. These few grow exceedingly large because the other sucrose molecules that precipitate do so on the crystals that first form. The crystals become so large that they can be seen by the unaided eye and their dimensions measured by a ruler. Crystals need not be this large for the graininess of crystalline candies to be detected, however. Crystals no larger than 45 microns across (1 micron equals 0.0001 or 10^{-4} centimeters) make fondant seem grainy on the tongue (18). In fact, crystals that are more than 25 microns across make fondant detectably crystalline; those no larger than 20 microns seem fine and creamy. This means that the tongue can detect a difference in the size of crystals of only 6 microns!

To obtain a large number of crystal nuclei, the syrup should be sufficiently supersaturated before any crystals begin to form. Crystals should be wiped from the sides of the pan as the syrup for fondant cooks. Syrup for fondant is cooled to 40°C (104°F) (2) and that for fudge, in which more interfering substances are present, is cooled to 50°C (122°F). Syrup for fudge is usually cooled in the pan; that for fondant is poured from the pan onto a flat surface to cool. The syrup is drained—not scraped—from the pan, and the thermometer is in position before the syrup is poured. Such syrups, as they cool, are unstable and should be undisturbed. Any agitation will start crystal formation before the syrup is sufficiently supersaturated. As a result, the few crystals that form initially grow larger as the syrup continues to cool. This is illustrated in Figure 8-3a. For this fondant, beating was initiated while the syrup was still hot (near 114°C or 237°F) and so only slightly supersaturated. Fondant syrup allowed to cool to 40°C (104°F) and become sufficiently supersaturated before beating is initiated forms numerous small crystals (Figure 8-3b).

131

■

CHAPTER 8
SUGARS,
ALTERNATIVE
SWEETENERS,
AND
CONFECTIONS

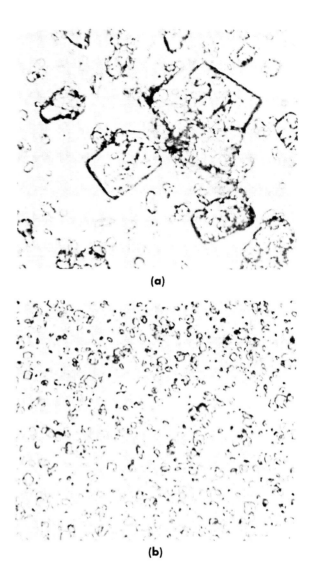

(a)

(b)

Figure 8-3. Sucrose crystals in fondant, for which beating was initiated a) when the syrup was still hot (near 114°C or 237°F), and b) after the syrup had cooled to 40°C (104°F). (Magnification approximately 240×.)

Once the syrup is supersaturated sufficiently and beating begins, it should be *continuous* until crystallization is complete, as shown in Figure 8-4. As beating proceeds, the moving surfaces of the spoon provide the stimulus that initiates the formation of innumerable crystal nuclei. If beating stops, no new crystals begin to form. Instead, sucrose molecules deposit on existing crystals. This makes them larger and the candy coarser. Thus sucrose crystals grow larger by the addition of sucrose molecules at the expense of the formation of many new and smaller sucrose crystals. Too, large crystals form if no interfering agent is present, if syrup is not cooled to make it supersaturated, and if cooled syrup is not beaten continuously as crystals form.

Agitation of the syrup incorporates air bubbles that make fondant opaque, rather than transparent like the syrup. Pulling taffy accomplishes the same thing. Air beaten into syrup for fudge lightens the color. The formation of sucrose crystals contributes to the

133

■

CHAPTER 8
SUGARS,
ALTERNATIVE
SWEETENERS,
AND
CONFECTIONS

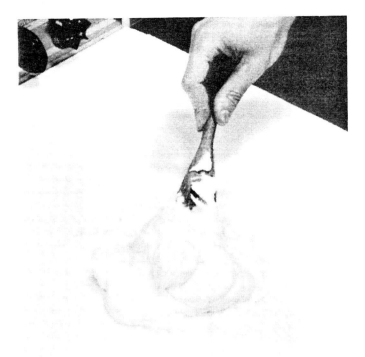

Figure 8-4. Supersaturated fondant syrup beaten until crystallization is nearly complete. Beating the syrup continuously is essential for the formation of fine crystals of sucrose. (Photograph by Wilbur Nelson.)

opaqueness of fondant and the lighter color of fudge, too. Fondant made with cream of tartar is snowy white, in contrast to that made with corn syrup which is creamy white. Impurities in the water may give the fondant a grayish cast. Fondant stored for 12 to 24 hours in a closed container becomes softer and more pliable. This ripening is due to the solution of extremely small crystals and the reduction in surface area to which the syrup can adhere.

Divinity

Syrup for divinity is cooked to the hard-ball stage because it will be diluted by water from the egg white. The hot syrup is beaten into the films of liquid around the air bubbles of beaten egg white. Beating the hot syrup favors the growth of large sucrose crystals. The formula for divinity calls for twice as much corn syrup per cup of sugar as that for fondant and fudge. This is to counteract the effect of beating the hot syrup as it is added to the egg white. In addition, the protein of the egg white serves as an interfering agent.

Even after the hot syrup is beaten into the egg white, divinity should be beaten continuously until crystallization has proceeded sufficiently for the candy to hold its shape. As this stage approaches, the candy temporarily loses its gloss as the utensil moves through it. At this point, the candy should be transferred to an oiled surface to harden. When divinity finally hardens, the egg white foam has been immobilized by the deposition of sucrose crystals in the films of syrup around each air bubble.

Another indication that crystalline candies have reached the stage of maximum sucrose crystal formation is a slight softening of the candy. Heat was required to dissolve the sugar in the first place and as sugar recrystallizes this heat is liberated. The trick is to stop beating a crystalline candy such as fudge and panocha and pour it from the pan after it softens and just before it crystallizes enough to set. Fondant should be kneaded after it hardens. For noncrystalline candies and confections such as caramels, brittle, and toffee, agitation of the syrup once it is removed from the heat is to be avoided.

Amorphous Candies

Some amorphous or noncrystalline candies are soft and chewy, for example, marshmallows, gum drops, and jellies. Marshmallows resemble divinity in that both are foams, but in the former the liquid that encloses the air bubbles is the syrup that contains gelatin. The gelatin prevents sucrose in the syrup from crystallizing. When the foam stands, the gelatin sets, or gels the liquid around the air bubbles (Chapter 30). When marshmallows are toasted (heated), the gel liquefies. In gum drops and similar candies, starch, or pectin converts the syrup to a gel. As was pointed out earlier, caramels are a very thick syrup with a high proportion of interfering substances.

The syrups for noncrystalline candies such as cinnamon balls, lemon drops, and lollipops that are boiled to the hard crack stage are so thick that sucrose molecules lack the mobility to unite as crystals. Instead, the viscous syrup becomes a glass when it cools below its glass transition temperature (17). Such confections are hygroscopic. Exposed to the atmosphere, the surface of the candy will take up moisture. This lowers its glass transition temperature and the surface changes from a glass to a rubber at room temperature. If the candy contains a high proportion of glucose or invert sugar, the candy becomes sticky or it even liquefies. Absent a high proportion of interfering sugars, sucrose molecules in the rubbery, more fluid portion can crystallize.

To prevent the surface of such amorphous confections from becoming either sticky or grainy (8), pieces of candy are wrapped in moisture-vapor-proof wrap. A wrap such as paper with a high number of —OH groups in the cellulose is avoided, because candies adhere tenaciously to such materials. Instead, waxed paper or other wrap incapable of participating in hydrogen-bond formation is used.

Comparison of Candies and Frozen Desserts

Fondant and fudge, like ices and ice creams, are a two-phase system of crystals in syrup—sucrose crystals in candy and ice crystals in frozen desserts. Both frozen desserts and fondant and fudge depend on the presence of interfering substances to limit the size of the crystals. Interfering substances in frozen desserts include milk solids, fat droplets, air bubbles, and sugars, plus stabilizers like gelatin and vegetable gums. In crystalline candies, the simple sugars, glucose and fructose, fat droplets, milk solids, and solids from cocoa and chocolate aid in the formation of small sucrose crystals.

Agitation of the mix as crystals form increases the number and decreases the size of ice crystals in frozen desserts and of sugar crystals in candies. Like amorphous candies, still-frozen desserts have a high ratio of interfering substances. However, interfering substances other than sugar should be increased in still-frozen desserts, as a high level of sugar depresses the freezing point and so makes freezing slower. This favors the formation of large crystals when the mix is not agitated as it freezes. Still-frozen desserts contain crystals of ice, unlike amorphous candies, which contain no crystals of sucrose. Air bubbles are incorporated in both crystalline candies and in frozen desserts by agitation of the syrup or of the mix. Preliminary incorporation of air bubbles in a whipped cream, beaten egg white, or liquid thickened by gelatin serves as a means of introducing air into still-frozen desserts.

Temperature of the boiling syrup for fondant and fudge and of the frozen dessert influences the ratio of crystals to syrup and so the consistency of the product. The ratio of crystals to syrup in frozen desserts is altered with alterations in temperature.

135

CHAPTER 8
SUGARS,
ALTERNATIVE
SWEETENERS,
AND
CONFECTIONS

REFERENCES

1. Andreas, H. J., A. B. Rizzuto, and S. E. Bichsel. 1990. Processing sugar from sugarcane and sugar beets. In *Sugar: A User's Guide to Sucrose*, N. L. Pennington and C. W. Baker, eds. New York: Van Nostrand Reinhold. Pp. 11–35. Details of the processing of the two raw materials.

2. Appl, R. C. 1991. "Confectionery ingredients from starch." *Food Technology* 45(3):148–49. Corn syrups, including high fructose syrup.

3. Carrick, M. S. 1919. "Some studies in fondant making." *Journal of Physical Chemistry* 23:589–92. Variables studied were amounts of water, cooking time, and temperature of syrup when beating started.

4. Daniels, A. L., and D. M. Cook. 1919. "Factors influencing the amount of invert sugar in fondant." *Journal of Home Economics* 11:65–69. Effects of varying proportions of water and cream of tartar.

5. Doner, L. W. 1977. "The sugars of honey—A review." *Journal of the Science of Food and Agriculture*. 28:443–56. Minor as well as major sugars; sources and formation.

6. Dziezak, S. 1989. "Ingredients for sweet success." *Food Technology* 43(10):94–116. Sugars and sugar substitutes; applications.

7. Giese, J. H. 1993. "Alternative sweeteners and bulking agents." *Food Technology* 47(1):114–26. Properties and functions.

8. Heiss, R. 1959. "Prevention of graininess and stickiness in stored hard candies." *Food Technology* 13:433–40. Technical treatment of the problem.

9. Homler, B., A. Kedo, and W. R. Shazer. 1987. "FDA approves four new aspartame uses." *Food Technology* 41(7):41–42, 44. Previous clearances included.

10. Hyvonen, I., P. Koivistoinen, and F. Vioril. 1982. "Food technological evaluation of xylitol." *Advances in Food Research* 28:373–403. Properties, including negative heat of solution.

11. Industry News. 1990. "Sun Up Foods to market Brazilian sweetener in the U.S." *Food Technology* 44(7):30. Stevioside as a potential alternative sweetener.

12. Jeffery, M. S. 1993. "Key functional properties of sucrose in chocolate and sugar confectionery." *Food Technology* 47(1):141–44. Importance in both the fat phase and the syrup phase in confections.

13. Johnson, R. R., E. D. Alford, and G. W. Kinzer. 1969. "Formation of sucrose pyrolysis products." *Journal of Agricultural and Food Chemistry* 17:22–24. Aldehydes, ketones, and cresols identified.

14. Mäkinen, K. K., and E. Söderling. 1980. A quantitative study of mannitol, sorbitol, xylitol, and xylose in wild berries and commercial fruits. *Journal of Food Science* 45:369–71, 374. Nineteen fruits and two wines analyzed.

15. Pepper, T., and P. M. Olinger. 1988. "Xylitol in sugar-free confections." *Food Technology* 42(10):98–106. Characteristics of the sweetener; formulas using it.

16. *Statistical Abstracts of the United States*, 116 edition. 1996. p. 147. Per-capita consumption of major food commodities: 1970–1994.

17. White, G. W., and S. H. Cakebread. 1966. "The glassy state in certain sugar-containing food products." *Food Technology* 1:73–82. Relation of the glass transition temperature to such defects as graininess and stickiness in confections.

18. Woodruff, S., and H. van Gilder. 1931. Photomicrographic studies of sucrose crystals. *Journal of Physical Chemistry* 35:1355–67. Level of acid (citric, tartaric, hydrochloric, and cream of tartar), invert sugar, and size of crystals in fondant.

PART III

Starches and Starchy Foods

Starches and Vegetable Gums

9

Starches and gums are colloids, polymers of sugars and sugar derivatives. The hydrophilic character of molecules of starches and gums comes from their numerous hydroxyl groups. Starch has been studied for more than a century, and its functional properties in foods is still being investigated. Although gums have been exploited as functional ingredients in foods more recently, they are now found in an array of foods as diverse as chocolate milk, whipped topping, ice cream, cake, and ground meat products. Starch is an important thickening and gelling component in a number of foods, and in many foods it is a major structure-forming constituent.

STARCHES

Starches are stored by plants as an energy reserve. They are especially abundant in cereals and are an important component of legumes and some vegetables. When such foods as rice, dried beans, or potatoes are cooked, the starch content makes a major contribution to the quality of the product. Starch, as a thickening or gelling agent, helps to achieve desired consistency in sauces, gravies, puddings, and soft pie fillings. Starch, as a major constituent in flour, contributes to the structure and texture of such baked products as biscuits, muffins, yeast breads, pie crusts, and cakes. The function of starch in each of these products is discussed in subsequent chapters.

At the outset it is well to keep in mind that the term starch is used with two different meanings. Certain types of molecules are referred to as starch. In the cells of plants these starch molecules are organized into microscopic packages or granules. These granules are referred to as starch, too. When a quantity of starch is specified, it is starch in the granular form that is meant. The functional properties of granular starch in foods stem from the nature of the starch molecules and their unique organization within the granule. To understand the fundamental role of starch in food preparation, some knowledge both of starch molecules and of their arrangement within the granule is essential.

Starch Chemistry

Glucose

Molecules of starch are polymers of the simple sugar, glucose, a monosaccharide. Glucose is a hexose, that is, a sugar with six carbon atoms in the molecule. The cluster of atoms that

139

make up each glucose molecule is tightly packed. Molecules of glucose in solution exist in both the aldehyde and the pyranose (ring) structures, as shown below. The ring structures of glucose predominate (16). The two ring structures, α-D-glucose and β-D-glucose, differ only in the orientation of the hydroxyl group at carbon 1. In the alpha (α) form, this hydroxyl group is shown oriented in the same direction as the hydroxyl at carbon 4. In the beta (β) form the hydroxyl groups at carbons 1 and 4 are oriented in opposite directions. A starch molecule is made of glucose with the pyranose structure, and in the alpha rather than the beta form.

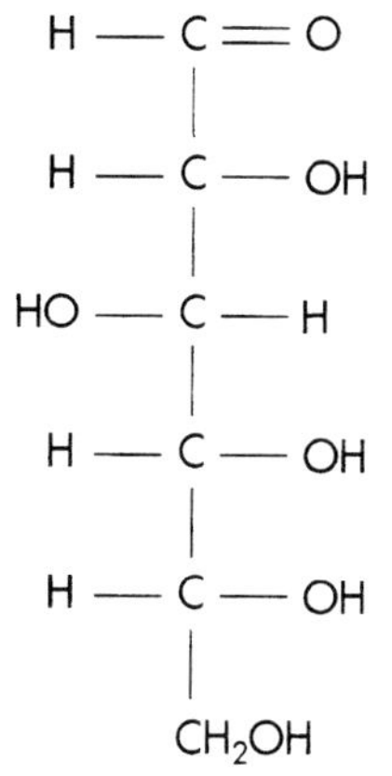

Aldehyde Form of Glucose 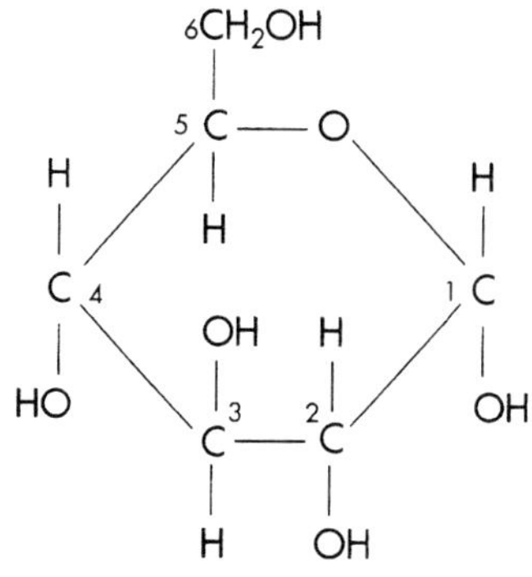   α-D-Glucose 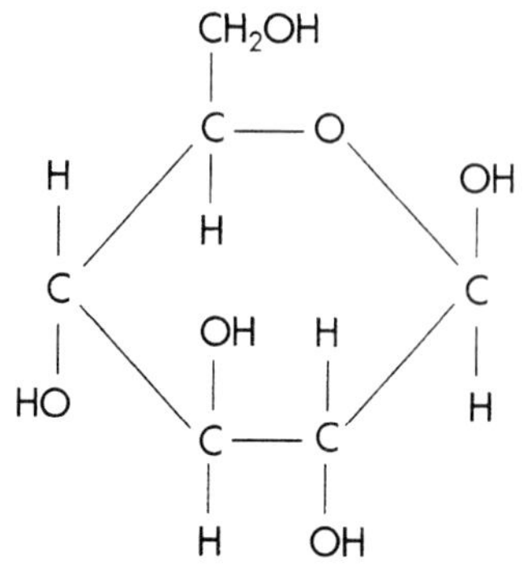   β-D-Glucose

As an alternative to depicting the ring of sugar such as glucose by the Haworth convention shown above, a chair conformation is used to indicate the spatial relationships of the atoms. Two such arrangements, denoted C1 and 1C, are possible, with C1 the favored conformation for glucose (34). In this conformation, carbons 2, 3, and 5 and the oxygen of the ring form the plane of the seat and carbon 1 is below the seat. The chair conformations of α-D-glucose and β-D-glucose are shown:

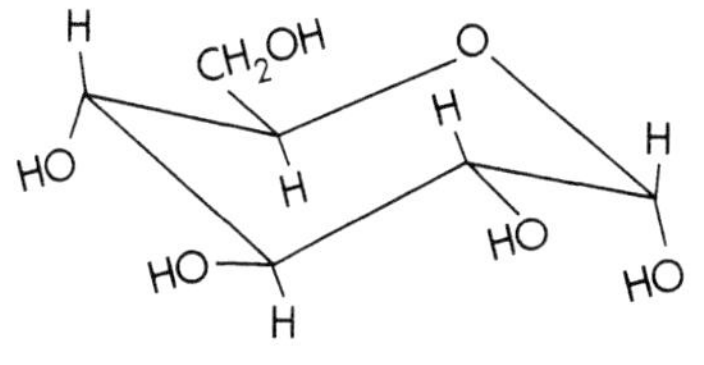

α-D-Glucose-C1 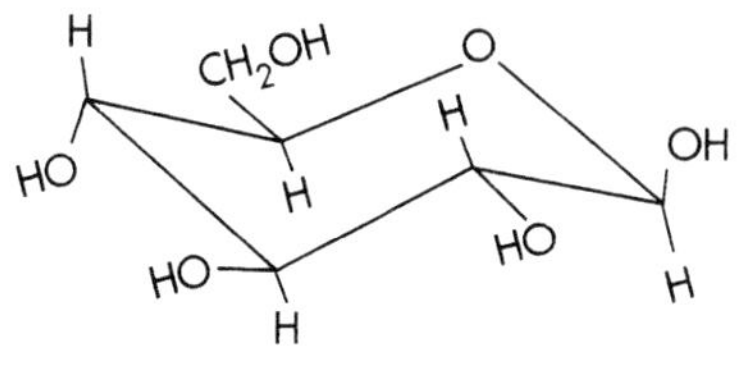   β-D-Glucose-C1

Maltose

Two α-D-glucose molecules linked through carbon 1 of one molecule and carbon 4 of the other (with a glycosidic linkage and the elimination of one molecule of water) give rise to a molecule of the disaccharide, maltose, as shown:

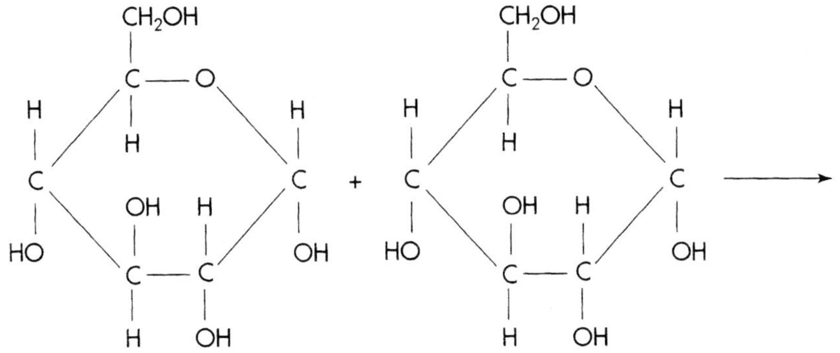

α-D-Glucopyranose + α-D-Glucopyranose →

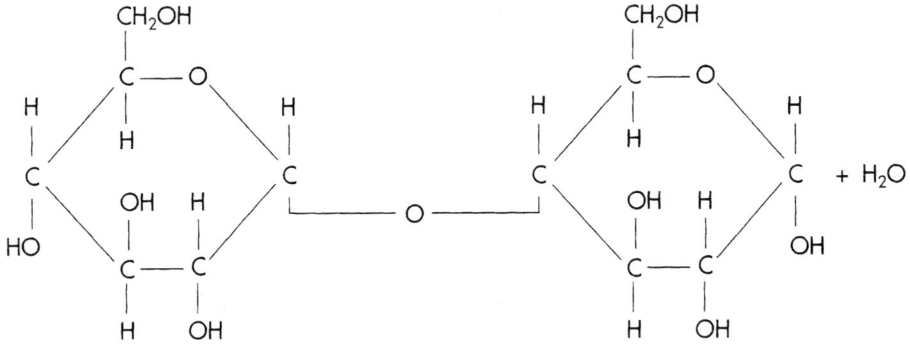

Maltose + Water

Three glucose molecules joined by this maltose-type linkage form a triose. Chains of several such glucose residues are called dextrins. When the glucose units in a molecule range from a few thousand to a million (38), the resulting high polymers are called *starch*.

Starch Molecules

Two types of starch molecules are synthesized by plants. In some molecules all the glucose residues are united through the 1,4-linkage as in maltose. Such a linear starch molecule is called *amylose*, a fragment of which is shown:

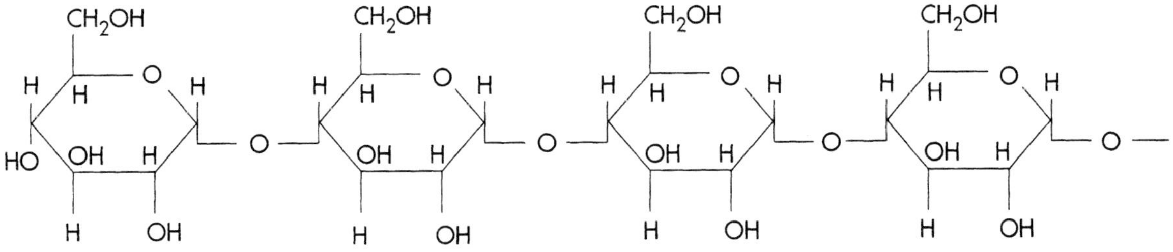

Unlike linear amylose, molecules of *amylopectin* are branched. The linkage is between carbon 1 of the branch and carbon 6 of the glucose residue in the α-1,4-linked main chain to which the branch is attached, as shown:

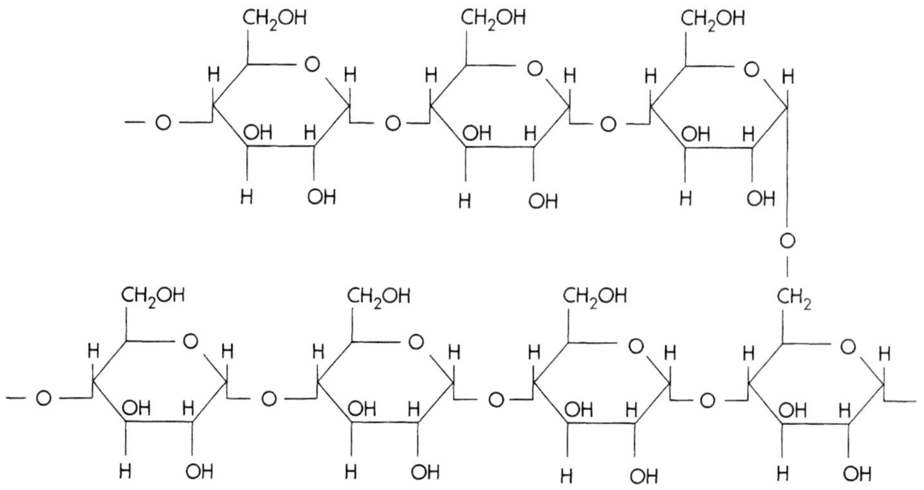

In the amylopectin molecule, several α-1,4 linked short chains of 15 to 30 glucose residues each may branch off near the same location on the α-1,4 main chain, giving rise to tuft-like clusters of short branches (38). As the molecule increases in size, a short branch in each cluster elongates, from which another cluster of short branches may arise. Elongation and branching is repeated, resulting in a molecule with a brushy shrub appearance. Molecules of amylopectin are large, some with degrees of polymerization in millions. Amylose is a smaller molecule, with the degree of polymerization measured in thousands.

Cellulose, like starch, is a polymer of glucose but β-D-glucose instead of α-D-glucose. When one α-1,4 linked glucose residue succeeds another in a starch molecule, a slight twist is built into it (38). For the β-1,4 linkage in cellulose, however, each glucose residue is rotated 180° about its molecular axis in relation to the glucose residue that precedes it. Instead of a twist in the molecule as in starch, the β-1,4 linkage gives a flat, ribbonlike shape to the cellulose molecule. Such molecules are readily aligned for maximum hydrogen bonding. In addition, intramolecular hydrogen bonds form between a hydroxyl on carbon 3 of one glucose residue and the oxygen of the ring of an adjacent glucose residue, due to their proximity in the C1 conformation. A seemingly minor difference in the glucose residues of starch and cellulose makes a great difference in the reactivity and properties of the two polymers.

Molecules of starch and especially amylose exist in water as random coils (1). In the presence of molecules of certain fatty substances or of iodine, starch assumes the shape of a helix, with six to seven glucose residues comprising each coil. The space inside each coil accommodates a molecule of iodine, and this complex makes possible the iodine test for starch. The color of the complex depends on the length of the helix and thus on the number of iodine molecules involved. If the helix is long, the iodine-starch complex is blue; if short, the complex is red.

Starch Granules

Size and Shape

As starch molecules are formed by the plant, they are deposited in the amyloplasts of the cell. These eventually become the starch granules. (Fig. 28-4) Starch granules from different plants have characteristic sizes and shapes. Diameters vary from 2 to 150 microns. Those from rice are the smallest of the granules of starch produced by plants; they average 3 to 8 microns in diameter and are polygonal in shape. Tapioca from the root of the cassava plant and cornstarch from the endosperm cells of corn average 12 to 25 microns. The former are round and the latter are either round or polygonal. Wheat starch granules are of two types. The small, spherical ones average 10 microns in diameter and the larger lentil- or discus-shaped ones are approximately 35 microns in diameter. Potato starch granules that are large (starch granules from canna are the largest) can be identified by their oyster shell shape and by the appearance of distinct concentric rings or striations. Photomicrographs of starches from different sources are shown in Figure 9-1. One pound of cornstarch contains an estimated 800 billion starch granules. A scanning electron micrograph of wheat starch is found in Figure 9-2.

Internal Organization

The starch granules of most plants consist of approximately ¼ amylose molecules and ¾ amylopectin molecules. However, certain plants have the ability to make starch granules that contain a high proportion of either amylose or amylopectin molecules. Amylomaize (high amylose cornstarch) is an example of the former, and waxy maize and waxy rice starches of the latter. Both the 1,4- and the 1,6- linkages that join glucose residues in starch molecules are under genetic control (29). The proportion of the two types of molecules that constitute the granules influences markedly the functional properties of the starch.

Microscopic examination of starch granules provides clues to the arrangement of starch molecules within. The cut cells of a potato are a readily available source of starch granules, which can be mounted in either water or glycerine for observation under the microscope. Concentric striations visible on the surface of some granules are beautifully illustrated in the photomicrograph of starch granules from the potato berry shown in Figure 9-3. These same granules viewed under crossed Nicol prisms are shown in Figure 9-4. As polarized light is transmitted through a starch granule, the granule appears to be divided into brilliantly colored quadrants. One pair of opposite quadrants is one color, the other pair a second color. This birefringence is a characteristic of highly ordered material.

Starch granules that have been partially digested either by acid or by enzymes show that all areas of the granules are not equally resistant to attack. Concentric striations and radial cracks and fractures that give rise to pie-shaped fragments are observed (29). (Fig. 9-5)

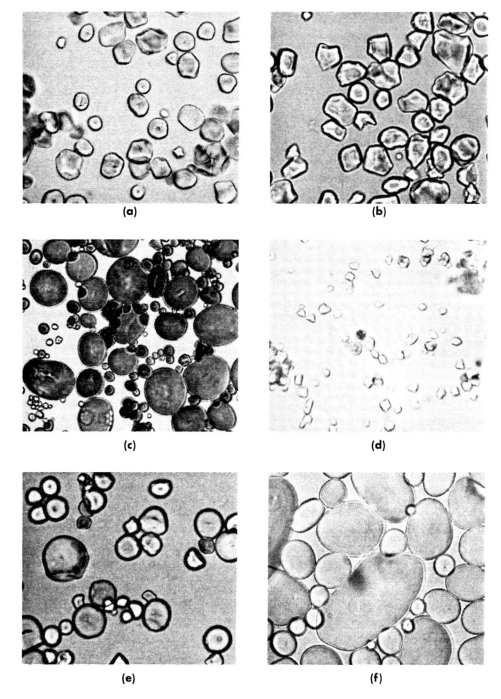

Figure 9-1. Photomicrographs of starch granules from different plants: (a) corn, (b) waxy corn, (c) wheat, (d) rice, (e) tapioca, (f) potato. Original magnification × 500. (Courtesy of R. J. Dimler. USDA Northern Regional Research Center. Peoria, IL.)

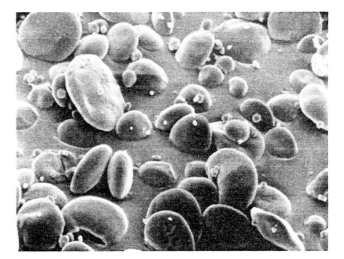

Figure 9-2. Scanning electron micrograph of wheat starch granules. (From R. C. Hoseney, W. A. Atwell, and D. R. Lineback. *Cereal Foods World* 22(2):57. 1977. Reprinted by permission.)

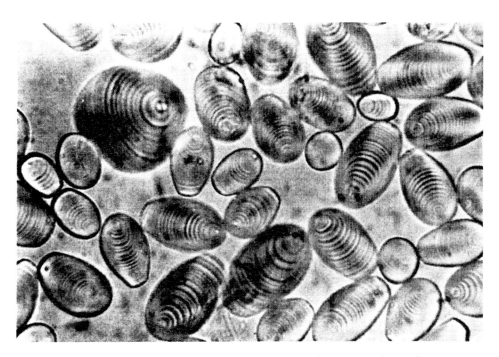

Figure 9-3. Concentric striations on starch granules of the potato berry. Original magnification × 750. (From C. T. Greenwood and S. MacKenzie. "An investigation of the starch of the fruit of the potato *Solanum tuberosum*." *Die Stärke* 15:251. 1963. Reproduced by permission.)

Figure 9-4. Photomicrograph of starch granules (of Figure 9-3) under polarized light, showing crosses that suggest a sphero-crystalline structure. (From C. T. Greenwood and S. MacKenzie. "An investigation of the starch of the fruit of the potato *Solanum tuberosum*." *Die Stärke* 15:251. 1963. Reproduced by permission.)

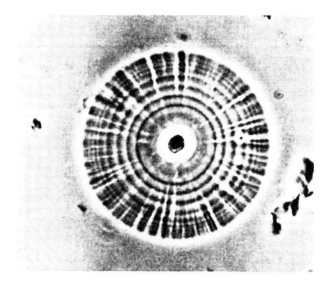

Figure 9-5. A starch granule digested with alpha amylase, showing radial cracks and concentric laminations. (From R. M. Sandstedt. *Cereal Science Today* 10:312. 1965. Reprinted by permission.)

These indicate that the starch molecules within a granule are not deposited in a uniform manner or that the bonding forces are unevenly distributed. Even so, the order within the granule is evident. The granules are believed to be made of starch molecules laid down in concentric rings, which in cross section look like the rings in a slice of onion. Starch molecules that make up a layer are deposited in a radial fashion and more or less parallel to each other. Certain parts of each ring are believed to be in a compact, highly ordered crystalline state. These radially arranged crystallites are linked by amorphous areas in which the starch molecules are deposited in a less orderly fashion.

The concepts of radial arrangement and concentric layers were embodied in an early model of the structure of a starch granule (Fig. 9-6). A current and more sophisticated model for the organization of molecules that constitute a starch granule (Figure 9-7) is based on x-ray and electron-microscopic studies and, more recently, on information from differential scanning calorimetry and nuclear magnetic resonance. The model shows branches of amylopectin as double helices that participate in the formation of crystallites, the latter with dimensions of 50 angstroms. Molecules of amylose are shown with a slight twist and also as a helix in an amylose-lipid complex. Molecules of amylose and those parts of amylopectin where branchings occur constitute the amorphous matrix of a starch granule. An amylopectin molecule may thus be part of a crystallite and also part of the amorphous material in which the crystallite is embedded (4).

Starch granules consist of water-compatible, amorphous, and partially crystalline polymers. The amorphous material may exist as a highly viscous glass or as a rubbery fluid, depending on whether it is below or above its glass transition temperature (T_g), which in turn is influenced by the amount of water present (17). The crystallinity of most starches is in the 35–40 percent range (38). Exceptions are potato starch with a crystallinity just under 30 percent and tapioca near 20 percent. Crystals of starch are classed as A, B, C, and V, based on their structure as deduced from X-ray diffraction (39). Native cereal starches have A-type crystals. Potato starch forms B-type crystals, as do pasted cereal starches when they retrograde, as when bread stales. B-type crystals contain water molecules as part of the

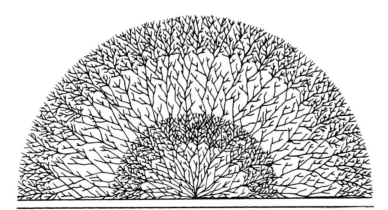

Figure 9-6. Organization of starch molecules within a granule, as originally conceived by the botanist, Arthur Meyer, in 1895. Branching trichitic crystals are pictured in radial orientation, with concentric layers in the granules attributed to alternate shells of dense and loose packing. (From T. J. Schoch. *Brewer's Digest* 37(2):43. 1962. Reprinted by permission.)

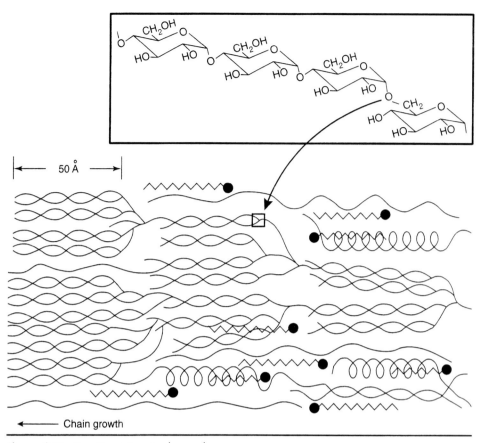

Figure 9-7. Constituents in a starch granule.

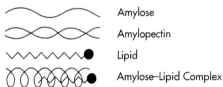

Amylose

Amylopectin

Lipid

Amylose–Lipid Complex

(From C. G. Biliaderis. "Molecular organization of starch constituents (amylose, amylopectin, monoacyl lipids) in granules." *Food Technology* 46(6):99. 1992. Reprinted by permission.)

crystal structure (12). Sweet potato starch and tapioca form C-type crystals. V-type crystals are characteristic of amylose-lipid complexes.

Starch as a Thickening Agent

Reversible Swelling of Starch

Starch granules are formed in the watery medium of the cells of plants. Commercial starches and flours, in which starch predominates, have been dried, as plants mature and/or during processing, to a moisture content of ten to sixteen percent (8). This level is low enough to maintain the amorphous material as a glassy polymer, stable at room temperature. The drying process causes some shrinkage of the granule. When undamaged, raw starch granules are combined with cold water, they absorb water and swell (29). The amounts of both the cold water absorbed and the swell are limited. The small increase in volume that takes place in water at room temperature is a true swelling and is reversible. Crystallinity and birefringence of the granules are unchanged. The uptake of water is exothermic.

Gelatinization and Pasting

Starch granules heated in water are capable of absorbing large amounts of water and swelling proportionately. Early changes that occur in the starch granule are designated gelatinization; later changes are termed pasting (1). Gelatinization involves irreversible changes in the structure of the granule. Once the amorphous glass of the granule is heated to the glass transition temperature (T_g), it becomes a rubbery fluid, molecules of which are now mobile (17). Portions of amylopectin molecules that constitute the crystallites are no longer restricted by the glass surrounding them. The crystallites are dismantled by heat, a melting process (3). The granules are no longer birefringent and swelling of the granules has begun.

Evidence that changes are occurring during gelatinization can be observed when a suspension of starch granules in cold water is heated. When the suspension reaches a certain temperature, depending on the starch, its appearance changes from opaque and white to translucent, and the liquid begins to thicken. The latter is caused by absorption of water and swelling of the granules. The translucency is due to the refractive index of the swollen granules being near that of water. Gelatinization of an individual starch granule occurs over a narrow range in temperatures (8). Frames (enlarged) from a motion picture sequence of the gelatinization of potato starch granules are shown in Figure 9-8 (26). Only 10 seconds elapse from frame A, where swelling is just beginning, to frame F where swelling completes. The increase in translucency and swelling is particularly evident between frames D and E.

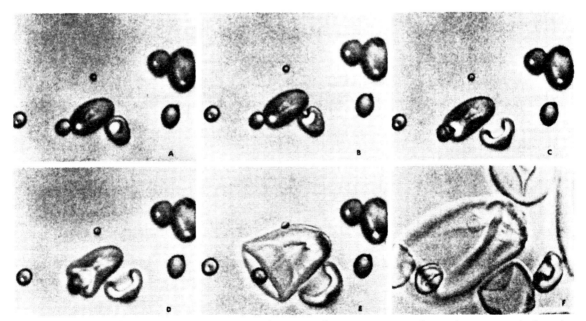

Figure 9-8. Frames from a motion picture sequence of pasting (gelatinizing) potato starch granules. Ten seconds elapse between frame A, where swelling is just beginning, to frame F, where swelling is complete. (From R. M. Sandstedt. *Cereal Science Today* 10:312. 1965. Reprinted by permission.)

Such water-inflated granules behave like deformable blobs. The enlarged granule in frame F has not disintegrated even though it has collapsed. Gelatinized granules of cornstarch, like those of potato (Fig. 9-8), retain the shape of the original; wheat starch granules swell radially at first and then tangentially so they become misshapen (35) (Fig. 26-4).

Pasting is the term used to designate the changes that take place when starch is heated subsequent to gelatinization (1). Additional uptake of water and additional swelling of granules accompany pasting. Soluble constituents move from the granules to the aqueous medium around them. Low molecular–weight amylose is the main exudate, with little amylopectin leaving the granule unless extended heating and/or manipulation causes its disintegration. Thickness is attributed to the enlarged granules that remain suspended and to the exudate around them, as shown in Figure 9-9 (22).

Starches from different plants differ in pasting behavior. Changes in viscosity as slurries of five common starches were heated are plotted in Figure 9-10. The left side of each curve shows the viscosity of the pasting starch as a function of temperature and time. Starch from potato, a tuber, begins to gelatinize at a lower temperature and reaches maximum paste viscosity at a lower temperature than do the other four starches. Viscosity of potato starch (maximum near 70°C or 158°F) declines rapidly with continued heating. Tapioca, a starch from the cassava or manioc plant, begins to gelatinize at a temperature only slightly higher (near 65°C or 149°F) than does potato starch. Viscosity of pasting tapioca starch reaches a maximum near 90°C or 195°F, after which viscosity of the paste decreases. The data plotted in Figure 9-10 are based on 25 grams of both potato and tapioca starches instead of the 35 grams used for the other three starches.

Both corn and wheat starch require higher temperatures to initiate gelatinization and higher temperatures to reach peak paste viscosity. Corn and especially wheat starch yield much less viscous pastes compared to potato starch. The viscosity profile of waxy corn starch

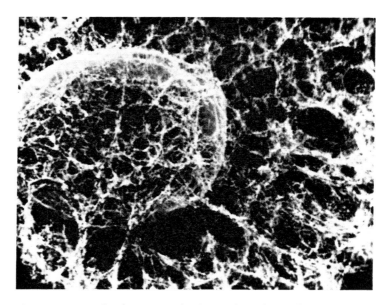

Figure 9-9. Exudate from a pasted (gelatinized) starch granule shown in a scanning electron micrograph × 1200). (From B. S. Miller, R. I. Derby, and H. B. Trimbo. *Cereal Chemistry* 50:279. 1973. Reprinted by permission.)

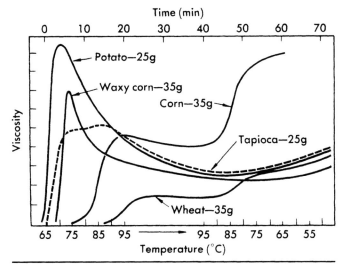

Figure 9-10. Changes in viscosity during heating, holding, and cooling of starch pastes. Concentration of starch in grams per 450 milliliters of water. (Reprinted from T. J. Schoch and A. L. Elder. "Starches in the Food Industry." In *Uses of Sugars and Other Carbohydrates in the Food Industry*, Advances in Chemistry Series No. 12. p. 24. 1955. Copyright © 1955 by the American Chemical Society and reprinted by permission of the copyright owner.)

resembles that of potato starch more than it does that of normal corn starch. Figure 9-10 thus shows that starches from different plants differ in the amount of energy required to disrupt the ordered packing of molecules that comprise the granule that leads to pasting of the starch.

A number of factors may contribute to differences in pasting behavior. Starches differ in their amylose/amylopectin ratios. Normal corn starch has an amylose content of 27 percent followed by wheat starch with 23 percent. Potato starch has an amylose content of 22 percent and tapioca 18 percent (38). Genetically modified waxy corn starch is essentially 100 percent amylopectin. The branched amylopectin molecules are more highly polymerized than are amylose molecules (a few million compared to a few thousand). Molecular weight of amylose ranges from a few hundred thousand in corn starch to a million in potato starch (38). The branches of amylopectin, which as double helices unite to form the crystalline areas of starch granules, vary in length. Those molecules with shorter branches form A-type crystals as in wheat and normal corn starch. Amylopectin molecules with longer branches, as in potato starch, form B-type crystals (11), with molecules of water an essential component of the crystal. Results of one study suggest that the molecular weight of amylose and the length of the branches of amylopectin in the granule influence pasting properties, especially the viscosity of the pasted starch (13). The phosphate content of starch affects its pasting properties (18). Phosphates linked chemically to starch molecules, as in potato starch granules, favor uptake of water and swelling of the granule and paste clarity. Phosphates united to lipids in the granule, as in wheat and normal cornstarch, associate with the starch and the lipids interfere with uptake of water and swelling of the granule. Such pastes are cloudy. In view of the above, it is not surprising that pasted starches differ in character in addition to gelatinization and pasting temperatures and viscosity. Potato and tapioca starches yield cohesive, sticky, stringy pastes that are translucent. Wheat and normal cornstarch form short, less cohesive pastes that are cloudy. Waxy cornstarch forms translucent pastes that become cloudy over time.

Setting or Gelation of a Pasted Starch

Changes in viscosity as the five pasted starches cool are shown in Figure 9-10. The gradual increase in viscosity of potato, tapioca, and waxy corn starch represents a typical cooling effect. Wheat and normal corn starch, however, show an abrupt rise in viscosity once the hot paste begins to cool. Low molecular weight amylose molecules that have escaped from the swollen granules of these two starches are responsible for the abrupt rise in viscosity. As the pastes cool, the kinetic energy is insufficient to counteract the tendency of amylose molecules to associate as double helices. If amylose is in sufficient concentration, segments of these helices unite as crystals that, together with enlarged granules, form a network or matrix that converts the cooled paste into a gel (21). This process of crystallization and matrix formation is termed retrogradation. Amylose retrogrades rapidly and it is irreversible, at least at 100°C (212°F) or below. Potato, tapioca, and waxy corn starch pastes do not form gels. Failure of amylose molecules to leave the granules of potato and tapioca starch is attributed to their high molecular weights and, in the case of potato starch, to the cocrystallization of amylose with amylopectin (38). Waxy corn starch contains no amylose. Amylopectin retrogrades as does amylose, but the process occurs over days. Retrogradation of amylopectin is reversible, a condition exploited when stale bread is heated to refresh it. It occurs only if enough water is present (27%) so that the starch molecules are mobile (17). The crystals that form are B-type, with molecules of water an integral part of the crystal (12, 39). The staling of bread is discussed in Chapter 14.

Starch is a basic component of many food products. In the preparation, handling, and storage of such products, the starch may undergo a number of changes, some desirable such as thickening a liquid, and some undesirable such as staling of baked goods. Promoting the one and preventing the other are desirable goals. A concept has been advanced that gelatinization, pasting, gelation, retrogradation, and staling are thermomechanical processes best understood and controlled by looking on starch as a polymer capable of a glassy rubbery transition controlled by moisture/temperature interaction (17).

Factors Affecting Starch-Thickened Products

Achieving Uniform Thickness

When starch is used as a thickening agent, a uniformly thickened liquid without lumps is desired. First the starch granules must be separated before they are heated in the liquid. This may be accomplished by suspending them in a small quantity of the cold liquid. Starch granules separate readily because they carry a negative charge and so repel each other in water. When conventional flour is used as a source of starch, separation is more difficult. Instantized flour, however (Chapter 11), disperses readily in cold liquid. Alternately, starch granules or flour particles may be separated with grains of sugar or with a coating of fat, either melted or plastic. This last is sometimes referred to as a *roux*.

Separating the starch granules is only the first step in getting a smooth starch-thickened paste. It is equally important that each starch granule swell independently of every other granule. When dry starch granules are blended with cold water, they remain suspended as long as the water is agitated. The temporarily suspended granules settle and pack when stirring stops. Heating must be slow so the suspension can be stirred fast enough to keep the starch granules suspended and the temperature uniform. In this way granules take up neither more nor less than their share of water. Otherwise, granules will swell unevenly and some will adhere. Lumps are the result.

Type of Starch

Wheat and normal cornstarch are the main thickening and gelling agents. Flour is frequently used as a source of wheat starch. Other starches, including arrowroot, potato, rice, tapioca, and waxy corn, are available. Each starch confers its unique character on the starch-thickened product, either before or after it is cooled. Cornstarch is an effective gelling agent, with six parts of starch by weight capable of immobilizing 94 parts of liquid (23, 27). The gel that forms when the paste is cooled behaves as a visco-elastic solid, but an easily deformable one. Liquid is confined within the network of the gel. When a gel is cut or as it ages and retrogradation continues, part of the liquid will leak or be squeezed from the gel. This expulsion of liquid from a gel is known as *syneresis*. It can be observed in starch-thickened puddings and soft pie fillings.

The structural framework responsible for the setting of a cooked starch paste as it cools can be demonstrated by freezing the paste and then allowing it to thaw (Fig. 9-11).

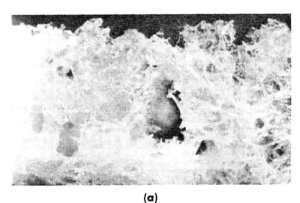

(a)

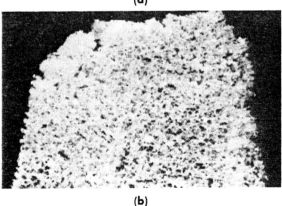

(b)

Figure 9-11. Cooked starch pastes after freezing and thawing show the structural framework responsible for the setting of a cooled, cooked paste: (a) a coarse textured starch sponge, originally magnified 7½ times; (b) similar view of a fine textured sponge. (From G. E. Hilbert et al. *Food Industries* 17:878. 1945. Courtesy of the Northern Regional Research Center, Peoria, IL. Reprinted by permission of Food Engineering.)

When a cooked starch paste freezes, water held in the starch network is converted into ice crystals. The starchy framework remains intact. When the ice crystals melt, the water regains its fluidity, but it is unable to associate with the starch as it did prior to freezing. The water now can be squeezed from the starch granule-amylose sponge and the sponge can reabsorb the water when pressure is released. The structure of a starch sponge is quite fragile and the sponge must be handled with care.

When pasted starch granules are dried, they do not revert to their pregelatinized condition. They do, however, retain the ability to reabsorb large amounts of liquid. This characteristic of pasted starches (referred to as pregelatinized) is utilized to make such convenience foods as instant rice, instant mashed potato, and instant puddings that are reconstituted with hot water. The slight graininess that may be observed in such products is due to high melting amylose crystals. Starches modified to be cold water-soluble are available. One derived from cornstarch yields a paste thick enough to hold its shape when turned from a mold or as a soft pie filling. It is acid- and freeze-resistant, unlike unmodified corn starch (26).

Starches exhibit some unwanted effects when they are used as thickening agents. Chemically modified starches, in which some of these defects are eliminated, are widely used by the food industry (20). Cross-bonding is one modification in which a substance such as phosphate is used to link adjacent molecules of starch through their hydroxyl groups and thus strengthen the granule. Cross-bonded starches are stable at high temperatures and they resist thinning when heated in the presence of acid and when the paste is stirred. Substituting a bulky group for the hydrogen of a hydroxyl group on the starch molecule is another modification. These bulky groups interfere with the recrystallization of amylose. This type of modification gives pastes with greater clarity and ones that resist syneresis when starch-thickened foods are refrigerated or frozen. Limited hydrolysis of starch by acid yields thin-boiling starch. The low viscosity of the hot paste permits it to be piped to molds where it gels. Gum drops are one confection made with thin-boiling starch.

Proportion of Starch to Liquid

In addition to the kind of starch, the viscosity of a starch-thickened hot food such as gravy or the stiffness of a cooled product such as soft pie filling is influenced by the proportion of starch to liquid. Flour, frequently used as a source of starch, has approximately half the thickening power of normal cornstarch. One tablespoon (15 milliliters) of flour per cup (250 milliliters) of liquid yields a thin product, two tablespoons (30 milliliters) one of medium thickness, and three tablespoons (45 milliliters) a thick product.

In puddings, sauces, and gravies the proportion of liquid is sufficient to permit gelatinization and pasting of the starch. In some doughs, however, the proportion of liquid may be too low to permit complete pasting of the starch (6), which may be as low as four percent in sugar cookies.

Effects of Sugar

That sugars interfere with the pasting of starch has been known since the 1950s. Of the three sugars—fructose, glucose, and sucrose—fructose inhibits gelatinization and pasting least, and sucrose most (2, 30). A number of papers report attempts to account for this phenomenon. Explanations tentatively put forward (19, 30, 32, 36) are that sugar competes with starch for water, that it binds water, leaving less for starch, that it interferes with the hydration of starch, that it interacts with starch, and that it interferes with the plasticizing effect of water by raising the average molecular weight of the sugar–water cosolvent (17). To date, no satisfactory explanation of the effect of sugars on the gelatinization of starch has been advanced (5, 14).

On a practical level, sugar (sucrose), except in low concentrations, in starch-thickened puddings, and in soft pie fillings decreases the thickness of the cooked product. It decreases the stiffness of the cooled product even more (11). Sugar in a layer cake controls the gelatinization temperature of the starch and this, in turn, influences the volume and texture of the cake. One problem in making a sugar-free cake is that the starch gelatinizes and the batter begins to set too early in the baking period.

Effect of Acid

Acids supplied by fruit juices and vinegar are present in some foods that are thickened with starch. When starch is heated in the presence of acid, some of the molecules are hydrolyzed to dextrins and low molecular compounds. The effect of the acid is to reduce the thickness of the hot paste and the firmness of the gel that forms (9). The effect of acid is more pronounced than that of sugar. However, with acid the decrease in thickness and stiffness has been attributed in part to fragmentation of swollen granules rather than to reduced swelling (2). No doubt hydrolysis of amylose exuded from the swollen granule contributes to the weak gel. Starch-thickened food that contains acid should be heated no more than necessary to complete gelatinization and pasting. When possible, as for lemon pie filling or the sauce for Harvard beets, acid should be added after the starch is cooked. For a lemon pie filling there is no advantage to waiting until the hot paste cools before the lemon juice is added. In fact, disturbing the filling once the gel starts to form makes the gel somewhat weaker (25). Both sugar and acid tend to make the cooked paste clearer.

Salts of phosphoric acid, usually disodium phosphate, hasten the cooking of starch. Phosphates are used in quick-cooking pasta and cereals and in packaged starch-thickened puddings. The phosphates in milk hasten the pasting of starch. Surface-active substances (Chapter 15) such as monoacyl glycerol delay pasting (16).

When flour is used as a source of starch, the liquid will be thicker if the flour is put into hot fat rather than dispersed in cold liquid. Heat inactivates the alpha-amylase of the flour, which would otherwise bring about some hydrolysis of the starch (31). A soft pie filling must be heated sufficiently after the egg yolk is added to inactivate the amylase or the filling will thin upon standing (24).

VEGETABLE GUMS

Substances known collectively as vegetable gums are complex polymers of several monosaccharides and their derivatives, unlike starch and cellulose, which are polymers of glucose. Because of their great affinity for water and their size, gums are referred to as hydrocolloids. Of course, starches are hydrocolloids, too. So are β-glucans, hemicelluloses, pectins, and gelatin, discussed in subsequent chapters. Gums are valued ingredients in a number of foods because they form viscous sols or plastic gels. As sols or gels, individual gums exhibit unique flow properties when subjected to force (technically, shear stress). These properties are reflected in the texture of foods that contain the gums.

Force (beating, stirring, gravity, or manipulation in the mouth) applied to a viscous liquid shears it. In the case of a liquid such as salad oil or sucrose syrup, viscosity is independent of shear rate. Such liquids are characterized as Newtonian. Most foods are non-Newtonian and exhibit either shear thinning or shear thickening when they are manipulated. Sols that undergo shear thinning are either pseudoplastic (regain their original viscosity as soon as shearing stops) or thixotropic (regain their original viscosity but need time to do so). Frosting that contains high viscosity cellulose gum is an example of a pseudoplastic material. The viscous frosting flows readily when applied with a knife or a spatula, a shearing action, to the surface of a cake. When spreading stops, the frosting at once reverts to its highly viscous state and so remains in place in the cake. Mayonnaise is an example of a thixotropic product. In the container, it has a gel-like consistency, but with manipulation it can be made to flow. Mayonnaise regains its gel-like consistency, but only after it is undisturbed for some time. Systems that undergo shear thickening are either dilatant or rheopectic. Dilatancy may be observed as syrup for fondant is beaten. As sucrose crystals accumulate in the syrup, a point is reached at which the fondant momentarily thickens and looses its gloss. Manipulation of the fondant forces sucrose crystals apart, forming voids that accommodate the syrup from which sucrose is yet to crystallize. If manipulation stops, syrup rises to the surface, the gloss returns, and the fondant regains some of its fluidity. This change in gloss and viscosity can be repeated several times before enough of the sucrose has crystallized to harden the fondant. A rheopectic substance increases in viscosity as the shear force or shear rate increases. Rheopectic behavior may be observed as egg whites are beaten or the gelatin-containing syrup for marshmallows is whipped. The flow behavior of gums contributes to the versatility of this group of ingredients (28).

Gums are widely used in the food industry, as a cursory examination of labels on food will attest. Individual gums are used in the formulation of specific foods to accomplish one or more of the following objectives (31). They are used to inhibit crystallization, to act as a whipping aid, to stabilize foams, to act as an adhesive and binding agent, to form and stabilize emulsions, to act as a coating agent, to prevent syneresis, to suspend solids, to act as a carrier for flavoring, and to replace fat in fabricated meat products.

Conventionally, gums are grouped into five categories: seaweed extracts, plant exudates, seed gums, biosynthetics, and chemically modified carbohydrates (7, 23, 31).

Seaweed Extracts

Alginates

Alginates are obtained from brown algae (Phaeophyceae) of which four species are major commercial sources. Alginates are harvested in a number of countries, including the United States. Giant kelp (*Macrocystis pyrifera*), which grows off the coast of California, is one source. The effective constituent in alginates is alginic acid, a linear polymer of D-mannuronic acid and L-guluronic acid. Blocks of residues of either one or the other monomer and blocks in which the two monomers alternate appear the length of the polymer. The distribution of the two monomers varies with the source and influences the functional properties of the gum. The potassium, sodium, and ammonium salts of alginic acid disperse in water, as does the chemically modified propylene glycol alginate. In the presence of calcium ions, alginates form gels in cold water; these do not liquefy below 100°C (212°F). Alginates are used to stabilize foams and to make simulated fruit items used in bakery products.

Agar

This gum comes from red seaweeds that grow off the coast of Japan, Mexico, Portugal, and Denmark. Agar consists of two fractions—agarose and agaropectin—both polymers of D-galactose and anhydro-L-galactose, agaro-pectin containing sulfate ester groups. Agar disperses readily in hot water. When the dispersion is cooled to 35° to 40°C (95° to 104°F), a gel begins to form that is stable up to 85°C (185°F). The main use of agar in foods is to stabilize icings, meringues, and pie fillings.

Carrageenans

These gums are obtained from red seaweed, the most important source being *Chondrus crispus,* known as Irish moss. It is harvested along the Atlantic coast of the United States, Canada, Ireland, and Brittany. Like agar, carrageenans are polymers of galactose and anhydrogalactose, but the latter are more highly sulfated. The main fractions of carrageenan, based upon increasing sulfate ester content, are kappa, iota, and lambda carrageenan. The negative charges on the sulfate ester groups favor dispersibility in water, but they make it more difficult for the molecules to approach and form gels unless the charges are neutralized. With potassium ions, kappa carrageenan forms strong gels with a tendency to syneresis. With calcium ions, iota-carrageenan forms elastic gels with no syneresis. Lambda-carrageenan is non-gelling. Carrageenans interact with proteins and they are used to stabilize the proteins in such products as canned evaporated milk.

Exudates

Gum Arabic (Acacia)

This complex, highly branched polysaccharide is obtained from acacia trees, mainly in the Sudan. Galactose, rhamnose, arabinose, and methylglucuronic acid are found in this gum along with calcium, magnesium, and potassium ions. Gum arabic is highly soluble in cold water. The sols are Newtonian and have low viscosity. Gum arabic is used to control crystals in ices and glazes, to stabilize emulsions, and to fix flavors.

Gum Tragacanth

This exudate comes from the *Astragalus* bush, several species of which grow in Asia Minor and in arid regions of Iran, Syria, and Turkey. The swelling and thickening properties of this gum come from the presence of highly branched polymers of galacturonic acid, with an occasional insert of rhamnose residue. Numerous side branches, in which xylose predominates, are attached to the backbone. Gum tragacanth forms highly viscous sols but it does not gel. It is used to impart a creamy texture, to suspend particles, to stabilize confections, and to give a glaze to fruit toppings.

Gums from the Endosperm of Seed

Locust Bean Gum

This gum comes from the endosperm of seeds of the carob tree (*Ceratonia silaqua*), which grows in the Mediterranean region. The gum is a polymer of mannose, with branches of single galactose residues attached to the mannose chain. The gum is insoluble in cold water and when heated to near boiling and then cooled the sol has maximum viscosity. This gum does not form a gel, but it reinforces gels formed by carrageenan. The gum is used as a stabilizer and as an inhibitor of syneresis.

Guar Gum

The endosperm of the guar plant (*Cyamopsis tetra gonolobus*) is the source of this gum. This annual grows in arid regions of India and Pakistan and is a minor agricultural crop in Texas and Arkansas. Like locust bean gum, guar gum is a linear polymer of mannose residues, with side chains of single galactose residues attached to alternate mannose residues. This gives a mannose/galactose ratio of 2:1, in contrast to locust bean gum in which the ratio is 4:1. Guar gum is highly soluble in cold water. The creamy sols are thixotropic. Alone, guar gum does not gel but it acts synergistically with gel-forming agar and carrageenan.

Biosynthetic Gums

Dextran

Organisms such as *Leuconostoc mesenteroides* form dextrans. These gums are polymers of glucose united primarily by 1,6 linkages. Dextran acts as a gelling agent in candies. Other functions are to inhibit crystals in icings and ice creams and to give desirable texture to pudding mixes.

Gellan Gum

Pseudomonas eleodea organisms produce gellan gum from carbohydrate substrates. Four saccharides, glucose, glucuronic acid, glucose, and rhamnose, in that order, appear as repeating units in the linear backbone of gellan gum. This gum disperses in hot water and when the sol cools it forms a gel but only with the aid of cations. The texture of the gel and the temperatures at which a gel forms and liquefies depend on the cation. In 1990, the FDA approved the use of gellan gum as a stabilizer in icings and glazes and for use in non-standardized jellies and jams.

Xanthan Gum

This gum is produced from a carbohydrate source by *Xanthomonas campestris,* an organism isolated originally from rutabagas. The molecule has a cellulosic backbone with side branches of oligosaccharides attached to alternate glucose residues along the polymer. Presence of these side chains accounts for the solubility of this gum. Xanthan gum forms viscous sols at low concentrations and the sols are stable over a wide range in temperatures and pH. Xanthan gum does not form a gel except with locust bean gum. Xanthan gum forms pourable emulsions, stabilizes egg white substitutes and the crystals in ice cream, and acts as a thickener and suspending agent.

Chemically Modified Carbohydrates

Cellulose Ethers

Insoluble cellulose can be converted to a water-dispersible form by treatment with alkali. A hydrogen of a hydroxyl group may be replaced by a carboxy group, with a cellulose ether the result. The type and number of constituents influence the solubility, viscosity, and gelling power of such modified celluloses. Methyl cellulose and carboxymethyl cellulose are two alkali-modified celluloses. Methyl cellulose forms gels when cold dispersions are heated. This makes them useful for coating food prior to deep fat frying to limit absorption of fat. These gels regain their viscous character when they cool. Methyl cellulose contributes to the viscosity of batters, strengthens cell walls, and limits loss of moisture during baking. Carboxymethyl cellulose—referred to as cellulose gum—forms pseudoplastic sols. It is used to suspend particles, to act as a binder and thickener, and to prevent syneresis. It is used also as a non caloric bulking agent.

Microcrystalline Cellulose

Hydrolysis of cellulose by acid yields microcrystalline cellulose, dispersions of which are thixotropic (subject to shear thinning and needing time to recover). This modification of cellulose is used to stabilize foams, icings, and emulsions and to suspend particles.

Propylene Glycol Alginate

When alginic acid is complexed with propylene oxide, the resulting propylene glycol alginate is dispersible in water in which it forms a viscous sol. Propylene glycol alginate aids in the emulsification of salad dressings and in the suspension of solids.

The many vegetable gums that are available offer numerous possibilities for modifying or improving texture, consistency, and other physical properties of foods. Gums are used in a variety of products, including frostings, glazes, frozen desserts, whipped toppings, sauces, puddings, salad dressings, packaged mixes for baked items, and fabricated meat products.

REFERENCES

1. Atwell, W. A., L. F. Hood, D. R. Lineback, E. Varriano-Marston and H. F. Zobel. 1988. "The terminology and methodology associated with basic starch phenomena." *Cereal Foods World* 33:306–11. Gelatinization, pasting, and retrogradation defined.
2. Bean, M. and E. M. Osman. 1959. "Behavior of starch during food preparation." II. "Effect of different sugars on the viscosity and gel strength of starch pastes." *Food Research* 24:665–71. Dextrose, fructose, invert syrup, sorbitol, lactose, maltose, and sucrose compared.
3. Biliaderis, C. G., T. J. Maurice and J. R. Vose. 1980. "Starch gelatinization phenomena studied by differential scanning calorimetry." *Journal of Food Science* 45:1669–74, 1680. Starch as an amorphous, semicrystalline polymer; and gelatinization as a solvent-assisted melting process.
4. Billiaderis, C. G., C. M. Page, T. J. Maurice and B. O. Juliano. 1986. "Thermal characterization of rice starches: A polymer approach to phase transition of granular starch." *Journal of Agricultural and Food Chemistry* 34:6–14. Attempts to clarify the mechanism of starch gelatinization.
5. Chinachoti, P., and T. R. Stengle. 1990. "Water mobility in starch/sucrose systems: An oxygen-17 NMR study." *Journal of Food Science* 55:1732–34. Explanations of effect of sugar on starch still incomplete.
6. Derby, R. I., B. S. Miller, B. F. Miller and H. B. Trimbo. 1975. "Visual observation of wheat-starch gelatinization in limited water systems." *Cereal Chemistry* 52:702–13. Moisture levels of 33 to 60 percent compared.
7. Dziezak, J. D. 1991. "A focus on gums." *Food Technology* 45(3):116–32. Individual gums and their uses in foods.

8. French, D. 1984. "Organization of starch granules." In *Starch Chemistry and Technology.* R. L. Whistler, J. N. BeMiller, and E. F. Paschall, eds. Orlando, FL: Academic Press. Pp. 183–247. Structure and functional properties.

9. Hansuld, M. K., and A. M. Briant. 1954. "The effect of citric acid on selected edible starches and flours." *Food Research* 19: 581–89. Thickening and gelling of pastes, made with cornstarch, wheat starches, and flours, compared.

10. Hester, E. E., A. M. Briant, and C. J. Personius. 1956. "The effects of sucrose on the properties of some starches and flours." *Cereal Chemistry* 33:91–101. Thickness of hot pastes and rigidity of cold pastes from cornstarch, wheat starches, and flour.

11. Hizukuri, S., T. Kaneko and Y. Takeda. 1983. "Measurement of the chain length of amylopectin and its relevance to the origin of crystalline polymorphism of starch granules." *Biochemica et Biophysica Acta* 760:188–91. Shorter chains associated with A-type crystals, longer chains with B-type.

12. Imberty, A., and S. Perez. 1988. "A revisit to the three-dimensional structure of B-type starch. *Biopolymers* 27:1205–21. Water molecules an integral part of B-type starch.

13. Jane, J.-L., and J.-F. Chen. 1992. "Effect of amylose molecular size and amylopectin branch chain length on paste properties of starch." *Cereal Chemistry* 69:60–65. Relation to viscosity of the paste.

14. Kim, C. S., and C. E. Walker. 1992. "Effects of sugars and emulsifiers on starch gelatinization evaluated by differential scanning calorimetry." *Cereal Chemistry* 69:212–17. Theories as to the action of sugars; Issue unsettled.

15. Kokini, J. L., L.-S. Lai and L. L. Chedid. "Effect of starch structure on starch rheological properties." *Food Technology* 46(6): 124–39. Pertinent papers reviewed.

16. Langley, R. W., and B. S. Miller. 1971. "Note on the relative effects of monoglycerides on the gelatinization of wheat starch." *Cereal Chemistry* 48:81–85. Length of fatty acid chain and delay in pasting.

17. Levine, H., and L. Slade. 1990. "Influence of the glassy and rubbery states on the thermal, mechanical and structural properties of doughs and baked products." In *Dough Rheology and Baked Product Texture,* H. Faradi and J. M. Faubion, eds. New York: Van Nostrand Reinhold. Pp. 227–75. Starch: a partially crystalline polymer system plasticized by water.

18. Lim, S.-T., T. Kasemsuwan and J.-L. Jane. 1994. "Characterization of phosphorus in starch by P-nuclear magnetic resonance spectroscopy." *Cereal Chemistry* 71:488–93. Role of phosphates in the pasting of starch.

19. Lineback, D. R., and E. Wongsrikasem. 1980. "Gelatinization of starch in baked products. *Journal of Food Science* 45:71–74. Effects of sugar on gelatinization; birefringence and scanning electron micrographs.

20. Luallen, T. E. 1988. "Structure, characteristics and uses of some typical carbohydrate food ingredients." *Cereal Foods World* 33: 924–27. Modified starches and their uses.

21. Miles, M. J., V. J. Morris, P. D. Orford and S. G. Ring. 1985. The role of amylose and amylopectin in the gelation and retrogradation of starch. *Carbohydrate Res.* 135: 271–81. A starch gel: a matrix of retrograded amylose with starch granules embedded in it.

22. Miller, B. S., R. I. Derby and H. B. Trimbo. 1973. A pictorial explanation for the increase in viscosity of a heated starch-water suspension. *Cereal Chemistry* 50:271–80. Evidence for presence of exudate.

23. Morris, V. J. 1990. "Starch gelation and retrogradation." *Trends in Food Science and Technology* 2:2–6. Processes from a molecular standpoint.

24. Murthy, G. K. 1970. "Thermal inactivation of alpha-amylase in various liquid egg products." *Journal of Food Science* 35:352–56. Whole egg and egg yolk compared; effects of salt and sugar.

25. Nielsen, H. J., J. D. Hewitt and N. K. Fitch. 1952. "Factors affecting consistency of a lemon pie filling." *Journal of Home Economics* 44:782–85. Effects of cooking time after addition of yolks, of cooling time before addition of lemon juice, and of acidity of lemon juice.

26. Osman, E. M. and P. D. Cummisford. 1959. "Some factors affecting the stability

of frozen white sauces compared. *Food Research* 24:595–604. Influence of the kind of starch and other ingredients on freeze-thaw stability.

27. Ring, S. G. 1985. "Some studies on starch gelation." *Starch* 37:80–83. A six-percent (w/w) starch paste can form a visco-elastic solid.

28. Sanderson, G. R. 1981. "Polysaccharides in foods." *Food Technology* 35(7):50–57, 83. Individual gums and their functions; shear thinning and shear thickening.

29. Sandstedt, R. M. 1965. "Fifty years of progress in starch chemistry." *Cereal Science Today* 10:305–15. Clear comprehensible presentation with many excellent photomicrographs.

30. Savage, H. L., and E. M. Osman. 1978. "Effects of certain sugars and sugar alcohols on the swelling of cornstarch granules." *Cereal Chemistry* 55:447–54. Three monosaccharides, three disaccharides and two sugar alcohols compared at levels of 5, 20, and 50 percent of the weight of the water.

31. Sharma, S. C. "1981. Gums and hydrocolloids in oil-water emulsions." *Food Technology* 35(1):59–67. Major gums included.

32. Spies, R. D., and R. C. Hoseney. 1982. "Effects of sugars on starch gelatinization." *Cereal Chemistry* 59:128–31. Attempts to account for elevation of the gelatinization temperature.

33. Trimbo, H. B., and B. S. Miller. 1971. "Factors affecting the quality of sauces (gravies)." *Journal of Home Economics* 63(1):48–53. Effects of the alpha-amylase of the flour.

34. Whistler, R. L., and J. R. Daniel. 1984. "Molecular structure of starch." In *Starch Chemistry and Technology*, R. L. Whistler, J. N. BeMiller and E. F. Paschall, eds. 153–82. Conformation, glycosidic linkage, and crystalline forms.

35. Williams, M. R., and P. Bowler. 1982. "Starch gelatinization: A morphological study of *Triticeae* and other starches." *Stärke* 34:221–23. Scanning electron micrographs of six starches heated to 20°, 60°, 75°, and 97°C.

36. Wootton, M., and A. Bamunuarachchi. 1980. "Application of differential scanning calorimetry to starch gelatinization." II. "Effect of sucrose and sodium chloride." *Stärke* 32:126–29. An attempt to account for the effect on pasting temperature.

37. Zeleznak, K. J., and R. C. Hoseney. 1987. "The glass transition in starch." *Cereal Chemistry* 64:121–24. Evidence for a glass transition in wheat starch.

38. Zobel, H. F. 1988. "Molecules to granules: A comprehensive review." *Stärke* 40:44–50. Composition, structure, properties.

39. Zobel, H. F. 1988. Starch crystal transformations and their industrial importance. *Stärke* 40:1–7. Crystalline types of starch discussed.

Cereals

10

The word cereal is derived from the name of the Roman grain or harvest goddess, Ceres, usually depicted with ears of barley braided in her hair. Cereals are the seeds of grasses. Plants that supply edible seeds or grains include wheat, corn, rice, oats, barley, sorghum, millet, and rye (2). Amaranth and quinoa (*keen wah*) are two other plants that yield edible seeds. Wild rice, unrelated to the other rice and once harvested only in the wild, is now grown commercially. Unlike the other grains, which evolved in nature, triticale, a wheat-rye hybrid, was crossed intentionally.

Cereal products made from grain include breakfast foods, rice, flours, and pasta. Discussion of flours and pasta is deferred to Chapter 11.

UTILIZATION OF CEREAL GRAINS

Wheat is the main grain consumed in the United States and Canada; rice the main cereal in China, Japan, and India; rye the chief one in Russia and Central Europe. Corn is used in Mexico, South America, and the United States. Oats are used to a limited extent for human food.

Not only does the main grain consumed vary from country to country, but so does the importance of cereals as a whole in the diet. The proportion of total calories that come from cereals is low in the United States, in contrast to parts of the Far East where the proportion is much higher (19). In this country the resources (land, climate, money, machinery, and agricultural know-how) for the production of food in relation to the number of people to be fed are high; in the Far East they are low. Where the food supply is inadequate, the population must eat grains to prevent starvation. Fruit and vegetables do not begin to approximate the calories contained in cereals from the same amount of land and labor. Furthermore, to produce milk, eggs, and meat, primary agricultural products are fed to animals that convert them into a more desirable form but waste much potential food for humans in the process.

The following comparison gives a rough idea of the effects of alternate uses of land resources. The estimated yield from 10 acres of land devoted to growing cattle is enough beef (in pounds) to feed one individual for one year. But the 10 acres of land could be used to produce enough wheat to feed 15 people for a year or enough rice to feed 24. The corn plant is an especially valuable food producer. It is one of the most efficient trappers of the sun's energy, sugar cane being another (21). Of course, filling an individual is not the sole function of food. But when one is hungry, getting enough food is an immediate objective.

Cereals provide almost half of the dietary protein worldwide (14), and they could make a greater contribution. In the United States we feed roughly 90 percent of our production of edible (for humans) plant proteins from cereals, legumes, and vegetables to animals. For each unit of animal protein obtained approximately five units of plant protein are fed. Consumption of cereal foods directly represents a more efficient use of arable land, fossil energy, and labor. Each hectare (2.47 acres) of corn planted in the United States will yield enough utilizable protein to feed 12 people 60 grams of protein per day for one year. For rice the figure is 10 and for wheat 8. True, cereals do not compare with animal foods for either quantity or quality of protein. Cereals are deficient in the essential amino acid lysine. Even so, yields of both protein and of essential amino acids per acre of cultivated land are several times greater from corn when the seed is used directly as food rather than from animals fed the same amount of corn (1). Calculated yield of protein from corn is 234 pounds per acre, and of essential amino acids 80 pounds per acre. Were this corn fed to animals, calculated yields of protein in pounds per acre are 87 for milk, 82 for broilers, 60 for eggs, 56 for hogs, 49 for mature chickens, and 26 for beef. Yields of essential amino acids in pounds per acre range from 37 for milk to 10 for beef. Interestingly, the yield of protein that can be extracted from the leaves of green corn is at least as great as that from the mature seed.

The economic advantage aside, cereal products merit a prominent place in the diet for their contributions to good health. In fact, cereals make up the broad base of the Food Pyramid, formulated as a guide for selecting a health-promoting diet. The annual per-capita consumption of cereal products and flour was 199 pounds in 1994 compared to 156 pounds in 1985, an increase of 27 percent over the decade (18).

STRUCTURE OF CEREAL GRAINS

The Cell

The cell is the basic structural unit of cereals as of all foods of plant origin. (Fig. 27-5). A plant cell is bound by a cell wall that encloses the protoplasm or actual living part of the plant. The cell wall contains celluloses and hemicelluloses. The protoplasm consists of water (in large quantities in the living plant), protein, starch grains, fat globules, and, in solution, water-soluble minerals, vitamins, and pigments.

Parts of a Cereal Grain

All cells in a cereal grain are not alike. Because of this, cereal grains can be separated into three different parts: the bran, the germ or embryo, and the endosperm. The parts of a wheat kernel are shown diagrammatically in Figure 10-1. The bulky *bran* consists of the outermost layer of cells of the grain. These cells have thick walls made mainly of cellulose and hemicellulose. The bran also contains minerals, chiefly iron. Water-soluble vitamins, which include thiamin, niacin, and riboflavin, together with some protein, are found in the bran. The bran accounts for about five percent of the entire grain. A single layer of cells (called the aleurone) separates the bran from the rest of the grain.

The *germ* or embryo makes up two to three percent of a cereal grain. Cells in this part of the grain are rich in unsaturated fat, the molecules of which are readily oxidized (*See* Chapter 15). The germ is removed from many of the cereal products on the market to prevent them from becoming rancid. Cells making up the germ also contain protein, iron, niacin, thiamine, and riboflavin.

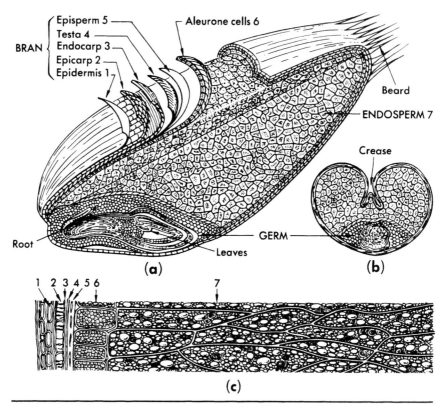

Figure 10-1. (a) Diagram of a grain of wheat enlarged approximately 17 times, with a wedge equal to approximately ¼ of the grain cut away. Layers 1 to 5 constitute the bran, separated from the endosperm by a layer of aleurone cells. (b) A cross section through the lower end of the kernel, the crease somewhat spread apart. (c) A section near the periphery of the grain enlarged approximately 238 times to show starch grains embedded in a protein matrix in the cells of the endosperm. Compare with Figure 9-2. (From J. Storck and W. D. Teague. *Flour for Man's Bread: A History of Milling.* University of Minnesota Press, Minneapolis. Copyright © 1952 by the University of Minnesota.)

The *endosperm* is the major portion of a cereal grain. It is made up of starch-storing parenchyma cells. These cells are packed full of starch granules, which are embedded in a matrix of protein. The walls of the cells of the endosperm are quite thin so there is less cellulose in this part of the grain. The two nutrients of any quantity in the endosperm of cereals are starch and protein. Cells in different parts of the endosperm vary somewhat in composition. However, differences among these cells are not so pronounced as between cells of different parts of the grain. Figure 10-2 shows a photomicrograph of cells of endosperm, aleurone layer, and inner layer of bran.

COMPOSITION AND NUTRITIVE VALUE OF CEREALS

Table 10-1 gives the energy value and the composition of representative cereal grains. Cereals are inexpensive sources of energy, furnishing from 1600 to 1700 calories per pound. Cereals

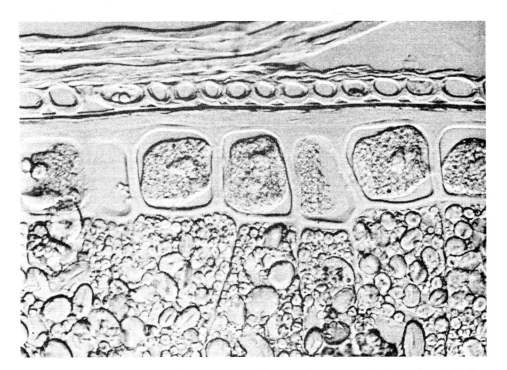

Figure 10-2. Photomicrograph of the outer layers of a grain of wheat. Note the layer of starch-filled endosperm cells. Original magnification × 1,000. (Photograph by R. I. Derby, General Mills, Inc.)

as a group are approximately 75 percent carbohydrates, 10 percent protein, 1 to 2 percent fat, 10 percent moisture, and 1 to 2 percent minerals. Starch accounts for the bulk of the carbohydrates in grains, but insoluble cellulose and soluble dietary fiber are present, too.

Grains are a fair source of protein of a quality somewhat lower (13) than that found in animal foods such as meat, milk, and eggs. Cereals as a group are deficient in lysine, and low in tryptophan and methionine. The level of these essential amino acids can be increased in cereals by the introduction of certain mutant genes. High lysine corn was developed some years ago. Two genes, opaque-2 and floury-2, enable the corn plant to synthesize more lysine and also more tryptophan (3) than the typical hybrid corn. Genes are available for improving the quality of the proteins in rice, barley, and wheat, too (21). Unfortunately, this genetic engineering that results in a higher lysine content also may result in lower total protein and lower yield. Functional properties of the cereal in food preparation are altered, too. The liming of corn in the preparation of such foods as tortillas paradoxically decreases a number of nutrients in the corn, at the same time improving its overall nutritive value by producing a better balance of amino acids (11). Triticale, the rye-wheat hybrid, is higher in lysine and in protein than wheat but the yield per acre is lower (17). Whole grains are good sources of iron, thiamin, and niacin and fair sources of riboflavin.

The high fiber content of cereals, especially whole grains, in addition to the other components, underlies the recommendation that the diet be based upon cereals. Promoting the rapid passage of toxic waste products has been added to the roles of insoluble cellulose in

TABLE 10-1
Composition and Energy Value of Selected Cereals (100-gram edible portion)

Cereal	Water (%)	Calories[a]	Protein (g)	Carbo-hydrates (g)	Fat (g)	Calcium (mg)	Phospho-rus (mg)	Iron (mg)	Vitamin A Value (I.U.)	Thiamin (mg)	Ribo-flavin (mg)	Niacin (mg)	Ascorbic Acid (mg)	Fiber Crude (g)	Fiber Total Dietary (g)
Amaranth	9.8	374	14.5	66.2	6.5	153	455	7.6	—	.08	.21	1.29	4.2	3.8	15.2
Barley, pearled	10.1	352	9.9	77.7	1.2	29	221	2.5	22	.19	.11	4.60	0	.7	15.6
Corn meal, de-germed[b] yellow	11.6	366	8.5	77.7	1.6	5	84	4.1	413	.72	.41	5.03	0	.6	5.2
Farina[b]	10.5	369	10.6	78.0	.5	14	88	3.7	—	.57	.36	4.05	—	.2	2.7
Macaroni[b]	10.3	371	12.8	74.7	1.6	18	150	3.9	—	1.03	.44	7.51	0	.3	3.9
Oats, rolled	8.8	384	16.0	67.0	6.3	52	474	4.2	—	.73	.14	.78	—	1.1	10.3
Quinoa	9.3	374	13.1	68.9	5.8	60	410	9.3	—	.20	.40	2.93	0	—	—
Rice															
Brown	10.4	370	7.9	77.2	2.9	23	333	1.5	—	.40	.09	5.09	0	1.3	3.5
White[b]	11.6	365	7.1	79.9	.7	28	115	4.3	—	.58	.05	4.19	0	.3	1.0
Flour															
All-purpose[b]	11.5	364	10.3	76.3	1.0	15	108	4.6	—	.79	.05	5.90	0	.3	2.7
Triticale	10.5	336	13.1	72.1	2.1	37	358	2.6	—	.42	.12	1.43	0	2.6	14.6
Whole wheat	10.3	339	13.7	72.6	1.9	34	346	3.9	—	.45	.22	6.37	0	2.1	12.6

[a] 1 kilocalorie = 4.185 kilojoules.
[b] Enriched
— = Data not available
Source: U.S. Dept. Agr. Handbook No. 8-20, Composition of Foods. Cereal Grains and Pasta. Raw, Processed, Prepared. Revised 1989.

the normal functioning of the large intestine. Equally important in justifying the greater utilization of cereals is the presence of soluble fiber. Included are hemicelluloses, mainly xylans that are polymers of the sugar xylose, and especially the β-glucans (4). The latter are polymers of β-D-glucose as in cellulose, but the 1,4 linkage is interrupted occasionally with a 1,3 linkage. This accounts for the solubility of the β-glucans (4) in contrast to the insolubility of cellulose. These dietary fibers, as they are called, are considered to have a role in lowering the lipid and cholesterol levels in the blood.

ENRICHMENT AND FORTIFICATION

The nutritive value of cereals can be improved by enrichment or by fortification. Cereals are enriched by replenishing certain nutrients removed in processing. Inclusion of thiamin, riboflavin, niacin, iron, and as of 1998, folic acid is mandatory if a cereal is labeled enriched. The use of calcium and vitamin D is optional. White flour, grits, farina, pasta, white rice, cornmeal, and white bread are routinely enriched. The objective of fortification is to use cereals as carriers of nutrients identified as likely to be deficient in the diet. The recommended level for fortification is approximately 25 percent of the Recommended Dietary Allowance (RDA), renamed Reference Daily Intake (RDI). Nutrients identified as appropriate to use in fortification include thiamin, niacin, riboflavin, vitamin B_6, folic acid (folacin), vitamin A, vitamin D, calcium, iron, magnesium, and zinc. Ready-to-eat cereals are considered appropriate vehicles for fortification. Ready-to-eat cereals are available fortified with different combinations of the nutrients above.

MARKET FORMS OF CEREALS

The intact grain of a cereal can be consumed, but this is not the usual practice. One disadvantage is the long cooking time required. Equally important, cereals with the germ left in may become rancid. Many individuals consider cereals more palatable without the outer, branny layer. For these reasons and for the sake of variety, grains are milled or otherwise processed before they are marketed. There are two general approaches to milling. The grain may be separated into its structural components, bran, germ, and endosperm. The other approach is to subdivide either the entire grain or its endosperm into particles of increasingly reduced size. Products made from the endosperm are referred to as refined cereals. Although some grains are marketed raw and so require cooking, heat is involved at some stage in the processing of the array of ready-to-eat products on the market.

CEREAL PRODUCTS THAT REQUIRE COOKING (6)

Rice

Three forms of uncooked rice are available. (5). The intact grain is known as brown rice. White or polished rice has had the bran removed. Converted or parboiled rice has been soaked and then steamed to drive nutrients from the bran into the endosperm, after which the grain is dried and the bran removed. The conversion process gives the grains a golden color and makes them translucent. Rice is marketed according to the length of the grain. Long-grain rice accounts for almost ¾ of the total, medium grain ¼ or less, and short grain rice constitutes no more than five percent. A number of specialty rices—some imported—are available, including glutinous rice, which is almost 100 percent amylopectin.

Wheat

Cracked wheat is made by subdividing the entire grain. Farina consists of middlings, the endosperm that is most resistant to cracking when wheat is milled to produce flour (Fig. 11-2). Bulgur is made from whole wheat. The grain is cooked, then dried and fractured. The product is not raw but time is required for it to rehydrate in hot water.

Corn

The hull of the corn kernel is removed by abrasion, as for polished rice, or it is loosened by soaking in water that contains lye. The hull and residual lye are rinsed away from the endosperm if the grain is soaked. Hominy consists of the whole endosperm; grits are broken pieces of it. Cornmeal is the finely ground pieces of either white or yellow corn.

Oats

The kernels of oats, called groats, are steel-cut to form a granular cereal similar to cracked wheat. Alternately, they are used to produce rolled oats. The groats are steamed to soften them before they pass between rollers that flatten them. Two types of rolled oats are available—regular and quick cooking. The entire grain is used for the former; the groat is subdivided to give quick cooking oats. Oat bran is rich in β-glucans (4).

Barley

This grain with the bran removed is marketed as pearl barley. It is used as a thickener in soups and as an ingredient in fabricated cereal products. Barley is a good source of β-glucans.

READY-TO-EAT CEREALS (6,7)

Flaked

For cornflakes, the endosperm of corn is divided in half and these grits are cooked under pressure with sugar, salt, malt, and water until the particles are translucent. Part of the water is removed before the grits are passed between rollers to flatten them. Toasting the flakes at high temperature produces blisters from the steam generated and reduces the moisture to below three percent so the flakes are shelf-stable.

Wheat flakes are made from intact grains. They are steamed and then slightly cracked to facilitate uptake of water, after which the grains are thoroughly cooked under pressure. Part of the moisture is removed before the grains are passed between rollers to flatten them. The flakes are dried to a low moisture level as are cornflakes.

Granular

Grape Nuts® are made from wheat and barley flours, salt, yeast, and enough water to form a stiff dough. The dough is allowed to ferment for a few hours after which it is shaped into loaves and baked. This compact loaf is then broken to yield the granules of Grape Nuts®.

Shredded

Shredded wheat is made from intact grains. They are boiled for an hour, after which the cooked grains are fed to pairs of grooved shredding rollers. A bank of pairs of rollers deposits parallel rows of these shreds, layer on top of layer. The layers are divided into biscuits. Baking begins at a high temperature to brown the surface and continues at a lower temperature to reduce the moisture to the desired level.

Puffed

Water vapor is used to puff cereals. In one procedure, the grains that are cooked until they are translucent are heated to a high temperature within a few seconds. Generation of steam enlarges the grains from two to five times. Alternately, a dough made from flour, middlings, or grits is cooked by steaming, after which the dough is shaped into pieces by forcing it through the die of an extruder. The pieces are sealed in a popping vessel or gun and heated to a high temperature and pressure. Release of the pressure inflates the pieces as much as 15 to 20 times. Milled rice and pearled wheat may be cooked and pressure puffed, too.

Extruded

For extruded cereal products, the dough is cooked under pressure and then forced to exit through the die at the end of the attached extruder barrel. The drop in pressure causes the product to expand.

Instant

Instant cereals are precooked and dried before they are marketed. They require no cooking. Addition of hot water converts an instant product into a hot cereal ready for serving. Farina, rice, and rolled oats are available as instant cereals.

When cereals are subjected to high temperature, as in pressure cooking, puffing, and toasting, the heat may destroy some thiamin and lower the nutritive value of the protein. Some of the starch may become indigestible, too (16).

COOKING CEREALS

Purposes

Cereals are cooked to increase their digestibility and their palatability. Chewing uncooked cereal is wearing on the molars. Cooking softens the cellulose, but mainly cooking increases the palatability of cereals by its effect on the major component, starch. From two to six volumes of water are required to cook one volume of cereal because of the uptake of water by the gelatinizing and pasting starch.

Precautions

One of the goals in cooking cereals, as with using starch itself in cooking, is to avoid lumps. When the dry cereal is added to boiling water, it should be stirred only enough to prevent the formation of lumps. Excessive agitation, either stirring or allowing the water to boil vigorously, results in an inferior product.

When grain is milled, the cells are fractured and some of the embedded starch granules are exposed on the surfaces of the individual particles. If the cereal is agitated during cooking, many of these starch granules are dislodged. These thicken the liquid around the individual particles of cereal. This gives a cooked cereal with individual pieces embedded in a thick starch paste, a consistency that many find unpalatable. Cooked cereal has a better consistency if the starch granules remain in place on the surface of the pieces of cereal. Flaked cereals are particularly susceptible to disintegration by agitation during cooking because flakes are inherently more fragile than granules. The β-glucans in rolled oats readily dissolve in the cooking water and form a viscous film around the cooked flakes. This is minimized when the cooking is started in boiling water (23) or when microwaves are used to cook the oats (22).

Proportions of Liquids

Proportion of water to cereal depends in part upon the size of the particles and their ability to absorb water. Fine granular cereals require five to six times their volume of water, coarse cracked cereals four times, and flaked cereals two times. The amount of water needed to cook a cereal is an indication of the approximate amount it will swell. However, rice increases more than twice in volume, even when it is steamed in only twice its volume of water. When this low proportion of water is used, the rice grains absorb all of it and the swell is limited. A pan with a tight-fitting lid and low heat should be used. If rice is cooked with a higher proportion of water, the increase in volume will be greater. The product will be more moist, also. Long-grain rice tends to swell more than short-grain rice; converted rice swells less than the same type polished. Brown rice swells somewhat less than polished. When cooked in milk, cereals swell more than when cooked in water. (Possibly phosphates from the milk are involved.)

Amount of Salt

The use of salt for flavor is optional. Approximately one teaspoon (5 milliliters) of salt per cup (250 milliliters) of dry cereal will season all except fine cereals, for which somewhat more salt, 1½ teaspoons (7 milliliters) per cup is suggested.

Cooking Time

A number of factors influence how long a cereal needs to be cooked. Size of the fragments (how much the grain is subdivided) and prior heat treatment are two such factors. Once water returns to a boil, cooking time varies from a minimum of 5 to 10 minutes on direct heat to 10 to 15 minutes over boiling water. When cooking is completed over boiling water, additional cooking does no harm.

The cooking time of rice depends upon the variety. Some need to be cooked only 15 minutes, but others may require up to 30. Quick-cooking rolled oats cook in less time than do regular rolled oats because the pieces are smaller. Directions on the package specify a cooking time of five minutes over direct heat for regular rolled oats and one minute for quick-cooking rolled oats. A number of quick-cooking cereal products, including rice, farina, and pasta, have had disodium phosphate, Na_2HPO_4, added to them. This phosphate salt speeds the cooking by enabling starch granules to reach gelatinization temperature sooner.

Effect of Alkaline Cooking Water

Polished rice or refined cereal may be cream colored or yellow tinted when cooked in alkaline water because of the presence of flavonoid compounds. A small amount of acid (vinegar, lemon juice, or cream of tartar) added to the cooking water, preferably late in the cooking period, will keep the pigments in colorless form.

Characteristics of Cooked Cereal

Pieces of cooked flaked cereal should be separate and distinct. They should be moist but not sticky. Cooked granular cereal should be free from lumps. It should not be so thin that it pours readily, but it should flow enough to assume the shape of the dish in which it is served. The cereal should not have a pasty consistency. The flavor of all cooked cereal should be mild and nutlike.

On the basis of cooked quality, rice falls into two categories. Most varieties of long-grain rice are slender and translucent and yield fluffy, dry grains that remain separate. Most medium- or short-grain varieties are soft and chalky and when cooked are moist and sticky and tend to adhere. A number of factors that might account for differences in the cooking quality of rice have been investigated. These include the amount of moisture the rice absorbs as it cooks, the amylose content of the starch, and its gelatinization temperature, and the anatomy of the kernel, particularly the amount and distribution of components that could limit the swelling of the starch. All of these factors point directly or indirectly to the starch component. The quality of cooked rice appears to stem more from characteristics inherent in the rice than from the cooking method used.

Leftover cooked cereal need not be wasted. It can be used to make polenta or tamale pie, as topping for meat pies, or as a lining for a casserole made from leftover stew or creamed meat—all ways to include more cereal in the diet.

POPCORN

The consumption of popcorn, one of the first snack foods, increased 72 percent over a 10 year period (10). Popularity of the microwaved product doubtless contributed to the increase (12). Successful popping begins with the grain. Corn kernels that can pop have a vitreous (glassy) rather than a chalky endosperm (8). Absence of voids around the tightly packed, angular-shaped, starch granules is essential. The pericarp (hull) must be able to withstand the pressure that builds as the water inside the grain is vaporized.

The kernels of popcorn are inflated by steam produced from moisture within the endosperm. Corn pops satisfactorily only when the moisture content is within a narrow range (10–14%), depending on the variety. A moisture content near the upper end of the range favors high volume; that near the lower end means fewer unpopped kernels (12). Quality popcorn has had the moisture content adjusted before it is put on the market, and it is sold in a moisture-vapor-proof package. Once a package is opened, popcorn should be stored in a sealed container.

The temperature to which the popper is preheated is another factor that influences the yield from popcorn (9). Optimum temperature varies somewhat with the size of the popper, its ability to hold heat, and the amount of corn popped at one time. If the popper is too hot, the corn scorches, and if not hot enough, the corn dries before it pops. Temperature inside the popper when the corn is popping should range from 173° to 198°C (343° to 388°F). The popper, itself, needs to be at a higher temperature (243° to 299°C or 470° to 570°F). A practical guide is to adjust the heat so that the corn begins to pop in one to three minutes after it goes into the popper. If, once popping begins, all the grains pop within two minutes, the yield of popped corn will be maximum. Properly engineered electric corn poppers eliminate the guesswork from attempts to maintain optimum temperature.

When the contents of the kernel reach a sufficiently high temperature (near 177°C), the accompanying high pressure ruptures the pericarp, exposing the interior of the grain to atmospheric pressure. Apparently, the superheated water in the starch granules vaporizes in the hilum (8). This has the effect of pushing the cooked starch to the periphery of the starch granule and at the same time inflating the grain. The volume of the corn may increase 20 to 30 times when it is popped. Films of gelatinized starch provide the structural framework of the porous popped kernels (15).

Thirty-six compounds have been identified in the volatiles from popped corn (20). Those considered important contributors to the aroma were pyrazines, furans, pyrroles, carbonyls, and substituted phenols. The odor of corn popped in a microwave oven does not differ materially from that popped conventionally in oil, but it does differ in tactile character.

REFERENCES

1. Akeson, W. R. and M. A. Stakmann. 1966. "Leaf protein concentrates: A comparison of protein production per acre of forage with that from seed and animal crops." *Economic Botany* 20:244–50. Alternate uses of natural resources for food production.

2. Caldwell, E. F., and R. B. Fast. 1990. "The cereal grains." In *Breakfast Cereals and How They Are Made*. R. B. Fast and E. F. Caldwell, eds. St. Paul: American Association of Cereal Chemists. Pp. 1–14. Corn, wheat, rice, oats, and barley included.

3. Christianson, D. D., U. Khoo, H. C. Nielsen, and J. S. Wall. 1974. "Influence of opaque-2 and floury-2 genes on formation of proteins in particulates of corn endosperm." *Plant Physiology* 53:851–55. High-lysine mutants.

4. Doublier, J. -L. 1990. "Rheological properties of cereal carbohydrates." In *Dough Rheology and Baked Products Texture*, H. Faradi and J. M. Faubion, eds. New York: Van Nostrand Reinhold. Pp. 111–55. Beta-glucans in oats and barley.

5. Dziezak, J. 1991. "Romancing the kernel: A salute to rice varieties." *Food Technology* 45(6):74–75, 78, 80. Forms of rice available, including specialty rice.

6. Fast, R. B. 1990. "Manufacturing technology of ready-to-eat cereals." In *Breakfast Cereals and How They Are Made*. R. B. Fast and E. F. Caldwell, eds. St. Paul: American Association of Cereal Chemists. Pp. 15–42. Flaked, puffed, granular, shredded, and extruded products.

7. Hoseney, R. C. 1986. "Breakfast cereals." In *Principles of Cereal Science and Technology*. St. Paul: American Association of Cereal Chemists. Pp. 293–304. Details of their manufacture.

8. Hoseney, R. C., K. Zeleznak and A. Abdelrahman. 1983. "Mechanism of popcorn popping." *Journal of Cereal Science* 1:43–52. Character of the kernel that favors popping.

9. Huelsen, W. A. and W. P. Bemis. 1954. "Temperature of the popper in relation to volumetric expansion of popcorn." *Food Technology* 8:394–97. Yields of popcorn at different temperatures.

10. Johnson, L. 1991. "Corn: Production, processing and utilization." In *Handbook of Cereal Science and Technology*. K. J. Lorenz and K. Kulp, eds. New York: Marcel Dekker. P. 65. Popcorn.

11. Katz, S. H., M. L. Hediger and L. A. Valleroy. 1974. "Traditional maize processing tech-

niques in the new world." *Science* 184:765–73. Effects of liming on nutritive value.

12. Lin, Y. E. and R. C. Anantheswaran. "1988. Studies on popping of popcorn in a microwave oven." *Journal of Food Science* 53:1746–49. Moisture content, volume, and unpopped grains.

13. Mertz, E. T. and L. S. Bates. 1964. "Mutant gene that changes protein composition and increases lysine content of maize." *Science* 145:279–80. Improvement in the nutritive value of corn.

14. Pimentel, D. W., J. K. Dritschilo, J. Krummel and J. Kutzman. 1975. "Energy and land constraints in food protein production." *Science* 190:754–61. Options for meeting the world's food needs.

15. Reeve, R. M. and H. G. Walker. 1969. "The microscopic structure of popped cereals." *Cereal Chemistry* 46:227–41. Structural changes when popped.

16. Ring, S. G., J. M. Gee, M. Whittam, P. Orford and I. T. Johnson. 1988. "Resistant starch: Its chemical form in foodstuffs and effects on digestibility in vitro." *Food Chemistry* 28:97–109.

17. Ruckman, J. E., F. P. Scheile and C. O. Qualset. 1973. "Protein, lysine, and grain yield of triticale and wheat as influenced by genotype and location." *Journal of Agricultural and Food Chemistry* 21:697–700. Improved nutritive value of the hybrid.

18. *U.S. Bureau of the Census, Statistical Abstracts of the United States, 1996, 116th edition.* Washington, D.C. 1996. P. 147. Per-capita consumption of major food commodities: 1970–1991.

19. United States Department of Agriculture, Economic Research Service. *National Food Situation.* NFS-115, February 1966. Per-capita consumption of major foods in different countries.

20. Walradt, J. P., R. C. Landsay and L. M. Libbey. 1970. "Popcorn flavor: Identification of volatile compounds." *Journal of Agricultural and Food Chemistry* 18:926–28. Popped conventionally in oil and dry by microwaves; aroma and tactile quality.

21. Woodbury, W. 1972. "Biochemical genetics and its potential for cereal improvement." *Bakers Digest* 46(5):20–24, 27, 63. Protein quality; photosynthetic efficiency.

22. Yiu, S. H., J. Weisz and P. J. Wood. 1991. "Comparison of the effects of microwave and conventional cooking on starch and β-glucan in rolled oats." *Cereal Chemistry* 68:372–75. More β-glucan released by conventional method.

23. Yiu, S. H., P. J. Wood and J. Weisz. 1987. "Effect of cooking on starch and β-glucan of rolled oats." *Cereal Chemistry* 64:373–79. Cold-*vs.* hot-water start.

Flour and Dough Formation

11

Wheat is the primary grain used to make flour, although a limited amount of flour is made from rye. The proteins of wheat flour are superior for making bread, but nutritionally they are incomplete. The limiting amino acid is lysine. The wheat-rye hybrid, triticale, yields a grain with a lysine content higher than that of the parent wheat. Information is available on the performance of triticale flour in bread making (24, 38) and also on the feasibility of using oil seed flours to supplement the proteins of wheat flour. Early work emphasized the use of soybean flour because of its high lysine as well as high protein content. Later, attention focused on other flours including cottonseed, cowpea, field pea, peanut, safflower, sesame, and sunflower (28, 32). Most will yield acceptable baked products if the amount of wheat flour replaced is limited, if the formula is modified, and in some cases if the manipulation is altered (37). Bread made with wheat flour is the standard against which breads made with nonwheat flours are measured.

Wheat flours differ from uncooked wheat cereal products such as cracked wheat and farina in that for flour the grain is more extensively subdivided or milled. Many more cells of the grain are fractured with their contents exposed. Too, wheat flours differ in functional properties due to the cultivar or blend of cultivars used when they are milled. Success in baking depends in part upon using the type of flour best for the product, so some consideration of how and why flours differ is pertinent.

TYPES OF FLOUR

Kind of Wheat

Flours are classed according to the type of wheat (26) from which they are milled. There are three common species of wheat grown in the United States. Two, the common (*Triticum aestivum*) and club (*Triticum compactum*) wheats, are used to make flour. The third, durum wheat, is used to make macaroni products. Wheats grown for flour can be classed according to color of the surface of the kernel (white or red), season when planted (winter or spring), and whether they are hard or soft. Red wheat varieties, some soft and others hard, predominate. Soft red wheat is planted in the fall and so is referred to as winter wheat. Hard red wheat is planted in either spring or fall, depending on the growing conditions in the area. The endosperm of hard wheat shows greater resistance to cracking during the milling process. The difference between soft and hard wheat had been attributed solely to the higher ratio of protein to starch in the latter. Recent evidence indicates, however, that the hardness of hard wheat comes from greater continuity of the protein matrix within the cells and the tighter bonding of starch granules to this matrix (20, 35). These differences are shown in the scanning electron micrographs (Fig. 11-1) of particles of flour milled from the two types of wheat. The protein matrix in the soft wheat lacks continuity and the structure appears more open. Many starch granules are exposed and some dislodged. Starch granules in hard wheat flour appear firmly embedded in a continuous protein matrix so that fracture of endosperm cells is more likely to crack starch granules. Soft wheat flour feels soft and powdery; hard wheat flour feels gritty.

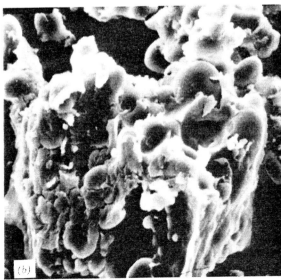

Figure 11-1. Scanning electron micrograph of (a) soft winter wheat flour and (b) hard red winter wheat flour. Magnified × 800. (From R. C. Hoseney and P. A. Seib. *Bakers Digest* 47(6):28. Reprinted with permission from the December 1973 issue of *Bakers Digest*. Chicago, IL.)

Effects of Milling

Flours differ not only in the kind of wheat from which they are made, but also in the way they are milled (40). The chart in Figure 11-2 shows in sequence the main steps in the conversion of wheat to flour. Whole wheat flours are made from the entire kernel. White flours come from the endosperm. White flour accounts for 97 percent of the total flour consumed. When the endosperm of wheat is reduced by milling to pieces of a size to qualify as flour, usually a maximum of 72 percent of the grain is utilized. The other 28 percent constitutes shorts that includes bran and germ, much of which is used as food for animals. A 72 percent–extraction flour is known as straight flour. However, millers do not put the last and more crush-resistant pieces of endosperm into high-quality flour. Those flours that are made of less than the entire endosperm are known as patent flours. The remainder of the endosperm yields lower-grade clear flours. The part of the endosperm from which clear flours come is also used to make breakfast cereals.

Long patent flours contain a high proportion of the endosperm. Short patent flours contain relatively less, with a higher proportion of the endosperm left as clear flour. The diagram in Figure 11-3 shows the percentage of the wheat kernel found in the different fractions of flour. That portion of the endosperm that most resists cracking is higher in protein and lower in starch. Thus longer patent flours have a higher percentage of protein than shorter patent flours made from the same type of wheat.

Air classification can be used to separate a flour into fractions with different ratios of protein to starch. A controlled flow of air is used to separate the particles of flour according to size and weight. Because heavier pieces are higher in protein, this technique provides flours from the same wheat differing widely in protein content (39). Before this innovation, the protein content of the flour had to be controlled by the kind of wheat used and to a lesser extent by the proportion of endosperm crushed to make the flour. By means of air classification, flours that vary in protein content over a range of 5 to 20 percent can be obtained from the same wheat. White flour averages 65 to 70 percent starch and 8 to 13 percent protein. Moisture content averages 12 percent. It can vary with the relative humidity of the air to which the flour is exposed. Flour contains approximately two percent pentosans and one to two percent lipids.

Particle Size

Pieces of endosperm in patent flour must be small enough for 98 percent to pass through a sieve with a mesh of 210 micrometers. (Fig. 11-4.) This is specified in the standard of identity for white wheat flour as promulgated by the Food and Drug Administration. But the range in size of particles is great. The heterogeneous character of conventional flour is shown in Figure 11-5a. Such flour packs and does not pour readily. In addition, its wettability is poor. Individual particles are too small to overcome the surface tension of water. The mass tends to float when combined with water, buoyed up by air trapped in the spaces between the finer particles. Uneven access of individual particles of flour to water results in lumps. To eliminate these disadvantages of conventionally milled flour, instantized flour (also called instant-blending or quick-mixing flour) was developed (29). Instantized flour is made from conventional all-purpose flour by bringing the particles into contact with moisture so that they adhere to each other. The clumps of flour are then dried. Particles of instantized flour must pass through a sieve with a mesh of 840 micrometers. Only 20 percent of the flour particles can be small enough to pass a mesh of 74 micrometers. Particles of instantized flours are not only larger than ordinary flour, but they are

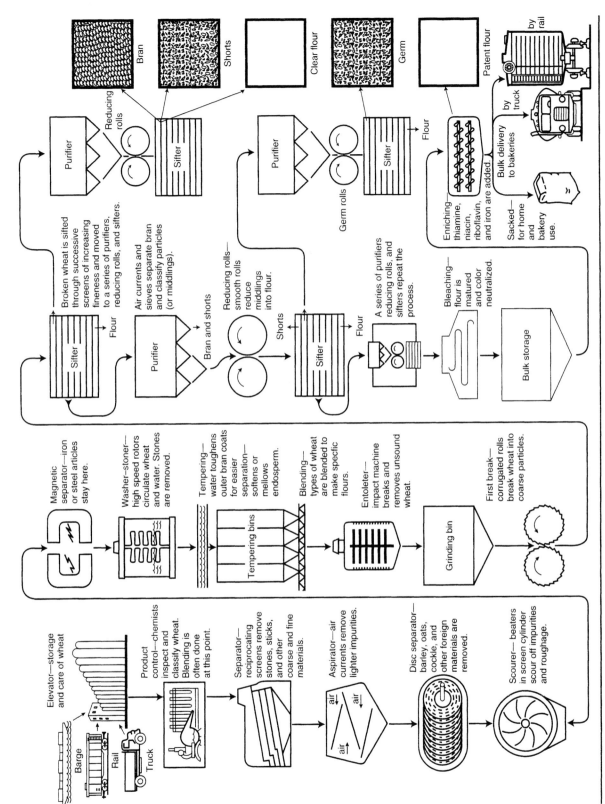

Figure 11-2. The milling of flour: Sequence of operations, greatly simplified. (Taken from *From Wheat to Flour.* Courtesy of Millers' National Federation.)

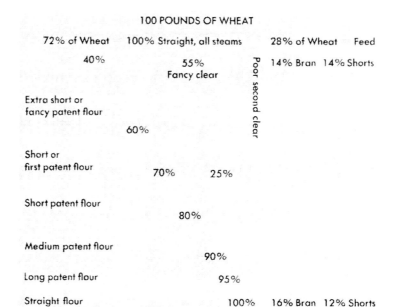

Figure 11-3. Milling of flour: yields of milled fractions from 100 pounds of wheat. (From C. O. Swanson. *Wheat Flour Quality.* Copyright © 1938, Burgess Publishing Company, Minneapolis, MN.)

more uniform in size, as the illustrations in Figure 11-5b show. Instantized flour does not pack, pours easily, and blends readily with cold liquid. Flour in this form is useful for thickening gravies and other liquids. Instantized flour absorbs moisture more slowly than conventional flour and can tolerate more mixing without making the product tough (27).

Classed by Use

A third classification of flours is according to use, as bread, all-purpose, pastry, cookie, and cake flour. Milled in the conventional way, bread flour is a long extraction of hard wheats. Cake flour, at the other end of the scale, is a short patent of soft wheats. Although the particles for all conventionally milled flours must fall within a certain size range, some flours are finer than others. Bread flour is coarse and gritty compared with cake flour, which is fine and powdery, with a greater tendency to pack. To obtain particles as small as those of cake flour, extensive crushing of the endosperm is required so the pieces of flour pass a very fine sieve. All-purpose flour is, as the latter term implies, an intermediate type, not as coarse as bread flour or as fine as cake flour. In a cup of all-purpose flour there are an estimated one hundred billion (10^{11}) pieces of endosperm. Pastry flour is not quite as short a patent as cake flour, but it resembles cake flour more than it does all-purpose flour in composition and in baking properties. Cookie flour is a long patent of a soft wheat.

Bread flour is eminently suited to making yeast breads. All-purpose flour makes biscuits, muffins, waffles, gingerbread, coffee cake, and even yeast bread of high quality. Recipes for muffins, biscuits, and pastry especially adapted for soft wheat flour have

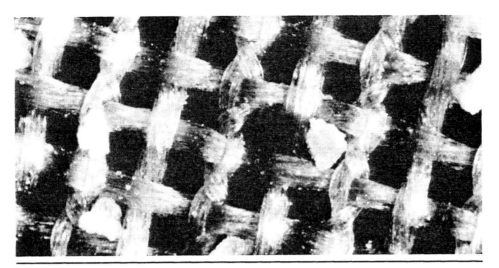

Figure 11-4. Photomicrograph of 16 ×× mesh silk bolting cloth with particles of flour adhering. Original magnification × 160. (Photograph by R. I. Derby, General Mills, Inc. From *Cereal Science Today.* October 1957. Reprinted by permission.)

been developed. Large quantities of soft wheat flour are used by the packaged mix industry.

As a consequence of differences in composition, flours vary in density. A cup of bread flour weighs more than a cup of all purpose flour, which in turn weighs more than a cup of cake flour. (See Chapter 3 or the A.H.E.A. *Handbook of Food Preparation* for the weights per cup of different flours.) Actually, a cupful of two brands of all-purpose flour may not weigh exactly the same. The weight of a cup of all-purpose flour of the same brand may differ slightly from year to year from variations in supply of wheat available to the miller. For substituting one flour for another, weight rather than measure is a better basis.

Durum wheat is harder than the hardest of hard wheats. When the endosperm of this type of wheat is milled, the product is called semolina. A dough of semolina and water is used to make all high-quality pasta products (macaroni, spaghetti, noodles). Pasta can be made from hard wheat bread flour, but the quality of the product is poor. Noodles differ from other pasta in that egg is added to the mix.

FORMATION OF DOUGH

When particles of flour are wetted and then manipulated, a viscoelastic dough forms, for which the protein complex, gluten, is essential. Wheat flour is unique in its ability to form such a dough (19). Evidence has been presented that wheat gluten is an amorphous polymer that exists in the glassy state at room temperature when the level of moisture is as low as that which prevails in flour (21). The high proportion of liquid to flour used to make dough is far in excess of that required to lower the glass transition temperature so that gluten becomes rubberlike. In the rubbery state, gluten can be manipulated to form dough. Much research effort has been expended to understand this dough-forming mechanism, as numerous papers on the subject attest (4–6, 10–12, 19, 22, 25, 33).

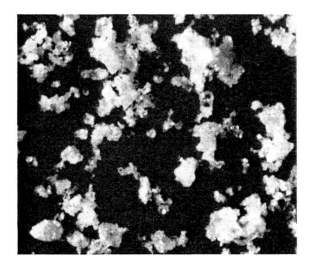

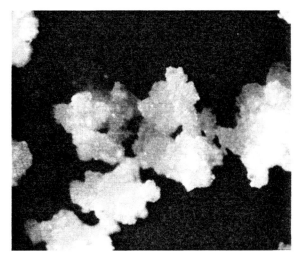

Figure 11-5. Photomicrographs of (*top*) conventional flour, showing unevenness of size of particles, and (*bottom*) instantized (agglomerated) flour, with particles of uniform size. (Photographs by R. I. Derby, General Mills, Inc.)

Components of Flour

Proteins

The assortment of amino acids that makes up the proteins of gluten is unique (9, 23). (The chemistry of proteins is discussed in Chapter 18.) A single amino acid, glutamic, makes up more than 40 percent of the total. Most of this amino acid is present, not with its second carboxyl group free, but as an amide, and as such it is available for hydrogen bonding with the oxygens of hydroxyl, carboxyl, and carbonyl groups of proteins and other molecules. Next in quantity is the amino acid proline, which makes up approximately 14 percent of the total amino acids in gluten. The presence of proline puts constraints on the shape that a polypeptide can assume. Other amino acids that affect the dough-forming potential of flour proteins are glycine, which contributes flexibility, and leucine, which is important for hydrophobic interactions. Approximately two percent of the amino acids contain sulfur either as a disulfide in cystine or a sulfhydryl group in cysteine. The low percentage of basic amino acids and the even lower content of acidic ones result in a low net charge on most of the molecules in the gluten complex.

Wheat flour contains small amounts of two classes of metabolic proteins, water-soluble albumins, and dilute salt-soluble globulins (10). The main portion of protein (85 to 90%), the part essential for the formation of dough, consists of reserve protein stored in protein bodies in the endosperm of the wheat grain (33). This reserve protein makes up the gluten complex, which can be separated into two fractions, gliadin and glutenin. Molecules of the gliadin fraction are single polypeptides. Gliadins are soluble in aqueous ethanol so they are classed as prolamins. The alcohol-insoluble residue contains the high molecular weight glutenins, which vary in the number of polypeptide subunits. Both the gliadin and the glutenin fractions can be further subdivided (10), the gliadins into four subgroups and the glutenins into a low molecular weight (LMW) component and a high molecular weight (HMW) one. Glutenins have an odd number of sulfhydryl groups, so reactive sulfhydryl groups are available for both intra- and intermolecular disulfide formation and for sulfhydryl ⇌ disulfide interchange believed essential for the dough-forming mechanism (25). Differences in the dough-forming and bread-making potential of different flours resides in the HMW glutenin.

A new system of nomenclature for the components of gluten has been introduced (34, 36), though not without controversy (11). When the complex molecules of glutenin are partially depolymerized, they become soluble in aqueous ethanol, as are the gliadins, hence the proposal to call all the proteins of gluten prolamins. According to this system, low-sulfur gliadins are prolamins; the other three gliadins and the LMW glutenins are sulfur-containing prolamins; and the HMW glutenins are high molecular weight prolamins.

The gliadins appear to have a compact, globular shape, attributed to the presence of numerous beta turns in the polypeptide. How polypeptide subunits of glutenins, especially the HMW component, are associated is still unsettled. Both linear and branched models have been proposed, with either secondary or covalent (disulfide) linkages between subunits. One model that shows how the subgroups might be arranged is shown in Figure 11-6 (22). Glutenin II of the scheme (HMW glutenin) is made of polypeptide subunits, each held in compact shape by intramolecular disulfide bonds. These subunits are linked, in turn, in more or less linear fashion by interpolypeptide disulfide bonds (13). Low molecular weight glutenins (glutenin I of the scheme) are believed to be united to each other and to glutenin II polypeptides by secondary bonds (hydrogen and Van der Waals linkages). In this scheme, glutenin II would contribute elasticity, and the mobile linkages of glutenin I would contribute the viscous element to gluten. A branched model has been proposed, based on fragments of polypeptides obtained when glutenin subunits are partially depolymerized (16). A linear model is shown in Figure 11-7 (33). The central portion of the polypeptide subunit is shown as a beta spiral (made of repeated hairpin or beta turns). Alpha helices are shown near either end of the polypeptide subunit and the polypeptides are linked head to tail by disulfide bonds between terminal cysteine residues. The fibrous character of glutenin is shown in the scanning electron micrograph of Figure 11-8.

Lipids

Lipids account for only a fraction of the weight of flour, but they are essential for the formation of dough and breadmaking (6). (Lipids are discussed in Chapter 15.) Most of the

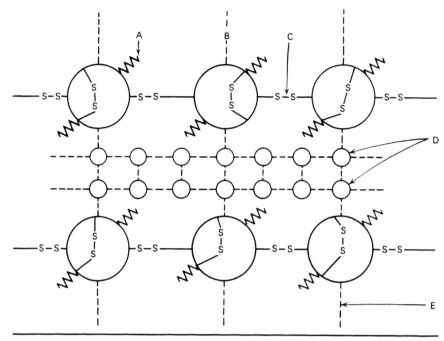

Figure 11-6. Model of glutenin: a scheme to account for its functional properties. (*a*) Glutenin II subunit with (*b*) intrapolypeptide disulfide bond and (*c*) interpolypeptide disulfide bond, (*d*) glutenin I subunits, and (*e*) secondary bonds (e.g., hydrogen bonds and hydrophobic interactions). (From K. Kahn and W. Bushuk. *Bakers Digest* 52(2):19. Reprinted with permission from the April, 1978, Issue of *Bakers Digest*, Chicago, IL.)

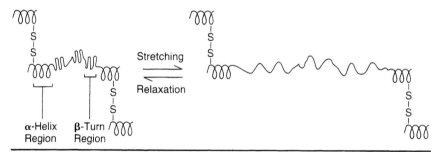

Figure 11-7. One polypeptide subunit of glutenin (shown schematically), linked head to tail by disulfide bonds to fragments of two other subunits. Alpha helices are shown near either end of the subunit and repeated beta turns that form a beta spiral occupy the central portion of the subunit. A beta spiral would allow for stretch and recovery (i.e., elasticity). (From J. D. Schofield. In *Chemistry and Physics of Baking*. J. M. V. Blanshard, P. J. Frazier and T. Galliard, eds. 1986. London: The Royal Society of Chemistry. P. 16. Reproduced by permission.)

lipids of flour can be removed by a nonpolar solvent. But once flour is formed into a dough, much of the fat can no longer be extracted (8). So dough formation involves the binding of lipids. The lipids of flour are known to be a complex mixture (6, 30, 31). They are classed on the basis of solubility as either free lipids or bound, and the two groups are present in roughly equal proportions. A high proportion of the bound lipids are polar and

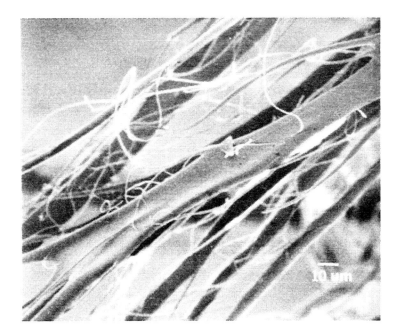

Figure 11-8. Scanning electron micrograph of purified glutenin from a gluten ball made from hard red spring wheat shows its fibrous character. (From R. A. Orth, B. L. Dronzek, and W. Bushuk. *Cereal Chemistry* 50:700. 1973. Reprinted by permission.)

a high proportion of the free lipids are nonpolar. The free nonpolar lipids are mainly triglycerides. The main polar lipids are phospholipids (i.e., have phosphoric acid as part of the molecule) and galactolipids (i.e., have the sugar, galactose, as part of the lipid molecule). The polar lipids are considered important in the formation of dough (30). There is evidence that polar lipids unite with gliadins by hydrogen bonds and with glutenins by hydrophobic interaction. Thus polar lipids could bind simultaneously with both gliadins and glutenins, possibly contributing to the gas-holding capacity of the gluten complex.

Role of Water

Water is essential for the conversion of flour into dough. Although the proteins of the gluten complex are insoluble in water, they are capable of absorbing large amounts of water. Exposed surfaces where water may contact the constituents of flour are great. Estimates are as high as 235 square meters of surface per gram of flour. Flour and water begin interacting the instant they are combined. When a drop of water came in contact with a particle of flour on a microscope slide, fibrils of protein were observed emerging from the surface of fractured endosperm cells (3), carrying with them granules of starch (Fig. 11-9). It was suggested that protein molecules may be deposited in the protein bodies of endosperm cells of wheat in laminar fashion (4) similar to that of starch molecules within the starch granule.

Another possibility is that the streaming fibrils are indicative of protein whose T_g is lowered by hydration so that it becomes rubberlike and mobile (19). Dough that contains only enough water to satisfy the numerous hydrogen bonding sites on the gluten complex

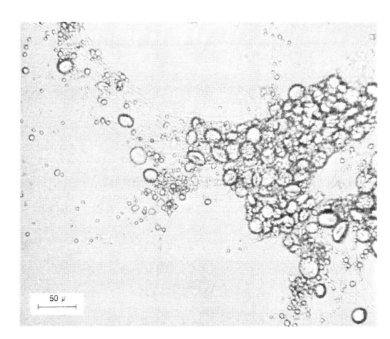

50 μ

Figure 11-9. Fibrils of protein (with starch granules adhering) that have emerged from a particle of flour wetted with a drop of water on a microscope slide. (From J. E. Bernardin and D. D. Kasarda. *Cereal Chemistry* 50:531. 1973. Reprinted by permission.)

(due in large measure to its high amide content) is stiff, inelastic, and lifeless. With increases in the ratio of water to flour, the water takes on the character of bulk water, which confers mobility on the mass. In this aqueous milieu flour can be converted into viscoelastic dough (25). The optimum ratio of water to flour increases with increase in the protein content of the flour, which may range from 10 to 18 percent. A difference of one percent in the water content of a dough above or below the optimum level results in a 5 to 15 percent difference in stiffness of the dough (5).

Manipulation

Manipulation is essential for the conversion of hydrated particles of flour into dough. Manipulation accomplishes two things. First, it strips away layer after hydrated layer from the surfaces of particles of flour (17). In addition, it brings these isolated masses into contact so glutenin fibrils unite to form longer elastic structures, and gliadins unite to form the viscous component of well developed gluten. The amount of manipulation required to develop dough fully varies with the flour (bread vs. all-purpose vs. cake) and with the presence of sugar and shortening, both of which interfere with the development of gluten.

Manipulation is done in an electric mixer with a dough hook attachment, in a home bread machine or by hand in a process called kneading. In any case, the mass of hydrated flour is stretched and folded repeatedly to develop the viscoelastic properties of the dough. Gluten forms an amorphous, continuous phase in fully developed dough in which starch granules are embedded and air bubbles are occluded. Figure 11-10 shows three stages in the development of a dough. At the left is shown dough immediately after water is stirred into the flour. In the center is incompletely developed dough. The satiny surface on the right denotes well-developed dough. Such dough is elastic and springy yet extensible. These qualities are essential in dough if it is to yield high-quality bread. The film of gluten that covers starch granules in the dough shown in the scanning electron micrograph of Figure 11-11 is typical of gluten films present in well-developed dough such as that illustrated in Figure 11-10.

Figure 11-10. Three stages in the development of dough: (left) dough immediately after water was stirred into the flour; (center) dough incompletely developed; (right) satiny surface of fully developed dough. (Courtesy of the Wheat Flour Institute.)

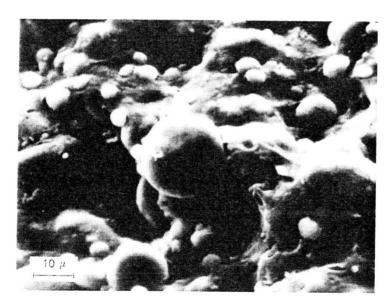

Figure 11-11. A veil-like film of gluten covers starch granules in this scanning electron micrograph of dough mixed to optimum development. (Reprinted from L. G. Evans, T. Volpe, and M. E. Zabik. *Journal of Food Science* 42:71. 1977. Copyright © by Institute of Food Technologists.)

The contributions of the gliadin and the glutenin fractions of gluten to the properties of dough are shown in Figure 11-12. The viscoelastic properties contributed by gluten in (a) are a composite of the elastic glutenin fraction in (b) and the viscous, cohesive properties contributed by the gliadin fraction in (c).

Harder wheat flours require more manipulation and yield doughs that are more elastic and extensible than softer wheat flours. In fact, doughs made from different all-purpose flour differ in this respect. Dough from rye flour lacks the elastic quality of wheat flour dough. Differences in the dough-forming potential of three types of flour—bread, all-purpose, and cake—are illustrated in the mixograms in Figure 11-13. These curves were made by an instrument that measures and records on a moving graph the force needed to manipulate flour and water as dough develops. The length of each vertical line in the curve indicates the resistance of the developing dough to the movement of the working parts of the instrument as they oscillate in the dough. The sharper the angle of the left side of the curve, the faster the dough develops; the higher the peak, the stronger the gluten. On the right, the steeper the slope, the faster the dough weakens with overmanipulation.

Once dough is developed gluten can be separated from other constituents of the flour, mainly starch granules and water solubles, by washing in water. Starch granules that are embedded in the gluten are dislodged by the water. The grayish mass that remains is crude gluten, which may still contain small adhering granules of starch and which is approximately ⅔ water. Harder wheat and longer patent flours yield more gluten than do softer wheat and shorter patent flours (Fig. 11-14). The yield of gluten from cake flour is small.

The ability of dough to retain gases and expand as they accumulate is due to gluten. When crude gluten is shaped into a ball and put into an oven and baked, it increases in volume several-fold (Fig. 11-13). The pressure of the expanding gas, coupled with the ability of the gluten to stretch and confine the steam, is responsible for the marked expansion of the gluten as it bakes. Once the gluten is inflated, pressure of the expanding steam maintains its volume until heat has had time to set the protein. If the gluten is removed from the oven before it has set, the steam condenses and the inflated gluten collapses. When the optimum volume has been reached or the gluten has expanded as much as it will or can, the oven temperature is lowered to avoid burning the exterior before the interior has had time to get hot enough to set. The interior of a baked ball of gluten shows pockets where bubbles of steam were once trapped by films of gluten.

Effects of Sugar and Fat on Gluten

Fat and sugar are two ingredients commonly combined with flour in baked products. Included in high proportions, they limit the development of gluten in dough. Fat is a more effective inhibitor than is sugar. Fat coats the particles of flour and thus prevents water from making contact with them. An early explanation for the effect of sugar was that it has more affinity for water than does flour (2). In any event, less gluten is developed in dough that contains either fat or sugar.

FLOUR IMPROVERS (DOUGH CONDITIONERS)

Oxidizing agents are added to flour to improve its dough-forming properties. Inclusion of an oxidant strengthens dough, reduces stickiness, and makes the dough easier to handle. An oxidizing agent is presumed to promote the formation of new disulfide bonds to replace those that are disrupted as dough is formed. Potassium bromate, azodicarbonamide,

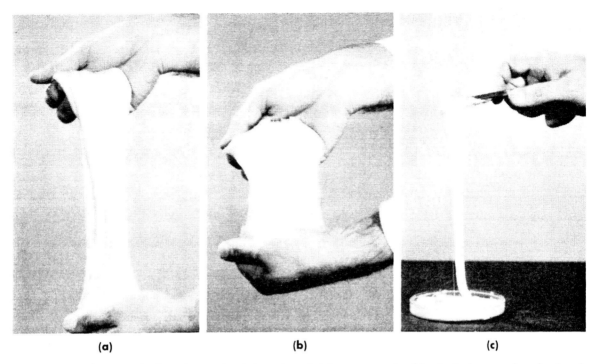

| (a) | (b) | (c) |

Figure 11-12. The unique rheological properties of gluten shown in (a) are a composite of the elastic character of one fraction of the protein molecules of the complex shown in (b) and the viscous character of the other molecules of the complex shown in (c). (From R. J. Dimler. *Bakers Digest* 37(1):52. 1963. Reprinted by permission.)

ascorbic acid, and calcium peroxide are used as flour improvers. The peroxide bleaches the xanthophyll pigments of the flour, too. When any bleaching agent is added to flour, the word bleached must appear on the label. Flour improvers (7) other than oxidizing agents that are used to give optimum rheological properties to dough include surface-active compounds such as sodium stearoyl lactylate, polysorbate 60, succinylated monoglycerides, and diacetyl tartaric acid esters of mono- and diglycerides.

ENRICHMENT OF FLOUR

Most of the wheat consumed as human food is in the form of flour and the major portion is refined white flour. Because enrichment of flour is mandatory in more than half of the states, practically all millers, because of competition, voluntarily enrich their flour. As a result, most of the flour on the market is enriched. Enriched flour is so labeled, and the inclusion of five nutrients—thiamin, riboflavin, niacin, iron, and folic acid (as of 1998)—is mandatory. Inclusion of calcium and vitamin D is optional.

PASTA

Pasta products were early convenience foods available to the consumer. Pasta comes in dozens of shapes and sizes, but the main ones are macaroni (hollow tubes) and spaghetti (solid rods)

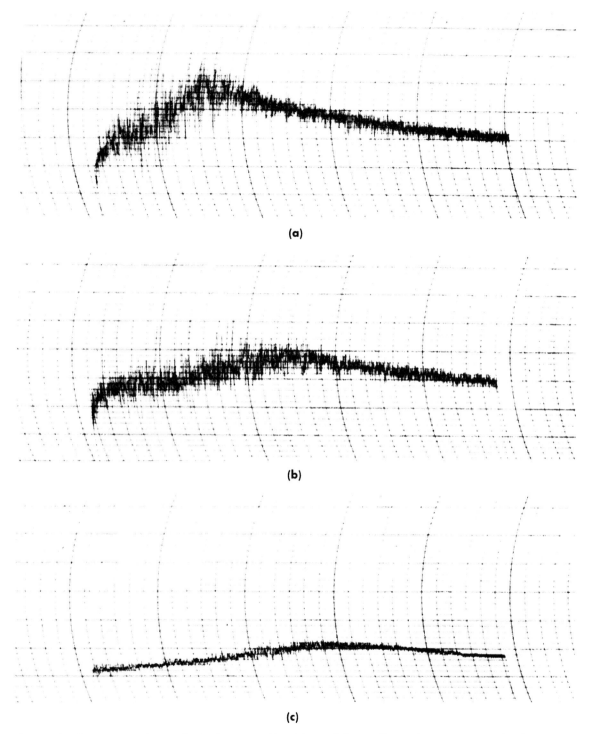

(a)

(b)

(c)

Figure 11-13. Mixograms showing the development and breakdown of gluten as flour and water are manipulated: (a) baker's hard wheat flour; (b) all-purpose or family flour; (c) cake or soft wheat flour.

Figure 11-14. Gluten balls from different flours before and after baking: (*left*) cake flour; (*center*) all-purpose flour; (*right*) bread flour. (Courtesy of the Wheat Flour Institute.)

(18). The dough for high quality pasta is made from the middlings, called semolina, of durum wheat. Water is combined with the semolina to form a stiff dough. The dough is forced along the barrel of an extruder and out through a die that determines the shape of the item. The dough for noodles contains eggs as well as semolina and water. The bulk of pasta products are dried to make them shelf-stable before they are marketed. High quality pasta is translucent and is a pale amber color due to the xanthophylls of the flour.

The accepted method for cooking pasta is to add the dried product to a surplus of boiling, salted water, approximately ¼ pound or 115 grams of pasta to one quart or liter of water. The optimum stage of doneness has been characterized as beyond the rubbery and before the mushy stage, or as *al dente*. Draining the cooked pasta in a colander removes excess water. A hot water rinse removes starch from the surface of the pasta so the pieces do not adhere. Macaroni may be cooked in twice its volume of boiling water or steamed like rice. A heavy container with a tight fitting lid and the unit turned low once the product is boiling are essential. Cooked in this way, the pasta swells somewhat less, is chewier, and has a more pronounced flavor. Nutrients are not discarded with the cooking water. A quality cooked pasta is firm and cohesive, characteristics contributed by low molecular weight glutenins (14). An intact surface with a sheen, another desirable quality, is associated with a high sulfhydryl—disulfide content of the glutenins of durum wheat (1).

REFERENCES

1. Alary, R., and K. Kobrehel. 1987. "The sulfhydryl plus disulfide content in the proteins of durum wheat and its relationship with the cooking quality of pasta." *Journal of the Science of Food and Agriculture* 39:123–36. Relationship to the surface condition of cooked pasta.

2. Baxter, A. J., and E. E. Hester. 1958. "The effect of sucrose on gluten development and the solubility of proteins of soft wheat flour." *Cereal Chemistry* 35:366–74. An attempt to account for the effects of sucrose on baked products made with flour.

3. Bernardin, J. E., and D. D. Kasarda. 1973. "Hydrated protein fibrils from wheat endosperm." *Cereal Chemistry* 50:529–36. Microscopic evidence for the formation of fibrils when flour is wetted.

4. Bernardin, J. E., and D. D. Kasarda. 1973. "The microstructure of wheat protein fibrils." *Cereal Chemistry* 50:735–45. Noncovalently linked fibrils as a basis for elasticity and viscous flow.

5. Bloksma, A. H., and W. Bushuk. 1988. "Rheology and chemistry of dough." In *Wheat Science and Technology*, Vol. 2. St. Paul: American Association of Cereal Chemists. P. 180. Water and consistency of dough.

6. Bushuk, W. 1986. "Protein-lipid and protein-carbohydrate interactions in flour-water mixtures." In *Chemistry and Physics of Baking*. J. M. V. Blanshard, P. J. Frazier and T. Gaillard, eds. London: The Royal Society of Chemistry. Pp. 147–54. Both galactolipids and an alpha-glucan involved.

7. CFR. 1990. "Dough conditioners." *Code of Federal Regulations, Title 21, 172.7.* Government Printing Office. Washington, D.C.

8. Chiu, C. M., and Y. Pomeranz. 1966. "Changes in the extractability of lipids during breadmaking." *Journal of Food Science* 31:753–58. Binding of lipids during mixing and baking.

9. Dimler, R. J. 1963. "Gluten—The key to wheat's utility." *Bakers Digest* 37(1):52–57. Chemical makeup and physical properties.

10. Eliasson, A.-C. 1990. "Rheological properties of cereal proteins." In *Dough Rheology and Baked Product Texture*. H. Faridi and J. M. Faubion, eds. New York: Van Nostrand Reinhold. Pp. 67–110. Metabolic and storage proteins: conformation and role of disulfide bonds.

11. Ewart, J. A. D. 1990. "Comments on recent hypotheses for glutenin." *Food Chemistry* 38:159–69. Linear *vs.* branched structure evaluated.

12. Ewart, J. A. D. 1972. "Recent research in dough visco-elasticity." *Bakers Digest* 46(4):22–28. Proteins of flour and the properties of dough.

13. Ewart, J. A. D. 1979. "Glutenin structure." *Journal of the Science of Food and Agriculture* 30:482–92. Disulfide-bonded linear structure reemphasized.

14. Feillet, P., O. Ait-Mouh, K. Kobrehel, and J. C. Autran. 1989. "The role of low molecular weight glutenin proteins in the determination of cooking quality of pasta products: An overview." *Cereal Chemistry* 66:26–30. Attributes of a quality product.

15. Fleming, S. E., and F. W. Sosulski. 1978. "Microscopic evaluation of bread fortified with concentrated plant proteins." *Cereal Chemistry* 55:373–82. Effects of soy flour and sunflower, fava bean, and field pea concentrate compared.

16. Graveland, A., P. Vosveld, W. J. Lichendonk, J. P. Marseille, J. H. E. Moonen, and A. Cheepstra. 1985. "A model for the molecular structure of the glutenins from wheat flour." *Journal of Cereal Science* 3:1–16. Proposed linkages of glutenin fractions and subfractions.

17. Hoseney, R. C. 1985. "The mixing phenomena." *Cereal Foods World* 30:453–57. Conversion of flour-to-dough, a hydration process.

18. Hoseney, R. C. 1986. "Pasta and noodles." In *Principles of Cereal Science and Technology*. St. Paul: American Association of Cereal Chemists. Pp. 277–90. Formulation of the products.

19. Hoseney, R. C. 1991. "Wheat gluten: Rheological and gas retaining properties." In *Water Relationships in Foods—Advances in the 1980s and Trends for the 1990s*. H. Levine and L. Slade, eds. New York: Plenum Press. Pp. 657–65. Unique features.

20. Hoseney, R. C. and P. A. Seib. 1973. "Structural differences in hard and soft wheat." *Bakers Digest* 47(6):26–28, 56. Shown by electron micrographs.

21. Hoseney, R. C., K. Zeleznak and C. S. Lai. 1986. "Wheat gluten: A glassy polymer." *Cereal Chemistry* 63:285–86. Evidence for the above.

22. Kahn, K. and W. Bushuk. 1978. "Glutenin: Structure and functionality in breadmaking." *Bakers Digest* 52(2):14–16, 18–20. Physico-chemical character; a working model.

23. Krull, L. H. and J. S. Wall. 1969. "Relationship of amino acid composition and wheat protein properties." *Bakers Digest* 43(4):30–34, 36, 38–39. Properties and interaction of component amino acids.

24. Lorenz, K. J., R. Welsh, N. Normann and J. Maga. 1972. "Comparative mixing and baking properties of wheat and triticale flour." *Cereal Chemistry* 49:187–93. Water absorption, mixing tolerance, and handling properties compared.

25. MacRitchie, F. 1992. "Physicochemical properties of wheat proteins in relation to functionality." *Advances in Food and Nutrition Research* 36:1–87. Technical review; minimum water level to plasticize dough.

26. Mangelsdorf, P. C. 1953. "Wheat." *Scientific American* 189(1):50–59. Origin and development of wheat varieties.

27. Matthews, R. H., and E. A. Bechtel. 1966. "Eating quality of some baked products made with instant flour." *Journal of Home Economics* 58:729–30. Adjustment recommended when instant flour is used in baked products.

28. Matthews, R. H., E. J. Sharp, and W. M. Clark. 1970. "The use of some oilseed flours in bread." *Cereal Chemistry* 47:181–89. Cottonseed, peanut, safflower, and soy flours compared.

29. Miller, B. S., H. B. Trimbo, and R. I. Derby. 1969. "Instantized flour—physical properties." *Bakers Digest* 43(6):49–51, 66. Structure, physical properties, and ease of dispersion in water.

30. Morrison, W. R. 1976. "Lipids in flour, dough and bread." *Bakers Digest* 50:29–34, 36, 47. In-depth summary of various aspects.

31. Pomeranz, Y., and O. K. Chung. 1978. "Interaction of lipids with proteins and carbohydrates in breadmaking." *Journal of the American Oil Chemists' Society* 55:285–89. Characterization of the lipids and evidence for their interaction.

32. Rooney, L. W., C. B. Gustavson, S. P. Clark, and C. M. Cater. 1972. "Comparison of the baking properties of some oilseed flours." *Journal of Food Science* 37:14–18. Cottonseed, peanut, sesame, and sunflower compared.

33. Schofield, J. D. 1986. "Flour proteins: Structure and functionality in baked products." In *Chemistry and Physics of Baking.* J. M. V. Blanshard, P. J. Frazier and T. Galliard, eds. London: The Royal Society of Chemistry. Pp. 14–29. Gliadins and glutenins; models and interactions.

34. Shewry, P. R., A. S. Tatham, J. Forde, M. Kreis, and B. J. Miflin. 1986. The classification and nomenclature of wheat gluten proteins. A reassessment. *Journal of Cereal Science* 4:97–106. Justification for the new nomenclature.

35. Stenvert, N. L. and K. Kingswood. 1977. "The influence of the physical structure of the protein matrix on wheat hardness." *Journal of the Science of Food and Agriculture* 28:11–19. Importance of continuity of the matrix and its bonding with starch.

36. Tatham, A. S., B. J. Miflin, and P. R. Shewry. 1985. "The beta-turn conformation in wheat gluten proteins: Relationship to gluten elasticity." *Cereal Chemistry* 62:405–12. New classification of the proteins; beta turns and secondary structure.

37. Tsen, C. C. and W. J. Hoover. 1973. "High-protein bread from wheat flour fortified with full-fat soy flour." *Cereal Chemistry* 50:7–16. Modifications that yield acceptable bread.

38. Tsen, C. C., W. J. Hoover and E. P. Farrell. 1973. Baking quality of triticale flours. *Cereal Chemistry* 50:16–20. Three triticale flours compared.

39. Wickser, F. W. 1958. "Baking properties of air classified flour fractions." *Cereal Science Today* 3:123–26. Photomicrographs of flour fractions and photographs of bread, layer cake, and angel cake made from each.

PART IV

Leavening Agents and Breads

Leavening Agents 12

The palatability of most baked products depends in part upon their being porous and light. The extent to which this is achieved depends upon the elasticity and the gas-holding capacity of the liquid-and-flour paste. Equally important is the availability of gas to inflate the elastic mass. Baked products made from flour would be heavy and compact without gas to leaven them. Air, steam, and carbon dioxide are the leavening gases. Most bakery products are leavened with more than one of the three gases. Some air bubbles are incorporated in all bakery products. Because all contain liquid, some steam is formed in all. Not all baked products are leavened with carbon dioxide, however.

STEAM AS A LEAVENING AGENT

As was pointed out in the preceding chapter, steam leavens a gluten ball when it is baked. The interior of a baked gluten ball contains thin films of gluten that once surrounded pockets of steam. Gluten balls do not appear on menus, but baked products leavened mainly by steam do. Cream puffs and popovers are hollow shells inflated by steam as the batter bakes. Yorkshire pudding is popover batter baked in a different shape. The flakes in pie crust result from blisters caused by steam that forms in the dough as it bakes. Steam, also, causes the blisters on the surface of Norwegian lefse and Indian chapati.

Proportions of Water to Flour

When steam is the chief leaven, the proportion of water to flour must be high enough so not all of the water is bound by the dry ingredients. The volume of liquid should equal the volume of flour (Chapter 13, Table 13-1). Vaporization of part of the liquid gives enough steam to make the product rise. This high ratio of water to flour gives a mixture with a fluid consistency that pours easily. Baked products leavened mainly by steam are baked in a hot oven for the first few minutes to convert the water to steam.

Gas-Holding Properties of a Batter or Dough

Although washed gluten has the ability to trap sufficient steam to make it rise (Fig. 11-14), the gluten in popovers and cream puffs is not concentrated enough for this purpose. It is too diluted with starch. However, both popovers and cream puffs contain eggs, and part of the ability of these two batters to trap steam is due to the protein supplied by the eggs, particularly the proteins of egg white. In baked products in which steam is not the main leaven it still contributes some leavening action.

AIR AS A LEAVENING AGENT

When ingredients are combined for baked products, some air bubbles are incorporated incidentally. In fact, it appears to be impossible to avoid trapping some air. This is fortunate because air appears to be an essential leaven in baked products (2, 6). This point is illustrated in the pound cakes in Figure 12-1. The ingredients (fat, sugar, flour, milk, and eggs) for the cake on the left were combined by a standard method that incorporates much air. The cake on the right was made in the same way, but all the air was evacuated before the cake was baked. The cake on the left rose; that on the right had essentially the same volume as the batter before it was baked. Thus the presence of air bubbles appears to be essential for the functioning of steam as a leaven. When the ingredients were combined for the cake in the center, precautions were taken to keep the incorporation of air to a minimum. However, the cake rose to a limited extent, presumably because some air was incorporated unintentionally.

Usually, attempts are made to incorporate air into baked products. In cakes made with fat, air is incorporated into the fat deliberately (Chapter 25, on shortened cakes). Beating air into egg white is another means of introducing air into shortened cake. A high proportion of beaten egg is used in angel and sponge cakes. These two products are leavened by air and by steam. Air incorporated into beaten eggs provides the leaven (along with steam) in such foods as soufflé, fondue, and puffy omelet.

CARBON DIOXIDE AS A LEAVENING AGENT

The third leavening gas used to make baked goods rise is carbon dioxide (CO_2). Baking soda, sodium bicarbonate ($NaHCO_3$) is the source of carbon dioxide in quick breads. Microorganisms are used to produce this gas in yeast breads. Yeast as a source of carbon dioxide is discussed later in this chapter.

Figure 12-1. The importance of air as a leaven in a baked product that contains no baking powder. (*Left*) The standard pound cake was made by creaming the fat with the sugar as in the conventional method for making shortened cake. (*Center*) The ingredients for this special pound cake were combined so as to minimize introduction of air into the batter. (*Right*) For this cake, part of the same batter for the standard cake was subjected to a vacuum to remove the air. (From J. A. Dunn and J. R. White. *Cereal Chemistry* 16:96. 1939. Courtesy of Lever Brothers Company. Reprinted by permission.)

Carbonates as a Source of Carbon Dioxide

Should sodium bicarbonate alone be heated, some carbon dioxide is released from the molecule. Sodium carbonate is formed concurrently. The reaction is

$$2NaHCO_3 \xrightarrow{\text{Heat } (\Delta)} Na_2CO_3 + CO_2 + H_2O$$

Sodium	Sodium	Carbon	Water
bicarbonate	carbonate	dioxide	

The sodium carbonate that is formed is markedly alkaline. It imparts to baked products an unpleasant, soapy taste, bitter if present in excess, and a yellowish color (attributed to the effect of the alkali on the flavonoid pigments of the flour). Thiamin is more susceptible to decomposition by heat when in an alkaline medium. Another reason sodium bicarbonate alone is undesirable as a source of carbon dioxide is that the gas is liberated too late in the baking period to be most effective as a leaven.

Ammonium bicarbonate is another source of carbon dioxide. In addition, it yields ammonia and water that can be converted to steam. The reaction is:

$$NH_4HCO_3 \xrightarrow{\text{Heat}} NH_3 + H_2O + CO_2$$

The use of ammonium bicarbonate as a source of leavening gas is limited to low moisture baked products such as cookies and crackers, which do not retain the ammonia (9).

Release of Carbon Dioxide from Sodium Bicarbonate by Acid

Sodium bicarbonate, as a salt of a strong base (sodium hydroxide) and a weak acid (carbonic), is alkaline. Because of this it reacts with acids. In solution, acids ionize, freeing hydrogen ions (H^+). Sodium bicarbonate in solution also ionizes, freeing sodium ions (Na^+) and bicarbonate ions (HCO_3^-). The positive sodium ion unites with the negative ion supplied by the acid to form the sodium salt of the acid. The positive hydrogen ion from the acid unites with the negative bicarbonate ion to give carbonic acid (H_2CO_3). The reaction, illustrated with hydrochloric acid, is

$$NaHCO_3 + HCl \xrightarrow{H_2O} NaCl + H_2CO_3$$

Sodium	Hydrochloric	Sodium	Carbonic
bicarbonate	acid	chloride	acid

Sodium chloride, an acceptable ingredient in baked products, is the salt formed. The carbonic acid dissociates to give carbon dioxide and water, as follows:

$$H_2CO_3 \rightleftharpoons H_2O + CO_2$$

Carbonic	Water	Carbon
acid		dioxide

This method of obtaining carbon dioxide as a leavening gas was first patented in 1837 by Dr. Whiting in England (1).

Hydrochloric acid is not used in baked products, but ingredients such as sour milk, vinegar, honey, and molasses, which contain one or more acids in solution, are used. Sour milk and buttermilk contain lactic acid, which is produced from the sugar in milk by certain bacteria. Vinegar contains five percent acetic acid and the main acid in honey is gluconic acid in equilibrium with gluconolactone (22). Molasses contains aconitic acid chiefly. The reaction that occurs when soda comes in contact with the acid in sour milk is typical although a different salt results with each acid.

$$NaHCO_3 + CH_3CHOHCOOH \xrightarrow{H_2O} CH_3CHOHCOONa + H_2O + CO_2$$

| Sodium bicarbonate | Lactic acid | Sodium lactate | Water | Carbon dioxide |

In products leavened by carbon dioxide small bubbles of air trapped in the batter seem to be essential for a proper leavening. It appears that adequate distribution of carbon dioxide depends upon numerous air cells previously incorporated in the batter, illustrated by observation of cake batter that contained a source of carbon dioxide as it baked on a microscope slide (2). It was noted that few if any new gas cells formed. The evolving gas appeared to collect in the existing air cells.

The relative importance of the three leavening gases—air, steam, and carbon dioxide—was studied in shortened cake (8). The percentage of the total leavening gas contributed by air was small, but essential (for reasons given above). Carbon dioxide made the major contribution to leavening action, but a considerable part of the expansion during baking was due to steam. In angel cake, which contains no source of carbon dioxide, ⅓ to ½ of the total expansion of ingredients is due to steam formed during baking and the remainder to air incorporated during mixing and its expansion during baking.

BAKING POWDER

When any food containing acid already in solution is combined with sodium bicarbonate, the bicarbonate dissolves in the cold liquid and the acid rapidly releases the carbon dioxide from it. A salt of the acid is formed along with the gas. Unless both the acid and the base are in solution and ionized, however, the two do not react. Baking powder, which is a mixture of dry sodium bicarbonate and dry acid, takes advantage of this fact: It is stable in a closed container because both reactants are dry. The first baking powder was marketed in 1853 in the United States (1). A selling point used to promote this new product was that it would decrease baking failures and so reduce nervous tension.

Yield of Carbon Dioxide

The yield of carbon dioxide from baking powder is set by law at a minimum of 12 percent, although most baking powders are formulated to yield 14 percent. This means that every 100 grams of baking powder must yield at least 12 grams of carbon dioxide. Because sodium bicarbonate is the source of this CO_2, all baking powder contains at least this minimum of sodium bicarbonate, which amounts to approximately ¼ teaspoon of sodium bicarbonate in each teaspoon of baking powder.

To formulate a baking powder, sufficient acid is added to neutralize the sodium bicarbonate. The amount of acid needed for each teaspoon of baking powder depends on the combining weight of the acid with the base. The difference between the volume of sodium bicarbonate plus the dry acid and one teaspoon is made up by an inert powder that serves as a means of standardizing the baking powder. If the acid has a high combining weight, less standardizing material is required. Cornstarch, which is inert, tasteless, and inexpensive, or calcium carbonate ($CaCO_3$) is commonly used. Cornstarch absorbs moisture and so keeps the reactants dry. Flour to which has been added sufficient sodium bicarbonate and acid for leaven and enough salt for flavor is called self-rising flour. This product, which has been on the market for many years, is the prototype of today's array of packaged mixes.

Acids Used in Baking Powders

Baking powders made with different acids are used by bakers and manufacturers of packaged mixes (3, 16), but only one type of baking powder is currently on the retail market. However, cream of tartar, the potassium acid salt of tartaric acid:

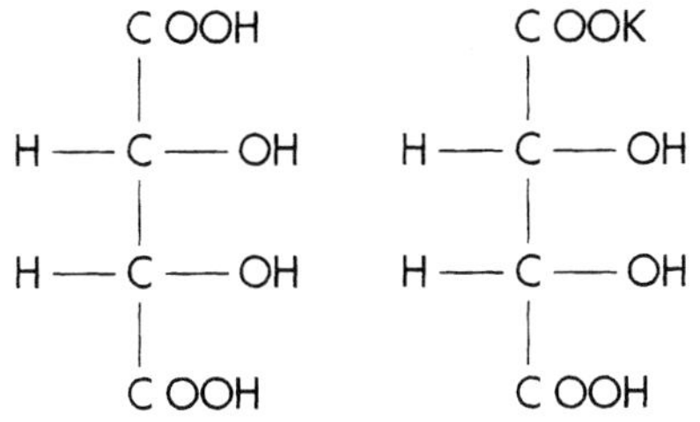

$$
\begin{array}{ccc}
\text{COOH} & & \text{COOK} \\
| & & | \\
\text{H}-\text{C}-\text{OH} & & \text{H}-\text{C}-\text{OH} \\
| & & | \\
\text{H}-\text{C}-\text{OH} & & \text{H}-\text{C}-\text{OH} \\
| & & | \\
\text{COOH} & & \text{COOH}
\end{array}
$$

It is available and can be combined with sodium bicarbonate to yield a homemade baking powder. A mix of ¼ teaspoon of sodium bicarbonate and ½ teaspoon of cream of tartar may be used in place of 1 teaspoon of baking powder.

The reaction when this acid releases carbon dioxide from sodium bicarbonate is:

$$NaHCO_3 + KHC_4H_4O_6 \xrightarrow{H_2O} KNaC_4H_4O_6 + CO_2 + H_2O$$

| Sodium bicarbonate | Potassium acid tartrate | Sodium potassium tartrate | Carbon dioxide | Water |

Cream of tartar dissolves readily in cold water, so this baking powder is fast acting (Fig. 12-2).

The baking powder now on the retail market is a slow or double-acting type. It is formulated with two acid-reacting ingredients, one of which is monocalcium phosphate monohydrate. An equation for one of several reactions believed to occur when this acid reacts with sodium bicarbonate is:

$$3CaH_4(PO_4)_2 + 8NaHCO_3 \longrightarrow Ca_3(PO_4)_2 + 4Na_2HPO_4 + 8CO_2 + 8H_2O$$

| Monocalcium phosphate | Sodium bicarbonate | Tricalcium phosphate | Disodium phosphate | Carbon dioxide | Water |

Monocalcium phosphate monohydrate is readily soluble in cold water.

The rates at which carbon dioxide is liberated from soda by this acid and by cream of tartar are shown in Figure 12-2. As the graph shows, almost 70 percent of the available carbon dioxide is evolved during the first two minutes. The hydrated form of monocalcium phosphate can react with soda and liberate a high proportion of the carbon dioxide as a batter or dough is mixed. When soda alone is used in a biscuit type dough, ⅓ of the CO_2 is released (Fig. 12-2) by the acidic constituents in the flour and milk (9).

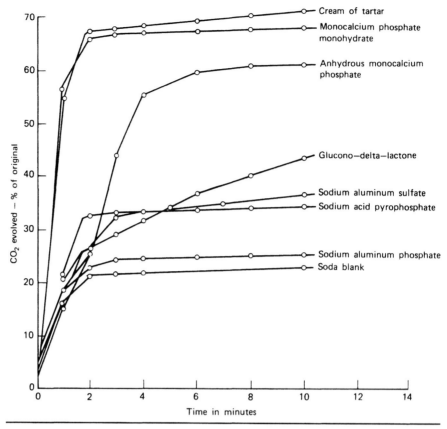

Figure 12-2. Rate of reaction in dough at 27°C of baking powder made with different acids (dough stirred three minutes). (From T. P. Kichline and J. F. Conn. *Bakers Digest* 44(4):37. Reprinted with permission from the August, 1970, issue of *Bakers Digest*. Chicago, IL.)

The second acid-reacting ingredient used in double-acting baking powder is sodium aluminum sulfate (abbreviated SAS). This ingredient is not an acid. However, it reacts with *hot* water to form sulfuric acid according to the following reaction:

$$Na_2Al_2(SO_4)_4 \ + \ 6H_2O \ \xrightarrow{\text{Heat}} \ 2Al(OH)_3 \ + \ Na_2SO_4 \ + \ 3H_2SO_4$$

Sodium aluminum sulfate	Water		Aluminum hydroxide	Sodium sulfate	Sulfuric acid

This sulfuric acid then liberates carbon dioxide from the soda left unneutralized by the calcium acid phosphate, as follows:

$$3H_2SO_4 \ + \ 6NaHCO_3 \ \xrightarrow[\text{H}_2\text{O}]{\text{Water}} \ 3Na_2SO_4 \ + \ 6H_2CO_3$$

Sulfuric acid	Sodium bicarbonate		Sodium sulfate	Carbonic acid

Double-acting baking powder that contains both SAS and monocalcium phosphate monohydrate (usually in a ratio of 2:1) is known as SAS-phosphate baking powder. The double action refers to the sequential release of CO_2, first in the dough by the cold-water soluble calcium acid phosphate and later during baking by the acid derived from sodium aluminum sulfate. This means that some CO_2 is released during mixing, but that the major portion is released only after the product is heated in the oven and the acid is formed.

A number of leavening acids are available commercially, each tailored to meet stringent requirements for release of carbon dioxide (3, 9, 16). Packaged mixes, packaged doughs, frozen batters, doughnuts from automatic doughnut machines, and bakery cake batters made in large batches all require specially formulated leavens.

The anhydrous form of monocalcium phosphate is less soluble in cold water than the monohydrate, made so in part by a coating of an insoluble material. The delay in release of CO_2 during the first few minutes of mixing means less loss of leavening gas from the batter and so greater mixing tolerance. Sodium acid pyrophosphate, $Na_2H_2P_2O_7$, is used commercially as a leavening acid. Forms of the acid that dissolve at different temperatures during baking are available. Sodium aluminum phosphate, $NaH_{14}Al_3(PO_4)_8 \cdot 4H_2O$, is a third acid-reacting ingredient with limited solubility in cold liquid. A high proportion of the self-rising flour on the market contains this compound as one of the acid-reacting ingredients. These three acids, anhydrous monocalcium phosphate, sodium aluminum phosphate, and sodium acid pyrophosphate, alone or in combination are used in packaged mixes.

The use of the acid, glucono-delta-lactone, with baking soda as a source of carbon dioxide was introduced in the early 1940s (12). This acid is the lactone of gluconic acid, a derivative of glucose. Quick bread leavened with this combination of soda and acid has the appearance, volume, grain, and texture of yeast bread (but not the flavor). No fermentation time is needed, but the batter can stand up to 50 minutes before it is baked.

Acids that form baking powder with a high reaction rate liberate as much as ¾ of the carbon dioxide in cold batter or dough compared to slightly more than ⅓ with sodium aluminum sulfate (13). Only 20 to 30 percent of the carbon dioxide liberated in cold batter or dough is retained at the end of the mixing period to leaven the product. For this reason, unnecessary stirring of flour mixtures leavened with soda and sour milk or cream of tartar should be avoided. The percentage of carbon dioxide retained varies with the thickness of the unbaked mixture. The amount of baking powder used in quick breads usually varies from one to two teaspoons per cup of flour. Less is needed to leaven a product when a large amount of air is incorporated into a batter or dough. A lower proportion of baking powder is required in cake batter in which air is incorporated by means of fat. An excess of baking powder gives a product with a porous, fragile crumb; too little yields a product with small cells but one that is compact (5).

The acid ingredient used to make baking powder influences the pH of the batter or dough (10). Those made with SAS-phosphate baking powder are neutral or slightly alkaline. Batters that are more acidic yield baked products with a finer, whiter crumb and a sweeter taste.

Each acid when it reacts with sodium bicarbonate leaves a different residue. For example, if hydrochloric were used, the salt would then be sodium chloride; with sour milk the salt is sodium lactate; with tartaric acid the salt is sodium tartrate; with cream of tartar it is sodium potassium tartrate; with calcium acid phosphate the salts include tricalcium phosphate and disodium phosphate; with sodium aluminum sulfate, both sodium sulfate and aluminum hydroxide are left in the baked product. Salts produced when sodium bicarbonate is neutralized by the various acids influence the taste of the baked product.

Difference in taste is more difficult to detect in muffins than in blander-tasting biscuits. However, differences in taste due to the type of baking powder can be detected in cakes.

The ions from the leavening acids influence viscosity and elasticity of batters and doughs and the grain, resilience, and moistness of the crumb of quick breads (9). This can be observed when biscuit dough made with baking soda and cream of tartar is compared with dough made with SAS baking powder. Cracks are more likely to appear along the sides of biscuits made with double-acting baking powder because of the greater elasticity and viscosity of the dough caused by the aluminum ions (3). The late release of part of the carbon dioxide during baking may be a contributing factor (1).

BAKING SODA AND SOUR MILK

When baking soda and sour milk or buttermilk are used in place of sweet milk and baking powder, the difficulty is in estimating the amount of acid present in the milk. One cup of very sour milk or buttermilk has enough lactic acid to neutralize and so release the carbon dioxide from ½ teaspoon of baking soda. If there is any question as to the sourness of the milk, the amount of soda per cup of milk should be limited to ¼ teaspoon. If a recipe calls for one cup of sour milk and only sweet milk is available, the equivalent of the sour milk is made by adding 1¼ teaspoons of cream of tartar to one cup of sweet milk. Or sour milk may be made by using one tablespoon of vinegar or lemon juice and enough milk to fill a one-cup measure. However, baking powder alone can be used with sour milk as well as with sweet, eliminating the danger of having unneutralized baking soda in the baked product. The small amount of acid in slightly sour milk will do no harm; in fact, the crumb will be whiter, finer, and more moist, as can be demonstrated by adding ⅛ to ¼ teaspoon of cream of tartar per cup of flour to biscuits made with baking powder and sweet milk. A disadvantage of this addition is that the crust does not brown as readily. Phosphated flours tolerate recipes with high proportion of soda because of the neutralizing effect of the phosphate.

One cup of fully sour milk together with ½ teaspoon of baking soda will yield carbon dioxide equivalent to the amount obtained from 2 teaspoons of baking powder. This amount of baking soda and sour milk in a batter or dough that contains two or more cups of flour will not yield enough carbon dioxide to leaven the product. For this reason many recipes using sour milk call for baking powder as well as soda. For example, to leaven 2 cups of flour, as in biscuits, 4 teaspoons of single-acting baking powder may be used. If one cup of very sour milk is used with ½ teaspoon of baking soda, 2 teaspoons of baking powder are needed in addition. To change a recipe from sour milk and soda to sweet milk requires an additional teaspoon of baking powder for each ¼ teaspoon of baking soda omitted. When soda is used, it should be sifted with the dry ingredients. If it is added to the sour milk instead, the lactic acid will release the carbon dioxide into the atmosphere instead of within the batter where it is needed. Excess soda in quick breads should be avoided because of greater destruction of thiamin in more alkaline products.

YEAST AS A SOURCE OF CARBON DIOXIDE

Market Forms of Yeast

Carbon dioxide produced by cells of the microorganism, *Saccharomyces cerevisiae* (Fig. 12-3), is utilized to leaven baked products. Active cells of yeast are available as a compressed cake or

Figure 12-3. Scanning electron micrograph of yeast cells
(*Saccharomyces cerevisiae*) multiplying by budding. One cell (*center*)
with large bud still attached. Magnification × 2,500. (Photo courtesy
of Martin W. Miller, Department of Food Science and Technology,
University of California, Davis.)

in dried form (7, 20). The compressed cake contains approximately 70 percent moisture so
it is highly perishable unless it is refrigerated, in which case the cells remain viable for three
to four weeks. If fresh compressed yeast is frozen and held in frozen storage, the yeast cells
will live and the cake of yeast will stay fresh for three to four months (19). Active dry yeast is
made by extruding cake yeast in fine strands that are then dried to a low moisture content
(near eight percent). The dried material is reduced to granular form. Instant (quick- or fast-
rising) yeast is made from more active strains of yeast (20) and dried faster and to a lower
level of moisture (near five percent). Both dried forms are marketed in seven-gram (¼ ounce)
packets that are flushed with nitrogen or carbon dioxide before they are sealed or in vacuum-
packed 115 gram (4 ounce) containers. The dried forms can be held at room temperature for
up to a year. The useful life of active dry yeast is indicated by an expiration date stamped on

the package. Once the package is opened, the unused portion should be stored in a closed container in the refrigerator.

Although active dry yeast has a long shelf life at room temperature, it has one disadvantage: It must be hydrated before it is incorporated with other ingredients, and the temperature of the water (43° to 46°C or 110° to 115°F) is critical (7, 15, 20). If the temperature is too high, the yeast is inactivated; if it is too low, substances leak from the cells, such as glutathione. As a reducing agent, glutathione is capable of breaking disulfide bonds and weakening dough. Instant dry yeast is in the form of short, porous rods that absorb water readily (21). Instant yeast can be incorporated with flour and other ingredients without prior hydration.

Production of Carbon Dioxide

As the cells of yeast metabolize fermentable sugars (11, 14), under anaerobic conditions that are present in dough, they produce carbon dioxide as a waste product. This waste can be utilized as a leavening agent in baked products. Yeast cells are able to ferment four sugars: glucose, fructose, sucrose, and maltose; they are unable to utilize the sugar from milk. The biochemical changes that take place when sugars are fermented by yeast are complex (11, 14). The main overall reaction, ignoring a number of intermediate steps, for the production of CO_2 with glucose as the sugar can be expressed by the Gay-Lussac equation:

$$C_6H_{12}O_6 \rightarrow 2C_2H_5OH + 2CO_2$$

Glucose   Ethyl alcohol   Carbon dioxide

Yeast cells also possess the enzyme invertase (sucrase) on or near the cell wall, which acts as a catalyst for hydrolysis of the dissaccharide, sucrose, to simple (and fermentable) sugars in the following reaction:

$$C_{12}H_{22}O_{11} + H_2O \xrightarrow{\text{Sucrase}} C_6H_{12}O_6 + C_6H_{12}O_6$$

Sucrose   Water   Glucose   Fructose

Maltose is fermented only after the supply of glucose and fructose is exhausted. Even then fermentation proceeds slowly.

Temperature is a major factor that controls the metabolism of sugar by yeast (4). Production of carbon dioxide increases slowly as the temperature rises from that of the refrigerator to near room temperature. It increases rapidly as the temperature rises from near 28° to 38°C (82° to 100°F). At temperatures much above this, inactivation of yeast out strips increased production of carbon dioxide from surviving cells. Two ingredients—sugar and salt—present in most baked products influence the ability of yeast to produce carbon dioxide. A high proportion of sugar limits the capacity of yeast to absorb water and sugar and so slows production. In the absence of salt, production of carbon dioxide by yeast is rapid, but an excess of salt is inhibitory.

As a generator of carbon dioxide, a packet of active dry yeast is equivalent to a cake of compressed yeast. Instant dry yeast cells are more active so the fermentation time is shorter when this form of yeast is used.

In Sour Dough Bread

Both bacteria and yeast are involved in the production of carbon dioxide that leavens sour dough bread (17, 18). A rod-shaped bacillus, *Lactobacillus sanfrancisco,* utilizes maltose preferentially to produce lactic and acetic acids. The latter may account for up to half the total acid in sour dough. The low pH (3.8–4.5) of the dough is favorable for the production of carbon dioxide by the yeast, *Saccharomyces exiguus.* This organism thrives also in the presence of an antibiotic elaborated by the bacillus and at the high concentration of acetic acid, conditions in which bakers' yeast cannot survive. Although lactic and acetic are the major acids, six minor acids, propionic, butyric, and two of its modifications, isovaleric, and valeric, also contribute to the flavor of sour dough bread.

REFERENCES

1. Barackman, R. A. 1954. "Chemical leavening agents." *Transactions of the American Association of Cereal Chemists.* 12:43–55. Leavening power and side effects of the various acids. Brief account of the introduction of the various acids.

2. Carlin, G. T. 1944. "A microscopic study of the behavior of fats in cake batter." *Cereal Chemistry* 21:189–99.

3. Conn, J. 1980. "Chemical leavening systems in food products." *Cereal Foods World* 26(3):119–23. Characteristics of the acids used; their neutralizing value.

4. Cooper, E. J., and G. Reed. 1968. "Yeast fermentation—effect of temperature, pH, ethanol, sugars, salt and osmotic pressure." *Bakers Digest* 42(6):22–24, 26, 28–29, 63. Summary of pertinent facts.

5. Davies, J. R. 1937. "The effect of formula and procedure variables upon cake quality." *Cereal Chemistry* 14:819–33. Major ingredients including leavens.

6. Dunn, J. A. and J. R. White. 1939. "The leavening action of air included in cake batter." *Cereal Chemistry* 16:93–100. Effects of evacuation of the batter and of modified mixing method on volume of pound cake.

7. Dziezak, J. D. 1987. "Yeast and yeast derivatives: Definition, characteristics and processing." *Food Technology* 41(2):104–21. Compressed, active dry, and instant active dry yeast compared.

8. Hood, M. P., and B. Lowe. 1948. "Air, water vapor, and carbon dioxide as leavening gases in cakes made with different types of fats." *Cereal Chemistry* 25:244–54. Relative contribution of each type of leaven.

9. Kichline, T. P., and J. F. Conn. 1970. "Some fundamental aspects of leavening agents." *Bakers Digest* 44(4):36–40. Neutralizing value and special characteristics of the various leavening acids.

10. McKim, E., and H. V. Moss. 1943. "Observations on the pH of chemically leavened products." *Cereal Chemistry* 20:250–59. The pH of biscuit dough, biscuits, cake batter, and cake made with common leavening agents.

11. Magoffin, C. D., and R. C. Hoseney. 1974. "A review of fermentation." *Bakers Digest* 48(6):22–23, 26–27. Utilization of sugars.

12. Miller, J. A., C. S. McWilliams, and S. A. Matz. 1959. "Development of the leavening system for an instant bread mix." *Cereal Chemistry* 36:487–97. Use of glucono-delta-lactone.

13. Noble, I. T., and E. G. Halliday. 1931. "A quantitative measurement of the carbon dioxide evolved in and lost from simplified muffin batters." *Cereal Chemistry* 8:165–67. Carbon dioxide evolved from three types of baking powder in water only and with three combinations of ingredients used in batters.

14. Pomper, S. 1969. "Biochemistry of yeast fermentation." *Bakers Digest* 4(2):32–33, 36–38. Effects of temperature, pH, and osmotic pressure on carbohydrate metabolism by yeast.

15. Ponte, J. G. Jr., R. L. Glass, and W. F. Geddes. 1960. "Studies on the behavior of

active dry yeast in bread making." *Cereal Chemistry* 37:263–79. Effects of rehydration temperature.

16. Reiman, Herbert M. 1977. "Chemical leavening systems." *Bakers Digest* 51(4):33–34, 36, 42. Emphasis on leavens for commercial products.

17. Saunders, R. M., H. NG, and L. Kline. 1972. "The sugars of flour and their involvement in the San Francisco sour dough French bread process." *Cereal Chemistry* 49:86–91. Substrates for the yeast and for the bacillus.

18. Sugihara, T. F., L. Kline, and L. B. McCready. 1970. "Nature of the San Francisco sour dough French bread process." II. "Microbiological aspects." *Bakers Digest* 44(2):51–53, 56–57. Bacillus and yeast identified.

19. Thiessen, E. J. 1942. "The effects of temperature upon the viability and baking properties of dry and moist yeast stored for various periods." *Cereal Chemistry* 19:773–84. Loss of activity when refrigerated and frozen.

20. Trivedi, N. B., E. J. Cooper, and B. L. Breunsma. 1984. "Development and applications of quick-rising yeast." *Food Technology* 38(6):51, 54–55, 57. Strains of yeast used; activity of the yeast.

21. Van Dam, H. W. 1986. "The biotechnology of bakers' yeast: Old and new business." In *Chemistry and Physics of Baking.* J. M. V. Blanshard, P. J. Frazier, and T. Galliard, eds. London: The Royal Society of Chemistry. Pp. 117–31. Compressed, active dry, and instant yeast included.

22. White, Jonathan W., Jr. 1978. "Honey." *Advances in Food Research* 24:304–5. Acids present.

Quick Breads

13

Quick breads are baked products made with flour that do not rely on microorganisms to produce carbon dioxide to leaven them. In the preparation of such products, flour is combined with liquid in such ratios as to form either a batter or a dough. Pour batters used for popovers and cream puffs have a ratio of liquid to flour of 1:1 and are, as the term implies, thin enough to pour. A drop batter has 2 parts flour and 1 part liquid, as for muffins. Doughs are stiff enough to handle. Soft doughs have 3 parts flour to 1 part liquid, as for biscuits and yeast bread. A higher ratio of flour to liquid yields a stiff dough as for cookies, pastry, and pasta. Most batters and doughs are foams. The size and shape of the gas cells determine the grain of the baked product. The texture is influenced mainly by the character of the material that defines and surrounds the gas cells.

INGREDIENTS IN QUICK BREADS AND THEIR FUNCTIONS

Flour

Flour gives to batters and doughs stretch or elasticity, a characteristic enabling them to hold leavening gas or gases. Flour also contributes structure or rigidity to baked products. Structure is contributed by starch when it is gelatinized and gluten when it is set by heat. Flours differ in the amount and quality of gluten they yield and so in their moisture-holding or -binding capacity. (Flours are discussed in Chapter 11.)

Liquid

A liquid ingredient is essential for dissolving sugar, salt, and the baking soda and acid in baking powder. In water, the soda and the acid ionize, after which they can react to release carbon dioxide. Water hydrates the protein of flour, a preliminary to the development of gluten. It also hydrates the starch and makes possible its gelatinization during baking. Water converted to steam serves as a leavening agent.

Salt

Salt is used in quick breads to improve the taste, but it also influences rate and degree of hydration of the flour. The usual proportion is ½ teaspoon per cup of flour unless the recipe includes a high proportion of salted table fat. The recipe for cream puffs (Table 13-1) specifies less than this amount of salt because of the large amount of butter or margarine. If unsalted butter or hydrogenated shortening is substituted, the amount of salt should be increased. It is possible to make a breadstuff from flour, salt, and water. Water is necessary to make the particles of flour adhere and salt to make the flour palatable. These three ingredients are basic to any quick bread.

Leavening Agent

Included in a batter or dough for a baked product is either a gas or a source of gas that can expand during baking and cause the product to rise. Air may be beaten into the batter directly or may be incorporated as beaten egg white. Steam, in addition to air trapped incidentally, can provide sufficient leaven if surplus water is available in the mixture. Steam contributes some leavening action in all baked products. Baking soda used with an acid already in solution (as in sour milk, honey, or molasses) or soda combined with dry acid (as in baking powder) is a source of leaven in most quick breads.

Leaven not only increases volume but is responsible in part for the grain of a baked product. The gas forms holes or pockets in a batter or dough and converts it into a foam. The amount and distribution of the leavening gas determine whether the holes in the crumb are big or little and round and intact or large and exploded. Of course the ability of the dough to stretch and also to retain the leavening gas as it is liberated and as it expands when heated is as important in determining both volume and grain of the baked products as is the amount of leaven that goes into the batter.

Fat

Fat is included in batters and doughs to tenderize the product. It accomplishes this in part by waterproofing the particles of flour. It thus limits the ease with which gluten is developed. Fat also lubricates the gluten strands already formed and permits them to slip past each other more readily. The function of fat as a tenderizing agent will be treated more fully in Chapter 17 on pastry.

Sugar

Aside from the obvious function of contributing sweetness, sugar is included in batters and doughs because it, too, contributes to the tenderness of baked products. Sugar decreases the uptake of water by flour and so interferes with the development of gluten, although to a lesser extent than does fat. Sugar serves also as a means of incorporating air into fat and so into the batter. Sugar performs this function in shortened cakes when it is creamed into the fat. Another reason for including sugar in baked products is that it aids in browning. The color is attributed to a reaction between reducing sugars and protein. In the absence of sugar, some browning results from dextrinization of starch. More acidic batters brown slowly. One popular homemade quick bread mix includes cream of tartar, which is added to delay the onset of rancidity (Chapter 15). Cream of tartar makes the mix more acid, too. A small amount of sugar is included in the mix (10) to compensate for the retarding effect of the acid on browning.

Eggs

Beaten eggs serve as a means of incorporating air into batters and doughs. Eggs contain protein, which contributes elasticity to the batter and structure to such baked products

TABLE 13-1
Formulas for Quick Breads

Ingredient	Popovers	Cream Puffs	Muffins	Biscuits	Waffles
Flour[a]	1 cup	1 cup	1 cup	1 cup	1 cup cake flour
Salt	½ tsp	¼ tsp	½ tsp	½ tsp	¼ tsp
Baking powder			2 tsp	2 tsp	2 tsp
Liquid	1 cup	1 cup	½ cup	⅓ to ⅜ cup	⅝ cup
Fat	1 Tbsp	½ cup	1–2 Tbsp	2½ Tbsp	¼ cup
Eggs	2	4	½		1
Sugar			1–2 Tbsp		

[a]All-purpose except where cake flour is specified.

as muffins, popovers, and cream puffs. Cream puff batter contains twice as many eggs as does popover batter for the same amount of flour and liquid (Table 13-1). More eggs are needed in cream puffs because of the high proportion of fat they contain. Egg yolk contains a fatlike material that can tie together or emulsify two incompatible liquids, water and melted fat.

BALANCING INGREDIENTS IN QUICK BREADS

Ingredients in any baked product need to be in reasonable balance. Structural ingredients, such as flour and egg, are balanced against tenderizing ingredients or those that weaken structure, such as fat and sugar. In addition, liquid ingredients, milk, egg, and fat, are balanced against dry ingredients, mainly flour. For example, when sugar, fat, or both are increased in the basic muffin recipe, the egg is increased to compensate. After these modifications are made, the recipe approaches that for a shortened cake. Ingredients do not need to be in perfect balance, a fact that makes possible the infinite number of new recipes. However, there are limits to the range in proportions of ingredients that will give an acceptable product. Proportions of ingredients in a product formulated at sea level may require modification if the product is to be baked at altitudes of 3,000 feet (915 meters) or above (1, 2, 9). Reduction of leavening agent may be indicated because the lower atmospheric pressure offers less resistance to expansion of the product; otherwise it may be overinflated. A lower boiling point and possibly greater evaporation at higher elevations may require an increase in the proportion of water. Formulas for packaged mixes are modified for the altitude of the area in which they are marketed.

MANIPULATION OF INGREDIENTS FOR QUICK BREADS

When ingredients for a batter or dough are combined, a number of factors have a bearing on the success of the operation. Techniques used to prepare quick breads should be appropriate for the ingredients used and for the results desired. Bowls and other utensils should be of appropriate size and shape. The distribution of ingredients brought about by manipulation and the resultant chemical and physical interaction among them are important factors. Each of these points is discussed below.

Techniques

A number of terms with fairly precise meanings are used in the directions for manipulating batters and doughs. To *beat* means to combine with a regular over-and-over or circular motion, either to make smooth (as for popover batter) or to incorporate air (as for beaten egg white). To *blend* means to combine thoroughly (as for melted chocolate in a batter). To *cream* applies to sugar and fat. The sugar crystals are worked into the fat to incorporate air that results in a foam (as for shortened cakes). To *cut* applies to fat and flour, with the fat progressively subdivided and coated with particles of flour (as for pastry). To *fold* means to use a knife, a spatula, or a flexible scraper to incorporate one ingredient within another (as beaten egg white into waffle batter, soufflés, or angel cake). Because the inexperienced have difficulty with this technique, it is given in detail. In folding, the edge of the implement leads. The first movement is down to the bottom of the bowl; the handle is rotated in the hand a quarter of a turn and the implement is moved across the bottom of the bowl; the handle is rotated another quarter turn and the spatula brought up through the mix, the edge of the implement leading; and finally the handle is given another quarter turn and the implement is moved across the top of the mixture (Figure 13-1). Using the utensil as a paddle should be avoided when ingredients are folded. To *knead* means to stretch, fold, and press dough gently to form and arrange strands of gluten (as for biscuit or yeast bread dough). To *mix* means to distribute ingredients using any technique suitable to the ingredients involved. To *stir* means to combine, usually with a spoon, with a circular motion. Liquid and dry ingredients are combined by stirring. To *whip* means to beat rapidly for the purpose of incorporating air.

Utensils

Bowls

Mixing bowls should have sides with a gentle slope rather than a pronounced curve. Although the base of the bowl should be wide enough to eliminate the danger of its overturning, the inside of the bowl at the base should be narrow. Otherwise it is difficult to combine ingredients thoroughly without much waste motion, and parts of some ingredients may be incompletely incorporated even after extensive mixing. The size of the mixing bowl or other utensil used to hold ingredients should be chosen with a view to what one intends to accomplish in manipulation. If the container is too large, ingredients are difficult to corner; if too small, ingredients are inadequately manipulated. If the volume of ingredients increases during manipulation, allowance must be made when selecting the container.

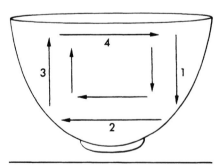

Figure 13-1. Technique of folding. Diagram shows the direction of movement of the implement used.

Spoons

Spoons shaped more like paddles than the conventional shape are superior for creaming and mixing batters. Some metal spoons used for stirring foods in aluminum pans discolor or give a peculiar taste to the food. Stainless steel and wooden spoons do not, but the latter are considered unsanitary by some.

Beaters

Hand beaters of different types—rotary, wire whip, and coiled spring—are available. The size of the handle on a rotary beater is important, as is its positioning. A handle either too large or too small or set at a wrong angle will cause the hands to cramp and tire quickly. Blades made from thin metal and whips made from thin wire will incorporate smaller bubbles of air and so produce finer foams. A spring-type whip is convenient for beating small volumes of liquids or for blending egg with milk. Too, it is easier to wash than the large rotary beater. A turbine-type beater has an advantage over a rotary type for beating small amounts of liquid. If gears on rotary beaters are exposed, they are easier to keep clean, dry, and free from rust. The blades of the beater should be washed and rinsed after use, but it is poor practice to submerge the gears of a rotary beater in water. If food does get on this part of the beater, it must be washed, of course. After it is washed the beater should be rinsed in very hot water and the exposed surfaces wiped dry. The gears should be rotated rapidly for a few seconds to remove moisture. A small drop of lubricant applied to the working parts when they are dry makes the handle turn easily.

Electric mixers are either hand-held or stationary. The working parts of a hand-held electric mixer work like a hand-operated rotary beater, with electricity replacing muscle power. Stationary electric mixers are of two types. In one the bowl revolves around the rotating blades. In the other the bowl is stationary and the blades, wire whip, or dough hook attachment move in a hypocycloidal, or planetary, fashion. The attachment not only rotates, but it also moves in an orbit around the inside of the bowl.

Scrapers and Spatulas

A flexible scraper is useful for getting the last of the batter out of a mixing bowl, for transferring the last bits of food from one utensil to another, and for otherwise eliminating waste. A scraper is useful also for folding and for some stirring operations. It is a good implement for scraping plates and other dishes preparatory to washing.

A metal spatula is helpful for folding beaten egg whites into batters, for turning pancakes, and for removing cookies from a baking sheet. The blade should be flexible enough to bend to form a right angle. Unless the blade is flexible, a kitchen knife would do almost as well; this would eliminate one more item cluttering the cutlery drawer.

Forks and Blenders

Pastry forks and pastry blenders are utensils made primarily for cutting fat into flour for biscuits and pastry. Both are dispensable, because the same operation can be performed with a kitchen fork, two table knives, or two spatulas.

Purposes

There are three main objectives of combining ingredients for batters and doughs. One is to achieve uniform distribution of the leavening gas throughout the batter. This objective is achieved by sifting the leaven with the flour and other dry ingredients. A second is to distribute the fat uniformly throughout the flour. Plastic fat can be cut in for biscuits and pastry and for muffins made by the biscuit method. It can be creamed with sugar as for cakes. Finally, it can be melted or an oil used and added to the flour along with the liquid ingredients. The distribution of fat by this last method is the least uniform of the three, but it is speedy. It is the way fat is incorporated in batters made by the muffin method. A third objective of the manipulation of batters is to achieve a uniform distribution of liquid. Liquid and dry ingredients are stirred to distribute the water. This also helps to dissolve the salt, the sugar, and the acid and soda in baking powder. Stirring gives cohesiveness to the mixture and actually forms the batter or dough. This should be accomplished with the minimum loss of leavening gas and without making the mixture too viscous.

Knowing how much to manipulate a batter or dough requires experience. Directions such as "stir until the ball of dough leaves the sides of the pan," "barely dampen the ingredients," or "cut until the mixture resembles coarse corn meal" require subjective criteria that can come only from experience. It is impossible to specify in directions the precise number of strokes to produce the best product. The optimum amount of manipulation is influenced by the volume of the mix, the size and shape of the bowl, the effectiveness of the mixing utensil, and whether the strokes are vigorous or weak. Specifying the number of strokes is preferable to specifying a time, as the number of strokes by hand in a given time varies. However, strokes are not equally vigorous. Even with a hand-operated rotary beater and the same number of strokes, the speed at which the beater is turned will make some difference in the results. The extent of manipulation may be duplicated by timing with an electric mixer, but bowls, beaters, and the efficiency of mixers differ.

BAKING QUICK BREADS

Before an oven is used, the accuracy of the setting of the thermostat should be checked by means of an oven thermometer. Directions for adjusting the thermostat are usually included in the operating instructions that come with the range. The temperature is likely to be most uniform in the center of the oven, although ovens are not precision instruments and small variations in temperature are to be expected.

Placement of the racks should be checked before the oven is turned on. (Fig. 4-2). The baking utensil (not the rack) should be centered in the oven to assure uniform heating. If the utensil is deep, the rack should be placed below the center position. Baking pans are usually oiled to keep food from sticking. Only that part of a baking utensil that will be in contact with the baked product should be oiled. Fat on exposed surfaces of the pan gets so hot that it polymerizes. The result is a thick, gummy layer. Scouring will remove this or the utensil may be soaked in hot water to which ammonia has been added. However, soaking with ammonia will discolor utensils made of aluminum. *Teflon** (a fluorocarbon resin) and similar coatings on baking utensils eliminate the need for oiling. The lining fills the pits in the metal that otherwise would cause baked products to stick.

---

*Registered trademark for DuPont's TFE nonstick finish.

Baking Time and Temperature

Most quick breads are baked in a hot oven, at least during the early part of the baking period. Aside from oven temperature, the baking time depends upon the material from which the baking utensil is made (Chapter 4) and upon the size and shape of the utensil. Heat moves to the center of the product mainly by conduction, a slow process at best, further slowed down by the innumerable bubbles of gas in the batter or dough. The temperature in the interior of a baked product only gets to approximately that of boiling water even though the food is baked in a hot oven.

Changes Effected in Batters and Doughs

Early in the baking period the fat begins to melt if it is not already liquid. The mix becomes more fluid. Substances soluble only in hot water begin to dissolve. Baking powder continues to form carbon dioxide. Heat causes both carbon dioxide and air in the batter to expand. Proteins of flour and eggs, if present, begin to set as the temperature in the mix rises. The starch begins to gelatinize. Part of the water is converted to steam that provides additional leaven and further inflates the product. When the heat penetrates the interior, the structure of the baked product is set because of the coagulation of the protein and the gelatinization of the starch. Finally, evaporation of water from the surface slows and the surface gets hot enough to brown.

INDIVIDUAL QUICK BREADS

Formulas

Formulas for five quick breads—popovers, cream puffs, muffins, biscuits, and waffles—are given in Table 13-1.

Popovers

Proportions

Equal parts flour and liquid used in popovers give a thin or pour batter. Such a batter can be used to make timbale cases and Yorkshire pudding as well as popovers or as a cover for apple fritters or French fried onion rings (Chapter 15, on fats). Crêpes are made from a similar batter except that the proportion of egg is slightly higher. The proportion of ingredients in popovers is far more critical than the technique of combining them. The protein of egg white is the ingredient that is essential if popovers are to pop, so size of the eggs is important. Proportion of liquid to flour is also important. Too much liquid produces a batter so weak that the protein is unable to hold the steam. Too little liquid yields a tight batter with insufficient steam to inflate it. Too much fat, either added to the batter or used to oil the baking utensil, will weaken the batter and cause loss of steam and poor volume.

Manipulation

No special technique or precautions are necessary to make popover batter. A spoon, spring whip, rotary beater, or blender may be used to combine the ingredients to form a smooth batter.

Baking

Special baking utensils are unnecessary for popovers. Muffin or custard cups may be used. The depth of the cup that holds the batter is important. This influences the amount of popover that the steam can support above the top of the utensil. Popovers baked in shallow utensils do not pop well.

A hot oven is used during the first part of the baking period to vaporize the water and inflate the batter. Then the heat is reduced to moderate to coagulate the protein and gelatinize the starch and so set the batter without unduly browning the popovers. Popovers will collapse if the oven is opened and the steam is permitted to condense before the batter gets hot enough to set. The photographs in Figure 13-2 illustrate six stages in the conversion of popover batter to the baked product.

Characteristics

Popovers are golden-brown, tender, crisp shells. The interior is divided by fairly thin, slightly moist, but thoroughly cooked partitions.

Cream Puffs

Proportions

Cream puffs are made with the same ratio of liquid to flour as popovers but contain eight times as much fat. The high proportion of fat makes cream puffs more tender and richer than popovers just as extra fat and sugar make a cake more tender and richer than muffins. More eggs are required in cream puffs than in popovers because of the large amount of fat in the former. Less salt is added to cream puffs to allow for the salt contributed by the large amount of salted table fat.

Manipulation

To make the paste for cream puffs, the flour is added to the rapidly boiling water–melted fat mixture in a sauce pan. The flour does not lump because the melted fat that floats on the surface of the water coats the flour before it comes in contact with the boiling water. When the liquid and flour are cooked to make cream puff paste, the mixture becomes thick, due to the gelatinization of the starch in the flour. The same thing happens in the thin popover batter when it is baked. Although cream puff paste does not have lumps, it does have a curdled appearance at this stage because the fat does not blend with the water. After the eggs are beaten into the cooked paste, the batter takes on a smooth, glossy appearance. Egg yolk contains emulsifier, mainly lipoproteins, molecules of which have an affinity for both water and fat and so effectively unite the two. Instead of being in two phases, the gelatinized starch in-water phase and the melted fat scattered-about-in-lakes phase, the two are intimately combined through the intermediary supplied by the egg yolk. In addition to emulsifier, eggs contribute protein, which confers on the cooked paste the ability to stretch (12) under the pressure of the evolving steam formed during baking. The proteins of egg white are particularly effective for this purpose.

If too much water is boiled away when cream puff paste is cooked, the flour will absorb most of the remaining water. This gives a paste that is too stiff, with little water free to form steam to leaven the product. As a result, the cream puff paste does not puff

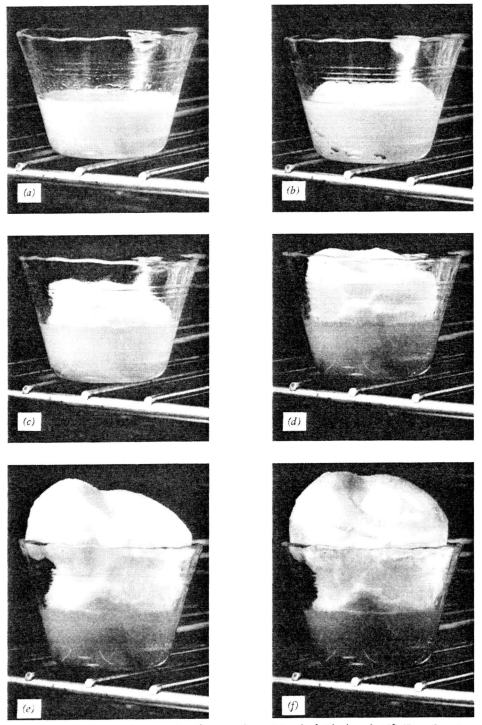

Figure 13-2. Stages in the conversion of popover batter (*a*) to the finished product (*f*). (From *Sunset*. May 1963. Darrow M. Watt, Photographer, 188 Felton Drive, Menlo Park, CA.)

during baking. Failure of the batter to lose its curdled appearance after the egg is added is an indication that too much water has been evaporated. To remedy this, hot water should be stirred in gradually until the paste appears glossy. Fat oozing from the paste during baking is another indication of a deficiency of water in the batter as is failure of the cream puffs to rise.

Too much water in the paste keeps it from rising, also, because the paste is too fluid to retain the steam. After the eggs are beaten into the cooked paste, it should be stiff enough to be transferred to the baking sheet with a spoon and should not flatten on the baking sheet. The proportion of fat is important, too. Fat enables the paste to give with pressure; with too little fat the paste cannot expand, whereas with excess fat too much steam escapes. Either way the paste fails to rise sufficiently.

Baking

Cream puffs, like popovers, are baked in a very hot oven for a few minutes so they will rise. Baking then continues in a slow oven to complete coagulation of the protein and gelatinization of the starch. Like popovers, cream puffs will collapse if the steam that inflated them condenses before the structure is set.

Characteristics

Cream puffs of high quality, like popovers, are hollow shells. The crust is crisp and more tender than that of popovers due to a large amount of finely dispersed fat. Interior partitions are thin, tender, and crisp.

Muffins

Proportions

Muffins are made from a drop batter of two parts all-purpose flour to one of liquid. A basic recipe contains one egg for each two cups of flour. Proportions of fat and sugar increase from a lean to a rich muffin. Most recipes call for 1½ to 2 teaspoons of baking powder for each cup of flour. Muffins made from cake or pastry instead of all-purpose flour should have the proportions of flour increased or the milk reduced, or both (5). Substituting legume flour—cowpea or peanut—for approximately 25 percent of wheat flour in muffins appears to be the upper limit to give an acceptable product (4). Flours that contained on a weight basis 25 percent dietary fiber (α-cellulose, oat hull, and bran from corn, rice, soy, and two varieties of wheat yielded acceptable muffins only with corn bran and the two wheat brans (9).

Manipulation

The baking powder should be sifted with the flour or stirred in thoroughly to ensure uniform distribution. This is essential for uniform gas cells, that is, grain, in the crumb of the baked muffin. The egg and milk should be blended thoroughly but without beating up a foam. The protein of the egg is needed primarily as a binding or structural ingredient and not as a means of incorporating air. If the egg is not blended thoroughly with the milk, it will be unevenly distributed and the crumb around part of the gas cells will be thick and tough. The muffin method of combining ingredients calls for the addition to the dry ingredients of fat in the liquid state at the same time that the milk and egg mixture is added. Alternately, plastic fat may be cut into the sifted dry ingredients before the liquids are added.

The ratio of liquid to flour in muffin batter is ideal for the development of gluten, especially when all-purpose flour is used. It is easy to overstir muffin batter and develop more gluten than is desirable. Muffins made from soft wheat flour (pastry or cake) tolerate more mixing and are still fine grained and tender. Muffin batter low in fat or sugar should be stirred only enough to barely dampen the dry ingredients. It will still be lumpy. Otherwise, too much gluten will be formed and the batter will be too elastic. Bubbles of carbon dioxide trapped in a too elastic batter will be retained and become very large (11). Confined by the walls of the muffin pan, the only way the bubbles can expand is upward. Thus they tend to be oriented from the bottom to the top of the muffin. These elongated gas cells are called tunnels (Fig. 13-3). When they form inside a muffin, it has a peaked top. Sometimes the unbaked batter pushes through the top crust that has begun to set.

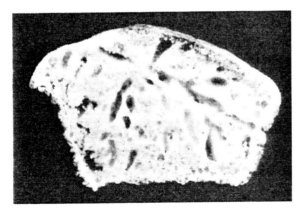

Figure 13-3. Structure of the crumb of muffins from batter stirred the optimum (top) and from overstirred batter (bottom). (From E. G. Halliday and I. T. Noble. *Hows and Whys of Cooking.* 1946. University of Chicago Press. Reprinted by permission of Isabel Noble.)

Because both fat and sugar interfere with the development of gluten, rich muffin batter not only can tolerate more manipulation but actually needs more. Muffin batter needs some gluten to give gas-retaining properties essential for a good volume in the baked product. It is an art to know by the look and feel of muffin batter at which stroke to stop stirring. The best way to acquire this art is to remove enough batter for a muffin, at successive stages in the mixing of the liquid and dry ingredients, and relate the characteristics of the baked muffin with those of the batter from which it came.

Once the muffin batter has been mixed, it should be transferred to oiled, paper-lined, or Teflon-coated baking cups at once; otherwise, more of the carbon dioxide liberated in the batter will be lost during the transfer. The batter can stand in the baking utensil for a few minutes before baking without detriment to the quality of the baked product.

Baking

Muffins are baked in a hot oven (218°C or 425°F). The baking time depends on the size of the muffin cups as well as the material from which the utensil is made. The small diameter of the cups of a muffin pan and the high baking temperature may contribute to the formation of tunnels.

Muffins can be removed from the pan more easily if they are allowed to stand for a minute or two after they come from the oven. The steam that condenses facilitates their removal. Leaving them in the tins too long, however, will cause them to be soggy. It is to avoid condensation of moisture as well as cooling that muffins and other hot breads are served on a plate or tray lined with a cloth napkin.

Characteristics

Muffins should have a thin, uniformly golden-brown crust. The top should be symmetrical, with a contour similar to a head of cauliflower (See center muffin in Fig. 13-4). The holes in the crumb should be round and medium sized and the cell walls fairly thin, like the upper muffin shown in Figure 13-3. The richer the batter, the smaller are the gas cells and the thinner the walls. The muffin should be light and the crumb tender. Indications

Figure 13-4. The cauliflower-shaped top of the muffin in the center indicates optimum manipulation and optimum amount of liquid in the batter. The rough top and lower volume of the muffin on the left indicates a deficiency of liquid or of manipulation. Overmanipulation or too much liquid could cause the slick top of the muffin on the right. The peak suggests overmanipulation. (Courtesy of Andrea Mackey and the Oregon Agricultural Experiment Station.)

of an understirred muffin are low volume, coarse crumb, flat, ricey top, and brown specks from undissolved baking soda. Tunnels, a peaked top, and pale, slick crust are indicative of overstirred muffin batter.

Biscuits

Proportions

Biscuits are from a soft dough, made with three parts flour to one of liquid. In addition to leaven and salt, biscuits contain from 2⅓ to 3 tablespoons of fat per cup of flour. For biscuits, a plastic fat apparently is a better shortening than a liquid fat (8). The ratio of liquid to flour in biscuits is a critical one. The softer the dough the better, provided the dough can be kneaded. Variations in the moisture-absorbing capacity of flours make it impossible to state in a recipe the precise amount of liquid. The amount of milk per cup of all-purpose flour falls between ⅓ cup and ⅜ cup.

Manipulation

For biscuits as for muffins, the baking powder is sifted with the flour to obtain a uniformly fine grain. Plastic fat is cut into the dry ingredients until the mixture resembles coarse cornmeal. A pastry fork, pastry blender, or two knives may be used to cut in the fat. Milk is added next, all at once, in the optimum amount for the moisture-absorbing capacity of the flour. The milk should be dispersed in the dry ingredients at once, with a fork. Stirring should continue until the mixture stiffens perceptibly. Stirring helps dissolve the salt and the acid and soda in the baking powder, dampens the flour, and forms the dough. For a dough made with two cups of flour approximately 20 to 30 strokes are necessary. The exact number depends on the size and shape of the mixing bowl, the quantity of dough, the kind of milk used, and the effectiveness of the stirring strokes.

Once the dough stiffens and loses some of its stickiness, it may be turned onto a *lightly* floured bread board or other suitable surface and kneaded 10 to 20 times to develop the desirable amount of cohesiveness. Because of the low ratio of liquid to flour in biscuit dough, gluten is slow to develop. Unlike muffin batter, where the common fault is overstirring, biscuit dough is likely to be undermanipulated. Biscuit dough not only tolerates but requires more manipulation. It is the total that counts: If biscuit dough is understirred in the bowl, it should be kneaded more.

The technique for handling biscuit dough is harder to acquire than is that for muffin batter. The ability to recognize when biscuit dough has been manipulated the optimum amount comes with experience. This can be achieved by removing a biscuit at a time from the dough as kneading proceeds. Again the object is to associate the characteristics of the baked biscuit with the way the dough handles and looks.

Biscuit dough with a high proportion of fat requires more manipulation, as does that slightly deficient in liquid. If the amount of milk is skimpy for the quantity of flour or for its moisture-absorbing capacity, the dough will be stiff. A stiff dough requires more manipulation to develop the desired amount of gluten. The dough is too tight to stretch, the biscuit does not rise as much as it should, and cracks appear on the sides. The crumb of the biscuit is dry, compact, and crumbly. Brown specks are likely to appear in the crust of the biscuit. The more milk in biscuit dough, the quicker the optimum amount of gluten develops. A slight excess of milk is preferable to too little. With too much liquid, the dough may be too sticky to handle. In this case, it may be stirred more in the bowl, instead of kneaded, and the dough dropped by the spoonful onto an oiled baking sheet.

Unless the dough is stirred and kneaded sufficiently to dissolve the acid and baking soda, part of the latter may be unneutralized. When this sodium bicarbonate is heated during baking, sodium carbonate is formed. This results in yellow spots in the crumb and brown spots on the crust.

When the dough is kneaded sufficiently, biscuits can be cut and placed on a baking sheet and allowed to stand at least 15 minutes before they are baked. Standing for this length of time at room temperature does no harm, and if held in the refrigerator the quality of the biscuits may be improved (6). They are not so likely to have brown spots on the crust, attributed to the reaction between undissolved monocalcium phosphate from the baking powder and carbohydrates in the flour. Unbaked biscuits should be covered with a cloth or waxed paper to prevent the surface from becoming dry.

Baking

Biscuits are baked in a hot oven (218°C or 425°F) for 12 to 15 minutes. Alternately, dough may be dropped in boiling liquid and steamed, in which case the product is called dumplings. The liquid may be meat broth, soups such as tomato and mushroom, or cooked fruit such as cherries, berries, or a medley of cooked, dried fruit.

Characteristics

If biscuits are made with sour milk and baking powder, the crumb in the interior will be snowy white, owing to the lowered pH, and it will be fine and moist. With an excess of baking soda the crumb of the biscuit is yellow; it tends to be coarse and have a slightly soapy taste because of the sodium carbonate produced from the unneutralized baking soda. Excess soda causes the crust to be too brown. A biscuit made with a high proportion of fat has a fine grain and a tender crumb. Biscuits made with SAS-phosphate baking powder frequently have deep cracks along the side (3), indicating some inability of the dough to stretch during baking.

A biscuit of high quality has a golden-brown crust without brown specks. The biscuit is symmetrical, with a smooth, level top and straight sides. (Fig. 13-5a). The crust is crisp and tender. The crumb should be white to creamy white, fine grained, moist, and fluffy, and should peel off in layers. A dry, crumbly crumb results from too little liquid or too little manipulation or both. In any case, the biscuit is likely to be low in volume. With too much liquid, the biscuit is likely to have a rounded top, which also may result from too much manipulation.

Griddle Cakes and Waffles

A pour batter is used for griddle cakes and waffles. Usually the ingredients are combined as for muffins. Frequently the beaten egg whites are folded into the batter at the end of the mixing. The same batter may be used for both griddle cakes and waffles. For the former, the batter is poured onto a preheated griddle, two tablespoons or more, depending on the diameter of the cake desired. The iron is hot enough to cook the griddle cakes when a drop of cold water snaps as it contacts the iron. If the batter contains fat, oiling the iron is

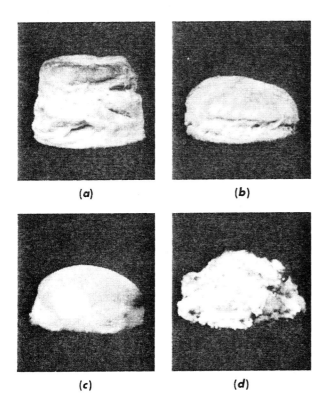

(a)

(b)

(c)

(d)

Figure 13-5. Variations in the quality of biscuits as affected by manipulation. (a) Optimum manipulation gives a biscuit with a flat top, straight sides, and good volume. (b) Low volume and rounded but rough top characterize biscuits from undermanipulated dough. (c) A biscuit with low volume and a smooth, rounded top results from overmanipulation of the dough, especially if a slight excess of liquid has been used. (d) Drop biscuits made intentionally or because the dough is too sticky to handle have a rough exterior and a crunchy crust. (Courtesy of the United States Department of Agriculture.)

unnecessary. Griddle cakes should be turned when the gas cells on the upper surface break. Griddle cakes should have a smooth, evenly browned surface with few pits. The crumb should be fine grained, moist, tender, and light.

Waffles should be baked in a preconditioned iron. The grids on a new waffle iron usually are preconditioned. Should batter stick to the grids, they should be removed, soaked in hot water, and then washed, rinsed, and dried. To recondition the grids, the waffle iron is heated and the grids brushed with unsalted fat. The iron is closed, heated to baking temperature, and left on for approximately 10 minutes. Heating polymerizes the fat that has filled the pores in the iron. This keeps the batter from sticking. The iron is allowed to cool naturally, after which it is ready for use. A griddle iron may be conditioned in the same way except that the iron is heated in a moderately hot oven for approximately 10 minutes.

The temperature of most waffle irons is thermostatically controlled. When the light on the preheated waffle iron indicates "Bake," batter is poured into the center of each section, with enough space around the edges for expansion of the batter as it bakes. The waffle should bake in approximately three minutes. It is done when steam no longer escapes from the iron. Waffles may stick to the iron if there is insufficient fat in the batter or if the waffle iron is either too hot or too cold when the batter is poured in. If the hinge on the iron is too stiff, the waffle will tend to be soggy. If the indentations on the iron are deep and close together, the waffle tends to be crisp; shallower ones far apart produce a softer waffle. Gingerbread batter, biscuit dough, and French toast may be cooked on a waffle iron.

REFERENCES

1. Bowman, F., and E. Dyar. 1951. "Quick mixes for high-altitude baking." *Colorado Agricultural Experiment Station Bulletin* 415-A. 34 pp. Recipes adapted for 5,000, 7,500, and 10,000 feet.

2. Boyd, S., and M. C. Schoonover. 1965. "Baking at high altitude." *Wyoming Agricultural Experiment Station Bulletin* No. 427. 71 pp. Cakes, cookies, and quick breads for 5,000 and 7,000 feet.

3. Briant, A. M. and M. R. Hutchins. 1946. "Influence of ingredients in thiamine retention and quality in baking powder biscuits." *Cereal Chemistry* 23:512–20. Effects of different types and levels of baking powder on hydrogen-ion concentration of biscuits, on quality of dough, and on retention of thiamine.

4. Holt, S. D., K. H. Mowatters, and A. V. A. Resurreccion. 1992. "Validation of predicted baking performance of muffins containing mixtures of wheat, cowpea, peanut, sorghum and cassava flours." *Journal of Food Science* 57:470–74. Composite flours with ⅔ vs ¾ wheat flour.

5. Mackey, A., M. Strauss, and J. Stockman. "Soft wheat flour muffins." *Oregon Agricultural Experiment Station Circular of Information* 547.

6. Maclay, E. 1926. "The effect of delayed baking on biscuits." *Journal of Home Economics* 18:157. Effects of holding temperature and time on unbaked biscuits and of holding time on refrigerated dough.

7. Matthews, R. M. and E. H. Dawson. 1963. "Performance of fats and oils in pastry and biscuits." *Cereal Chemistry* 40:291–302. Tenderness and flavor of products made with five levels each of three oils and three fats.

8. Peterson, M. W. 1930. "Baking flour mixtures at high altitudes." *Colorado Agricultural Experiment Station Bulletin* 365. 180. Report of experimental work on baking from the high-altitude laboratory; recipes for elevations of 3000 to 11,000 feet.

9. Polizzotto, L. M., A. M. Tinsley, C. W. Walker, and J. W. Berry. 1983. "Dietary fiber in muffins." *Journal of Food Science* 48:111–13, 118. Seven dietary fibers compared.

10. Sunderlin, G. 1952. "Master mix." *Purdue University Agriculture Extension Bulletin* 344. 16 pp. Proportions for the mix and recipes for its use.

11. Trimbo, Henry B. and Bryon S. Miller. 1973. "The development of tunnels in cakes." *Bakers Digest* 47(4):24–26, 71. Contributing factors.

12. Wheeler, F. G. 1946. "Cream puff troubles are overcome by test studies." *Food Industries* 18:88–90. Functions of ingredients; common faults and their causes.

Yeast Breads ## 14

Yeast breads are made from soft dough leavened with carbon dioxide formed by microorganisms. Yeast dough is a foam. Bubbles of carbon dioxide are surrounded by or trapped in the dough. The ingredients, their proportions, and the way they are handled all interact to influence the characteristics of the dough in which the bubbles of gas are generated. These, in turn, influence the quality of the product obtained when heat converts a mobile foam into a rigid yet deformable sponge.

INGREDIENTS AND THEIR FUNCTIONS

Flour, liquid, yeast, and salt are essential ingredients in yeast dough. Sugar and fat, although not absolutely necessary, are usually included. Eggs are optional.

Yeast

In addition to producing carbon dioxide (Chapter 12), which inflates dough, yeast modifies the rheological properties of the dough. Carbon dioxide dissolves in the aqueous phase of dough, forming carbonic acid. As yeast ferments the sugar in dough, bacteria associated with the yeast produce lactic and acetic acids (14) in a ratio of 3:1. Some acid in yeast dough is desirable because it favors both fermentation and the action of amylases. Acids produced during fermentation lower the pH of yeast dough from near 6.0 to 5.6 to 5.0, shifting the pH closer to the isoelectric point (Chapter 18) of gluten. At this pH, gluten is less soluble, less sticky, and more elastic. Yeast dough is easier to handle after it has fermented.

In addition to producing carbon dioxide, yeast produces an enzyme that can hydrolyze the phytin of flour. The end products, unlike phytin, do not bond with and so make unavailable minerals such as calcium, iron, and zinc (10).

Flour

Both the quality and quantity of gluten that a flour yields are important in bread making. Harder wheat flours tolerate and even require more manipulation than do softer wheat flours. Bread flour produces bread of superior grain and texture and maximum volume, especially when made under commercial conditions. All-purpose flour makes excellent yeast breads or rolls, although the dough has less tolerance to mixing and to the stress of over-fermentation compared to dough from hard wheat flour. Dough conditioners, such as sodium stearoyl lactylate, strengthen dough and increase its resistance to mixing and its ability to retain leavening gases and yield a symmetrical loaf of high volume (32, 37).

Although the gluten-forming potential of wheat flour is emphasized in bread making, the importance of the starch should not be overlooked. Unlike gluten, no satisfactory substitute has been found for starch. The starch granules from wheat and those from rye and barley appear uniquely suitable for the formation of yeast dough and bread (15). Starch granules in bread dough are embedded in the gluten around the gas cells, an estimated twenty thousand or more per gas cell (6). In bread, these starch granules, now gelatinized, give rigidity to the crumb. Starch has another role in breadmaking. It is a source of fermentable sugar.

Yeast cells need sugar to produce carbon dioxide, but too much sugar (above 10 percent based on the weight of the flour) in the dough at one time retards fermentation (4). Yeast cells do best with a continuously replenished supply of fermentable sugar. Ability of flour to support fermentation depends upon the presence of two starch-hydrolyzing enzymes—alpha amylase and beta amylase (25). Most wheats contain sufficient beta-amylase. This enzyme frees molecules of the disaccharide maltose by catalyzing the hydrolysis of the α-1,4 glycosidic linkages, beginning at the reducing end of the starch polymer (24). Once the branching points in amylopectin are reached, hydrolysis by beta-amylase, known as an exoenzyme, stops. The resulting polymer, a stubbier, shrubby-looking residue, is called limit dextrin. Alpha amylase, unlike beta amylase, can attack undamaged starch granules, but the amount of alpha amylase in flour is variable and insufficient. When flour is milled, it is tested for alpha amylase activity (gassing power) and a sufficient quantity of this enzyme from malted grain is added. Both amylases catalyze the hydrolysis of the α-1,4 glycosidic linkage but alpha amylase does so at random in both amylopectin and amylose molecules. Beta amylase can then hydrolyze molecules of maltose from the amylopectin fragments. Alpha amylase thus makes more of the starch available for fermentation by yeast. Cooked potato starch is readily attacked by amylases, which explains why water in which potatoes have been cooked is sometimes used in making yeast dough. Other nutrient substances leached from cells of the potato favor fermentation, too. The flour itself provides nutrients needed by the yeast.

Liquid

Water may be used as the liquid in yeast dough, although milk, either fluid or nonfat dry milk plus water, is usually used. Milk increases food value and also delays staling of bread. Liquid dissolves salt and sugar and aids in dispersing the yeast cells through the flour. It also serves as a means for transporting food to yeast through cell membranes. Water is essential for the hydrolysis of both starch and sucrose. Water lowers the glass transition temperature of gluten, which changes from a rigid glass to a flowable rubber at room temperature (15, 17). Water also makes possible the manipulation of flour to form a viscoelastic dough. Water is essential for the gelatinization of starch when the dough is baked, and the steam it provides contributes to expansion in the oven.

Salt

Salt has more important functions in yeast dough than improving the taste of the baked product. Some salt in dough favors the action of amylases and thus helps to maintain a supply of maltose as food for the yeast. Salt inhibits the action of proteases (protein splitting enzymes) of the flour, which otherwise would depolymerize proteins of the gluten complex. In addition, salt acts directly on gluten. Sodium ions interact with amide groups and strengthen the polypeptide polymer (15). Yeast dough without salt is sticky and difficult to manipulate. The weak gluten permits gas cells to overexpand during fermentation. Additional expansion of the cells and extensive rupture as the dough bakes give a moth-eaten appearance to the bread. Salt does, however, slow the production of carbon dioxide by the yeast. Presumably it is an osmotic effect that limits the net flow of water into the yeast cells (5). For this reason a lower proportion of salt to flour is used in yeast dough compared with quick breads. If yeast dough rises very rapidly and it is sticky and hard to handle, it is possible that salt was omitted. However, both stickiness and rapid rising may result from allowing the dough to rise at too high a temperature. Bread made without salt for individuals on a salt-free diet is inferior in grain and texture.

Sugar

Sugar is included in dough for yeast bread mainly to serve as a readily available source of fermentable sugar (5). Flour contains only a small amount of sucrose (approximately one percent). During the first few minutes after a dough is mixed a high percentage of the sucrose is hydrolyzed to invert sugar (4, 29). In the absence of added sugar, production of carbon dioxide by yeast cells is limited and delayed, pending hydrolysis of starch in the flour to maltose by amylases (5). Reducing sugars that remain in the dough when it goes into the oven aid in browning and also flavor the product.

Fat

The glycolipids of flour are essential for the formation of gluten. (Chapter 11). Including fat in yeast dough is optional because bread can be made without it. Fat does make the product more tender, the crust brown better, and the volume larger. One explanation for the increased volume is that the added fat slows the early loss of carbon dioxide from dough as it bakes, apparently by counteracting the deleterious effects on gluten of one fraction of flour lipids (13). Another explanation is that fat acts as a plasticizer for gluten, enabling dough to remain mobile longer and so expand more as it bakes (35). Vegetable oils rather than plastic shortening are widely used in commercial breads and similar bakery products. A dough conditioner or a combination of conditioners included in the formula adequately substitutes for the solid phase of plastic shortening (21).

Yeast

A certain amount of carbon dioxide is needed to make dough rise. The more yeast cells added to the dough, the sooner will the required amount of carbon dioxide be produced. The amount of yeast used for each 125 milliliters (½ cup) of liquid may vary from ⅓ to 1⅓ cakes or packages. When one cake or package of dry yeast is used with 125 milliliters (½ cup) of liquid and 375 milliliters or 175 grams (1½ cups) of flour, dough needs approximately one hour to rise the first time and approximately ½ hour after it has been shaped and placed in the baking pan (Table 14-1). The fermentation time may be shorter (up to 50 percent) when instant dry yeast is used.

Too little yeast and the dough takes a long time to rise; too much yeast and the dough is inflated before other essential changes take place in the dough. An excess may make the product taste yeasty. A higher proportion of yeast is used when the time available for making

TABLE 14-1
Approximate Fermentation Schedule at 27°C (80°F)

Yeast	Liquid	First Rising[b]	Second Rising[c]	Rising in Pan[b]
⅓ cake or package yeast[a]	½ cup (125 ml)	2 hr	1 hr	1 hr
⅔ cake or package yeast	½ cup (125 ml)	1½ hr	45 min	45 min
1 cake or package yeast	½ cup (125 ml)	1 hr	15 min	35 min
1⅓ cakes or packages yeast	½ cup (125 ml)	25 min	5 min	30 min

[a]One package of dry yeast weighs 7 grams.
[b]Fermentation time for instant dry yeast may be 50 percent shorter.
[c]Omit for soft wheat flour; optional for all-purpose flour; recommended for hard wheat flour.
Source: Adapted from Belle Lowe. Experimental Cookery. Copyright © 1955 by John Wiley & Sons, Inc. New York. Reprinted by permission.

yeast bread is limited. Time permitting, less yeast and a somewhat longer fermentation time makes better bread unless the flour yields weak gluten. Cells from a cake of compressed or active dry yeast do not produce carbon dioxide readily at the start of fermentation. Dough is slow to rise at first, but it picks up momentum as fermentation proceeds because the cells become more active. A higher proportion of yeast is indicated in sweet dough to compensate for the effect of high concentrations of sugar on rate of fermentation. If a package of dry yeast is opened, the unused portion should be stored in a closed container in the refrigerator. The useful life of dry yeast is indicated by an expiration date stamped on the package.

Eggs

Many yeast breads are made without eggs. When eggs are included in dough, they make the product look and taste richer. The protein of the egg gives additional stretchability to the dough without making it sticky.

PROPORTIONS OF INGREDIENTS

Flour to Liquid

Approximately three volumes of flour to one of liquid are used to make the soft dough for yeast breads. The optimum amount of flour depends upon its moisture-holding capacity. Bread dough contains approximately 40 percent water. Doughs from strong flours can carry more liquid than can those from weak flours. If the milk for yeast dough is measured before it is scalded, the volume that remains is unknown; loss of moisture by evaporation may be as high as 25 percent if the starting volume is low. In this event, the flour should be reduced to compensate. A dough that contains too much flour is stiff, inelastic, and slow to rise. Expansion of the dough during baking is limited. Cells in the bread are small with thick cell walls. The volume is small as a consequence. The higher the ratio of liquid to flour the better, provided the dough is not too sticky to handle.

Salt and Sugar

For reasons explained earlier, the ratio of salt to flour is critical in yeast dough. Less salt per cup of flour is used in yeast dough than in quick breads. The amount of salt usually does not exceed two percent of the weight of the flour (5).

When only the small amount of fermentable sugar supplied by the flour is available to the yeast, fermentation is slow to start. As the amount of sugar included in yeast dough increases fermentation proceeds more rapidly. Yeast dough made with ½ tablespoon (7 milliliters or 2 grams) of sugar per 1½ to 1¾ cups (375 milliliters or 175 grams) of flour (a ½-pound loaf of bread) has approximately four percent of sugar. For rolls the amount of sugar may be doubled, and for sweet rolls it may be quadrupled. When the level of sugar in yeast dough exceeds 10 percent, the production of carbon dioxide by the yeast is inhibited (4). Dough for sweet rolls is slow to rise. Presumably a high concentration of sugar limits the entry of water and nutrients into the yeast cells by an osmotic effect. Reducing the amount of salt in a very sweet dough will help to compensate for the effects of high levels of sugar (greater than 10 percent of the weight of flour) on the rate of fermentation. Increasing the yeast is another means of maintaining a desirable rate of fermentation in sweet dough. A high proportion of sugar in dough delays the uptake of water by flour (4). Sweet doughs should be mixed or kneaded longer as a consequence. Fat may be increased in yeast dough without prolonging fermentation unduly.

MANIPULATION OF YEAST DOUGH

Basic Methods

Ingredients for yeast dough may be combined by the straight-dough or the sponge method (13). When bread is made by the straight-dough method, all of the ingredients are combined and the dough is kneaded before it is allowed to rise. The short-time method is a variation of the straight-dough method. A faster mixing speed and higher levels of both oxidant and yeast are used. As a result, fermentation time can be reduced or eliminated (39). When dough is made by the sponge method, the yeast, dispersed in the liquid, and part of the flour are combined. Addition of part of the sugar is optional. This batter is allowed to rise until it becomes spongy and light. The remainder of the ingredients are stirred into the sponge and the dough is then kneaded and allowed to rise as in the straight-dough method. The yeast cells while they are in the sponge adjust to fermenting maltose.

Scalding the Milk

Milk used to make yeast dough should be heated; otherwise, the dough is slack and sticky and the bread is coarse and of poor volume. One or more constituents of the serum proteins of milk are believed to be responsible (18), but neither the loaf-depressant factor nor the protein(s) responsible for the slackness of dough have been identified unequivocally (38). (Milk proteins are discussed in Chapter 19.) Nonfat dried milk available for commercial baking has had more severe heat treatment than has that available at the grocery store (23). When fluid milk is used to make breads, it should be scalded. Scalding may be accomplished by heating milk to a high temperature for a short time (92°C or 198°F, for one minute) or for a longer time at a lower temperature (85°C or 185°F, for seven minutes) (23). Insufficient heating of milk for bread making does more harm than good (18). Sugar and salt dissolve more quickly while the milk is hot and the fat melts more readily. Scalded milk should be cooled to near 37°C (98°F) and, preferably, to near 27°C (80°F) before the yeast is added because the cells are quite sensitive to heat. Yeast cells are unable to survive a temperature of 54.4°C (130°F), known as the thermal death point.

Dispersing the Yeast

One objective in combining ingredients for yeast dough is to distribute the cells of yeast evenly through the dough. To this end, the yeast, compressed cake, or active dry, is put into liquid to separate the cells, which can then be distributed via the water. The liquid should be no hotter than 37°C (98.6°F) when compressed yeast is used. Active dry yeast is put in water instead of milk to permit the cells of yeast to rehydrate. Yeast cells have an outer membrane that encloses the living protoplasm. When the moisture content of active dry yeast cells is reduced to eight percent, the permeability of this membrane is altered so constituents that diffuse from the cells make the dough soft and sticky (30). The temperature of the water used to rehydrate active dry yeast is critical. Directions on the package specify a range in temperature of 40° to 46°C (105° to 115°F) for the water. This range is optimum for returning to the cell membrane its normal and original permeability. Water much hotter will harm the yeast. If the water is cooler than 40°C (105°F), a substance detrimental to the quality of the dough diffuses from the cells. The offender appears to be glutathione, a reducing substance that breaks disulfide bonds in glutenin. Instant dry yeast rehydrates so rapidly that it can be added directly to flour without prior soaking. Dead yeast cells from compressed yeast cake held too long or at too high a temperature affect dough in the same way as active dry yeast hydrated below 40°C (104°F).

Combining Flour and Liquid

Once yeast is dispersed in liquid (or distributed in flour), enough flour to form a soft dough is combined with the liquid in the straight-dough method, or approximately half that amount for the sponge method. The sponge batter is allowed to stand until it becomes foamy and light, after which the remainder of the flour is added (14). The last portions of flour should be added only if needed to prevent the dough from being too sticky to handle. The constituents of flour take up water at different rates. If dough is permitted to stand for five minutes after the last addition of flour, it will lose some of its stickiness. Excess flour yields a stiff, lifeless dough. A minimum of flour produces superior bread with fine grain and texture, and large volume.

Dough Development

A coherent but sticky mass forms when water is first combined with flour. Absorption of plasticizing water by particles of flour lowers the glass transition temperature of gluten so at room temperature the gluten has changed from a rigid glass to a flexible rubber that can be manipulated (7, 15). Work is required to convert the hydrated particles of flour into viscoelastic dough (24). Resistance of wetted flour particles to manipulation increases as dough develops up to a point (36), as shown by the mixogram curve in Figure 11-13. This peak indicates that the dough is fully developed. Manipulation beyond this point leads to breakdown of the dough, as shown on the right hand side of the curve.

Whether done mechanically or by hand, kneading involves stretching and folding—a shearing process, the object of which is to bring order to the random distribution of components of gluten so they make contact (24). Gliadins unite by hydrogen bonds and Van der Waals forces to form an amorphous matrix that provides cohesiveness to dough. Glutenin fibrils, aligned and moved past one another, unite to form elongated fibrils that give elasticity to dough. Oxidizing agents promote formation of disulfide bonds, strengthening the elastic component of dough; reducing agents cause scission of glutenins, weakening the dough. Development of viscoelasticity in dough is essential for the production of high quality bread. Dough must be able to expand and at the same time retain enough leavening gas over the extended fermentation period and during the early part of baking to prevent collapse of the dough until heat sets the structure.

An equally important function of manipulation is to incorporate bubbles of air into dough (1). These serve as nuclei for the accumulation of carbon dioxide as the dough ferments and for gases evolved and expanded as the dough bakes (15). Gas cells originate only from manipulation of the dough; without occluded air bubbles dough would not rise. One theory is that only hydrated gluten defines the cells of trapped air (15), but evidence has been presented that an aqueous film is present between the air and the supporting gluten–starch matrix (8).

When dough is to be kneaded by hand, flour and water are stirred until the mixture loses some of its stickiness (Fig. 14-1) before it is turned onto a lightly floured surface. Dusting the surface of the dough with flour helps prevent the dough from sticking to fingers and the surface on which it is kneaded. No more flour than is absolutely necessary should be used. Should dough stick to the fingers, rubbing dry flour onto them will remove it. Water should not be used, because dough will adhere to a damp surface. Scraping all of the dough from the pan or bowl before kneading is started eliminates waste and makes it possible to put the dough to rise in the same utensil in which it was mixed.

When dough is kneaded (Fig. 14-2), firm, short, rhythmic strokes with time between each for the dough to relax are best to develop springiness in the dough. When gluten is sufficiently developed, the dough loses its stickiness and becomes stretchy yet elastic. Numerous tiny bubbles appear just below the surface. Obvious changes that take place in

Figure 14-1. Yeast dough ready for kneading. The last portions of flour should be added cautiously to avoid an excess, and each addition should be stirred in thoroughly. With the optimum amount of flour and adequate mixing, little dough adheres to the mixing bowl. (Photograph by Wilbur Nelson.)

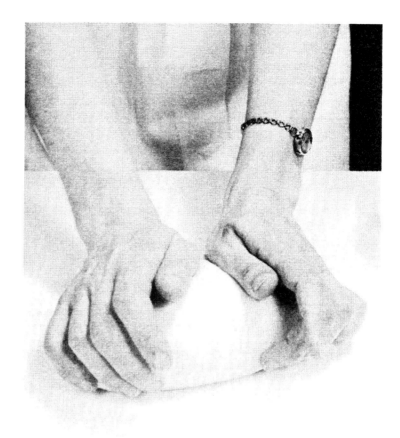

Figure 14-2. Yeast dough is kneaded by stretching and folding with short, firm, rhythmic strokes. (Photograph by Wilbur Nelson.)

yeast dough when it is kneaded properly are convincing evidence that there is indeed some magic in the stretching of dough (1). A common problem when dough is kneaded by hand is for the bread maker to tire before the gluten is developed. Increasing the kneading time or the number of strokes 50 to 100 percent above what one considers optimum is not likely to harm, and frequently improves, the quality of the product.

When kneaded by hand, more dough is ruined by faulty technique than by excessive kneading done skillfully. It is possible to overwork yeast dough so the gluten loses its cohesiveness and springiness, the cells leak gas, and they coalesce, but this is unlikely with hand kneading. Sweeter doughs require longer kneading to hydrate the flour adequately. The ability to recognize signs that indicate that a dough has been adequately kneaded can be developed in this way. A quantity of dough can be kneaded until the gluten seems sufficiently developed (eight to ten minutes). One-third of the dough is then removed and put to rise. The remainder of the dough is kneaded another three or four minutes and half of this put to rise. The third portion is then kneaded for an additional three to four minutes before it is put to rise. At no time should the dough be handled roughly. No flour should be put on the board when the last two portions of the dough are kneaded. Should the dough stick to the board, oiling the board lightly should eliminate the problem. In this way one may learn to associate characteristics of feel and appearance in the dough with a satisfactory baked product. If as kneading proceeds the surface of the dough looks rough and lumpy, it probably means that the dough is being mistreated and that gluten strands are being broken instead of developed and arranged in an orderly fashion.

FERMENTATION OF YEAST DOUGH

After the dough is kneaded it is ready to rise. It should be put into a utensil with a tight-fitting lid to keep the surface from drying. Alternately, the surface may be oiled lightly and the dough covered with waxed paper or a clean towel.

Temperature

Temperature of the dough as it ferments influences markedly the speed of fermentation and the quality of the final product. When the temperature is increased from 20° to 30°C (68° to 86°F) the fermentation rate increases threefold and the rate is twice as great at 55°C (95°F) as at 25°C (77°F) (29). Below 24°C (75°F) fermentation is slow and the dough is slow to rise. Optimum temperature for the growth and reproduction of yeast ranges from 24°C (75°F) to 35°C (95°F). For fermentation of bread dough the optimum range in temperature is narrower, lying between 25° and 27.7°C (78° and 82°F). Yeast dough at 37°C (98.6°F) rises rapidly, but the dough may become light before it has a chance to mellow, and undesirable byproducts of fermentation may give a soured or off odor. Furthermore, dough that is too warm is soft and likely to be sticky and hard to handle. Directions to ferment yeast dough in a warm place should not be taken literally. Because the optimum temperature is lower than body temperature, the dough should feel cool to the touch.

Fermentation of yeast dough may be retarded by chilling the dough. However, there are problems attendant upon holding yeast dough in the refrigerator. The dough cools slowly, and as long as it is warm fermentation continues. Unless the dough is punched periodically, it will get too light. Yeast cells may die if they exhaust the nutrients in their immediate vicinity in the dough. Contents of dead cells bring about changes in the dough that lower volume as well as quality of the crumb. A rich dough, especially one high in sugar (to retard fermentation and to maintain a supply of sugar for the yeast) is recommended for dough for refrigerated storage. A limited increase in salt may also prove beneficial. Refrigerated dough should be used within three or four days.

Inflating the Dough

Carbon dioxide dissolves in the aqueous phase of dough from which it diffuses into the air bubbles incorporated in the dough when it was kneaded (15). This converts the dough into a foam. Expansion of these bubbles stretches the films of gluten surrounding them; this stretching is essential if the dough is to expand as it should during baking. The extent to which the dough needs to be stretched varies with the flour that supplies the gluten. Dough from harder wheat flour can rise more than that from softer wheat flour without unduly weakening the gluten.

Yeast dough should never be allowed to become overlight. Once gluten strands are overstretched, like rubber bands stretched beyond their elastic limit, they are unable to recover their original elasticity. Dough allowed to become overlight before it is punched is unable later to retain as well the gas produced by the yeast. Such dough is slow to rise the second time and does not regain the volume it had at the end of the first rising. The result is a heavy, compact loaf of low volume and poor texture.

Dough is sufficiently light when it has approximately doubled in bulk. Slightly less is better for dough from all-purpose flour and somewhat more is better for hard wheat flour. A second criterion for lightness is that the dough barely springs back when touched lightly with the finger. The time required for yeast dough to rise depends mainly on the proportion of yeast in the dough and on the fermentation temperature (Table 14-1). The proportion of salt and sugar and the stiffness of the dough are contributing factors.

Punching the Dough

When the dough is sufficiently light, it should be punched down gently. One object of punching dough is to keep the films of gluten around gas cells from being overstretched. A second object is to subdivide the gas cells that have enlarged during the fermentation period. Lifting the dough, now an inflated foam, from the sides of the utensil will cause it to collapse. Dough made from hard wheat flour may be allowed to rise and be punched a second time. Should a dough become light sooner than anticipated, it should be punched and allowed to begin rising again, not allowed to become too light. The dough can be shaped any time and does not have to reach its full volume a second time. A second rising needs no more than half the time for the first rising (Table 14-1). After the dough is punched, it should be manipulated but handled in such a way as to avoid tearing or matting the gluten strands which are separated by bubbles of carbon dioxide. Working the dough at this stage divides and increases the number of gas cells (1). The larger the number of gas cells, the better is the distribution of carbon dioxide in the dough and the more even the grain in the baked product. Apparently, carbon dioxide produced by yeast collects in gas cells formed in the dough as it was mixed, kneaded, and shaped. New gas cells do not form. As fermentation proceeds, the yeast cells use the nutrients in the immediate vicinity. Punching the dough replenishes the supply. Also, if the yeast cells have multiplied, manipulating the dough distributes these cells more uniformly throughout. Heat is evolved during fermentation, so another reason for punching yeast dough is to equalize the temperature. The dough is warmer in the interior than on the surface. This condition is not so noticeable with a small quantity of dough, but with a large quantity, as in a bakery, the amount of heat evolved is appreciable and means must be provided to dissipate it. The optimum amount of manipulation of the dough at this stage can be determined in the same way as the optimum amount of kneading.

When the dough has been punched sufficiently, it is ready to be shaped. Dough is easier to shape if it is allowed to rest for a few minutes after it is punched. To produce bread with a good contour, the dough should be so manipulated that the strands of gluten are made parallel. Shaping should be done with the minimum of tearing and matting of gluten strands. If the dough has a tendency to stick, the surfaces with which it comes in contact may be oiled. Unfermented flour should not be used at this stage to keep the dough from sticking.

PROOFING

After the dough is shaped and in the baking pan, it is proofed, that is, allowed to rise again, this time so the baked product will be light (Fig. 14-3). Temperature of the dough during

Figure 14-3. Yeast dough at the end of proofing. Bubbles of carbon dioxide trapped in strands of gluten convert the dough into a foam. (Courtesy of Millers' National Federation.)

proofing should be near 27°C (80°F) or possibly a few degrees higher at this stage. Proofing should be terminated when the dough again has approximately doubled in bulk and when it holds a slight depression if pressed gently with a finger.

BAKING

Temperature

Yeast dough is put to bake in a hot oven at 204° to 218°C (400° to 425°F). Temperature may be lowered after the first 10 to 15 minutes if the crust appears to be getting too brown. Rich dough that browns readily may be baked in a moderate oven, 177° to 190°C (350° to 375°F).

Changes Affected

The volume of bread dough increases rapidly during the first few minutes in the oven. This phenomenon, known as oven spring, may be observed if the oven has a glass window. The increase in volume may approach 80 percent of proofed volume in good dough from hard wheat flour. A number of factors contribute to this oven spring. Lightness of the dough when it goes into the oven is one factor. Dough of optimum lightness expands just enough to give a baked product with thin cell walls and a fine grain. If the dough is overlight, oven spring is magnified. Overblown cells that give bread crumb a moth-eaten appearance result. (The top of the loaf tends to flatten and to balloon over the sides of the pan.) If the dough is underlight when it goes into the oven, gas cells will be small with thick cell walls and oven spring will be low. Production of carbon dioxide by yeast is accelerated temporarily and the gas is less soluble in hot water. Amylases are more active. Heat expands the gases within the cells, and starch granules are oriented around them (33, 34). The ability of cells to retain gases at this stage is important. Viscosity of the dough decreases to a minimum ($\frac{1}{6}$ of that at room temperature) as the temperature of the dough rises to near 60°C (140°F) (3).

Additional heating begins the conversion of closed-celled, inflated, mobile foam to open-celled, compressible, sponge-like bread (12). As internal temperature rises above 60°C (140°F), gelatinization of starch occurs and viscosity of the dough rises rapidly. Rapid loss of carbon dioxide begins near 72°C (162°F) and is at a maximum at 88°C (190°F) (12). An explanation for this rapid loss of gas is that starch from swollen granules interacts with gluten and reduces its extensibility. Expanding gas then ruptures the less mobile films of gluten that define the gas cells, thus establishing the texture of the crumb.

In addition to gelatinizing and pasting the starch in dough, heat also causes permanent disulfide bonding between glutenin polymers (3). These bonds are unlike the transient bonding that occurs as dough is kneaded. These heat-setting bonds effect the final step in the conversion of closed-celled dough to open-celled bread (Fig. 14-4).

Doneness

At the end of the baking period the temperature in the interior of bread is approximately that of boiling water. Evaporation of moisture from the surface of the bread keeps it cool during the early part of the baking period. When the surface dries, the temperature rises and may go as high as 150°C (302°F). Heat effects the formation of a complex between reducing sugars and protein that causes browning of the crust. Doneness of bread is difficult to assess, and brownness is not always a criterion. A loaf of bread may sound hollow when thumped, even when it is not done. Baking for a specified time is probably the best way to assess doneness, but the size of the loaf influences baking time. Doubling the size of the loaf does not double the baking time, because the distance from the outside to the center of the loaf is not doubled.

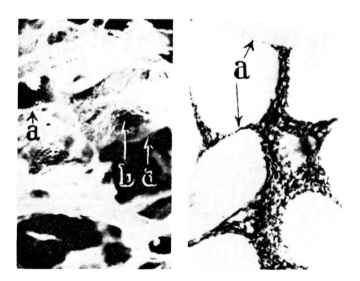

Figure 14-4. Bread crumb as it appears under the microscope: (*left*) untreated crumb; (*right*) embedded and stained crumb. Areas marked *a* are cuts across films of crumb that define gas cells; those marked *b* are surface views. Original magnification × 30. (From R. M. Sandstedt, L. Schaumburg, and J. Fleming. *Cereal Chemistry* 31:45. 1954. Reprinted by permission.)

The Baking Pan

The shape of the pan in which bread is baked influences the product. A shallow pan is preferred, because a deep one appears to put maximum strain on the dough. The comparative shallowness of muffin cups may explain why rolls baked in them have better grain and texture than does a loaf of bread baked from the same dough. Possibly, faster heat penetration in the muffin cups contributes to the better quality of the rolls, too. Of course, more extensive manipulation of the dough and the formation of many more gas bubbles as the dough is shaped for rolls may be contributing factors.

QUALITY OF BREAD

Aroma

The aroma of baking and freshly baked bread is appreciated by everyone. Fermentation by yeast appears to be essential for the development in bread of substances that contribute to aroma. Bread made to rise by an excess of oxidizing agent with no time for fermentation lacks aroma. Because a ferment of water, yeast, and sugar has the characteristic aroma of bread, sugar appears to be essential, too. Sugar contributes to aroma in another way. Bread cooked in such a way that it has no crust lacks aroma. Apparently odorous compounds are formed in the crust as it browns and these diffuse into the crumb. The mixture of compounds that contributes to the odor of baked yeast products is complex. More than 60 volatile components are considered possible contributors to the aroma of bread (19). Included are organic acids, alcohols, and esters as well as carbonyl compounds from the crust. It appears that a combination of volatiles is responsible for the tantalizing aroma of freshly baked bread.

Other Characteristics

Quality yeast bread is light without being overinflated. The top crust is thin, well-rounded, symmetrical, and a uniform golden brown. The crumb is moist and resilient. Films of baked dough that constitute the cell walls are thin and the surfaces have a silky sheen (Fig. 14-5). The flavor is pleasant and nutlike without traces of soured or yeasty odor.

STALING OF BREAD

When bread first comes from the oven, it is a moist, highly compressible sponge with a pliable crumb. As it cools to room temperature, it passes through a series of rubbery states (2) but still retains the character of fresh bread. Once bread cools to room temperature, staling begins and continues over several days. The nature of bread staling has long been a puzzle (20). The symptoms are clear enough. The crust becomes tough and leathery; the crumb becomes rigid, harsh, and crumbly. These changes occur in bread even though it is sealed in a moisture-vapor-tight wrap.

Firmness is used by consumer and research worker alike as a criterion of staleness. An estimated three to five percent of baked products are discarded because of staleness (11)—a serious economic loss. The number of papers on the subject that continues to appear attests to the importance attached to understanding the phenomenon (20, 22, 40).

Crystallinity observed in stale bread points to the involvement of starch. Monoglycerides (Chapter 15), if included in dough, form a complex with amylose as starch is

Figure 14-5. Fine texture, even grain, and good volume characterize homemade bread at its best. (From *Sunset.* October 1962. Darrow M. Watt, Photographer, 188 Felton Drive, Menlo Park, CA.)

pasted and act as crumb softeners by limiting the amount of retrogradable amylose. Unlike the rapid retrogradation of amylose, staling continues over several days (9) once the bread has cooled. Staling is attributed to retrogradation of amylopectin in the pasted granules. However, increasing crystallinity does not always parallel increasing firmness of bread. For example, bread made soft with antistaling enzyme has increased crystallinity (2). A low-moisture bread firms rapidly without a corresponding increase in crystallinity (31). These and similar reports indicate that factors in addition to retrogradation of amylopectin influence staling. One theory is that interaction between pasted starch and gluten that begins during baking continues as bread ages (27). Starch molecules from pasted granules link adjacent gluten fibrils and firms bread crumb.

Staling can be prevented by freezing fresh bread and storing it at $-18°C$ ($0°F$) (28). At this temperature, the gelatinized starch is in the glassy state and retrogradation cannot occur.

Stale bread can be refreshed by heating it to $60°C$ ($140°F$), a fact known since 1852 (27). At this temperature the crystals of retrograded amylopectin melt. Fresh bread will remain fresh if held at this temperature. However, precautions must be taken to prevent drying. Bread is likely to mold at high storage temperatures unless it contains a compound, such as calcium propionate, that retards the growth of mold. Bread reheated by microwaves becomes tough and leathery unless exposure is brief. This effect on the texture of bread is attributed to a continuation of the thermosetting of gluten that was interrupted at the end of the baking period (35).

The development of off flavor in bread is another aspect of staling. Oxidation is considered a contributing factor.

REFERENCES

1. Baker, J. C., and M. D. Mize. 1941. "The origin of the gas cell in bread dough." *Cereal Chemistry* 18:19–34. Effects of mixing, punching, molding, and oxidizing agents on crumb structure.

2. Blanshard, J. M. V. 1986. "The significance of the structure of the starch granule on baked products." In *Chemistry and Physics of Baking*. J. M. V. Blanshard, P. J. Frazier and T. Galliard, eds. London: The Royal Society of Chemistry. Pp. 1–13. Rubbery states of fresh bread; antistaling enzymes and crystallinity.

3. Bloksma, A. H. 1986. "Rheological aspects of structural changes during baking." In *Chemistry and Physics of Baking*. J. M. V. Blanshard, P. J. Frazier and T. Galliard, eds. London: The Royal Society of Chemistry. Pp. 170–78. Viscosity of dough; effects of heat on starch and gluten.

4. Bohn, R. T. 1959. "How sugar functions in high sugar yeast dough." *Cereal Science Today* 4:174–76. Effects of sugar on fermentation and on water uptake by dough.

5. Cooper, E. J., and G. Reed. 1968. "Yeast fermentation—effect of temperature, pH, ethanol, sugars, salt, and osmotic pressure." *Bakers Digest* 42(6):22–24, 26, 28–29, 63. Summary of pertinent facts.

6. Ewart, J. A. D. 1989. "Hypothesis for how linear glutenin holds gas in dough." *Food Chemistry* 32:135–50. Factors affecting the viscoelastic properties of dough.

7. Faubion, J. M., and R. C. Hoseney. 1990. "The viscoelastic properties of wheat flour doughs." In *Dough Rheology and Baked Product Texture*. H. Faridi and J. M. Faubion, eds. New York: Van Nostrand Reinhold. Pp. 29–60. Mixing and unmixing of dough; proportions of water.

8. Gan, Z., R. E. Angold, M. R. Williams, E. R. Ellis, J. G. Vaughn, and T. Galliard. 1990. "The microstructure and gas retention in bread dough." *Journal of Cereal Science* 12:15–24. Evidence (indirect) of an aqueous gas bubble film.

9. Ghiasi, K., R. C. Hoseney, K. Zeleznak, and D. E. Rogers. 1984. "Effect of waxy barley starch and reheating on firmness of bread crumb." *Cereal Chemistry* 61:281–85. Firming and crystallization not synonymous.

10. Harland, B. F. and J. Harland. 1980. "Fermentative reduction of phytate in rye, white and whole wheat breads." *Cereal Chemistry* 57:226–29. Elimination of mineral binding sites.

11. Hebada, R. E., L. K. Bowles, and M. W. Teague. 1990. "Developments in enzymes for retarding staling of baked goods." *Cereal Foods World* 35(5):453–54. Estimate of stale baked goods discarded; fungal and bacterial enzymes.

12. He, H., and R. C. Hoseney. 1991. "Gas retention in bread dough during baking." *Cereal Chemistry* 68:521–25. Role of gelatinizing starch in the rupture of gas cells.

13. Hoseney, R. C. 1986. "Component interaction during baking and storage of baked products." In *Chemistry and Physics of Baking*. J. M. V. Blanshard, P. J. Frazier and T. Galliard, eds. London: The Royal Society of Chemistry. Pp. 216–27. One explanation of the improving effect of fat on bread volume.

14. Hoseney, R. C. 1986. "Yeast leavened products." In *Principles of Cereal Science and Technology*. St. Paul: American Association of Cereal Chemists, Inc. Pp. 203–41. Bread, from formula, through baking, to staling.

15. Hoseney, R. C. 1991. "Wheat gluten: Rheological and gas retaining properties." In *Water Relationships in Foods—Advances in the 1980s and Trends for the 1990s. Advances in Experimental Medicine and Biology*, Vol. 302. H. Levine and L. Slade, eds. New York: Plenum Press. Pp. 657–64. Dough formation, gas retention, and conversion of dough to bread.

16. Hoseney, R. C., K. F. Finney, Y. Pomeranz, and M. D. Shogren. 1971. "Functional (breadmaking) and biochemical properties of wheat flour components." VIII. "Starch." *Cereal Chemistry* 48:191–201. Effects on loaf volume and bread crumb of starches from various sources.

17. Hoseney, R. C., and D. E. Rogers. 1990. "The formation and properties of wheat flour doughs." *Critical Reviews in Food Science and Nutrition* 29:73–93. Current concepts; straightforward presentation.

18. Jenness, R. 1954. "Milk proteins. Effect of heat treatment on serum proteins." *Journal of Agricultural and Food Chemistry* 2:75–81. Discussion of the loaf-depressant factor in unheated milk. Or see R. Jenness. 1954. "Recent work on the effects of milk in bread." *Bakers Digest* 28:87–91, 103.

19. Johnson, J. A., and C. R. S. Sanchez. 1973. "The nature of bread flavor." *Bakers Digest* 47(5):48–50. Constituents involved.

20. Kim, S. K., and B. L. D'Appolonia. 1977. "The role of wheat flour constituents in bread staling." *Bakers Digest* 51(1):38–42, 44, 57. Conflicting evidence summarized.

21. Knightly, W. H. 1981. "Shortening systems: Fats, oils, and surface-active agents—Present and future." *Cereal Chemistry* 58(3):171–74. Oils and dough conditioners in bakery products.

22. Kulp, K., and J. G. Ponte. 1981. "Staling of white pan bread." *CRC Critical Reviews in Food Science and Nutrition* 15:1–48. An extended review.

23. Larson, R. A., R. Jenness and W. F. Geddes. 1949. "Effect of heat treatment of separated milk on the physical and baking properties of doughs enriched with dry milk solids." *Cereal Chemistry* 26:189–200. Heat treatment required for milk used to make yeast bread.   ·

24. MacRitchie, F. 1986. "Physicochemical processes in mixing." In *Chemistry and Physics of Baking*. J. M. V. Blanshard, P. J. Frazier, and T. Galliard, eds. London: The Royal Society of Chemistry. Pp. 132–46. Wetting of flour, development of dough, and occlusion of air.

25. Magoffin, C. D., and R. C. Hoseney. 1974. "A review of fermentation." *Bakers Digest* 48(6):22–23, 26–27. Utilization of sugars; starch and the function of amylases; effects on dough development.

26. Martson, P. E., and T. L. Wannan. 1976. "Bread baking—the transformation from dough to bread." *Bakers Digest* 50(4):24–28, 49. A review of chemical and physical changes.

27. Martin, M. L., K. J. Zeleznak, and R. C. Hoseney. 1991. "A mechanism of bread firming." I. "Role of starch swelling." *Cereal Chemistry* 68:498–503. Starch-gluten crosslinks; mechanism of bread firming.

28. Pence, J. W., N. N. Standridge, T. M. Lubisich, D. K. Mecham, and H. S. Olcott. 1955. "Studies on the preservation of bread by freezing." *Food Technology* 9:495–99. Optimum temperatures for maintaining freshness.

29. Pomper, S. 1969. "Biochemistry of yeast fermentation." *Bakers Digest* 42(2):32–33, 36–38. Effects of pH, temperature, and osmotic pressure on carbohydrate metabolism by yeast.

30. Ponte, J. G. Jr., R. L. Glass, and W. F. Geddes. 1960. "Studies on the behavior of active dry yeast in breadmaking." *Cereal Chemistry* 37:263–79. Effect of rehydration temperature on functional properties.

31. Rogers, D. E., K. Zelesnak, C. S. Lai, and R. C. Hoseney. 1988. "Effect of native lipid, shortening and bread moisture on bread firming." *Cereal Chemistry* 65:398–401. Retrogradation and firming not parallel.

32. Rusch, D. T. 1981. "Emulsifiers: Uses in cereals and bakery foods." *Cereal Foods World* 26(3):110–15. Dough conditioners and crumb softeners.

33. Sandstedt, R. M. 1961. "The functions of starch in the baking of bread." *Bakers Digest* 35(3):36–43. Review of the importance of starch.

34. Sandstedt, R. M., L. Schaumburg, and J. Fleming. 1954. "The microscopic structure of bread and dough." *Cereal Chemistry* 31:43–49. Illustrations and interpretation.

35. Slade, L., H. Levine, and J. W. Findley. 1988. "Protein–Water interactions: Water as a plasticizer of gluten and other protein polymers." In *Protein Quality and the Effects of Processing.* D. Phillips and J. W. Findley, eds. Pp. 9–124. Gluten, a thermosetting polymer, plasticized by lipid; effect of microwaves.

36. Spies, R. 1990. "Application of rheology in the bread industry." In *Dough Rheology and Baked Product Texture.* H. Faridi and J. M. Faubion, eds. New York: Van Nostrand Reinhold. Pp. 343–61. As related to mixing, baking, and the baked product.

37. Tamstorf, S., T. Jonsson, and N. Krog. 1986. "The role of fats and emulsifiers in baked products." In *Chemistry and Physics of Baking.* J. M. V. Blanshard, P. J. Frazier and T. Galliard, eds. London: The Royal Society of Chemistry. Pp. 75–88. Fats in bread, cakes, and puff pastry: emulsifiers as dough conditioners and crumb softeners.

38. Volpe, T. and M. E. Zabik. 1975. "A whey protein contributing to loaf volume depression." *Cereal Chemistry* 52:188–97. A proteose-peptone identified.

39. Wu, J. Y., J. I. Maningat, J. P. Ponte, Jr., and R. C. Hoseney. 1990. "Short-time breadmaking systems. Effects of formulation, temperature and flour quality." *Journal of Food Science* 53:535–39. High-speed mixing, and increased yeast and oxidant mimic effects of fermentation.

40. Zobel, H, F. 1973. "A review of bread staling." *Bakers Digest* 47(5):52–53, 56, 61. Role of starch; action of surfactants.

PART V

Fats and Fat-Rich Foods

Fats and Oils

15

Fats and oils are important ingredients in a variety of foods. They confer desirable characteristics on cheese, sour cream, salad dressings, fabricated meats, and baked products. Fats contribute tenderness to pastry crust and shortened cake, as well as biscuits and muffins. By aerating batter, fats aid in establishing texture in cakes. They contribute flavor to foods and influence the order in which components of flavor are released when foods are eaten (34). Fats have a lubricating effect and they produce a sensation of moistness in the mouth. They are a medium for transferring heat to foods.

The fats and oils that constitute shortening, salad and cooking oils, and margarine are obtained from both plants and animals. Oils—fats that are liquid at room temperature—are obtained from the seeds of a number of plants. Fats from the adipose tissue of animals are tallow from beef and lard from pork. Crude fat is either expelled under pressure, extracted with suitable solvent or, in the case of lard, rendered from fat tissue by heating until the melted fat drains from the cells. Crude fat or oil so obtained undergoes a series of manufacturing processes before it is marketed. These include treatment with alkali to remove certain impurities, removal of pigments by adsorption on clay or carbon, deodorization by steam distillation, hydrogenation if a plastic fat is desired instead of an oil, and plasticizing to give fat a creamy smoothness. Butter is made from the emulsified fat of cream.

Some knowledge of the chemistry of fats is essential to understand their functional properties in foods. Fats of special interest in food preparation are classed on the basis of their chemical makeup as phospholipid, glycolipids, and neutral lipids. Phospholipids, important in forming emulsions, occur in egg yolk, milk fat, and in the seeds of soybeans. They are present also in lean meat and poultry where they may give rise to undesirable odors. Phospholipids are discussed in Chapters 22 and 23. Galactolipids, members of the glycolipid group of fats, are important in the development of gluten in bread dough (Chapter 11). The neutral fats make up the bulk of food fats. These fats and their low- and noncaloric substitutes are discussed in this chapter.

CHEMISTRY OF FATS

Chemically, fats belong to the class of organic compounds known as esters (7), which are formed by the reaction of an alcohol with organic acids. The alcohol that participates in the formation of each molecule of fat is the water-soluble trihydric glycerol:

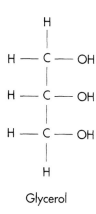

Glycerol

The acids are the fatty acids.

Fatty Acids

Fatty acids, like all organic acids, characteristically contain a carboxyl group:

$$-C\overset{O}{\underset{OH}{\diagup}}$$

In addition, each fatty acid contains a chain of —CH_2 groups denoted by the symbol R. Thus,

$$R-C\overset{O}{\underset{OH}{\diagup}}$$

represents any fatty-acid molecule. What the R stands for is the feature that distinguishes one fatty acid from another. The particular fatty acids found in the molecules of a fat influence the chemical and physical properties of the fat and its functional properties in food preparation.

Molecules of most fatty acids contain an even number of carbon atoms, from 4 to 24. Some are saturated, that is, each carbon atom with a valence of four is linked to two other carbon atoms and to two atoms of hydrogen:

$$-\underset{|}{\overset{|}{C}}-\underset{|}{\overset{H}{\underset{|}{C}}}-\underset{|}{\overset{|}{C}}-$$

Other fat molecules are unsaturated, that is, one or more carbon atoms are linked to a second carbon by a double bond, thus:

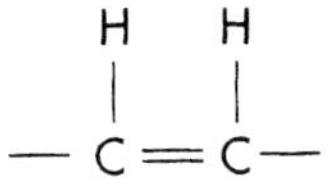

$$
\begin{array}{cc}
H & H \\
| & | \\
-C & = C-
\end{array}
$$

Unsaturated fatty acids differ in the number and position of the double bonds. They also differ from saturated fatty acids in the overall shape of the molecule. Saturated fatty-acid molecules are linear in shape as shown diagrammatically for stearic acid:

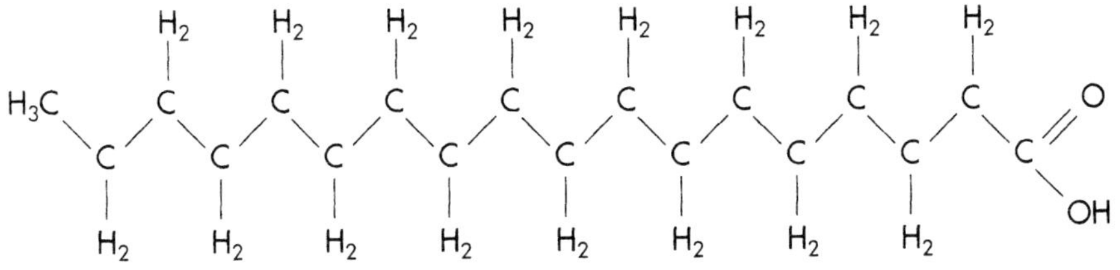

Linear form of a saturated fatty acid (stearic)

Unsaturated fatty acids usually exist in the *cis* form. The presence of a double bond linking two carbon atoms in an unsaturated fatty acid puts a kink in the molecule, interrupting its linearity, as shown:

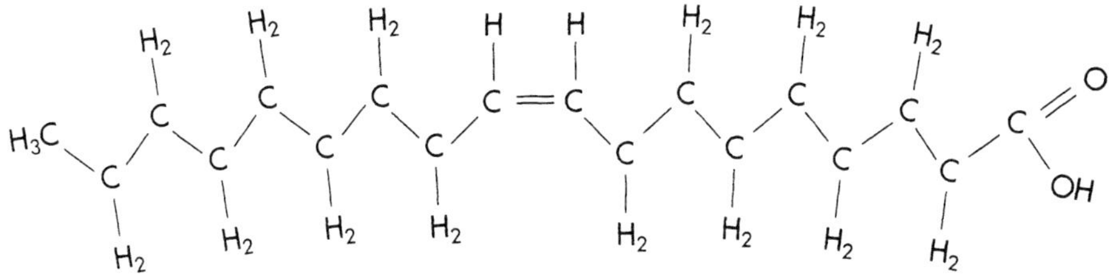

Cis form of an unsaturated fatty acid (oleic)

Unsaturated fatty acids, under certain conditions, may change from a *cis* to a *trans* configuration at the double bond, thus eliminating much of the bend in the molecule, as shown.

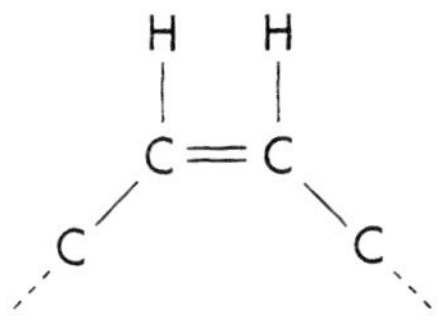

cis 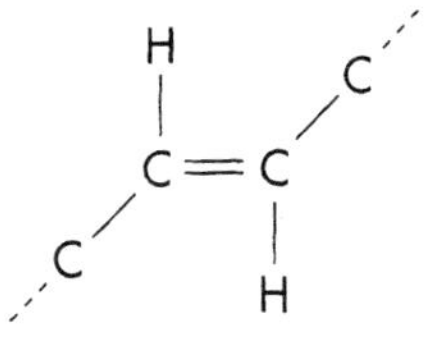   *trans*

The fatty acid with the shortest chain, four carbons, is butyric. When the carbon chain is so long that it is tedious to write all the —CH_2 groups, a shorthand form, $CH_3(CH_2)_xCOOH$, may be used. The x may stand for two such groups, as in butyric acid, or 14, as in palmitic acid.

Some fatty acids and their chemical makeup follow:

Butyric	$CH_3CH_2CH_2COOH$
	also written $CH_3(CH_2)_2COOH$
Caproic	$CH_3(CH_2)_4COOH$
Caprylic	$CH_3(CH_2)_6COOH$
Capric	$CH_3(CH_2)_8COOH$
Lauric	$CH_3(CH_2)_{10}COOH$
Myristic	$CH_3(CH_2)_{12}COOH$
Palmitic	$CH_3(CH_2)_{14}COOH$
Stearic	$CH_3(CH_2)_{16}COOH$
Arachidic	$CH_3(CH_2)_{18}COOH$
Behenic	$CH_3(CH_2)_{20}COOH$
Oleic	$CH_3(CH_2)_7CH=CH(CH_2)_7COOH$
Linoleic	$CH_3(CH_2)_3(CH_2CH=CH)_2(CH_2)_7COOH$
Linolenic	$CH_3(CH_2CH=CH)_3(CH_2)_7COOH$
Arachidonic	$CH_3(CH_2)_3(CH_2CH=CH)_4(CH_2)_3COOH$

An even more streamlined way to indicate a specific fatty acid is to give the number of carbon atoms and the number of double bonds in the molecule. Thus stearic acid with 18 carbons and no double bond is 18:0; oleic acid with 18 carbons and one double bond is 18:1; and linoleic acid with two double bonds is 18:2. The position of any double bond can be indicated, too, and again by number. The carbon atoms in a fatty acid are numbered consecutively from 1 to 18. In one system, numbering begins with the carboxyl carbon as number 1 and ends with the carbon in the methyl group as number 18. In oleic acid the first carbon that is involved in a double bond is carbon 9, designated Δ9. Oleic acid thus is 18:1Δ9. With this numbering system, linoleic acid is 18:2Δ9,12 and linolenic acid is 18:3Δ9,12,15. An alternate numbering system begins with the carbon of the methyl group as number 1 and ends with the carboxyl carbon as number 18. The ninth carbon from the methyl end of the molecule of oleic acid is involved in a double bond and this carbon is denoted omega-9 (also ω-9 or n-9). With this numbering system, oleic acid is 18:1ω-9 (or n-9). In linoleic acid, the carbon nearest the end that is involved in a double bond is number 6, designated omega-6. Linoleic acid is thus 18:2ω-6 (or n-6). In linolenic acid, the third carbon, omega-3, from the methyl end of the molecule is the first involved in a double bond. Linolenic acid is represented as 18:3ω-3 (or n-3).

Glycerides

Glycerides are esters of fatty acids and the polyhydric alcohol, glycerol. The carbons at either end of glycerol are indicated by numbers 1 and 3 or α and α′, with the central carbon designated β. One fatty acid united with a molecule of glycerol yields a monoacylglyceride, as shown:

| Glycerol | Fatty acid | A monoacylglyceride | Water |

Because the end carbon, α or 1, of glycerol is involved, the monoacylglyceride shown is an α- or 1-monoacylglyceride. Esterification that involves the middle carbon of glycerol yields a β-monoacylglyceride. Diacylglycerides can involve the two end carbons, α and α', (or 1 and 3) or the β-carbon and either the α or the α' carbon. The unesterified part of the glycerol of monoacyl- and diacylglycerides retains its water-soluble character while the fatty acids confer on the glycerides the ability to unite with fat. When three fatty acids are esterified to the same molecule of glycerol, a molecule of fat (a triacylglyceride) results, as shown:

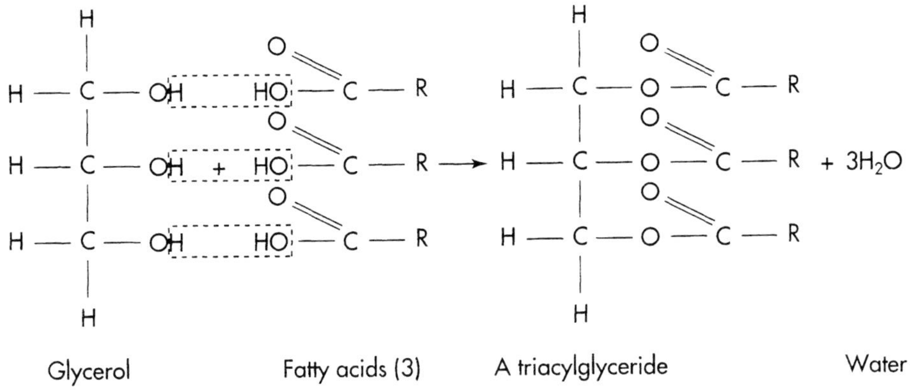

Glycerol | Fatty acids (3) | A triacylglyceride | Water

Many different molecules of fat are possible, depending on the fatty acids involved and their position of attachment on the glycerol. If all three fatty acids are alike (which is rare), a simple triacylglyceride results. All may be different (which is rarer) or two may be alike and one different, which is the usual pattern. In either of the last two cases, the fat molecule is a mixed triacylglyceride. With two fatty acids alike, the odd one may be attached to the middle or beta carbon, which gives a symmetrical molecule, as shown:

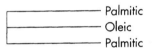

Palmitic
Oleic
Palmitic

Or the odd fatty acid may be attached at either the alpha (α) or alpha prime (α') carbon, as the end carbons are designated, which gives rise to an unsymmetrical molecule, thus:

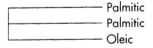

Palmitic
Palmitic
Oleic

A triacylglyceride with stearic acid only is called (tri)stearin, with palmitic only (tri)palmitin, and with oleic only (tri)olein. Mixed glycerides such as palmityl diolein, oleyl dipalmitin, or dipalmityl stearin are more common.

Considering food fats as a whole, the most abundant and widely distributed saturated fatty acid is palmitic, although fats of animal origin, in contrast to those from plants, have appreciable quantities of stearic acid. Oleic acid is the most ubiquitous unsaturated fatty acid. Most fats of vegetable origin contain appreciable amounts of linoleic acid. Natural fats like olive oil, lard, and corn oil are mixtures of mixed triglycerides.

The formula for a triglyceride molecule is customarily written as shown above. Due to steric hindrance when all three fatty-acid radicals are oriented in the same direction, a tuning fork arrangement, with the fatty acid at the middle carbon positioned in the opposite direction from the fatty acids on the end carbons,

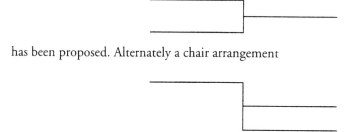

has been proposed. Alternately a chair arrangement

with the fatty acid on the alpha carbon oriented in a direction opposite the other two has been suggested.

CRYSTALS OF FAT

When liquid fat is cooled, removal of heat slows down the movement of the molecules. When they approach within five angstroms, they are attracted to each other by van der Waals forces (16). Such attraction has been likened to a zippering effect. If the molecular chain is long enough, as in the higher fatty acids, the cumulative attractive forces may be appreciable. As a result of this attraction, fatty-acid radicals in fat molecules are aligned in parallel fashion, the molecules overlapping thus (16):

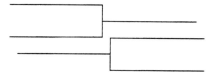

They bond to form crystals.

Symmetrical molecules and those with fatty acids that are similar in chain length can align themselves more readily to form crystals. Compare the close packing of a saturated glyceride such as palmitin in Figure 15-1a with that of less symmetrical molecules in b, c, and d. Fats that contain such asymmetrical molecules have low melting points.

Polymorphism

Most fats are polymorphic, that is, they can exist in more than one of four crystalline forms depending on alignment of molecules in the crystal (15). If a fat is chilled very rapidly, it forms small, transparent alpha crystals. Alpha crystals of most fats seldom last. Instead, they change rapidly to the β′ form, which exists as delicate needles not more than one micrometer long. Those fats, the β′ crystals of which are stable, remain fine-grained. The β′ crystals of other fats change into the intermediate form, three to five micrometers in size, and finally transform to the coarse beta crystals. The latter range from 25 to 30 micrometers up to 100 micrometers in length (15). Figure 15-2 shows photomicrographs of three of the polymorphic forms in which crystals of fats may exist. The particular polymorphic

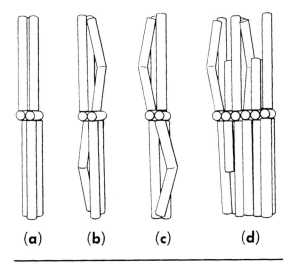

(a)   (b)   (c)   (d)

Figure 15-1. Arrangement of triglyceride molecules in a crystal of fat, shown by models. (a) Close packing of fatty acid chains in a triglyceride such as palmitin. (b, c) Unsaturated fatty acids on the central or on the terminal carbon atoms of glycerol interfere with the close packing shown in (a). (d) Variations in the chain length and presence of *cis* forms make crystal formation more difficult. (From C. W. Hoerr and D. F. Waugh, *Journal of the American Oil Chemists' Society* 32:40, 1955. Reprinted by permission.)

form in which a fat exists depends on the conditions under which the crystals were formed, the treatment of the fat after crystallization, and the fatty-acid makeup of the fat molecules.

Rapid cooling and agitation, which favor the formation of small crystals in frozen desserts and candies, promote the formation of small alpha crystals in fats. Slow cooling of melted fat favors the formation of coarser crystalline forms. For example, butter, with crystals so small that one is unaware that they exist, when melted and allowed to cool, forms crystals so large they are readily seen. The butter is not only coarser, but it appears oily because the few large crystals have much less surface area for the unsolidified phase to coat. This same butter can be made fine-grained again by melting it, cooling it rapidly, and agitating it as it cools.

The fatty acid makeup of the molecules of a fat influence which crystalline form will be stable. The more heterogeneous the fatty acid makeup, the more likely are the crystals to stabilize in the beta-prime crystalline form and the texture of the fat remain fine-grained. Acetoglycerides (acetic acid replacing one or two fatty acids in a molecule) stabilize in the alpha crystalline form (24).

Homogeneity in the molecules that make up a fat favors transformation to coarser crystalline forms. Crystals in lard readily transform to the coarse β form, which tends to associate in large clusters as the fat is stored. The instability of the finer crystalline forms in lard is attributed to the high proportion of molecules that are similar in chemical makeup. More than ¼ of the molecules of lard contain one unsaturated fatty-acid (usually oleic), one stearic acid, and one palmitic acid, the last attached at the central carbon of the glycerol.

Melting Points

The melting point of a fat is a measure of the strength of the bonding forces between fatty acids within the crystals. The greater the attraction between molecules, the less they need to be slowed down (by removal of heat) in order to crystallize. Fats that contain such molecules have high melting points. Those fatty acids that do not fit so well must have more heat removed before they crystallize. Much less energy in the form of heat is needed to melt

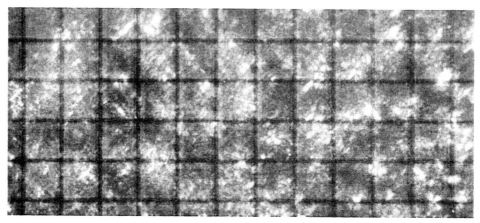

Beta prime

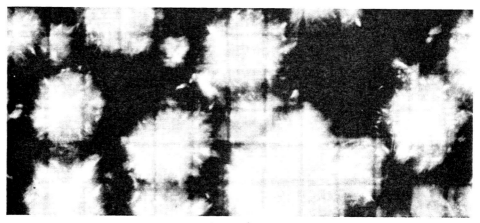

Intermediate

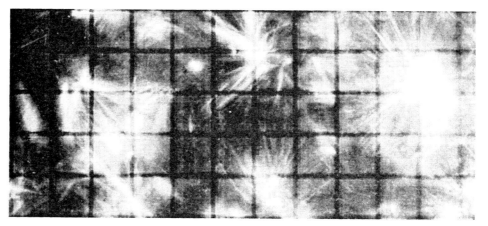

Beta

Figure 15-2. Photomicrographs (in polarized light) of polymorphic forms of crystals of fat. Original magnification × 200. Grid lines represent 18 microns. (From C. W. Hoerr, *Journal of the American Oil Chemists' Society* 37:542, 1960. Reprinted by permission.)

the crystals of the latter; that is, they have a lower melting point. The melting points of the glycerides that make up a fat determine whether the fat will be a liquid, a plastic solid, or hard and brittle at room temperature. The consistency of a fat influences its functional properties in preparation. Characteristics of fatty acids that influence the attractive forces between adjacent molecules of fat within the crystal are the length of the carbon chain, the number of double bonds in the chain, and whether the unsaturated fatty acid is in the *cis* or *trans* form.

The longer the carbon chain, the higher is the melting point of the compound.

Fatty Acid	Number of Carbons	Melting Point, °C (5)
Butyric	4	−4.5
Stearic	18	71.2

Butyric acid liquefies at a temperature below the freezing point of water, yet stearic acid is still in crystalline form at room temperature.

The melting point decreases with an increase in the number of double bonds. Unsaturated fatty acids do not fit together well enough for maximum attraction because of the bends in the carbon chain at the double bonds. The greater the number of double bonds, the poorer is the fit.

Fatty Acid	Number of Double Bonds	Melting Point, °C
Stearic	0	71.2
Oleic	1	16.3
Linoleic	2	−5
Linolenic	3	−11.3

The *trans* form of a fatty acid has a higher melting point than the *cis* form. Linear molecules are more readily zippered into crystals than are molecules that are bent.

Fatty Acid	Geometrical Form	Number of Double Bonds	Melting Point, °C
Elaidic	trans	1	45.0
Oleic	cis	1	16.3

The melting point of a triglyceride is conditioned by the melting point of the component fatty acids. Monoglycerides have higher melting points than the corresponding triglycerides.

Saturated	Melting Point, °C	Unsaturated	Melting Point, °C
Stearic acid	71.2	Oleic acid	16.3
Glyceryl monostearate	81.0	Glyceryl monooleate	35.0
Tristearin	73.0	Triolein	5.5

The melting point of a fat increases with each shift in polymorphic form from alpha crystals to beta. For example, the melting point of alpha crystals of tristearin is 55°C; for the beta form the melting point is 73°C.

CONSISTENCY OF FATS

The consistency of a fat influences its functional properties in food preparation. Fats are either liquid at room temperature (oils) or they are plastic (so-called solid fats). Plastic fats are a two-phase system, as are fondant, fudge, and ice creams. The solid phase consists of crystals of fat surrounded by a liquid phase of oil. The consistency of a plastic fat depends mainly on the ratio of the volume of crystals to the volume of oil. As the temperature of a plastic fat rises, the crystals melt. Those formed from triglycerides with lower melting points melt first. The fat softens and eventually becomes liquid. Cooling a liquid fat may cause crystals to form. Salad oil placed too near the freezing coils of the refrigerator may appear milky if the temperature of the oil is below the melting point of some of the fat molecules. Most salad oils have been chilled to remove those molecules that would crystallize at refrigerator temperature, a process called winterizing (23). A heat-oxidized saturated fat, oxystearin, has been approved as a crystal inhibitor for salad oils by the Food and Drug Administration.

Fats with a wide plastic range have some glycerides that remain in the crystalline form at elevated temperatures and others that remain liquid at low temperatures. A wide plastic range and small crystals (17) are desired in fats that are to be creamed, as for shortened cakes. On the other hand, one of the desirable attributes of butter as a table spread is its mouthfeel as it melts and this is due to its narrow plastic range. This characteristic is a disadvantage when butter is served on a very warm day. Manufacturers of margarine have found it difficult to produce a product with the unique melting characteristics of butter. Some of the crystals in the fat of beef and lamb have high melting points. Such fats that melt above body temperature are said to be tallowy.

The fat in chocolate has a unique melt-down. A high proportion of the triglyceride molecules in cocoa fat are identical, that is, they contain palmitic, oleic, and stearic acid radicals, with oleic positioned at the central carbon of glycerol (POS) (25). Oleoyldistearin (SOS) is another major component. These two triglycerides in their stable crystalline form have melting points within a few degrees of each other and just below body temperature (25). This gives to chocolate its sharp melting point and freedom from chewiness. Cocoa butter is solid below 31°C (88°F). Heated above 34°C (93°F), it melts sharply (17). Chocolate for dipping is first melted and then cooled and agitated so as to develop many crystal nuclei in the stable beta form. If unstable crystals are present in chocolate used to coat a center, they eventually melt and the fat migrates to the surface where it recrystallizes. These crystals dull the chocolate coating, which is said to bloom. Coconut fat with its high percentage of two short-chain saturated fatty acids—lauric and myristic—has a sharp melt-down, too.

Crystal size, as well as ratio of crystals to oil, also influences the consistency of a fat. In hydrogenated fat (see p. 253) the crystals may be only two to three microns long; those in lard may measure 20 to 30 microns. Hydrogenated fats have more than 100 times the number of crystals that lard does, with the ratio between the volumes of crystals and liquid in both fats the same. When crystals of fat are large, so are the spaces between crystals. Spaces that are too large are unable to hold the liquid portion of the fat, which tends to leak from the pores between the crystals. Such fats are coarse and oily, and they are softer than fats with the same ratio of solid to liquid glycerides that contain many smaller crystals. A fat may be plastic (workable) at room temperature when the solid phase accounts for as little as 5 percent of the total or as much as 35 percent, depending mainly on the size and type of crystals involved.

Most of the so-called visible fats that are consumed are pure fats. In this group are lard (rendered from the fatty tissue of pork), vegetable oils (coconut, corn, cottonseed, olive, peanut, safflower, sesame, soya, and sunflower), and hydrogenated vegetable shortenings. Butter and margarine are approximately 80 percent fat. Water and milk solids account for the other 20 percent. Invisible fats are consumed in larger quantities than visible ones. A number of foods contain appreciable quantities of invisible fat. Included are meats, poultry, certain fish, whole milk cheese, chocolate, egg yolk, avocados, as well as pastries, cakes, cookies, salad dressings, nuts, and fried foods.

The fatty-acid makeup of some of the more common food fats is given in Table 15-1 and is shown graphically in Figure 15-3. Fats from beef and butter contain a higher proportion of saturated fatty acids and those from plants (chocolate and coconut excepted) a higher proportion of unsaturated fatty acids. Chicken fat has a higher proportion of unsaturated fatty acids than the fat from beef or pork. Aside from chocolate, stearic acid is found in greatest concentration in beef, pork, and butter fat. Linoleic, an unsaturated fatty acid with two double bonds, predominates over oleic acid in safflower (one type), sunflower, corn, cottonseed, and soy bean oil, and in the fat from English walnuts and from wheat. In other fats oleic acid predominates. The oil from sunflowers grown in northern states has a higher proportion of linoleic to oleic acid than those grown in a warmer climate (29). Oleic acid makes up ¾ the total fatty acids in olive oil. Chicken fat contains a higher proportion of linoleic acid than does beef or pork. Soybean oil, canola, and the fat from English walnuts contain appreciable amounts of linolenic, an omega-3 fatty acid.

Marine oils are noted for their content of even more highly unsaturated fatty acids, with chains of 20 and 22 in addition to 18 carbon atoms, and with 3, 4, 5, or 6 double bonds. The possible beneficial effect of fish oils in the diet is an area of current research interest. Polyunsaturated fatty acids account for approximately ⅓ of the total fatty acids in the oils of sardines and menhaden, for example. Eicosapentaenoic acid, a 20:5 omega-3 unsaturated fatty acid and docosahexaenoic acid, a 22:6 omega-3 unsaturated fatty acid account for approximately ⅔ of the polyunsaturated fatty acids in each of these marine oils.

MODIFICATION OF NATURAL FATS

Plants supply the raw material from which not only salad and cooking oils are made, but the bulk of shortenings and margarines also. Soybeans are the chief source of oil, but corn, cotton, olive, peanut, palm, safflower, sunflower, coconut, and canola are other sources (20). For plastic shortenings and margarines, the oils are hardened.

Hydrogenation

Oils that are fluid at room temperature can, by a process known as hydrogenation (6,33), be changed to fats that are plastic and workable. Fat that contains unsaturated fatty acids is exposed to hydrogen gas in the presence of a catalyst. Double bonds in the fatty acids open, and one atom of hydrogen unites to each of the two carbon atoms formerly joined by a double bond. If the fatty acid is oleic, stearic acid results, in a reaction as shown:

$$CH_3(CH_2)_7CH = CH(CH_2)_7COOH \ + \ 2H \longrightarrow CH_3(CH_2)_7CH_2CH_2(CH_2)_7COOH$$

Oleic acid　　　　　　　Hydrogen　　　　　　Stearic acid

TABLE 15-1
Fatty Acid Content of Selected Food Fats (grams per 100 grams of ether extract or crude fat)

Food Source	SATURATED			UNSATURATED			
	Palmitic	Stearic	Total	Oleic	Linoleic	Linolenic	Total
Meats							
Beef	24.9	18.9	49.8	36.0	3.1	0.6	45.8
Lamb	21.5	19.5	47.3	37.6	5.5	2.3	48.4
Chicken	21.6	7.6	29.8	37.3	19.5	1.0	65.6
Fats							
Butter	21.3	9.8	50.5	20.4	1.8	1.2	26.4
Cocoa butter	25.4	33.2	59.7	32.6	2.8	0.1	35.9
Lard	23.8	13.5	39.2	41.2	10.2	1.0	56.3
Margarine,[a] hard	10.9	8.6	19.8	32.0	23.6	1.5	57.1
Margarine,[a] soft	7.2	4.9	12.8	16.1	47.6	0.4	64.1
Shortening[a]	14.1	10.6	25.0	44.5	24.5	1.6	70.6
Oils							
Canola	4.0	1.8	7.1	56.1	20.3	9.3	88.5
Coconut	8.2	2.8	86.5	5.8	1.8	—[d]	7.6
Corn	10.9	1.8	12.7	24.2	58.0	0.7	82.9
Cottonseed	22.7	2.3	25.9	17.0	51.5	0.2	69.7
Olive	11.0	2.2	13.5	72.5	7.9	0.6	82.1
Palm	43.5	4.3	49.3	36.6	9.1	0.2	46.3
Peanut	9.5	2.2	16.9	44.8	32.0	—	78.2
Safflower[b]	6.2	2.2	9.1	11.7	74.1	0.4	86.6
Safflower[c]	4.8	1.3	6.1	75.3	14.2	—	89.5
Sesame	8.9	4.8	14.2	39.3	41.3	0.3	81.4
Soybean	10.3	3.8	14.4	22.8	51.0	6.8	81.2
Sunflower	5.9	4.5	10.3	19.5	65.7	—	85.2
Walnuts	7.0	2.0	9.1	22.2	52.9	10.4	86.1
Wheat germ	16.6	0.5	18.8	14.6	54.8	6.9	76.8
Menhaden	15.1	3.8	30.4	14.5	2.2	1.5	60.9

[a]Varies widely with the fats used in manufacture
[b]High linoleic acid
[c]High oleic acid
[d]— = Data not available
Source: U.S. Dept. Agr. Handbook No. 8-4. *Composition of Foods. Fats and Oils. Raw, Processed, Prepared.* 1979, 1990 supplement.

Double bonds not only decrease in number but also migrate during hydrogenation. In the case of polyunsaturated fatty acids, only certain of the double bonds may become saturated. As a result, isomers of unsaturated fatty acids that do not occur naturally are formed. Temperature, pressure, and amount of agitation during hydrogenation influence which unsaturated fatty acid and which double bonds on polyunsaturated acids will be saturated.

During hydrogenation some of the unsaturated fatty acids change from the *cis* to the *trans* form (29). This shift, in addition to a decrease in unsaturated fatty acids, accounts for the conversion of an oil to a plastic fat. *Trans* fatty acids are found in hydrogenated shortenings and

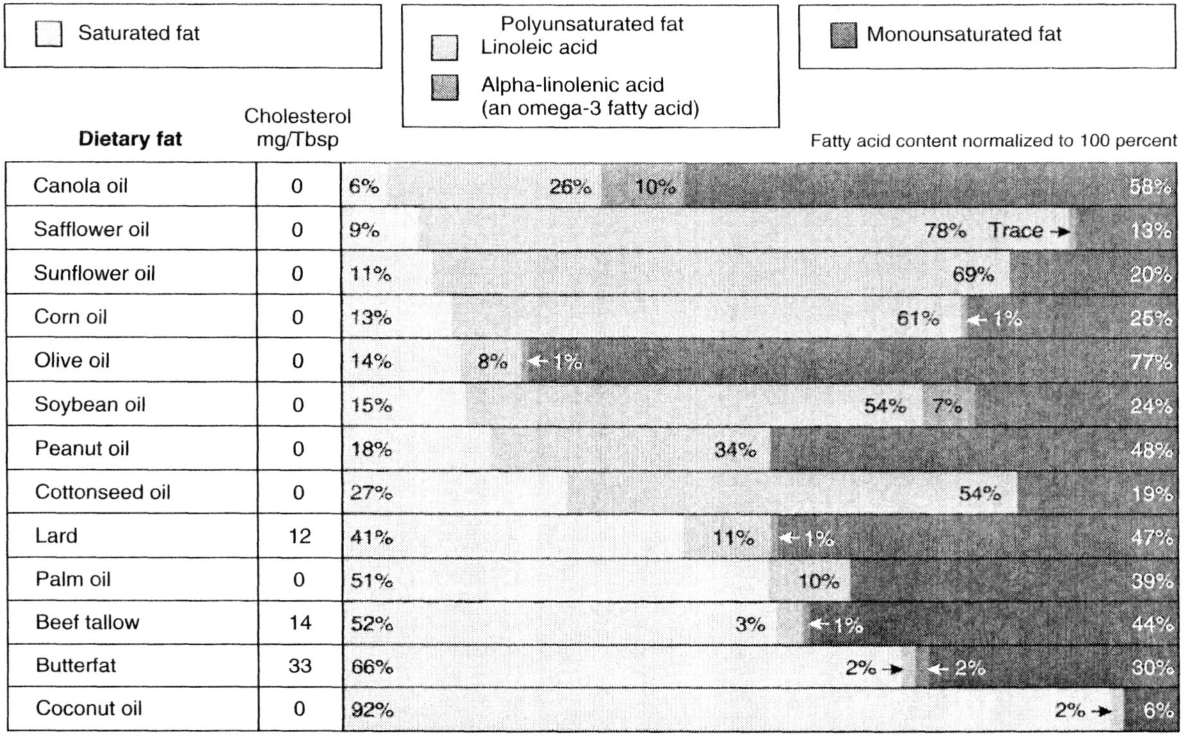
Saturated fat
Polyunsaturated fat
Linoleic acid
Alpha-linolenic acid
(an omega-3 fatty acid)
Monounsaturated fat
Dietary fat
Cholesterol mg/Tbsp
Fatty acid content normalized to 100 percent
Canola oil 0 6% 26% 10% 58%
Safflower oil 0 9% 78% Trace 13%
Sunflower oil 0 11% 69% 20%
Corn oil 0 13% 61% 1% 25%
Olive oil 0 14% 8% 1% 77%
Soybean oil 0 15% 54% 7% 24%
Peanut oil 0 18% 34% 48%
Cottonseed oil 0 27% 54% 19%
Lard 12 41% 11% 1% 47%
Palm oil 0 51% 10% 39%
Beef tallow 14 52% 3% 1% 44%
Butterfat 33 66% 2% 2% 30%
Coconut oil 0 92% 2% 6%

Figure 15-3. Fatty acids and cholesterol in edible fats. (From J. Dziezak, *Food Technology* 43(7):68, 1989. Graph courtesy of Calgene Chemicals, Inc.)

margarines. Of the 10 margarines analyzed in one study (both hard and soft types represented), eight had more than 15 percent monounsaturated fatty acids in the *trans* configuration and nine contained smaller amounts (less than five percent) of diunsaturated fatty acids in the *trans* form (4). In another study, seven samples of margarine had monounsaturated fatty acids that ranged from 25 to 64 percent, 6 to 33 percent of which were in the *trans* configuration (29). There is some indication that *trans* fatty acids may act in the body much as cholesterol-raising saturated fatty acids (28). Butter fat may contain up to 10 percent *trans* unsaturated acids, formed by bacteria in the rumen of the cow from *cis* forms of fatty acids in the cow's feed.

After an oil has been hydrogenated but while it is still in liquid form, it is charged with nitrogen gas under pressure. The fat is cooled rapidly to 18°C (65°F), at which point it is agitated for a few minutes to effect crystallization (33). With the sudden release in pressure, the gas is dispersed throughout the mass of plastic fat. The fat is then tempered, that is, warmed sufficiently so that the crystals first formed change over to the most stable crystalline form. After a hydrogenated fat has been tempered, the crystals are stable and the consistency of the fat does not change appreciably even though the storage temperature may fluctuate from 4° to 32°C (40° to 90°F). Hydrogenated shortenings are superior to butter or regular lard in this respect.

An alternate method of producing a plastic fat from a vegetable oil is to add highly hydrogenated fat to the oil. Fats so formed are called compound shortenings in contrast to the former, known as hydrogenated all-vegetable shortening.

Interesterification

When fat is heated under nitrogen and in the presence of a suitable catalyst, the fatty acids migrate and recombine with the glycerol in a more random fashion (16,18). As a result of this shuffling of fatty acids, new glycerides form. Molecules of a fat after such interesterification are more heterogeneous. For example, lard, normally quite coarse and grainy, after rearrangement contains smaller crystals. Photomicrographs of crystals of lard before and after rearrangement are shown in Figure 15-4. Rearrangement alters the consistency of a fat, and it remains plastic over a wider range of temperature.

Interesterification can be used to produce what are called structured lipids (21). Medium chain triacylglycerides (MCT) formed by esterifying caprylic (8:0) and capric (10:0) acids with glycerol have been used in clinical nutrition for some time. When these unconventional triacylglycerides are interesterified with long chain fatty acids, a structured lipid results. If behenic acid replaces one of the medium chain fatty acids, the structured triacylglyceride caprenin is the result (21). The physical properties of caprenin resemble those of cocoa butter. Caprenin has been approved as a coating agent in confections by the Food and Drug Administration (34).

Acetylation

When acetic acid replaces a fatty acid in a fat molecule, acetylated or acetin fats are formed (24). Acetin fats may be liquid or plastic at room temperature, depending on the fatty acids present in the molecule. Oils advertised as edible lubricants are acetin fats. The presence of acetic acid in a glycerides has the advantage of lowering the melting point, as does an unsaturated fatty acid, without the instability of the latter. A second advantage is that acetin fats crystallize and remain in the alpha form. Acetin fats appear translucent and waxy rather than grainy when they crystallize. The crystals form a ribbonlike, unordered but interlocking network, as shown in Figure 15-5. Acetin fats are considered safe and currently

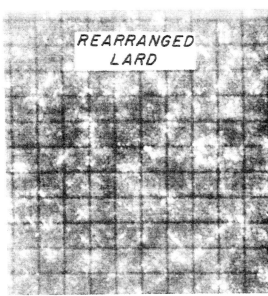

Figure 15-4. Effect of rearrangement (interesterification) on the size of the crystals of lard. Original magnification approximately × 200. (From C. W. Hoerr and D. F. Waugh, *Journal of the American Oil Chemists' Society* 32:37, 1955. Reprinted by permission.)

are permitted in edible fats. Acetin fats form flexible films and are used as coating agents for such foods as dried raisins, prepared meats, cheese, and nuts (24).

A number of shortenings on the market contain from two to three percent glyceryl monostearate (which is usually accompanied by smaller amounts of the diacylglyceride). Fats that contain monoacylglyceride are advantageous in cake making (Chapter 25).

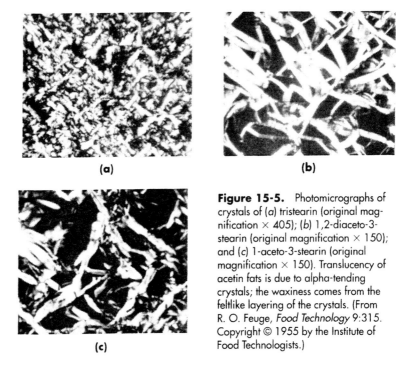

(a)   **(b)**

(c)

Figure 15-5. Photomicrographs of crystals of (*a*) tristearin (original magnification × 405); (*b*) 1,2-diaceto-3-stearin (original magnification × 150); and (*c*) 1-aceto-3-stearin (original magnification × 150). Translucency of acetin fats is due to alpha-tending crystals; the waxiness comes from the feltlike layering of the crystals. (From R. O. Feuge, *Food Technology* 9:315. Copyright © 1955 by the Institute of Food Technologists.)

FUNCTIONS IN FOODS

Fats function in a number of ways in foods as different as ice cream, French fries, pastry, ground beef, and mayonnaise. They modify crystals in ice cream (Chapter 5) and in fudge (Chapter 6). Fats serve as a medium for the transfer of heat when foods are cooked by frying. The long hydrocarbon chains of fatty acids are hydrophobic; that is, they have limited affinity for water and other polar compounds. Lipids that have made contact with flour block its accessibility to water. The limited development of gluten that results has a tenderizing effect on such products as biscuits and muffins (Chapter 13), on pastry (Chapter 17), and on cakes (Chapter 25). Fats contribute flavor and tenderness to protein-rich foods such as cheese (Chapter 20) and ground beef (Chapter 22). In emulsified form, fats contribute to the velvety smoothness of cream, cream cheese, and mayonnaise. Crystals in a fat give it a workable consistency at room temperature; as they melt in the mouth they produce a sensation of moistness. Fats are valued ingredients because of the body and mouthfeel they contribute to foods.

FAT SUBSTITUTES

Emphasis on the positive health effects of controlling caloric intake and especially of limiting the intake of fat prompted a search for low- or noncaloric fat substitutes. A number of substitutes currently available mimic the body and mouthfeel that fats contribute to foods (12). The maltodextrins are one group of fat replacers. They are formed by limited hydrolysis of starch by acid or enzymes to give a dextrose equivalent (DE) near 20 versus a high DE (near 100) when corn syrup is the end product (1,34). Maltodextrin fat substitutes made from corn, potato, and tapioca starches are available. Oatrim consists of maltodextrins from oat starch plus the viscous beta-glucans present in the oat grain (19). Maltodextrins are dispersed in water at a ratio of three grams of water per gram of dextrin (34). The resultant gel at one kilocalorie per gram is used to replace one gram of fat at nine kilocalories per gram. The ability of starch derivatives to substitute for fat comes from their association with water. In fact, water is the essential ingredient and the dextrins hold the water (40). Maltodextrin gels can replace fat in sour cream, cheese spread, margarine-type spreads, frozen dairy products, layer cakes, and muffins.

Hydrocolloids and the viscosity they impart to water are especially effective in mimicking the effects of fat in salad dressings. Carrageenan, with water, is used to give tenderness and juiciness to reduced-fat ground beef patties that are commercially available. Although such substitutes may mimic the mouthfeel of fat, other attributes normally supplied by fat may be missing (12).

Fat substitutes may be made from protein as well as from carbohydrates. Proteins of milk and egg whites are heated to form a gel that is sheared into spheroids less than three microns in size by a process called microparticulation. These microparticles move over the tongue like so many miniature ball bearings, giving the impression of fluidity. Simplesse® is such a product (1). It is dispersed in water in a ratio of two grams of water to one gram of protein before it is used. So one gram of the hydrated product supplies 1⅓ calories instead of the nine calories from one gram of fat. When egg white is used to manufacture the product, it is not stable to heat. Simplesse®, first approved for use in frozen dairy products, is now used in products such as cheese spread, cream cheese, salad dressings, sour cream, and yogurt.

Synthesis of fat-based compounds that have physical properties similar to those of natural fats represents another approach. Fatlike compounds are formed when fatty acids are esterified with the OH groups of sucrose. Olestra is the generic term for a mixture of hexa- to octa-sucrose esters (1). These sucrose polyesters function much as do glycerol esters of fatty acids. They are heat-stable and so can be used in baking and frying. However, they are noncaloric because they resist hydrolysis and so are not absorbed. The use of Olestra in the commercial production of potato chips and other salty snack foods, in place of conventional, calorie-laden fats and oils, has been approved by the Food and Drug Administration.

In most cases, instead of a single replacer a combination of ingredients that varies with the product is required for adequate substitution of fat. N-FLATE® is a blend of ingredients developed for use in place of fat in low-calorie cake mix (39). It consists of a combination of emulsifiers for adequate aeration of the batter, of a modified, pregelatinized starch that absorbs water and thickens on contact, and of guar gum, a hydrocolloid that contributes viscosity to the batter. Nonfat dry milk solids are included as a carrier for the other ingredients when the fat replacer is manufactured. N-FLATE® at six to eight percent of the mix can replace fat at a level of 10 to 12 percent of the mix, yielding a cake with no fat and reduced calories. N-FLATE® is a dry powder and is combined with other dry ingredients when a cake is made.

It is unlikely that a single ingredient will be developed that can duplicate all of the functions of fat. However, combinations of ingredients, each providing partial replacement, can be used to simulate fat in varied products.

DETERIORATION OF FATS

Absorption of Odors

Fats absorb odors because they dissolve odorous gases to which they are exposed. This type of spoilage is quite obvious when fat is held in an open container in a refrigerator in which cantaloupe is stored. But there are many more subtle instances of spoilage of fat due to absorption of odors.

Rancidity

Fats may spoil because they have become rancid. Rancidity in fats is due to either hydrolysis or oxidation (11). In hydrolytic rancidity, the triglyceride reacts with water and for each molecule of water involved one molecule of fatty acid is released. When a molecule of fat reacts with three molecules of water, glycerol, and three fatty acids are formed, as shown below:

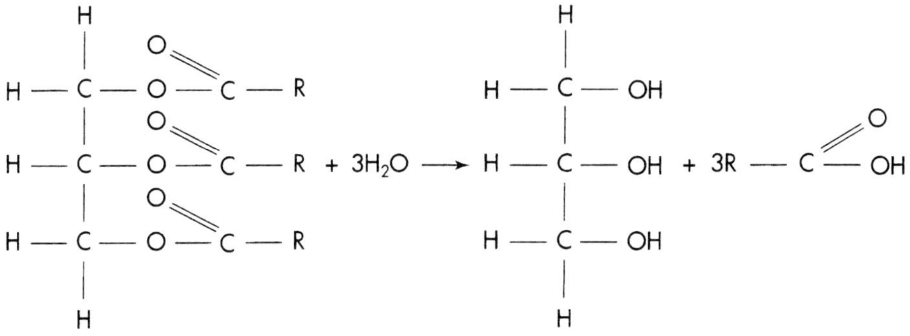

$$
\begin{array}{ccc}
\text{A triglyceride} & + 3H_2O \longrightarrow & \text{Glycerol} & + 3R - C(=O) - OH
\end{array}
$$

| A triglyceride | Water | Glycerol | Fatty acid |

Heat acts as a catalyst for this reaction, so hydrolysis takes place in fat used for deep-fat frying. Cold, wet food placed in hot fat favors hydrolysis of the fat. If the molecule of fat reacts with the base NaOH instead of water, glycerol and three molecules of the sodium salt of the fatty acid are formed. The latter, of course, is soap. Ammonium hydroxide will react with fat in the same way as the stronger base. It is for this reason that ammonia in hot water effectively removes fat from the surface of utensils and an open container of ammonia placed in a hot oven in which fat has been spattered aids in its removal.

Fat-splitting enzymes known as lipases, also act as catalysts for the hydrolysis of fats when present in foods. For example, butter becomes rancid when stored in a warm place, which favors the activity of the enzyme. Keeping fats cold delays the beginning of hydrolytic rancidity. The odor of rancid butter comes from butyric acid, which has been liberated according to the reaction above. Aged whipping cream, particularly that which clings to the edges of the container, may have a bitter taste from the butyric acid liberated by hydrolysis.

Molecules of fat that contain unsaturated fatty acids are subject to oxidative rancidity. The unpleasant odor of such rancid fats is attributed to the formation and subsequent breakdown of hydroperoxides (11,35). According to the theory held currently, a hydrogen on a carbon adjacent to one carrying a double bond is displaced by a quantum of energy to give a free radical:

$$
\begin{array}{ccccc}
\text{H} & \text{H} & \text{H} & \text{H} \\
| & | & | & | \\
-\text{C}- & \text{C}= & \text{C}- & \text{C}- \quad + \quad \text{a quantum of energy} \longrightarrow \\
| & & & | \\
\text{H} & & & \text{H}
\end{array}
$$

Unsaturated
fatty acid

$$
\begin{array}{ccccc}
\text{H} & \text{H} & \text{H} & \text{H} \\
| & | & | & | \\
-\text{C}- & \text{C}= & \text{C}- & \text{C}- \quad + \qquad \text{H} \\
\bullet & & & | \\
& & & \text{H}
\end{array}
$$

Free radical   Labile hydrogen

Both heat and light are common sources of the energy that gives rise to free radicals. Molecular oxygen can unite with the carbon that carries the free radical to form an activated peroxide as follows:

$$
\begin{array}{ccccccccc}
\text{H} & \text{H} & \text{H} & \text{H} & & & \text{H} & \text{H} & \text{H} & \text{H} \\
| & | & | & | & & & | & | & | & | \\
-\text{C}- & \text{C}= & \text{C}- & \text{C}- & + \; O_2 \longrightarrow & -\text{C}- & \text{C}= & \text{C}- & \text{C}- \\
\bullet & & & | & & & | & & & | \\
& & & \text{H} & & & \text{O}-\text{O}\bullet & & & \text{H}
\end{array}
$$

Free radical   Oxygen   Activated peroxide

The energy from this activated peroxide can displace a hydrogen from another unsaturated fatty acid and thus activate it. The latter becomes a free radical. The displaced hydrogen unites with the activated peroxide to form a hydroperoxide. This part of the reaction is:

$$
\begin{array}{ccccccccc}
\text{H} & \text{H} & \text{H} & \text{H} & & \text{H} & \text{H} & \text{H} & \text{H} \\
| & | & | & | & & | & | & | & | \\
-\text{C}- & \text{C}= & \text{C}- & \text{C}- & + & -\text{C}- & \text{C}= & \text{C}- & \text{C}- \longrightarrow \\
| & & & | & & | & & & | \\
\text{O}-\text{O}\bullet & & & \text{H} & & \text{H} & & & \text{H}
\end{array}
$$

Activated peroxide   Unsaturated fatty acid

$$
\begin{array}{ccccccccc}
\text{H} & \text{H} & \text{H} & \text{H} & & \text{H} & \text{H} & \text{H} & \text{H} \\
| & | & | & | & & | & | & | & | \\
-\text{C}- & \text{C}= & \text{C}- & \text{C}- & + & -\text{C}- & \text{C}= & \text{C}- & \text{C}- \\
| & & & | & & \bullet & & & | \\
\text{O}-\text{OH} & & & \text{H} & & & & & \text{H}
\end{array}
$$

Hydroperoxide   Free radical

In this way the energy that catalyzes the oxidation of a fatty acid is not squandered but is passed on to another fatty acid where it repeats the process. A free radical is particularly troublesome because it is the beginning of a self-perpetuating reaction whereby the oxidation of many unsaturated fatty acids is catalyzed. A hydroperoxide is very unstable, decomposing into compounds with shorter carbon chains. These include fatty acids, aldehydes, and ketones, which are volatile and contribute to the unpleasant odor of rancid fat.

The more unsaturated the fatty acid, the greater is its susceptibility to oxidative rancidity. Hydrogenation makes a fat more stable in this respect. However, hydrogenated fats after extended storage, especially at elevated temperatures, undergo a change called reversion. An aldehyde—6-nonenal—has been identified as responsible for the off odor. Oxidation of two isomers of linoleic acid, formed during hydrogenation, gives rise to the aldehyde (22).

Because of the prooxidant effect of light, fats should be stored in a dark as well as a cold place. Printed on potato chip packages are directions to avoid placing the package where sunlight can reach it. Certain frequencies of the light spectrum, especially the ultraviolet, are more harmful than others. Certain metals also catalyze the reaction leading to oxidative rancidity in fats. Both copper and iron are prooxidants (11). For this reason stainless steel or aluminum utensils are preferred for fats. Oxidation of unsaturated fats may be catalyzed by the enzyme lipoxygenase (38) as well as by heat, light, and certain metals. Iron freed from the pigment hemoglobin catalyzes rancidity in cooked meats. Reactions similar to those outlined above for autocatalytic oxidative rancidity occur in unsaturated fats when the enzyme lipoxygenase is present (11,38). Less energy is needed for the reaction so low temperatures are less effective in preventing lipoxygenase-catalyzed than autocatalytic rancidity (11).

Antioxidants

Substances that delay the onset of oxidative rancidity in fats have been sought because of the unpalatability of rancid fats. These substances are known as antioxidants. One of them was known to the pioneers, who added the bark of the slippery elm tree to pork fat when lard was rendered. A substance derived from the inner bark acted as an antioxidant. Lard so rendered could be stored longer before it became rancid.

Most of the antioxidants in use today are phenolic compounds (35). Four phenolic antioxidants approved for use in fats are butylated hydroxyanisole (BHA), butylated hydroxytoluene (BHT), propyl gallate (PG), and tertiary butylhydroquinone (TBHQ). Labels on containers for margarine and many rich crackers indicate the presence of one or more of these antioxidants. Flavonoid compounds with a minimum of two hydroxyl groups in the *ortho* position (on adjacent carbons) or *para* position (on carbons opposite each other) are good antioxidants. Many oils derived from seeds of plants contain tocopherols, naturally occurring antioxidants. Vegetable oils keep as well as they do at room temperature because of the presence of these naturally occurring antioxidants.

Phytic acid—inositol hexaphosphate—is a naturally occurring antioxidant present in cereals, legumes, oil seeds, and nuts. It is particularly effective in preventing iron-catalyzed rancidity of phospholipids in cooked meat and poultry (9). Presence of phytic acid may account for the fact that development of rancid odor is suppressed when cooked meat or poultry is reheated in flour-thickened sauce or gravy.

A molecule of antioxidant functions by replacing an unsaturated fatty acid as the source of labile hydrogen to unite with a free radical or an activated peroxide. The molecule of antioxidant is oxidized instead of another fatty acid. In the process, the antioxidant siphons off the energy that would otherwise be available for the formation of a new fatty acid free radical and that would perpetuate the chain reaction that occurs in the autoxidation of fats. The phenolic hydroquinone illustrates how the more elaborate molecules of phenolic antioxidants act as hydrogen donors:

Hydroquinone   Quinone   Hydrogen

Certain organic acids that act as synergists may be added to fats along with a phenolic antioxidant (34). A synergist is a substance that increases the effectiveness of the primary antioxidant. Di- or tricarboxylic acids are effective because they bind or sequester metal ions. A molecule of citric acid used as a synergist may bind prooxidant iron thus:

Ethylenediaminetetraacetate (EDTA) is a metal-sequestering agent used in some salad dressings.

In one homemade quick bread mix, cream of tartar is included to act as a synergist and increase the effectiveness of the tocopherol present in the vegetable oil from which the fat was made. Other synergists keep the primary antioxidant in reduced form and thus maintain its ability to act as a hydrogen donor. The effectiveness of one antioxidant may be increased by using it in combination with another. A combination of butylated hydroxyanisole and propyl gallate is more effective than the sum of the effectiveness of the two used separately. Use of antioxidants and synergists in foods that contain fat are responsible for improved keeping qualities of many foods.

Cereals, especially whole grain ones, are likely to become rancid from the polyunsaturated fat they contain. Baked products such as crackers and cookies and fried foods are subject to oxidative rancidity. For these and similar foods, an antioxidant that is stable at the high temperatures used in baking and frying is desirable. One such antioxidant with high carry over is butylated hydroxyanisole. Sugar cookies that contain a small amount of the reducing sugar glucose, in addition to sucrose, resist rancidity more than do cookies made from sucrose alone (13). The greater stability of the former is attributed to the antioxidant properties of the products of the sugar-amine reaction that contribute to browning of the cookies.

FATS AS A MEDIUM FOR THE TRANSFER OF HEAT

Foods are cooked in hot fat or oil by sautéing or by deep-fat frying. A fat used for frying should be odorless and bland tasting, a neutral medium for the transfer heat. An advantage of fat as a cooking medium is that the temperature attained is not limited by boiling as is that of water. Foods heated in fat are not only cooked, but the surface is browned due to caramelization of sugars and to reducing sugar-protein reaction. Because it is desired to brown fried food, the fat used must be able to withstand high temperatures. Recommended frying temperatures vary from 177° to 201°C (350° to 395°F). A thermometer suspended in the fat, or a fryer with a thermostat, permits monitoring of the temperature. The crisp surface of fried foods adds to their appeal, as does their flavor. Unsaturated gamma-lactones have been identified as contributing to the flavor of deep fat fried foods (26).

The Frying Process

Frying is a dehydration process involving transfer of water from the interior of an item to the surface where it is converted to steam (3). Steam dissipates heat from the surface and so maintains its temperature at 100°C even though the surrounding fat is 180°C. At the same time that water is being drawn from the interior to the surface, heat from the periphery of an item is conducted to the interior. The temperature of the oil should be balanced against the movement of water from the food and the conduction of heat into it. The balance is different for (a) potato chips in which the original water content is reduced from approximately 80 percent to 2 percent, for (b) fried chicken for which cooking the chicken, not loss of moisture, is the main objective, and for (c) a precooked product such as fish croquettes for which bringing the product to serving temperature, browning, and crisping of the breaded surface are the effects desired. A temperature that is too low prolongs contact of food with oil and retards browning. A high temperature may cause crossbonding of carbohydrates and proteins (case-hardening) of the surface, result in excessive browning before heat is conducted to the center of the item, and accelerate deterioration of the oil. In any case, only after water is unavailable to move to the surface and change into steam does the surface's temperature rise enough to brown and crisp it.

When a food with its hydrophilic surface is lowered into fresh oil, actual contact of the food with the hydrophobic oil may be as little as 10 percent (3), even though the food is submerged in the oil. This condition changes slowly as heating of the oil continues during its early, break-in stage. This stage is followed by a build-up of decomposition products of the oil. The combination of high temperature and moisture causes hydrolysis of triacylglycerides to mono- and diacylglycerides. These partly hydrophilic and partly lipophilic (fat-like) compounds act at surfaces where oil and food meet to bring about increased contact between them. This, in turn increases the conduction of heat from the oil to the food. An extended period follows during which surface active compounds continue to accumulate and the oil is at optimum frying performance. After contact between the oil and the food is approximately 50 percent, performance of the oil begins a slow decline. In commercial frying operations, fresh oil is added to the fryer at regular intervals to keep the concentration of surface active material at the optimum level for frying.

At length, exposure of the oil to oxygen and to substances from foods during frying, plus accumulation of breakdown substances of the fat and the prolonged heating at high temperatures combine to bring about its rapid deterioration. The color changes from pale yellow, to amber to shades of brown. Molecules unite in long chains or polymers (32). Unsaturated molecules may give rise to cyclic compounds. The oil becomes more viscous and has an increased tendency to foam. Fatty acids and glycerol accumulate as well as mono- and diacylglycerides. The latter are readily hydrolyzed to yield glycerol. Glycerol, when heated, is converted to acrolein by dehydration. Acrolein is a blue gas that is irritating to mucous membranes.

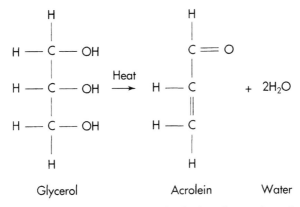

Glycerol   Acrolein   Water

The lower the percentage of glycerol in an oil the higher the smoke point (the higher the temperature to which the oil can be heated before the appearance of acrolein (4). Starting with an oil that has a high smoke point, avoiding overheating (in terms of temperature or time) and using a container with a small diameter increases the temperature to which it can be heated before it smokes (4).

Absorption of Fat

Although fat contributes to the sensory properties desired in fried foods, a fat-soaked food is neither palatable nor desirable from a health standpoint. Absorption should be kept to a minimum. A number of factors influence the amount of oil absorbed. Oil should be kept at optimum temperature during the entire period. Overloading the fryer causes the temperature to drop and prolongs the cooking time. A food fried in a deteriorating oil absorbs more of it because of the accumulating surface active compounds (32). The more viscous the oil the greater its absorption (37). Addition of silicones (dimethyl polysiloxanes) reduces foaming, which limits exposure to oxygen (10). Batters cause more rapid deterioration of the oil used for deep frying than do french fries (2). Baking powder, egg, and milk are responsible for the greater decomposition. Doughnuts from leaner dough absorb less fat, but those from richer dough are more tender (7). Absorption is greater in dough that contains lecithin (27). A survey of fried snack and convenience items (41 brands included) found average percentages of fat for the items included as follows: potato chips 40, cheese puffs 38, corn chips 35, cheese chips 25, tortilla chips 24, cake doughnuts 22, chicken thighs 14, french fried potatoes 14, and fish pieces 10 (36).

Hazards in Using Fats for Frying

Burns are one hazard. Fat may be hotter than it appears because it does not boil. A burn from hot fat may be severe not only because of the high temperature, but also because of its tendency to cling to the skin. Fire is another hazard. The specific heat of oil is approximately half that of water, so a volume of oil will come up to temperature faster than an equal volume of water. If left on a hot unit, the temperature will continue to rise until it reaches the flash point when the volatiles from the fat ignite.

When cold, wet food comes in contact with hot fat, the water as it sinks is converted into steam, the bubbles of which may cause the fat to overflow the container. The surface of the uncooked food should be as dry as possible, overloading the container should be avoided, and the wire basket or slotted spoon that holds the food should be lifted momentarily to prevent overflow. Use of a deep container reduces the hazard. Fat splashed on the unit may ignite, and thus set the contents of the container on fire. Should this happen, a lid should be put on the container and the heat turned off. The container should be removed from a hot electric unit. A deep fat fryer with thermostat control minimizes this hazard and also frees one to concentrate on the food rather than on maintaining the temperature of the oil.

When butter is heated for sautéing, it does not spatter even though it contains appreciable water. A surfactant (Chapter 16) present in butter keeps the water in the form of an emulsion so it does not separate from the fat. Instead, the butter foams as the water boils away. Most margarines contain an antispattering agent, usually lecithin (14).

For heating frying fats, stainless steel containers are preferable to those made of iron for two reasons. In addition to iron's being a prooxidant, fat is more easily removed from the smooth surface of stainless steel. Foods stick to iron because of the pits in the surface. One reason that oiling a baking pan prevents sticking is that it partly fills and coats the pits.

Cleaning the container after foods have been fried presents problems. Stainless steel is easiest to clean, because only hot water and detergent are required. The fat and the gummy material on the exterior of an aluminum pan can be removed by scouring with steel wool or other aluminum cleanser. Iron utensils may be soaked in ammonia to dissolve the gummy film of polymerized fat, which can then be washed away.

REFERENCES

1. Anon. 1990. "Fat substitute update." *Food Technology* 44(4):92, 94, 97. Protein-based, carbohydrate-based, and synthetic fats.
2. Bennion, M. and F. Hanning. 1956. "Decomposition of lard in the frying of french-fried potatoes and of fritter-type batters." *Journal of Home Economics* 48:184–88. Effects of the two products on smoke point and on discoloration of fat; effects of ingredients in the batter on smoke point and on fat absorption.
3. Blumenthal, M. M. 1991. "A new look at the chemistry and physics of baking." *Food Technology* 45(2):68–71, 94. Heat transfer, role of surfactants, and deterioration of fats.
4. Blunt, K., and C. M. Feeney. 1915. "The smoking temperature of edible fats." *Journal of Home Economics* 7:535–41. Analysis of the main factors that affect the smoking point of fats.
5. Carpenter, D. L., and H. T. Slover. 1973. "Lipid composition of selected margarines."

American Oil Chemists Society Journal 50:372–76. Fatty acids in the oils used.

6. Coenen, J. W. E. 1976. "Hydrogenation of edible oils." *American Oil Chemists' Society Journal* 53:382–89. Details of the process.

7. Denton, M. C., E. Wengel, and L. Pritchett. 1920. "Absorption of fat by fried batters and doughs, and causes of variations." *Journal of Home Economics* 12:111–27. Variations in doughnut type batters that affect fat absorption.

8. Dziezak, J. D. 1989. "Fats, oils and fat substitutes." *Food Technology* 43(7):66–74. Fatty acids in fats; main replacers.

9. Empson, K. L., T. P. Labuza, and E. Graf. 1991. "Phytic acid as a food antioxidant." *Journal of Food Science* 56:560–63. Effectiveness in model systems and in refrigerated chicken.

10. Freeman, I. P., F. B. Padley, and W. L. Sheppard. 1973. "Use of silicones in frying oils." *American Oil Chemists' Society Journal* 50:101–3. Antifoaming agents.

11. Glass, R. L. 1966. "Food rancidity: Its nature and prevention." *Bakers Digest* 40:34–35, 38–39. Clear, concise presentation.

12. Glicksman, M. 1991. "Hydrocolloids and the search for the 'oily grail.'" *Food Technology* 45(10):94–103. Fat replacers; applications.

13. Griffith, T., and J. A. Johnson. 1957. "Relation of browning reaction with storage stability of sugar cookies." *Cereal Chemistry* 34:159–69. Effects of glucose.

14. Harris, B. H., A. K. Epstein, and F. J. Kahn. 1941. "Fatty interface modifiers. Composition, properties, and uses in the food industry." *Oil and Soap* 18:179–82. Antispattering and other roles of surfactants.

15. Hoerr, C. W. 1960. "Morphology of fats, oils, and shortenings." *Journal of the American Oil Chemists' Society* 37:539–46. Polymorphic forms of crystals in fats.

16. Hoerr, C. W., and D. F. Waugh. 1955. "Some physical characteristics of rearranged lard." *Journal of the American Oil Chemists' Society* 32:37–41. Effects of molecular rearrangement on crystal formation and the functional properties of lard.

17. Hoerr, C. W., and J. V. Ziemba. 1965. "Fat crystallography points way to quality."

Food Engineering 37(5):90–95. Tailoring fats for different food uses.

18. Husted, H. H. 1976. "The interesterification of edible oils." *American Oil Chemists' Society Journal* 53:390–92. Nature of the process; advantages.

19. Inglett, G. E., and S. B. Grisanore. 1991. "Maltodextrin fat substitute lowers cholesterol." *Food Technology* 45(6):104. Oatrim.

20. Institute of Shortening and Edible Oils. 1994. *Food Fats and Oils.* Washington D.C. 28 pp. Chemistry, processing, and oil-rich products.

21. Kennedy, J. P. 1991. "Structured lipids: Fats of the future." *Food Technology* 45(11):76, 78, 80, 83. Interesterification of long chain with medium chain triglycerides.

22. Keppler, J. G., M. M. Horikx, P. W. Meijboom, and W. H. Feenstra. 1967. "Isolinoleic acids responsible for the formation of hardening flavor." *American Oil Chemists' Society Journal* 44:543–44. Identity of the compounds.

23. Kreulen, H. P. 1976. "Fractionation and winterization of edible fats and oils." *American Oil Chemists' Society Journal* 53:393–96. Nonchemical modification of edible lipids.

24. Luce, G. T. 1967. "Acetylated monoglycerides as coatings for selected foods." *Food Technology* 21:1462–63, 1466, 1468. Unique properties.

25. Lutton, E. S. 1957. "On the configuration of cocoa butter." *Journal of the American Oil Chemists' Society* 34:521–22. Triglyceride make up of the fats in chocolate.

26. May, W. A., R. J. Peterson, and S. S. Chang. 1978. "Synthesis of some unsaturated lactones and their relationship to deep-fat fried flavor." *Journal of Food Science* 43:1248–52. An attempt to pin-point the source of the deep-fat fried flavor.

27. McComber, D., and E. M. Miller. 1976. "Differences in total lipid and fatty acid composition of doughnuts as influenced by lecithin, leavening agent, and use of frying fat." *Cereal Chemistry* 53:101–9. Absorption of frying fat.

28. Mensink, R. P., and M. B. Katan. 1990. Effects of dietary *trans* fatty acids on high-density and low-density lipoprotein cholesterol levels in healthy subjects. *New*

England Journal of Medicine 323:439–45. Unfavorable effects on both HDL and LDL serum levels.

29. Ottenstein, D. M., L. A. Wittings, G. Walker, V. Mahadevan, and N. Pelick. 1977. "*Trans* fatty acid content of commercial margarine samples determined by gasliquid chromatography on OV-275." *American Oil Chemists' Society Journal* 54:207–9. Seven retail samples analyzed.

30. Robertson, J. A. 1972. "Sunflower: America's neglected crop." *American Oil Chemists' Society Journal* 49:239–44. Fatty acid make-up.

31. Roth, H., and S. P. Rock. 1972. "The chemistry and technology of frying fats." 1. "Chemistry." *Bakers Digest* 46(4):38–45, 66. Autoxidation reviewed; technical.

32. Roth, H., and S. P. Rock. 1972. "The chemistry and technology of frying fats." 2. "Technology." *Bakers Digest* 46(5):38–40, 41–44. Changes in fats brought about by frying.

33. Sanders, J. H. 1959. "Processing of food fats—a review." *Food Technology* 13:41–45. Brief outline of main steps in preparing shortenings from vegetable oils; alkali refining, hydrogenation, deodorization, plasticizing, interesterification, and winterizing discussed.

34. Setser, C. S., and W. L. Racette. 1992. "Macromolecule replacers in food products." *Critical Reviews in Food Science and Nutrition* 32:275–97. Carbohydrate-, protein-, and lipid-based products; their effectiveness.

35. Sherwin, E. R. 1976. "Antioxidants for vegetable oils." *American Oil Chemists' Society Journal* 53:430–36. Rancidity; types and function of antioxidants.

36. Smith, L. M., A. J. Clifford, A. K. Creveling, and C. L. Hamblin. 1985. Lipid content and fatty acid profiles of various deep-fat fried food. *American Oil Chemists' Society Journal* 62(6):996–99. Nine snack and convenience food products analyzed.

37. Stern, S., and H. Roth. 1959. "Properties of frying fat related to fat absorption in doughnut frying." *Cereal Science Today* 4:176–79. Relation between fat absorption and development of viscosity.

38. Wagenknecht, A. C., and F. A. Lea. 1956. "The action of lipoxidase in frozen raw peas." *Food Research* 21:605–10. Oxidation of fat and chlorophyll in frozen peas catalyzed by lipoxidase.

39. Waring, S. 1988. "Shortening replacement in cakes." *Food Technology* 42(3):114, 116–18. A free-flowing fat substitute.

40. Yeckel, W. C., and C. Cox. 1992. "Application of starch-based fat replacers." *Food Technology* 46(6):146–48. Effectiveness due to association with water.

Emulsions

16

An emulsion is defined as a colloidal dispersion of one liquid in another, molecules of the two liquids immiscible. In foods the liquids are basically oil and water. Milk, cream, and coconut milk are naturally occurring emulsions. Mayonnaise and French dressings, as well as butter, margarine, cheese, cream cheese, cake batter, cream soups, and gravies are fabricated emulsions. The oil may be partly solidified as in butter; and the water may contain air bubbles or be partly crystallized as in ice cream.

NATURE OF AN EMULSION

Phases

Water and oil do not blend because the attraction of water molecules for each other excludes the oil, molecules of which likewise are attracted to each other. If oil and water are mixed, they separate with a definite, sharp line, once shaking or beating stops. As Aeschylus has Clytemnestra say

> Pour oil and vinegar into the same jar,
> You would say they stand apart unlovingly.*

To keep droplets of one liquid suspended in another in which it is immiscible requires a third substance—an emulsifier. Thus an emulsion has three parts or phases. One—the dispersed phase—consists of suspended droplets, usually oil. Another—the continuous phase or dispersions medium—is usually water in foods. The third is the emulsifier, which not only segregates droplets of the dispersed phase but also anchors them in the continuous phase.

Functions of an Emulsifier

Work is required to bring about the great increase in surface area between oil and water in an emulsion. The force of the blades of a beater can shear the two liquids, portions of which assume a spherical shape. Surface tension accounts for the tendency of liquids to form droplets. The beads on a splashed drop of milk (Fig. 16-1) illustrate the effects of surface tension. Molecules in the surface of a liquid do not have the same freedom of movement as those in the interior. The diagram in Figure 16-2 shows this. The *net* attractive force on

---

*From *Agamemnon of Aeschylus*, Louis MacNeice, translator, Faber and Faber, Ltd., publishers, London.

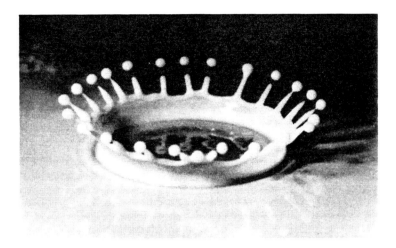

Figure 16-1. Photomicrograph at 1/100,000 of a second of a drop of milk splashing onto a flat surface. The beads of liquid of the crown form because of surface tension. (From Harold Edgerton, MIT, Cambridge, MA.)

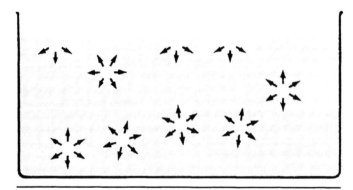

Figure 16-2. Forces acting on molecules in the interior and on the surface of a liquid. (Reproduced from Paul Becker, *Principles of Emulsion Technology,* by permission of Reinhold Book Corporation, a subsidiary of Chapman-Reinhold, Inc., New York, 1955.)

a molecule in the main body of a liquid surrounded on all sides by the same kind of molecules is zero. But the pull on molecules in the *surface* of a liquid is unbalanced and toward the interior. To conserve energy, molecules at the surface take on the character of an elastic skin. Droplets of oil and water are maintained only by continuous agitation. Once agitation stops, droplets of each liquid coalesce and oil, being lighter, rises to the top, and the denser water settles to the bottom of the container. The liquids return to the original two phases; the plane at which the two meet is called the interface.

An emulsifier aids in the formation and maintenance of both the dispersed and the continuous phases of an emulsion. An emulsifier has two functional areas—one nonpolar or hydrophobic (lipophilic) with an affinity for oil, and one polar or hydrophilic with an affinity for water. If an emulsifier is present when oil and water are agitated, it will parti-

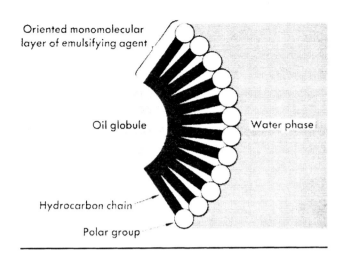

Figure 16-3. Diagram showing the orientation of emulsifying agent in an oil-in-water emulsion. (Reproduced from J. R. Hartman, *Colloid Chemistry*, 1947, by permission of Houghton Mifflin Company, Boston.)

tion between the two liquids according to its solubility in each. The liquid whose surface tension is lowered most will become the continuous phase, the other the dispersed phase. Most food emulsions are oil-in-water (O/W) type. A three-part protective layer surrounds each fat droplet. It consists of molecules of the emulsifier aligned at the interface where oil droplets meet the aqueous phase. It includes the hydrophobic part of the emulsifier and the layer of oil in which it is dissolved plus the hydrophilic portion of the emulsifier and the water in which it is dissolved. A diagram of a droplet of oil with its protective layer is shown in Figure 16-3. This three-part protective layer of emulsifier prevents droplets of oil already emulsified from uniting with oil as it is added. Should two oil droplets already emulsified collide, the protective film prevents their coalescence.

In addition to the three-part protective film around dispersed droplets of an emulsion, other factors contribute to stability (3, 4, 7). Small droplets of the dispersed phase and a viscous continuous phase favor stability. When the continuous phase is water, hydration of polar groups of the emulsifier help to keep the droplets apart. Charged groups on the emulsifier attract opposite charges, thus building up an electric double layer that makes fat-to-fat contact between adjacent droplets less likely. Finally, bulky parts of the emulsifier that project into the aqueous phase can prevent close approach of dispersed fat droplets.

EMULSIFYING AGENTS

Manufactured

The production of a number of specialized surfactants, as these emulsifiers are called, makes possible a great variety of manufactured foods such as icings, frostings, coffee whitener, low-calorie spreads, and prepared mixes. Soap, the sodium salt of a fatty acid, was an early manufactured surfactant. Soap markedly lowers the surface tension of water and, by emulsifying fat, enhances the cleansing power of water. A series of low molecular weight, edible compounds, chiefly fatty acid esters of polyhydric alcohols such as glycerol, are used as emulsifiers in foods (5, 11). A mixture of mono- and diacylglycerides has been used for a number of years, first as an antispattering agent in margarine. A distilled monoacylglyceride, glycerol monostearate, that is approximately 90 percent monoester is available, also. Acids such as acetic, citric, lactic, succinic, and tartaric esterified with monoacylglycerides constitute another group of emulsifiers, of which sodium stearoyl-2-lactylate is an example. Glycol can replace glycerol, as in propylene glycol monostearate. Fatty acid esters of sorbitan, called SPANS, and of polyoxyethylene sorbitan, called TWEENS, are still another group of surfactants. Fatty acid esters of sucrose are available also as surfactants. Esterification usually involves one, two, or three of the primary hydroxyl groups instead of the six to eight hydroxyl groups when the polyester is to be used as a fat substitute.

The fatty acid portion of each molecule of surfactant contributes its lipophilic character and the remainder its hydrophilic property. The chain length of the fatty acid(s) involved and the presence or absence of double bonds and the properties of the polyhydric portion of the surfactant influence the type of emulsion formed. In some surfactants the hydrophilic aspects predominate; in others it is the lipophilic quality. A scale of 1 to 20 has been devised to denote the hydrophilic/lipophilic balance (HLB). Emulsifiers at the low end of the scale have a greater affinity for oil and so form water-in-oil (W/O) emulsions. Those near the high end of the scale have more affinity for the aqueous phase and so form oil-in-water (O/W) emulsions. The HLB of common food surfactants can be found in Table 16-1 (5).

An HLB range from three to six is considered best for the formation of water-in-oil emulsions and a range from 8 to 18 is best for oil-in-water emulsions (8). Most emulsions in foods are oil-in-water type, although butter and margarine are water-in-oil emulsions. Glycerol monostearate and sorbitan fatty acid esters (SPANS) form water-in-oil emulsions. Polyoxyethylene sorbitan esters (TWEENS) form oil-in-water emulsions. Acid esters of monoacylglycerides can form either O/W or W/O emulsions, depending on the HLB, as can lecithin, discussed in the section that follows. Proteins form oil-in-water emulsions.

Naturally Occurring

Proteins as a group are widely utilized as emulsifiers (3, 13). Those from milk, eggs, and meat act as emulsifiers in many of the food products in which they are used. Plant proteins, especially those from soybeans, are also used as emulsifiers. When a surface-active protein molecule is adsorbed at an interface, polar amino acid residues are oriented toward the aqueous phase and nonpolar residues toward the lipid phase. Such surface-active mol-

TABLE 16-1
Common Food Surfactants and HLB

Surfactant	HLB
Propylene glycol monostearate	1.8
Glycerol monostearate	3.7
Sorbitan monostearate (SPANS 60)	4.7
Succinylated monoglycerides	5.3
Diacetyl tartaric acid esters of monoglycerides	9.2
Polyoxyethylene sorbitan monostearate (TWEENS 60)	14.4
Sodium stearoyl-2-lactylate	21.0
Sucrose esters	1–18
	(Varies with the ester)
Lecithin	(Varies with the substituents)

ecules lower interfacial tension. Individual macromolecules of protein can extend over more of the interface than can low molecular weight surfactants. Sections of protein molecules lying in the interface have been referred to as trains. Sections between trains, essentially either hydrophilic or hydrophobic, may form loops in either the aqueous or the lipid phase, while the ends of the molecules, referred to as tails, may project into the aqueous phase. Protein molecules are not only surface active, but they also stabilize emulsions. They contribute viscosity to the aqueous phase and they form flexible, elastic films around the oil droplets. Gums also form viscous sols that stabilize emulsions.

Phospholipids are another type of naturally occurring emulsifier found in egg yolk and soybeans. They are derivatives of fat in which, instead of a fatty acid, phosphoric acid is esterified with glycerol at one of the terminal carbon atoms. The particular fatty acids attached to the other two carbon atoms of the glycerol depend on the source of the phospholipid. Usually one of the two fatty acids is unsaturated. Attached to the phospholipid molecule at one of the hydroxyl groups of the phosphoric acid residue is either choline, which gives rise to lecithin, or ethanolamine or serine, which give rise to phosphatidyl ethanolamine or phosphatidyl serine, the last two phospholipids called cephalins.

Formulas for lecithin and for phosphatidyl ethanolamine are:

Lecithin (phosphatidyl choline)

Phosphatidyl ethanolamine

Usually R denotes an unsaturated fatty acid, oleic, linoleic, or linolenic. R′ usually stands for a saturated fatty acid. Stearic acid predominates in the phospholipids of animal origin, and palmitic in those from plants. Molecules of phospholipids contain both nonpolar fatty acids and the polar phosphoric acid with the nitrogen-containing fragment.

Lecithin, together with small quantities of other phospholipids, is extracted from soybeans and is available commercially. For preparing foods at home, egg yolk is a ready and excellent source of emulsifier (14). Lecithin, plus some cephalin, is present in the lipovitellin of the granules of egg yolk and in the low-density lipoprotein found mainly in the plasma of the yolk. The superior role of egg yolk as an emulsifier derives from both its protein and its lecithin contents. The importance of egg yolk as an emulsifier is indicated by the ratios of egg and fat in cream puffs compared to popovers and in a rich compared to a lean cake formula:

	Popovers	Cream Puffs	Lean Cake	Rich Cake
Fat	1 Tbsp	½ cup	¼ cup	1½ cups
Egg	2	6	1	6

Figure 16-4 shows schematically the orientation of some common emulsifiers at the oil–water interface.

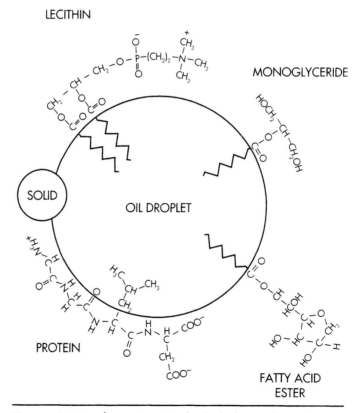

Figure 16-4. Surface-active materials adsorbed at an oil–water interface. Hydrocarbon chains are shown in the oil, polar moieties in the continuous phase. (From L. R. Fisher and N. S. Parker, *Food Research Quarterly* 45:33, 1985. Reproduced by permission.)

French Dressing

Proportions of ingredients typical of French dressing are ½ to ¾ cup of oil, ¼ cup of vinegar or lemon juice, ½ teaspoon each of paprika and mustard, plus salt and sugar for flavor. This type of dressing is made by agitating the oil and acid (lemon juice or vinegar) in the presence of the paprika and mustard.

The emulsion that forms is temporary. The ¾ cup of oil yields the upper limit of fat droplets of uniform size that can be accommodated by the ¼ cup of acid. Less than ½ cup of oil would yield so few droplets that the emulsion would be even more temporary. The emulsion is formed by agitating the oil and the acid is stabilized by the solids of the two powders that collect at the interface between the oil and the acid, as shown in Figure 16-5. Aside from providing solid particles, mustard contains a surface-active constituent that lowers markedly the surface tension of the water and the interfacial tension between the water and the oil (15). Mustard promotes the formation of an oil-in-water emulsion so the oil becomes the disperse phase and the water the continuous phase (2). Mustard powder stabilizes an emulsion, too (6).

The fat droplets in a French-type dressing are large when they are formed by shaking the oil and vinegar. When shaking ceases, the droplets of fat soon coalesce, because the protective film of emulsifier is too weak to protect the dispersed phase. Some French-type dressings do not separate into two phases because the emulsion has been stabilized either by a vegetable gum or by gelatin. These act by making the aqueous phase so viscous that the fat globules are unable to rise. Vegetable gums used for this purpose include agar, acacia, carrageenan, karaya, propylene glycol, alginate, tragacanth, and xanthan. Gums are also used in cream cheese, another food with a high fat (33%) and high moisture content (55%).

Mayonnaise

Basic proportions of ingredients for mayonnaise are one egg yolk and ⅛ cup of vinegar or lemon juice (plus seasonings) per cup of oil. Mayonnaise is an example of a relatively stable emulsion. The technique for making it a permanent emulsion is more complicated than that for making a temporary one. For making mayonnaise, the acid plus seasoning and egg yolk are combined. The shape of the container, which should be narrow and deep, and the

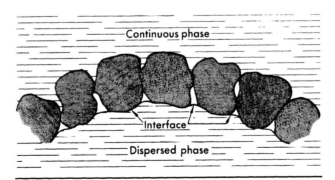

Figure 16-5. Particles of finely divided solid acting as an emulsifying agent. (From A. W. Thomas. *Journal of the American Leather Chemists Association* 22:171. 1927. Reprinted by permission.)

blades of the beater used to incorporate the oil are important in making a good emulsion. In addition, both mustard and egg yolk lower interfacial tension between water and oil. The livetin fraction of egg yolk proteins (16) and the low-density lipoproteins are the most effective surface-active agents. As each portion of the oil is added, the mixture is beaten sufficiently to break up the fat into small droplets. It is important that small portions of oil be added at first and that each portion of oil be thoroughly emulsified before the next is added. Beating can be either continuous or intermittent. After some of the oil has been emulsified, the next portions are more readily emulsified. To avoid breaking the emulsion, no more oil should be added at one time than the quantity that is already emulsified.

Mayonnaise thickens as more oil is beaten into it. The question arises as to why adding fluid oil to egg yolk and acid—both fluid—results in a product as thick as mayonnaise. First, consider what happens to the oil. By the cupful, it pours. When separated into droplets which are surrounded by a film of emulsifier, the oil is immobilized and loses its fluidity. As more oil is incorporated, the droplets become more numerous and the interfacial area between oil and acid increases. The following example will serve to illustrate the magnitude of the increase in surface area when oil is emulsified. Assume a cylinder with a diameter of one square centimeter that contains 10 milliliters of oil and a quantity of water. The interfacial area between the oil and water is one square centimeter. If this oil is emulsified in the water as droplets 0.1 micrometer in diameter, the interfacial area has increased three million fold (to 300 square meters). This is shown graphically in Figure 16-6. The water in the mayonnaise, which separates the droplets of oil, is reduced to a very thin film, much of it bound to the surface of the fat droplets. The flow of any unbound water in these films is impeded by the droplets of fat. The more oil added and the more finely it is divided, the thicker the mayonnaise. In fact, it may become stiff enough to cut and hold a sharp edge. One egg yolk contains sufficient emulsifier to coat the fat droplets from two or possibly three cups of oil.

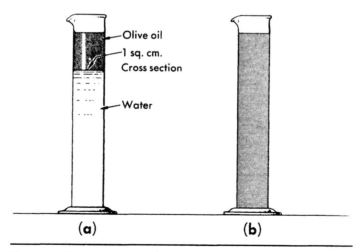

Figure 16-6. Increase in interfacial area when an emulsion is formed. (a) Ten milliliters of oil in contact with water with an interfacial area of one square centimeter. (b) Ten milliliters of oil emulsified in water as droplets 0.1 micron in diameter with an interfacial area 300 meters square. (Reproduced from Paul Becker. *Principles of Emulsion Technology,* by permission of Reinhold Book Corporation, a subsidiary of Chapman-Reinhold, Inc., New York, 1955.)

Figure 16-7. Scanning electron micrograph of layers of electron-dense particles around droplets of fat from mayonnaise. (From C. M. Chang, W. D. Powrie, and O. Fennema, *Canadian Institute of Food Science and Technology Journal* 5:136, 1972. Reprinted by permission.)

Electron micrographs of mayonnaise made with only egg yolk as the emulsifier show droplets of fat surrounded by layers of electron-dense particles (Fig. 16-7). Their size suggests that they came from the low density lipoprotein of the yolk, but lipovitellins may have contributed some of the electron-dense particles observed (1).

Cooked Dressing

Cooked salad dressings are acidified liquids (water, milk, or fruit juice) thickened with starch alone or with egg. Such products involve basic principles of starch cookery (Chapter 9) or of egg cookery (Chapter 21). The amount of fat included in cooked dressings is so small as to be readily emulsified by the proteins present. When cooked salad dressing is added to mayonnaise in amounts to reduce the vegetable oil content below 65 percent, the product must be labeled salad dressing.

Other Emulsions

Mayonnaise-type salad dressings in which the concentrated emulsion of fat has been diluted by cooked starch dispersion have been on the market for a number of years. The health benefits of limiting the amount of fat in the diet spurred interest in the development of low fat or fat-free salad dressings. Ingredients are selected for these modified dressings for their ability to mimic the flow properties and the mouthfeel of the innumerable droplets of fat found in conventional products. Hydrocolloids such as xanthan gum and alginates fill this role, as do maltodextrins and microparticulates.

Emulsions play an important role in foods other than salad dressings. The importance of a good emulsion in cream puff batter is emphasized in Chapter 13. Cake batters as emulsions are discussed in Chapter 25, cream and milk as emulsions in Chapter 19, and ice creams in Chapter 7.

Margarine and butter are examples of water-in-oil emulsions. Each contains a minimum of 80 percent fat with much of the remainder as water. When either is used for sautéing, spattering is minimal compared to that which occurs when other fats are heated with any water present. In butter and margarine, conversion of the emulsified droplets of water to steam causes the fats to foam. Rupture of the film of emulsifier around the bubbles releases the steam in small jets.

STABILITY OF EMULSIONS

Emulsions are unstable colloidal dispersions. Instability is manifested as creaming, phase inversion, or coalescence. Creaming occurs when less dense oil droplets rise and form a fat-rich layer above the more aqueous phase below. It is to prevent creaming that milk is homogenized (Chapter 19). Creaming accounts for the thicker upper layer in a carton of whipping cream that has been held in the refrigerator for a few days. The emulsion is not broken and the two layers can be redistributed by stirring the cream. The conversion of cream to butter is an example of phase inversion. When cream—an oil-in-water emulsion—is churned the emulsion breaks. At the same time, a water-in-oil emulsion is formed with the freed butter fat. Coalescence involves rupture of the protective film around the dispersed phase of an emulsion. Oil then unites with oil, water with water.

A number of factors may cause an emulsion to break. Adding salt may do so because salt increases the surface tension of water, decreasing its spreadability. Violent or continuous jarring, as when a product is shipped, may break an emulsion. Allowing the surface to dry removes one part of the protective layer around dispersed droplets. Freezing may cause an emulsion to break, too. Conversion of water to crystals removes the continuous phase of the emulsion and sharp edges of ice crystals may puncture the layer of emulsifier. Freezing may cause the fat to crystallize, too. Stability to freezing is an issue for salad dressings used in prepared frozen foods. Salad dressings withstand freezing and frozen storage better if the oil used does not crystallize at low temperature, if relatively high levels of either egg yolk or salt are used, and if waxy rather than regular starch is used as a thickening agent (9).

A broken emulsion may be reformed by adding it slowly to liquid (one tablespoon of water for mayonnaise made with one cup of oil), or beating the mixture after each addition. The broken emulsion also may be gradually stirred into a stable emulsion. When a good emulsion is emulsifying a broken one, the force involved can be felt as a drag on the spoon or spatula used to combine the two.

Destabilization of an emulsion is at times desirable. In fact, partial and controlled destabilization of the emulsion is necessary to stiffen the foam in whipped cream, whipped toppings, and ice cream. When these products are agitated, low molecular weight surfactants displace just enough of the protein that forms the emulsion originally to allow fat from adjacent droplets to adhere.

VINEGAR

Vinegar is a common ingredient in salad dressings. Cider, wine, malt, and distilled vinegar are four types. The characteristic constituent of vinegar (literally, *vin aigre,* or sour wine) is acetic acid, which is produced by fermentation (12). Vinegar is fermented in two stages. First, a sugar solution is converted to alcohol by yeast and then this alcoholic brew is converted to an acetic acid solution. Microorganisms responsible for the second stage in the conversion of sugars to acetic acid are those of the *Acetobacter* group. Cider vinegar is made from apple juice, wine vinegar from grape juice, malt vinegar from malted grain, the starch in the last converted to sugar by malt, or sprouted barley. Distilled vinegar is made by fermentation of a dilute solution of alcohol. Other acids besides acetic form during fermentation, and these react with the alcohol to yield esters that contribute aroma to the vinegar. Vinegar from each source has a characteristic flavor. Vinegars on the market are standardized at five percent (50 grains) or four percent (40 grains) acetic acid. Lemon juice is approximately five percent citric acid and so is comparable to vinegar in acidity. The pH of distilled vinegar tends to be lower than that of other forms (10).

REFERENCES

1. Chang, C. M., W. D. Powrie and O. Fennema. 1972. "Electron microscopy of mayonnaise." *Canadian Institute of Food Science and Technology Journal* 53:(3):134–37. Electron micrographs of protective layer surrounding droplets of emulsified oil.

2. Corran, J. W. 1934. "Emulsification by mustard." *Spice Mill* 57:175–77. Effectiveness of mustard demonstrated.

3. Das, K. P., and J. E. Kinsella. 1990. "Stability of food emulsions: Physicochemical role of protein and nonprotein emulsifiers." *Advances in Food Science and Nutrition* 34:81–201. Technical treatment.

4. Dickinson, E., and G. Stainsby. 1988. "Emulsion stability." In *Advances in Food Emulsions and Foams.* E. Dickinson and G. Stainsby, eds. New York: Elsevier Science Publishing Company. Pp. 1–44. Factors involved.

5. Dziezak, J. D. 1988. "Emulsifiers: The interfacial key to emulsion stability." *Food Technology* 42(10):172, 174–80, 182–83, 185–86. Surfactants, structure, and formulas: applications.

6. Fishback, R., and J. L. Kokini. 1987. "Effect of aging and mustard flour on rheological properties of model O/W emulsions." *Journal of Food Science* 52: 1748–49. Effectiveness of mustard flour as a stabilizer.

7. Fisher, L. R., and N. S. Parker. 1988. "Effect of surfactants on the interaction between emulsion droplets." In *Advances in Food Emulsions and Foams.* E. Dickinson and G. Stainsby, eds. New York: Elsevier Science Publishing Company. Pp. 45–90. Types of surfactants; stabilizing action.

8. Friberg, S. E., R. E. Coubran, and I. H. Kayali. 1990. In *Food Emulsions.* K. Larsson and S. E. Friberg, eds. New York: Marcel Dekker. P. 21. HLB and emulsion type.

9. Hansen, H. and L. R. Fletcher. 1961. "Salad dressings stable to frozen storage." *Food Technology* 15:256–62. Factors that increase stability of emulsions to freezing.

10. Kintner, T. C., and M. Mangel. 1952. "Variation in hydrogen ion concentration and total acidity in vinegar." *Food Research* 17:456–59. Cider, wine, malt, peach, pear, apricot, and distilled vinegars compared.

11. Krog, N. J. 1990. Food emulsifiers and their chemical and physical properties. In *Food Emulsions.* K. Larsson and S. E. Fribeg, eds. New York: Marcel Dekker. Pp. 127–80. Chemistry and structure of surfactants: Behavior at the interface.

12. Mayer, Ernst. 1963. "Historic and modern aspects of vinegar making." *Food Technology* 17:582–84. Fermentation process in the production of vinegar.

13. Phillips, M. C. 1981. "Protein conformation at liquid interfaces and its role in stabilizing emulsions and foams." *Food Technology* 35(1):50–51, 54–57. Mechanism of stabilization.

14. Snell, H. M., A. G. Olsen, and R. E. Kremers. 1935. "Lecitho-protein. The emulsifying ingredient in egg yolk." *Industrial and Engineering Chemistry* 27:1222–23. Identification of the effective emulsifier in egg yolk.

15. Ury, R. 1962. Unpublished data. Class in Experimental Food Studies, Oregon State University.

16. Vincent, R., W. D. Powrie, and O. Fennema. 1966. "Surface activity of yolk, plasma and dispersions of yolk fractions." *Journal of Food Science* 31:643–48. Surface activity and emulsifying capability of various egg yolk fractions.

Pastry

17

Pastry includes conventional pie crust and the less frequently made puff pastry. Conventional crust is used to make such popular desserts as double-crust fruit pies, single-crust soft pies, and fruit tarts. The single crust pie may be baked, the cooked filling added, and then topped with meringue or whipped cream, as for cream pie. For custard and pumpkin pie the raw filling is cooked in the crust as the latter bakes. Conventional crust is used also in such entrées as meat pie and Quiche Lorraine. Puff pastry is used for patty shells, tarts, and as top crust for meat pies.

Pastry crust is one of the simplest of the batters and doughs in terms of the number of ingredients. Making high-quality pastry should be a simple matter, because only four ingredients—flour, fat, salt, and water—are used. That it is not simple is attested by the wide variation in the quality of pastry and the lack of confidence of many cooks.

An important characteristic of good pastry is tenderness. Pastry should cut easily with a fork and should disintegrate readily when bitten into, but it should not crumble. High-quality pastry is flaky. Flakes are due to layers of gluten that have been raised in blisters by steam formed as the crust bakes. If the layers are thick and the blisters few, the pastry will be tough. If the layers are thin and the blisters numerous, the pastry will be tender as well as flaky. Pastry should be crisp, not doughy or soggy. The edge of the pastry crust should be a golden brown and the center a paler brown (6).

The degree to which each characteristic is actually obtained in a pastry depends upon the ingredients, their proportions, and the way they are manipulated. Crusts made from crumbs and softened table fat are simpler to make and are essentially fail-proof, which in part accounts for their popularity.

INGREDIENTS AND THEIR FUNCTIONS

Flour

Flour is the main ingredient in pie crust. Two kinds of flour may be used: Each affects the characteristics of the pastry (4). All-purpose flour, because of its higher protein content, yields more gluten, and the more gluten developed the more cohesive the dough. The result is either a tough or a flaky pastry, depending on how extensively the gluten is distributed. In contrast to all-purpose flour, pastry flour does not yield as much gluten and tends to make a tender but crumbly pastry (4).

Salt

Salt is used to season the flour. Omitting the salt makes no difference in pastry except in taste.

Fat

Fat contributes tenderness (shortness) to pastry. Part of the toughness (lack of shortness) in pastry comes from the cooked starch paste. A cup of flour is about ¾ starch. If ¾ cup of starch were combined with two tablespoons of water—as used in pastry—and the mixture then rolled and baked, the product would be hard even without the protein of the flour. If a ball of dough made from flour and water were rolled and baked, it would be tough and hard. The protein in the flour yields gluten wherever the flour is dampened with water and manipulated. When the dough is rolled and baked, the gluten is denatured by heat and this contributes additional toughness.

Fats tenderize pastry by waterproofing the particles of flour (15). Both the protein and the starch in flour have an affinity for water, that is, contain polar groups. In a molecule of

fat, the carbonyl $\left(\diagdown C = O \diagup \right)$ groups are polar as are the double bonds in unsaturated

fatty acids. These particular groups in a molecule of fat make it possible for the fat to unite at strategic spots with polar groups on the surface of particles of flour. The remainder of the molecule of fat (the major part of it) with no affinity for the flour (or the water) acts as a mechanical barrier to prevent contact of the water molecules with the protein of the flour. It is in this way that fat waterproofs flour and so limits the development of gluten.

Pure fats have more shortening power than do those that, like butter and margarine, contain moisture. Even with pure fats such as lard, hydrogenated shortenings, and edible oils, the characteristics of pastry depend upon the particular fat used (6, 8). Liquid fats have more covering or spreading power than do plastic fats so a high proportion of flour particles become coated with fat. Softer fats spread more readily and contact more flour particles than do firmer ones. The higher the ratio of liquid to crystals, the greater is the covering power of fat (8). This is influenced by the temperature of the fat as well as by its fatty acid makeup.

In addition to making pastry tender, fats also contribute desirable flakiness by separating the dough into layers. Oils, on the other hand, tend to coat each particle of flour. As a result, water contacts the flour with difficulty, little gluten is developed, and a tender but crumbly or even greasy pastry results. Plastic fats tend to make a more flaky product. Lard is considered a superior fat for making pastry (12).

Liquid

The liquid used in pastry is usually water, but pastry made with oil by the stir-and-roll method contains milk. Without liquid, the flour particles would not adhere to form a dough. Liquid is needed to hydrate the flour so that during the mixing the gluten can be developed sufficiently to give a certain amount of cohesion to the dough. How extensively gluten is distributed throughout pastry and, of course, the amount of gluten, determine whether pastry is (a) crumbly with a tendency to be too brown, (b) compact, tough, and browning with difficulty, or (c) crisp, flaky, and tender. To produce the third type, gluten should be distributed throughout the mass of the dough in hundreds of small areas. A third purpose for the liquid in pastry dough is to provide steam to leaven it and so actually produce the flakes.

PROPORTIONS OF INGREDIENTS

Salt

As for biscuits, muffins, and most other quick breads, ½ teaspoon of salt per cup of flour is usually recommended.

Fat

The proportion of fat customarily recommended varies from ¼ to ⅓ cup for each cup of flour. In one study (13) pastry made with plastic fat was nearest optimum in quality when the volume of fat was ¼ the volume of flour. When liquid fat was used, the optimum volume was less (3½ tablespoons per cup of flour). A later study verified the greater effectiveness of oil versus shortening in producing satisfactory pastry (2). When less than ¼ cup of plastic fat is used, it is difficult to stir in the water and make a dough without at the same time developing so much gluten as to make the pastry tough. When more than ⅓ cup of fat is used for each cup of flour, the pastry tends to be crumbly and greasy. Within the recommended range, the smaller the proportion of fat, the greater is the likelihood of the development of too much gluten as the dough is worked after the addition of water. If cut into the flour adequately, ¼ cup of fat per cup of flour will give tender, flaky pastry.

Liquid

Only a minimum of water should be used. That small amount is necessary if the pastry is to be flaky. If pastry has too little water, it tends to be crumbly and browns very quickly, as does understirred pastry made with the optimum amount of water. Two tablespoons of water per cup of flour are sufficient to make the dough adhere and contribute flakiness with minimum risk of the pastry being tough. With the small amount of liquid used in pastry, errors in measuring in percentage can be large and so make a great difference in the quality of the pastry. A difference of ½ teaspoon (three milliliters) of water per cup of flour can make a noticeable difference in the tenderness of the pastry. When more than two tablespoons of water per cup of flour are used, the chances of developing too much gluten in the dough and so making the pastry tough are great (7). The smaller the proportion of fat to flour, the more important it is to avoid excess water; otherwise, the pastry is likely to be tough.

MANIPULATION OF INGREDIENTS

One cause for lack of confidence in making pastry is that considerable skill is required for the manipulation of ingredients. Even though ingredients are in correct proportion, the method and extent of manipulation determine whether pastry will be tender or tough, flaky, or mealy (7, 14, 17). The proportions suggested above put the minimum demands on skill in making pastry. Until one's technique is perfected, however, it is difficult to achieve the particular combination of tenderness and flakiness desired.

In a certain respect tenderness and flakiness in pastry are opposing characteristics, which is probably the reason it is difficult to achieve both in the same pastry. Gluten toughens pastry, yet to obtain flaky pastry some gluten is necessary. The secret, of course, is in its distribution. Even though two samples of pastry contain the same amount of gluten, they may differ in tenderness, owing to differences in the distribution. If the flakes are large and exist as a few thick layers, the pastry will be tough; if the layers are numerous and tissue-paper thin, the pastry will be crisp yet tender.

Cutting Fat into the Flour

The first step in making pastry is to sift the salt with the flour to distribute the salt evenly. A plastic fat may be distributed throughout the flour by cutting it in with a pastry blender, a pastry fork, two knives, or two spatulas manipulated with a cutting motion like the blades of scissors. The technique is the same as that employed for biscuits (Chapter 13). The purpose of this cutting is to subdivide the fat and to increase its surface area so that more of the flour particles make contact with it. The mixture resembles coarse cornmeal when the fat is cut into the flour sufficiently. Some of the pieces of flour are embedded in the fat, but between small chunks of fat are layers of flour particles untouched by fat. Where pieces of flour are in contact with fat or embedded in it, the water cannot reach the flour. The finer the fat is cut, the more flour particles are waterproofed and the less likely is an excessive development of gluten, which would result in a tough pastry. Gluten in the pastry in the photomicrograph in Figure 17-1 is stained to show its distribution.

Stirring the Dough

Water is added to the flour–fat mixture all at once and in such a way as to distribute the water over the mixture as evenly as possible. The mixture should be stirred *at once* and with a wide circular motion. Otherwise, part of the dough will absorb more than its share of water. Some very wet, sticky spots result, whereas some flour gets no water. When this happens, spots that are too damp are overworked to get the spots that are too dry worked into the dough; the excessive stirring makes tough pastry. Stirring should be discontinued when the dough adheres in large lumps.

INTERRELATIONS OF INGREDIENTS AND MANIPULATION

To achieve the desired characteristics in pastry, the kind of ingredients, their proportions, and the extent to which they are manipulated are interrelated. Different conditions necessitate varying the amount of manipulation before and after the water is added.

EFFECTS OF KIND OF FAT AND TYPE OF FLOUR

When oil is used instead of plastic fat, the flour is more readily waterproofed. In this case the dough needs to be manipulated more after the liquid is added to develop enough gluten to make the pastry flaky and not too tender. The warmer a plastic fat, the more flour it can contact and the more tender is the pastry. Pastry flour, because it is low in gluten, tends to make a pastry that is so tender it is mealy (4). Dough made from pastry flour not only can tolerate more mixing but needs more after the water is added to develop some cohesiveness in the dough.

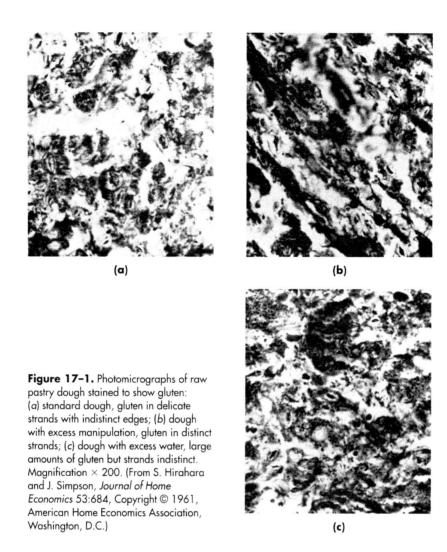

Figure 17–1. Photomicrographs of raw pastry dough stained to show gluten: (a) standard dough, gluten in delicate strands with indistinct edges; (b) dough with excess manipulation, gluten in distinct strands; (c) dough with excess water, large amounts of gluten but strands indistinct. Magnification × 200. (From S. Hirahara and J. Simpson, *Journal of Home Economics* 53:684, Copyright © 1961, American Home Economics Association, Washington, D.C.)

Effects of Proportions of Fat and Water

When a high proportion of fat is used, the fat should be cut into the flour less or the dough should be manipulated more after the water is added so the pastry will be flaky and not too tender. When a low proportion of fat to flour is used, the fat should be cut into the flour more to limit the development of gluten. When a slight excess of water is added, stirring the dough should be kept to a minimum to prevent excessive development of gluten and tough crust. When the water is skimped, the dough not only tolerates more stirring, but requires more to prevent its being too tender and crumbly and lacking flakiness. Limiting the amount of water and the manipulation of the dough after the water is added can compensate for a low ratio of fat to flour, too.

Effect of the Extent to Which Fat Is Cut into the Flour

The extent to which the fat is cut into the flour determines the tolerance of the dough to mixing after the water is added. The thicker the layers of flour between the pieces of fat, the thicker are the layers of gluten developed in the dough subsequently. The less the fat is cut into the flour, the trickier it is to distribute the water evenly throughout the dough without developing so much gluten that the pastry is tough. If the fat is cut in more and better distributed at this point, then the areas of flour not waterproofed by fat and so free to be dampened by water will be smaller. It is in this flour that gluten is developed. Obviously, the more the fat is cut into the flour, the more the dough can be handled after the water is added without developing so much gluten that the dough is excessively cohesive and the pastry tough. In fact, the more such dough is stirred at this point, the more flaky and tender is the pastry. For example, pastry made by cutting in the fat with 100 strokes and incorporating the liquid with 60 strokes is at least as flaky and as tender as pastry made by cutting the fat into the flour with 50 strokes and incorporating the water with 30 strokes. If minimum proportions of both fat and liquid are used, and if, in addition, the fat is cut into the flour extensively, the dough has a high tolerance to handling after the water is added.

The discussion above applies to the standard method of combining ingredients in making pastry. Other methods for making pastry have been developed (16). When ingredients are combined by the water–paste method, for example, an attempt is made to control the amount and distribution of gluten in another way. In this method all of the liquid is combined with enough of the fat–flour mixture to tie up most of the water. This lumpy paste in which gluten develops is combined with the remainder of the fat–flour mixture. Tender, flaky pastry can be made by this method, but no better than by the standard method (outlined above). For pastry made by the stir-and-roll method, melted fat or oil is used and milk is the liquid. The two are combined and then stirred into the flour to form a dough. Ingredients combined by this method require more manipulation to develop enough gluten so the pastry will be flaky and not excessively tender.

ROLLING AND SHAPING PASTRY

After pastry dough is stirred sufficiently in the bowl, it is shaped into a ball. Then it is rolled to a desirable thickness (slightly less than ⅛ inch) on a clean, flat surface. A minimum of flour should be used on the rolling surface, because it increases the toughness of pastry (14). A pastry cloth under the dough facilitates rolling, but the cloth is difficult to launder and keep sanitary. Rolling pastry between two sheets of waxed paper eliminates the need for flour. Lifting the rolling pin as it approaches the edge of the circle of dough prevents the formation of a beveled edge. In addition to flattening the ball of dough into a sheet large enough to fit into a pie pan, rolling flattens out the small masses of gluten into very thin layers. The lumps of fat are also spread into layers. A cut down through a sheet of rolled raw dough properly stained would show thin layers of gluten with embedded starch granules alternating with and superimposed upon layers of fat. The thinner and more numerous the layers, the flakier and more tender is the pastry.

After the dough is rolled into a sheet, it should be transferred, without stretching, to a pie pan, and the excess dough trimmed away. For a single-crust pie, the pastry may be baked on either the inside or the outside of the pie pan. Pricking the dough helps prevent steam pockets forming between crust and pan.

BAKING PASTRY

A hot oven (218°C) [425°F] is usually recommended for baking pastry. A moderately hot oven is also satisfactory if the baking time is lengthened. The baking time is influenced, too, by the material from which the pan is made. A pan made of highly emissive dark or dull metal or glass favors rapid and uneven browning of the crust. Lowering the temperature approximately 15°C (25°F) and increasing the baking time a few minutes will yield a more evenly browned crust.

During baking, the fat melts and the gluten begins to set. Starch granules appear little altered in appearance due to the low level of moisture (9) (Fig 17-2). Part of the water in the layers of gluten in which the starch granules are embedded is converted to steam. Steam from layers of dough that are separated by layers of fat forms pockets around the fat and puffs up the layers of gluten. When these are coagulated by heat, the bubbles break, and layers of gluten with embedded starch granules, the whole coated with layers of fat, are left. Pockets of steam that form in dough as it bakes make the pastry porous and flaky. Some of the steam pockets show as large blisters in the crust; others are quite small.

It is interesting to watch pastry as it bakes if an oven with a glass window is available. After the pastry has been in the oven for approximately five minutes, the dough becomes quite agitated. A pocket of steam forms in a particular area and lifts the dough until it no longer can stand the strain, at which point the inflated dough collapses and steam escapes. Thousands of miniature explosions, side by side, superimposed on each other, in unison, and in sequence, occur in the dough during the next five minutes in the oven. Gradually the number of explosions decreases and the agitation of the dough ceases as most of the water boils away. At this point the dough begins to set and the surface begins to brown. If all has gone well, the result is a light, crisp, tender product that can be handled, cuts easily with a fork, and collapses with slight pressure in the mouth—in short, a perfect pastry.

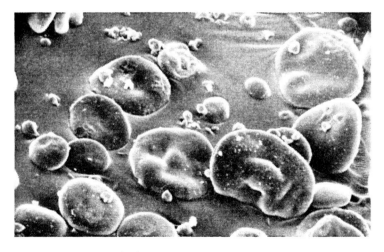

Figure 17-2. Incompletely pasted (gelatinized) starch granules isolated from pastry. Low moisture and high fat sharply restrict the pasting of starch in pie crust. (From R. C. Hoseney, W. A. Atwell, and D. R. Lineback, *Cereal Foods World* 22(2):57, 1977. Reprinted by permission.)

Tenderness versus Toughness

Tenderness in pastry is determined by the amount and the distribution of gluten. The amount of gluten developed in the pastry is a composite of many factors: The kind of flour, the temperature of the ingredients, the kind of fat, the proportion of fat to flour and of liquid to flour, the extent to which the fat is cut into the flour, and the extent to which the dough is stirred after the water is added. If pastry is too tender, it is mealy. Factors that contribute to mealiness include use of an oil or warm plastic fat, use of pastry flour, cutting the fat in excessively, using too little water, and undermanipulating the dough after the water is added. Tough pastry is the result of too little fat, too much water, cutting fat into the flour insufficiently, or too much manipulation of the dough after the water is added. Use of flour on the board or pastry cloth makes pastry tougher. Because pastry is crisp, an objective way to assess its tenderness (really the crispness or friability) is to measure the force used to break the pastry by an instrument known as a shortometer (1) (Fig. 17-3). Because pastry is not homogeneous, the breaking strength of a number of samples must be measured to arrive at an average figure representative of the pastry.

Flakiness

Flakiness in pastry is due to layers of gluten with embedded starch granules separated by fat and puffed up by steam. Plastic fats favor the development of flakiness. The better the fat is distributed, the finer the flakes. Some manipulation of the dough after the water is added is necessary to develop gluten. Tender, flaky pastry is desired, but it should not be so tender that it will not hold together. Small, thin sheets of gluten distributed throughout the pastry make crisp, flaky, yet tender pastry (Fig. 17-4). The same amount distributed less widely might give a tough crust. Puff pastry differs from conventional pastry in the greater numbers of layers of gluten separated by layers of fat (10).

Crispness

Crispness in pastry results when sufficient water is evaporated from the layers of dough during baking. It is influenced by how thick the dough is when rolled, how long the pastry is

Figure 17-3. A shortometer used to measure the breaking strength of crisp, baked products such as pie crusts, cookies, and crackers. (Photograph by John Woodward.)

CHAPTER 17

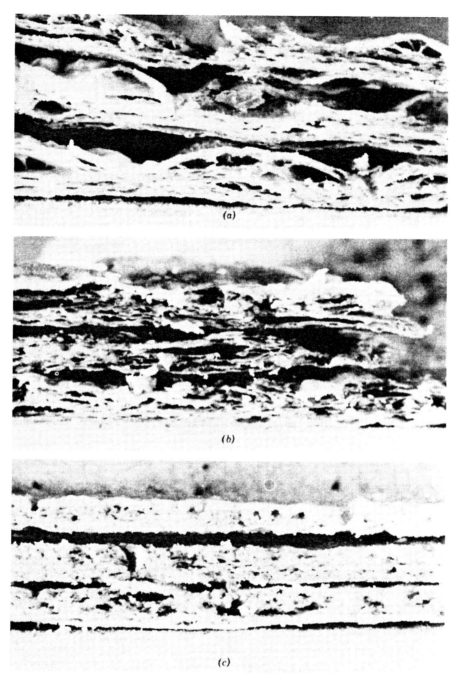

Figure 17-4. Pastry (3-layer stacks) varying in flakiness from (*a*) most to (*c*) least. (From D.Preonas, A. I. Nelson, and M. P. Steinberg, "Continuous Production of Pie Dough," *Bakers Digest* 41(6):34–40. Reprinted with permission from the December 1967 issue of *Bakers Digest,* Chicago, IL.)

baked, and whether the crust is an upper or a lower one. Making a pie that has a crisp lower crust is a real achievement, especially if the filling is fluid when it is poured into the unbaked crust as it is for custard and pumpkin pie. Having the baking temperature too low at first or allowing the pie to stand before it is put to bake is likely to give a soggy crust. Keeping the amount of water in the pastry crust to a minimum reduces the tendency of the lower crust to be soggy. If the filling is warm (not hot!) so that it does not take too long to begin to thicken, the lower crust is less likely to be soggy. Increasing the proportion of egg in a filling lowers the setting temperature. Another way to eliminate a soggy crust in custard pie (not as fantastic as it sounds) is to bake the crust in one pan and the filling in another and transfer the cooked filling to the baked crust. The baked filling needs to be cooled before an attempt at transfer is made. Brushing the surface of the unbaked pastry crust with slightly beaten egg white and placing it in a hot oven for a few minutes to coagulate the protein and waterproof the crust before adding the filling reduces sogginess. For fruit pies, the juice may be thickened before it is poured into the unbaked pie crust.

PUFF PASTRY

Puff pastry, like conventional pie crust, is made from flour, fat, and water, plus salt for flavor. Conventional pie crust has many small layers of dough (flakes) distributed throughout, while puff pastry consists of tissue-paper thin layers of dough stacked layer above layer (Fig. 17-5). This laminated effect in puff pastry is achieved by the way the fat is incorporated. Unlike conventional crust in which many small pieces of fat are distributed randomly in the dry flour, the fat in puff pastry is distributed by spreading it on preformed dough, which is then folded and rolled repeatedly to form numerous thin layers of fat alternating with thin layers of dough. A high ratio of fat to flour (1:2 v/v) is used in puff pastry. Butter freed of milk solids and water is a satisfactory fat for making puff pastry, as are certain margarines (3). It is essential that the fat spreads to form continuous layers without extensive penetration into the layers of dough. Steam collects at these layers of fat and puffs the pastry (10). A hard wheat, high-protein flour that forms an elastic dough is essential for puff pastry (11). Layers of dough should be cohesive enough to resist rupture when the dough is folded and stretched to form the many layers to be separated and lifted by steam as the dough bakes.

To make puff pastry, the water is first combined with the flour (⅓ cup per cup of flour) to form a stiff dough that coheres in a ball. This dough is kneaded on a floured

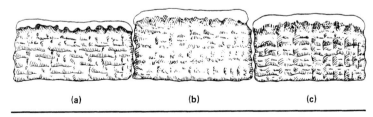

(a)   (b)   (c)

Figure 17-5 Effects of folding on volume of puff pastry: (a) under-; (b) optimum; and (c) overfolding. (Adapted from J. T. Colburn and G. R. Pankey, *Bakers Digest* 38(2):72, 1964. Reprinted with permission from the April 1964 issue of *Bakers Digest*, Chicago, IL.)

board (approximately five minutes) until it is smooth and elastic. The dough is then rolled into a rectangle or square approximately ¼-inch thick. The fat, cut into pieces, is spread over half the dough and the other half of the dough folded to cover the fat. The dough is sealed securely by pressing the edges. Then the dough, wrapped to prevent drying, is chilled in the refrigerator for at least half an hour. The chilled dough is rolled to a thickness of ¼ inch, after which it is folded in thirds, one third above and the other below. The dough is given a quarter turn on the board and again rolled and folded. Chilling of the dough should follow to keep the fat from melting and so maintain the continuity of the layers. The rolling-folding, rolling-folding, plus chilling, routine repeated two more times forms enough thin layers to yield a flaky, tender pastry of optimum volume.

After the last folding, the layered dough is rolled to a thickness to give the height desired in the baked product. An eight-fold increase in height is possible. Cream horns are made by winding thin, one-inch wide strips of dough, edges overlapping slightly, around conical forms. For patty shells, a three-inch cookie cutter is used to shape rounds, half of which have the centers cut out by a smaller cutter. The latter are used to make the rims and tops of the patty shells. The plain rounds are placed on a baking sheet lined with heavy paper and the edges moistened so the rings set on top of them will adhere. The assembled patty shells and the horns are chilled one last time.

Puff pastry is baked in a very hot oven (232° to 246°C or 450° to 475°F) for approximately five minutes, after which the temperature is lowered approximately 10°C (50°F). The high initial temperature results in the rapid production of steam at the fat/dough interface, which separates and lifts the layers of dough. After 10 minutes, the oven temperature is again lowered 10°C (50°F) for completion of baking. Total baking time varies with the thickness of the pastry.

REFERENCES

1. Bailey, C. H. 1934. "An automatic shortometer." *Cereal Chemistry* 11:160–63. Instrument devised to measure the breaking strength of pastry.

2. Berglund, P. T., and D. M. Hertsgaard. 1986. "Use of vegetable oils at reduced levels in cake, pie crust, cookies and muffins." *Journal of Food Science* 51:640–44. Two oils at two levels in pastry.

3. Colburn, J. T., and G. R. Pankey. 1964. "Margarines, roll-ins, and puff pastry shortenings." *Bakers Digest* 38(2):66–68. Desirable characteristics of fats for puff pastry.

4. Denton, M. C., B. Gordon, and R. Sperry. 1933. "Study of tenderness in pastries made from flour of varying strengths." *Cereal Chemistry* 10:156–60. Breaking strength of pastries made from low-, from medium-, and from high-protein flour.

5. Fisher, J. D. 1933. "Shortening value of plastic fats." *Industrial and Engineering Chemistry* 25:1171–73. Breaking strength of pastries made with different fats; congealing points of fat and shortening value.

6. HEIB. 1962. "Finished foods—a third report. Pie crusts—from recipe and mix." *Journal of Home Economics* 54:767–71. Desirable characteristics; factors for success; defects and their causes.

7. Hirahara, S., and J. I. Simpson. 1961. "Microscopic appearance of gluten in pastry dough and its relation to the tenderness of baked pastry." *Journal of Home Economics* 53:681–86. Standard pastry dough, dough with excess manipulation, and dough with excess water compared; photomicrographs of raw dough.

8. Hornstein, L. R., F. B. King, and F. Benedict. 1943. "Comparative shortening value of some commercial fats." *Food Research* 8:1–12. An attempt to account for differences in the shortening value of fats.

9. Hoseney, R. C., D. R. Lineback, and P. A. Seib. 1978. "Role of starch in baked foods." *Bakers Digest* 52(4):11–14, 16, 18, 40. Scanning electron micrographs of starch in baked products, including pastry.

10. Lagendijk, J., and J. van Dolfsen. 1965. "Classification of puff-pastry fats and margarines based on dough firmness." *Cereal Chemistry* 42:255–63. Nature of the fat and characteristics of the pastry.

11. Levine, H., and L. Slade. 1990. "Influence of the glassy and rubbery states on the thermal, mechanical and structural properties of doughs and baked products." In *Dough Rheology and Baked Product Texture.* H. Faridi and J. M. Faubion, eds. New York: Van Nostrand Reinhold. P. 309. Demands on flour used to make puff pastry; one page of a long, involved discourse.

12. Lowe, B., P. M. Nelson, and J. H. Buchanan. 1938. "The physical and chemical characteristics of lard and other fats in relation to their culinary value." *Iowa Agricultural Experiment Station Research Bulletin* 242:1–52. Iodine value and refractive index of fats and the breaking strength of pastry.

13. Matthews, R. H., and E. H. Dawson. 1963. "Performance of fats and oils in pastry and biscuits." *Cereal Chemistry* 40:291–302. Three oils, lard, and two hydrogenated vegetable oils compared.

14. Noble, I. T., H. McLaughlin, and E. G. Halliday. 1936. "Factors influencing the apparent shortening value of a fat." *Cereal Chemistry* 11:343–46. Effects of manipulation and of flour used to roll the dough on the breaking strength of shortbread.

15. Platt, W., and R. S. Fleming. 1923. "The action of shortening in the light of the newer theories of surface phenomena." *Industrial and Engineering Chemistry* 15:390–94. An attempt to relate the tenderizing effects of fat in pastry to fundamental work by Harkins and coworkers on the orientation of molecules at film interfaces.

16. Rose, T. S., M. E. Dressler, and K. A. Johnston. 1952. "Effect of fat and water incorporation on the average shortness and uniformity of tenderness of pastry." *Journal of Home Economics* 44:707–9. Comparison of pastry made by the water-in-fat emulsion and by the conventional method.

17. Swartz, V. N. 1943. "Effects of certain variables in techniques on the baking strength of lard pastry wafers." *Cereal Chemistry* 20:121–26. Effects of increasing the water, of increasing the mixing time after the water was added and of having ingredients at room *vs.* refrigerator temperature.

PART VI

Proteins and Protein-Rich Foods

Introduction to Proteins

18

Proteins are nitrogen-containing organic compounds that constitute one group of essential nutrients. Both plants and animals are sources of protein in the diet. Plants supply proteins via seeds, with legumes and cereals as the main sources. Animals obtain protein from plants or from other animals that have fed on plants from which they form new proteins of a higher biological value. Proteins from animal sources include milk, cheese, eggs, meat, poultry, and fish. Proteins are important not only for their nutritive value but also because of the functions they perform in many food preparation processes.

Proteins are polymers of amino acids. The amino acids in a protein molecule and the order in which they appear in the polymer influence the three-dimensional arrangement of the polymer and the functional properties of the protein macromolecule. A brief account of the amino acids found in proteins and their structure and characteristics precedes a discussion of the structure and properties of proteins. The functions of proteins in the preparation of foods follows.

AMINO ACIDS

Structure

Amino acids are organic acids with the following characteristic carboxyl group

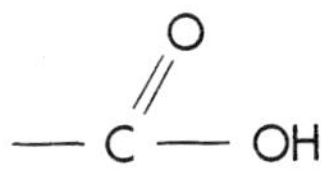

$$-\overset{\displaystyle\overset{O}{\parallel}}{C} - OH$$

Attached to this carboxyl carbon is another carbon atom, designated the alpha carbon. To this alpha carbon is joined, in addition to an atom of hydrogen, an amino group ($-NH_2$), the feature that distinguishes an amino acid from a fatty acid. One of some twenty different groups of atoms may be attached at the fourth position of the alpha carbon. The symbol R is used to represent such groups. Thus the type formula

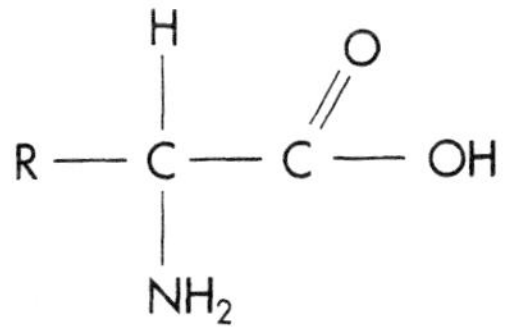

$$R - \overset{\displaystyle\overset{H}{|}}{\underset{\displaystyle\underset{NH_2}{|}}{C}} - \overset{\displaystyle\overset{O}{\parallel}}{C} - OH$$

can represent any amino acid. The carboxyl group ionizes as an acid and the amine group as a base, so an amino acid has both acidic and basic properties.

The ionic form that prevails depends on pH.

| Low pH | Intermediate pH | High pH |

When the positive and negative charges are in balance, the amino acid is at its isoelectric point, in which condition it is least soluble. An R group may contribute acidic or basic properties that affect the ionization of an amino acid at a given pH.

R Groups

The chemical makeup of the R group distinguishes one amino acid from another (Table 18-1). An R group may be a single hydrogen at the fourth position of the alpha carbon, as in glycine, a chain of four $(-CH_2)$ groups plus a $(-NH_2)$ group, as in lysine, or a complex ring structure, as in tryptophan. Although each R group is different, certain groups do have characteristics in common. Six of the R groups consist of hydrocarbons, which are nonpolar or hydrophobic. All but three of the remaining R groups contain polar $(-OH)$ or $(-NH_2)$ groups that make them hydrophilic. The three R groups that are classed as amphiphilic consist of a single hydrogen (glycine), a methyl group (alanine), or a heterocyclic ring (tryptophan). The amino acids that have hydrophilic R groups are acidic, basic, or neutral.

Hydrophobic	Amphiphilic
Valine	Glycine
Leucine	Alanine
Isoleucine	Tryptophan
Methionine	
Proline	
Phenylalanine	

Acidic	Basic
Aspartic acid	Arganine
Glutamic acid	Histidine
	Lysine

Groups that contain a carboxyl are acidic and those with nitrogen are basic. Asparagine, an amide derivative of aspartic acid, and glutamine, an amide derivative of glutamic acid, are found in foods. In either case, a $(-NH_2)$ group replaces a $(-OH)$ group of the carboxyl at the free end of the R group. The R groups of methionine, cystine, and cysteine contain sulfur. The unique feature of cystine is the disulfide group $(-S-S-)$, which may be broken by reducing agents. This frees sulfhydryl groups $(-SH)$

TABLE 18-1
Structure of Amino Acids

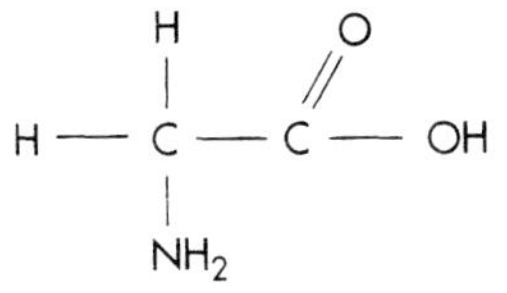

Structural formulas of amino acids:

- Glycine
- Alanine 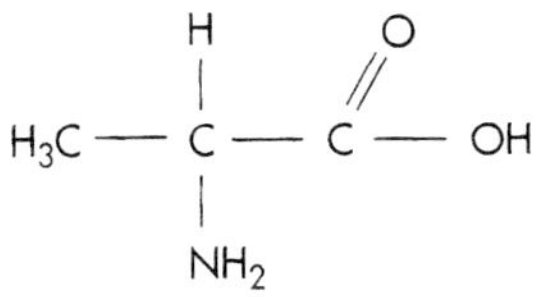
- Serine 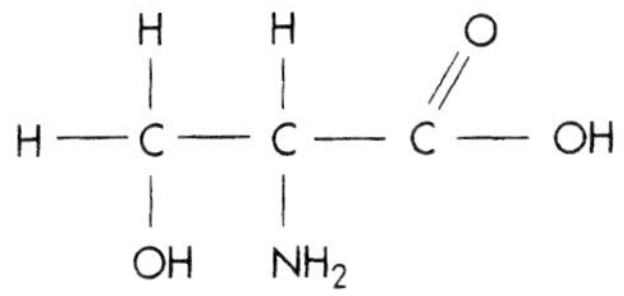
- Threonine* 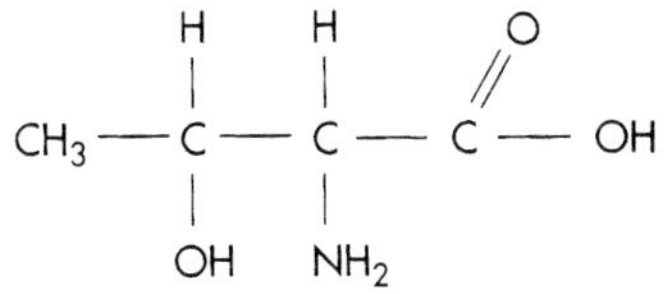
- Valine* 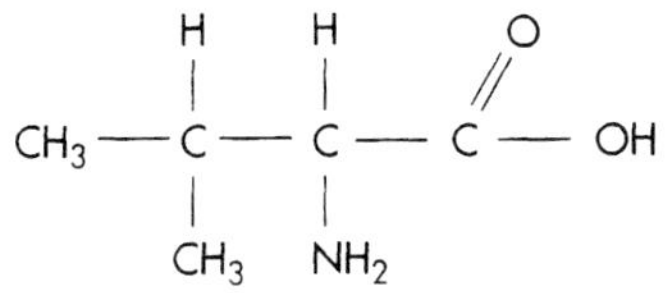
- Leucine* 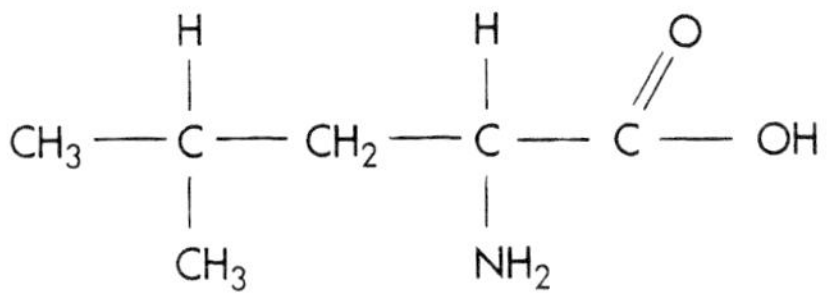
- Isoleucine* 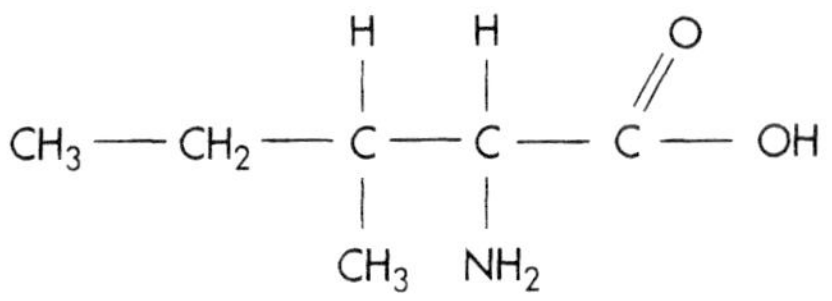
- Aspartic Acid 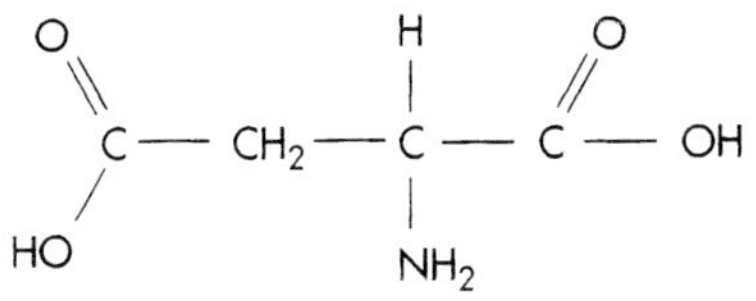
- Glutamic Acid 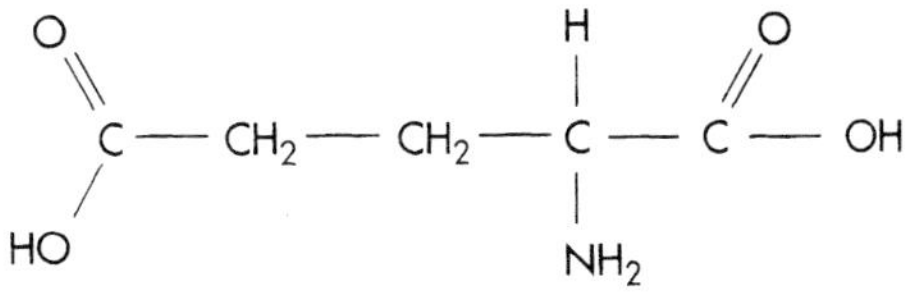
- Methionine* 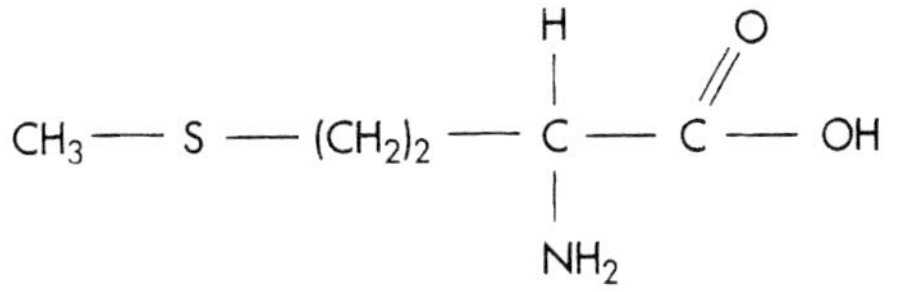
- Cysteine 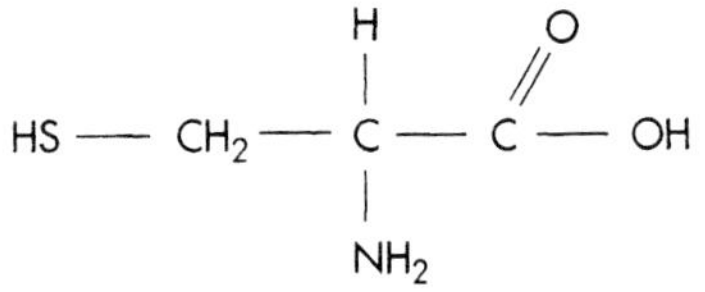
- Cystine 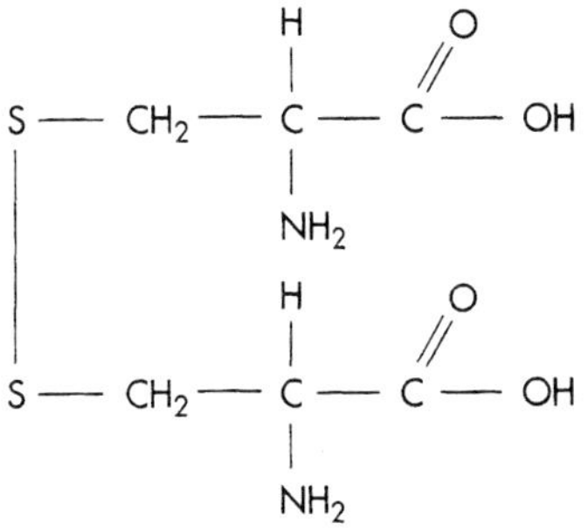
- Arginine 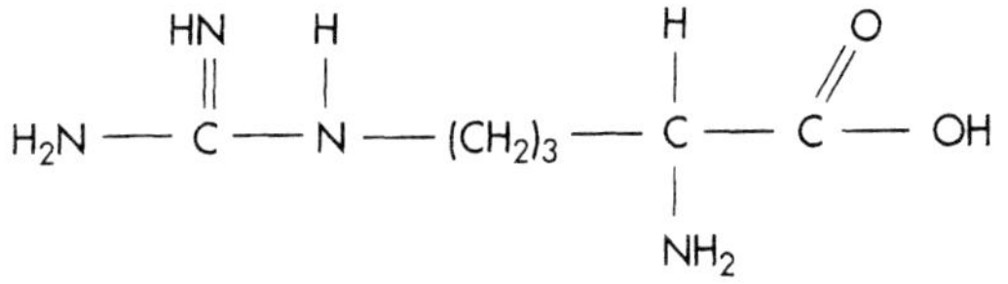
- Lysine* 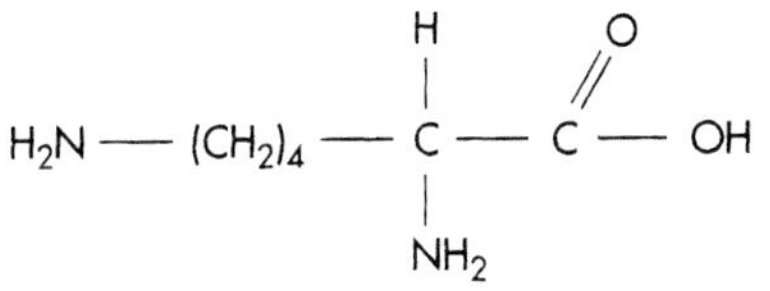

*Essential amino acids

TABLE 18-1 (*continued*)
Structure of Amino Acids

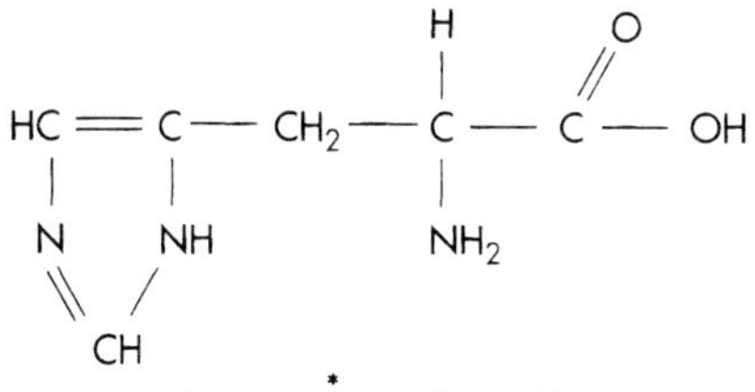

Histidine*

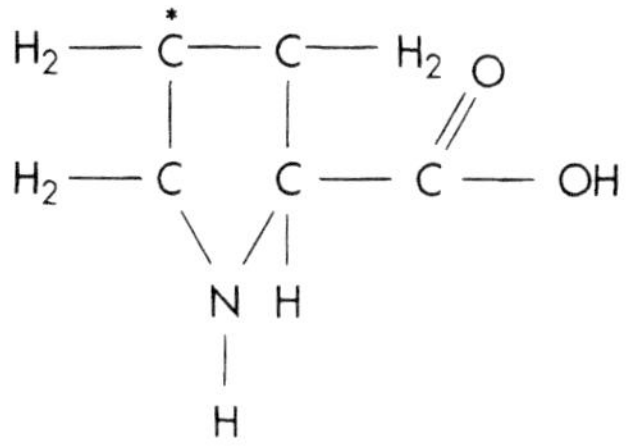

Hydroxyproline has an —OH group in place of one of the hydrogens at the carbon marked.*

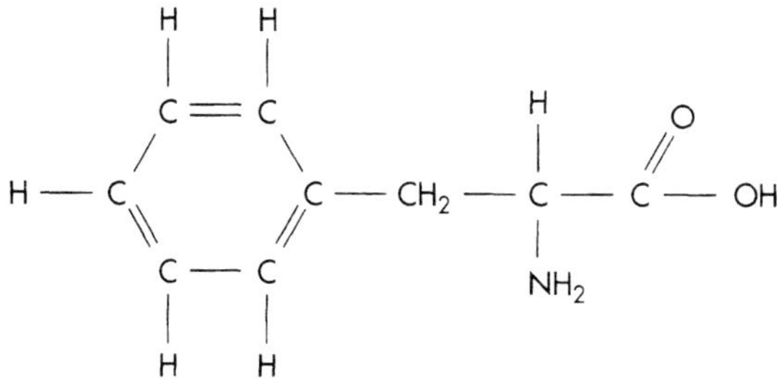

Proline

Phenylalanine*

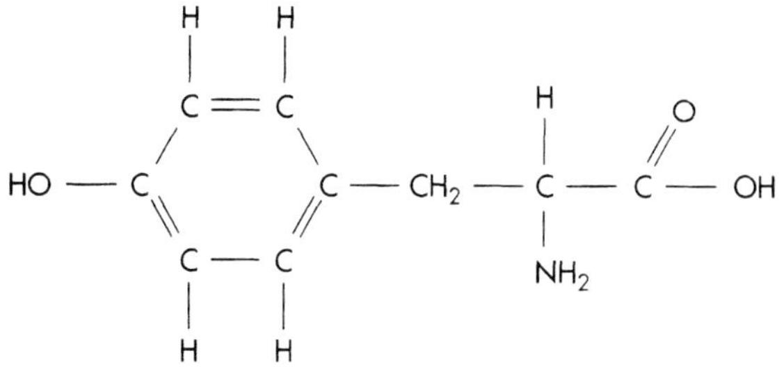

Tyrosine

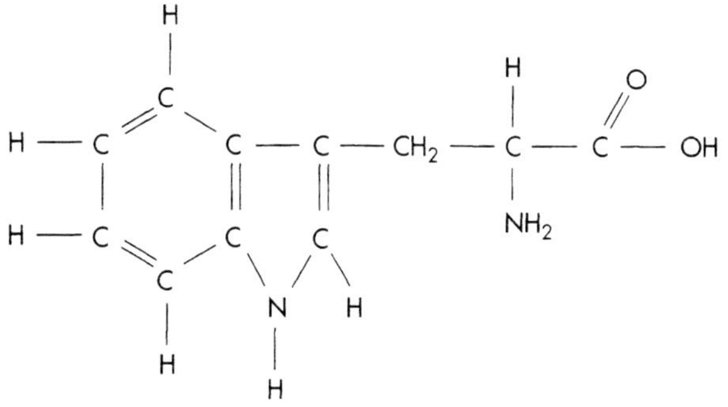

Tryptophan*

*Essential amino acids

as in cysteine, which can be converted to a disulfide by oxidizing agents. In addition, sulfhydryl-disulfide interchange

$$(-SH) \rightleftharpoons (-S-S-)$$

is possible when both sulfhydryl and disulfide groups are present. Proline and hydroxyproline are imino rather than amino acids. The nitrogen is linked to the end of the hydrocarbon side chain to form a cyclic structure. Presence of either imino acid in a polypeptide puts restrictions on the flexibility of the polymer. The R groups of constituent amino acids are major determinants of both shape and properties of a protein molecule.

STRUCTURE OF PROTEINS

Primary Structure

When the carboxyl of one amino acid unites with the amino group of another, with the elimination of one molecule of water,

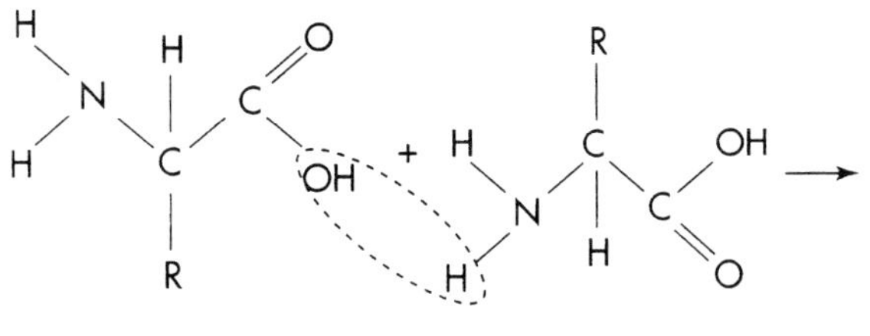

Amino acid   Amino acid

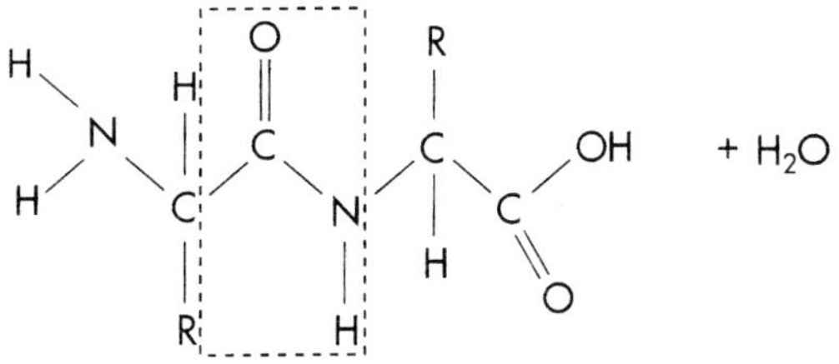

Peptide bond (a dipeptide)   Water

the bond that unites the two amino acids is called a peptide bond and the substance formed a dipeptide. Union of three amino acids gives a tripeptide; a number of amino acids so united form a particular kind of polymer, a polypeptide, a fragment of which is shown:

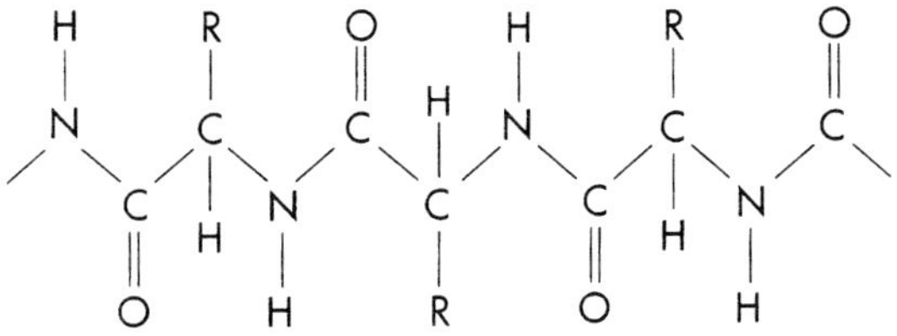

The main chain of atoms, which consists of repeating units of $-C-C-N-$ is known as the backbone of the protein molecule. Projecting alternately from either side of the main chain, like balls of fringe, are the R groups. One protein molecule differs from another in the particular R groups (amino acids) it contains and in the order in which they are united in the polypeptide. The kind, number, and sequence of amino acids in a protein molecule constitute its primary structure (7).

Secondary Structure

These high molecular weight polymers, unwieldy if fully extended, occupy space in a number of different shapes. Although rotation at the peptide bond is restricted because of its partial double bond character, the bond that links the alpha carbon in the backbone of the molecule is free to rotate (12). More than one kind of secondary structure is possible. Where and how a portion of a polypeptide chain twists or bends is influenced by the amino acid–side chains that are present. The alpha helix is the predominant secondary structure in many proteins. The portion of a molecule in this conformation exists as a tight, right-handed coil, with 3.7 amino acid residues per turn of the spiral (5, 10). Holding the polypeptide in this arrangement are hydrogen bonds, which form when a carbonyl group

$$\left(\begin{array}{c} \diagdown \\ \diagup \end{array} C = O \right)$$ at one point along the molecule approaches an imido group $$\left(\begin{array}{c} \diagdown \\ \diagup \end{array} N - H \right)$$

farther along the polypeptide backbone (Fig. 18-1). An imaginary line between the two atoms linked by a hydrogen bond would parallel the major axis of the helix, as shown in Figure 18-1. The beta-pleated sheet is the favored conformation where the molecule is very hydrophobic (4). Those segments assume an extended, rippled, or wavy shape, unlike the compact coil of the alpha helix. At intervals a beta turn, involving four amino acid residues, effects a 180° change in direction of the polypeptide (12). Hydrogen bonds between carbonyl and imido groups of parallel sections of the molecule stabilize the conformation. The random coil is another secondary structure. This term is used to characterize those molecules that undergo rapid fluctuation in bond angles. Most proteins, depending on their amino acid makeup, contain varying proportions of these three secondary structures (7).

One secondary structure, the poly-L-proline helix, is a loose, left-handed coil characteristic of those segments of a molecule that contains a high proportion of proline or hydroxyproline. The alpha carbon and the nitrogen in these acids are part of the pyrolidine ring. This restricts the flexibility of the polypeptide and influences its secondary structure (7). A molecule of gelatin exists as a poly-L-proline helix. Another secondary structure, the beta spiral (Fig. 11-7), has been proposed to account for the elasticity of gluten in bread dough (8). Repeated beta turns account for the spiral shape. The beta spiral with 13.5 residues per turn is a less compact coil than is the alpha helix.

Tertiary Structure

At a still higher level of structural organization, designated tertiary, protein molecules are arranged to give compact, three-dimensional complexes that are globular shaped, such as ovalbumin of egg white and lactalbumin of milk. Proteins originate in the watery medium

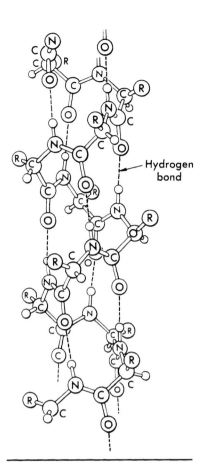

Figure 18-1. A drawing of a portion of the alpha helix of a protein molecule. (From R. B. Corey and L. Pauling, "The configuration of polypeptide chains in proteins," In *Proceedings of the International Wool Textile Research Conference,* Volume B. *Chemical Physics and Physical Chemistry of Wool and Proteins.* Copyright © 1955, by the Commonwealth Scientific and Industrial Research Organization, Melbourne.)

of the cell. Folding or twisting of the molecule to form the tertiary structure tends to orient the hydrophobic side chains to the interior of the structure to avoid contact with water. Hydrophobic groups that are within a distance of three to five angstroms are subject to van der Waals attraction (7). Bonding of polar amino acid residues that project from the backbone stabilize the tertiary structure of protein molecules, also. Such forces include hydrogen bonds between neighboring hydroxyl and carboxyl groups or between hydroxyl and amino groups. Or the attractive force may be due to salt bridges (ionic bonds) that form between the —COO⁻ groups of an acidic amino acid radical and the—NH₃⁺ group of a basic amino acid radical, thus:

$$ -\mathrm{NH_3^+} \quad {}^-\mathrm{OOC}- $$

Covalent bonds may also serve to stabilize the tertiary structure of protein molecules. These include the disulfide bond (—S—S—) that links two cysteine residues. Or two R groups along the polypeptide backbone may be esterified to phosphoric acid, which serves as a cross link.

Quaternary Structure

Proteins that consist of more than one polypeptide are characterized as having quaternary structure. Such is the molecule of collagen from the connective tissue of meat. A molecule of collagen consists of three strands of gelatin wound like three-ply yarn, with a right hand twist, to form a super helix (Fig. 18-2). Myosin found in the muscle fibers of meat is another example of a protein with quaternary structure. One part of the molecule, referred to as the tail, consists of two alpha helical polypeptides twisted together as a helix. Each polypeptide terminates at one end of the myosin molecule as a globular-shaped head. Both myosin and collagen are asymmetric molecules, as is the gelatin that forms collagen. The casein micelles of milk have quaternary structure (Chapter 19). Three different casein molecules are assembled as submicelles and these, in turn, are linked to form the micelles. Unlike the asymmetric myosin and collagen, casein micelles are roughly spherical in shape.

Conjugated Proteins

Some proteins are combined with nonamino acid substances. Glycoproteins, such as the main one in egg white, contain small amounts of carbohydrates. Proteins complexed with lipids include lipovitellin and low-density lipoproteins of egg yolk. The micelles of casein in milk and phosvitin in the granules of egg yolk are examples of protein conjugated with phosphorus.

PROPERTIES

The highly polymerized protein molecules are within the size range of colloidal particles. Molecules of such dimensions form colloidal dispersions in water. Such dispersions when they are in the liquid state are called sols. Repulsion due to like charges on such dispersed particles favors the stability of colloidal dispersions. Repulsion may be due to an excess of negative charges on ionized carboxyl groups of acidic amino acid residues or to an excess

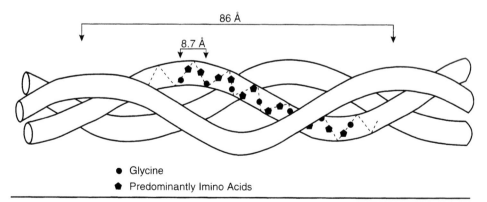

86 Å

8.7 Å

● Glycine
⬟ Predominantly Imino Acids

Figure 18-2. Segment of a right-handed collagen triple helix with three left-handed poly-L-proline helices. (Reprinted from M. E. Nimni, "The molecular organization of collagen and its role in determining the biophysical properties of the connective tissues," *Biorheology* 17:52. Copyright © 1990, with kind permission from Elsevier Sciences Ltd, The Boulevard, Langford Lane, Kidlington OX5 1GB, UK.)

of positive charges on nitrogen-containing groups of basic amino acid residues. Dispersions of polypeptides stabilized by electrical charge are sensitive to changes in the pH of the medium in which they are dispersed. If the protein is brought to its isoelectric point, the dispersion is destabilized. Thus the acid from a tart fruit such as peaches may thicken or curdle the cream served with it.

Hydration of a protein macromolecule is another source of stability of a protein sol. Water molecules hydrogen bond to polar groups of the backbone and to those of the amino acid side chains. Other water molecules that are hydrogen bonded to those directly associated with the polypeptide form a protective layer that prevents protein–protein contact when they are jostled about by Brownian motion or by agitation. Both heat and salts may destabilize such dispersions.

When the bonds that maintain the tertiary and secondary structures of a protein molecule are disrupted, the polypeptide loses its characteristic spatial arrangement. This denaturation, as it is termed, exposes reactive groups that were concealed in the native state. Included are acidic, basic, hydrophobic, and sulfhydryl groups. Their exposure and their interactions subsequently may have unwanted effects as well as others that are desired. In fact, many of the functions that proteins perform in foods depend on denaturation as a preliminary step. Heating is used frequently to denature proteins. Surface denaturation is effective, also. Tertiary and secondary structures that are stabilized by salt bridges may be denatured by altering the pH. Salts in high concentration may denature protein. Breaking disulfide bonds by reducing agents may alter the conformation of a protein molecule. The poor quality of yeast bread from dough that contains dead yeast cells is attributed to the detrimental effects of the reducing agents from the yeast on the disulfide bonds in the gluten. The compactness of a loaf of whole wheat bread is attributed to the action on gluten of glutathione, a reducing agent found in the germ.

FUNCTIONS

Proteins as sources of essential amino acids are important constituents of the diet. Protein-rich foods from animal sources have a higher biological value than do those from plants such as legumes and cereals. Proteins make important contributions to the sensory qualities and to the acceptability of foods, too.

As Enzymes

Proteins as enzymes catalyze a variety of reactions that affect color, flavor, and texture of foods (9). An enzyme acts on a specific compound known as a substrate. To the suffix *ase*, which denotes an enzyme, is attached a prefix that indicates the substrate for the enzyme or the type of reaction, such as hydrolytic or oxidative, that the enzyme catalyzes. Thus lipase indicates an enzyme that acts on fat, amylase an enzyme that acts on starch, and polyphenol oxidase an enzyme that catalyzes oxidation of polyphenolic compounds.

Enzymes are responsible for numerous desirable changes in foods, but they produce some unwanted effects, too. Enzyme activity that contributes to the ripening of fruits also contributes to their senescence and decay. The action of starch-hydrolyzing enzymes is desirable in yeast bread dough but undesirable in cold-stored potatoes used for potato chips. Enzymes tenderize meat but they also lead to rancidity of fats. Destabilization of the casein of milk in the production of cheese is the result of enzyme action, as is the ripening of cheese during storage. The enzyme that causes discoloration of fresh fruits and vegetables contributes to the color of black tea, cocoa, raisins, and prunes. Enzyme activity is temperature-dependent. An increase in temperature speeds the reaction until the temperature is high enough to inactivate the enzyme. Enzyme activity is pH-dependent, too, which explains why a coating of tart lemon juice delays browning of such fresh fruit as peaches, pears, and bananas.

Nonenzymatic Browning

Proteins may participate in nonenzymatic browning in certain foods. Proteins react with reducing sugars in a complex series of reactions, known as the Maillard reaction, which result in the production of unsaturated, volatile products and brown colored pigments called melanoidins. The amino acids that yield the most highly pigmented products are lysine, glycine, tryptophan, and tyrosine, in descending order. The most reactive sugars are lactose, ribose (a pentose), fructose, and glucose, again in descending order (1). Such reactions involving essential amino acids, especially lysine, lower the nutritive value of a protein. Factors that influence the rate and extent of browning, which may vary in color from light cream to dark brown, are temperature and pH. Browning increases with increase in pH above six and it increases with increase in temperature. Sugar–amine reactions contribute to the brown color of chocolate and cocoa and to browning of the crust of bread. The light tan color of heat-processed evaporated and of condensed milk is due to these reactions, as is browning of dried milk and dried egg white after extended storage at ambient temperature. Browning of the latter is prevented by treatment of egg white with an enzyme that eliminates glucose prior to dehydration.

Modifiers of Texture

Proteins make possible a variety of fabricated foods with unique textural properties. They contribute to the texture of foods through their action as gelling, foaming, and emulsifying agents (6).

Gels

The conversion by heat of sols of globular proteins to gels that vary in consistency from soft and jelly-like to rubbery, firm, or hard is one way that proteins affect the texture of foods. A gel consists of two phases, a three-dimensional network of macromolecules and a liquid phase immobilized by the network. Thermal denaturation of a globular protein disrupts the intramolecular bonds that stabilize the tertiary and secondary structures of the molecule. This exposes reactive groups that can then form intermolecular disulfide and noncovalent bonds, including the beta sheet, that establish the network of the gel (17). Opposing forces that affect the integrity of a gel are protein–protein attraction as opposed to protein–water affinity and elasticity of the macromolecules of the network against the pressure of movement of ions released from the network (14). Shrinkage of the network or mechanical disruption reduces its ability to retain liquid, a phenomenon known as syneresis. Heat denatured gel-forming proteins include whey proteins from milk, chiefly beta-lactoglobulin; egg white proteins, mainly ovalbumin; myosin of the muscle fibers of meat, poultry, and fish; and soy proteins (11, 16, 17). Some denaturation is necessary for gelation, but many globular proteins form gels with only limited unfolding. Gelation is a complex process only partly understood (3).

Proteins are less susceptible to denaturation by heat when sugar is present. Interaction between pairs of hydrophobic groups is stronger in a solution of sucrose or other polyol. The theory is that this strengthening is due to the effect of the polyol on the structure of water, which is a function of spacing and orientation of the —OH groups on the polyol (2).

Two proteins that do not require heat denaturation in order to form gels are casein of milk (Chapter 19) and gelatin (Chapter 30).

Foams

The foam-forming ability of proteins influences the texture of such items as whipped toppings, whipped cream, meringues, ice cream, marshmallows, soufflés, bread dough, and cake batter. A foam is a two-phase system of bubbles of gas surrounded by a continuous film of liquid. In foods, usually the gas is air and the liquid is a protein sol.

The first bubbles of air whipped or beaten into a protein sol are round and they remain so until the phase volume of the gas exceeds 0.74 (4). As more air is incorporated, the aqueous film that separates neighboring air cells thins. A thin interfacial film is a denaturing environment (6). Exposed hydrophobic groups, essential if a protein is to function as a foaming agent (15), orient toward and are associated with the gas phase. Hydrophilic groups are dissolved in the aqueous film. This surface activity lowers surface tension of water, facilitating foam formation (4). Molecules of protein can make multiple contacts with the interface, sections of the polypeptide between contacts forming loops that project from the interface (11). Ends of the polypeptides may project from the interface, too. Proteins are more effective foaming agents at the isoelectric point. Repulsion is less and interaction of molecules at the interface is favored (11). This interaction helps to stabilize the aqueous film around air cells (6).

Even so, foams are unstable dispersions, as evidenced by the accumulation of liquid below air cells when a foam is allowed to stand. Drainage is due in part to gravity. In addition, pressure of water in the spaces formed by the curved surfaces where three or more air cells meet is lower than is that in the thin film, called lamella, in the interface between adjacent air cells (13). The ensuing siphoning effect not only contributes to drainage but it exerts a pull on the denatured protein film that may result in its rupture. Drainage is less when the interfacial film is viscous. Sugar, which increases the viscosity of water, makes for a more stable foam (4). Overbeating makes some foams stiff, inelastic, and less able to retain liquid. When such foams are combined with other ingredients, air cells break and the foam loses volume.

Emulsions

In addition to their foam-forming ability, surface active proteins with their hydrophilic/lipophilic character contribute to the texture of foods by their emulsifying action (7, 11, 13). Emulsification, including the role of proteins as emulsifiers, is discussed in Chapter 16. Proteins are a part of the layer of emulsifier around the droplets of fat that contribute the smooth, thick creaminess to cream. As an emulsifier around the many new droplets of fat that are formed when milk is homogenized, proteins contribute to the viscosity of milk. Emulsification of fat by the proteins of flour, milk, or eggs in such products as gravies, sauces, and soft pie fillings contributes to the desirable tactile sensations these items produce in the mouth. The higher proportion of fat and the increase in egg protein, especially the low density lipoprotein, for emulsifying the increased fat, account for the difference in texture of cream puffs compared to popovers and cake compared to muffins.

In themselves, proteins are essential dietary components. Equally important, proteins have major impacts on the sensory properties of foods. They help make nutritious food more palatable, contributing to the pleasure of eating.

REFERENCES

1. Ashoor, S. H., and J. B. Zent. 1984. "Maillard browning of common amino acids and sugars." *Journal of Food Science* 49:1206–7. Effectiveness of five sugars with eighteen amino acids.

2. Back, J. P., D. Oakenfull and M. B. Smith. 1979. "Increased thermal stability of proteins in the presence of sugars and polyols." *Biochemistry* 18:5191–96. Attempt to account for the effect.

3. Clark, A. H., and C. D. Lee-Tuffnell. 1986. "Gelation of globular proteins." In *Functional Properties of Food Macromolecules.* J. R. Mitchell and D. A. Ledward, eds. London and New York: Elsevier Applied Science Publishing Co. Pp. 203–72. A complex process only partially understood.

4. Damodaran, S. 1990. "Interfaces, protein films and foams." *Advances in Food and Nutrition Research* 34:1–79. Energetics of film formation.

5. Doty, P. 1957. "Proteins." *Scientific American* 197(3):173–78, 180, 182, 184. Amino acids, polypeptides, and protein molecules; illustrated.

6. German, J. B., T. E. O'Neil, and J. E. Kinsella. 1985. "Film forming behavior of food proteins." *Journal of the American Oil Chemist Society* 62:1358–66. Foam development and stability.

7. Kinsella, J. E. 1982. "Relationship between structure and functional properties of food proteins." In *Food Proteins.* P. F. Fox and J. J. Condon, eds. London and New York: Distributed by Elsevier Science, Applied Science Publishers. Pp. 51–103. General properties, three-dimensional structures, stabilizing forces.

8. Miles, M. J., et al. 1991. "Scanning tunneling microscopy of a wheat seed storage protein reveals details of an unusual supersecondary structure." *Proceedings of the National Academy of Science U.S.A.* 88: 68–71. Evidence for the beta spiral conformation.

9. Ory, R. L., G. J. Flick, Jr., and R. Y. Cook. 1989. "Enzymes that affect protein quality in foods." In *Protein Quality and the Effects of Processing.* R. D. Phillips and J. W. Findley, eds. New York: Marcel Dekker. Pp. 291–314. Action of common hydrolases and oxidases.

10. Pauling, L., R. B. Corey and R. Hayward. 1954. "The structure of protein molecules." *Scientific American* 191(1):51–59. Development of the knowledge of the structure of protein molecules; many excellent illustrations.

11. Phillips, M. C. 1981. "Protein conformation at liquid interfaces and its role in stabilizing emulsions and foams." *Food Technology* 35(1):50–51, 54–57. Proteins in the aqueous films (lamellae) that separate air bubbles.

12. Richards, F. M. 1991. "The protein folding problem." *Scientific American* 264(1): 54–63. Factors that affect folding; secondary and tertiary structures.

13. Stainsby, G. 1986. "Foaming and emulsification." In *Functional Properties of Food Micromolecules.* J. R. Mitchell and D. A. Ledward, eds. London and New York: Elsevier Applied Science Publishing Company. Pp. 315–53. Action of macromolecules at interfaces.

14. Tanaka, T. 1981. "Gels." *Scientific American* 244:124–36, 138. Liquid/network relationship; expanding and contracting forces.

15. Townsend, A., and S. Nakai. 1983. "Relationship between hydrophobicity and foaming characteristics of food proteins."

Journal of Food Science 48:588–94. Foaming mechanism.

16. Wang, C.-H., and S. Damodaran. 1991. "Thermal gelation of globular proteins: Influence of protein conformation on gel strength." *Journal of Agricultural and Food Chemistry* 39:433–38. Involvement of the beta-pleated sheet.

17. Ziegler, G. R., and E. A. Foegeding. 1990. "The gelation of proteins." *Advances in Food and Nutrition Research* 34:203–98. Gelation mechanisms: gelatin, soy proteins, whey proteins, myosin, and egg proteins.

Milk

19

Milk is the raw material used in the manufacture of butter, cheese, yogurt, and frozen dairy desserts. Fluid milk is widely used as a beverage, either plain or flavored, especially with chocolate or cocoa. Milk is the main ingredient in some sauces, soups, and puddings. Items such as meat, poultry, eggs, vegetables, and cereals may be cooked in or with milk. Milk is valued for the functional properties of its components, especially the proteins that act as binding, emulsifying, or foaming agents. Many of the problems encountered in the use of milk for making such products as cream of tomato or cream of asparagus soup, cheese sauce, macaroni and cheese, or even yeast bread dough stem from the proteins in milk. Milk is valued not least for its nutrients.

COMPOSITION

The composition of different forms of milk is found in Table 19-1. The values are for 100 grams, or slightly less than ¼ pound. This weight of fluid milk measures somewhat more than 100 milliliters (⅖ cup).

Because milk has a high percentage of water, it is used as the source of water in foods such as cakes and bread. Milk is less sweet than its approximate five percent sugar content might lead one to expect, because of the low sweetness of lactose (Chapter 2). Milk is a good source of high quality protein. The cow converts feed protein to food protein with an efficiency of 31 percent, the highest conversion for any animal protein (23). The fat content of milk as drawn varies with the breed of the cow. It can be separated from the aqueous phase of milk by centrifugation. Milk is sold on the basis of fat content. Glycerides of milk fat differ from others of animal origin in that they contain short-chain (C_4–C_{10}) saturated fatty acids. These may give rise to desirable flavors in such products as cheese and to off flavors in rancid butter or dried whole milk. The color of the fat is influenced by the carotenoids in the feed. Milk is a poor source of the mineral iron, a good source of phosphorus and magnesium, and an excellent source of calcium.

Milk contains vitamin A (carried by the fat) and some thiamin (derived from bacteria that thrive in the rumen). It is a good source of niacin and an excellent source of riboflavin. The latter, which gives the greenish yellow fluorescence to whey (the watery part of milk from which much of the protein has been removed), is influenced by the feed of the cow and by the flow of milk. The latter is influenced by somatotropin, a hormone synthesized in the cow's pituitary. Cows given a supplement of microbe-produced bovine somatotropin

TABLE 19-1
Composition of Different Forms of Milk (per 100 grams)

Milk	Water (%)	Calories[a]	Protein (g)	Lipid (g)	Carbo-hydrate (g)	Calcium (mg)	Phosphorus (mg)	Iron (mg)	Vitamin A Value (I.U.)	Thiamin (mg)	Riboflavin (mg)	Niacin (mg)	Ascorbic Acid (mg)
Whole milk	87.69	64	3.28	3.66	4.65	119	93	.05	138	.038	.161	.084	1.47
Low fat (2%) milk	89.21	50	3.31	1.92	4.80	122	95	.05	205[b]	.039	.165	.086	.95
Skim milk	90.80	35	3.41	.18	4.85	123	101	.04	204[b]	.036	.140	.088	.98
Dried nonfat, instant	3.96	358	35.10	.72	52.19	1,231	985	.31	2,370[b]	.413	1.744	.891	5.58
Evaporated, whole	74.04	134	6.81	7.56	10.04	261	202	.19	243	.047	.316	.194	1.88
Cream													
Half and half	80.57	130	2.96	11.50	4.30	105	95	.07	434	.035	.149	.078	.86
Light whipping	63.50	292	2.17	30.91	2.96	69	61	.03	1,127	.024	.125	.042	.61
Sour, cultured	70.95	214	3.16	20.96	4.27	116	85	.06	790	.035	.149	.067	.86
Yogurt													
plain	87.90	61	3.47	3.25	4.66	121	95	.05	123	.029	.142	.075	.53
lowfat	85.07	63	5.25	1.55	7.04	183	144	.08	66	.044	.214	.114	.80

[a]1 kilocalorie = 4.185 kilojoules.
[b]Vitamin A added (2,000 I.U. per quart).
Source: U.S. Dept. Agr. Handbook No. 8-1. Composition of Foods. Dairy and Egg Products. Raw, Processed, Prepared. Revised 1976, 1989 Supplement.

consume more feed and produce more milk (10). The ascorbic acid content of milk varies with the feed of the cow and the procedures used to prepare different forms of milk for the market.

DISPOSITION OF CONSTITUENTS IN MILK

Solution

As is true of most foods, milk is complex from the standpoint of its physical organization. For one thing, milk is a solution. Dissolved in the 87 parts of water per 100 of milk is the milk sugar, lactose. The water-soluble vitamins thiamin, riboflavin, niacin, and ascorbic acid are in solution in milk. Part of the minerals in milk are in solution. Included are chlorides, citrates, potassium, magnesium, and sodium ions. Part of the calcium phosphate is in solution.

Colloidal Dispersion

Dispersed in the aqueous phase, colloidally rather than in solution, are calcium and magnesium phosphates and citrates. The proteins of milk (8) are colloidally dispersed, too. These consist of the caseins that are precipitated by acidifying milk to a pH of 4.6 and the whey or serum proteins that remain dispersed (30). Caseins, which account for approximately 80 percent of the proteins of milk, consist of alpha$_s$, beta-, and kappa-casein. The α_s-casein consists of two fractions, α_{s1}- and α_{s2}- casein. The four caseins—α_{s1}-, α_{s2}-, β-, and κ-casein—are present in an average weight ratio of 3:0.8:3:1 (25). The proteins that remain in the whey after the caseins are precipitated with acid include β-lactoglobulin, α-lactalbumin, serum albumin, and immunoglobulins. β-lactoglobulin is the main whey protein, present in a concentration similar to that of κ-casein.

Casein Micelles

The caseins of milk are associated with each other and with part of the salts of milk in structures called micelles (25) (Fig. 19-1). These micelles are responsible for the opalescent whiteness of milk. This micellar complex is often referred to simply as casein. Exactly how the caseins are arranged in the micelle has been the subject of much research and various models have been proposed (19, 25, 28, 29). The model that most nearly accounts for the properties of the casein complex is shown schematically in Figure 19-2. Micelles are roughly spherical structures made of submicelles. The submicelles consist of aggregates of molecules of α_{s1}-, α_{s2}-, β-, and κ-casein. The amino acid makeup of molecules of the caseins, with their high proline content (30), limits formation of alpha helix or beta sheet. Instead, the polypeptides, with their numerous β turns, assume a compact, ellipsoidal shape, with a length-to-diameter ratio of 4:1 for α_s-casein, for example (28). Polar amino acid residues are clustered at one end of the molecule and hydrophobic ones at the other. At the polar ends of the caseins are serine residues esterified with phosphate. The polar end of κ-casein contains a complex trisaccharide unit in addition. When these casein molecules assemble to form a submicelle, they are oriented radially, hydrophobic ends toward the center of the submicelle and polar and charged ends toward the periphery (Fig. 19-2a). In the formation of a casein micelle, colloidal calcium phosphate, chiefly, links adjacent submicelles by way of phosphate groups on the surface of the submicelles (Fig. 19-2b). Hence,

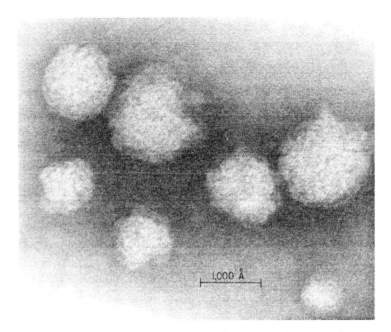

Figure 19-1. Casein micelles from cow's milk. (Courtesy of R. S. Carroll, USDA, Regional Research Center, Philadelphia. From *Fundamentals of Dairy Chemistry*, B. H. Webb, A. H. Johnson, and A. J. Alvord, ed, p. 443, 1974. Avi Publishing Company. 250 Post Road East, Westport, CT, publisher.)

the casein micelles are sometimes referred to as calcium phosphocaseinate. Submicelles that contain κ-casein are oriented so that the calcium-insensitive κ-casein portion is on the surface of the micelle (Fig. 19-2c). The resulting hydrophilic and charged surface of the micelle keeps it colloidally dispersed.

Emulsion

Milk typifies not only a solution and a colloidal dispersion (a sol), but it is also an emulsion. The fat in milk is present as small droplets or globules with an average diameter of three to six microns (14). Fat globules may range in size from less than one to 10 microns, the size influenced by the breed of cow. Jersey and Guernsey cows secrete larger fat globules than do Holsteins. Fat droplets in milk are prevented from coalescing by a thin coating of emulsifier (a few millimicrons thick) around the fat globules at the liquid–fat interface. Emulsions are discussed in Chapter 16.

The layer of emulsifier around the fat globules of milk is more complex (14) than is the alignment of solid particles of mustard and paprika around droplets of oil in French dressing or the orientation of lecithoprotein around fat droplets in mayonnaise. The structure for this membrane is pictured schematically in Figure 19-3. Lipids and proteins are the main components of the membrane. Triacyl glycerols are the main lipids, but phospholipids and sterols are present, too. The proteins have a high content of hydrophobic leucine and of aspartic and glutamic acids. The enzymes alkaline phosphatase and lipase are associated with the membrane. The components of the membrane are deposited in an

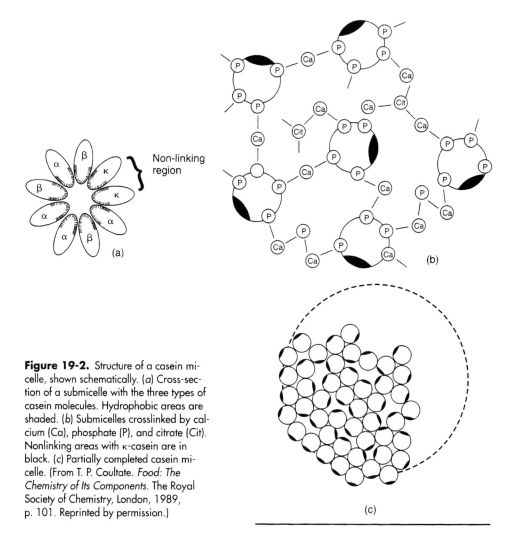

Figure 19-2. Structure of a casein micelle, shown schematically. (*a*) Cross-section of a submicelle with the three types of casein molecules. Hydrophobic areas are shaded. (*b*) Submicelles crosslinked by calcium (Ca), phosphate (P), and citrate (Cit). Nonlinking areas with κ-casein are in black. (*c*) Partially completed casein micelle. (From T. P. Coultate. *Food: The Chemistry of Its Components.* The Royal Society of Chemistry, London, 1989, p. 101. Reprinted by permission.)

orderly fashion, with high melting triacyl glycerols at the periphery of the oil droplet and with carbohydrate side chains that are associated with lipids and proteins at the outer surface of the membrane (13).

Fat globules are suspended throughout freshly drawn milk, but they do not remain so. The globules associate in clusters that become so large the forces binding them to the water phase are insufficient to counteract the effect of the difference in density between the oil phase and the water phase. A globulin, one of the serum proteins, promotes clustering. When whole milk stands, clusters of fat droplets, being lighter, rise to the top of the milk, a process known as creaming. Cream is milk that is extra rich in emulsified fat droplets. Fat droplets contribute viscosity to milk and cream, the greater the number, the more viscous the product. In goat's milk the fat globules are so small that they are unable to float to the top of the milk. As a result, goat's milk does not cream. Carotene dissolved in the fat globules gives the creamy tint to milk and cream.

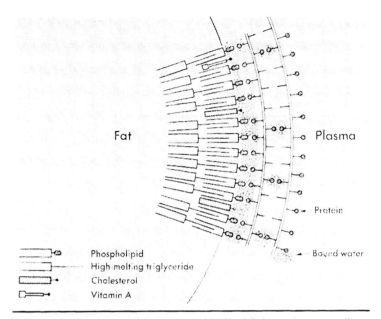

Figure 19-3. Diagram of the structure of the fat globule membrane in milk. (From Nicolai King. *The Milk Fat Globule Membrane.* 1955. Reprinted by permission of the Commonwealth Agricultural Bureau, Bucks, U.K.)

Homogenization

To eliminate creaming, milk is homogenized. Milk is forced under pressure through fine orifices that reduce the fat globules to an average diameter of less than two micrometers (Fig. 19-4). The higher the pressure used to force the milk through the orifices, the smaller the fat globules. With the formation of many smaller fat droplets, the surface of the fat increases enormously. As the fat droplets are subdivided by homogenization, the original emulsifying material is supplemented by proteins from the aqueous phase of the milk. These differ from the original protein and consist of casein subunits and serum proteins (11). The small size of the fat droplets and their greater density because of adsorbed casein eliminate visible creaming.

Homogenization affects milk in other ways. Homogenized milk is whiter, more opaque, and more viscous than unhomogenized milk with the same fat content. A starch thickened product is slightly thicker if made with homogenized milk and added fat blends less readily (32). These effects are due, at least in part, to greater surface area of the fat globules and to the composition of the new fat globule membranes.

PASTEURIZATION OF MILK

Although market milk is produced under sanitary conditions, it is routinely pasteurized (33) to eliminate pathogens that might have contaminated it at any stage from drawing the raw milk to bottling the product. In fact, the cow can be the source of pathogens such as those that cause tuberculosis, undulant fever, and listeriosis. Pasteurization is a mild heat treatment that eliminates pathogens, some spoilage microorganisms, and enzymes in milk.

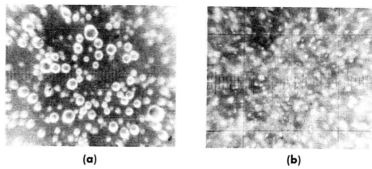

(a)　　　　　　　　　**(b)**

Figure 19-4. Fat globules in (a) nonhomogenized milk and (b) homogenized milk. Smallest gradation on the scale is two microns. Photomicrographs taken with dark field illumination. (Courtesy of CP Division, St. Regis, Chicago, IL.)

To effect pasteurization milk may be heated to 62°C (145°F) and held at that temperature for 30 minutes or heated to 72°C (161°F) and held for 15 seconds. The latter, known as high-temperature-short-time pasteurization, does less damage to the flavor of milk. Ultrapasteurized milk has been heated to 138°C (280°F) for two seconds, which gives it a longer shelf life under refrigeration. The enzyme, phosphatase, serves as a built-in indicator by which the adequacy of pasteurization may be gauged. Pasteurized milk gives a negative test for phosphatase. So sensitive is this test that the presence of 0.1 percent raw milk added to pasteurized milk can be detected, as can the fact that the pasteurization temperature was off by one degree Fahrenheit. The enzyme lipase is inactivated by pasteurization, which prevents homogenized milk from becoming rancid. Spoilage bacteria may survive pasteurization, so milk is cooled promptly and should be held under refrigeration. An outbreak of listeriosis traced to the consumption of pasteurized milk raises questions about the adequacy of pasteurization should milk be heavily contaminated with a pathogen (9).

Milk heated to 138°C (280°F) and then aseptically packaged may be held at room temperature for up to three months or until the seal is broken. The milk should then be refrigerated. Certified milk is produced under sanitary conditions that keep the bacterial count low. Unless the milk is pasteurized, it may contain pathogens that cause foodborne illness.

Milk is graded on the basis of bacterial count (number of bacteria per milliliter of milk). Grade A milk must have a low bacterial count (a maximum of 20,000 per milliliter). Most of the fluid milk on the retail market is Grade A. To keep the bacterial count low, milk and milk products must be stored at refrigerator temperature.

Milk may be fortified with vitamins A and D. For the former, the level is 2000 International Units per quart (946 milliliters), Vitamin D milk must have 400 International Units added per quart (946 milliliters).

TYPES OF DAIRY PRODUCTS

Fluid Milk

Federal standards specify a minimum fat content of 3.25 percent for whole milk. This may be raised at the option of a state. Fat can be separated from milk, and milks that differ in fat content can be formulated. Milk is marketed with fat contents of 2, 1½, 1, and ½ percent in addition to whole and skim milk. The latter contains less than ½ percent fat. Milk treated with the enzyme lactase, that hydrolyzes lactose to glucose and galactose, is available for lactose-intolerant individuals.

Cream

The heavier the cream, the higher is the proportion of fat droplets to milk. The fat content increases from half and half with approximately 10 percent fat, to coffee cream with approximately 18 percent fat, to light whipping cream with a minimum butterfat content of 30 percent, and to heavy whipping cream with a minimum fat content of 35 percent.

Evaporated Milk

Evaporated milk is prepared from whole milk by preheating it to facilitate evaporation of moisture and then removing 60 percent of the water under vacuum. The resultant concentrate is then homogenized, sealed in a tin, and sterilized. Carrageenan, a vegetable gum, added to evaporated milk before it is sterilized, stabilizes the α_s- and β-caseins against precipitation by either calcium ions or by the high temperature even more effectively than does the κ-casein present in the milk. The effectiveness of the carrageenan (kappa form) is attributed to the ester sulfate groups and the 3,6-anhydrogalactose units in the molecule (17). The distinctive flavor and tan color of evaporated milk result from the reaction between the proteins and the lactose of milk at the high sterilization temperature. Evaporated milk does not cream, and because it has been sterilized, it keeps indefinitely as long as the can is unopened. Once the seal is broken, the contents become contaminated with microorganisms and the milk should be refrigerated and handled like fresh milk. To reconstitute evaporated milk, usually equal parts of the concentrate and water are used. Vitamin D is added to evaporated milk in an amount to give 400 International units per quart (946 milliliters).

Condensed Milk

The market form of milk called condensed is made from whole milk by removing half the water. Sugar is added in sufficient quantity (approximately 44 percent) to preserve the milk, which is then canned. The milk is not sterilized, but because of the high concentration of sugar it keeps well.

Dried Milk Solids

Whole milk, buttermilk, and skim milk are available in the form of dried powders. The last is called nonfat dry milk. Milk used to make dried milk is pasteurized. That destined for the manufacture of cottage cheese gets no additional heating. For the bread-making industry, which uses the bulk of the dried milk produced, the milk is heated sufficiently (usually to 85°C or 185°F, for 20 minutes) to inactivate the loaf-depressant factor. Milk to be dried for general purposes receives a less severe heat treatment before it is dried (5).

To evaporate the moisture from milk, it is first condensed under reduced pressure. This concentrate is then blown as a fine spray into a preheated vacuum chamber. The resulting powders have a moisture content of approximately two to three percent. To reconstitute these powders, 4½ ounces of dried whole milk or 3½ ounces of nonfat dry milk solids are made to a volume of one quart with water. Reconstituting milk powder is unnecessary for a number of products. This is especially true of batters and doughs for which the milk powder may be sifted with the dry ingredients and water (equivalent to the amount of milk specified) added when the milk normally would be.

Dried milk solids added to water as a fine powder tend to lump. To eliminate this problem some milk powder is exposed to water vapor, which causes the fine pieces to clump or agglomerate in much the same way that instantized flour is agglomerated. Water can then more easily find its way in the interstices that separate adjacent particles. Not only are the particles in instant-dispersing milk powder larger, but their exposure to moisture has brought lactose to their surface. Lactose is the more water-soluble constituent of the dried milk solids, which facilitates reconstituting the dried milk powder (3).

Butter

Butter is obtained from cream by a process called churning. The cream is agitated or whipped, which disrupts the membranes around the fat droplets. As the fat droplets continue to coalesce, the milk eventually separates into two phases—the butterfat, and the aqueous phase with its dissolved and dispersed constituents. The membranes around some of the fat droplets remain. The clumps of fat are removed from the milk and the butterfat washed in several changes of cold water to remove the milk. Butter is usually salted and is worked to remove excess water. However, butter contains approximately 15 percent water, a part of which is emulsified. The minimum fat content of butter is 80 percent. The high moisture content of butter makes it prone to hydrolytic rancidity if it is stored in a warm place. One fatty acid so released is butyric, a molecule with a short chain. It is volatile and has an unpleasant odor.

Cultured Buttermilk

This form of soured milk is produced by treating pasteurized skim or part skim milk with a bacterial culture that converts lactose to lactic acid. The acid, a minimum of 0.5 percent, thickens the product through its action on the colloidally dispersed proteins. In addition, organisms in the culture produce compounds that contribute aroma to the buttermilk. One such compound is diacetyl, derived from citrate (24).

Yogurt

Yogurt is a custardlike or semifluid product made by fermenting pasteurized milk with *Lactobacillus bulgaricus* and *Streptococcus thermophilus* cultures (12, 31). The milk is usually fortified by adding powdered milk, which increases the viscosity of the mix and the nonfat milk solids above the minimum of 8.25 percent. The mix is heated for 30 minutes at 80° to 85°C (176° to 185°F) before it is incubated with the cultures. Heat denatures the β-lactoglobulin, which reacts with the casein. The fine protein network that forms when acid accumulates constitutes a stable coagulum that resists syneresis. Fermentation of the citrate in milk yields acetaldehyde, diacetyl, and acetic acid. Incubation time and temperature influence the contribution of the two organisms to the fermentation process and determine whether the product will be predominantly sour or have an agreeable balance between sour taste and aroma (16). Federal standards specify milk fat contents of 3.25 percent minimum for yogurt, of 0.5 to 2 percent for low fat yogurt and less than 0.5 percent for nonfat yogurt. The acidity calculated as lactic acid is 0.9 percent minimum. In addition to the product that must be held under refrigeration, yogurt is available in frozen form. Sweetener, flavoring, and fruits are optional ingredients. Federal standards for the frozen product are yet to be established.

Sour Cream

Sour cream is light cream cultured as is yogurt. Half-and-half sour cream produced in the same manner is available.

Caseins, Caseinates, and Whey Proteins

These products manufactured from milk are available in dried form. They are used by the food industry as ingredients in a variety of foods, including baked products, cereals, cheese analogs, comminuted meats, snack foods, and whipped toppings. Casein micelles, destabilized by either acid or enzyme, form a coagulum also referred to as a curd. This curd, after removal of the serum or whey, is washed, dried, ground, and sieved to yield commercial caseins. If the washed curd that is formed by acidification of milk is treated with alkali before it is dried, the sodium, potassium, or calcium salts of individual casein molecules (caseinates) are the result. Whey, a byproduct of the manufacture of either caseins or cheese, is available as either whey protein concentrate (up to 50 percent protein) or whey protein isolate (up to 90 percent protein) (20).

Filled and Imitation Dairy Products

These range from filled milk in which part or all of the milk fat has been replaced by fat of plant origin to nondairy creamers or coffee whiteners made with sodium caseinate or soy protein and vegetable oil.

MILK FOAMS

Foam Formation

Foam formation, including the role of proteins as foaming agents, is discussed in Chapter 18. The caseins are proteins with a nonuniform distribution of charged and hydrophobic groups (30). β-casein is the most hydrophobic of the caseins, and it has the most nonuniform distribution of both acidic (hydrophilic) and hydrophobic groups. Such molecules collect at the air–water interface, lowering surface tension and facilitating foam formation (18). When milk is secreted, β-casein molecules are present in the casein submicelles, held there by hydrophobic interaction. Chilling milk or cream weakens hydrophobic interaction, and some of the β-casein molecules may dissociate from the submicelles (1) and disperse in the aqueous phase together with the serum proteins. The serum proteins are less hydrophobic than are the caseins, but they participate in the foaming of milk. When the ghosts of bubbles of milk foams were analyzed, β-lactoglobulin, α-lactalbumin, and β-casein were the chief components (1), suggesting that these proteins serve as the primary foaming agents.

Fluid milk foams readily but the bubbles are large and rise to the surface of the milk and soon disappear. It is one thing for a liquid to foam and another for the foam to be stable. A viscous liquid can more easily retain bubbles of air that are incorporated. Increasing the concentration of milk solids, as in evaporated milk or in only partially reconstituted nonfat milk solids, provides the increased viscosity that enables the milk to retain gas bubbles better. Fat globules in sufficient concentration, as in whipped cream, are more effective in stabilizing a milk foam.

Evaporated Milk Foams

Evaporated milk whips best if it has been chilled to the point where ice crystals have formed from part of the water in the milk. This serves to further increase the concentration of solids and make the milk more viscous. Addition of acid in the form of lemon juice increases the viscosity of the milk through its effect on the dispersibility of the proteins. Whipped evaporated milk yields a glossy foam with fine cells and a large volume (three times the unwhipped volume). The milk thickens as more air cells are whipped into it. The film of liquid around the air cells gets thinner and the many air cells impede flow, much as mayonnaise thickens as more oil is beaten into it. Although a whipped evaporated milk foam becomes very thick, it does not set. Such a foam must be served or used promptly. Upon standing,the milk drains from around the bubbles of air, which coalesce and then rise to the surface. In less than an hour the milk regains its fluid state, leaving little sign that it was once a foam. Chilling a whipped evaporated milk foam makes it last longer.

Dried Milk Foams

If dried milk solids are combined with much less water than would be needed to reconstitute the milk, the viscosity of the milk concentrate is sufficient to retain bubbles of air whipped into it. Nonfat dry milk yields a more stable foam than does dry whole milk. A whipped milk foam made with nonfat dry milk resembles beaten egg white more than it does either whipped evaporated milk or whipped cream. Some of the protein in the milk is denatured in the foam so that the foam sets. The structure is fragile, however. Upon standing, liquid drains from around the gas cells, leaving behind fragile films of denatured protein. Lemon juice beaten into a milk foam increases its stability. Increasing the viscosity of a milk concentrate by dispersing in it either gelatin or one of a number of vegetable gums (algin, karaya, locust bean, or tragacanth) gives a more stable foam. Addition of lemon juice or calcium sucrate also increases the viscosity of milk and improves the foam.

Whipped Cream

In contrast to milks, cream with sufficient fat whips to a fine, fairly stable foam. Cream thickens when air bubbles are whipped into it, as does evaporated milk, but, in addition, the foam of whipped cream stiffens. The rigid but fragile structure of the foam results when fat globules aligned at the periphery of an air bubble make physical contact. A transmission electron micrograph of one air bubble or foam cell (FC) with milkfat globules aligned at the air/serum interface is shown in Figure 19-5.

The basic concept of why cream can be whipped to a stiff foam was arrived at almost ¾ of a century ago (2, 6). Elaboration of details of the process became possible with the availability of more sophisticated instruments. Cream is a two-phase system of emulsified fat dispersed in a sol of milk proteins. Converting cream to a foam is a dynamic process that involves action at interfaces (4). Air bubbles, many of which are incorporated early in the whipping process, are thought to be stabilized temporarily by a protective film of β-lactoglobulin, α-lactalbumin, and β-casein. Milkfat globules are in the aqueous layers that define the air bubbles. As beating or whipping continues, subdivision of air bubbles increases their surface areas and the aqueous film that separates the bubbles becomes thinner and thinner. This has the effect of orienting the fat globules around the air bubbles. In

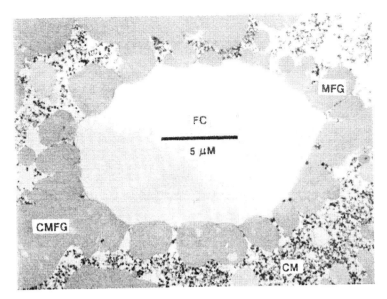

Figure 19-5. Transmission electron micrograph of a foam cell (FC) in whipped cream. Milk fat globules (MFG) are aligned at the air/serum interface through which they protrude. Coalesced milk fat globules (CMFG) are at the lower left. Casein micelles (CM) are stained dark. (Micrograph courtesy of C. V. Moor. From S. Y. Lee and C. V. Moor, *Journal of Food Science* 58:125, 1993. Reproduced by permission.)

chilled cream, sharp crystals of fat disrupt the milkfat globule membrane and the outflow of unsolidified fat from adjacent globules unites the globules. Breaks in the milk fat globule membrane make possible a network of clumped fat globules at the air–serum interface around foam cells. As a result, the foam stiffens. Controlled disruption of the milk fat globule membrane, essential for stiffening a foam, is the first step in churning cream to make butter. For this reason, the amount of whipping or beating should be closely monitored. Shearing a stiff foam with the blades of a beater dislodges clumped fat globules, resulting in collapsed foam cells and loss of foam volume. Additional beating may cause complete collapse of the foam and its separation into butterfat and buttermilk.

A number of factors influence the ease with which cream is converted to a foam. An important one is the concentration of fat globules. Figure 19-6 illustrates the effect of the percentage of fat on the volume, stiffness, and stability of whipped cream (6). Heavy whipping cream whips in less time than regular whipping cream, but the latter whips to a larger volume (1). Cream with less than 30 percent fat requires excessive whipping and more serum drains from the foam. Addition of lemon juice thickens the cream and can help compensate for fewer fat globules.

Temperature of the cream when it is whipped should be no higher than 7° to 10°C (45° to 50°F). Chilling makes the cream more viscous, but, more important, it causes part of the fat in the globules to crystallize. Only when the fat is at least partly solidified are the globules able to stiffen the foam. Presence of the enzyme that promotes clustering of fat globules and creaming also favors foam formation. This enzyme is denatured by the heat of pasteurization so pasteurized cream does not whip as readily as raw cream. The more severe heat treatment used to prolong the shelf life of ultrapasteurized whipping cream increases whipping time even more.

Figure 19-6. Effects of percentage of fat on the volume and stability of whipped cream (cream pasteurized and aged 24 hours at 4.4°C (40°F). (From A. C. Dahlberg and J. C. Hening. New York Agricultural Experiment Station Bulletin No. 113. 1925. Reproduced by permission.)

Cream that has been homogenized must be whipped longer to form a stiff foam. The proteins of the new fat globule membranes differ from those of the original membranes. As a result, the new globules are not so readily adsorbed at the air–liquid interface that surrounds the air bubbles and globule–globule clumping is reduced (1). With the inclusion of a low molecular weight surfactant, a fabricated product homogenized with milk protein whips to a foam that is indistinguishable in structure from that of unhomogenized dairy cream (1). For reasons that are not clear, low molecular weight surfactants such as acylated and lactylated monoacyl glycerols modify the interaction of homogenized milk fat globules.

Sugar added to whipped cream before it reaches maximum stiffness delays the clumping of fat. There is somewhat less danger of overbeating cream once the sugar is added, however. The whipped cream must be beaten longer to make it equally stiff.

Instant-foaming cream as an aerosol packed under pressure is available. As well as cream the mixture contains sweetener, vegetable gum (usually carrageenan), low molecular weight surfactant, and flavoring. Nitrous oxide is usually used as propellant. Instant-foaming, pressure-packed, nondairy toppings are also available.

MILK PROTEINS AS EMULSIFIERS

The proteins of milk function as emulsifiers of food emulsions. Both α_{s1}- and especially the more hydrophobic β-casein are effective emulsifiers (7). Their high surface activity makes possible their adsorption at an oil–water interface of an emulsion as it does at an air–water interface of a foam. Of the two main whey proteins, β-lactoglobulin is more hydrophobic than is α-lactalbumin (15). In addition to their surface activity, proteins form flexible films that contribute to the stability of an emulsion. Emulsions are discussed in Chapter 16.

Effects on Casein Micelles

The colloidally dispersed casein micelles are relatively insensitive to heat at the pH of fresh milk. Moderate heat as used in cooking fails to alter the stability of the casein micelles enough for the protein to precipitate. In fact, sweet fluid milk may be held for four hours at the boiling point before the casein complex is destabilized enough for clotting to occur. The high temperature used to sterilize evaporated milk may destabilize the casein micelles, however. Decrease in the pH of milk by the action of lactic acid bacteria or by combination with an acidic food may sufficiently neutralize charges on the casein micelles so that they are sensitive to denaturation by heat. Thus, milk that is not obviously sour may curdle when it is heated.

Milk sometimes curdles when cream of tomato soup is made. The pH of processed tomatoes may be as low as 4.0. A number of techniques have been recommended to protect casein from the acid and so prevent curdling of tomato soup. Included are adding the tomato to the milk rather than the opposite, having both milk and tomato hot when combined and serving the soup promptly, and thickening either the tomato juice or milk before they are combined.

If cooked tomatoes are thickened with a paste made from flour and milk or cream, the acid from the tomatoes causes the milk to curdle as soon as the cold paste is combined with the hot tomatoes. As cooking continues, however, the curds disappear. The great surplus of acid from the high proportion of tomato to milk causes a reversal of charge on the protein molecules of the milk, making it possible for them to be again colloidally dispersed.

Milk or cream used to make caramels sometimes curdles. Acid from brown sugar, the dehydrating effect of the high concentration of sugar, and the high temperature in the boiling syrup all no doubt contribute to the instability of the casein.

When milk is heated with foods that contain appreciable quantities of certain polyphenolic substances, the milk may curdle. These polyphenolic compounds are sometimes referred to as tannins. Foods that contain such compounds produce an astringent, puckery sensation in the mouth. The precipitation of the proteins in milk by polyphenolic compounds is attributed to dehydration. The curdling of cream of asparagus soup and of scalloped potatoes is attributed to the presence of polyphenolic constituents in these foods. Salt in high concentration can cause milk proteins to precipitate, for example, cured ham baked in milk.

Effects on Skin Formation

When milk is heated in an uncovered utensil, a skin forms on the surface. This is attributed to evaporation of water from the surface and concentration of casein that occludes some milk fat and calcium salts. If milk is heated uncovered for some time and the skin removed as it forms, appreciable amounts of milk solids are removed from the milk. Another disadvantage of the formation of a skin is that it tends to hold steam and thus makes the milk more likely to boil over. A foam on the surface of hot milk minimizes the formation of a skin. It is for this reason that hot cocoa and hot chocolate are served topped with marshmallow or whipped cream or the beverage itself is whipped to induce a foam.

Effects on Serum Proteins

Heat denatures the serum proteins of fresh milk, making them precipitate (20). Inactivation of phosphatase by the mild heat treatment used to pasteurize milk has been mentioned. The enzyme lipase, a protein, is inactivated during pasteurization also. Were it not, this enzyme would rapidly bring about hydrolytic rancidity in homogenized milk (14). The factor (or factors) in unheated milk that causes slackness and stickiness in yeast bread dough and low loaf volume (Chapter 14) requires more drastic treatment for denaturation than do most of the other serum proteins of milk.

In the preparation of a number of food products milk is preheated before it is combined with other ingredients. When milk is heated, the denatured and coagulated serum proteins settle to the bottom of the container, carrying some of the colloidal calcium phosphate that is precipitated by heat too. Settling of this precipitate is one of the reasons milk scorches so readily when it is exposed to high heat. Milk should be heated at a moderate or slightly lower setting in a steam-jacketed vessel or in a pan with a thick bottom.

Of the two main serum proteins, β-lactoglobulin is more heat sensitive than is α-lactalbumin. Both contain disulfide groups, but β-lactoglobulin also contains a reactive sulfhydryl group. Sulfur-containing serum proteins are the source of hydrogen sulfide and methyl sulfide, major components of the flavor of heated milk (22). Reaction products of protein with the lactose of milk contribute to the flavor of heated milk, as well as its color. Also contributing to the cooked flavor, but from the heated fat, is δ-decalactone, a compound with a buttery, coconutlike flavor characteristic of foods cooked in butter (22).

HANDLING MILK AND FOODS MADE WITH MILK

Holding Temperature

The shelf life of fluid milk can be prolonged by keeping it at 4°C (40°F) or lower. Milk and foods made with high proportions of milk, such as whipped cream, sauces, puddings, and soft pie fillings, not only nourish humans but also provide good media for the growth of microorganisms. Such foods have been implicated in a number of cases of illness (Chapter 4). One microorganism that is widely distributed is *Staphylococcus aureus*. Food may become contaminated by contact with work surfaces, utensils, and hands. If such food is held in a warm place, these microorganisms grow and in the process develop a metabolic product that is toxic to humans. Consumption of the food that contains the enterotoxin results in gastrointestinal upsets of variable severity and duration. Prompt cooling of such foods to at least 4°C (40°F) will limit the growth of these (and most other) microorganisms. Even so, such foods should be eaten soon after they are prepared for best quality.

Exposure to Light

Light may have a deleterious effect on two vitamins in milk. Milk exposed to fluorescent light of an intensity of 300 foot-candles at a temperature of 4.4°C (40°F) for 48 hours loses approximately 11 percent of its riboflavin in glass or regular plastic containers and 3 percent in paper or gold-tinted plastic containers (27). Loss is low in all containers at a light intensity of 150 foot-candles and a temperature of 1.7°C (35°F). The loss of retinyl palmitate (vitamin A) in fortified milk when it is exposed to 1076 1× fluorescent light is significant in plastic containers but less so than in glass. No loss occurs in milk in paperboard containers (21). Plastic containers are widely used, so extended holding of milk in lighted display cabinets should be avoided.

REFERENCES

1. Anderson, M., and B. E. Brooker. 1988. "Dairy foams." In *Advances in Food Emulsions and Foams.* E. Dickenson and G. Stainsby, eds. New York: Elsevier Applied Science Pp. 221–55. Role of proteins and fat in whipped cream.

2. Babcock, C. J. 1922. "The whipping quality of cream." *U.S. Department of Agriculture, Bulletin Number 1075.* 22 pp. Basic information about factors that affect the quality of whipped cream.

3. Bockian, A. H., G. F. Stewart, and A. L. Tappel. 1957. "Factors affecting the dispersibility of instant dissolving dry milks." *Food Research* 22:69–75. Why instant milks disperse so readily.

4. Brooker, B. E., M. Anderson, and A. T. Andrews. 1986. "The development of structure in whipped cream." *Food Microstructure* 5:277–85. Interfacial changes as cream is whipped.

5. Choi, R. P. 1959. "Dry milk-processing for specific uses." *Cereal Science Today* 4:39–42. Manufacture and uses of different forms of dried milk.

6. Dahlberg, A. C., and J. C. Hening. 1925. "Viscosity, surface tension and whipping properties of milk and cream." *New York State Exp. Sta. Tech. Bull. No. 113.* 42. Factors affecting the quality of whipped cream.

7. Dickenson, E. 1989. "Surface and emulsifying properties of caseins." *Journal of Dairy Research* 56:471–77. Effectiveness of α_{s1} – and β-casein as emulsifiers.

8. Eigel, W. N., J. E. Butler, C. A. Ernstrom, H. M. Farrel, Jr., V. R. Harwalkar, R. Jenness and M. R. Whitney. 1984. "Nomenclature of proteins of cow's milk: Fifth revision." *Journal of Dairy Science* 67:1597–1631. Nomenclature updated.

9. Fleming, D. W. et al. 1985. "Pasteurized milk as a vehicle of infection in an outbreak of listeriosis." *New England Journal of Medicine* 312:404–7. Documentation of the outbreak.

10. Hecht, D. W. 1991. "Bovine somatotropin safety and effectiveness: An industry perspective." *Food Technology* 45(4):118, 123–24, 126. Summary of papers in support of its safety and effectiveness.

11. Henstra, S., and D. G. Schmidt. 1970. "On the structure of the fat-protein complex in homogenized cow's milk." *Netherland Milk and Dairy Journal* 24:45–51. Evidence for subunits of casein micelles in new fat globule membranes.

12. Kalab, M., P. Allan-Wojtas, and B. E. Phillips-Todd. 1983. "Development of microstructure of set-style nonfat yogurt: A review." *Food Microstructure* 2:51–66. Factors affecting the microstructure.

13. Keenan, T. W., D. P. Dylewski, T. A. Woodford, and R. H. Ford. 1988. "Origin of milk fat globule and the nature of the milk fat globule membrane." In *Developments in Dairy Chemistry.* Vol 2. *Lipids.* P. F. Fox, ed. London and New York: Applied Science Publishers. Pp. 83–118. Components and structure of the membrane.

14. King, N. 1955. *The Milk Fat Globule Membrane and Some Associated Phenomena.* Farnham Royal, Bucks, England: Commonwealth Agricultural Bureau. 99 pp. Monograph summarizing information about the nature of the fat globule membrane.

15. Klemaszewski, J. R., K. P. Das, and J. E. Kinsella. 1992. "Formation and coalescence stability of emulsions stabilized by different milk proteins." *Journal of Food Science* 57:366–71, 379. Effectiveness of β-lactoglobulin and sodium caseinate.

16. Kroger, M. 1976. "Quality of yogurt." *Journal of Dairy Science* 59:344–50. Microbiological activity and flavor; body.

17. Lin, C. F., and P. M. T. Hansen. 1968. "Stabilization of calcium caseinate by carrageenan." *Journal of Dairy Science* 51:945. Effective groups on the hydrocolloid.

18. Lorient, D., B. Class, and J. L. Courthaudon. 1989. "Surface properties of the bovine casein components: Relationship between structure and function." *Journal of Dairy Research* 56:495–502. Qualities of β-casein that favor foaming; β-lactoglobulin foams more stable.

19. McMahon, D. J., and R. J. Brown. 1984. "Composition, structure and integrity of ca-

sein micelles: A review." *Journal of Dairy Science* 67:499–512. Detailed and technical.

20. Morr, C. V. 1982. "Functional properties of milk proteins and their use as food ingredients." In *Developments in Dairy Chemistry—1. Proteins.* P. F. Fox, ed. London and New York: Applied Science Publishers. Pp. 375–99. Caseins, caseinates, and whey proteins.

21. Murphy, P. A., R. Engelhardt, and S. E. Smith. 1988. "Isomerization of retinyl palmitate in fortified skim milk under retail fluorescent lighting." *Journal of Agricultural and Food Chemistry* 36:592–98. Paperboard, glass, and plastic compared.

22. Patton, S. 1958. "Review of the organic chemical effects of heat on milk." *Journal of Agricultural and Food Chemistry* 6:132–35. Color and flavor developed in milk by heat and the flavor of heated milk fat.

23. Pimentel, D., W. Dritschilo, J. Krummel, and J. Kutzman. 1975. "Energy and land constraints in food protein production." *Science* 190:754–61. Options for use of resources to meet the world's food needs.

24. Sandine, W. E., and P. R. Elliker. 1981. "Flavor in fermented dairy products." *Journal of Agricultural and Food Chemistry* 18:557–62. Commodities; organisms, substrates, and flavoring components.

25. Schmidt, D. G. 1982. "Association of caseins and casein micelle structure." In *Development in Dairy Chemistry—1. Proteins.* P. F. Fox, ed. London and New York: Applied Science Publishers. Pp. 61–86. Critique of casein micelle models; stabilizing forces.

26. Shimada, K., and J. Claude-Chaftel. 1988. "Texture characteristics, protein solubility, and sulfhydryl group/disulfide bond contents of heat-induced gels of whey protein isolate." *Journal of Agricultural and Food*

Chemistry 36:1018–25. Hydrophobic interaction and disulfide bonds predominate in neutral and alkaline gels.

27. Singh, R. P., D. R. Heldman, and J. R. Kirk. 1975. "Kinetic analysis of light-induced riboflavin loss in whole milk. *Journal of Food Science* 40:164–67. Effects of container, temperature, and intensity of light.

28. Slattery, C. W. 1976. "Review: Casein micelle structure; An examination of models." *Journal of Dairy Science* 59:1547–56. Evidence for and against various proposed models.

29. Slattery, C. W., and R. Evard. 1973. "A model for the formation and structure of casein micelles from subunits of variable composition." *Biochimica et Biophysica Acta* 317:529–38. Porous micellar model proposed.

30. Swaisgood, H. E. 1982. "Chemistry of milk proteins." In *Developments in Dairy Chemistry—1. Proteins.* P. F. Fox, ed. London and New York: Applied Science Publishers. Pp. 1–59. Levels of structure of individual proteins and their physical–chemical characteristics.

31. Tamine, A. Y., and H. C. Death. 1980. "Yogurt technology and biochemistry." *Journal of Food Protection* 43:939–77. Extensive treatment of both aspects.

32. Towson, A. M., and G. M. Trout. 1946. "Some cooking qualities of homogenized milk." II. "White sauces." *Food Research* 11:261–73. Effect of milk on thickness of sauce and apparent curdling due to poor incorporation of added fat.

33. Westhoff, D. C. 1978. "Heating milk for microbial destruction: A historical outline and update." *Journal of Food Protection* 41:122–30. Pasteurization standards for milk.

Cheese

20

Cheese is the curd of milk, basically a gel of casein from which more or less of the whey has been removed by heating, stirring, and pressing. Varieties of natural cheeses numbering in the hundreds are made, with names ranging from Abertam to Zomma (1). Figure 20-1 shows some of the more common varieties. Only a cheese expert or a connoisseur of cheese would be familiar with all. One is entitled to wonder how the curd from milk could give rise to so many varieties.

TYPES OF NATURAL CHEESE

One factor that contributes to the great variety of cheeses is the kind of milk used. Cow's milk is used almost exclusively in this country, but the milk from sheep is used in French Roquefort, goat's milk in Norwegian gjetost, and buffalo milk was originally used for Italian mozzarella. Whole milk is usually used, but some cheese is made from cream as well as milk, some from skimmed milk, and some from whey. The type of curd is a second factor that contributes to differences among cheeses. For cream cheese and for cottage cheese, the curd is formed by acidifying the milk. For most, however, the curd is made with rennet. Whether the cheese is ripened and, if it is, the kind of microorganisms used constitutes a third distinguishing factor. The temperature to which the cheese is exposed as it ripens, the humidity in the air, and the length of the ripening period also confer unique characteristics on cheese of different types. Production of cheese with lowered fat contents (2) has the potential for increasing the varieties of cheese available. Cheese analogs made with milk proteins and vegetable oil and lower in calories also are now marketed.

Cheese is a solid with both elastic and viscous properties that vary from one type of cheese to another. Texture of cheese is an important aspect of quality. It has an impact even before the taste of cheese is sensed (12). Based primarily on moisture content and ripeness, the texture of cheese may range from soft to semisoft, hard to very hard, to grating cheese.

Unripened Cheese

Unripened cheese is ready to eat as soon as it is made. Cottage cheese, cream cheese, and Neufchâtel are examples of unripened cheese. These are characterized by high moisture content. Cottage cheese has the highest (maximum of 80 percent), followed by Neufchâtel with a maximum of 65 percent. Neufchâtel (milkfat content less than 33 percent but not less than 20 percent) is a leaner cousin of cream cheese, which has a minimum fat content

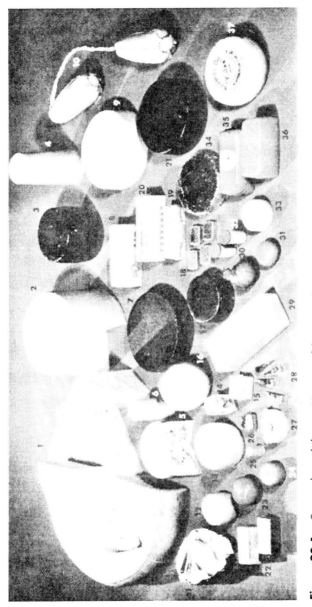

Figure 20-1. Commonly used cheeses. (Courtesy of the National Dairy Council.)

1—Swiss	14—Gjetost	27—Brie
2—American (Cheddar Style)	15—Primost	28—Sectors of Blue
3—Romano	16—Bel Paese	29—American (10-lb. Print)
4—American (Daisy Style)	17—Sardo	30—Apple
5—Gorgonzola	18—Cream	31—Baby Gouda
6—Cottage	19—Process Cheese Food	32—Process Cheese Spread
7—Asiago	20—Process American	33—Camembert
8—Brick	21—Parmesan	34—Port du Salut (Oka)
9—American (Daisy Style)	22—Limburger	35—Nokkelost
10—Provolone	23—Edam (Cannonball)	36—Block Edam
11—Blue	24—Baby Edam	37—Nordlands-Ost
12—Kumminost	25—Sapsago	
13—Muenster	26—Hand	

of 33 percent and a maximum moisture content of 55 percent. If dry curd cottage cheese is creamed, the minimum fat content is four percent. Any of the following ingredients may be added to cream cheese to give it its characteristic consistency: algin, carob bean gum, gelatin, gum karaya, gum tragacanth, or guar gum. These ingredients are permitted in amounts not to exceed 0.5 percent of the weight of the finished cheese.

Not all unripened cheese is soft. Gjetost and mysost, made from whey, are unripened cheeses that are firm because of their low moisture content. Lactose makes them sweet. Unripened cheese low in moisture may be stored for some time, in contrast to high-moisture cheese, which must be consumed soon after it is made.

Soft Ripened Cheese

Ripened cheeses vary in consistency from soft to very hard. Three soft ripened cheeses are Brie, Camembert, and Limburger. All three have a moisture content of approximately 50 percent. All three are surface-ripened cheeses, the first two by white or grayish-white molds that together with bacteria grow on the surface, followed by the growth of yellow and reddish molds that impart a creamy yellow translucency to the interior of the cheese. Yeasts and a species of bacteria are the curing agents for Limburger cheese. Limburger is creamy white on the interior and has a characteristic high aroma.

Semisoft Ripened Cheese

Semisoft ripened cheeses have a moisture content that ranges from 35 to 45 percent. Bel Paese, Brick, and Muenster are semisoft cheeses ripened primarily by bacteria. Gorgonzola, Roquefort, and Stilton, also semisoft, are cured by blue mold as well as by bacteria. Blue cheeses are mellow and have a piquant flavor. The flavor is due in part to hydrolysis of fat and liberation of free fatty acid (caproic, caprylic, and capric).

Firm and Hard Ripened Cheese

Both firm and very hard ripened cheeses are cured by bacteria. Cheddar, Edam, Gouda, Gruyère, and Swiss are examples of firm ripened cheeses. The holes in Swiss cheese are due to gas formed by bacteria as the cheese ripens. Very hard or grating cheeses include Parmesan, Romano, and Sap Sago. These are characterized by a low moisture content.

American cheese, including cheddar style, is the main type consumed in the U.S., with mozzarella a close second. The main cheese-producing states are Wisconsin, New York, Missouri, Illinois, and Minnesota. Detailed information about some of the more commonly used varieties of cheese is given in Table 20-1.

FORMATION OF COTTAGE CHEESE

Pasteurized skim or reconstituted nonfat milk is used to make cottage cheese. The milk is acidified either by a culture of bacteria that converts the lactose of milk to lactic acid or by the addition of acid (with or without a milk clotting enzyme) that lowers the pH of milk from approximately 6.6 to between 4.5 to 4.7. Acid makes the calcium phosphate associated with the micelles soluble (10). It also neutralizes the negative charge on the micellar surface, lowering the pH to the isoelectric point. The explanation

TABLE 20-1
Characteristics of Some Popular Varieties of Natural Cheeses

Kind or Name	Place of Origin	Kind of Milk Used in Manufacture	Ripening or Curing Time	Flavor	Body and Texture	Color	Retail Packaging	Uses
Soft, Unripened Varieties								
Cottage, plain or creamed	Unknown	Cow's milk skimmed; plain curd, or plain curd with cream added	Unripened	Mild, acid	Soft, curd particles of varying size	White to creamy white	Cup-shaped containers, tumblers, dishes	Salads, with fruits, vegetables, sandwiches, dips, cheese cake
Cream, plain	U.S.	Cream from cow's milk	Unripened	Mild, acid	Soft and smooth	White	3- to 8-oz. (85 to 226 g) packages	Salads, dips, sandwiches, snacks, cheese cake, desserts
Neufchâtel (Nū-shä-tĕl')	France	Cow's milk	Unripened	Mild, acid	Soft, smooth, similar to cream cheese but lower in milkfat	White	4- to 8-oz. (113 to 226 g) packages	Salads, dips, sandwiches, snacks, cheese cake, desserts
Ricotta (Rĭ-co-ta)	Italy	Cow's milk, whole or partly skimmed, or whey from cow's milk with whole or skim milk added. In Italy, whey from sheep's milk	Unripened	Sweet, nutlike	Soft, moist, or dry	White	Pint and quart (473 and 946 ml) paper and plastic containers, 1.3 kilograms (3 lb) metal cans	Appetizers, salads, snacks, lasagne, ravioli, noodles and other cooked dishes, grating, desserts
Firm, Unripened Varieties								
Gjetost[a] (Yĕt'ôst)	Norway	Whey from goat's milk or a mixture of whey from goat's and cow's milk	Unripened	Sweetish, caramel	Firm, buttery consistency	Golden brown	Cubical and rectangular	Snacks, desserts, served with dark breads, crackers, biscuits, or muffins

Name	Country	Kind of Milk	Ripening	Flavor	Body and Texture	Color	Shape	Uses
Mysost (Müs-ôst) also called Primost (Prēm'-ôst)	Norway	Whey from cow's milk	Unripened	Sweetish, caramel	Firm, buttery consistency	Light brown	Cubical, cylindrical, pie-shaped wedges	Snacks, desserts, served with dark breads
Mozzarella (Mŏ-tsa-rel'la) also called Scamorza	Italy	Whole or partly skimmed cow's milk. In Italy, originally made from buffalo's milk	Unripened	Delicate, mild	Slightly firm, plastic	Creamy white	Small round or braided form, shredded, sliced	Snacks, toasted sandwiches, cheeseburgers, cooking, as in meat loaf, or topping for lasagne, pizza, and casseroles
Soft, Ripened Varieties Brie (Brē)	France	Cow's milk	4 to 8 weeks	Mild to pungent	Soft, smooth when ripened	Creamy yellow interior; edible thin brown and white crust	Circular, pie-shaped wedges	Appetizers, sandwiches, snacks, good with crackers and fruit, dessert
Camembert (Kăm'ĕm-bâr)	France	Cow's milk	4 to 8 weeks	Mild to pungent	Soft, smooth; very soft when fully ripened	Creamy yellow interior; edible thin white, or gray-white crust	Small circular cakes and pie-shaped portions	Appetizers, sandwiches, snacks, good with crackers, and fruit such as pears and apples, dessert
Limburger	Belgium	Cow's milk	4 to 8 weeks	Highly pungent, very strong	Soft, smooth when ripened; usually contains small irregular openings	Creamy white interior; reddish yellow surface	Cubical, rectangular	Appetizers, snacks, good with crackers, rye or other dark breads, dessert

(continued)

TABLE 20-1 (continued)
Characteristics of Some Popular Varieties of Natural Cheeses

Kind or Name	Place of Origin	Kind of Milk Used in Manufacture	Ripening or Curing Time	Flavor	Body and Texture	Color	Retail Packaging	Uses
Semisoft, Ripened Varieties								
Bel Paese[b] (Běl Pä-ā´-zě)	Italy	Cow's milk	6 to 8 weeks	Mild to moderately robust	Soft to medium firm, creamy	Creamy yellow interior; slightly gray or brownish surface sometimes covered with yellow wax coating	Small wheels, wedges, segments	Appetizers, good with crackers, snacks, sandwiches, dessert
Brick	U.S.	Cow's milk	2 to 4 months	Mild to moderately sharp	Semisoft to medium firm, elastic, numerous small mechanical openings	Creamy yellow	Loaf, brick, slices, cut portions	Appetizers, sandwiches, snacks, dessert
Muenster (Mün´stĕr)	Germany	Cow's milk	1 to 8 weeks	Mild to mellow	Semisoft, numerous small mechanical openings. Contains more moisture than brick	Creamy white interior; yellow-tan surface	Circular cake, blocks, wedges, segments, slices	Appetizers, sandwiches, snacks, dessert
Port du Salut (Por dü Sä-lü´)	France	Cow's milk	6 to 8 weeks	Mellow to robust	Semisoft, smooth, buttery, small openings	Creamy yellow	Wheels and wedges	Appetizers, snacks, served with raw fruit, dessert
Firm Ripened Varieties								
Cheddar	England	Cow's milk	1 to 12 months or more	Mild to very sharp	Firm, smooth, some mechanical openings	White to medium-yellow-orange	Circular, cylindrical loaf, pie-shaped wedges, oblongs, slices, cubes, shredded, grated	Appetizers, sandwiches, sauces, on vegetables, in hot dishes, toasted sandwiches, grating, cheeseburgers, dessert

Name	Place of Origin	Kind of Milk	Ripening or Curing Time	Flavor	Body and Texture	Color	Retail Packaging	Uses
Colby	U.S.	Cow's milk	1 to 3 months	Mild to mellow	Softer and more open than Cheddar	White to medium-yellow-orange	Cylindrical, pie-shaped wedges	Sandwiches, snacks, cheeseburgers
Caciocavallo (Kä′chō-kä-val′lō)	Italy	Cow's milk. In Italy, cow's milk or mixtures of sheep's, goat's, and cow's milk	3 to 12 months	Piquant, similar to Provolone but not smoked	Firm, lower in milkfat and moisture than Provolone	Light or white interior; clay or tan colored surface	Spindle or ten-pin shaped, bound with cord, cut pieces	Snacks, sandwiches, cooking, dessert; suitable for grating after prolonged curing
Edam (Ē′dam)	Netherlands	Cow's milk, partly skimmed	2 to 3 months	Mellow, nutlike	Semisoft to firm, smooth; small irregularly shaped or round holes; lower milkfat than Gouda	Creamy yellow or medium yellow-orange interior; surface coated with red wax	Cannon ball shaped loaf, cut pieces, oblongs	Appetizers, snacks, salads, sandwiches, seafood sauces, dessert
Gouda (Gou′-dá)	Netherlands	Cow's milk, whole or partly skimmed	2 to 6 months	Mellow, nutlike	Semisoft to firm, smooth; small irregularly shaped or round holes; higher milkfat than Edam	Creamy yellow or medium yellow-orange interior; may or may not have red wax coating	Ball shaped with flattened top and bottom	Appetizers, snacks, salads, sandwiches, seafood sauces, dessert
Provolone (Prō-vō-lō′-nē) also smaller sizes and shapes called Provolette, Provoloncini	Italy	Cow's milk	2 to 12 months or more	Mellow to sharp, smoky, salty	Firm, smooth	Light creamy interior; light brown or golden yellow surface	Pear shaped, sausage and salami shaped, wedges, slices	Appetizers, sandwiches, snacks, soufflé, pasta dishes, pizza, suitable for grating when fully cured and dried
Swiss, also called Emmentaler	Switzerland	Cow's milk	3 to 9 months	Sweet, nutlike	Firm, smooth with large round eyes	Light yellow	Segments, pieces, slices	Sandwiches, snacks, sauces, fondue, cheeseburgers

(continued)

TABLE 20-1 (continued)
Characteristics of Some Popular Varieties of Natural Cheeses

Kind or Name	Place of Origin	Kind of Milk Used in Manufacture	Ripening or Curing Time	Flavor	Body and Texture	Color	Retail Packaging	Uses
Very Hard, Ripened Varieties								
Parmesan (Pär′mē-zăn) also called Reggiano	Italy	Partly skimmed cow's milk	14 months to 2 years	Sharp, piquant	Very hard, granular, lower moisture and milkfat than Romano	Creamy white	Cylindrical, wedges, shredded, grated	Grated for seasoning in soups, or vegetables, spaghetti, ravioli, breads, popcorn, used extensively in pizza and lasagne
Romano (Rō-mä′-nō) also called Sardo Pecorino Romano	Italy	Cow's milk. In Italy, sheep's milk (Italian law)	5 to 12 months	Sharp, piquant	Very hard granular	Yellowish-white interior, greenish-black surface	Round with flat ends, wedges, shredded, grated	Seasoning in soups, casserole dishes, ravioli, sauces, breads, suitable for grating when cured for about one year
Sap Sago° (Săp′-sä-gō)	Switzerland	Skimmed cow's milk	5 months or more	Sharp, pungent cloverlike	Very hard	Light green by addition of dried, powdered clover leaves	Conical, shakers	Grated to flavor soups, meats, macaroni, spaghetti, hot vegetables; mixed with butter makes a good spread on crackers or bread

Blue-Vein Mold-Ripened Varieties

Blue, spelled Bleu on imported cheese	France	Cow's milk. In France, cow's milk or sheep's milk or mixtures of these	2 to 6 months	Tangy, peppery	Semisoft, pasty, sometimes crumbly	White interior, marbled or streaked with blue veins of mold	Cylindrical, wedges, oblongs, squares, cut portions	Appetizers, salads, dips, salad dressing, sandwich spreads, good with crackers, dessert
Gorgonzola (Gôr-gŏn-zō'-lá)	Italy	Cow's milk. In Italy, cow's milk or goat's milk or mixtures of these	3 to 12 months	Tangy, peppery	Semisoft, pasty, sometimes crumbly, lower moisture than Blue	Creamy white interior, mottled or streaked with blue-green veins of mold. Clay colored surface	Cylindrical, wedges, oblongs	Appetizers, snacks, salads, dips, sandwich spread, good with crackers, dessert
Roquefort[a] (Rŏk'-fèrt) or (Rŏk-fôr')	France	Sheep's milk	2 to 5 months or more	Sharp, slightly peppery	Semisoft, pasty, sometimes crumbly	White or creamy white interior, marbled or streaked with blue veins of mold	Cylindrical, wedges	Appetizers, snacks, salads, dips, sandwich spreads, good with crackers, dessert
Stilton[a]	England	Cow's milk	2 to 6 months	Piquant, milder than Gorgonzola or Roquefort	Semisoft, flaky; slightly more crumbly than Blue	Creamy white interior, marbled or streaked with blue-green veins of mold	Circular, wedges, oblongs	Appetizers, snacks, salads, dessert

[a]Imported only.
[b]Italian trademark—licensed for manufacture in U.S.; also imported.
Source: U.S. Dept. Agriculture. Marketing Bulletin No. 17. *Cheese Buying Guide for Consumers.* 1961.

usually given for the gel that results is that chains or clusters of these altered micelles form a three-dimensional network that immobilizes the liquid. The gel-forming process by acid is shown in simplied form as follows:

$$\text{Casein micelles} + \text{H}^+ \rightarrow \text{Neutral casein} + \text{Ca}^{++}$$
$$\text{(Colloidally} \quad \text{(Hydrogen} \quad \text{(Gel)}$$
$$\text{dispersed)} \quad \text{ions)}$$

However, gel formation by acid may be more complex (10). Not only is the stabilizing calcium phosphate dissolved by acid, but weakly bound β-casein dissociates from the micelle. As the pH is lowered further, the β-casein becomes positively charged and can then reassociate with the negatively charged α_{s1}-casein and so form new aggregates. These gel-forming entities would thus differ from the original micelles. Once the gel or clabber (as soured milk is called) forms, it is cut, stirred, and may be warmed slightly to shrink the curd. This frees part of the liquid that contains noncoagulable whey proteins. The curds are then allowed to drain.

PRODUCTION OF CHEDDAR CHEESE

Curd Formation

Whole milk, usually pasteurized, is used to make cheddar cheese. Rennet is used as a co-agulant. The milk is brought to a temperature of 30° to 31°C (86° to 88°F), and a culture of lactic acid-forming bacteria, called a starter, is added. Chymosin, a protease and the main component in rennet, acts slowly in fresh milk but can be accelerated if the pH is lowered (7). Traditionally, rennet was obtained from calf stomachs, but the supply of calves became inadequate to meet the increased demand for cheese. Rennets obtained from other animals (cows and swine), and especially from microbial sources (*Mucor miehei, Mucor pusillus,* and *Endiothia parasitica*) that contain proteases other than chymosin, are used extensively (21). Calf rennet is preferred because of its high proportion of chymosin and low percentage of pepsin. Recombinant DNA technology is now used to insert the gene that codes for the production of bovine chymosin into organisms that includes nonpathogenic *Escherichia coli* bacteria and *Saccharomyces cerevisiae* yeast (3), with the potential for relieving the shortage of chymosin. Bovine chymosin produced by *E. coli* was approved for use in food by the Food and Drug Administration in 1990 (8).

Chymosin is responsible for the first step in the conversion of the casein of milk into cheese. The enzyme catalyzes the hydrolysis of the peptide bond between phenylalanine and methionine (residues 105–106) of κ-casein. The specificity of the attack by chymosin on this bond is attributed both to the particular amino acid residues on either side of the bond that cause it to stand out (7) and especially to the presence of two predicted β-turns, one on either side of the bond (19). Chymosin and other proteases that are chymosin substitutes have two lobes separated by a cleft that contains the bonding site, which presumably accommodates the part of κ-casein with the 105–106 bond (7). Heating milk, depending on time and temperature above 60°C (140°F), may slow or prevent the action of the enzyme even if the temperature is reduced subsequently so the enzyme will not be denatured. This effect of heat is attributed to the formation of a complex between heat-denaturable β-lactoglobulin and κ-casein (16) that makes the 105–106 bond inaccessible to the enzyme (7).

When chymosin acts on κ-casein, the hydrophobic part of the molecule, *para*-κ-casein, remains with the micelle while the detached hydrophilic and charged part floats away. This has the effect of reducing the charge on the surface of the micelle (7). The micelles can then unite in a three-dimensional network that immobilizes the aqueous phase of the milk and traps the fat globules. Although the details of the mechanism of gel formation are not fully understood, hydrophobic interaction between destabilized casein micelles is believed to be involved. This is supported by the temperature dependence of gel formation (7). No gel forms at a temperature below 15°C (58°F), and gel formation is speeded as the temperature is increased to 45°C (113°F). Unlike the casein micelles that are altered by acid, those modified by chymosin retain calcium phosphate and are therefore better sources of calcium.

Once the gel is formed it is cut into cubes and stirred to facilitate drainage of whey from the curds. The curds are warmed slightly to a temperature near 40°C (104°F) to shrink the protein network so that more whey can be expelled. The curds are salted and a food coloring is added to give the typical yellow of most cheddars, in contrast to the creamy white of uncolored Swiss cheese. The curds are then placed in molds under pressure to release still more whey. Even so, the moisture content of even a firm cheese such as cheddar is approximately 37 to 38 percent.

Ripening

When cheese is first formed, it is tough, rubbery, and bland tasting. This freshly made green cheese is held in storage for a time to bring about changes in both texture and flavor. A major change in the texture of cheese occurs during the first week or two of ripening (12). Chymosin retained by the curd, and to a lesser extent plasmin, a protease of milk, bring about cleavage of the 23–24 peptide bond of α_{s1}-casein, forming a short fragment and the main α_{s1}-I polypeptide (5). This action requires more time than does the original attack of chymosin on κ-casein. It results in a weakening of the casein network and a loss of rubberiness of the curd. Unless this break in the α_{s1}-casein occurs, subsequent alteration of the texture of the curd does not take place (12).

Once the initial break in the α_{s1}-casein occurs, enzymes from microorganisms of the starter bring about a more general proteolysis of the peptides, further altering the texture. The extent to which the casein network of the curd is hydrolyzed is influenced by the salt/water content and the pH of the curd, as well as by the ripening time and temperature. The texture of the finished cheese can vary from crumbly or granular to cohesive or plastic, depending on the final pH. The pH affects the character of the curd in two ways. Acid makes the calcium that stabilizes the micelles soluble, favoring their fragmentation (12). When the pH is lowered near the isoelectric point of casein, attraction between casein fragments makes the curd compact and the moisture unevenly distributed, with much of it in the interstices. Such cheese tends to be crumbly. In cheese with a high pH, water can associate with (solvate) the charged caseins, in effect forming a concentrated casein dispersion that contains the fat. Such cheese tends to be cohesive (6). Camembert cheese has a high pH because mold on the surface has metabolized the lactic acid (12).

The percentage of milk fat affects the texture of cheese by diluting the protein of the curd. If the fat content is too low, the cheese is compact and bricklike. A cheddar-type cheese with a milkfat content of 16 percent (compared to 33 percent fat in the control) had poor texture, but one with 25 percent fat had texture that was much improved. More extensive proteolysis of the casein can partially compensate for the lower level of fat (2), as can a higher percentage of water.

Ripening of the curd, with milkfat an essential component, results in the development of flavor in cheese. The aroma of cheese is attributed to the free fatty acids, ketones, aldehydes, and lactones, all derived from fat (2). A fat content of 25 percent is needed to yield a cheese with a mild cheddar flavor. Milk fat with the fat globule membrane intact yields a superior product (14). Salt in the curd promotes the formation of desirable flavor components (20) and limits the proteolysis of β-casein, which otherwise might yield bitter products (9). Free fatty acids from the milk fat and H_2S liberated from cysteine residues of β-casein must be in balance for good flavor (11). So too must be the ratio of fatty acids to acetate (0.55:1.0) (13). If short-chain fatty acids equal or exceed the acetate, the cheese may have a fruity or rancid aroma. The breakdown products of fat, as well as those from lactose, citrates, and proteins and the products of their interaction, are essential for converting a bland-tasting curd into a flavorful, ripened cheese.

Federal regulations require that cheese made from unpasteurized milk be ripened for not less than 60 days at a temperature no lower than 1.7°C (35°F). During this holding period pathogenic bacteria that might be present in the milk die. This regulation applies, of course, only to cheese that enters interstate commerce. The adequacy of this treatment has been questioned should the raw milk be heavily contaminated with a pathogen such as *Listeria monocytogenes* (17).

Some cheeses are marketed with the age stamped on them; others are labeled mild, mellow, sharp, or very sharp—terms that indicate progressively longer aging periods. Providing storage space while cheese ripens adds to the cost.

White deposits found occasionally on fully ripened cheeses are sometimes mistaken for mold. They may be crystals of the amino acid tyrosine. This accumulates as the proteins in the cheese are hydrolyzed. Because of its low solubility, tyrosine precipitates if enough accumulates.

PASTEURIZED PROCESS CHEESE

Any natural cheese can be made into process cheese. A high proportion of the cheese marketed is in the form of process cheese. The natural cheese is grated or shredded, and an emulsifier, usually disodium phosphate, is added. The cheese is then blended and heated to pasteurize it. The moisture content of a process cheese can be only one percent greater than the maximum allowed for the natural form. More moisture is allowed in cheese spread, and for cheese food even more is permitted. The minimum fat content is lower for process than for natural, lower still for cheese food, and lowest for cheese spread. Thus the cheese in cheese food is more dilute than in process cheese and still more dilute in cheese spread. The money spent for these items buys less cheese but more convenience, such as greater spreadability. The intimate blending of constituents in process cheese diminishes the strength of the cheese flavor. Too, the emulsifier contributes a taste of its own. Advantages of cooking with cheese in processed form are that it blends readily with liquid and is less likely to curdle or become stringy or matted if it is overheated.

The presence in process cheese of conjugated linoleic acid, an isomer of the natural 9,12 form of the fatty acid (Chapter 15) is of interest. At least one conjugated linoleic acid has been shown to have anticarcinogenic properties in experimental animals (18). Heat used in the manufacture of process cheese appears to cause a shift in the double bonds of linoleic acid from the 9,12 to new positions. One such isomer, 9,11 linoleic acid, is conjugated; that is, the two double bonds in the molecule are separated by only one single bond. Instead of the all-*cis* natural form of the molecule, the *cis*-9,*trans*-11 geometric isomer is presumed to be the active form. This conjugated linoleic acid acts as an inducer of an enzyme that is an effective inhibitor of carcinogenesis.

COMPOSITION OF CHEESES

Table 20-2 gives the composition of a few of the varieties of cheeses commonly used. Figures are based on 100 grams, or slightly less than ¼ pound.

Cheese retains a high proportion of most of the nutrients of the milk from which it was made and supplies these in a more concentrated form. Cheese is a rich source of high-quality protein, has a high percentage of fat (cottage cheese excepted), and is an excellent source of calcium and phosphorus (cottage and cream cheese excepted) (3, 4). Cheese is an excellent source of riboflavin, and if made from whole milk, contributes vitamin A to the diet. Primost and Gjetost are high in lactose.

USES OF CHEESE

Cheese is a versatile food found in menus from appetizers to desserts. As appetizers, cheese may appear as dips, spreads, or wedges. Cheese soufflé, fondue, omelet, casserole dishes, or sandwiches make a main course. Cottage, cream, and Neufchâtel cheeses are used in salads, as are shredded or grated hard cheeses. Cheeses that are preeminently for dessert include Bel Paese, Brie, Camembert, Port du Salut, and Roquefort. Camembert, Edam, Gouda, and Liederkranz are popular for cheese trays with crackers and fruit.

CHEESE IN COOKING

The bulk of the cheese used in cooking is American cheese or some modification of it. Problems in melting cheese and in blending cheese with liquid are discussed below.

Melting Cheese

As cheese is heated, it softens until it becomes a viscous liquid that can flow. This softening is due in part to the fat in the cheese. At refrigeration temperature the fat in cheese is solid; at room temperature it softens. When cheese is heated, the fats liquefy. The more fat in the cheese the more readily the cheese softens. When cheese is heated beyond a certain temperature, coagulation and shrinkage of the protein offset the tendency of the cheese to soften because of the melting of the fat. The fat may separate from the curd.

The presence of water in cheese permits the curd to shrink due to evaporation of moisture. Cheese melted in the oven or under the broiler may shrink and toughen because of loss of moisture to the air and because of the effect of heat on the protein. Overexposure to hot, dry atmosphere is one of the greatest indignities that cheese suffers at the hands of cooks.

TABLE 20-2
Composition of Cheeses (per 100 grams)

Cheese	Water (%)	Calories[a]	Protein (g)	Lipid (g)	Carbohydrate (g)	Calcium (mg)	Phosphorus (mg)	Iron (mg)	Vitamin A Value (I.U.)	Thiamin (mg)	Riboflavin (mg)	Niacin (mg)	Ascorbic Acid (mg)
Natural													
Blue	42.41	353	21.40	28.74	2.34	528	387	.31	721	.029	.382	1.016	0
Brick	41.11	371	23.24	29.68	2.79	674	451	.43	1,083	.014	.351	.118	0
Cheddar	36.75	403	24.90	33.14	1.28	721	512	.68	1,059	.027	.375	.080	0
Cottage, creamed	78.96	103	12.49	4.51	2.68	60	132	.14	163	.021	.163	.126	Trace
Cream	53.75	349	7.55	34.87	2.66	80	104	1.20	1,427	.017	.197	.101	0
Gjetost	13.44	466	9.65	29.51	42.65	400	444	—[b]	—	—	—	.813	0
Limburger	48.42	327	20.05	27.25	.49	497	393	.13	1,281	.080	.503	.158	0
Parmesan, grated	17.66	456	41.56	30.02	3.74	1,376	807	.95	701	.045	.386	.315	0
Swiss	37.21	376	28.43	27.45	3.38	961	605	.17	845	.022	.365	.092	0
Process, Pasteurized													
American	39.16	375	22.15	31.25	1.60	616	745	.39	1,210	.027	.353	.069	0
American cheese food	43.15	328	19.61	24.60	7.29	574	459	.84	913	.029	.442	.140	0
American cheese spread	47.65	290	16.41	21.23	8.73	562	712	.33	788	.048	.431	.131	0

[a] 1 kilocalorie = 4.185 kilojoules.
[b] — = Data not available.

Source: U.S. Dept. Agr. Handbook No. 8-1. Composition of Foods. Dairy and Egg Products. Raw, Processed, Prepared. Revised 1976, 1990 supplement.

338

Blending Cheese with Liquid

Often cheese is combined with liquid as in cheese sauce, pasta and cheese, and cheese soufflé. The higher the moisture and fat content of the cheese, the more readily it blends with liquid (15). To take advantage of the high fat content, the temperature of the liquid is important. If it is not hot enough to melt the fat, the cheese will not blend with the liquid. If the liquid is too hot, the cheese shrinks excessively and moisture is forced from the curd. An overheated cheese sauce is watery and either stringy and matted or grainy. More highly ripened cheese (15), because the protein of the curd is more readily dispersed, blends better with liquid. The riper the cheese, the higher the temperature it can tolerate. Cheese does not disperse well at a pH below 5.6; it tends to string and mat (15). A Swiss fondue for dipping is a special type of cheese sauce made by melting grated Swiss cheese in dry white wine heated in a chafing dish until it is bubbling hot. The boiling point of the alcohol in the wine is low enough so that the cheese does not become overheated. The sauce is eaten by dipping cubes of French bread or other edibles into it.

A final factor favoring the blending of cheese with liquid is the presence of emulsifier in the cheese. It is for this reason that process cheese presents less of a problem in making cheese dishes. A cheese sauce made from process cheese is less likely to curdle. The texture of a cheese sauce made from process cheese is very smooth, although it has an adhesive, tacky, rubbery consistency that some find objectionable. Cheese sauce made with natural cheese seems grainy by comparison, but the cheese flavor is more pronounced. Using part process and part natural cheese gives the advantages of both.

Hard cheese is usually grated before an attempt is made to incorporate it in liquid. It is impossible to grate process cheese; instead, this type should be cut into very thin slices or shredded to facilitate blending. Process cheese, if thinly sliced, blends readily with white sauce if the liquid is hot enough. Grated sharp cheese blends readily, too, because the cheese is in such small pieces and is fully ripened. Ordinarily, mild, less highly ripened grated cheese blends more slowly than does sharp cheese.

REFERENCES

1. Anon. 1978. "Cheese varieties and descriptions." *U.S. Department of Agriculture Handbook No. 54.* 151 pp. A listing of varieties of cheese with descriptions.
2. Banks, J., M. E. Y. Brechany, and W. W. Christie. 1989. "The production of low fat cheddar-type cheese." *Journal of the Society of Dairy Technology* 42:6–9. Fat level and texture and flavor.
3. Barach, J. T. 1985. "What's new in genetic engineering of dairy starter cultures and dairy enzymes." *Food Technology* 39(10): 73–74, 79, 84. Calf chymosin from microorganisms.
4. Blunt, K., and E. Summer. 1928. "The calcium of cheese." *Journal of Home Economics* 20:587–90. Analysis of cottage, cheddar, and Swiss cheese (commercial source).
5. Carles, C., and B. R. Dumas. 1985. "Kinetics of the action of chymosin (rennin) on a peptide bond of bovine α_{s1}-casein. *FEBS Letters* 185:282–86. Cleavage of bond 23–24.
6. Creamer, L., and N. F. Olson. 1982. "Rheological evaluation of maturing cheddar cheese." *Journal of Food Science* 47:631–36, 646. Relation between pH and cheese texture.
7. Dalgleish, D. G. 1982. "The enzymatic coagulation of milk." In *Developments in Dairy Chemistry*—1. *Proteins.* P. F. Fox, ed. London and New York: Applied Science Publishers. Pp. 157–87. Details of the clotting process.
8. Flamm, E. L. 1991. "How FDA approved chymosin: A case history." *Biotechnology* 9:349–51. Details of the process.

9. Guinee, T. P., and P. F. Fox. 1987. "Salt in cheese: Physical, chemical and biological aspects." In *Cheese: Chemistry, Physics, and Microbiology.* P. F. Fox, ed. London and New York: Elsevier Applied Science Publishers. Pp. 251–97. Effects on proteolysis.

10. Heertje, I., J. Visser, and P. Smits. 1985. "Structure formation in acid milk gels." *Food Microstructure* 4:267–77. Network formation with newly formed particles, not with casein micelles.

11. Kristoffersen, T. 1967. "Interrelationship of flavor and chemical changes in cheese." *Journal of Dairy Science* 50:279–84. Constituents in the flavor of ripened cheese.

12. Lawrence, R. C., L. K. Creamer, and J. Gilles. 1987. "Texture development during cheese ripening." *Journal of Dairy Science* 70:1748–60. Interrelations of pH, moisture, and salt on texture.

13. Ohren, J. A., and S. L. Tuckey. 1969. "Relation of flavor development in cheddar cheese to chemical changes in the fat of the cheese." *Journal of Dairy Science* 52:598–607. Role of fat in cheese flavor.

14. Olson, N. E., and M. E. Johnson. 1990. "Light cheese products: Characteristics and economics." *Food Technology* 44(10):93–6. Importance of fat and of intact fat globule membrane.

15. Personius, C. J., E. Boardman, and A. R. Ausherman. 1944. "Some factors affecting the behavior of cheddar cheese in cooking." *Food Research* 9:308–11. Effect of fat content, moisture content, and ripening on the melting characteristics and the blending of cheese with liquid.

16. Reddy, I. M., and J. E. Kinsella. 1990. "Interaction of β-lactoglobulin with κ-casein in micelles as assessed by chymosin hydrolysis: Effect of temperature, heating time, β-lactoglobulin concentration, and pH." *Journal of Agricultural and Food Chemistry* 38:50–8. Interaction increased above 60°C and release of the charged peptide by chymosin decreased.

17. Ryser, E. T., and E. H. Marth. 1987. "Behavior of *Listeria monocytogenes* during the manufacture of ripening cheddar cheese." *Journal of Food Protection* 50:7–13. Adequacy of FDA's rules for ripening cheese made from raw milk questioned.

18. Shantha, N. C., E. A. Decker, and Z. Ustunol. 1992 "Conjugated linoleic acid concentration in processed cheese." *Journal of the American Oil Chemists Society* 69:425–28. Effects of processing conditions and presence of whey protein concentrate.

19. Swaisgood, H. E. 1982. "Chemistry of milk proteins." In *Developments in Dairy Chemistry*—1. *Proteins* P. F. Fox, ed. London and New York: Applied Science Publishers. Pp. 1–59. Much detail including structure around the chymosin-sensitive bond of α_{s1}—casein.

20. Thakur, M. K., J. R. Kirk, and T. I. Hedrick. 1975. "Changes during ripening of unsalted cheddar cheese." *Journal of Dairy Science* 58:175–80. Effect of salt on flavor and texture.

21. Winwood, J. 1989. "Rennet and rennet substitutes." *Journal of the Society of Dairy Technology* 42:1–2. Microbial proteases as chymosin substitutes.

Eggs

21

Eggs served fried, scrambled, poached, or cooked in the shell add variety to meals and are a source of high quality protein. In addition, eggs are important functional ingredients in many prepared foods. They act as emulsifiers in mayonnaise, cream puffs, cheese soufflé, Hollandaise sauce, and shortened cake. They function as a coating material for croquettes, a thickening agent in soft pie filling, a gelling agent in custard, and a structural material in shortened cake. Whipped to a foam, eggs serve as a means of incorporating air into meringues, divinity candy, puffy omelets, and sponge and angel cakes. In shortened cake, eggs make possible the aeration of the batter by beating or stirring without prior creaming of the fat and sugar. Eggs are thus polyfunctional ingredients in foods.

STRUCTURE

Shell

The egg is unique in a number of ways, not least of which is its elaborate structure (Fig. 21-1). The shell of an egg, constituted mainly of crystals of calcium carbonate deposited in an organic matrix, surrounds and supports the part that is used for food. An egg shell is brittle and rigid, but it is not impervious (44). It contains thousands of pores so small that they are invisible and a few just large enough to be seen without magnification. Spots of color that appear on the white of a colored Easter egg are evidence of the porosity of the shell. Some egg shells are white; others are brown. Pigmentation of the shell depends on the breed of the hen and has no bearing on the quality of the egg. Eggs with white shells are preferred in some areas, whereas in other markets those with brown shells are first choice.

Shell Membranes

Inside the shell of an egg are two shell membranes, one of which adheres tenaciously to the shell. These membranes are made mainly of keratin (a protein also found in human hair), together with mucin (44). After an egg is laid the contents shrink more than the shell and the two membranes are separated by a small air cell. This usually appears at the large end of an egg.

Albumen

The egg proper consists of the white, known as the albumen, and the yolk. The albumen is present in three layers, an outermost layer of thin white, a layer of thick white,

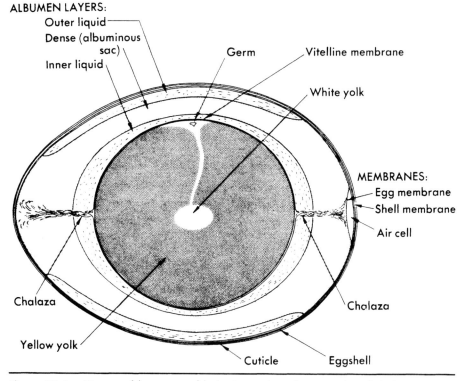

ALBUMEN LAYERS:
Outer liquid
Dense (albuminous sac)
Inner liquid
Germ
Vitelline membrane
White yolk
MEMBRANES:
Egg membrane
Shell membrane
Air cell
Chalaza
Chalaza
Yellow yolk
Cuticle
Eggshell

Figure 21-1. Diagram of the structure of the hen's egg, shown by section through the long axis. (From A. L. Romanoff and A. J. Romanoff, *The Avian Egg,* copyright © 1949 by John Wiley & Sons, Inc., New York, p. 112. Reprinted by permission.)

and another layer of thin white that lies adjacent to the yolk (44). Some hens secrete a higher ratio of thick to thin white than do others. Storage conditions also affect the thickness of the albumen and the ratio of thick to thin egg white.

Yolk

Separating the egg white from the yolk, and enclosing the latter, is the yolk sac, called the vitelline membrane. Projecting from either side of the yolk are ropelike structures called chalazae. These serve to anchor the yolk in the thick white and keep it centered in the egg but permit the yolk to rotate.

An egg yolk consists of a small sphere of white yolk surrounded by yellow yolk. In some eggs thin bands of white yolk alternate with thicker bands of yellow around this central core. The germ spot on the surface of the yolk is attached to the white yolk in the center by the tubelike latebra. The color of an egg yolk is influenced mainly by the xanthophyll content of the ration fed the hen. Because most carotenoid pigments deposited in the yolk are not precursors of vitamin A, more highly colored egg yolks are not necessarily richer in potential vitamin A activity.

The shell contributes 11 percent of the weight of an egg, the white 58 percent, and the yolk 31 percent. Egg white accounts for ⅔ and the yolk ⅓ of the weight of the edible portion of an egg.

Table 21-1 gives the constituents of a whole egg, an egg white, and an egg yolk. The white and the yolk differ markedly in composition, as the table shows.

Egg White

The chief constituents in egg white, aside from water, are proteins. They are secreted into the oviduct as the mature yolk traverses it, after which the egg is encapsuled by the shell (50). Ovalbumin is the main protein in egg white, more than half the total. Ovalbumin contains a high proportion of the sulfhydryl groups of the white. It exists in three fractions that vary in phosphate content. Next in quantity are conalbumin (ovotransferrin), that forms complexes with such divalent ions as iron and copper, and ovomucoid, which account for 12 and 11 percent, respectively. These three glycoproteins (or protein fractions) constitute more than 75 percent of the total protein in egg white. Globulins account for approximately eight percent, lysozyme less than four percent, and ovomucin less than two percent (9). Avidin, minor in amount, is of interest because of its ability to bind biotin and make it unavailable to microorganisms. Avidin is easily denatured when eggs are cooked. Also present is a small amount of a protein to which the riboflavin of the egg white is bound.

Egg Yolk

Egg yolk is approximately ½ water, ⅓ lipid, and ⅙ protein (8). The high lipid content of the yolk accounts for the fact that roughly ¾ of the calories supplied by an egg come from the yolk. Triacylglycerols make up almost ¾ of the total lipids of the yolk and phospholipids slightly less than ¼, with cholesterol accounting for four to six percent. The fatty acids esterified with glycerol are oleic, palmitic, stearic, and linoleic, in descending order. The main phospholipid is lecithin (phosphatidyl choline) with some phosphatidyl ethanolamine and a small amount of phosphatidyl serine.

Proteins of the yolk include vitellin, present as a complex with lipid and referred to as lipovitellin. Phosvitin, a phosphoprotein, as is vitellin, binds more than 80 percent of the iron of the yolk. Livetin, a sulfur-containing globular protein, and low-density lipoproteins are found in the yolk, too (8).

The protein and lipid components of egg yolk are associated in a complex way (8). The yolk consists of an aqueous phase called plasma in which are dispersed discrete particles, the globules and granules. The large globules (50 to 100 μm in diameter) can be readily seen in a smear of egg yolk viewed with a light microscope. The more numerous, irregularly-shaped, and smaller (diameter 0.3 to 1.6 μm) granules appear in the background. Granules constitute ¼ of the yolk on a dry weight basis. Lipovitellins are found in the granules, as is phosvitin. Some low-density lipoprotein is in the granules, too. The presence of phosphoproteins and divalent ions, plus the effects of pH and ionic strength on the granules led to the suggestion that the granules are structured much like the casein micelles of milk (10).

The plasma of yolk, which is 50 percent water, contains protein (8%) and low-density lipoproteins (30%). Livetins constitute the nonlipid-bound protein dispersed in the plasma. The low-density lipoproteins contain approximately 12 percent protein, with the remainder neutral lipids and phospholipids (8). A model proposed for the assembly of constituents

TABLE 21-1
Constituents in Whole Egg, Egg White, and Egg Yolk

Item	Weight (g)	Water (%)	Calories[a]	Protein (g)	Lipid (g)	Carbo-hydrate (g)	Calcium (mg)	Phos-phorus (mg)	Iron (mg)	Vitamin A (I.U.)	Thiamin (mg)	Ribo-flavin (mg)	Niacin (mg)	Ascorbic Acid (mg)
Egg	50	37	75	6.3	5.0	.61	25	89	.72	317	.03	.25	.037	0
Egg white	33.4	29	17	3.5	0.0	.34	2	4	.01	—[b]	—	.15	.031	0
Egg yolk	16.6	8	59	2.8	5.1	.30	23	81	.59	323	.03	.11	.002	0

[a] 1 kilocalorie = 4.185 kilojoules
[b] — = Data not available.

Source: U.S. Dept. Agr. Handbook No. 8-1. Composition of Foods. Dairy Products and Egg Products. Raw, Processed, Prepared. Revised 1976, 1990 supplement.

in low-density lipoproteins shows triacylglycerols and cholesterol esters at the center of the globular-shaped structure, with protein, cholesterol, and phospholipids on the periphery. Low-density lipoproteins account for 60 percent of the yolk on a dried weight basis. This fraction of the yolk contributes many of the functional properties of eggs in food preparation (31,48).

QUALITY OF EGGS

A freshly laid egg has a high proportion of thick white that resists spreading when the egg is broken from the shell. Thick white appears to be a weak, transparent gel in which parallel, translucent bands are embedded (Fig. 21-7). There is general agreement that ovomucin contributes to the physical properties of thick white, but the role of lysozyme is still at issue. The height of thick egg white, that is, its resistance to spreading, can be measured objectively by a micrometer as shown in Figure 21-2. The yolk of a fresh egg is upstanding and it remains centered in the white. Changes in an egg leading to a deterioration in quality may occur as soon as an egg is laid.

Deteriorative Changes

Enlargement of the air cell because of loss of moisture spoils the appearance of an egg cooked in the shell. More important from the standpoint of maintaining quality is loss of carbon dioxide, which permits the egg white to become more alkaline. The pH of the

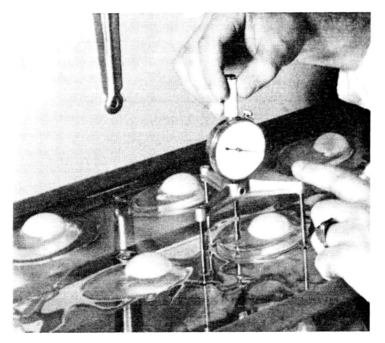

Figure 21-2. Micrometer or gauge for measuring the height of thick egg white, shown in position over an egg. (Courtesy of the United States Department of Agriculture.)

white may increase from about 7.6 in a freshly laid egg to as high as 9.0 to 9.7 in a few days (44). The white becomes thinner, so it spreads more when the egg is broken out. Thinning of the white has been attributed to (a) breakup of a lysozyme–ovomucin complex when loss of carbon dioxide results in a higher pH (12), (b) disruption of an ovomucin gel when lysozyme reacts with ovomucin (43), and (c) disruption of disulfide bonds in ovomucin (7). In addition to thinning, the white may eventually become yellow and even cloudy. When the vitelline membrane that confines the yolk weakens, the yolk flattens. The thinner white is unable to keep the yolk centered in the egg.

Handling Eggs to Maintain Quality

The temperature of an egg when it is laid is that of the body of the hen, 40°C (105°F). To maintain the high quality of a freshly laid egg it must be cooled promptly, preferably to 4°C (40°F), and held in a cool place. The effect of storage temperature on the quality of egg albumen (15) is shown graphically in Figure 21-3.

Storage of eggs in a closed container retards the loss of both moisture and carbon dioxide, as does submerging the eggs in a solution of waterglass (sodium silicate). This is a viscous liquid that plugs the pores of the shells. Eggs so treated and stored in a cool place will keep from four to six months and may be higher in quality than eggs only a few days old that have been improperly handled. Coating eggs with mineral oil (15) fills the pores and makes the shell less permeable to water vapor and carbon dioxide and so delays deterioration in quality of eggs during storage. Thermostabilizing eggs (dipping in warm mineral oil for a few minutes) is particularly effective in maintaining quality of stored eggs.

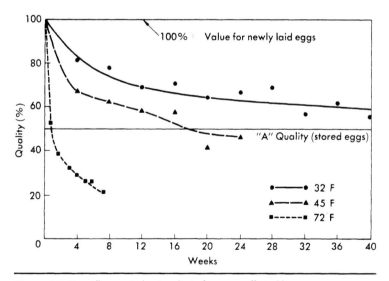

Figure 21-3. Albumen index (quality) of eggs as affected by storage temperature. Albumen quality declines rapidly in eggs held at room temperature. (From E. H. Dawson, C. Miller, and R. A. Redstrom, United States Department of Agriculture Bulletin No. 164, 1956.)

Candling Eggs to Determine Quality

Candling is the method used to assess the quality of an egg without removing it from the shell. The appearance of the egg is observed as it is rotated with a strong light behind it (50). The electronic eye is replacing the human eye for this examination. Factors used as an index to the grade of an egg when it is candled are size and position of the air cell, clearness of white, position and mobility of the yolk, the shadow cast by the yolk, and the condition of the shell. On the basis of the above characteristics eggs may be assigned to U.S. quality grades AA, A, B, and C. Break out characteristics of eggs for the different grades (50) are shown in Figure 21-4. Note that the quality of eggs for any one grade may be high, medium, or low. And due to difficulties inherent in assessing quality of eggs by candling, 20 percent of the eggs may actually grade lower than labeled.

Uses of Eggs of Different Quality Grades

The grade of an egg is more important for some uses to which eggs are put than for others. Eggs of AA grade are essential for high quality in fried or poached egg (17). A fried or poached egg of high quality is compact, and the yolk is centered in and covered by a thick layer of coagulated white (Fig. 21-5). The lower the grade of the egg the flatter is the cooked product, the thinner the coating of white over the top of the yolk, and the more ragged the edges of the white. If the egg is of lower grade, the yolk moves off center in eggs hard cooked in the shell, just as it does in those poached or fried. Differences in scrambled eggs, muffins, shortened cakes, and soft pie fillings due to the quality of egg are not detectable. However, the volume, tenderness, and acceptability of angel food cake is less when made with eggs of lower quality (15). Off flavor associated with storage eggs of lower quality is more noticeable in soft cooked eggs than in either custard or angel food cake, no doubt because other ingredients partially mask the off flavor of the eggs.

Resistance of Eggs to Spoilage

Eggs are unique among foods of animal origin in that, with minimum precautions, they may be kept in common storage for an appreciable time without spoiling (although deteriorating in *quality*) even though the shell may be contaminated. A number of factors contribute to the superior keeping quality of eggs. Although the shell of an egg is porous, the pores normally are filled with organic material that hinders the entrance of microorganisms into the egg unless the surface is damp. The two membranes inside the shell, and particularly the inner one, act as the first effective line of defense against microbial invasion of the egg proper (34). Equally important, the white itself contains substances with antibacterial action (20). The most effective germicidal agent in the white is lysozyme, which lyses (dissolves) the cell membranes of some bacteria. The lower the pH of the egg the more effective is lysozyme, an added reason for preventing loss of carbon dioxide from eggs. Avidin, which binds biotin, curtails the growth of certain microorganisms. A third constituent in the white of an egg that enables it to resist microorganisms that might invade it is conalbumin, which unites with iron and makes it unavailable. Thus microorganisms for which iron is essential are unable to grow. Should salmonella penetrate the inner membrane, however, these microorganisms can multiply in the white (1).

Once an egg is broken from the shell, the contents are heavily contaminated and the natural defenses of the egg no longer are able to cope with the load of microorganisms.

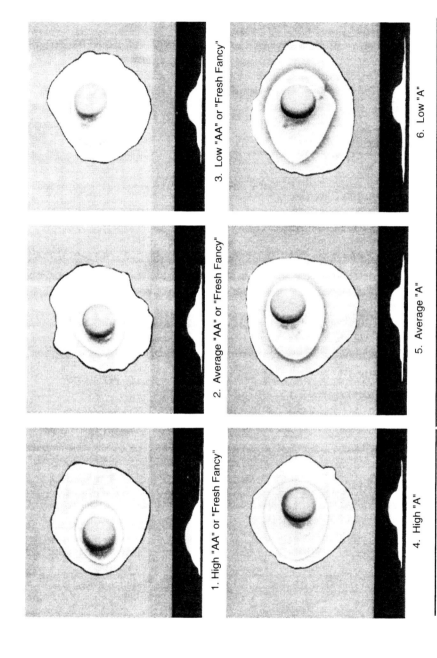

1. High "AA" or "Fresh Fancy"   2. Average "AA" or "Fresh Fancy"   3. Low "AA" or "Fresh Fancy"

4. High "A"   5. Average "A"   6. Low "A"

Figure 21-4.   Characteristics of eggs of the four quality grades. (Courtesy of the United States Department of Agriculture.)

348

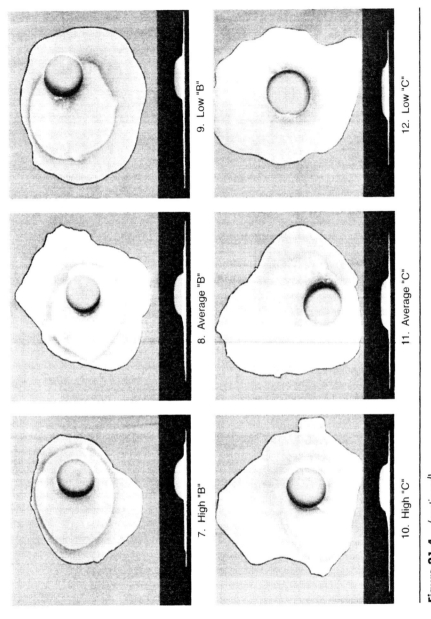

7. High "B"   8. Average "B"   9. Low "B"

10. High "C"   11. Average "C"   12. Low "C"

Figure 21-4. *(continued)*

349

Figure 21-5. A poached egg of high quality has an upstanding yolk and a thick, compact white. (Courtesy of the Poultry and Egg National Board.)

Eggs out of the shell are highly perishable, must be kept cold at all times, and used promptly. Eggs sold broken out are pasteurized.

Preserving Eggs by Freezing and Drying

Eggs, in addition to storage in the shell, may be preserved either by freezing or by drying. Egg whites freeze satisfactorily without preliminary treatment. Egg yolk and blended whole egg untreated are not satisfactory after frozen storage. The egg, after thawing, is thick, pseudo plastic, and lumpy. The undesirable consistency is attributed to aggregation of lipoproteins, possibly due to change in the structure of water brought about by freezing (11). Addition of salt, sugar, or corn syrup to egg yolk prior to freezing yields thawed yolk with near normal fluidity (35). Once thawed, frozen eggs should be used promptly.

Whole egg, egg yolk, and egg white are available in dried form, the latter as freeze, foam-spray, and spray dried. Eggs in dried form are used extensively in packaged mixes. Recipes using dried eggs are available. Pasteurization of the broken-out eggs (3.5 minutes at 60°C (140°F) for whole egg and at 57°C (134°F) for egg white) prior to drying eliminates the possibility of their being carriers of pathogenic bacteria, especially of the salmonella group. Glucose is removed from egg white prior to drying.

SIZE OF EGGS

Eggs vary markedly in size and are classed according to one of six sizes, jumbo, extra large, large, medium, small, and peewee. Successive sizes differ in weight by three ounces per dozen. The smallest eggs, peewee, which weigh 15 ounces (425 g) per dozen, are half as large as jumbo, which weigh 30 ounces (850 g) per dozen. Eggs of medium size weigh 21 ounces (595 g) per dozen. Each medium egg white has a volume of 30 milliliters and the yolk a volume of 18 milliliters, giving a total of 48 milliliters for a medium-sized whole egg.

EGGS AS EMULSIFIERS

This function of eggs is discussed in Chapter 16 on emulsions and Chapter 25 on shortened cakes.

EGGS AS BINDING, THICKENING, AND GELLING AGENTS

Effects of Heat on Egg Proteins

Eggs are useful as binding, thickening, and gelling agents because they contain proteins that are denatured by heat. Alteration of the native conformation of a protein molecule by heat exposes reactive groups that make intermolecular association possible. As a result of this aggregation, molecules are no longer dispersed as a sol. The change in state that occurs is referred to as coagulation or gelation. Coagulation involves a random aggregation in which protein–protein interaction predominates, while gelation denotes an orderly aggregation in which protein–solvent as well as protein–protein interactions are involved (23).

Heat changes egg white from a viscous, transparent sol to an opaque, elastic solid. Egg yolk, a thick liquid, increases in thickness as it is heated, becoming either a pasty or mealy solid, depending on the extent of heating. Egg white is more sensitive to heat than is egg yolk. Coagulation of undiluted egg white may begin near 60°C (140°F), with the white no longer able to flow near 65°C (149°F). Coagulation of the yolk begins near 65°C (149°F), and the yolk no longer flows when the temperature nears 70°C (158°F) (36). Heating undiluted egg much beyond this temperature shrinks and toughens the coagulum of the white. The range in coagulation temperatures is influenced by such factors as pH of the dispersion, presence of salts, and how fast the temperature rises. A protein heated slowly begins to coagulate at a lower temperature and the process continues over a wider temperature range than does one heated rapidly. In the case of ovalbumin an increase in temperature of 10 degrees increases the rate of coagulation more than 600 times. At high temperatures the rate of coagulation is so rapid that it is almost instantaneous. Eggs exposed to heat of high intensity are overcoagulated before they can be removed.

Individual proteins of egg white differ in sensitivity to heat. In one study, each of the proteins of the white was dispersed in a model custard mixture and denaturation temperature of the protein determined (28). Conalbumin was the most heat-sensitive, with a denaturation temperature of 57.3°C (161°F). That of ovalbumin and globulins was next with denaturation temperatures of 71.5°C (161°F) and 72°C (162°F), respectively. Lysozyme was the most stable to heat, with a denaturation temperature of 81.5°C (179°F). Neither ovomucin nor ovomucoid was coagulated by heat. When conalbumin, ovalbumin, globulins, lysozyme and ovomucoid were combined as in native egg white and the mixture used in model custard, coagulation occurred at two different temperatures, one near 62°C (144°F) and the other near 72°C (162°F). The coagulum, as shown in a scanning electron micrograph, appears to consist of grapelike clusters of molecules crosslinked to form a porous network.

In another study, heat denaturation of egg white was accompanied by changes in the secondary structure of the proteins. Little change had occurred when egg white was heated to 60°C (140°F) but at 70°C (158°F) the alpha-helical content of egg white had decreased by nearly ⅓ and the beta-sheet structure had almost doubled (41). Ovalbumin is the main heat-denaturable protein in eggs. The formation of a coagulum or a gel that follows its denaturation has been attributed to electrostatic interaction (16, 37), to hydrophobic interaction (37, 41) and to sulfhydryl ⇌ disulfide interchange (37, 40, 41). Hydrogen bonds are involved in both the alpha helix and the pleated sheet conformations.

When blended whole egg was heated (52), its appearance began to change when the temperature reached 60°C (140°F). At 63°C (113°F) a slight opaqueness was observed, that increased as the temperature continued to rise. At 75°C (135°F) a soft coagulum formed that increased in firmness as the temperature increased. Presence of egg yolk influenced the denaturation temperature of two of the proteins, especially. Lysozyme heated with the yolk present had a lowered denaturation temperature of 63°C (113°F). Conalbumin, more heat-stable when heated in whole egg, had a denaturation temperature of 78°C (172°F). Its greater stability to heat was attributed to a complex of the protein with the iron of the yolk. Denaturation of ovalbumin was unaffected by presence of the yolk.

METHODS OF COOKING EGGS

Eggs and foods made with eggs are heated in such a way as to give the desired textural quality to the finished products. Equally important, eggs are heated to make such products safe to eat. Poultry is known to carry *Salmonella,* a pathogen for humans, that lives in the fowl's intestinal tract. An infected hen can contaminate an egg as it is laid. Before eggs are marketed in the shell, they are washed in an alkaline solution and given a sanitizing rinse (32). However, Grade A shell eggs have been implicated in a number of cases of salmonellosis (46). Consumption of raw eggs, as in eggnog and Caesar salad, carries risks, as does the consumption of undercooked eggs. Adequate heating can make eggs safe to eat.

The effectiveness of common methods of preparing eggs for elimination of pathogens that might be present has been investigated (5). Eggs were cooked in the shell, poached, fried, and scrambled. For the tests, the egg yolks were inoculated with two pathogens, *Salmonella typhimurium* and *Staphylococcus aureus.* The heating time required to eliminate each pathogen is noted in the description of cooking methods that follows.

Cooked in the Shell

Cooking eggs in the shell is the simplest method, with the intensity of the heat applied and the time of exposure critical factors. The eggs are covered with water that is brought to a boil. The heat is turned off and the eggs are left in the hot water for 20 to 25 minutes, depending on the size of the egg and its starting temperature. Heat from the hot water is conducted through the coagulating white into the yolk, a process that takes time. At best, egg white is somewhat overcoagulated by the time heat has reached the yolk to cook it. This effect is magnified if the water around the egg continues to boil. Like shell eggs, egg yolk with the vitelline membrane intact may be cooked in hot water. As soon as eggs are done, they should be transferred to cold water for rapid cooling.

The white of a cooked egg should be an opaque, tender coagulum. The yolk should be a pale yellow color and have a mealy rather than a pasty consistency. The yolk should be centered and there should be little evidence of an air cell.

Occasionally a greenish gray layer may be observed on the surface of the yolk of an egg that has been cooked in the shell. The iron sulfide responsible for this discoloration is attributed to a reaction between the iron of the yolk and hydrogen sulfide liberated from sulfur-containing proteins. The alkalinity of the white that is in contact with the yolk favors the reaction (4). The discoloration is similar to that on the tines of a silver fork used to eat eggs, except that on the fork the deposit is silver sulfide. Discoloration is less likely if the eggs are fresh and if hot, not boiling, water is used to cook the eggs. Prompt cooling of the eggs and removal of the shell lowers pressure at the periphery of the egg, which helps to draw hydrogen sulfide from the surface of the yolk.

Removal of the shell without some of the white adhering is sometimes a problem. This is likely to happen if the egg is fresh (less than 48 hours old) or if the shell has been dipped to prevent the loss of carbon dioxide. Ease of removing the shell from a hard-cooked egg is associated with a pH of 8.7 or above. In fact, the white of a fresh egg (less than two hours old) made alkaline by exposure to ammonia vapor for 10 minutes parts with the shell cleanly (49). Cooling the egg in ice water for one minute followed by 10 seconds reheating facilitates removal of the shell (24).

Cracking may be a problem when eggs are cooked in the shell. In one study, fewer shells cracked when eggs were put in water already boiling instead of in cold water brought to a boil subsequently (27). The shells were easier to remove, too. For some reason, more shells cracked when a hole was drilled in the large end of the egg.

Heat not only affects the quality of a cooked egg, but it can determine whether an egg is safe to eat. In the study referred to above (5), eggs cooked in the shell by immersion in boiling water required seven minutes and an internal temperature of 75.4°C (168°F) to destroy *Salmonella* and 12 minutes and an internal temperature of 87.2°C (189°F) to eliminate *Staphlycocci*.

Poached Egg

An egg to be poached is turned from the shell and promptly slipped into water that has been brought to a boil and then the heat turned off. The egg is left in the hot water until the white is jellylike and uniformly coagulated and the yolk semiliquid and covered by a thick coating of white. Ideally, a poached egg should be compact with no ragged edges (Fig. 21-5). This necessitates an egg of top quality. The technique used to put the egg in the water influences somewhat how much the white will spread. The closer the egg to the hot water when it slips into it the less likely is the egg to spread. Swirling the hot water and slipping the egg into the vortex is a technique that works in experienced hands. A Grade AA egg is the best guarantee of a quality poached egg. Eggs of lower grade may be confined in the cups of an egg poacher or, better still, scrambled. In the study referred to earlier (5), eggs poached five minutes were free from both pathogens.

Fried Egg

A nonstick frying pan or one lightly oiled is used to fry eggs. The frying pan is preheated to begin coagulation of the white and limit its spreading. If the pan is too hot, however, bubbling, popping, and spattering occur. Edges of the white become crisp and brown and the layer of white next to the pan is toughened. A frying temperature of 137°C (278°F) is recommended (2). An egg is turned to cook the side not in contact with the frying pan. As an alternative, a small amount of water may be added and the pan covered so that steam can cook the upper surface of the egg. The white of a fried egg should be compact, uniformly coagulated, and tender. The yolk should be centered and covered with a layer of coagulated white. A fried egg that is neither turned nor cooked covered, called sunny-side, has an upper layer that is undercooked. Eggs fried in this way for 7.5 minutes still contained both pathogens referred to above (5). Eggs cooked covered for four minutes were free of both. Eggs fried three minutes on one side and two on the other had no Salmonella, but three minutes on each side were needed to eliminate the Staphylococcus.

Scrambled Egg

For scrambled egg, the yolk and white are blended with or without the addition of a small amount (15 milliliters or one tablespoon) of milk or cream per egg. The mixture is then heated to effect coagulation of the proteins. The secret of making scrambled egg that is moist (but not watery), tender, and fluffy is to heat the mix slowly and scrape the egg from the edges and bottom of the pan as it coagulates. This prevents the cooked part from being overcoagulated and allows the uncoagulated part to contact the hot pan. Once the coagulum forms, the egg should be removed from the heat. If scrambled eggs are overheated, excessive shrinkage of the coagulum squeezes out liquid temporarily. The heat soon evaporates this, with the result that the product is shrunken, tough, and dry. If scrambled eggs are not served promptly, they either cool or, if kept hot, they are likely to be overcooked. They can be held for a short time over hot water if the partially cooked eggs are combined with a medium white sauce (⅓ to ½ cup for six eggs). Scrambled eggs cooked in a frying pan set at 121°C (250°F) were free of *Salmonella* in one minute but two minutes were needed to eliminate the *Staphlycoccus* (5).

A French or plain omelet differs from scrambled egg in the way it is cooked. The mixture for a French omelet is cooked in an oiled frying pan. Instead of scraping the coagulum from the frying pan as it forms, it is lifted from the pan only enough to allow uncooked egg to come in contact with the pan. A French omelet, unlike a puffy omelet (discussed near the end of this chapter), is flat, in one piece, and the size and shape of the pan. It is customary to roll a French omelet as it is turned from the pan onto the serving plate, so the coagulum should be soft and flexible. One egg will yield a French omelet six inches in diameter.

Custards

The ingredients in custard are egg, sugar, and milk, plus salt and vanilla for flavor. The egg, sugar, and salt are blended before the milk is added. The milk is usually scalded (heated to approximately 85°C, or 185°F) because this improves the flavor and may shorten the cooking time. The coagulable protein from one whole egg or two egg yolks is sufficient to thicken or gel one cup of milk. Less than one percent of the gel is due to proteins from the milk. However, salts supplied by the milk are essential for gelation of a custard mixture (36).

Heat converts this fluid mixture into a gel or a thickened liquid, depending on whether it is heated in an oven or on a surface unit. In either case, the container that holds the mixture is surrounded by hot water that cushions the mixture from heat that is too intense. Baked, the mixture becomes a tender, quivery solid (a gel) because it is undisturbed as it is heated. A custard mixture heated on a surface unit is stirred continuously to equalize the temperature. This breaks up the coagulum as it forms, making a continuous network impossible. The numerous gel fragments with their surface areas thicken the liquid.

Temperature and timing are critical factors in making custard. A moderate oven (177°C or 350°F) is used to bake custard. The water used to heat a stirred (soft) custard should be above 85°C (185°F) but below boiling. There are advantages to having the temperature rise slowly in a stirred custard, especially after the mix reaches 75°C (167°F). A custard heated slowly begins to thicken at a lower temperature, thickens gradually over a wider temperature range, and is done at a lower temperature (36). If the mix is heated rapidly, it must be heated to a higher temperature before it begins to thicken and a difference of only one to three degrees may separate the beginning of thickening and the appearance of curds. Ten to twelve minutes for the temperature of the mix to rise from 75°C (167°F) to 83° to 85°C (181° to 185°F), near which temperature the custard should be done, provides an adequate margin of safety between the initiation of thickening and the appearance of curds. The temperature of the mix within this range may remain stationary or even drop momentarily as the proteins coagulate. A baked custard from the same mix as a soft custard can tolerate a somewhat higher internal temperature.

The temperature to which a custard must be heated for it to thicken (or gel) is influenced by a number of factors. It is higher than that required to coagulate the egg because the protein of the egg is diluted with milk. Whether sugar is omitted or doubled in a standard recipe makes no difference in gel strength or firmness (sensory) of a baked custard; but sugar does make the custard more translucent and the crust more tender (51). Acid, on the other hand, lowers the setting temperature. Because of the acid supplied by the fruit, baked custard that contains slices of dried figs or dates gets done sooner than one without fruit. The higher the proportions of egg to milk, the lower the temperature at which the custard sets. But two egg yolks in the place of one egg raises the coagulation temperature.

A stirred custard heated beyond gelation temperature is likely to curdle, as is one held at gelation temperature for a time. For this reason, once a custard has reached the consistency desired, the utensil that contains it should be removed from the hot water at once. Overheating a custard shrinks the gel. An overheated stirred custard separates into curds and serum. The texture and consistency of a curdled custard can be improved by removing it from the heat and beating it as soon as the curds appear. An overheated baked custard becomes porous, the pores filled with watery serum. This expulsion of liquid from a gel is an example of syneresis. A stirred custard is more sensitive to overheating than is a baked one.

A stirred custard is done when it forms a thick, velvety coating on the spoon or other utensil used to stir it (Fig. 21-6). A stirred custard should be smooth and have the consistency of heavy whipping cream. It will thicken somewhat as it cools. A baked custard is done when a silver knife inserted in the center comes out free of milky fluid. An alternate way to assess the doneness of a baked custard is to tilt the container to see whether the milk at the center still flows. A baked custard of high quality is a tender gel, uniformly coagulated and with no signs of porosity.

Baking a custard pie filling in an unbaked pie shell presents unreconcilable conditions. If the pie is baked at the high temperature recommended for the crust, the filling is likely to be porous and to weep. If baking temperature is low, delay in setting the filling permits absorption of liquid by the crust. Either way a soggy lower crust is likely. The only sure way to avoid this is to bake crust and filling separately and then transfer baked, cooled filling to the crust. This has hazards, too, and requires steady nerves and some dexterity.

A quiche Lorraine is a baked entrée made with unsweetened custard filling poured over cheese and cooked bacon bits in an unbaked pastry shell. The quiche is then baked like a custard pie.

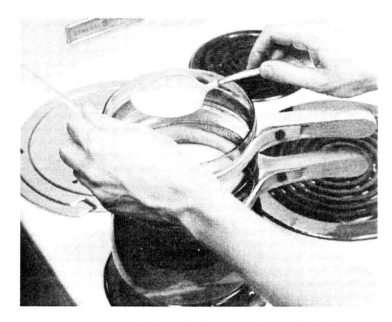

Figure 21-6. A soft cooked custard is done when it forms a thick, velvety coating on a spoon. (Photograph by Wilbur Nelson.)

Soft Pie Filling

Egg yolk is used in cooked salad dressing and in many soft pie fillings to supplement the thickening power of the starch. The usual practice in making pie filling is to incorporate the yolk into the hot cooked starch paste. Unless the filling is heated sufficiently after the yolk is added, the filling will thin as it stands in the baked pie shell. Eggs contain α-amylase, the enzyme content of the yolk being much higher than that of the white (30). Heating whole egg 3.5 minutes at 60°C (140°F) inactivates less than 50 percent of the enzyme; heating the yolk, approximately 25 percent. Only 6 percent was inactivated at 63°C (145°F) when yolks contained 10 percent sucrose (42). The higher the proportion of sugar in a pie filling, the higher the temperature needed to prevent thinning. Heating a cream pie filling that has approximately ⅓ as much sugar as liquid (v/v) to 85°C (185°F) will prevent thinning, whereas a butterscotch filling in which the ratio of sugar to liquid is twice as high must be heated to a higher temperature.

EGG FOAMS

Foams are essential for angel food and sponge cakes, soft and hard meringues, puffy omelets, and divinity candy. They contribute to the production of a number of other foods. The functional value of eggs derives in part from the ease in which the whites are made to foam.

Foam-Forming Properties of Egg White Proteins

General information on foams and foam formation is found in Chapter 18. Egg white is a colloidal dispersion of proteins in water. Bubbles of air are incorporated in this viscous liquid with a wire whip or the blades of a beater. Individual proteins of the white contribute aspects of its film-forming potential. Presence of hydrophobic groups with an affinity for air and hydrophilic groups that are soluble in water are essential to lower surface tension, thus making incorporation of air possible. Surface denaturation of protein molecules in the lamellae alters their native conformation. Exposed reactive groups make possible sufficient protein–protein association to stabilize the aqueous film around the air cells. If a foam is to be usable, however, it must retain some flexibility. To give permanance to a foam, some of the proteins must be coagulated by heat.

The importance of globulins in egg white foams was established early. Duck eggs, deficient in globulins, do not foam well, nor do hen's eggs from which globulins have been removed (38). Laminations observed in thick egg white (Fig. 21-7) are attributed to ovomucin (18). When egg white is first beaten, layers of ovomucin are sheared from the white. These coil to form hollow tubes, with the appearance of fibers. Egg white beats to a better foam when these fibers do not exceed 300 to 400 microns in length. Perhaps rapid initial beating of egg white, which results in a foam with larger volume, does so because it shears layers of ovomucin to an optimum length. In one study, egg white was separated into its component proteins, each of which was tested singly and in combination for foam-forming ability (29). Dispersions of globulins had good foaming properties, due in part to the ability of these proteins to lower surface tension. A dispersion of ovalbumin required extended beating for a foam to form. A dispersion of ovomucin alone yielded an unstable foam. One with lysozyme and ovomucin foamed less readily but the foam was more stable, attributed to formation of an ovomucin–lysozyme complex. With lysozyme present, a continuous layer of protein was observed in the films that enveloped the included air. In an earlier study, ovomucin was less concentrated in the drainage from egg white foam than in the unbeaten white and together with conalbumin, lysozyme, and globulins was retained in the drained foam (13). Conalbumin and ovalbumin supply heat-denaturable protein to a foam.

Stages to Which Egg Whites Are Beaten

Egg whites are beaten to different stages for incorporation into various products. It is important to have clearly in mind the stage to which the egg white should be beaten before starting. Equally important is the ability to recognize when the beaten egg has reached the stage desired. As air is beaten into egg whites, the mass becomes foamy, but it remains transparent and can still flow. If beating is stopped at this stage, the liquid drains from around the large air cells and the bubbles coalesce. If beating continues, large air cells incorporated at the foamy stage are subdivided and additional air is introduced. As the number of air cells increases, the film of liquid around each becomes thinner and thinner. The result is that egg white thickens as it is beaten.

As beating continues the foam gets thicker, finer, and whiter. Soon it begins to form peaks as the beater is withdrawn. The peaks become more definite and more permanent as beating continues. They progress from soft peaks with rounded tops (Fig. 26-3) to stiff peaks with sharp points. This gradual stiffening of the foam is attributed to surface denaturation of protein in the lamellae (38).

Up to a point the volume of an egg foam increases with continued beating. Should the foam be beaten beyond the stiff peak (but still shiny) stage, it takes only a few additional revolutions of the blades of the beater to make the foam stiff, dry, and opaque and curdled

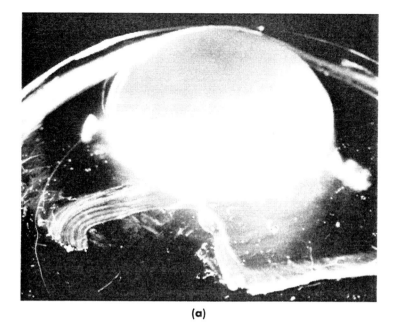

(a)

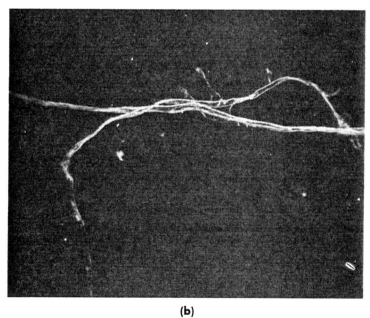

(b)

Figure 21-7. Structure of thick egg white. (*a*) Cross section of thick white. Whole egg placed in distilled water; layering revealed by cutting thick white. Oblique illumination. (*b*) Blending or beating egg white shears off layers that curl to give fibers, usually several centimeters long. Dark field illumination. (From R. H. Forsythe and D. H. Bergquist, *Poultry Science* 30: 305, 1951. Reprinted by permission.)

I   **II**

(a)

(b)

(c)

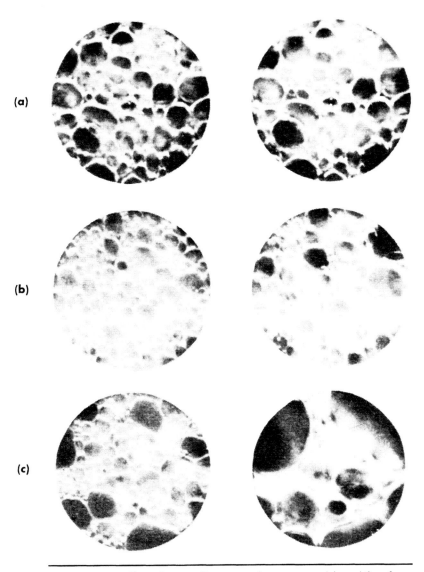

Figure 21-8. Effects of extent of beating on the structure and the stability of egg white foams. Photomicrographs in column I are of foams taken two minutes after beating stopped. Note the finer cells in I*b* (foam beaten for two minutes) compared with the underbeaten foam in I*a* and with the overbeaten foam in I*c*. Coalescence of cells after foams stood for 10 minutes (column II) is especially marked in the overbeaten foam in II*c*. Magnification × 27. (From Mark Barmore, *Colorado Agricultural Experiment Station Technical Bulletin 9*, 1934.)

in appearance. The surface-denatured protein in the film is rendered insoluble and the film around the air cells is no longer elastic (6). The protein in such an overbeaten foam behaves as though it had been cooked. Liquid drains from the film and the bubbles coalesce (Fig. 21-8). Thus coagulation of egg proteins can be caused by both beating and heating.

Once egg whites are beaten to the stage desired, they should be combined with other ingredients *at once*. If egg white foam beaten no more than to the soft-peak stage stands for more than a few seconds, the foam stiffens and loses its elasticity. When it is combined with other ingredients, air cells are ruptured.

Factors Affecting Egg White Foams

A number of factors influence the quality of an egg foam. The utensils used to produce the foam are important. The bowl should be large enough to allow for the expansion in volume. If it is too large, however, especially at the base, the blades of the beater will whip more air than egg.

A good foam can be obtained by beating eggs with either a rotary beater or a wire whip, but the construction of the implement is important. The finer the wire or the thinner the blade, the smaller are the cells and the finer is the foam. If beating is done by hand, thin whites whip faster and give foams slightly larger in volume than do thick whites (45). There is some advantage in using a hand beater for thin whites because the likelihood of overbeating them is not so great. If the egg white is very viscous, it is difficult to shear it fast enough with a hand-operated beater to get the best volume. When the blades of the beater are propelled by electric rather than muscle power, thick whites whip to a foam with good volume and fine texture (3) and are somewhat less likely to be overbeaten than are thin whites.

Egg whites whip more readily at room temperature (21°C or 70°F) than at refrigerator temperature (45). The volume of the foam is greater and the texture finer. Egg whites are too viscous to whip readily when cold. Egg whites that have been frozen and then thawed whip as well or better than unfrozen (3).

Reconstituted dried egg whites require a longer time to whip than do fresh egg whites. This has been attributed to the effects of heat on the proteins of egg white when they are pasteurized prior to being dried (33). Heat denaturation of the lysozyme–ovomucin complex, which results in a dry foam that tends to break as the blades of the beater are incorporating additional air bubbles, has been suggested as a factor contributing to the longer beating time for dried egg whites (21). The fact that conalbumin is heat-labile may be a factor, too (28).

The presence of fat, even in small amounts, interferes with the foaming of egg whites and reduces the foam volume (3, 45). The directions on packages of angel food cake mix specify use of a bowl other than plastic because of the difficulty of removing traces of fat that cling tenaciously to a plastic surface. Should a yolk be broken when the white and yolk are being separated, it is difficult to remove traces of the yolk from the white. To identify the foam depressant(s) in egg yolk, yolk fractions—lipovitellin and livetin—were isolated and each added separately to egg whites used to make angel food cake. The lipoprotein but not the livetin reduced cake volume (14). Data from the study appeared to suggest that the lipoprotein interfered with the foaming potential of ovomucin and lysozyme.

Salt is used for flavor in recipes that contain egg white. Acid, usually cream of tartar or lemon juice, is used to make the foam more stable (6). Both ingredients delay the formation of a foam. For this reason, egg whites are beaten to the foamy stage before acid and salt are added. In addition to delaying foam formation, acid reduces somewhat the volume of the beaten egg white.

Dilution of egg white with water, up to 40 percent of the volume of the egg, increases the volume of the foam as much as would an equivalent volume of egg. Addition of liquid to eggs used to make omelet and sponge cake makes both products more tender too. However, water added to egg whites used in meringues increases drainage.

If sugar is added to egg white before beating begins, extensive beating is needed to produce a foam (25). Once formed, the foam is stable and very fine although the volume may be lower. The shininess of egg white foam with added sugar is due in part to the prevention of coagulation of the protein with the accompanying opaqueness. Once sugar is added to egg white beaten to the foamy stage, to the soft-peak, or even to the stiff-peak stage, beating can continue longer without the foam being overbeaten. After sugar has been beaten into a foam, it can stand for some time without becoming coagulated and losing its elasticity. The foam can be manipulated and spread without rupturing the air cells.

Beating egg whites in a copper bowl delays foam formation. In one study, it took twice as long to beat the whites to a stiff peak stage in a copper bowl than it did in a glass bowl (39). The foam from the copper bowl was more stable, with drainage of one milliliter compared to 10 milliliters after 20 minutes, starting with 60 milliliters of unbeaten whites. Adding a trace of a copper salt to the egg whites in the glass bowl had the same effects as did beating them in the copper bowl. Formation of a conalbumin–copper complex analogous to a conalbumin–iron complex referred to earlier presumably accounts for the delay in foaming and the improved stability of the foam from the copper bowl.

Egg Yolk Foams

Although egg white foams are far more common, yolk too may be converted into a foam. Two foods in which egg yolk foams are used are puffy omelet and sponge cake (Chapter 26). Yolks require more extensive beating than do the whites. Yolks become lighter in color and thicker as air bubbles are beaten in, but yolk proteins are not surface-denatured and the foam does not stiffen or set as does one made from egg whites. Egg yolk foam should be used without undue delay because the larger gas bubbles tend to rise to the surface and liquid drain to the bottom of the foam.

Meringues

Meringues are egg white foams into which sugar has been incorporated. There are two kinds of meringue: soft ones used as toppings for cream, lemon, and chocolate pies, and hard meringues used as confections or to make a base for the filling in lemon angel pie. Soft meringues are made with a minimum of 2 tablespoons (30 milliliters) of sugar per egg white, with 2½ tablespoons (38 milliliters) per egg white possibly giving a meringue of superior appearance and one that cuts more readily (22). Because an average egg white measures 2 tablespoons (30 milliliters), the water in the egg white is converted into a fairly concentrated syrup.

To make meringue, egg whites are beaten to the foamy stage and then salt is added. Beating is continued until the foam barely flows in the bowl, at which point portions of sugar are added without delay and beaten into the foam. After the last portion of sugar is added, the meringue is beaten until it is fine grained and fairly thick, but will still form peaks with rounded tops. A meringue is more stable when sugar is beaten rather than folded in.

Meringues may be of poor quality because of faulty manipulation. If the egg white is overbeaten before sugar is added, the volume of the meringue will be low and it will have a curdled look. If the meringue is underbeaten after the sugar is added, it will have a low volume, will shrink unduly, and will have a slick and shiny surface. Meringues beaten until they are very stiff after the sugar is added have fine cells, but the surface looks dull after the meringue is baked.

Soft meringues are spread on soft pie fillings and baked. The object of baking is to coagulate the protein and stabilize the foam without causing undue shrinkage. Baking may cause defects in soft meringues, two of which are difficult to avoid. One is the accumulation of liquid where the meringue and the filling meet. This is attributed to leakage (drainage) from the meringue due to undercoagulation of the foam (26). Leakage is likely to be least when the meringue is baked on a hot filling (60° to 77°C or 140° to 170°F). The second defect, the appearance of amber-colored droplets of syrup on the surface of baked meringues, is attributed to overcoagulation of the protein in the foam (26). Beading is more likely to occur on meringues baked on hot fillings. If a meringue is baked on a hot filling to minimize leakage, beading can be minimized by baking the meringue in a hot oven for a short time (218°C or 425°F for 4½ minutes). Too, a baking temperature of 425°F gives more tender and less sticky meringues.

A soft meringue of high quality is fluffy, slightly moist, and tender. The surface should be a light brown with little contrast in color between peaks and depressions. The surface should be fine grained and have a glossy sheen. The meringue should cut cleanly.

Hard meringues contain ¼ cup (60 milliliters) of sugar per egg white. The egg whites are beaten to the soft peak stage, the sugar is added, and beating is continued until the foam forms stiff peaks. The meringue mixture may be spooned onto an oiled baking sheet. Hard meringues are baked at a lower temperature (120°C or 250°F) and for a longer time (60 minutes or more) than are soft meringues. Hard meringues should be dry, crisp, yet puffy, and tender.

Puffy Omelet

To make a puffy omelet, the egg yolks with the added liquid should be beaten first and until they are very *thick* and light lemon in color. The yolks will not stiffen as do the whites, but they should be beaten thoroughly. Then the whites are beaten until they are stiff but not dry. Without delay the two foams should be combined with a gentle folding technique until the mixture is homogeneous. This mixture is unstable and will separate into a more dense layer below and a lighter foamy layer above unless it is cooked promptly.

The oiled pan in which the mixture is cooked should be preheated. It should not be too hot, however, because this produces a hard layer on the surface of the omelet next to the cooking utensil. Omelets may be cooked on a surface unit or in a slow oven. When an omelet that is cooking on a surface unit begins to set around the edges, the pan may be covered and the heat lowered to complete cooking. It will cook faster covered, but should the omelet touch the lid it is likely to fall when the lid is removed. Alternately the omelet can be placed under the broiler for a short time to coagulate the uppermost layers. Heat penetrates the omelet mainly by conduction. The slow transfer of heat by conduction is doubly slow in puffy omelet because of the air bubbles that act as insulators. Baking a puffy omelet in an uncovered pan in a slow oven (163°C or 325°F) presents less of a problem than cooking it on a surface unit.

A puffy omelet should be light and puffy, uniformly cooked throughout, and have no islands of unblended white. It should be tender, slightly moist, and a delicate uniform brown.

A fondue is a less concentrated protein dish than a soufflé, as the following listing of ingredients shows:

Ingredients	Cheese Fondue	Cheese Soufflé
Milk	1 cup	½ cup
Grated cheese	1 cup	1 cup
Eggs	3–4	3–4
Salt	½ tsp	½ tsp
Butter	1 Tbsp	2 Tbsp
Bread	1 cup, cubed	—
Flour	—	2 Tbsp

Quantities of cheese, eggs, and salt are the same in both the fondue and the soufflé, but the fondue has twice as much milk as the soufflé. The milk for a fondue is thickened with bread cubes instead of being made into a white sauce with flour. The hot milk-bread mixture for a fondue is blended with the egg yolk, the cheese is added and blended, and then the beaten egg whites are folded in. A very thick white sauce is used in a soufflé. The white sauce need not be cooked beyond the point of maximum thickness as it will finish cooking as the soufflé bakes. Egg yolks with their emulsifiers are added to the white sauce before the cheese to aid in blending. The white sauce should be warm enough to melt the fat in the cheese when the latter is added. Egg whites beaten to form stiff peaks that remain shiny are folded into the white sauce-egg-cheese mixture. If the sauce is too thick or the egg white foam too stiff from standing or from overbeating, extensive folding is needed to blend the two and much air is lost from the beaten whites.

Both soufflé and fondue are baked in a moderate oven (177°C or 350°F). The casserole that contains the mix is placed in a pan of hot water to protect the contents, especially the part next to the baking utensil, from a too rapid rise in temperature before the heat has time to penetrate to the interior. As these products bake, heat expands the air bubbles incorporated via the egg foam and both the soufflé and the fondue rise. Heat coagulates proteins of both egg yolk and egg white and these help to give structure to the soufflé and fondue. A high proportion of egg is needed to provide enough structure to keep the product from falling as it cools. A very thick white sauce base helps too. Baking should be timed so that the product can be served as soon as it comes from the oven. Some shrinkage may be expected in both a soufflé and a fondue when they are removed from the oven, but they should not collapse. A soufflé should be fluffy, light, slightly moist, and tender. The top should be a delicate brown (Fig. 21-9). A Swiss fondue (Chapter 20) differs from the type of fondue discussed above. A soufflé used as an entree may contain cooked meat, fish, poultry, or vegetables instead of cheese. Made with cooked fruit or melted chocolate, soufflé is suitable as a dessert.

EGG SUBSTITUTES

Although eggs are important functional ingredients in foods, the high cholesterol content of the yolk inhibits the use of eggs in products for individuals who must limit cholesterol intake. Commercial egg substitutes are available in dehydrated, frozen, and fluid form. The dried product contains albumen solids, approximately ⅛ as much yolk solids as in intact egg, plus nonfat dried milk. Both fluid and frozen products are yolk-free. They contain egg

Figure 21-9. A perfect soufflé, handsome yet fragile, light, tender, and steaming hot. (From *Sunset.* August 1962. Darrow M. Watt, Photographer, 188 Felton Drive, Menlo Park, CA.)

albumen, nonfat dried milk, and instead of yolk, cholesterol-free vegetable oil, emulsifier, and antioxidant. Flavoring substance and coloring agent (carotenoid pigments) are included. In one study (19), these three substitutes were compared with fresh eggs in scrambled eggs, custard, and yellow cake (boxed mix). Custards made from the substitutes sagged less and cakes had larger volumes. Missing from all three products was the delicate flavor supplied by yolk. Custard made from the dried substitute had an unpleasant aftertaste. Whole eggs scrambled were more tender, and they yielded custards with a smoother texture. Thus egg substitutes function well in some ways, but they do not duplicate the delicate texture and especially the superior flavor supplied by egg yolk.

REFERENCES

1. Adler, H. E. 1965. "Salmonella in eggs—An appraisal." *Food Technology* 19:623–25. A review of the hazards.

2. Andross, M. 1940. "Effect of cooking on eggs." *Chemistry & Industry* 59:449–54. One of the early studies of simple egg cookery.

3. Bailey, M. I. 1935. "Foaming of egg whites." *Industrial and Engineering Chemistry* 27: 973–76. A study of some factors that influence foam formation.

4. Baker, R. C., J. Darfler, and A. Lifshitz. 1967. "Factors affecting the discoloration

of hard-cooked egg yolks." *Poultry Science* 46:664–72. Compound responsible and factors favoring its formation.

5. Baker, R., C. S. Hogarty, W. Poon, and D. V. Vadehra. 1983. "Survival of *Salmonella typhimurium* and *Staphylococcus aureus* in eggs cooked by different methods." *Poultry Science* 62:1211–15. Poached, fried, scrambled, and in the shell.

6. Barmore, M. A. 1934. "The influence of chemical and physical factors on egg white foams." *Colorado Agricultural Experiment Station Technical Bulletin No. 9.* 58 pp. Effects of beating time, addition of acid, type of beater, and traces of egg yolk on stability of egg white foams.

7. Beveridge, T., and S. Nakai. 1975. "Effects of sulfhydryl blocking on the thinning of egg white." *Journal of Food Science* 40:864–68. An attempt to account for the thinning of egg white.

8. Burley, R. W., and D. V. Vadehra. 1989. "Egg yolk: Structure and properties." In *The Avian Egg—Chemistry and Biology.* New York: John Wiley and Sons. Pp. 171–93. Constituents and their organization; organized and readable.

9. Burley, R. W., and D. V. Vadehra. 1989. "The albumens: Chemistry." In *The Avian Egg—Chemistry and Biology.* New York: John Wiley and Sons. Pp. 65–128. Detailed treatment.

10. Causeret, D., E. Matringe, and D. Lorient. 1991. "Ionic strength and pH effects on composition and microstructure of yolk granules." *Journal of Food Science* 56:1532–36. Tentative proposal for structure of the granules.

11. Chang, C. H., W. D. Powrie, and O. Fennema. 1977. "Studies on the gelation of egg yolk and plasma upon freezing and thawing." *Journal of Food Science* 42:1658–65. Factors involved.

12. Cotterill, O. J., and A. R. Winter. 1955. "Egg white lysozyme." 3. "The effect of pH on the lysozyme-ovomucin interaction." *Poultry Science* 34:679–86. Possible role of lysozyme in the consistency of thick white.

13. Cunningham, F. E. 1976. "Properties of egg white drainage." *Poultry Science* 55:738–43. Proteins essential for foaming.

14. Cunningham, F. E., and O. J. Cotterill. 1972. "Performance of egg white in the presence of yolk proteins." *Poultry Science* 51:712–14. An attempt to pinpoint the foam depressant in yolk.

15. Dawson, E. H., C. Miller, and R. A. Redstrom. 1956. "Cooking quality and flavor of eggs as related to candled quality, storage conditions and other factors." *U.S. Department of Agriculture Information Bulletin No. 164.* 44 pp. Relationship of candled characteristics of eggs and their functional properties; research from three state experiment stations summarized graphically.

16. Egelandsal, B. 1980. "Heat-induced gelling in solutions of ovalbumin." *Journal of Food Science* 45:570–73, 581. Electrostatic forces and gel formation.

17. "Egg buying guide for consumers." 1954. *U.S. Department of Agriculture, Home and Garden Bulletin No. 26.* 8 pp. Official grades for eggs; weight classes.

18. Forsythe, R. H., and D. H. Bergquist. 1951. "The effect of physical treatments on some properties of egg white." *Poultry Science* 30:302–11. The structure of thick white and the effect of its breakdown during foam formation.

19. Gardner, F. A., M. L. Beck, and J. H. Denton. 1982. Functional quality comparison of whole egg and selected egg substitutes." *Poultry Science* 61:75–78. Three egg substitutes in custard, scrambled eggs, and yellow cake.

20. Garibaldi, J. A. 1960. "Factors in egg white which control growth of bacteria." *Food Research* 25:337–44. Bactericidal action of various components of egg white.

21. Garibaldi, J. A., J. W. Donovan, J. G. Davis, and S. L. Cimino. 1968. "Heat denaturation of the ovomucin-lysozyme electrostatic complex—a source of damage to the whipping properties of pasteurized egg white." *Journal of Food Science* 33:514–24. An attempt to account for the longer whipping time.

22. Gillis, J. N., and N. K. Fitch. 1956. "Leakage of baked soft meringue topping." *Journal of Home Economics* 48:703–7. Effects of level of sugar, beating time before sugar is added, and baking time.

23. Gossett, P. W., S. S. H. Rizvi, and R. C. Baker. 1984. "Quantitative analysis of gelation in egg protein systems." *Food Technology* 38(5):67–68, 70, 72–74, 96. Terms defined; factors involved in gelation.

24. Hale, K. K., Jr., and W. M. Britton. 1974. "Peeling hard cooked eggs by rapid cooling and heating." *Poultry Science* 53:1069–77. One suggestion for alleviating the problem.

25. Hanning, F. M. 1945. "Effect of sugar or salt upon denaturation produced by beating and upon the ease of formation and the stability of egg white foams." *Iowa State College Journal of Science* 20:10–12. Beating time, foam volume, and drainage from egg foams with and without sugar; effect of salt.

26. Hester, E. E., and C. J. Personius. 1949. "Factors affecting the beading and leakage of soft meringues." *Food Technology* 3:236–40. Temperature of the filling, baking time, and temperature; addition of acid and quality of egg investigated.

27. Irmiter, T. F., L. E. Dawson, and J. R. Reagen. 1970. "Methods of preparing hard cooked eggs." *Poultry Science* 49:1232–36. Boiling- *vs.* cold-water start.

28. Johnson, T. M., and M. E. Zabik. 1981. "Gelation properties of albumen proteins, singly and in combination." *Poultry Science* 60:2071–83. Effects of heat on the main proteins; interactions.

29. Johnson, T. M., and M. E. Zabik. 1981. "Ultrastructural examination of egg albumen protein foams." *Journal of Food Science* 46:1237–40. TEM and SEM of the foams.

30. Kaga, T. 1923. "Uber die fermente in Huhnerei." *Biochemische Zeitschrift* 141: 439. Amylase in egg yolk.

31. Kamat, V. B., G. A. Lawrence, C. J. Hart, and R. Yoell. 1973. "Contribution of egg yolk lipoproteins to cake structure." *Journal of the Science of Food and Agriculture* 24:77–88. Role of micelles and granules in sponge and pound cakes.

32. Kinner, J. A., and W. A. Moats. 1981. "Effect of temperature, pH and detergent on survival of bacteria associated with shell eggs." *Poultry Science* 60:761–67. Effectiveness of the washing procedure.

33. Kline, L., T. F. Sugihara, M. L. Bean, and K. Ijichi. 1965. "Heat pasteurization of raw liquid egg white." *Food Technology* 19:1709–18. Effect of different temperatures on salmonella and on foaming of egg white.

34. Lifshitz, A., R. C. Baker, and H. B. Naylor. 1964. "The relative importance of chicken egg exterior structures in resulting bacterial penetration." *Journal of Food Science* 29:94–99. Shell, outer and inner membranes compared.

35. Lopez, A., C. R. Fellers, and W. D. Powrie. 1954. "Some factors affecting gelation of egg yolk." *Journal of Milk and Food Technology* 17:334–39. Effect of temperature and additives.

36. Lowe, B. 1955. *Experimental Cookery.* New York: John Wiley & Sons. 573 pp.

37. Ma, C. Y., and J. Holme. 1982. "Effect of chemical modification on some physico-chemical properties and heat coagulation of egg albumen." *Journal of Food Science* 47:1454–59. Possible role of electrostatic interactions.

38. MacDonnell, L. R., R. E. Feeney, H. L. Hanson, A. Campbell, and A. T. Sugihara. 1955. "The functional properties of egg white proteins." *Food Technology* 9:49–53. The role of globulins, ovomucin, and ovalbumin in egg white foams.

39. McGee, H. J., S. R. Long, and W. R. Briggs. 1984. "Why whip egg whites in copper bowls?" *Nature, London* 308:667–68. The question answered.

40. Margoshes, B. A. 1990. "Correlation of protein sulfhydryl groups with the strength of heat-formed egg white gels." *Journal of Food Science* 55:1753, 1756. Evidence for direct relationship.

41. Mine, Y., T. Noutomi, and N. Haga. 1990. "Thermally induced changes in egg white proteins." *Journal of Agricultural and Food Chemistry* 38:2122–25. Forces involved in aggregation.

42. Murthy, G. K. 1970. "Thermal inactivation of alpha-amylase in various liquid egg products." *Journal of Food Science* 35:352–56. Whole egg and yolk compared; effects of added salt and sugar.

43. Robinson, D. S., and J. B. Monsey. 1972. "Changes in the composition of ovomucin during the liquefaction of egg white: The effects of ionic strength and magnesium

salts." *Journal of the Science of Food and Agriculture* 23:893–904. Possible role of lysozyme in the thinning of egg white.

44. Romanoff, A. L., and A. J. Romanoff. 1949. *The Avian Egg.* New York: John Wiley & Sons. 918 pp. A comprehensive treatment of the subject.

45. St. John, J. L., and I. H. Flor. 1931. "A study of whipping and coagulation of eggs of varying quality." *Poultry Science* 10:71–82. Thick *vs.* thin, fresh *vs.* aged, and warmed *vs.* chilled whites, and the effect of egg yolk.

46. St. Louis, M. E., D. L. Morse, M. E. Potter, I. M. Demeifi, J. J. Guzewich, J. J. Tauxe, and P. A. Blake. 1988. "The emergence of Grade A eggs as a major source of *Salmonella enteritidis* infections." *American Medical Association Journal* 259:2103–07. Prevalence of the organism; controls.

47. Sauter, E. A., and J. E. Montoure. 1972. "The relation of lysozyme content of egg white to volume and stability of foam." *Journal of Food Science* 37:918–20. Lysozyme content and foaming properties.

48. Schultz, J. R., and R. H. Forsythe. 1967. "The influence of egg yolk lipoprotein-carbohydrate interactions on baking performance." *Bakers Digest* 41(1):56–57, 60–62. Proposed structure of egg yolk lipoprotein micelles and their function.

49. Swanson, M. H. 1959. "Some observations on the peeling problem of fresh and shell treated eggs when hard cooked." *Poultry Science* 38:1253–54. pH of egg white and ease of peeling.

50. U.S. Department of Agriculture. 1978. "Egg grading manual." *U.S. Department of Agriculture, Handbook No. 75.* 64 pp. Brief account of the formation of an egg, its structure and composition; egg grades and grading.

51. Wang, A. C., K. Funk, and M. E. Zabik. 1974. "Effect of sucrose on the quality characteristics of baked custard." *Poultry Science* 53:807–13. Effects on firmness, gel strength, flavor, translucence, and tenderness of crust.

52. Woodward, S. A., and O. J. Cotterell. 1983. "Electrophoresis and chromatography of heat-treated plain, sugared and salted whole egg." *Journal of Food Science* 48:501–6. Protective effects of the additives; influence of yolk on denaturation of individual proteins.

Meat

22

The word meat in its broadest sense means any food taken for nourishment. In common usage, however, the term refers to those parts of animals that are used for food. In this chapter meat refers to the flesh of beef animals, of sheep, and of pigs. Most of the beef on the market comes from unsexed, young male animals called steers; some comes from young females called heifers; a limited amount of lower quality comes from mature females (cows); and veal comes from immature animals. Pork is not differentiated by age and sex of the pig.

CONSUMPTION OF MEAT

The annual per-capita consumption of meat in the U.S. was 52 kilograms (115 pounds) in 1994, down from 57 kilograms (126 pounds) in 1980. Consumption of beef decreased from 33 kilograms (72 pounds) to 29 kilograms (64 pounds) and pork from 24 kilograms (52 pounds) to 23 kilograms (50 pounds) over the same period (117). Per-capita consumption of veal and of lamb and mutton is approximately 0.5 kilograms (1 pound) annually. The amount of beef in ground form available at retail in 1992 was 30 pounds per capita compared to 31 pounds available in the form of beef cuts (2).

Decrease in consumption of meat in recent years not withstanding, a much higher proportion of dietary protein in the U.S. comes from livestock than the 25 percent of animal origin worldwide (102). To support this high consumption of meat, we feed to livestock plant proteins that could be eaten directly by humans. Where population is dense and the amount of arable land and the supply of moisture is limited, a country cannot afford to feed animals food fit for human consumption. Animals get protein from plants, concentrate it, and resynthesize proteins with combinations of amino acids more suitable for humans. In the process much potential human food is wasted. Where the food supply is limited, humans must garner from plants the proteins and other nutrients instead of feeding animals to do this for them, which wastes potential human food.

COMPOSITION

The approximate composition of some common cuts of meat is given in Table 22-1. Meats contain from 15 to 20 percent protein. They are valued for the quantity of this nutrient that they provide in the diet. The proteins in meats, like those in eggs and milk, are of high

TABLE 22-1
Composition of Selected Cuts of Meat (100-gram edible portion, raw)

Cut of Meat	Water (%)	Calories[a]	Protein (g)	Lipid (g)	Carbohydrates (g)	Calcium (mg)	Phosphorus (mg)	Iron (mg)	Vitamin A Value (I.U.)	Thiamin (mg)	Riboflavin (mg)	Niacin (mg)	Ascorbic Acid (mg)
Beef													
Arm pot roast	61.1	255	18.4	19.6	0	7	173	2.1	0	.11	.18	3.22	0
Flank	8.6	180	19.7	10.6	0	5	191	1.9	0	.11	.15	4.55	0
Rib, 10–12	64.2	315	16.6	27.1	0	10	158	1.7	0	.08	.12	3.05	0
Round	64.8	203	20.4	12.8	0	4	197	1.9	0	.10	.17	3.71	0
T-bone	59.2	272	17.6	21.9	0	6	163	1.8	0	.10	.17	3.43	0
Top sirloin													
Choice	62.7	227	19.0	16.2	0	8	184	2.3	0	.12	.20	3.20	0
Select	64.2	207	19.3	13.7	0	7	187	2.4	0	.12	.21	3.24	0
Ground													
Regular	56.1	310	16.6	26.6	0	8	130	1.7	—[b]	.04	.15	4.48	0
Extra lean	63.2	234	18.7	17.1	0	7	141	1.9	—	.06	.25	4.53	0
Heart	75.6	117	17.1	3.8	2.6	2	173	4.6	0	.19	1.02	9.46	6.3
Liver	69.0	143	20.0	3.5	5.8	6	318	6.8	35,346	.26	2.78	12.78	22
Pork													
Center loin	66.7	200	20.1	12.7	0	24	192	0.8	7	1.10	.21	4.7	0.9
Ham													
Cured, center cut, country style	55.9	195	27.8	8.3	0.3	—	—	—	0	.57	.24	3.9	—
Shoulder, cured													
Blade Boston	65.9	218	17.7	15.8	0	25	175	1.1	7	.81	.22	3.7	0.7
Fresh ground	61.1	263	16.9	21.2	0	14	175	0.9	7	.73	.24	4.3	0.7
Bacon, cured	31.6	556	8.7	57.5	0.1	7	142	0.6	0	.37	.10	2.8	21.7
Heart	76.2	118	17.3	4.4	1.3	5	169	4.7	25	.16	1.19	6.8	5.3
Liver	71.1	134	21.4	3.7	2.5	9	288	23.3	6,495	.28	3.01	15.3	25.3
Lamb													
Leg	54.3	230	17.9	17.1	0	9	170	1.7	—	.13	.23	6.3	—
Loin	56.6	310	16.3	26.6	0	15	152	1.6	—	.01	.21	6.5	—
Veal													
Top round	74.8	117	21.0	3.1	0	5	220	0.8	—	.08	.27	9.4	—

[a] 1 kilocalorie = 4.185 kilojoules
[b] — = Data not available

Source: U.S. Dept. Agriculture Handbook No. 8-13. *Beef Products. Raw, Processed, Prepared.* Revised 1990. Handbook No. 8-10. *Pork Products. Raw, Processed, Prepared.* Revised 1992. Handbook No. 8-19. *Lamb, Veal and Game Products. Raw, Processed, Prepared.* 1989.

369

quality. The fat content of meat, which ranges from under 5 percent to near 30 percent, varies with the type of animals and with the breed, feed, and age of the animal. Pigs tend to convert a high proportion of their feed to fatty tissue. In response to the preference of health-conscious consumers for foods lower in calories and especially lower in fat, producers have not only switched to leaner breeds, but also modified the feeding regimen to give leaner, less fatty meat. The possibility of altering the metabolism of the animal to increase deposition of protein at the expense of fat has been explored. As the animal is finished for market, injection with porcine somatotropin—a growth hormone normally synthesized in the pituitary gland (104) or the addition of ractopamine, an analog of epinephrine (adrenaline), as a supplement to the feed (129) has been shown to yield leaner meat. Closer trimming of external fat, now the practice, eliminates nine calories for each gram of fat removed. A study conducted in the 1980s found that consumers, given a choice of beef with 13 millimeters (0.5 inch) *vs.* 8 millimeters (0.3 inch) of exterior fat, or 8 millimeters (0.3 inch) *vs.* essentially no exterior fat, were more likely to purchase meat with the lesser amount of external fat (110).

Most of the calcium in the body of an animal is found in the bones, so the edible portion of meat is low in this mineral. Lean muscle meats are excellent sources of phosphorus and iron. Liver is an especially rich source of iron and a concentrated source of vitamin A. Meats are excellent sources of niacin and riboflavin and are good sources of thiamin. Pork is richer in thiamin than is beef. Lean meats are deficient in ascorbic acid. The water content of lean meat is approximately 75 percent.

STRUCTURE OF MEAT

A cut of meat consists of lean tissue, which, aside from water, is chiefly protein, with some fatty tissue and bone. The lean part of meat consists of one or more muscles, each of which is made up of many bundles of muscle fibers. Muscle fibers are the basic structural unit of the lean of meat.

Muscle Fibers

Muscle fibers are long, thin structures, cylindrical in shape and sheathed by a delicate, transparent membrane, the sarcolemma. They range in diameter from 10 to 100 micrometers and in length from a few millimeters to several centimeters (6). Fibers of beef (semitendinosus) imaged by a scanning electron microscope are shown in Figure 22-1. Minerals, vitamins, enzymes, and the pigment myoglobin are in the sarcoplasm within the fibers. Each muscle fiber is made of threadlike structures, the myofibrils, of one to two micrometers in diameter (6, 59, 65). Longitudinal striations seen in muscle fibers viewed with the light microscope (Fig. 22-2) are due to these myofibrils. Visible the length of the muscle fiber are alternating dark and light bands known as cross striations (59). These are due to the way the myofibrils are structured. Myofibrils are made of substructures called myofilaments. The latter are of two types: thick (diameter: 100 angstroms); and thin (diameter: 50 angstroms). Rows of thick myofilaments alternate with rows of thin myofilaments the length of the myofibril. The long axis of both the myofibrils and the myofilaments parallels the long axis of the muscle fiber. A thin longitudinal section of a muscle fiber much magnified by an electron microscope (Fig. 22-3) shows the myofilaments that make up the myofibrils (59). The striations (banding) observed in Figure 22-3 are the result of the differential staining of

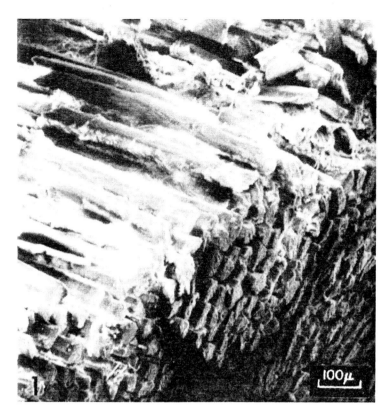

Figure 22-1. A three-dimensional view of muscle fibers (beef semitendinosus) embedded in connective tissue, imaged at low magnification by scanning electron microscopy. (Courtesy of S. B. Jones. USDA Eastern Regional Research Center, Philadelphia. Reprinted from *Food Technology* 31(4):82. 1977. Copyright © by Institute of Food Technologists.)

components of the muscle fiber, which are present in an orderly, repeating pattern. The narrowest, darkest bands have been designated the Z-lines, from either side of which emerge rows of thin filaments. The space occupied by the Z-line and the attached thin filaments is designated the I-band. Two neighboring Z-lines mark the outer limits of one sarcomere. The middle section of the sarcomere that contains the dark-staining, thick filaments is called the A-band. In the middle of the A-band is a narrow white (unstained) space, the H-zone, which is bisected by a narrow, dark (M) line (7).

Thick filaments approximately 1.5 μm long are made chiefly of the protein myosin, each molecule of which consists of a long, thin rod (the tail) terminating at one end in a pair of small structures that constitute the globular-shaped head. A thick filament consists of bundles of these myosin molecules joined head end to tail end, head ends oriented outward in both directions from the center of the filament and with the heads (cross linkages) projecting from the surface of the filament in a six-fold screw axis. Thin filaments, somewhat shorter than thick filaments, are made chiefly of the protein actin, individual molecules of which are approximately spherical in shape. Monomers of actin can unite like beads on a string to form polymers, two strands of which are twisted in a helix to form a

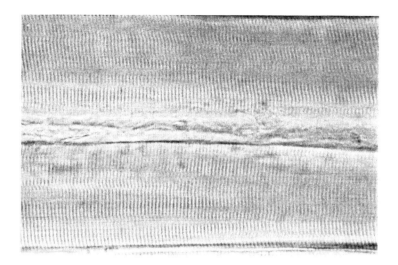

Figure 22-2. Microscopic view of a longitudinal section of two muscle fibers from uncooked round of beef showing longitudinal and cross striations. Magnification × 450. (From Belle Lowe and Joseph Kastelic, Iowa Agricultural Experiment Station Research Bulletin 465, 1961. Reprinted by permission.)

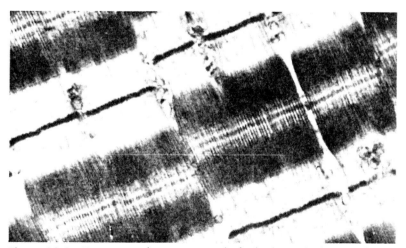

Figure 22-3. Transmission electron micrograph of a thin longitudinal section of a muscle fiber. The darker bands that alternate with lighter ones are due to overlap of thick and thin filaments. Original magnification × 24,000. (Courtesy of H. E. Huxley, from *Scientific American* 199(5):69, 1958.)

thin filament. Rows of thick and thin filaments are positioned in such a way that each thick filament is surrounded by six thin filaments and each thin filament is surrounded by three thick filaments. The structural components of muscle are shown schematically in Figure 22-4. A surface view of a longitudinal fracture of a muscle fiber as viewed by a scanning electron microscope is shown in Figure 22-5b. The image, a topographical view of

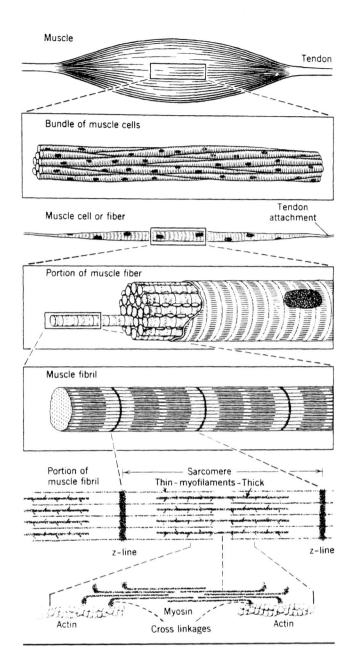

Muscle

Tendon

Bundle of muscle cells

Muscle cell or fiber

Tendon attachment

Portion of muscle fiber

Muscle fibril

Portion of muscle fibril

Sarcomere

Thin - myofilaments - Thick

z-line

z-line

Actin

Myosin

Cross linkages

Actin

Figure 22-4. Structural components of muscle, shown schematically.

the surface, shows A-bands, I-bands, and Z-lines. A transmission electron micrograph of the muscle fiber is shown in Figure 22-5a for comparison.

According to Huxley's sliding filament theory (60), the thin actin filaments slide from each end of a sarcomere toward its center as a muscle contracts. A polypeptide at the myosin head first extends and then unites momentarily with a thin filament, and finally contracts, thereby inching the thin filaments on either side toward the center of the

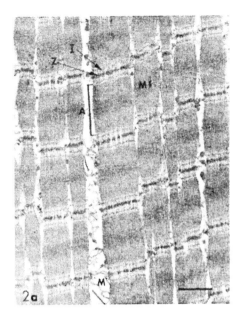

Figure 22-5. Two views of the fine structure of aged beef muscle (semitendinosus) fibers. (*a*) Transmission electron micrograph. (*b*) Scanning electron micrograph. A, A-band; I, I-band; Z, Z-line. Bar represents one micrometer. (Courtesy of S. B. Jones, USDA Eastern Regional Research Center, Philadelphia. Reprinted from *Food Technology* 31(4):83. 1977. Copyright © by Institute of Food Technologists.)

sarcomere. Repetition of the cycle results in shortening of the sarcomere and contraction of the muscle (61). When a muscle relaxes, the actomyosin complex breaks, the thin filaments are free to slide back to their original position, and the sarcomeres return to their relaxed length, a condition that prevails in the muscles immediately after an animal is slaughtered.

Regulatory proteins, tropomyosin and the three subunits of troponin, lie in the grooves of the two-stranded helix of molecules that form the actin filament. These proteins mediate the contraction $\rightleftharpoons$ relaxation process in muscle, either facilitating crosslinkages of myosin heads with actin or blocking them (7).

Other filamentous structures have been identified in muscle in addition to the actin and myosin filaments that are involved in contraction. The first of these cytoskeletal filaments, as they are called, are observed in the spaces (gaps) that open between the ends of the actin and myosin filaments when muscles (sarcomeres) are stretched. These thin, elastic gap filaments run parallel to those of actin and myosin and link Z-disc to Z-disc, giving longitudinal integrity to the sarcomeres. Two cytoskeletal proteins, titin and nebulin, are considered components of these longitudinal filaments (126). Other cytoskeletal filaments appear to provide lateral linkage of Z-disc to Z-disc (in the Z-line) and so keep features of the myofibrils in register. The cytoskeletal protein, desmin, has been identified as a component of these filaments (110).

Connective Tissue

Connective tissue provides support for the muscle fibers, fat, and bones of meat. A layer of connective tissue called endomysium surrounds individual muscle fibers. This con-

Figure 22-6. Scanning electron micrograph of raw beef semitendinosus muscle fractured perpendicular to the muscle fiber axis, showing (*E*) endomysial and (*P*) perimysial connective tissue. (Courtesy of S. B. Jones, USDA Eastern Regional Research Center, Philadelphia. Reprinted from *Journal of Food Science* 43:1182. 1978. Copyright © by Institute of Food Technologists.)

nective tissue merges with the perimysium that surrounds muscle fibers in bundles (Fig. 22-6). Bundles of fibers, in turn, give rise to muscles that are surrounded by epimysial connective tissue. Connective tissue consists chiefly of an undifferentiated matrix called ground substance, made mainly of mucopolysaccharides, in which collagen and, if present, elastin are embedded.

The textural quality of meat is influenced by the collagen in the muscle. The main fiber-forming collagens in muscle are Types I and III, as well as some Type V (79). Type IV collagen is nonfibrous. Collagen fibers are made of tropocollagen monomers, which, in turn, are made of three polypeptide chains. The amino acid glycine occupies every third position over much of the polymer. It is usually followed by proline or hydroxyproline. These last two constitute approximately ¼ of the amino acid residues. Lysine, hydroxylysine, glutamine, and asparagine are present, too, as is cysteine in Type III collagen. Thus, the polypeptide is largely a repeat pattern of glycine–proline–lysine or another basic or acidic amino acid.

Each polypeptide exists over much of its length as a poly-L-proline II helix; nonhelical areas exist at both the carboxyl and amino ends. Three of these chains twisted about each other with a right-hand twist form the triple helix of collagen.

Two of the three chains in Type I collagen are identical; all three chains in Type III collagen are identical. In the assembly of collagen fibers, the three coiled chains are joined end to end and aligned side by side, ends staggered ¼ of their length. This positions the nonhelical carboxyl and amino ends near sites on the helical portions of adjacent units where cross links are possible. The endomysium has Types I and III collagen with small amounts of Type IV. Type I collagen is a major and Type III a minor component of the perimysium and the endomysium (79). Collagen fibers predominate over those of elastin in connective tissue of most muscles, two exceptions being the semitendinosus of the round and the latissimus dorsi of the chuck, muscles involved in moving the legs (11).

Although collagen fibers are flexible, they do not stretch as do those of elastin. Collagenous connective tissue is found in tendons that attach muscle to bone, in the skin, in the bones, and in the dentine of the teeth. A collagen-rich tendon may be observed at the end of muscles in the leg of a chicken. Connective tissue that contains collagen fibers is pearly white in contrast to yellow connective tissue in which elastic fibers predominate. The neck ligament from the beef animal is made mainly of elastic fibers. This structure may be seen in the meat from the shoulder region of the animal. Collagen fibers can be disintegrated in hot water, whereas those of elastin are affected little if at all. From the standpoint of tenderizing meat during cooking, it is fortunate that collagen fibers predominate over elastic fibers in the connective tissue in muscle.

FAT

When an animal eats more food than it needs to maintain itself and provide the energy it needs to live and move about, the surplus is converted into fat that begins to accumulate in body tissues. Fat is deposited in the connective tissue within the muscle—where it is known as marbling—around and between muscles, under the skin, and in other connective tissue that contains special fat storage cells. Globules of fat may be packed so tightly in these cells that they appear angular. Fat is deposited in the connective tissue around organs in the abdominal cavity. For example, the kidney which is cushioned and protected by a moderate coating of fat. Age, feed, and exercise influence the fat content of meat. Meat from well-fed animals with limited exercise and past the period of most rapid growth tends to contain more fat. Pigs accumulate fat more readily than do other meat-producing animals. A moderately well-fed pig may have a thick layer of fat-filled cells over the entire surface of the body.

IDENTIFICATION OF MEAT

A high proportion of the money spent for food goes toward meat. Knowing the best method and technique for cooking meat to make it most palatable is important. To choose an appropriate cooking method, however, one must be able to identify meats. This involves the ability to distinguish beef, veal, lamb, or pork by sight and to know the part of the animal from which the meat comes. Both factors have a bearing on the most suitable cooking methods.

Types of Meat

Color of the lean and the character and amount of fat are the two best indices for identification of the animal from which the meat comes. The color of beef when freshly cut is a dark, purplish red. This changes to a bright, cherry red when the meat is exposed to oxygen. The change in color from purplish red to bright red is reversible. With prolonged exposure to oxygen, the pigment is oxidized and loses its bright red color. Veal, too young to have accumulated as much pigment as the older beef animals, is grayish pink and the bones have a pinkish tinge. The lean of lamb is a darker, deeper red than beef. The paler rose-pink of fresh pork is due at least in part to the high proportion of white, myoglobin-free muscle fibers interspersed among the red, myoglobin-rich ones (21). The species difference in this regard is illustrated by the whale, which is so richly endowed with oxygen-storing red muscle fibers that it can stay submerged without breathing for many minutes. Conversely, the rabbit has a high proportion of white glycolytic muscle fibers that provides not only rapid take-off but also early oxygen depletion, and thus a biochemical basis for the scared-rabbit reputation.

The fat of pork, with its higher unsaturated fatty acid content, is much softer than that from either beef or lamb (Table 15-1). Lamb fat is the hardest of all, in fact, quite brittle. It is usually whiter than beef fat, which tends to be more yellow especially if the animal has been fattened for market by grazing.

In addition to the color of the lean and the character of the fat, the size and contour of a cut are also a clue to the source of the meat. The size and shape clearly differentiate a loin chop of lamb, a center cut pork chop, and a T-bone steak from beef.

Cuts of Meat

Identification of a cut of meat is more important than identification of the animal source for choosing an appropriate cooking method. Distinguishing features of a cut of meat are the size, shape, and location of bone; the size and shape of muscles found in the cut; and the amount and distribution of fat. Bone, if present, is one of the best identifying features. For this reason, familiarity with the skeletal structure of meat animals is essential.

The skeletal structure of beef, veal, lamb, and pork is basically the same, as shown by the charts in Figure 22-7, which depict the bones in the four meat animals. Not only are bones and muscles similar in shape in cuts from analogous parts of different animals, but the meat is likely to be comparable in tenderness, too. A carcass is disassembled first by splitting it down the center of the backbone into right and left sides. In the case of beef, the sides are divided between the twelfth and thirteenth rib into fore and hind quarters. Then the carcass is subdivided into primal cuts.

Primal Cuts of Beef

Primal cuts of beef from the fore quarters (starting at the head end of the animal) include the chuck and rib above, and the brisket and plate below (Fig. 22-7). The chuck contains the neck bones, the shoulder blade, part of the backbone, the upper part of the first five ribs, the arm bone, and the muscles attached to these bones. The rib wholesale cut contains part of the backbone and the upper part of the ribs. The brisket contains the breast bone and the lower ends of the first five ribs. The foreshank is attached to the brisket. The plate contains the lower ends of ribs 6 to 12.

From the hind quarter and adjoining the rib cut is the short loin, which contains the mid-section of the backbone, and below it the flank, which is boneless. To the rear of the short loin is the sirloin, which contains part of the hip bone and the tail bone. The final wholesale cut of beef is the round, which includes the rump. The latter is a triangular-shaped piece that contains the remainder of the tail bone and the aitch (or rump) bone. The round is named for the round bone (femur) it contains.

Primal Cuts of Veal and Lamb

Primal cuts of veal and lamb (Fig. 22-7) differ from primal cuts of beef in the following way. The shoulder of veal or lamb corresponds to the chuck of beef and the hotel rack to the rib of beef. Breast of veal or lamb includes the parts called brisket and short plate in beef. The leg of veal or lamb comprises the equivalent of both round and sirloin of beef.

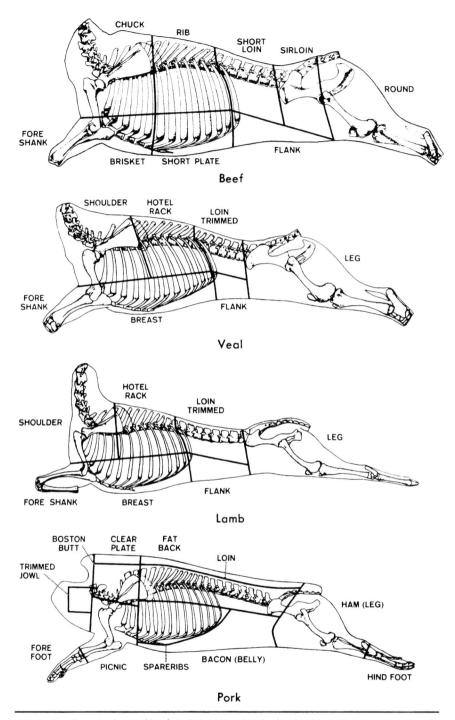

Figure 22-7. Primal cuts of beef, veal, lamb, and pork, showing bone structure. (Courtesy of the National Live Stock and Meat Board.)

Primal Cuts of Pork

Primal cuts of pork (Fig. 22-7) differ somewhat from those of beef, veal, and lamb. Beginning at the head end of the pork carcass, primal cuts include the jowl, the Boston butt, which corresponds to the upper part of the shoulder of lamb and veal or the chuck of beef, and the picnic (shoulder) of pork, which corresponds to the lower part of the shoulder of lamb or veal or to the chuck of beef. The picnic includes the foreshank of the pig. The loin of pork includes almost all of the backbone, the upper part of most of the ribs, and part of the hip bone. Sliced off the outside of the loin and parallel to the backbone is a layer of fatty tissue known as fat back. Similar tissue sliced off the upper part of the exterior of the Boston butt is known as clear plate. Both fat back and clear plate consist of connective tissue in which fat is deposited. Both are used as sources of lard. The lower part of most of the ribs of pork, called spare ribs, is peeled away from the walls of the abdominal cavity. When fresh, the latter is called side pork, and when cured and smoked, bacon. Ham corresponds to round of beef and to the leg of lamb and veal minus the sirloin part of the last two.

Retail Cuts

When a carcass of meat is subdivided into both primal and retail cuts, an attempt is made to separate thicker from thinner pieces and tender meat from less tender. Whenever possible the cut is made across the grain of the muscle, that is, perpendicular to the long axis of the muscle fibers. The first two objectives are easier to accomplish than the third, because muscles run in more than one direction, especially in certain parts of an animal. This is illustrated in Figure 22-8. Partly on this account, meat from the chuck is less desirable than that from the round. At the meat market, primal cuts are further subdivided into pieces suitable for cooking. These are the retail cuts.

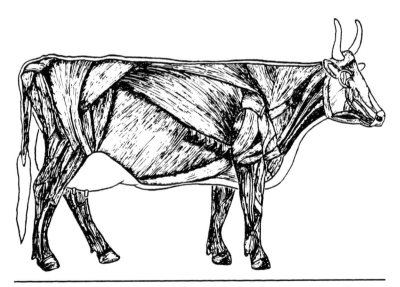

Figure 22-8. Orientation of muscles in different parts of a beef animal, shown schematically. (Courtesy of the Ohio Art Company, Brian, OH.)

In many instances the retail cut is named for the primal cut from which it came. Thus sirloin steak comes from the sirloin, round steak from the round, and rib roast from the rib of beef. Loin chops come from the loin and sliced ham from the ham of pork, and rib chops from the rib and loin chops from the loin of lamb.

Some cuts of meat are named for the bones that they contain. In an attempt to simplify identification of cuts of meat on the basis of bones, the following charts have been devised. Shown in Figure 22-9 are the basic retail cuts of meat and their location on the carcass. In Figure 22-10 are shown the seven basic shapes of the bones by which these basic retail cuts may be identified. The round arm bone is found in the lower part of the shoulder or chuck. Cuts that contain this bone are known as shoulder arm steaks, shoulder arm chops, or shoulder arm pot roasts. Cuts from the upper part of the shoulder or chuck contain cross sections of the blade bone. Cuts from this part of the animal are called blade or 7-bone steaks, chops, or pot roasts. Rib chops, steaks, or roasts contain the backbone and the rib bone. Cuts from the short loin contain cross sections of the backbone or vertebrae, which are usually but not always T-shaped. These cuts are called club, T-bone, porterhouse steaks, or simply loin steaks. Cuts of meat from the sirloin or the hip of the animal contain cross sections of the hip bone, which vary in shape. The hip bone appears in cuts nearest the short loin as the pin bone, in the center as the flat bone, and nearest the leg as the wedge bone. Cuts from the leg or round contain a round bone. These cuts can be distinguished from those of the shoulder arm where the bone is round, too, by the size and the shape of the muscles in the two cuts (Fig. 22-11). Cuts from the breast or brisket contain the breast bone (or sternum) and the ends of the rib bones.

Although bones may aid in distinguishing one retail cut from another, shape, size, and location of muscles serve as identifying features, too. Many cuts contain cross sections of

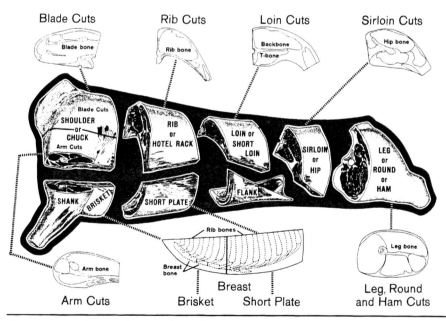

Figure 22-9. The seven basic retail cuts of meat and the primal cuts from which they come, as illustrated with a side of beef. (Courtesy of the National Live Stock and Meat Board.)

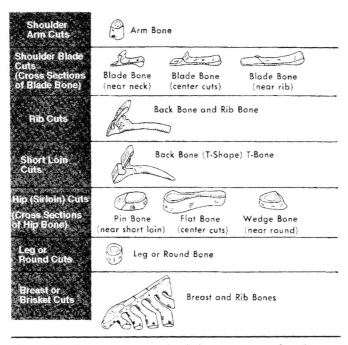

Figure 22-10. Bones serve to identify the seven groups of retail cuts. Cuts from the sirloin contain either the pin bone, the flat bone, or the round bone, and the last may appear round on one side of the cut. (Courtesy of the National Live Stock and Meat Board.)

several muscles (Figs. 22-11, 22-12), and the same muscle, differing somewhat in size, shape, and location, may appear in consecutive cuts. The *longissimus dorsi* (Fig. 22-12b) appears in cuts, made perpendicular to the backbone, from chuck, rib, and loin. The *psoas major* muscle is found in cuts from the loin. The *biceps femoris* muscle originates in the sirloin, is a prominent muscle in the rump, and forms part of the bottom round (Fig. 22-12a). A publication is available that reproduces from tracings minor as well as major muscles found in 39 retail cuts of beef (124).

The variety of popular names under which the same retail cut of beef is marketed is often confusing to the consumer at the meat display counter. To bring some order out of this confusion, recommended names for 314 retail cuts of beef, pork, and lamb have been proposed for adoption by retailers (63). The list is called the Uniform Meat Identity Standards. Information recommended for the label on each retail cut includes (a) the kind of meat, (b) the wholesale cut from which it comes, and (c) the name recommended for the cut.

TENDERNESS OF MEAT

Tenderness in meat is highly prized. Meat that is hard to cut and hard to chew is unpalatable. The texture of meats can vary from tender to extremely tough. Tenderness varies not only from carcass to carcass but from one part of a carcass to another. Meat

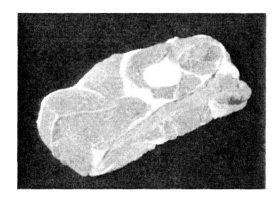

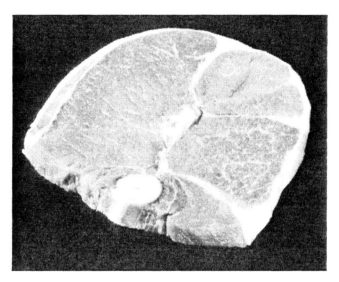

Figure 22-11. Shapes of the muscles and location of the fat differentiate two cuts that contain a round bone, (*top*) chuck arm pot roast and (*bottom*) round steak. (Courtesy of the National Live Stock and Meat Board.)

from the upper part of a carcass along the backbone is more tender than that from the lower part. Meat from the chuck is more tender than that from the brisket, and that from the rib more tender than that from the plate of beef. Meat from the rib is more tender than that from the chuck, and that from the loin more tender than that from the round. Meat from the lower part of the legs and from the neck and flank is toughest of all.

Although a carcass is divided to separate more-tender from less-tender parts, different muscles within a cut are not equally tender. Figure 22-12 shows by diagram the muscles in the round and in the loin of beef. Numbers in the diagrams indicate the amount of force required to shear individual muscles after the meat is cooked (107). Muscles of the loin, except the internal oblique, are more tender (have lower shear values) than the most tender muscle of the round. Differences in tenderness among the other muscles of the loin are not great. The two muscles for which cuts from the short loin are prized are the *longissimus dorsi* (backstrap) and the *psoas major* (tenderloin). In round steak the *semimembranosus* (top round) is only slightly tougher than the *semitendinosus* or the *biceps femoris* (bottom round). The *rectus femoris* and the three smaller muscles next to the bone have somewhat

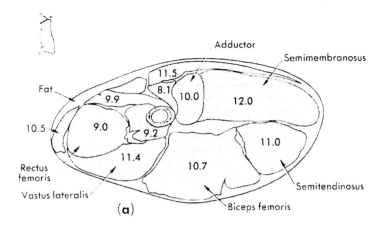

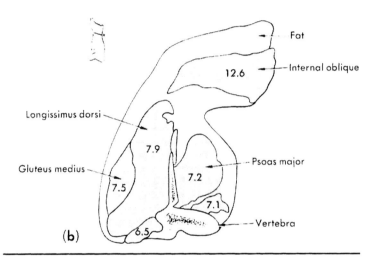

Figure 22-12. Different muscles within a cut vary in tenderness. Numbers indicate the force needed to shear the cooked meat: (a) round; (b) short loin. (From J. M. Ramsbottom and E. J. Strandine, *Food Research* 13:322, 324. 1948. Copyright © by Institute of Food Technologists.)

lower shear values. Marked differences among three muscles of the rib of beef have been documented (97).

Basis of Toughness

Underlying causes of toughness in meat and why meats differ so markedly have been the subject of a number of studies. Fat deposited in the connective tissue of lean meat appears as white flecks that is called marbling. It is of questionable value in predicting tenderness in meat (27, 94). However, well-marbled meat tastes juicier, doubtless because the melted fat lubricates the lean. Early work considered the relation between the collagen of intramuscular connective tissue and toughness of meat (108). Later studies focused on contributions of the myofibrillar component to toughness of muscle. Both are now considered as contributing factors.

Connective Tissue Toughness

Toughness of meat contributed by collagen is sometimes referred to as background toughness, to distinguish it from that due to the myofibrillar component (84, 85). There is evidence that the type of cross links between collagen monomers that make up the fibers is as important as the content of collagen (78). The lability of collagen to heat decreases with increasing age. The more heat-labile cross links of collagen fibers from younger animals are believed to be replaced by more thermally stable links in older animals (8). The tendency of meat from older animals to be tougher may thus reflect the changing ratio of heat-stable to heat-labile cross links of collagen (116). This may account for the fact that veal is more readily tenderized by cooking than beef even when veal is higher in collagen. Although one study showed the percentage of soluble collagen in five different muscles of beef to be related to the contribution of the connective tissue component to toughness (31), another study showed that differences in the number or nature of the cross links in the collagen of active versus less-active muscles failed to account for the former being judged as less tender and the latter more tender (116). Intramuscular collagen influences the fracture properties of meat when stress is applied, as in biting and chewing (105). Collagen makes a difference in the toughness of meat, but just how it acts has been hard to pin down. This topic is the subject of an extensive view (78).

Actomyosin Toughness

Muscles potentially tender because connective tissue contributes little to toughness may become tough because of the condition of the myofibrillar component. Immediately after an animal is slaughtered muscles are in a relaxed state, with sarcomeres extended. Actin and myosin filaments overlap little if at all and they are joined by few cross links. The warm flesh is soft and pliable. Cooked in this state, the meat is tender. Muscles remain in this relaxed condition from a few hours up to 24 hours, depending on the animal, its physiological condition, and certain environmental conditions. After this time rigor develops. The development of rigor is analogous to contraction of muscle in the live animal. Muscles become rigid and inelastic. Cross links form between the myosin and the actin filaments to the extent that they have overlapped (61), and these cross links are locked in place during rigor. Rigidity is attributed to the shortening of sarcomeres that occurs during onset of rigor, and the loss of extensibility maintains that rigidity (58). In the live animal, energy is available to uncouple the filaments so muscles can relax, but depletion of energy reserves in postmortem muscle leaves actin and myosin filaments cross-linked as actomyosin. Meat in this condition is tough.

Changes that take place in the myofibrils after the animal is slaughtered but before rigor develops influence the extent to which meat is tenderized by aging. Rapid chilling of prerigor meat by exposure to temperature below 15°C (59°F) may bring about cold shortening of the muscles. An excised muscle induced to shorten by rapid chilling to the extent of 35 to 40 percent of its resting length is at peak toughness (86). Viewed microscopically, a cold shortened muscle resembles one that has contracted (121). All fibers in a muscle are not subject to cold shortening, even those lying side by side. When a fiber shortens actively, adjoining fibers are passively shortened and appear crumpled and wavy. A fiber that cold shortens does not do so over its entire length. In areas where shortening is severe, breaks may occur across muscle fibers (125). When a muscle shortens near 35 percent of its resting length, the sarcomeres are shortened to the approximate length of the myosin filaments (33). This overlap of thick and thin filaments makes possible extensive cross linking between myosin and actin filaments and also eliminates areas along the fiber (the I-bands) where resistance to shear should be less (85).

A muscle cooled while still attached to bone will be more tender than if it had been excised, but muscles left on the carcass are not equally restrained from shortening. If a carcass is suspended by the aitch bone rather than by the achilles tendon (the usual practice), more of the muscles are maintained near their relaxed length in the live animal and tenderness of a number of the muscles is improved (54). Holding a carcass at elevated temperature (16°C or 61°F) for 16 to 20 hours postmortem rather than chilling it immediately increased tenderness of longissimus muscle 47 percent and also avoided the irregular shape of a carcass hung by the aitch bone (119). Hanging a carcass by the aitch bone rather than the conventional way, however, made more difference in the tenderness of nine major muscles of beef than did conditioning the carcass at 16°C (61°F) for 20 hours prior to chilling (52). In general, muscles with less connective tissue show greater response in tenderness and in length of sarcomeres to the way a carcass is hung than do muscles in which connective tissue is prominent (54).

Conditioning (Aging) of Meat

Meat is conditioned to counteract the toughness induced by rigor mortis. Meat held under chilling conditions (near 4°C or 40°F) for a period of time will become tender. In one study, 8 out of 20 muscles of beef had reached maximum tenderness when aged 5 to 8 days, but the remaining 12 muscles required 11 days or more, leading to the recommendation of an aging period of 11 days as optimum for both tenderization and overall palatability of the four major wholesale cuts of beef (chuck, rib, loin, and round) (120). A high conditioning temperature (15°C or 59°F), with provision to control microbial growth, yields tender meat in a short time. Electrical stimulation of meat speeds the development of rigor (30). This permits meat to be chilled early postmortem without inducing cold shortening of sarcomeres and the toughness that would result (98). Electrical stimulation also makes possible separation of muscle from bone while the flesh is still warm. This hot boning has economic advantages (115). Less refrigerated space and less refrigerant are required for boneless cuts. Rapid turnover of meat is cost-effective. Handling and shipping costs are less.

A number of studies have attempted to explain how conditioning tenderizes meat. Two proteolytic enzyme systems, the cathepsins and calcium-activated proteases, presumably are responsible for tenderization of meat when it is conditioned (70). No measurable proteolysis of collagen fibers occurs during conditioning, but subtle structural changes may make collagen more vulnerable to dissolution when meat is cooked (38). Conditioning has its major impact on the myofibrillar component of muscle. Sarcomeres lengthen but not to their relaxed, prerigor dimension (121). A muscle stretched to twice its resting length (at which point little if any overlap of actin and myosin filaments should exist) and held in that position during onset and resolution of rigor was still tenderized by aging, a result that appears to rule out weakening of linkages between actin and myosin filaments as a cause of tenderization (35). An increase in the α-actinin that can be extracted and disappearance of desmin from the Z-line (134) result from conditioning, which could account in part for weakening and disintegration of the Z-line (33). Nebulin and titin are altered by conditioning (81), the latter degraded more in meat that becomes more tender (3). The subunit, troponin-T, that is associated with the actin filament is degraded (101). The ease with which myofibrils are fragmented when tissue from loin steaks is homogenized is reported to be a good index to tenderness (32). Future additions of data to these bits and pieces no doubt will provide a coherent explanation of how conditioning tenderizes meat.

Meat Tenderizers

Meat that is tough may be tenderized by treatment with certain enzymes that catalyze the hydrolysis of one or more of the proteins of muscle. Proteolytic enzymes that attack the sarcolemma and the muscle fibers are available. Other enzymes also attack either the collagen or elastin (89). Enzymes from tropical plants that are effective meat tenderizers are bromelain from pineapple, ficin from figs, actinidin from kiwi fruit, and proteases from the latex of the green papaya fruit (68), including papain, chymopapain (the main enzyme), and a peptidase. Bromelain is more active toward collagen than toward the proteins of the myofibrils, but the reverse is true for papain, ficin, actinidin, and the fungal enzyme, Rhozyme P-11 (67). All three papaya enzymes can hydrolyze the proteins of the myofibrils extensively, but connective tissue is attacked only after it has been heated to disrupt the triple helix. All three enzymes are unaffected by heating to 60°C (140°F), but chymopapain is the most stable of the three at 70°C (158°F) (68).

A preparation of papaya enzymes as a dry powder diluted with salt and referred to as papain has been on the market as a meat tenderizer for some time. Sprinkled on the surface of meat, it must then be forked into the interior to be effective. It is essentially inactive in meat at room temperature, is increasingly active as meat is heated from 55° to 75°C (131° to 167°F), and is very active after meat reaches 80°C (176°F). Once meat is heated to the optimum temperature, digestion of the proteins will continue. A temperature a few degrees higher (85°C or 185°F) will inactivate the enzyme. Tenderization of meat by enzymes appears to be different from that effected by either aging or cooking. Meats tenderized by enzymes tend to have a mushy consistency due to the loss of structure of the muscle fibers.

INSPECTION

The Federal Meat Inspection Act of 1906 makes inspection mandatory for all meat packing plants that slaughter and process meat to be marketed in interstate commerce. Federal inspection is done by or under the supervision of a trained veterinarian under the auspices of the United States Department of Agriculture. The live animal, the carcass and certain parts where disease is likely to be evident, and the packing plant are scrutinized, the meat

Figure 22-13. Meat inspection stamps. The stamp on the left, used on fresh and cured meats, shows that the meat was inspected and passed as clean, wholesome food. The stamp on the right is used on canned and packaged meat products. The number indicates the meat packing establishment. (Courtesy of the U.S. Department of Agriculture.)

for signs of disease and the plant from the standpoint of sanitation. Carcasses that pass federal inspection are identified on each wholesale cut by a round, purple stamp bearing the legend "U.S. INSP'D & P'S'D" together with the official number of the packing plant (Fig. 22-13). A harmless purple fluid is used to stamp meat that passes inspection. The wording, "U.S. Inspected and Passed by Department of Agriculture," is used on labels of processed meats that pass inspection. The Wholesome Meat Act of 1967 made inspection of all meat mandatory including that slaughtered and marketed within a state. Inspection may be done under federal or state auspices. If the latter, the same standards apply as for federally inspected meat.

GRADES OF MEAT

Quality Grades

Meat inspected for wholesomeness may be graded for quality and for yield. Because of the great variation among beef carcasses in the quality of the lean, eight quality grades have been established: Prime, Choice, Select, Standard, Commercial, Utility, Cutter, and Canner. Presumably these grades reflect differences in the palatability of the meat, although there is some question as to their predictive value (18). The four top-quality grades, Prime through Standard, are reserved for the two youngest maturity classes (A and B) of beef. These younger animals have pinker, less ossified bones and the color and texture of the lean differ from that in more mature animals. C-, D-, and E-maturity carcasses are graded Commercial or lower.

Both marbling and firmness and texture of the lean are considered when a quality grade is assigned to a carcass. Marbling, abundant in beef graded Prime decreases through Choice and Select to Standard, which has little if any intramuscular fat. Choice beef predominates on the market (Figure 22-14). The grade is indicated by a shield-shaped purple stamp (Figure 22-15). The four lower grades are used in ground beef and in fabricated meat products. Quality grades have been established for lamb and veal but not for pork. A high proportion of beef on the market has been graded for quality, although grading, unlike inspection, is voluntary. In addition to these federal grades for quality, individual meat packers may use their own grading system along with brand names to indicate the grade of their products, hence Armour's Star and Safeway's Lean.

Yield Grades

Meat that is officially graded for quality is graded also for yield. Thickness and fullness of muscle and the amount of fat (both external and in the body cavity) that must be trimmed away are considered when a yield grade is assigned. Yield grades for beef are numbered 1

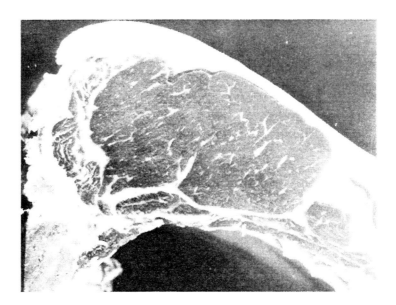

Figure 22-14. Marbling (intramuscular fat) in beef rib of Choice grade, before it was trimmed. (Courtesy of the U.S. Department of Agriculture.)

Figure 22-15. The grade of meat is indicated by a shield-shaped stamp. (Courtesy of the U.S. Department of Agriculture.)

through 5. Carcasses that yield the highest proportion of boneless, closely trimmed meat qualify for yield grade 1. Those with the lowest proportion for yield qualify for grade 5. Yield grades for pork are 1 (highest yield) to 4 (lowest yield).

COLOR OF MEAT

Fresh Meat

Differences in the color of lean meats are due mainly to differences in concentration of the pigment myoglobin, which accounts for approximately ¾ of the total pigment of red meat, the remainder due to the hemoglobin of the blood (39). Beef contains more myoglobin than does either veal or pork. The more exercised muscles tend to be deeper in color. For example, the heel of the round is a deeper color than cuts from the loin or rib of beef. Pork shoulder steak is a deeper color than is a chop from the loin.

At times puzzling changes may occur in the color of fresh meat, especially noticeable in lean beef. The change in color is due to a change in the pigment myoglobin. Molecules of myoglobin (and hemoglobin) contain the iron porphyrin ring as shown:

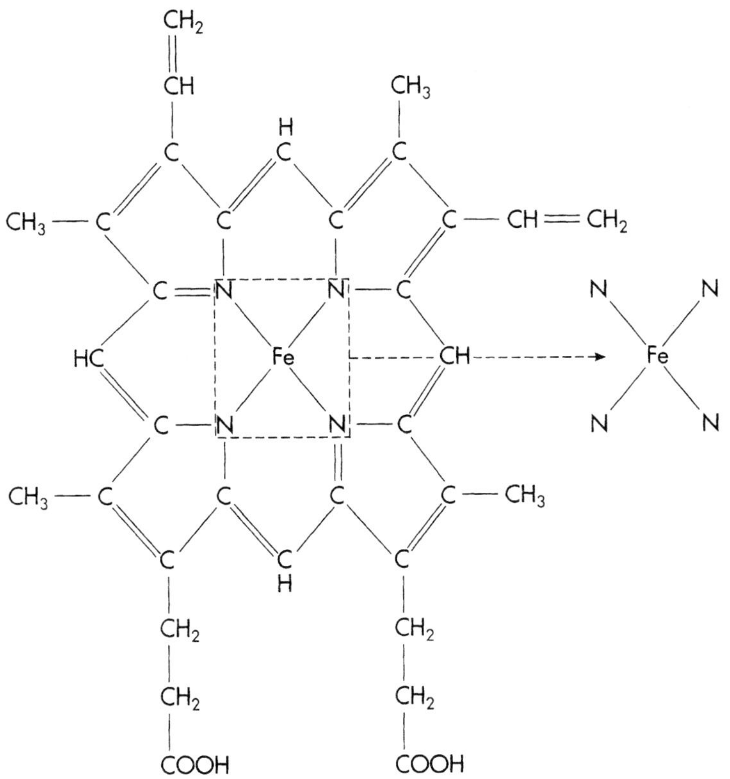

Formula for heme

Resonance of the conjugated double bonds in the porphyrin ring gives rise to the color of meat pigments. In the center of the porphyrin ring is an atom of iron linked covalently to the nitrogens of the four pyrrole groups. In the molecule of myoglobin the nitrogen of the protein moiety, a globin, is attached to the ferrous iron at the fifth coordination site (92), as shown:

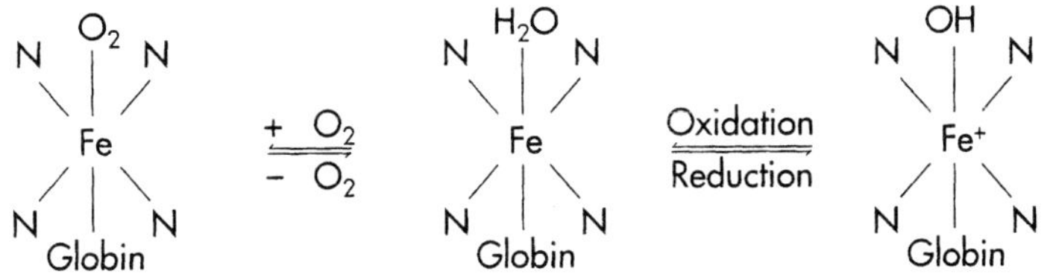

Oxymyoglobin (bright red)   Myoglobin (purplish red)   Metmyoglobin (brownish red)

Pigment in fresh, uncooked meats

Myoglobin, like hemoglobin, can unite temporarily and reversibly with oxygen, as shown above. In the live animal the myoglobin of muscle takes from hemoglobin of the blood the oxygen that the latter transports from the lungs to the tissues where it is needed. As soon as an animal stops breathing, its supply of oxygen is cut off and the tissues are depleted of oxygen. Myoglobin in unoxygenated form with the iron in the ferrous state gives to freshly cut beef its purplish-red color. Upon exposure to air the pigment in the cut surface of meat becomes oxygenated to form oxymyoglobin, which is a bright, cherry red color. This difference in color of the pigment, depending on whether or not it is oxygenated, explains why the outer layer of ground meat on display for sale at a meat counter may be a bright red, whereas the interior is purplish red. It also accounts for the fact that a slice of beef that has been partly covered by another may be two colors, purplish red where the two overlapped and bright red on the exposed part.

When oxygen pressure is high, the pigment is maintained in the oxygenated form. Exposed to low levels of oxygen, the oxygen–myoglobin complex dissociates, the iron is oxidized to the ferric state, and brownish red metmyoglobin is the result, as shown above. Reducing conditions that continue for a time in the meat will convert any metmyoglobin formed back to myoglobin. Thus in raw, uncured meat three forms of the pigment may exist in dynamic equilibrium (39). For prepackaged meats to retain a bright red color, the packaging film must be permeable to oxygen (106).

The pH of muscle influences the color of meat. At death the tissues are slightly alkaline, but lactic acid derived from glycogen accumulates in muscle postmortem. The final pH affects both the water-holding capacity of muscle and its color. The abnormally pale flesh from stress-susceptible pigs and the dark-cutting flesh of some beef animals are associated with abnormally low and high pH values, respectively (64).

Cured Meat Pigments

Myoglobin has the ability to unite loosely not only with oxygen but also with nitric oxide, which occurs when meats such as bacon, ham, and corned beef are cured. The nitric oxide myoglobin (nitrosylmyoglobin) is a light red (pink) rather than the purplish red of myoglobin. When meat is exposed to low heat during curing, part of the nitric oxide myoglobin is changed to a more stable complex, the iron still in the ferrous state. The pigment is now considered to be nitric oxide hemochrome (dinitrosylhemochrome) (77), as shown:

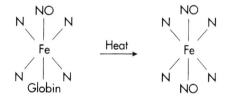

Nitric Oxide Myoglobin (pink) Nitric Oxide Hemochrome
(more intense pink)

Pigment in cured meats

Although heat is not detrimental to the color of cured meat, exposure to light when the meat is in contact with oxygen will cause the color to fade. Light accelerates the dissociation of nitric oxide from the pigment after which oxidation takes place (106). The iron is changed from the ferrous to the ferric form. Slices of ham are turned with the liner uppermost in meat display counters to protect the pigment and the color of the meat from the harmful effects of light. Photo-induced fading can be prevented by vacuum packaging in an oxygen-impervious wrap (105). Under certain circumstances oxidation of the porphyrin ring rather than of the iron may result in the formation of yellowish or greenish fluorescing compounds. The iridescence sometimes observed in cured ham and dried beef is attributed to the refraction of light by structural components of the meat rather than to changes in the pigment.

The practice of using nitrites in the curing of meat became an issue when it was learned that nitrites could give rise to nitrosamines that are carcinogenic (55). As a result, the amount of nitrite that is allowed in cured meat has been sharply reduced. However, nitrites do more than stabilize the color of meat. They are antimicrobial and prevent the growth of *Clostridium botulinum* and the production of toxin. Other ingredients are now used in the curing mix to supplement the low level of nitrite. Nitrosamines form in bacon because, as it cooks, the tissue is heated after moisture has evaporated. The nitrosamine content of the cooked-out fat, mainly nitrosopyrrolidine, is approximately twice that of the fried bacon. When this fat is used in cooking, nitrosamines are volatilized and little remains in either the fat or the food cooked in it (56).

STORING MEAT

Meats are highly perishable. Prompt refrigeration at 4°C (40°F) or lower reduces the growth of microorganisms on the cut surfaces and maintains freshness. Unless cuts of fresh meat are to be cooked within three days, they should be frozen. Ground meat and variety meats should be held no longer than one to two days before they are cooked. Raw meats may carry pathogens (Chapter 4), so surfaces they contact should be washed thoroughly to prevent cross-contamination. Processed meats such as slices of ham, frankfurters, and luncheon meat may be held in the refrigerator three to five days. Bacon, smoked sausage, and smoked ham may be held up to one week.

COOKING MEAT

Meats are usually served cooked for a number of valid reasons. Heat destroys microorganisms that may have contaminated the surface of steaks, chops, and roasts. Grinding meat distributes any surface contaminants throughout the mass, so heating only the surface of a ground meat patty, for example, is insufficient. It should be heated to a temperature of 70°C (155°F) throughout or until juice pressed from the meat is clear and without pink color. In addition to making the meat safer to eat, cooking also changes the color, alters the water-holding capacity, affects the tenderness, and develops the flavor and especially the characteristic aroma of meat. Some methods of cooking yield a more flavorful product than others. Heat brings about changes in the fat, the protein and, in the case of cured meats, the sugar that contribute to cooked meat flavor. The presence of sugar in cured meats and of glycogen in liver accounts for the ease with which these meats brown and even scorch if the cooking temperature is too high.

Effects on Meat Pigment and Color

Meat may be cooked for esthetic reasons. Heat brings about changes in the pigment that alter the color of the meat. The color of beef is changed more by cooking than is the less highly pigmented pork. Much of the pigment in the interior of a cut of raw beef is present as reduced and unoxygenated purplish red myoglobin. When the meat is heated, the pigment is converted first to oxymyoglobin, as evidenced by the bright red color of the meat when cut (12). With further heating the protein moiety of the pigment is denatured, the ferrous iron is oxidized, and the meat takes on the grayish brown color of denatured globin hemichrome. Attributes of the pigment in cooked meat are not inconsistent with the structure as shown (40):

Pigment of uncured, cooked meats

Because heat brings about a change in the color of the pigment in meat, the color of cooked meat, especially tender cuts of beef, is used as an index to doneness, that is, the extent to which the meat proteins have been coagulated. The three stages of doneness to which tender cuts of beef may be cooked are characterized as rare, medium, and well done. For rare beef the internal temperature is 60°C (140°F). Rare meat is plump and juicy. The interior of rare beef is bright red and the surface is covered with a thin brown layer containing denatured globin hemichrome. Beef cooked to an internal temperature of 71°C (160°F) has reached the medium-done stage. The meat is less juicy and not so plump in appearance as rare meat. The interior of beef at the medium-done stage is pink rather than the bright red of rare beef because more of the myoglobin has been denatured, and the surface layer of brown is deeper. Tender beef heated to an internal temperature of 77°C (170°F) is considered well done. The meat no longer looks plump. It is less juicy than that cooked to the medium-done stage, although it need not be dried out. Beef cooked to the well-done stage is a uniform grayish brown throughout. However, the color of cooked meat is not a precise index to its exposure to heat. Paired cuts of meat heated to the same internal temperature may vary somewhat in doneness, as assessed by color of the lean, if they are heated at different rates either in different media or in the same medium but at different temperatures (27). For example, one-inch steaks cooked on a broiler rack in an oven at 177°C (350°F) to an internal temperature of 80°C (176°F) had the color of well-done beef, whereas steaks braised in steam to an internal temperature of 85°C (185°F) were still slightly pink (27). Cooking time for the former was approximately an hour and for the latter approximately 15 minutes. Myoglobin is less sensitive to heat if the pH of the muscle is high, in which case some undenatured pigment (and color) may remain when meat approaches the well-done state (118).

Occasionally a pink color is apparent in well-done meat, especially light-colored pork loin after one to two days of refrigeration. This phenomenon has long been a puzzle. Heat-resistant cytochrome C, a heme-containing molecule like myoglobin, may be involved

(42). Complexes of cytochrome C with the amino acids, cysteine, methionine, and histidine, and with derivatives of vitamin B_6, all of which could be liberated during cooking, exhibit a pink color upon reduction (1). More recent evidence points to denatured globin hemochrome as the pigment (41). Regardless of the cause, a pink color in refrigerated cooked meat does not in itself indicate that the meat is undercooked.

The color of well-done meat from different animals is influenced by the amount of pigment in the raw meat. Well-done beef is darker than well-done pork. Pork loin changes from a pale, grayed pink to a near white. Pork shoulder steak and uncured ham, a dull rose red when raw and a deeper color than the loin, are grayish brown when cooked. Veal changes from pink to brownish gray. Cooking intensifies the color of the pigment in cured meats.

Although doneness of tender beef may be assessed reasonably well by the color of the meat, tough cuts may not be tender when they reach an internal temperature of 77°C (170°F), the well-done stage for tender beef. So color is not a good criterion for doneness of less tender meat. The character of the connective tissue in a cut of meat influences how and how long the meat should be heated to make it tender. Collagen fibers in tough cuts should be sufficiently solubilized by cooking that the meat is fork-tender and the muscle fibers and bundles of fibers can be separated with relatively little pressure of the teeth.

Effects on Meat Proteins and Tenderness

Two of the attributes desired in cooked meat are juiciness and tenderness, both qualities determined in large measure by the effects of heat on the proteins of meat. The potential for altering the inherent tenderness or toughness of meat by cooking is great. The number of studies attempting to relate the two attests to the complexity of the issue. Early studies emphasized the beneficial effects of low cooking temperature and low internal temperature on cooking losses, shrinkage, and tenderness of meat. Advantages of a low cooking temperature were attributed to the resultant longer cooking time (26). Later it was pointed out that what is considered a high cooking temperature depends on how the heat is transferred, with 204°C (400°F) judged high for roasting but low for broiling, and 121°C (250°F) judged low for roasting but 100°C (212°F) considered high for braising (27). Greater tenderness of beef cooked at lower temperatures (i.e., heated more slowly) has been verified by a number of workers, and the time the meat is held near 60°C (140°F) has been proposed as a decisive factor (16).

Tenderness of cooked meat may be evaluated by taste panel, by the force required to shear the tissue, and by the force required to compress it. Both the rate of heat penetration in meat as affected by the temperature of the cooking medium and the final internal temperature have been investigated for their effects on connective tissue as well as on myofibrillar proteins, both of which influence tenderness.

Effects on Connective Tissue

In respect to the connective tissue component of meat, the overall effect of cooking is decreased toughness. Much of the tensile strength of muscle comes from fibers of collagen that are a part of connective tissue. Tenderization of tough meat involves disassembly of the ordered arrangement of collagen monomers in the fibers. In tough cuts of meat, particularly from mature animals, covalent bonds are broken first. Then disruption of hydrogen bonds and unwinding of the triple helix of collagen yield three individual strands of water-soluble gelatin. As this takes place, connective tissue is weakened, muscle fibers are separated more easily, and toughness is decreased.

When meat is exposed to heat, collagen fibers shrink. This puts pressure on bundles of muscle fibers and causes them to appear humped. Meat at this stage is tougher than it was before any heat was applied. Both temperature and time are involved in tenderizing tough cuts of meat. In one study, a decrease in shear was observed when muscle (semi-tendinosus of the round) was held for an extended time at temperatures that ranged from 55° to 65°C (131° to 149°F). There is some evidence that proteolytic activity may occur when the tissue is held for some time near 60°C (140°F) (74, 96). Tenderness of meat (top round) was related to the time the internal temperature of the meat stayed in the 55° to 60°C (131° to 140°F) range (130). The greater tenderness of meat (beef semitendinosus) when it was heated at 93°C (199°F) instead of 149°C (300°F) was attributed to the longer (3½ times) cooking time needed to bring the meat to an internal temperature of 70°C (158°F) (99).

The time required to convert collagen to gelatin varies inversely with the temperature. Conversion is negligible at 60°C (140°F) and requires considerable time when the temperature of the meat is no higher than 65°C (149°F). Between 65°C (149°F) and 80°C (176°F) conversion is more rapid (132). Within this range of temperatures, the rise in internal temperature in tough cuts of meat is retarded, as flattening of the heating curves in Figure 22-16 illustrates (25). If muscle is held at a temperature near 80°C (176°F), shear declines as collagen is converted into gelatin. Heating tough cuts of meat at a temperature near simmering requires appreciable time to convert enough of the collagen to gelatin so that muscle fibers can be separated with ease. Conversion is faster at 100°C (212°F) and faster still at 121°C (250°F), the temperature in a pressure cooker operating at 103 pKa (15 pounds) steam pressure. Ease in separation of fibers and bundles of fibers is not the only consideration when less tender meats are cooked. The effects of heat on the proteins of muscle fibers of tender as well as tough cuts of meat should be considered, too.

Effects on Muscle Fibers

The proteins of muscle fibers are denatured by heat as is collagen. Unlike collagen, however, they are not solubilized. Instead, they lose their ability to associate with water, and the higher the temperature the greater the loss. Shrinkage of fibers and firmness of tissue result. When tender cuts of meat are cooked, avoidance of excessive coagulation is the main objective. In the case of tough cuts, the objective is to keep overcoagulation to a minimum as connective tissue is tenderized.

Two stages in the temperature-dependent toughening of meat have been identified (34). The first increase in the force needed to shear the tissue occurred early in the heating sequence when the temperature of the tissue rose from 40° to 50°C (104° to 122°F). This increase in shear was accompanied by a sharp decrease in the solubility of myosin. A marked decrease in the hydration of the proteins of muscle when they were heated from 40° to 50°C (104° to 122°F) had been reported (46) earlier. Hardening of meat tissue has been observed when muscle was heated at temperatures between 65° and 75°C (149° and 167°F) (82). Identified as the second phase of toughening (34), meat heated in this temperature range had an additional increase in the force needed to shear it. Shortening of muscle fibers induced by shrinkage of collagen and the resultant loss of meat juice may account for this second stage in heat-induced toughening (34), although the effects of heat on the proteins of muscle fibers may be directly involved.

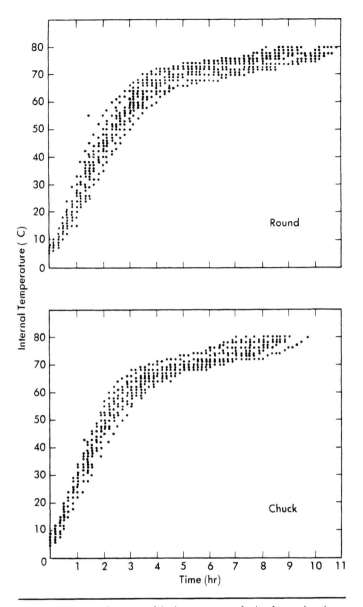

Figure 22-16. Flattening of the heating curves for beef (round and chuck) cooked in an oven at 125°C (257°F). (Courtesy of Sylvia Cover and Texas Agricultural Experiment Station, *Food Research* 6:236. Copyright © 1941 by Institute of Food Technologists.)

Proteins of the muscle fibers are not equally sensitive to heat. The most labile, α-actinin becomes insoluble near 50°C (122°F) (24). Myosin is denatured near 55°C (131°F) and actin in the 70° to 80°C (158° to 176°F) range. A temperature near 80°C (176°F) is required to denature tropomyosin and troponin. Proteins of the sarcoplasm are denatured over a range of temperatures of 40° to 90°C (104° to 194°F). Denaturation of gap filaments begins near 60°C (140°F) (80).

The firming of meat tissue as it is heated is attributed to denaturation (unfolding) of the protein molecules of the muscle fibers and the subsequent formation of hydrogen, hydrophobic, and finally disulfide linkages between peptide chains (17). The reduction in water-holding capacity that results decreases the tenderness of meat. Liquid expelled from the tissue collects in the cooking utensil and this with fat from the connective tissue constitutes the drippings. Cooking makes meat less juicy even when the meat is covered with water.

The loss of weight as meat is cooked is considered a rough index to the water-holding capacity of the tissues. Loss of weight and of water from longissimus and biceps femoris steaks were reported to increase with each increase in internal temperature (61°, 68°, 74°, and 80°C or 142°, 154°, 165°, and 176°F) (109). The increase from 74° to 80°C (165° to 176°F) made the greatest difference in retention of water and in dimensions of the steaks. Softness and juiciness of the steaks decreased as internal temperature increased. Beef longissimus sealed in plastic and heated in a water bath programmed for a rise in temperature of 0.1°C per minute to a maximum of 60°C or 140°F (rare) and held at that temperature for a total heating time of 10 hours contained twice as much uncoagulated protein as did samples of the muscle heated to 80°C (176°F) in one hour and held at that temperature for an additional hour. Weight loss for the sample held at 60°C (140°F) averaged 21.9 percent compared with a loss of 38.7 percent for samples held at 80°C (176°F) (75). These results led to the suggestion that greater retention of juices due to reduced coagulation of myofibrillar proteins as well as alteration of the collagen fibers may account for the greater tenderness of meat cooked for a long time at a low temperature.

Effects on the Fine Structure of Muscle

The way cooking alters the fine structure of muscle and the relationship of the latter to tenderness have been studied using the light microscope. More recently and in greater detail, the transmission electron microscope, which gives a greatly magnified view through the tissue, and the scanning electron microscope, which gives a three-dimensional image or topographical view of the tissue, have also been used.

Early work using the light microscope shows dimensional changes in muscle fibers brought about by heat. A gradual decrease in the width of muscle fiber fragments occurs up to 45°C (113°F) and a rapid decrease from 45° to 62°C (113° to 145°F), at which point the decrease is essentially complete. Shrinkage in length does not begin until 55°C (131°F), is very rapid and extensive between 55° and 65°C (131°F and 149°F), and continues but less markedly between 65° and 80°C (149° and 176°F) (53). Longitudinal shrinkage is accompanied by a loss of the brilliant birefringence characteristic of the raw tissue.

Changes in the fine structure of beef longissimus shown by transmission electron microscopy include initiation of shortening of sarcomeres and some degradation of structure of the Z-line when the tissue is heated to 50°C (122°F) (113). Heated to 60°C (140°F), the thin filaments begin to disintegrate and the thick filaments to coagulate, possibly accounting for the loss of birefringence observed when tissue is heated to this temperature. At 70°C (158°F) changes in both thick and thin filaments are more marked. At 80°C (176°F) and especially at 90°C (194°F) filaments become amorphous but banding that corresponded to the original sarcomeres remain (113). The transmission electron micrographs of Figure 22-17 illustrate changes in the fine structure of beef semitendinosus muscle heated to internal temperatures of 63°C, 68°C, and 73°C (145°, 154°, and 163°F)

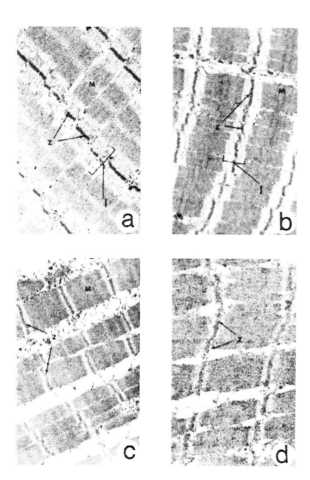

Figure 22-17. The effects of heating on the structure of aged beef muscle (semitendinosus) shown by transmission electron microscopy: (*a*) unheated; (*b*) heated to 63°C or 145°F; (*c*) heated to 68°C or 154°F; and (*d*) heated to 73°C or 163°F. Magnification × 9,260 for *a, b,* and *c* and 13,900 for *d.* I—I-band; M—M-line; Z—Z-line. (Reprinted from R. C. Leander, H. B. Hedrick, M. F. Brown, and J. A. White, *Journal of Food Science* 45:5, 1980. Copyright © by Institute of Food Technologists.)

(76). Disappearance of material from the I-band and coagulation of material in the A-band are evident in tissue heated to 63°C (145°F). Some disorder appears in the Z-line. Reduction in the length of the sarcomeres is due mainly to shrinkage of the I-band. At 68°C (154°F), additional shortening of the I-band occurs, but some actin filaments still remain. Heating to 73°C (163°F) results in further shortening of the sarcomeres, some disruption of the Z-disks, and some breaks where the filaments of the I-band joined the Z-line. Changes in the fine structure of longissimus muscle heated to the three internal temperatures are more marked than were those in the semitendinosus. The progressive toughening of the muscle, measured by shear, as the internal temperature increases is attributed to the contracted and possibly hardened material of the A-band (76).

Changes in the fine structure of beef semimembranosus muscle, as imaged by a scanning electron microscope, are slight when the tissue is held at 50°C (122°F) for 45 minutes (66). When held at 60°C (140°F), the A-bands appear more compact and breaks were observed at the junction of the A- and I-bands, which left rigid blocks corresponding to the A-bands of the raw tissue. Little change in length of the sarcomeres is evident. When the tissue is held at 90°C (194°F), the sarcomeres shorten and extensive detachment of Z-disks occurs, but banding of the sarcomeres persists.

Some changes in the connective tissue of meat when heated have been reported. Viewed by the light microscope, shrinkage of endomysial connective tissue was observed first near 50°C (122°F) and was complete near 70°C (158°F), at which temperature changes in the perimysial fibers were first observed (113). Increases in both interfiber and interfibrillar spaces have been demonstrated in beef longissimus heated to 60°C (140°F) (23). The endomysial sheath, closely associated with the muscle fibers in the raw state appears detached and wavy after being heated to 70°C (158°F) (Fig. 22-18), indicative of shrinkage of the muscle fibers. Granular material appears between the endomysial connective tissue and the fibers of longissimus muscle heated to 70°C (158°F), but was more evident when the internal temperature is 80°C (176°F). Degradation of perimysial connective tissue of longissimus and psoas major muscles of beef begins near 70°C (158°F) and occurred rapidly at 80°C (176°F) (23), but perimysial connective tissue in semitendinosus of beef still retains some of its fibrous character even after it had been heated at 90°C (194°F) for 45 minutes (20).

The preceding discussion indicates that although heat may tenderize meat through its action on collagen, it may also toughen through its effect on coagulation and shrinkage of muscle fibers. These opposing effects are illustrated graphically in Figure 22-19. If tender cuts are heated only to the collagen melting temperature (near 60°C or 140°F) or slightly above, coagulation of muscle fiber proteins will be incomplete, excessive shrinkage of muscle fibers will be avoided, and less of the meat juices will be lost. The meat will be as tender as cooked meat can be. Meat with background toughness because of collagen fibers is entirely different. Heating such meat at low temperature for a long time will eliminate connective tissue toughness and minimize toughening caused by overcoagulation of muscle fiber proteins (75). However, even meat that was originally tender can be made rubbery, tough, and stringy by overheating. Toughness is due to the effects of high temperature on proteins of the muscle fibers and stringiness to almost complete conversion of collagen to gelatin.

Effects on Flavor

The effects of cooking on the flavor of meat is another consideration. Evidence suggests that cooking decomposes one or more precursors in the lean of meat to give the basic cooked meat taste. Less tender cuts that get much exercise have more extractives and thus are more flavorful. Lactones and sulfur-containing compounds, including sulfides, mercaptans, and cyclic compounds such as pyrazine, are thought to make important contributions to the flavor of cooked meats (22). Hydrogen sulfide, a prominent component, has been shown to be formed from the amino acid cystine (87). None of the numerous compounds isolated has been identified as uniquely meaty (127). Less tender cuts cook in less time in a pressure saucepan, but the flavor is not so well developed (45). Components identified in the aroma of beef cooked by microwave radiation have been characterized as less desirable than those identified in the aroma of beef heated conventionally (83). Apparently, long cooking is needed to develop a full, meaty flavor. The aroma from the heated adipose tissue differentiates beef from pork from lamb (51). Precursors of the aroma appear to be water soluble because when the fats are extracted with water before they are heated, they have only a basic meaty odor, not the aroma characteristic of the kind of meat (128).

The odorous compound in the fat of uncastrated male pigs, particularly noticeable in cooked, uncured pork, has been identified as the volatile steroid 5-α-androst-16-ene-3-one

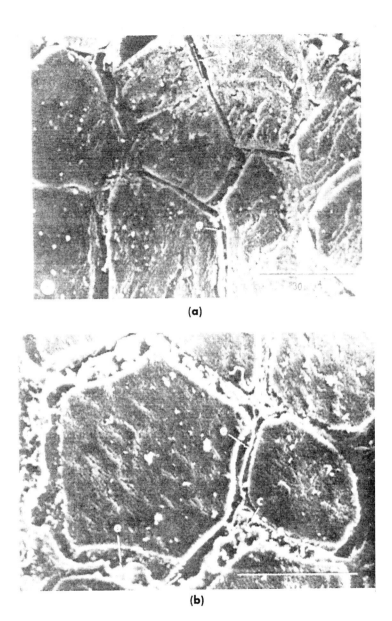

(a)

(b)

Figure 22-18. Effects of heating on the ultrastructure of beef longissimus muscle fibers, shown by scanning electron micrographs of cross-sectional fractures: (a) unheated (× 730); (b) heated to 70°C (158°F) internal temperature (× 900). (Reproduced from C. S. Cheng and F. C. Parrish, *Journal of Food Science* 41:1452, 1976. Copyright © by Institute of Food Technologists.)

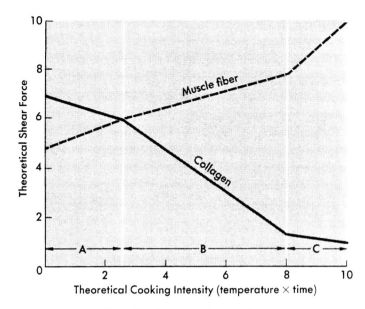

Figure 22-19. Effects of cooking on tenderness of meat. (From H. H. Wang et al., *Food Research* 19:320. Copyright © 1954 by Institute of Food Technologists.)

(95). Women can detect the odor better than men (92 percent vs. 56 percent of the subjects tested); and with the same odor thresholds women found the odor more unpleasant than did men (43).

Cooked meats are susceptible to oxidative rancidity, which gives rise to stale and rancid odors. The term warmed over is used to characterize the oxidized flavor that develops in cooked meat (132). Warmed-over flavor is present in cooked meat after one to two days of refrigeration. Phospholipids associated with the lean of meat, rather than the neutral lipids of adipose tissue, are believed to be the main precursors of warmed-over flavor. The fatty acids of the phospholipids are highly unsaturated, with two to four or more double bonds. The hydroperoxides that form when unsaturated fatty acids are oxidized are unstable and decompose to form short chain, volatile compounds that contribute off flavors. Both nonheme iron and hydrogen peroxide-activated metmyoglobin are catalysts for oxidative rancidity of unsaturated fatty acids (5, 47). Curing makes meat less susceptible to development of warmed-over flavor. Nitrite used in the curing is an effective antioxidant, but how it operates is still unclear (62). Oxidative rancidity in beef is less the higher the cooking temperature and the longer the cooking time (57). The suggested cause is the production of antioxidants as the meat browns. The aroma of cooked pork is judged better when it is reheated in a microwave rather than in a conventional oven (100).

Effects of Initial Fat Content

The effects of the fat content of raw meat on the cooked product have been investigated. Pork loin chops trimmed of subcutaneous fat before cooking have less fat in the lean than those trimmed after cooking. Preliminary trimming makes little difference in the amount of fat retained in pork rib chops and blade steaks (90). Broiled or pan fried patties from regular (30% fat) and lean (20% fat) ground beef differ little in fat content (50). Beef patties with an initial fat content of 14 percent lose 8.5 percent of it as they cook, and those with an initial fat content of 24 percent lose 27.6 percent (14). Patties from the leaner beef lose more moisture when cooked. Juiciness, tenderness, and flavor ratings decrease with decreasing fat content (13).

A ground beef product that contains only 10 percent fat is available commercially. The product is formulated with 10 percent water for juiciness and tenderness and iota carrageenan for retention of the water. Hydrolyzed vegetable protein contributes flavor (37).

Effect on Nutritive Value

Cooking does not appreciably lower the nutritive value of the proteins of meat (44). Retention of the B vitamins (thiamin, riboflavin, niacin, and pantothenic acid) when meat is cooked is good (28, 71, 123). Loss of thiamin tends to be somewhat greater. Retention of the B vitamins is somewhat greater in rare compared to well-done meat (28). When meat is cooked by moist heat, an appreciable quantity of each vitamin is found in the cooking liquid (88). Whether lamb roasts are cooked slowly in a microwave or in a conventional oven makes no difference in the retention of thiamin and riboflavin (93). Retentions of the two vitamins are essentially the same when top rounds of beef are cooked slowly in a portable oven broiler and in a conventional electric oven (71).

Methods

Methods of cooking meat are classed as either dry- or moist-media methods. Actually, changes that take place in the interior of a piece of meat occur in a watery medium regardless of the cooking method used. Methods are described as moist or dry media on the basis of the medium that surrounds the meat as it cooks. Dry-media cooking encompasses those methods in which the meat is cooked without added water and uncovered so that moisture from the meat can evaporate. The meat is exposed to radiant energy or is in contact with hot air, a hot frying pan, or hot fat from which heat is conducted rather than with hot water or steam. Roasting, broiling, panbroiling, and frying are classed as dry-media methods for cooking meat. Dry-media methods are usually recommended for tender cuts of meat for which coagulation of meat fiber proteins to the preferred stage of doneness is the object. Ground meat may be cooked by dry-media methods.

Moist-media cooking includes those methods in which the meat is cooked in a covered utensil (pan, pressure saucepan, foil wrap, or plastic bag), whether water is added or the meat is cooked in the steam or liquid released from the meat as the proteins coagulate. Braising and cooking in water are moist-media cookery methods. Pot roasting and breading are forms of braising. Less tender cuts of meat are usually cooked by moist-media methods, especially on a surface unit. In this way the meat may be cooked long enough to be tenderized without danger of its cooking dry and scorching.

Tender cuts of meat are usually cooked by dry-media methods and tough cuts by moist-media methods. However, tender cuts may be cooked by moist-media and some tough cuts can be tenderized by dry-media methods. For example, a tough cut of beef may be made tender by roasting if the oven temperature is kept very low (80°C or 176°F) and the cooking time is long (several hours) (27).

Roasting

Roasting is one of the simplest methods of cooking meat. The cut is placed with the fat side up on a rack, unless the bone will support it, and in a shallow pan. A meat thermometer, if available, is placed in the cut with the bulb in the center of the largest muscle and not touching bone or fat. The oven need not be preheated but may be set to bake and turned on when the roast is put to cook. An oven temperature of 163°C (325°F) is satisfactory for all except very small cuts, for which a higher temperature (177°C or 350°F) is recommended, or for very large cuts, for which a lower temperature (149°C or 300°F) gives more uniform doneness.

Roasts are cooked to the degree of doneness desired as indicated by the internal temperature or for the time specified in a timetable. Timetables for roasting give the approximate cooking time in minutes per pound. Differences in the size and shape of the cut, in the temperature of the meat when it is put to cook, and in oven temperature will influence the roasting time. Frozen roasts need not be thawed before they are put to cook, but the cooking time may be increased by 50 percent, so thawing saves energy. The fat content of meat influences the roasting time, which is longer for muscle low in fat or with coarse, uneven marbling (29). Use of a meat thermometer is a more accurate way to assess doneness. Allowance should be made for the fact that, because of conduction from hotter outer layers, the temperature will continue to rise 5 to 10 degrees after the meat is removed from the oven, especially in larger roasts. Roasts carve better if allowed to stand a few minutes after they are cooked. In one study that compared beef ribs roasted at an oven temperature of 107°C (225°F) with the customarily recommended 163°C (325°F), cooking losses were usually lower for the former even though the cooking time was longer. As might be anticipated, cooking losses increased as the internal temperature increased from 60° to 70° to 77°C (140° to 158° to 170°F) (10). Roasts cooked at the lower temperature and those heated to the rare stage at the higher oven temperature were judged more tender than the others.

Roasting is a good method for cooking large, tender cuts of meat. Ham, rib or rump roast of beef, leg or loin of veal, loin or shoulder of pork, or leg or shoulder of lamb are frequently roasted. Cuts from the round or chuck of Choice or Select grade beef may be roasted, especially if the oven temperature is reduced to 149°C (300°F) or lower so that meat is heated a longer time to reach the stage of doneness desired. Tender cuts of beef are roasted to the rare, medium, or well-done stage. Pork roasts should be heated beyond the rare stage to 71° or 77°C (160° or 170°F). Flesh of pigs may be infected with the parasitic worm *Trichinella spiralis,* which causes trichinosis in humans. These worms, which are embedded in the muscles of the animal, are microscopic in size, and their presence may go undetected when the meat is inspected. A temperature of 58.3°C (137°F) is lethal for the parasite (73). Therefore an end point of 71°C (160°F) provides a safety factor of 13°C (23°F), and one of 77°C (170°F) a safety factor of 18°C (33°F). When fresh pork roasts are cooked in a conventional oven at 163°C (325°F) to four endpoint temperatures, endpoints of 71.1°C (160°F) and 76.7°C (170°F) were judged minimum and maximum, respectively, for yielding cooked roasts of maximum sensory qualities (49).

Broiling

Broiling is cooking by radiant energy. On an electric range the door to the broiler or oven is left partly open so the thermostat will not turn the current off; on a gas range the door is usually closed. Meat to be broiled is placed on a rack in the broiler pan and the oven regulator set at broil. The broiler pan is adjusted so that the meat is from 5 to 12 centimeters (2 to 5 inches) from the source of heat. The shorter distance is used for thin cuts of meat, 2 to 2½ centimeters (¾ to 1 inch) thick, whereas those 2½ to 5 centimeters (1 to 2 inches) thick are placed farther from the heat. Broiled meat is more uniformly done the farther the cut is placed from the source of the heat. Also, less spattering and smoking occur. The aroma of meat broiled nearer the unit may be somewhat greater, owing to cracking of proteins and decomposition of fat by heat.

When the meat is approximately half done and the top surface is brown, it is then salted, turned, and broiled on the other side. Salt on raw meat draws liquid from tissues to the surface by osmosis, and this moisture delays browning. Tongs, rather than a fork that pierces the lean, are recommended for turning the meat. Cooking is continued until the desired stage of doneness is reached. Doneness can be observed by making a slit near the bone and noting the color of the juice. A more accurate way of assessing doneness of broiled meat is with a meat thermometer, but only on thicker cuts.

The approximate total cooking time for broiling cuts of meat of different thicknesses to both rare and medium-done stages are given in timetables for cooking meats. Most cuts require an additional five minutes to progress from rare to medium done. A 1-centimeter (½-inch) difference in thickness of a cut to be broiled makes a difference of approximately five minutes in broiling time. Thicker cuts yield plumper and juicier cooked meat. A broiled steak 4 to 5 centimeters (1½ to 2 inches) thick, cut into two servings, is superior to two 4- to 5-centimeter (¾- to 1-inch) broiled steaks. Broiled meat should be served immediately once it has reached the desired doneness.

Tender steaks and chops, ground meat, and cubed meat for kabobs are suitable for broiling. Broiling is a faster method of cooking than is roasting because the transfer of energy (chiefly radiant) is more rapid. The estimated cooking time for a 1- to 1½-kilogram (2- to 3-pound) loin roasted to the rare stage in a hot oven is 5 to 10 minutes longer than that for a 5-centimeter (2-inch) porterhouse steak weighing 1 to 1½ kilograms (2½ to 3½ pounds) broiled to the rare stage.

One study compared roasting top round (semimembranosus) in an oven at 177°C (350°F) versus broiling (177°C or 350°F at the top surface) of top round to internal temperatures of 60° and 71°C (140° and 160°F) (9). Roasting required twice as much time as did broiling but used less than half the kilowatts of electricity. Cooking losses were greater from steaks that were broiled and greater in steaks heated to the higher temperature. Roasted steaks were ranked juicier and more tender than those broiled to the same temperature, but neither the method nor the doneness had a marked effect on the shear force. Steaks heated to 60°C (140°F) by roasting appeared not as well done as did those heated to 60°C (140°F) by broiling. Roasted steaks needed less attention and the oven had less spatter.

Panbroiling

In panbroiling, energy is transferred from a surface unit to the meat primarily by conduction from the heated frying pan or griddle, although some energy radiates from the utensil. Meat is placed in a cold skillet or griddle and the heating unit is adjusted to moderate so the meat cooks slowly. It is turned occasionally, and any fat that accumulates is poured off so the meat will continue to panbroil rather than panfry. When the meat appears to be done, its color may be checked by making a cut in the thickest part or in the meat next to the bone. Cuts suitable for panbroiling have a fair amount of fat and include those recommended for broiling. Ground beef patties and pork chops are often panbroiled.

Panfrying and Deep-Fat Frying

Meat may be cooked in fat by panfrying or by deep-fat frying. Panfried meat is cooked in a small amount of added fat or in the fat that accumulates as the meat cooks. The temperature is adjusted so the fat is hot enough to brown the meat but no so hot that the fat decomposes and smokes. The meat is turned occasionally. Panfried meat is crisp and flavorful at some sacrifice of tenderness and juiciness. Thin cuts of tender meat or tough cuts tenderized by slashing or cubing are best for panfrying.

For deep-fat frying, enough fat is used to cover the meat completely, thus ensuring a rapid transfer of heat into the meat. Fat used to fry meat is preheated to a temperature of 177° to 190°C (350° to 375°F).

Braising

Braising is the more commonly used of the two methods of moist-media cookery. The meat may first be browned on a surface unit of the range. A heavy utensil is used. If the cut is lean or the meat has been floured, a small amount of fat in the utensil is essential for browning the meat. The temperature should be high enough that the meat browns, but not so high that the fat smokes. The meat is turned to brown on all sides. A small quantity of liquid may be added at the beginning and during cooking to keep the meat from becoming dry. The utensil is covered with a tight-fitting lid and the surface unit adjusted to keep the cooking liquid between simmering temperature and a gentle boil. Alternately, braised meat may be cooked in an oven set at 121° to 149°C (250° to 300°F).

The feasibility of using a portable oven broiler to cook less tender cuts has been studied (71). Top round of beef in a covered dish heated to 88°C (190°F) in an oven broiler with the heat setting low has greater cooking losses, but is more tender (shear value and panel scores) than top round cooked in an electric oven preheated to 135°C (275°F). Flavor, juiciness, and retention of thiamin and riboflavin are essentially the same for the two methods. The meat will cook in less time in a pressure saucepan; but the meat fibers tend to be tough and stringy and the flavor of the meat is not fully developed. A comparison of top round of beef braised in an oven at 149°C (300°F) and in a pressure saucepan at 115°C (10 psi or 69 pKa) with samples of the same muscle cooked in deep fat or roasted in an oven at 149°C (300°F) shows that cooking losses are greatest from meat cooked in a pressure saucepan and least from meat that is roasted. The method of cooking makes little difference in flavor, tenderness, and overall acceptability (114). Doneness of braised meat can be tested by piercing it with a fork. The cooking liquid from braised meat is very flavorful and can be used for making gravy or sauce.

Rolled shoulder of lamb or veal and large pieces of meat from the chuck and the heel of the round of beef are usually cooked by braising. When vegetables are cooked with the meat, the product is called pot roast. Smaller cuts of meat that are suitable for braising include pork liver, kidney, flank steak, short ribs, and round and shoulder arm steak of beef. The last two cuts of beef when braised are called Swiss steak. Shoulder chops of lamb, shoulder steaks of pork and veal, and veal loin, rib chops, and round steaks (called cutlets) are cooked successfully by braising. Pork chops, although tender cuts, are frequently braised with or without water added. Cubed stew meat from beef, veal, or lamb is braised also. Flank steak is often stuffed, rolled parallel to the grain of the fibers, and cooked by braising. When the meat is carved, it can be cut across the grain of the fibers.

Cooking in Water

Large pieces of less tender meat may be cooked in water to cover. The meat may or may not be browned before it is covered with water or broth. The utensil is covered and the meat simmered until it is tender when tested with a fork. If the meat is to be served cold, allowing it to cool in the broth is recommended to make it juicy and flavorful. Cooling should be hastened by placing the uncovered utensil in cold water. Cuts cooked in liquid include heart, tongue, kidney, smoked ham shank or picnic, corned beef, and heel of round. Meat for stew may be cooked by this method as well as by braising. Meat (and bone) for soup is cooked in water. The bone contributes no flavor but the gelatin obtained from it contributes body to the soup stock. Pieces of neck and the heel of round make especially flavorful soup stock and stews. Vegetables should be added to stews as well as to boiled dinners only after the meat is nearly done.

Soup stock may be clarified for esthetic purposes. The cool stock is blended with egg white and then heated. The fine particles that float in the broth and make it cloudy are trapped by the coagulating egg, which may be strained out. Chilling meat broth to be used as soup stock hardens the fat so it can be removed easily. The layer of fat that hardens on the surface of the broth protects it from contamination by bacteria. The fat should be removed just before the broth is reheated. Soup stock as in vegetable soup should not have a film of fat floating on the surface.

Microwaving

Tender cuts of meat are most suitable for cooking in microwave ovens. Pieces of uniform shape and without bone (bone deflects microwaves) cook more evenly. Steaks, chops, and ground beef patties are cooked at full power (wattage) and are turned once during the cooking period. Roasts cook more evenly if the cooking power (wattage) is reduced by 50 percent. Turning or rotating the roast evens the heating, also. Siphoning off fat that accumulates reduces spattering in the oven. Depending on the size of the roast and the cooking power, the oven should be turned off 10 to 20 minutes before the meat is done. This standing time allows heat from the surface of the meat to be conducted to the center. If a thermometer is used to assess doneness, the oven should be turned off 5° to 8°C (9° to 14°F) before the desired final temperature. A thermometer designed for a microwave oven should be used. Microwaving roasts shortens cooking time markedly, but it also leads to increased cooking losses and shrinkage (48, 72, 136).

If pork is cooked in a microwave oven, an end point of 77°C (170°F) is recommended (103). Heating pork to this well-done stage makes it more likely that all areas will be hot enough to devitalize any trichinae that might be present. In addition to the uneven temperature demonstrated when meat loaves are heated in a microwave oven (19), evidence suggests that devitalization of trichinae depends not only on the temperature reached but also on the time required to reach that temperature (73, 135). Thus using a medium low (30 percent) power setting is recommended. Covering the meat with foil once it is out of the oven and allowing it to stand for 10 minutes promotes equalization of temperature, especially important for microwaved pork.

Less tender cuts of meat, such as pot roast, are cooked at low power. Until heat is conducted to the center of the meat, a slow process, tenderization does not begin. Heating is speeded if a large piece of meat is cut into smaller chunks. The meat is cooked covered and the addition of 50 milliliters (¼ cup) of water should suffice.

Cooking Frozen Meat

Frozen steaks can go directly into the broiler or skillet to cook without preliminary thawing. At least partial thawing of large tender cuts of meat like roasts may be desirable to shorten the time the cut remains in the oven. Frozen meat should be thawed in the wrapper and, preferably, in the refrigerator. Tough cuts may be thawed in the water in which the meat is to be cooked. The cooking time for frozen meat is longer than for unfrozen cuts of the same kind and size to allow for the thawing of the cut.

Storage of Cooked Meat

Leftover cooked meat should be cooled promptly and then refrigerated at 4°C (40°F). If leftovers are not to be used within 3 or 4 days, they may be frozen and held in frozen storage at −18°C (0°F) for two to three months. If left over cooked meat is not chilled promptly, it should be heated to a temperature of 60°C (140°F) and held for 10 minutes or at 74°C (165°F) for a few seconds before it is eaten.

Liquid in which tough cuts of meat have been cooked until tender often solidifies when chilled. Molecules of gelatin derived from collagen fibers of connective tissue convert the broth into a gel when it cools:

$$\text{Gelatin sol} \rightleftharpoons \text{Gelatin gel}$$
$$\text{(Hot)} \qquad\qquad \text{(Cold)}$$

The gelation of a gelatin sol is discussed in Chapter 30.

REFERENCES

1. Ahn, D. U., and A. J. Maurer. 1990. "Poultry meat color: Kinds of heme pigments and concentration of the ligands." *Poultry Science* 69:157–65. Possible roles of cysteine, histidine, and methionine in appearance of pink color in well-done meat.

2. American Meat Institute. 1993. *Meat and Poultry Facts*. Chicago: American Meat Institute. P. 25. Hamburger and beef: disappearance and prices, 1970–1992.

3. Anderson, T. J., and F. C. Parrish, Jr. 1989. "Postmortem degradation of titin and nebulin in beef steaks varying in tenderness." *Journal of Food Science* 54:748–49. Greater degradation in more tender meat.

4. Asghar, A., and A. R. Bhatti. 1987. "Endogenous proteolytic enzymes in skeletal muscle: The significance in muscle physiology and during postmortem aging events in carcasses." *Advances in Food Research* 31:343–451. Detailed summary of changes effected.

5. Asghar, A. J., J. Gray, D. J. Buckley, A. M. Pearson, and A. M. Boorer. 1988. "Perspectives on warmed-over flavor." *Food Technology* 42(6):102–8. An excellent summary, including the nonheme iron *vs.* metmyoglobin issue.

6. Bailey, A. J. 1972. "The basis of meat texture." *Journal of the Science of Food and Agriculture* 23:995–1007. A review.

7. Bailey, A. J. 1982. "Muscle proteins and muscle structure." In *Food Proteins*, P. F. Fox and J. J. Condon, eds. London and New York: Applied Science, distributed by Elsevier Science Publishers. Pp. 245–59.

Organization of the sarcomeres: Connective tissue component.

8. Bailey, A. J., C. M. Peach, and L. J. Fowler. 1970. "Chemistry of collagen cross-links. Isolation and characterization of two intermediate cross-links in collagen." *Biochemistry Journal* 117:819–31. Lysine-derived reducible and permanent cross links.

9. Batcher, O. M., and P. A. Deary. 1975. "Quality characteristics of broiled and roasted beef steaks." *Journal of Food Science* 40:745–46. Cooking times, cooking losses, press fluid, shear, and panel scores.

10. Bayne, B. H., M. B. Allen, N. F. Large, B. H. Meyers, and G. E. Goertz. 1973. "Sensory and histological characteristics of beef rib roasts heated at two rates to three end point temperatures." *Home Economics Research Journal* 2:29–34. Oven temperatures of 107°C and 163°C (225° and 325°F) and end points of 60°C, 70°C, and 77°C (140°, 158°, and 170°F) compared.

11. Bendall, J. R. 1967. "The elastin content of various muscles of beef animals." *Journal of the Science of Food and Agriculture* 18:553–58. Muscles grouped for high, medium, and low elastin content.

12. Bernofsky, C. J., B. Fox, Jr., and B. S. Schweigert. 1959. "Biochemistry of myoglobin." VII. "The effects of cooking on the myoglobin of beef muscle." *Food Research* 24:339–43. Changes in the pigment of meat induced by heat.

13. Berry, B. W. 1992. "Low fat level effects on sensory, shear, cooking and chemical properties of ground beef patties." *Journal of Food Science* 57:537–40, 574. Tenderness, juiciness, and flavor ratings decrease as fat levels decrease.

14. Berry, B. W., and K. Leddy. 1984. "Beef patty composition: Effects of fat content and cooking method." *Journal of the American Dietetic Association* 84(6):654–58. Effects of three fat levels on loss of fat and loss of water by cooking.

15. Bowers, J., J. A. Craig, D. H. Kropf, and T. J. Tucker. 1987. "Flavor, color and other characteristics of beef longissimus muscle heated to seven internal temperatures between 55° and 85°C." *Journal of Food Science* 52:533–36. Marked change in color, flavor, and juiciness between 60° and 65°C (140° to 149°F).

16. Bramblett, V. D., R. L. Hostetler, G. E. Vail, and H. N. Draudt. 1959. "Qualities of beef as affected by cooking at very low temperatures for long periods of time." *Food Technology* 13:707–11. Five muscles of the round cooked at 63°C (145°F) versus 68°C (154°F).

17. Buttkus, H. 1974. "On the nature of the chemical and physical bonds which contribute to some structural properties of protein foods: A hypothesis." *Journal of Food Science* 39:484–89. Bonding involved when protein foods are cooked.

18. Campion, D. R., J. R. Crouse, and M. E. Dikeman. 1975. "Predictive value of USDA beef quality grade factors for cooked meat palatability." *Journal of Food Science* 40:1225–28. Low predictive value for young steers.

19. Carlin, F., W. Zimmerman, and A. Sundbery. 1982. "Destruction of trichina larvae in beef-pork loaves cooked in microwave ovens." *Journal of Food Science* 47:1096–99, 1118. Live trichinae in 8 out of 30 loaves tested.

20. Carroll, R. J., F. P. Rorer, S. B. Jones, and J. R. Cavanaugh. 1978. "Effect of tensile stress on the ultrastructure of bovine muscle." *Journal of Food Science* 43:1181–87. Connective tissue and muscle fibers of raw and heated (90°C or 194°F) beef semitendinosus viewed by transmission and scanning electron microscopy.

21. Cassens, R. G., and C. C. Cooper. 1971. "Red and white muscle." *Advances in Food Research* 19:1–74. Characterization of the two types; importance to meat science.

22. Chang, S., and R. J. Peterson. 1977. "Symposium: The basis of quality in muscle foods. Recent developments in the flavor of meat." *Journal of Food Science* 42:298–305. Summary of current knowledge.

23. Cheng, C.-S., and F. C. Parrish. 1976. "Scanning electron microscopy of bovine muscle: Effects of heating on ultrastructure." *Journal of Food Science* 41:1449–54. Micrographs of longissimus muscle, raw and heated to 60°, 70°, and 80°C (140°, 158°, and 176°F).

24. Cheng, C. S., and F. C. Parrish. 1979. "Heat-induced changes in myofibrillar proteins of beef longissimus muscle." *Journal of Food Science* 44:22–25. Effects of internal temperature on proteins of thick and thin filaments and of Z-disks.

25. Cover, S. 1941. "Effect of metal skewers on cooking time and tenderness of beef." *Food Research* 6:233–38. Rate of heat penetration and tenderness of beef; heating curves during cooking.

26. Cover, S. 1943. "Effects of extremely low rates of heat penetration on tenderizing of beef." *Food Research* 8:388–94. Oven temperatures of 80°C (176°F) and 125°C (357°F) compared.

27. Cover, S., and R. L. Hostetler. 1960. "Beef tenderness by new methods: An examination of some theories." *Texas Agricultural Experiment Station Bulletin No. 947.* 24 pp. A review of theories; data on the effect of dry *vs.* moist heat and on the degree of doneness as it affects tenderness of loin and round steaks.

28. Cover, S., B. A. McLaren, and P. B. Peters. 1944. "Retention of the B-vitamins in rare and well-done beef." *Journal of Nutrition* 27:363–75. Rib roasts of beef analyzed for thiamin, riboflavin, niacin, and pantothenic acid.

29. Cross, H. R. 1977. "Effect of amount, distribution and texture of marbling on cooking properties of beef longissimus." *Journal of Food Science* 42:185–88. Cooking times of longissimus steaks differing widely in marbling.

30. Cross, H. R. 1979. "Effects of electrical stimulation on meat tissue and muscle properties. A review." *Journal of Food Science* 44:509–14. Summary of papers on the topic.

31. Cross, H. R., Z. L. Carpenter, and G. C. Smith. 1973. "Effects of intramuscular collagen and elastin on bovine muscle tenderness." *Journal of Food Science* 38:998–1003. Five muscles compared.

32. Culler, R. D., F. C. Parrish, Jr., G. C. Smith, and H. R. Cross. 1978. "Relationship of myofibrillar fragmentation index to certain chemical, physical and sensory characteristics of bovine longissimus dorsi." *Journal of Food Science* 43:1177–80. Sarcomere length, soluble collagen, and myofibrillar fragmentation as indices to tenderness.

33. Davey, C. L., and K. V. Gilbert. 1967. "Structural changes in meat during aging." *Journal of Food Technology* 2:57–59. Effects on the Z-line.

34. Davey, C. L., and K. V. Gilbert. 1974. "Temperature-dependent cooking toughness in beef." *Journal of the Science of Food and Agriculture* 25:931–38. Two phases of heat-induced toughening.

35. Davey, C. L., and A. E. Grafhaus. 1976. "Structural changes in beef muscle during aging." *Journal of the Science of Food and Agriculture* 27:301–6. Another attempt to learn what happens when meat is aged.

36. Dutson, T. R., and M. W. Orcutt. 1984. "Chemical changes in proteins produced by thermal processing." *Journal of Chemical Education* 61(4):303–7. Summary of the effects of heat on the proteins of muscle.

37. Egbert, W. R., D. L. Huffman, C. M. Chen, and D. P. Dylewski. 1991. "Development of low-fat ground beef." *Food Technology* 45(6):64–73. Rationale for modifications of the commercially available product.

38. Etherington, D. J. 1987. "Collagen and meat quality: Effects of conditioning and growth rate." In *Advances in Meat Research,* Vol. 4, *Collagen as a Food.* A. M. Pearson, T. R. Dutson, and A. J. Bailey, eds. New York: Van Nostrand Reinhold. Pp. 351–60. Only subtle changes due to conditioning.

39. Fox, J. B., Jr. 1966. "The chemistry of meat pigments." *Journal of Agricultural and Food Chemistry* 14:207–10. Fresh and cured meat pigments and the color of meat.

40. Giddings, G. G. 1977. "Symposium: The basis of quality in muscle foods. The basis of color in muscle foods." *Journal of Food Science* 42:288–94. A review; technical.

41. Ghorpade, V. M., and D. P. Cornforth. 1993. "Spectra of pigments responsible for pink color in pork roasts cooked to 65° or 82°C." *Journal of Food Science* 58:51–52, 89. Identification of the pigment in well-done pork.

42. Girard, B., J. Vanderstoep, and J. F. Richards. 1990. "Characterization of the

residual pink color in cooked turkey breasts and pork loin." *Journal of Food Science* 55:1249–54. Cytochrome C as a possible factor in appearance of pink color in well-done meat.

43. Griffiths, N. M., and R. L. S. Patterson. 1970. "Human olfactory response to 5-α-androst-16-ene-3-one—principal component of boar taint." *Journal of the Science of Food and Agriculture* 21:4–6. Odor thresholds of men *vs.* women.

44. Griswold, R. M. 1951. "Effect of heat on the nutritive value of proteins." *Journal of the American Dietetics Association* 27:85–95. A review article.

45. Griswold, R. M. 1956. "The effect of different methods of cooking beef round of commercial and prime grades." I. "Palatability and shear force values." *Food Research* 20:160–70. Braising, cooking in a pressure saucepan, and roasting at two oven temperatures.

46. Hamm, R., and F. E. Deatherage. 1960. "Changes in hydration, solubility and charges of muscle proteins during heating of meat." *Food Research* 25:587–610. An early study of the effects of heat on muscle proteins.

47. Harel, S., and J. Kanner. 1985. "Muscle membrane lipid peroxidation initiated by H_2O_2-activated metmyoglobin." *Journal of Agricultural and Food Chemistry* 33:1188–92. Evidence that heme is involved as well as iron.

48. Headley, M. E., and M. Jacobson. 1960. "Electronic and conventional cookery of lamb roasts." *Journal of the American Dietetics Association* 36:337–40. Cooking time, cooking losses, and palatability.

49. Heymann, H., H. B. Hedrick, M. A. Karrasch, M. K. Eggeman, and M. R. Ellersieck. 1990. "Sensory and chemical characteristics of fresh pork roasts cooked to different endpoint temperatures." *Journal of Food Science* 55:613–17. Endpoints of 65.6°, 71.1°, 76.7°, and 82.2°C (150°, 160°, 170°, and 180°F) compared.

50. Hoelscher, L. M., J. W. Savell, J. M. Harris, H. R. Cross, and K. S. Rhee. 1987. "Effect of initial fat level and cooking method on cholesterol content and calorie value of ground beef patties." *Journal of Food Science* 52:883–85. Fat levels of 0 to 30 percent compared.

51. Hornstein, I., and P. F. Crowe. 1963. "Meat flavor: Lamb." *Journal of Agricultural and Food Chemistry* 11:147–49. Source of the characteristic aroma of meats.

52. Hostetler, R. L., Z. L. Carpenter, C. C. Smith, and T. R. Dutson. 1975. "Comparison of postmortem treatments for improving tenderness of beef." *Journal of Food Science* 40:223–26. Two methods of hanging a carcass with and without preliminary conditioning at 16°C (61°F) prior to chilling.

53. Hostetler, R. L., and W. A. Landmann. 1968. "Photomicrographic studies of dynamic changes in muscle fiber fragments." 1. "Effects of various heat treatments on length, width, and birefringence." *Journal of Food Science* 33:468–70. Changes attributed to coagulation of proteins of the muscle fibers.

54. Hostetler, R. L., B. A. Link, W. A. Landmann, and H. A. Fitzhugh, Jr. 1973. "Effect of carcass suspension method on sensory panel scores for some major bovine muscles." *Journal of Food Science* 38:264–67. Nine muscles varying in connective tissue compared.

55. Hotchkiss, J. H., and R. G. Cassens. 1987. "Nitrate, nitrite and nitroso compounds in foods." *Food Technology* 41(4):127–34, 136. Nitroso compounds as carcinogens; limits on nitrites in bacon.

56. Hotchkiss, J. H., and A. J. Vecchio. 1985. "Nitrosamines in fried-out bacon fat and its use as a cooking oil." *Food Technology* 39(1):67–73. Fate of nitrosopyrrolidone.

57. Huang, W. H., and B. E. Green. 1978. "Effect of cooking method on TBA numbers of stored beef." *Journal of Food Science* 43:1201–3, 1209. Beef semitendinosus heated by roasting, braising, in a pressure saucepan, in a microwave oven, and by canning.

58. Hultin, H. O. 1984. "Postmortem biochemistry of meat and fish." *Journal of Chemical Education* 61:289–98. Structure and functioning of muscle in the live animal and postmortem changes that affect meat quality.

59. Huxley, H. E. 1958. "The contraction of muscle." *Scientific American* 199(5):67–82. The structure of striated muscle; electron micrographs and diagrams.

60. Huxley, H. E. 1969. "The mechanism of muscular contraction." *Science* 164: 1356–66. Details of the sliding filament theory.

61. Huxley, H. E. 1971. "The structural basis of muscular contraction." *Proceedings of the Royal Society B.* 178:131–49. The Croonian lecture on the topic.

62. Igene, J. O., K. Yamauchi, A. M. Pearson, J. I. Gray, and S. D. Aust. 1985. "Mechanism by which nitrite inhibits the development of warmed-over flavor (WOF) in cured meat." *Food Chemistry* 18:1–18. Three possible mechanisms proposed.

63. Industrywide Cooperative Meat Identification Standards Committee. 1973. *Uniform Meat Identity Standards.* National Live Stock and Meat Board. A proposal for standardizing the names and labeling of retail cuts of meat.

64. Janicki, M. A., J. Kortz, and J. Rozyczka. 1967. "Relationship of color with certain chemical and physical properties of porcine muscle." *Journal of Food Science* 32:375–78. The pH, water-holding capacity, and color.

65. Jones, S. B. 1977. "Ultrastructural characteristics of beef muscle." *Food Technology* 31(4):82–85. Beef semitendinosus muscle imaged by a scanning electron microscope.

66. Jones, S. B., R. J. Carroll, and J. R. Cavanaugh. 1977. "Structural changes in heated bovine muscle: A scanning electron microscope study." *Journal of Food Science* 42:125–31. Beef semitendinosus muscle heated at 50°, 60°, and 90°C (122°, 140°, and 194°F).

67. Kang, C. K., and E. E. Rice. 1970. "Degradation of various meat protein fractions by tenderizing enzymes." *Journal of Food Science* 35:563–65. Effects of collagenase, bromelain, trypsin, ficin, and Rhozyme P-11 on myofibrillar, sarcoplasmic, and stroma proteins.

68. Kang, C. K., and W. D. Warner. 1974. "Tenderization of meat with papaya latex proteases." *Journal of Food Science* 39: 812–18. Stability of the proteases to heat; substrates.

69. Kastner, C. L. 1983. "Optional hot processing systems for beef." *Food Technology* 37(5):96–100, 102. Electrical stimulation and feasibility of hot boning.

70. Koohmaraie, M., A. S. Babiker, R. A. Merkel, and T. R. Dutson. 1988. "Role of Ca^{++}-dependent proteinases and lysosomal enzymes in postmortem changes in bovine skeletal muscle." *Journal of Food Science* 53:1253–57. Evidence that supports the role of Ca^{++}-dependent enzymes.

71. Korschgren, B. M., and R. E. Baldwin. 1978. "Sensory qualities, cooking losses, shear values, and B-vitamins of beef roasts cooked by slow heat." *Home Economics Research Journal* 7:116–20. Top rounds braised in a portable oven broiler versus a household electric oven.

72. Korschgren, B. M., R. E. Baldwin, and S. Snider. 1976. "Quality factors in beef, pork, and lamb cooked by microwaves." *Journal of the American Dietetics Association* 69:635–39. Low- and high-powered ovens compared.

73. Kotula, A. W., K. D. Murrell, L. Acosta-Stein, L. Lamb, and L. Douglass. 1983. "Destruction of *Trichinella spiralis* during cooking." *Journal of Food Science* 48: 765–68. Effectiveness of a number of procedures including microwave cooking.

74. Laakkonen, E., J. W. Sherbon, and G. H. Wellington. 1970. "Low-temperature, long-time heating of bovine muscle." 3. "Collagenase activity." *Journal of Food Science* 35:181–83. Evidence for a collagenase-like enzyme in the water-soluble fraction.

75. Laakkonen, E., G. H. Wellington, and J. W. Sherbon. 1970. "Low-temperature, long-time heating of bovine muscle." 1. "Changes in tenderness, water-holding capacity, pH and amount of water-soluble components." *Journal of Food Science* 35:175–77. Effect of programmed, slow rise in internal temperature.

76. Leander, R. C., H. B. Hedrick, M. F. Brown, and J. A. White. 1980. "Comparison of structural changes in beef longissimus and semitendinosus muscle during cooking." *Journal of Food Science* 45:1–6, 12. Transmission and scanning electron microscopy

of muscle fibers and connective tissue heated at 177°C (350°F) to internal temperatures of 63°, 68°, and 73°C (145°, 154° and 163°F).

77. Lee, S. H., and R. G. Cassens. 1976. "Nitrite binding sites on myoglobin." *Journal of Food Science* 41:969–70. Evidence for the dinitrosyl structure of cooked cured meat pigment.

78. Light, N. D. 1987. "The role of collagen in determining the texture of meat." In *Advances in Meat Research*, Vol. 4, *Collagen as a Food*. A. M. Pearson, T. R. Dutson, and A. J. Bailey, eds. New York: Van Nostrand Reinhold. Pp. 87–107. A summary of the sometimes conflicting evidence of the role of collagen in meat quality.

79. Light, N., and E. Champion. 1984. "Characteristics of muscle epimysium, perimysium and endomysium collagen." *Biochemical Journal* 219:1017–26. Types of collagen in each.

80. Locker, R. H. 1984. "The role of the gap filaments in muscle and in meat." *Food Microstructure* 3:17–32. A lengthy review.

81. Lusby, M. L., J. F. Ridpath, F. C. Parrish, Jr., and R. M. Robson. 1983. "Effect of postmortem storage on degradation of the myofibrillar protein titin in bovine *longissimus* muscle." *Journal of Food Science* 48:1787–90, 1795. Evidence that conditioning degrades titin and nebulin.

82. Machlik, S. M., and H. N. Draudt. 1963. "The effect of heating time and temperature on the shear of beef semitendinosus muscle." *Journal of Food Science* 28: 711–18. Muscle heated at one degree intervals between 50° and 90°C (122° and 194°F).

83. MacLeod, G., and B. M. Coppock. 1976. "Volatile flavor components of beef boiled conventionally and by microwave radiation." *Journal of Agricultural and Food Chemistry* 24:835–42. Identification and characterization of the compounds.

84. Marsh, B. B. 1977. Symposium: "The basis of quality in muscle foods. The basis of tenderness in muscle foods." *Journal of Food Science* 42:295–97. A readable summary of the concept.

85. Marsh, B. B., and W. A. Carse. 1974. "Meat tenderness and the sliding-filament hypothesis." *Journal of Food Technology* 9:129–39. An attempt to account for the effects of shortening of the sarcomeres on tenderness.

86. Marsh, B. B., and N. G. Leet. 1966. "Studies in meat tenderness." III. "The effects of cold-shortening on tenderness." *Journal of Food Science* 31:450–59. The concepts of background and actomyosin toughness.

87. Meschi, E. P., E. L. Pippen, and H. Lineweaver. 1964. "Origin of hydrogen sulfide in heated chicken muscle." *Journal of Food Science* 29:393–99. Identification of the sulfur-containing precursor.

88. Meyer, B. H., W. F. Hinman, and E. G. Halliday. 1947. "Retention of some vitamins of the B-complex in beef during cooking." *Food Research* 12:203–11. Niacin and pantothenic acid retention in braised, broiled, and fried beef.

89. Miyada, D. S., and A. L. Tappel. 1956. "The hydrolysis of beef proteins by various proteolytic enzymes." *Food Research* 21:217–25. Enzymes and their substrates.

90. Morgan, J. B., C. R. Calkins, and R. W. Mandigo. 1988. "Effects of trim level, cooking method and chop type on lipid retention, caloric content and cholesterol level in cooked pork." *Journal of Food Science* 53:1602–9, 1630. Fat retention in cuts trimmed before or after cooking.

91. Murray, J. M., and A. Weber. 1974. "The cooperative action of muscle proteins." *Scientific American* 230(2):58–71. The assemblage of protein molecules in the muscle fiber; their interaction during contraction; illustrated.

92. Nobbs, C. L., H. C. Watson, and J. C. Kendrew. 1966. "Structure of deoxymyoglobin." *Nature* 209:339–41.

93. Noble, I., and L. Gomez. 1962. "Vitamin retention in meat cooked electronically. Thiamine and riboflavin in lamb and bacon." *Journal of the American Dietetics Association* 41:217–20. Meat cooked in microwave range at low setting and in conventional oven at 149°C (300°F).

94. Parrish, F. C., Jr., D. G. Olson, B. E. Minor, and R. E. Rust. 1973. "Effect of degree of marbling and internal temperature of doneness on beef rib steaks." *Journal of Animal*

Science 37:430–34. Three degrees of marbling and three internal temperatures compared.

95. Patterson, R. L. S. 1965. "5 α-androst-16-ene-3-one: Compound responsible for boar taint." *Journal of the Science of Food and Agriculture* 19:31–37. Identification of the compound.

96. Paul, P., L. Buchter, and A. Wierenga. 1966. "Solubility of rabbit muscle proteins after various time-temperature treatments." *Journal of Agricultural and Food Chemistry* 14:490–92. Longissimus dorsi muscle heated at five-degree intervals from 40° to 80°C (104° to 176°F) for up to 10 hours.

97. Paul, P. C., R. W. Mandigo, and V. H. Arthud. 1970. "Textural and histological differences among three muscles of the same cut of beef." *Journal of Food Science* 35:505–10. Longissimus dorsi, spinalis dorsi, and trapezius of beef rib compared.

98. Pearson, A. M., and T. R. Dutson. 1985. "Scientific basis for electrical stimulation." In *Advances in Meat Research,* Vol. 1. *Electrical Stimulation.* A. M. Pearson and T. R. Dutson, eds. Westport, CT: Avi Publishing Company, Inc. Pp. 185–218. Effects of electrical stimulation on muscle.

99. Penfield, M., and B. M. Meyers. 1975. "Changes in tenderness and collagen of beef semitendinosus muscle heated at two rates." *Journal of Food Science* 40:150–54. Heated at 93°C and 149°C to end points of 40°, 50°, 60°, and 70°C (104°, 122°, 140° and 158°F).

100. Penner, K. K., and J. A. Bowers. 1973. "Flavor and characteristics of conventionally and microwave reheated pork." *Journal of Food Science* 38:553–55. Flavor, moistness, and TBA values.

101. Penny, I. F., and F. Dransfield. 1979. "Relationship between toughness and troponin T in conditioned beef." *Meat Science* 3:135–41. Troponin T loss as meat is conditioned.

102. Pimentel, D., W. Dritschilo, J. Krummel, and J. Kutzman. 1975. "Energy and land constraints in food protein production." *Science* 190:754–61. Options for use of re-sources for meeting the world's food needs.

103. Pork Industry Board of the National Live Stock and Meat Board. 1993. *Facts about Pork.* Chicago: Pork Industry Group and the National Pork Board. P. 20. Microwaving pork.

104. Prusa, K. J., J. A. Love, and L. F. Miller. 1989. "Composition and sensory analysis of rib chops from pigs supplemented with porcine somatotropin (pSt)." *Journal of Food Quality* 12:455–65. Analyzed for crude fat, thiamin, and cholesterol; evaluated for tenderness, juiciness, and flavor.

105. Purslow, P. P. 1985. "The physical basis of meat texture: Observations on the fracture behaviour of cooked bovine *M. semitendinosus.*" *Meat Science* 12:39–60. Fracture patterns in response to stress; illustrated.

106. Ramsbottom, J. M., P. A. Goeser, and H. W. Schultz. 1951. "How light discolors meat: What to do about it." *Food Industries* 23(2):120–24, 222. Effect of display lighting on visual perception of meat color; instability of cured meat pigments to light.

107. Ramsbottom, J. M., and E. J. Strandine. 1948. "Comparative tenderness and identification of muscles in wholesale cuts of beef." *Food Research* 13:315–30. Tenderness (shear force) of 50 of the most important muscles of beef.

108. Ramsbottom, J. M., E. J. Strandine, and C. H. Koonz. 1945. "Comparative tenderness of representative beef muscles." *Food Research* 10:497–509. Histological rating for content of connective tissue and tenderness of raw and cooked tissue of 25 muscles of beef.

109. Ritchey, S. J., and R. L. Hostetler. 1964. "Relationship of free and bound water to subjective scores for juiciness and softness and to changes in weight and dimensions of steaks from two beef muscles during cooking." *Journal of Food Science* 29:413–19. Steaks from longissimus and biceps femoris heated to four internal temperatures from rare to well done.

110. Robson, R. M., and T. W. Huiatt. 1983. "Cytoskeletal proteins desmin, titin and neb-

ulin in muscle." *Reciprocal Meat Conference Proceedings* 36:116–24. Tentative location of the three in the sarcomere.

111. Savell, J. W., H. R. Cross, J. J. Francis, J. W. Wise, D. S. Hale, D. L. Welkes, and G. C. Smith. 1989. "National consumer retail beef study. Interaction of trim level, price and grade on consumer acceptance of beef steaks and roasts." *Journal of Food Quality* 12:251–74. Preference for meat severely trimmed.

112. Savell, J. W., G. C. Smith, and Z. L. Carpenter. 1978. "Beef quality and palatability as affected by electrical stimulation and cooler aging." *Journal of Food Science* 43:1666–68. Effects on aging time and tenderness.

113. Schmidt, J. G., and F. C. Parrish, Jr. 1971. "Molecular properties of postmortem muscle." 10. "Effect of internal temperature and carcass maturity on structure of bovine longissimus." *Journal of Food Science* 36:110–19. Light, phase, and transmission electron microscopic views of muscle heated to temperatures from 50°C to 90°C (122° to 194°F).

114. Schock, D. R., D. L. Harrison, and L. Anderson. 1970. "Effect of dry and moist heat treatments on selected beef quality factors." *Journal of Food Science* 35:195–98. Top round cooked by deep fat frying, roasting, and braising in a household oven and in a pressure saucepan.

115. Seideman, S. C., and H. R. Cross. 1983. "The economics and palatability attributes of hot boned beef: A review (advantages and disadvantages)." *Journal of Food Quality* 5:183–201. Summary of pros and cons.

116. Shimokomaki, M., D. F. Edsen, and A. J. Bailey. 1972. "Meat tenderness: Age related changes in bovine intramuscular collagen." *Journal of Food Science* 37:892–96. Stable and labile cross-links as influenced by age and by activity of muscle.

117. *Statistical Abstracts of the United States,* 1996. 116th edition. Washington, D.C. P. 147. Per-capita consumption of major food commodities: 1970–1994.

118. Trout, G. R. 1989. "Variation in myoglobin denaturation and color of cooked beef, pork and turkey meat as influenced by pH, sodium chloride, sodium tripolyphosphate and cooking temperature." *Journal of Food Science* 54:534–44. Elevation of denaturation temperature by high pH.

119. Smith, G. C., T. C. Arango, and Z. L. Carpenter. 1971. "Effects of physical and mechanical treatments on the tenderness of beef longissimus dorsi." *Journal of Food Science* 36:445–49. Methods of hanging the carcass and elevated cooling temperatures compared.

120. Smith, G. C., G. R. Culp, and Z. L. Carpenter. 1978. "Postmortem aging of beef carcasses." *Journal of Food Science* 43:823–26. Aging time for optimum tenderness of four major wholesale cuts of beef.

121. Stromer, M. H., and D. E. Goll. 1967. "Molecular properties of post-mortem muscle." 3. "Electron microscopy of myofibrils." *Journal of Food Science* 32:386–89. Effects of aging time and temperature on microscopic appearance.

122. Suzuki, A., D. E. Goll, I. Singh, R. E. Allen, R. M. Robson, and M. H. Stromer. 1976. "Some properties of purified skeletal muscle α-actinin." *Journal of Biological Chemistry* 251:6860–70. Substantiating evidence that α-actinin is present in the Z-line.

123. Tucker, R. E., W. F. Hinman, and E. G. Halliday. 1946. "The retention of thiamine and riboflavin in beef cuts during braising, frying and broiling." *Journal of the American Dietetics Association* 22:877–81. Heel of round, chuck, round steak, and loin compared.

124. Tucker, H. Q., H. M. Voegeli, and G. M. Wellington. 1952. *A Cross Sectional Muscle Nomenclature of the Beef Carcass.* 41 pp. East Lansing, MI: Michigan State College Press. Reproduction of tracings of the muscles in 39 retail cuts.

125. Vogle, C. A. 1969. "Some observations on the histology of cold-shortened muscle." *Journal of Food Technology* 4:275–81. Optical, transmission, and scanning electron microscopy of muscle cold shortened (2°C or 36°F) compared with muscle held at 18°C or 64°F.

126. Wang, K. 1985. "Sarcomere-associated cytoskeletal lattices in striated muscle." In *Cell and Muscle Motility.* Vol. 6. J. W. Shay, ed. London: Plenum Press. Pp. 315–69. Evidence for cytoskeletal structures; illustrated.

127. Wasserman, A. E. 1972. "Thermally produced flavor components in the aroma of meat and poultry." *Journal of Agricultural and Food Chemistry* 20:737–40. A review.

128. Wasserman, A. E., and A. M. Spinelli. 1972. "Effects of some water-soluble components on aroma of heated adipose tissue." *Journal of Agricultural and Food Chemistry* 20:171–74. Essential for development of aroma characteristic of meats from different animals.

129. Watkins, L. E., D. J. Jones, D. H. Mowery, D. B. Anderson, and E. L. Veenhuizen. 1990. "The effects of various levels of ractopamine hydrochloride on the performance and carcass characteristics of finishing swine." *Journal of Animal Science* 68:3588–95. Repartition of dietary energy from fat to lean.

130. Williams, J. R., and D. L. Harrison. 1978. "Relationship of hydroxyproline solubilized to tenderness of bovine muscle." *Journal of Food Science* 43:464–467, 492. Beef top round cooked in oven film bags at 94° and 194°C (201° and 381°F) to internal temperatures of 70° and 80°C (158° and 176°F).

131. Wilson, B. B., A. M. Pearson, and F. B. Shorland. 1976. "Effect of total lipids and phospholipids on warmed-over flavor in red and white muscles from several species as measured by TBA analysis." *Journal of Agricultural and Food Chemistry* 24:7–11. Beef, pork, lamb, and poultry compared.

132. Winegarden, M. W., B. Lowe, J. Kastelic, E. A. Kline, A. R. Plagge, and P. S. Shearer. 1952. "Physical changes in connective tissue of beef during heating." *Food Research* 17:172–84. Effect of heating on connective tissue and its relation to tenderness of cooked meat.

133. Younathan, M. T. 1985. "Causes and prevention of warmed-over flavor." *Reciprocal Meat Conference Proceedings* 38:74–80. Readable review of factors involved.

134. Young, C. A., A. E. Graafhaus, and C. L. Davey. 1980. "Postmortem changes in cytoskeletal proteins of muscle." *Meat Science* 5:41–55. Degradation of desmin as meat ages.

135. Zimmerman, W. J., and P. J. Beach. 1982. "Efficacy of microwave cooking procedures for devitalizing trichinae in pork roasts and chops." *Journal of Food Protection* 45:405–9. Procedures tested varied in effectiveness.

136. Ziprin, Y. A., and A. F. Carlin. 1976. "Microwave and conventional cooking in relation to quality and nutritive value of beef and beef soy loaves." *Journal of Food Science* 41:4–8. Cooking time, cooking losses, and thiamin retention.

Poultry

23

Poultry includes ducks, geese, guineas, pigeons, turkeys, and chickens. The last two account for the bulk of the poultry consumed. The annual per-capita consumption of ready-to-cook chicken has increased from 15 kilograms (32.5 pounds) in 1980 to 21.4 kilograms (49.5 pounds) in 1994, an increase of 52 percent (33). The increase in the per-capita consumption of turkey was lesser, from 4 kilograms (8 pounds) in 1980 to 6 kilograms (14.1 pounds) in 1994. De-emphasis on red meat and the availability of a dependable supply of ready-to-cook poultry on a year-round basis due to streamlined production and marketing procedures no doubt account for the spectacular increase in the use of poultry. Poultry products constitute an important source of farm income.

MARKET CLASSES OF POULTRY

The different classes of poultry are marketed on the basis of age. Age influences tenderness and fat content and so dictates the cooking methods that are appropriate. Signs of youth in poultry are smooth leg skin, supple wing joint, pliable keel or breast bone, and the presence of pin feathers. Young birds have no hairs on the skin and little subcutaneous fat. The weight of the bird varies with age. Rock Cornish hens are marketed at less than six weeks of age and at ready-to-cook weights of less than 1 kilogram (2 pounds). Broiler-fryer chickens are marketed at six to eight weeks and at ready-to-cook weights of 1 to 1½ kilograms (two to three pounds). Roasters weigh in at one to two kilograms (2½ to 4½ pounds) at 2½ to 5 months of age. A capon (unsexed male) may weigh from 2 to 4 kilograms (4 to 8 pounds) and is usually marketed under eight months of age. Birds nearing one year or older, called hens, laying hens, or fowl, may weigh from 1 to 2½ kilograms (2½ to 5½ pounds) or more when ready to cook. Very young broiler-fryer turkeys, under four months of age, weigh from two to four kilograms (4 to 8 pounds) ready-to-cook. Fully grown young turkeys suitable for roasting may weigh from 3 to 10 kilograms (6 to 24 pounds). Broiler-fryer ducklings, less than two months of age, and roasting duckling, under four months of age, weigh from 1 to 2 kilograms (2½ to 5 pounds). The ready-to-cook weight of goose may vary from 2 to 5 kilograms (4 to 12 pounds), of pigeon from 0.2 to 0.5 kilogram (½ to 1 pound), and of guinea from 0.3 to 0.6 kilogram (¾ to 1 ½ pounds).

PREPARING POULTRY FOR MARKET

Poultry is marketed ready-to-cook, i.e., head, feet, and entrails are removed. Birds are customarily fasted for eight hours prior to slaughter. They are killed by a method that minimizes struggle. The jugular vein is cut so that the bird bleeds well. As an aid to removing the feathers the bird is scalded, that is, dipped in hot water briefly. A dip in water at a temperature as low as 52° to 54°C (126° to 130°F) will loosen the feathers on chickens and turkeys without damaging the outer layer of skin (the cuticle). However, water at 59° to 60°C (138° to 140°F) and a scalding time of 45 seconds may be used (32). This is a few degrees lower than the minimum temperature (66°C or 150°F) recommended for water used to rinse dishes. Although this removes the cuticle and allows the flesh to show through the transparent skin below (particularly noticeable in frozen poultry), the higher temperature facilitates removal of feathers as well as pin feathers (feathers that have not quite emerged). Any time-saving technique is important in an enterprise in which profit is measured in fractions of a cent per pound. Feathers are removed from the scalded poultry by a machine equipped with rubberlike projections that rub or brush the feathers from the skin. Ducks and geese are scalded in water at 66° to 71°C (150° to 160°F) for 1½ to 2½ minutes. Water above 71°C (160°F) damages the skin of poultry.

Evisceration of the bird usually follows scalding and picking. The abdominal cavity is slit and the entrails removed. Head, feet, and oil gland are removed from the drawn bird. The weight after drawing is approximately ¾ that of the live bird.

The bird is chilled either before or after the entrails are removed. The latter is preferable from the standpoint of flavor. Also, prompt cooling is essential to control growth of bacteria that contaminate the bird. The use of a solution of trisodium phosphate as a spray or dip to follow chilling was approved by the U.S. Department of Agriculture in 1992 for use on chicken (3). This step, optional for the processor, reduces but does not eliminate bacterial contamination on the birds.

Chilling poultry is important for another reason. The time of onset of rigor, its duration, and the tenderness of the meat once rigor has passed are influenced by the way the bird is cooled (12). Muscle from poultry cooled rapidly in ice water is more tender than that from poultry cooled slowly in air (13). Prompt cooling from body temperature to 15°C (59°F) before the pH is lowered to 6.3 by accumulation of lactic acid is essential if toughening of the muscles is to be avoided (12, 22). Poultry goes into and out of rigor more rapidly than other meats. Aging longer than 24 hours results in no additional tenderizing (12). Weakening of the Z-line of breast muscle and lengthening of the sarcomeres of leg muscle were observed in poultry as a result of aging (19).

Eviscerated birds are marketed whole, disjointed, or less commonly, as halves or quarters. Parts are available boneless and skinless. A bird left whole usually costs a few cents less per pound, and disjointing is not difficult.

INSPECTION AND GRADING

Practically all poultry is now marketed in a ready-to-cook form. This means that the consumer has few if any clues as to the health of the bird and the wholesomeness of the meat. In a live bird signs of health (bright eyes, red comb, sleek feathers, and good posture) are easily recognized. Since 1971 inspection of all poultry has been mandatory. Federal inspection (USDA) is mandatory for poultry in interstate commerce. Inspection of poultry slaughtered and marketed intrastate may be done under the state system. A label or tag bearing a round purple stamp that says "Inspected for Wholesomeness by the United States Department of Agriculture" (Fig. 23-1) assures the consumer of the health of the bird and the sanitary conditions in the plant in which it was slaughtered (34).

Figure 23-1. This mark on poultry indicates that the bird has been inspected for wholesomeness. (Courtesy of the U.S. Department of Agriculture.)

Poultry that has been graded for quality as well as inspected for wholesomeness is available (34). Characteristics that are considered in assigning the grade are shape and meatiness, distribution of fat, and general appearance of the bird. Breaks in the skin, bruises, and pin feathers lower the grade. Quality grades for poultry are A, B, and C. Grade A and Grade B fryers are shown in Figure 23-2. A shield-shaped mark similar to the grading (or grade) mark for meats shows the quality of an inspected bird (Fig. 23-3). Poultry may be inspected without being graded but not the reverse. A combination grading (or grade) and inspection mark showing the market class may be used as a wing-tag.

HANDLING RAW POULTRY

Raw poultry, like other foods of animal origin, spoils readily. Poultry should be held in the coldest part of a refrigerator and cooked within two or three days. Frozen, raw poultry should be thawed in the refrigerator or in changes of *cold* water. Once thawed, it should be cooked promptly. The incidence of *Salmonella* on raw poultry is high, 34.8 percent in one study (14), so when raw poultry is handled cross-contamination of other foods may occur. Any surface contacted by poultry should be washed with warm water containing detergent and rinsed thoroughly. This includes knives, counters, and hands. Cutting boards should be rinsed with dilute chlorine bleach or other sanitizer. Without these precautions, food prepared subsequently may be contaminated. Hazards are great, for example, if ingredients such as those for a salad, uncooked before they are eaten, come in contact with contaminated surfaces. Rinsing poultry does not eliminate all of the bacteria that are present, but it is likely to spread contamination (36).

COMPOSITION AND STRUCTURE

Poultry is comparable to beef, lamb, and pork in composition and nutritive value (Table 23-1). The proteins in poultry, approximately ⅕ the edible portion, are of high quality. Poultry is a good source of iron and phosphorus. Poultry, like all lean meat, is a good source of B vitamins. Dark meat of chicken is richer in riboflavin than the light, but light meat is richer in niacin. The fat content varies with the age of the bird from under five percent in young chicken to near 25 percent in mature fowl. A feeding ration high in corn favors the deposition of fat. The fat content also varies with the type of poultry. It is higher in duck than in chicken and higher still in goose. Dark meat has more fat and more connective tissue than white; it also contains the pigment myoglobin missing from white meat. Xanthophyll and carotene in the feed are responsible for the yellow color of the fat of poultry.

Figure 23-2. Quality grades for ready-to-cook young chicken: (top) A quality; (bottom) B quality. (Courtesy of the U.S. Department of Agriculture.)

Figure 23-3. The USDA grade shield for use on poultry that has been graded for quality as well as inspected for wholesomeness. (Courtesy of the U.S. Department of Agriculture.)

The muscles of poultry, like those of beef, pork, and lamb, are constructed of muscle fibers and connective tissue. The fibers consist of thick (myosin) and thin (actin) contractile myofilaments, with the associated regulatory proteins, tropomyosin and the troponins. The myofilaments of the cytoskeleton consist mainly of the proteins, titin, nebulin, and desmin.

COOKING POULTRY

Principles for cooking poultry are basically those for cooking meat. The cooking method is selected on the basis of the tenderness of the poultry and its fat content, both influenced mainly by the age of the bird. Young, tender birds are cooked by methods recommended for tender cuts of meat and older and less tender birds by methods suitable for less tender meat. In addition to altering the appearance and flavor, heat alters the texture of poultry. Denaturation of myosin is completed at 60°C (140°F), that of the sarcoplasmic proteins at 70°C (158°F) and denaturation of actin is completed at 80°C (176°F) (23). Denaturation of the collagen occurs when the temperature reaches 66°C (151°F), at which point shrinkage of the network of perimysial connective occurs. Additional heating is required to convert the collagen to soluble gelatin.

Methods

Young tender poultry can be cooked by broiling. Halves, quarters, or pieces are placed on a broiler rack, skin side down to prevent the flesh from sticking to the rack. The uppermost surface may be basted with melted fat or oil to keep the meat from drying out, because young birds tend to have little fat. When broiler halves were heated to an internal temperature of 95°C (203°F) in the breast muscle, at broiling temperatures of 177°C (350°F), 190°C (375°F), and 204°C (400°F), the lowest temperature gave broilers somewhat closer to optimum doneness (18). As was pointed out in the chapter on meat, doneness is influenced not only by the temperature attained but also by the length of the heating period.

Because of the small amount of fat present, frying and deep-fat frying are particularly suitable methods for cooking young tender poultry. Coating serving-sized pieces with flour or dipping in batter before frying yields a crisp crust. Pieces coated with flour and rolled in fat and placed in a shallow baking pan may be oven-fried at 177° to 204°C (350° to 400°F). Broiled and fried poultry should be turned with tongs rather than a fork to avoid loss of juices.

Somewhat older but still immature birds are suitable for roasting. They are still tender but have more fat than a fryer or broiler. Capons are usually roasted. The bird, as it cooks breast side up on a rack, may be basted with drippings that accumulate in the roasting pan or with melted table fat, rendered chicken fat, or salad oil. An oven temperature

TABLE 23-1
Composition and Nutritive Value of Selected Poultry (100-gram edible portion)

Food	Water (%)	Calories[a]	Protein (g)	Fat (g)	Carbohydrates (g)	Calcium (mg)	Phosphorus (mg)	Iron (mg)	Vitamin A Value (I.U.)	Thiamin (mg)	Riboflavin (mg)	Niacin (mg)	Ascorbic Acid (mg)
Chicken, broiler-fryer													
Breast	69.5	172	20.9	9.3	.0	11	174	0.7	83	.06	.09	9.9	1.0
Breast, meat only	74.8	110	23.1	1.2	.0	11	196	0.7	21	.07	.09	11.2	1.2
Drumstick, with skin	72.5	161	19.3	8.7	.0	11	154	1.0	95	.07	.18	5.4	2.7
Thigh, with skin	67.7	211	17.3	15.3	.0	10	145	1.0	145	.06	.15	5.4	2.3
Liver	73.6	125	18.0	3.9	3.4	11	272	8.6	20,549	.14	1.96	9.3	33.8
Gizzard	76.2	118	18.2	4.2	.6	8	135	3.5	217	.02	.18	4.7	3.2
Chicken, stewing	61.8	258	17.6	20.3	.0	10	172	1.0	178	.11	.17	6.3	2.4
Turkey, young hen	69.5	168	20.2	9.1	.0	15	175	1.6	4	.06	.16	3.8	0.0
Turkey, young tom	71.0	154	20.5	7.4	.0	15	180	1.4	7	.07	.15	4.3	0.0
Duck, domesticated	48.5	404	11.5	40.0	.0	11	139	2.4	168	.20	.21	3.9	2.8
Goose	49.7	371	15.9	33.6	.0	12	234	2.5	55	.09	.25	3.6	—[b]

[a] 1 kilocalorie = 4.185 kilojoules.
[b] — = Data not available.
Source: U.S. Dept. Agr. Handbook No. 8-5. Composition of Foods. Poultry Products. Raw, Processed, Prepared. Revised 1979, 1989 supplement.

of 163°C (325°F) is most often recommended for roasting poultry. The bird may be trussed before it is put into the oven. A foil wrap on a large bird such as turkey prolongs roasting time and in one study resulted in less juicy meat than in an open pan, the cooking method preferred by the taste panel (11). In another study, however, dark muscle cooked in foil had more moisture than that cooked in an open pan, in ovenproof film, or paper bag, and light meat had more moisture cooked in open pan or in foil (20). Cooking time was longest in a paper bag, more browning occurred, and dark meat was more tender cooked in either an open pan or paper bag. The four treatments made no difference in tenderness of light meat.

Stuffing a bird prior to roasting is not recommended. Poultry has been implicated in outbreaks of foodborne illness traced to *Staphylcoccus* and *Salmonella* organisms. Temperature of the stuffing rises slowly and microorganisms multiply during the warm-up. A major portion of the roasting period serves as an incubator for microbial growth, including that of any pathogens present, and increases the hazards should the stuffing fail to reach lethal temperature (8).

A microwave oven is not recommended for cooking poultry. The high incidence of pathogens on poultry, the nonuniform distribution of microwaves in the oven and the nonuniform response to microwaves of constituents in poultry make microwave cooking of poultry risky. Two studies (2, 25), one with chicken and the other with turkey, showed that pathogens such as *Clostridium perfringens, Staphylococcus aureus,* and *Salmonella* can survive microwave cooking.

For mature birds moist-media methods allow time to tenderize the meat without its becoming dry. Stewing (simmering) whole birds in water and braising disjointed ones are common practices. Smothering and fricasseeing are modifications of braising. Braising may be done in a covered pan on a surface unit or in an oven at 163°C (325°F).

Fatty tissue from the body cavity and under the skin, especially of older birds, may be cut into small pieces and rendered over low heat to expel the fat. This may be used to baste broiled or roasted poultry, to make sauce for creamed chicken, to brown chicken for braising, or as part of the fat for frying. The crisp tissue that remains can be used in the same way as bacon bits.

Doneness of Poultry

Poultry is cooked to the well-done stage. The juice should be free of pink color. Cooking times given in timetables serve as a guide to the length of time to cook poultry. A flexible knee joint in a bird stewed whole or one that is roasted is a sign that the meat is tender. The internal temperature may be used as an index to doneness, too, if thigh or breast muscle is large enough to cover the bulb of a thermometer. In one study, optimum doneness was achieved by roasting turkey halves at 163°C (325°F) to an end-point temperature of 95°C (203°F) in the thigh muscle or 90°C (194°F) in the breast muscle (17). The meat was considered underdone when the internal temperature was five degrees lower than specified in either muscle. On the other hand, whole turkeys weighing 16 to 21 pounds as purchased were considered neither undercooked nor overdone when they were roasted in an oven at 163°C (325°F) to an end-point temperature in the thigh of 85°C (185°F) (21). In a third study, whole turkeys roasted at 163°C (325°F) to an end-point temperature in the thigh of 82°C (180°F) were considered overall more desirable than were those foil-wrapped and cooked either at 232°C (450°F) to an end-point temperature of 82°C

(180°F) in the thigh or at 93°C (200°F) to a temperature in the thigh of 73°C (163°F) (7). In the last study birds were of three weight classes that ranged from 12 to 24 pounds.

Cooking Losses

Losses for young, tender chicken cooked by five methods increase in the following order: baking, broiling, microwaving, panfrying, and pressurized deep-fat frying (31). Total cooking losses are essentially the same whether boneless turkey breasts are roasted in a conventional, a forced convection, or a microwave oven (10).

Cooking appears to have little effect on the total retention of vitamin B_6 of poultry, although the proportions of the three forms of this vitamin differ in the cooked version compared to the raw (6). Retention of riboflavin (90%) is higher than that of thiamin (80%) (5).

Frozen Poultry

Frozen poultry to be broiled, fried, or roasted may be thawed at least partially and in the refrigerator. Thawing time varies from one day for a small (four-pound) bird to three days for a turkey that weighs 20 pounds. Frozen poultry may be thawed at room temperature if the bird in its plastic wrap is overwrapped with a double-walled paper bag, which keeps the thawed exterior cool. Thawed this way a four- to six-pound bird thaws in approximately 15 hours and a 12 to 20 pound bird in up to 20 hours at 21°C (70°F) or above (24). Thawing of frozen poultry sealed in the freezing wrap may be speeded also by placing the sealed package in changes of cold (not warm) water. Approximate thawing times in cold water are one to two hours for a four-pound chicken and eight hours for a 20-pound turkey. Once thawed, poultry should not be refrozen.

When frozen young chickens are cooked, discoloration may occur in the meat next to the larger bones (15). Freezing and thawing release hemoglobin from the red cells in the bone marrow. The porosity of bones in young chickens allows seepage of the pigment into the flesh next to the bones. Heating denatures the pigment and this is responsible for the discoloration. Darkening is not a problem in older birds because the bones are more dense. No completely satisfactory way to prevent this discoloration in frozen young birds has been found.

Flavor of Cooked Poultry

Volatile carbonyls are responsible for the chickeny aroma of cooked poultry (28). Without them, the sulfur compounds that are present give only a meaty or beeflike aroma. Hydrogen sulfide is a prominent constituent (30).

Freshly cooked poultry has a higher meaty-brothy taste and a higher aroma than that reheated after frozen storage. The latter tastes stale and somewhat rancid in comparison, but somewhat less so when reheated in a microwave oven as opposed to a conventional one (4).

YIELD

The edible portion of turkey and of roasting chicken and hen is 73 percent of the ready-to-cook weight. In broiler-fryer chickens the percentage of bone and refuse averages somewhat higher (32 percent). One pound of ready-to-cook poultry will yield approximately two servings.

Cooked poultry that is leftover should be cooled promptly and refrigerated at 4°C (40°F) or lower. If leftovers are not chilled promptly, they should be reheated to 74°C (165°F) before they are eaten. Unless the chilled product will be eaten within two or three days, it should be frozen and held at −18°C (0°F).

A pink color is observed occasionally in well done poultry, especially noticeable in white meat, after it has been refrigerated. Attempts to identify the pigment (1, 9, 16), observed also in refrigerated, cooked pork loin, are summarized in Chapter 22.

Cooked poultry is more susceptible to oxidative rancidity than is red meat (35). Oxidation of the polyunsaturated fatty acids (many with 4–6 double bonds) that are present in the phospholipids of poultry meat are the source of compounds (e.g., malonaldehyde) that contribute to the rancid odor of the cooked product (29). Chicken meat is less susceptible to this warmed-over flavor than is that of turkey because the chicken deposits more tocopherol in fatty tissue (27). The warmed-over flavor, detectable in refrigerated, cooked poultry, is intensified when the product is reheated. Turkey reheated by microwaves was reported to have less warmed-over flavor than that reheated conventionally (4). Turkey rolls reheated in a forced convection oven had better flavor than did those reheated in either an infrared or a microwave oven (10). Even better were those reheated in broth or in starch-thickened sauce.

REFERENCES

1. Ahn, D. O., and A. J. Maurer. 1990. "Poultry meat color: Kinds of heme pigments and concentration of the ligands." *Poultry Science* 69:150–65. Identification of complex-forming ligands.

2. Alexio, J. A. G., B. Swaminathan, K. S. Jamesen, and D. E. Pratt. 1985. "Destruction of pathogenic bacteria in turkeys roasted in microwave ovens." *Journal of Food Science* 50: 873–75, 880. Pathogens tested: *Staphylococcus aureus, Salmonella,* and *Clostridium perfringens.*

3. Anonymous. 1993. "Salmonella reduction process receives approval." *Food Technology* 47(1):110. Dip or spray to reduce bacterial contamination of poultry.

4. Bowers, J. 1972. "Eating quality, sulfhydryl content and TBA values of turkey breast muscle." *Journal of Agricultural and Food Chemistry* 20:706–8. Fresh cooked and that reheated conventionally and by microwaves compared.

5. Bowers, J., and B. A. Fryer. 1972. "Thiamin and riboflavin in cooked and frozen reheated turkey." *Journal of the American Dietetics Association* 60:399–401.

Heating in a microwave and a gas oven compared.

6. Bowers, J., and J. Craig. 1978. "Components of vitamin B_6 in turkey breast muscle." *Journal of Food Science* 43:1619–21. Effects of cooking.

7. Bramblett, V. D., and K. W. Fugate. 1967. "Choice of cooking temperature for stuffed turkeys. Part I. Palatability factors." *Journal of Home Economics* 59:180–85. Three oven temperatures and two internal temperatures in the thigh compared.

8. Castellani, A. G., R. R. Clarke, M. I. Gibson, and D. F. Meisner. 1953. "Roasting time and temperature required to kill food poisoning microorganisms introduced experimentally into turkeys." *Food Research* 18:131–38. Factors affecting attainment in stuffing of temperature lethal for food poisoning microorganisms.

9. Cornforth, D. P., F. Vahabzadeh, C. E. Carpenter, and D. T. Bartholomew. 1986. "Role of reduced hemochromes in pink color defect of cooked turkey rolls." *Journal of Food Science* 51:1132–35. Attempt to account for pink color in the cooked product.

10. Cremer, M. L., and S. K. Hartley. 1988. "Sensory quality of turkey rolls roasted at two temperatures and reheated in varying sauces in three types of institutional ovens." *Journal of Food Science* 53:1605–9. Forced convection, infrared, and microwave ovens compared.

11. Deethardt, D., L. M. Burrill, K. Schneider, and C. W. Carlson. 1971. "Foil-covered vs. open-pan procedures for roasting turkey." *Journal of Food Science* 36:624–25. Juiciness, tenderness, flavor, and cooking losses reported.

12. De Fremery, D. 1966. "Relationship between chemical properties and tenderness of poultry muscle." *Journal of Agricultural and Food Chemistry* 14:214–17. Relation of post mortem handling, metabolic changes, and tenderness of poultry.

13. Dodge, J. W., and W. J. Stadelman. 1959. "Post mortem aging of poultry and its effect on the tenderness of breast muscle." *Food Technology* 13:81–83. Cooling in air and in water at the same temperature and in ice water compared.

14. Duitschaever, C. L. 1977. "Incidence of salmonella in retail raw cut-up chicken." *Journal of Food Protection* 40:191–92. Slightly more than 1/3 of samples contaminated.

15. Ellis, C., and J. G. Woodruff. 1959. "Prevention of darkening in frozen broilers." *Food Technology* 13:533–38. Review of causes and treatment to prevent darkening; illustrated.

16. Girard, B., J. Vanderstoep, and J. F. Richard. 1990. "Characterization of the residual pink color in cooked turkey breast and pork loin." *Journal of Food Science* 55:1249–54. Cytochrome C possibly involved.

17. Goertz, G. E., K. Cooley, M. E. Ferguson, and D. L. Harrison. 1960. "Doneness of frozen and defrosted turkey halves roasted to several end point temperatures." *Food Technology* 14:135–38. Flavor, tenderness, juiciness, and doneness of birds roasted to different end point temperatures.

18. Goertz, G. E., D. Meyer, B. Weathers, and A. S. Hooper. 1964. "Effect of cooking temperature on broiler acceptability." *Journal of the American Dietetics Association* 45:526–29. Three broiler temperatures and three oven temperatures compared.

19. Hay, J. D., R. W. Currie, F. H. Wolfe, and E. J. Sanders. 1973. "Effects of postmortem aging on chicken muscle fibrils." *Journal of Food Science* 38:981–86. Electron micrographs of breast and leg muscles 0, 3, 48, and 162 hours postmortem.

20. Heine, N., J. Bowers, and P. G. Johnson. 1973. "Eating quality of half turkey hens cooked by four methods." *Home Economics Research Journal* 1:210–14. Open pan, oven-proof film, foil wrap, and paper bag compared.

21. Hoke, I. M., and M. K. Kleve. 1966. "Heat penetration, quality and yield of turkeys roasted to different internal thigh temperatures." *Journal of Home Economics* 58:381–84. Three endpoint temperatures compared.

22. Kahn, A. W. 1971. "Effect of temperature during post-mortem glycolysis and dephosphorylation of high energy phosphates on poultry meat tenderness." *Journal of Food Science* 36:120–21. Importance of temperature when muscle goes into rigor.

23. Kijowski, J. M., and M. G. Mast. 1988. "Thermal properties of chicken broiler tissue." *Journal of Food Science* 53:303–6. Denaturation temperatures of the proteins of dark and light meat.

24. Klose, A. A., and H. H. Palmer. 1968. "Thawing turkeys at ambient air temperature." *Food Technology* 22(10):108–12. Thawing of plastic-bagged birds overwrapped in double-walled paper bag at 13°, 21° and 29°C (55°, 70°, and 85°F).

25. Lindsay, R. E., W. A. Krissinger, and B. F. Fields. 1986. "Microwave vs. conventional oven cooking of chicken. Relationship of internal temperature to surface contamination by *Salmonella typhimurium*." *Journal of the American Dietetics Association* 86:373–74. Survival of organisms on more than half the birds heated to 85°C (185°F) by microwaves.

26. McNeil, M., and M. P. Penfield. 1983. "Turkey quality as affected by ovens of varying energy costs." *Journal of Food Science* 48:853–55. Conventional, forced convection, and microwave ovens compared.

27. Mecchi, E. P., M. F. Pool, G. A. Behman, M. Hamachi, and A. A. Klose. 1956. "The role of tocopherol content in the comparative stability of chicken and turkey fat." *Poultry Science* 35:1238–46. Greater deposition of tocopherol in chicken muscle.

28. Minor, L. J., A. M. Pearson, L. E. Dawson, and B. S. Schweigert. 1965. "Chicken flavor: The identification of some chemical components and the importance of sulfur compounds in the cooked volatile fraction." *Journal of Food Science* 30:686–96. Contribution of carbonyls and sulfur compounds.

29. Pikul, J., D. E. Leszczynski, and F. A. Kummerow. 1984. "Relative role of phospholipids, triacylglycerols, and cholesterol esters on malonaldehyde formation in fat extracted from chicken meat." *Journal of Food Science* 49:704–8. Unsaturated fatty acids of phospholipids the main source of warmed-over flavor.

30. Pippen, E. L., and E. P. Mecchi. 1969. "Hydrogen sulfide a direct and potentially indirect contributor to cooked chicken aroma." *Journal of Food Science* 34:443–46. Importance of H_2S.

31. Proctor, V. A., and E. E. Cunningham. 1983. "Composition of broiler meat as influenced by cooking method and coating." *Journal of Food Science* 48:1696–99. Five methods compared.

32. Shannon, W. G., W. W. Marion, and W. J. Stadelman. 1957. "Effect of temperature and time of scalding on the tenderness of breast meat of chicken." *Food Technology* 11:284–85. Interrelation of scalding time and temperature and tenderness.

33. *Statistical Abstracts of the United States:* 1996. 116th edition. Washington, D.C. P. 147. Per-capita consumption of major food commodities: 1970–1994.

34. United States Department of Agriculture. Consumer and Marketing Service. 1971. *Inspection, Labeling, and Care of Meat and Poultry.* Agr. Handbook 416. 46 pp.

35. Wilson, B. R., A. M. Pearson, and F. B. Shorland. 1976. "Effect of total lipids and phospholipids on warmed-over flavors in red and white muscle from several species as measured by thiobarbituric acid analysis." *Journal of Agricultural and Food Chemistry* 24:7–11. Chicken, turkey, beef, pork, and mutton analyzed.

36. Woodburn, M. 1989. "Myth: Wash poultry before cooking." *Dairy, Food and Environmental Sanitation* 9:65–67. Greater chance for cross-contamination.

Seafood

24

Seafoods are an excellent source of protein of high quality. They provide an appreciable share of the available food protein worldwide. The annual commercial world catch of fish (marine and fresh water) has approached 100 million metric tons (live weight) in recent years (31). Cultured fish supply an increasing share of the U.S. market, aquatic farming accounting for an estimated 11 percent of the edible fish and shellfish in the U.S. (17).

Although several thousand species of fish exist, only about 200 are of commercial importance. Some species are underutilized, but others are heavily exploited. The typical consumer in the United States is familiar with only a few species. Those six species most frequently served, according to a recent survey, are the same six species reported in a similar survey done in 1950 (24). Cultural factors, in addition to economic ones, influence the acceptability of seafoods and their place in the diet (20). Annual per capita consumption of fish (fresh, frozen, canned, and cured) is approximately 6.8 kilograms (15 pounds) edible meat (31).

TYPES OF FISH

To bring some order to the great number of species (30), fish are sometimes classed on the basis of anatomical differences, for example, as fish with vertebrae and fins or shellfish. Fin fish can be grouped further into lean (fat content under five percent) and fat fish (fat content 5 to 20%). Bass, flounder, halibut, perch, and sole are examples of lean fish. Fat fish include albacore, herring, mackerel, salmon (Chinook and red), shad, sardines, smelt, and tuna. Fin fish are also classified on the basis of the kind of water in which they spend their adult lives as either fresh or salt water types.

Such broadbased categories of fin fish are of little help to the consumer who is unlikely to be familiar with the edible quality of most species. Work is in progress to formulate marketing categories for fish based on edibility characteristics, irrespective of species (19). Of eight edibility characteristics tentatively considered, two—flavor and flakiness—are considered of primary importance. Ultimately, categories could be adopted reflecting various combinations of strength of flavor from mild to strong and texture from flaky to nonflaky. Aspects of the texture of 17 species of North American fish and their flavor profiles have been determined as a basis for the adoption of informative marketing categories (21).

Shellfish have, instead of a skeleton, a hard shell on the outside of the soft tissues. The crustaceans, one group of shellfish, are encased in a chitinous armor that, being segmented,

426

gives the creatures freedom for locomotion. Crabs, crayfish, lobsters, prawn, and shrimp are such. Mollusks constitute another group of shellfish. These creatures have a soft, un-segmented body in a calcified shell. Most mollusks are bivalves. Included are abalone, clams, mussels, oysters, and scallops. The snail is a mollusk although not a bivalve. Other mollusks include octopus, squid, and periwinkle.

COMPOSITION AND NUTRITIVE VALUE

Composition of representative fish is given in Table 24-1. Fish are an excellent source of protein. They are interchangeable with meat in both quantity and quality of protein. Shellfish have a slightly sweet taste due to glycogen, which in meat and poultry is found in the liver only. Salt water fish contain iodine. Fish are an excellent source of phosphorus but are low in iron compared with red meats. Fish, like meats, are low in calcium. Canned salmon is the exception because the fish is processed long enough to weaken the bones so they are edible. Fish with vertebrae tend to be lower in thiamin, riboflavin, and niacin than are red meats. The fat in most fish is highly unsaturated. Salt water species are known to contain both n-3 and n-6 polyunsaturated fatty acids, and the ratio of the two types (n-3/n-6) is especially favorable (above 10) for sea bass, cod, haddock, herring, sardines, and smelt (10). Fresh water fish (eight species from Lake Superior) are excellent sources of polyunsaturated fatty acids, although the n-3/n-6 ratio is not as favorable as is that in certain salt water species (32).

PURCHASING FISH

Market Forms

Fresh and frozen fin fish can be purchased in the round (whole fish as landed), drawn (entrails removed), dressed (minus entrails, head, tail, fins and scales), as steaks (cross section from 1¼ to 2.5 cm or ½ to 1 inch thick), and as fillets (slices parallel to the backbone). Clams, oysters, and mussels purchased in the shell should be alive, as indicated by a tightly closed shell or one that closes when tapped lightly. Crabs and lobsters uncooked in the shell should be alive, evidenced by movement of the legs. These crustaceans are available cooked in the shell or as meat. Shrimp may be purchased in the shell or peeled (raw or cooked). Clams, scallops, and oysters are available shucked. Oysters are surrounded by a slightly milky or light gray liquor. Surimi-based shellfish analogs, such as crab or shrimp, are fabricated products (13). The deboned, minced flesh of fin fish, typically Alaskan pollock, is washed free of all constituents except actomyosin, the basic ingredient in surimi. Actomyosin, with the addition of flavoring, a cryoprotectant (4% sucrose and 4% sorbitol are included if the product is to be frozen), plus egg white and starch (both optional) are used to fabricate structures that simulate the texture and chewiness of the fibers of shellfish. Most shellfish are available in a breaded, frozen form. Tuna, salmon, sardines, and mackerel are marketed canned, as are clams. Cured fish, either salted or smoked, include herring, mackerel, salmon, chub, and whitefish.

Freshness in Fish

Fish and shellfish are highly perishable foods, and icing or refrigeration is essential for marketing high-quality raw or lightly processed products. Both odor and appearance are clues to freshness. The sniff test is a readily available way to tell whether the fish has been

TABLE 24-1
Composition of Representative Fish (100-gram edible portion, raw)

	Water (%)	Calories[a]	Protein (g)	Carbo-hydrate (g)	Lipid (g)	Calcium (mg)	Phos-phorus (mg)	Iron (mg)	Vitamin A Value (I.U.)	Thiamin (mg)	Ribo-flavin (mg)	Niacin (mg)	Ascorbic Acid (mg)
Fin fish													
Bass, striped	79.2	97	17.7	0	2.3	—[b]	—	0.8	—	—	—	—	—
Catfish	76.4	116	18.2	0	4.3	40	213	1.0	—	.05	.11	2.14	—
Cod	81.2	82	17.8	0	0.7	16	203	0.4	40	.08	.07	2.06	1.0
Haddock	79.9	87	18.9	0	0.7	33	188	1.1	55	.04	.04	3.80	—
Halibut	77.9	110	20.8	0	2.3	47	222	0.8	155	.06	.07	5.85	—
Herring, Pacific	71.5	195	16.4	0	13.9	—	—	1.1	106	—	—	—	—
Mackerel, Atlantic	63.6	205	18.6	0	13.9	12	217	1.6	165	.18	.31	9.08	0.4
Ocean perch, Atlantic	78.7	94	18.6	0	1.6	107	216	0.9	40	—	.11	2.00	—
Orange roughy	75.9	69	14.7	0	0.7	—	—	0.2	—	—	—	—	—
Salmon, pink	76.4	196	19.9	0	3.5	—	—	0.8	118	—	—	—	—
Smelt	78.8	97	17.6	0	3.4	60	230	0.9	—	—	.12	1.45	—
Snapper	76.9	100	20.5	0	1.3	32	198	0.2	—	.05	.003	0.28	—
Swordfish	75.6	121	19.8	0	4.0	4	263	0.8	119	.04	.10	9.68	1.1
Trout, rainbow	71.5	118	20.6	0	3.4	67	250	1.9	65	.07	.19	—	3.6
Tuna, yellowfin	71.0	108	23.4	0	1.0	16	191	0.7	59	.43	.05	9.80	—
Shellfish													
Abalone	74.6	105	17.1	6.0	0.8	31	—	3.2	—	—	—	—	—
Clam	81.8	74	12.8	2.6	1.0	46	169	14.0	300	—	.21	1.77	—
Crab, king	79.6	84	18.3	—	0.6	47	219	0.6	24	.04	.04	1.10	—
Lobster, northern	76.8	90	18.8	0.5	0.9	—	—	—	—	—	.05	1.46	—
Oyster, eastern	84.1	69	7.1	3.9	2.5	45	139	6.7	—	—	.17	1.31	—
Shrimp	75.9	106	20.3	0.9	1.7	52	205	2.4	—	.03	.03	2.55	—

[a]1 kilocalorie = 4.185 kilojoules.
[b]— = Data not available or too low to measure (ascorbic acid).
Source: U.S.D.A. Agr. Handbook No. 8-15. Fin fish and Shellfish Products. Composition of Foods. Raw, Processed, Prepared. 1987, 1990 supplement.

temperature abused or too long out of water. The surface of a freshly caught fish is shiny, iridescent, and covered with a moist, transparent film. The eyes are full and bright, the pupils jet black, and the corneas transparent. Gills are bright pink. The flesh, once rigor has passed, springs back and does not pit when pressed with the finger. The flesh is translucent when cut, and shimmering rather than dull and milky appearing. A fresh fish has a not unpleasant odor described as seaweedy in contrast to the dead-fish odor of one too long out of water. Evidence indicates that the flesh of freshly caught fish is sterile (22). Spoilage occurs rapidly in fish that is not drawn promptly because of powerful digestive enzymes, but bacterial spoilage does not begin until the fish has gone into and passed out of rigor. Rigor takes place sooner and is of shorter duration in fish than in mammals. The onset of rigor can be delayed and the period of rigor prolonged by minimizing the struggling that the fish does and by prompt chilling once the fish is dead. Either will prolong the period of freshness. Halibut has a long rigor and it stores better than most fish.

Marine microorganisms are in the slime, the gills, and the intestinal tract of fish (22). Most marine bacteria that cause fish to spoil grow best at 10° to 20°C (50° to 68°F). In fact most can grow at 0°C (32°F) and some flourish at −7.5°C (18.5°F). Nevertheless, lowering the temperature of fish from 10° to 0°C (50° to 32°F) delays the beginning of the rapid growth phase for the microorganisms that are present and cuts the spoilage rate by a factor of five to six (27). Even so, as a rule fish can be kept in good condition by icing for not more than a week to 10 days. When fresh fish is purchased, it should be refrigerated (near 0°C or 32°F) promptly. If fish is to be kept for more than a few days, other means of preservation must be utilized.

ISSUES OF SAFETY IN SEAFOOD CONSUMPTION

Seafoods were the cause of 10.5 percent of the outbreaks of foodborne illness reported to the Centers for Disease Control during a recent 10-year period (14). Safe consumption of seafood involves being aware of potential hazards and taking elementary precautions to avoid them.

Marine Toxins

Under certain circumstances, both fish and shellfish may contain toxins (29). Scombroid fish poisoning is caused by histamine, a toxic amine produced in fish by microorganisms when fish is temperature abused. Prompt icing or refrigeration of fish when it is caught eliminates this hazard. Ciguatera fish poisoning is caused by eating reef-feeding species after they have consumed toxic dinoflagellates. This hazard is greater if the fish are taken from tropical or subtropical waters in which dinoflagellates abound. Paralytic shellfish poisoning may result from eating clams, mussels, and scallops. These shellfish may contain toxins if they feed on dinoflagellates that proliferate (form a red tide) when the temperature of the water is between 5° and 8°C (41° to 46°F). Several species of dinoflagellates on both the West and the East Coasts may be involved. These shellfish should not be harvested when a red tide is present. Neurotoxic shellfish poisoning is caused by another red-tide-forming organism that sometimes proliferates in the Gulf of Mexico and off the coast of Florida. Fish are rarely the source of the toxin that causes botulism, a potentially fatal food poisoning (14). Canned products are processed to destroy any *Clostridium botulinum* present and the odor of mishandled raw fish caused by the action of spoilage organisms warns of inedibility. However, processing of fish to lengthen shelf life (light smoking, irradiation, modified atmosphere) may eliminate spoilage microorganisms that otherwise could provide a safety factor against botulism (7). Temperature abuse of such products is hazardous; they should not be held at a temperature above 3.3°C (37°F) for more than a few days.

Bacterial and Viral Hazards

The production of safe and wholesome shellfish, particularly oysters, requires stringent sanitary controls. Oysters, which require salt water but are unable to tolerate the concentration of salt in undiluted sea water, grow in protected bays and inlets near the mouths of rivers. There, surface water from the land drains into the ocean and dilutes the salt water to an acceptable level. If the water contains untreated sewage, contamination of the oysters with pathogenic microorganisms can occur. An oyster filters large volumes of water, as much as five quarts a day by one 18 months old. In this filtering process many microorganisms are retained. For oysters to be safe to eat requires high standards for the water in the beds where they are cultivated. Sanitary control of the growing areas and of the harvesting and processing of shellfish are under the control of the state in which the shellfish originates. Inspection of shellfish growing areas and licensing of shellfish shucking plants have eliminated many of the hazards of contamination of shellfish with pathogens. *Vibrio parahaemolyticus* organisms are present in the marine environment (9). Outbreaks of illness have occurred from eating oysters taken from the Gulf of Mexico, the south Atlantic, and the Pacific Northwest coastal waters (14). High temperature when the bivalves are harvested or as they are transported allows the *Vibrio* to multiply to a level high enough to cause illness. *Vibrio* die off at 0° to 5°C (32° to 41°F), and they are destroyed by mild heat (55°C or 131°F). Clams taken from water along the Northeast and Mid-Atlantic Coasts have caused outbreaks of illness attributed to viruses. Sewage treatment plants are at times unable to cope with the load of viruses from densely populated areas along the East Coast. Illness of both bacterial and viral origins can be prevented by eating only cooked shellfish. Eating raw or undercooked shellfish is hazardous. Shellfish may be contaminated with more traditional, land-based pathogens and the presence of psychotropic organisms (Chapter 4) may make such seafoods unsafe to eat even when held at refrigerator temperature.

Fishborne Parasites

Fish and shellfish may be a source of worms that are parasitic to humans (11). Salmon from Alaska and wall-eyed pike and burbot from the Great Lakes region have been contaminated with tapeworms. The larvae can be eliminated by freezing fish and holding at −18°C (0°F) for 24 to 48 hours or by heating at a minimum of 56°C (133°F) for five minutes. Roundworms (nematodes) have been identified in such fish as red snapper and salmon marketed in the United States. Holding frozen fish at −18°C (0°F) for 24 to 48 hours or heating the fish to 60°C (140°F) for one minute makes fish safe to eat. Crustaceans and mollusks may contain parasites, too. In most cases, heating shellfish at 60°C (140°F) for one to five minutes will eliminate parasites.

Illness associated with eating seafoods could be reduced an estimated 60 percent or more by (a) eating no raw or undercooked mollusks and (b) foregoing certain tropical reef fish (14). Knowing the hazards associated with eating fish and taking elementary precautions should permit the safe consumption of this tasty and nutritious food.

STRUCTURE OF FIN FISH MUSCLE

Two types of muscle are found in vertebrate fish. The main one, the great lateral muscle, makes up the bulk of the edible part of most such fish. The lateral muscle of most fish is essentially colorless. Salmon is an exception, but the pink color is due not to myoglobin but to a carotenoid, astaxanthin. Outside the lateral muscle of many fish is a small superficial muscle that fans out on each side of the lateral line. This muscle, which is dark reddish brown, is rich in myoglobin in contrast to the main muscle, which is practically devoid of it. A high proportion of fat is found in this superficial dark muscle. The fatty acids in the fat of fish are more highly unsaturated than are those of warm-blooded animals. When fish are held, rancidity develops, particularly in the heme-rich, dark muscle. Lipoxygenase, present in the skin of fish (8), gives rise to radicals that lead to rancidity.

The muscles of fish, like those of meat and poultry, consist of muscle fibers and connective tissue. Myofibrils are embedded in the sarcoplasm of the fibers defined by the sarcolemma. Some of the myofibrils are cylindrical in shape like those in red meats. Others, especially those just inside the sarcolemma, are flat and ribbonlike in cross section. Both types of myofibrils appear to be made up of overlapping thick (myosin) and thin (actin) filaments just as in red meats. The contractile proteins—actin and myosin—make up about ⅔ of the total protein of the muscle of fish (4). This is a higher proportion than in red meats. Values of three to five percent are given for the connective tissue content of bony fish (6), much lower than that in the most tender cut of beef.

Aside from a higher proportion of actin and myosin and a lower proportion of connective tissue, fish muscle differs from that of meat and poultry in other ways. The muscle fibers of fish are short—usually not more than two centimeters (¾ inch) long—and thick (4), unlike those of meat, which are thin and hairlike. These short fibers, their long axes parallel to the backbone of the fish, are embedded at either end in thin layers of connective tissue, the myocommata (Fig. 24-1). Layers of these short fibers—the myotomes—separated by myocommata, are repeated the length of the lateral muscle, giving fish a segmented body (Fig. 24-2). The connective tissue of fish, more abundant in the skin, fins, and skeleton than in the muscle (26), appears to lack one type of collagen found in the connective tissue of warm-blooded animals (23). The collagen of fish has a lower percentage of proline and hydroxyproline, which affects its thermal properties. Both the collagen and actomyosin of fish are more labile to heat than are these constituents in meat (25).

INSTABILITY OF FISH IN FROZEN STORAGE

The muscle of fish differs from that of warm-blooded animals in its ability to withstand frozen storage. Fast freezing and thawing of fish cause no undue damage (4). It is during frozen storage that undesirable changes in texture occur. The uncooked fish loses its springiness and becomes friable. Cooked, the fish is dry, tough, stringy, and tasteless. The instability of frozen fish muscle and its undesirable textural changes are believed to be associated with the myofibrillar proteins rather than with those of the sarcoplasm or the connective tissue. Specifically the myosin of fish appears to be the labile component. Much work has been done and many words have been written on the instability of fish in frozen storage. To date no satisfactory explanation is forthcoming. Damage to the texture of frozen fish diminishes the lower the temperature at which the frozen product is stored. Fish purchased frozen should be stored at $-18°C$ ($0°F$) and thawed just before it is cooked.

Figure 24-1. Photomicrograph of muscle tissue of salmon. Ends of fibers from one myotome (left) with the intervening layer of connective tissue called myocommata separating it from another myotome, the ends of a few fibers of which are seen on the right. Original magnification × 112. (From H. Charley and G. E. Goertz, *Food Research* 23:21. Copyright © 1958 by Institute of Food Technologists.)

COOKING FISH

Early studies on the cooking of fish focused on losses of weight and nutrients. Baking, broiling (both at 190°C or 375°F), and simmering (85°C or 185°F) had no adverse effect on the nutritive value of the proteins of cod fillets (16). Whether croaker fillets are baked in a moderate (190°C or 375°F) or in a hot (260°C or 500°F) oven makes no difference in the nutritive value of the protein or in the thiamin, riboflavin, or niacin contents of the cooked fish (18). The loss of weight at the higher temperature is ⅔ that at the lower temperature. In neither study was internal temperature controlled or sensory qualities assessed. One study investigated the effects of internal temperature of the flesh on both loss of weight and sensory qualities of the cooked fish (3). Salmon steaks, one-inch thick, were

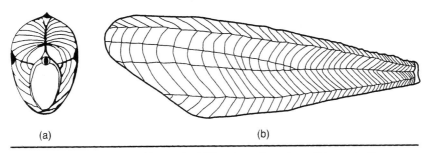

Figure 24-2. Cross (a) and longitudinal (b) sections of vertebrate fish muscle. Lines represent layers of connective tissue (myocommata) that divide muscle into segments (myotomes). (From E. Dunajski, *Journal of Texture Studies* 11:302. 1980. Reproduced by permission.)

baked in an oven at 204°C (400°F) to internal temperatures of 70°, 75°, 80°, and 85°C (158°, 167°, 176°, and 185°F). The two higher internal temperatures resulted in significantly higher evaporation and total cooking losses. Steaks baked to the lowest internal temperature ranked high for moistness but low in flavor and in desirability, and were judged underdone. Steaks heated to the highest internal temperature had almost twice the loss of weight of steaks heated to 70°C (158°F). Steaks baked to the highest temperature were ranked most flavorful. In the same study, steaks were baked to an internal temperature of 75°C (167°F) at oven temperatures of 177°, 204°, 232°, and 260°C (350°, 400°, 450°, and 500°F). Oven temperature made no difference in the palatability characteristics of the baked fish or in total cooking losses, although the drip at the highest oven temperature contained more fat. In contrast to the results above, rainbow trout and cod baked in covered glass baking dishes to internal temperatures of 55°C (131°F) were ranked higher for tenderness, juiciness, surface moistness, and "intensity of fresh fish flavor," compared with the same species heated to internal temperatures of 65° and 75°C (149° and 167°F) (12). However, heating fish to an internal temperature of only 55°C (131°F) raises the issue of safety, as the investigators noted. Proteins of fish muscle have been shown to be more heat labile than are those of chicken or beef (25). Heated to 60°C (140°F), little change can be observed in the scanning electron microscopic appearance of longissimus dorsi of beef or semitendinosus of chicken, but the dorsal muscle of rainbow trout shows extensive damage. Breaks across the fibers, particularly at the Z-discs, and disruptions of fibrils in the H-zone can be observed.

Three studies compare fish (fillets or sections) cooked in a microwave versus a conventional oven (1, 15). The oven makes no difference in most of the sensory attributes of the cooked fish. The retention of thiamin is essentially the same, too (1). Retentions of both thiamin (87.2 percent) and riboflavin (92.6 percent) when salmon steaks are broiled is essentially the same as when steaks are baked in a forced convection oven. Color and appearance of the baked fish are better, but the steaks are less tender and less juicy. The cooking method makes no difference in flakiness, flavor, or overall acceptability (28).

Methods

Fish is cooked to alter the texture, develop flavor, and destroy pathogens. Methods used to cook fish include baking, broiling, pan- or deep-fat frying, microwaving, poaching, and steaming. Baking and broiling are good methods for cooking fat fish that are self-basting.

Steaks or whole fish, with or without stuffing, may be baked. Removal of the backbone from the latter gives a pocket for stuffing and makes carving easier. Moist-media methods such as steaming or poaching are particularly appropriate for lean fish. The latter is done in simmering liquid (water, stock, or milk). Slices of lemon may be added to the poaching water. Such herbs as basil, bay leaf, capers, caraway, chives, dill, fennel, marjoram, or parsley, judiciously used, complement the flavor of fish. Steaks, fillets, or whole fish may be poached. Pan- and deep-fat frying are methods used to cook breaded and battered fish.

Assessing Doneness

The muscle fibers of raw fish are not tough and the collagen in the small amount of connective tissue present in fish is readily solubilized to gelatin (near 60°C or 140°F) (5). Instead of cooking fish to tenderize it, the objectives are to heat it enough to make it safe to eat, and to alter the texture without overcoagulating and toughening the proteins of the muscle fibers. Doneness may be assessed by the end point temperature, with a minimum of 60°C (140°F) usually recommended. At this point, the flesh loses its translucency and becomes milky-looking and opaque. So appearance is a rough index to doneness. When fish collagen in the myocommata is degraded to gelatin, the myotomes (layers of muscle fibers) separate readily and give rise to the flakes of cooked fish. Fish is done as soon as heat has coagulated the muscle fiber proteins (and solubilized the collagen) so that the flesh can be separated into flakes. Fish cooked beyond this stage shrinks excessively and becomes tough and dry. An allowance of 10 minutes per inch of thickness, measured at the thickest part, is suggested as a way to estimate cooking time.

When lobster is cooked, it undergoes a pronounced change in color. The dull olive green of the shell changes to bright red. When heat denatures the protein of the green carotenoid-protein complex, the bright red astaxanthin is freed. A comparable but less pronounced change in color occurs in shrimp when they are cooked.

REFERENCES

1. Brady, P. L., P. E. Haughey, and M. F. Rothschild. 1985. "Microwave and conventional heating effects on sensory quality and thiamin content of flounder and haddock fillets." *Home Economics Research Journal* 14(2):236–40. Thiamin content, appearance, flavor, and acceptability essentially the same.

2. Cardello, A. V., F. M. Sawyer, O. Maller, and L. Digman. 1982. "Sensory evaluation of the texture and appearance of 17 species of North American fish." *Journal of Food Science* 47:1818–23. Categories of fish, based on textural attributes.

3. Charley, H. 1952. "Effects of internal temperature and of oven temperature on the cooking losses and the palatability of baked salmon steaks." *Food Research* 17:136–43.

Oven temperatures of 350° to 500°F and internal temperatures of 70° to 85°C (158° to 185°F) compared.

4. Connell, J. J. 1964. "Fish muscle proteins and some effects on them of processing." In *Symposium on Foods: Proteins and Their Reactions.* Westport, CT.: Avi Publishing. Pp. 255–93.

5. Dunadski, E. 1979. "Texture of fish muscle." *Journal of Texture Studies* 10:301–18. A review paper.

6. Dyer, W. J., and J. R. Dingle. 1961. "Fish protein with special reference to freezing." In *Fish as Food.* Vol. 1. Georg Bergstrom, ed. 275–320. Structure of fish muscle, behavior of fish proteins, and theories of freezing damage.

7. Eklund, M. W. 1982. "Significance of Clostridium botulinum in fishery products

preserved short of sterilization." *Food Technology* 36(12):107–12. Risks involved in products treated to lengthen shelf life.

8. German, J. B., and J. E. Kinsella. 1985. "Lipid oxidation in fish tissue. Enzymatic oxidation via lipoxygenase." *Journal of Agricultural and Food Chemistry* 33:680–83. Endogenous enzyme and oxidation of fish lipids.

9. Hackney, C. R., and A. Dicharry. 1988. "Seafood-borne bacterial pathogens of marine origin." *Food Technology* 42(3):104–9. *Vibrios* emphasized.

10. Hearn, T. L., S. A. Sgoutas, J. A. Hearn, and D. S. Sgoutas. 1987. "Polyunsaturated fatty acids and fat in fish flesh for selecting species for health benefits." *Journal of Food Science* 52:1209–11. The n-3 and n-6 polyunsaturated fatty acid contents of a number of species.

11. Higashi, G. I. 1985. "Foodborne parasites transmitted to man from fish and other aquatic foods." *Food Technology* 39(3): 69–74, 111. Emphasis on tape and round worms.

12. Johansson, L., H. Ruderus, and R. I. Beilby. 1992. "Optimum internal temperature established by sensory evaluation of fish prepared in conventional and microwave ovens." *Home Economics Research Journal* 21(2):192–205. Internal temperatures of 55°, 65°, and 75°C (131°, 149°, and 167°F) compared.

13. Lee, C. M. 1984. "Surimi process technology." *Food Technology* 38(11):69–80. Details of its manufacture; use in shellfish analogs.

14. Liston, J. 1990. "Microbial hazards of seafood consumption." *Food Technology* 44(12):56, 58–62. Seafood toxins, bacteria, viruses, and land-based pathogens.

15. Maderia, K., and M. P. Penfield. 1985. "Turbot fillet sections cooked by microwaves and conventional heating methods: Objective and sensory evaluation." *Journal of Food Science* 50:172–77. Method makes no difference in flakiness or moistness; microwaved softer and chewier.

16. Marks, A. L., and H. W. Nilson. 1946. "Effect of cooking on the nutritive value of the proteins of the cod." *Commercial Fisheries Rev. 8, No. 12.* 6 pp. Baking, broiling, simmering, and boiling compared.

17. Martin, R. E. 1988. "Seafood products, technology and research in the U.S." *Food Technology* 42(3):58, 60. Fish supplied by aquatic farming.

18. Martinek, W. A., and C. G. Goldbeck. 1947. "Nutritive value of baked croaker." *Commercial Fisheries Review, Sep. No. 171.* Pp. 9–13. Thiamin, riboflavin, and niacin in fish baked in a moderate and in a very hot oven.

19. National Marine Fisheries Service. 1978 (March). *A Model Retail Plan for Seafood Species.* U.S. Department of Commerce, National Oceanic and Atmospheric Administration, Washington, D.C.

20. Pariser, E. R., and O. A. Hammerle. 1966. "Some cultural and economic limitations on the use of fish as food." *Food Technology* 20:629–32. Food prejudices and taboos as they affect the consumption of fish.

21. Prell, P. A., and F. M Sawyer. 1988. "Flavor profiles of 17 species of North Atlantic fish." *Journal of Food Science* 53:1036–42. Data for establishing market categories of fish.

22. Reay, G. A., and J. M. Shewan. 1949. "The spoilage of fish and its preservation by chilling." *Advances in Food Research* 2:343–92. A review.

23. Sato, K., R. Yoshinaka, Y. Itoh, and M. Sato. 1989. "Molecular species of collagen in intramuscular connective tissue of fish." *Comparative Biochemistry and Physiology* 92B:89–91. Types I and V but no Type III in fish.

24. Sawyer, F. M., A. V. Cardello, and P. A. Prell. 1988. "Consumer evaluation of the sensory properties of fish." *Journal of Food Science* 53:12–18. Survey of consumers' familiarity with fish (32 species).

25. Schaller, D. R., and W. D. Powrie. 1972. "Scanning electron microscopy of heated beef, chicken, and rainbow trout muscle." *Canadian Institute of Food Science and Technology* 5:184–90. Effects of heating to 60° and 97°C (140° and 199°F) recorded.

26. Schikorski, Z. E., D. N. Scott, and D. H. Busson. 1984. "The role of collagen in the quality and processing of fish." *CRC Critical Reviews in Food Science and Nutrition* 20:301–43. Distribution in fish, amino acid makeup; response to heat.

27. Spencer, R., and C. R. Baines. 1964. "The effect of temperature on the spoilage of wet white fish." *Food Technology* 18:769–73. Fluctuations in temperature of fish from catch to consumer and effects on quality.

28. Takahashi, Y., and M. A. Khan. 1987. "Impact of infrared broiling on the thiamin and riboflavin retention and sensory quality of salmon steaks for food service use." *Journal of Food Science* 52:4–6. Effects compared with those of baking.

29. Taylor, S. L. 1988. "Marine toxins of microbial origin." *Food Technology* 42(3): 94–98. Scombroid, ciguatera, paralytic, and neurotoxic poisoning.

30. United States Congress. 79th, 1st Session. 1945. *Fishery Resources of the United States.* Senate Document No. 51. 135 pp. Major and minor aquatic species, illustrated; distribution, utilization, and conservation.

31. U.S. Department of Commerce. *Fisheries of the United States,* 1994. Current Fisheries Statistics No. 9400. p. 27, 69. Data on world fisheries and U.S. per-capita consumption.

32. Wang, Y. J., L. A. Miller, M. Perrin and P. B. Addis. 1990. "Omega-3 fatty acids in Lake Superior fish." *Journal of Food Science* 55:71–73, 76. Eight commercial species analyzed.

PART VII

Cakes

Shortened Cakes

25

Shortened cakes are, by definition, ones that contain fat. The fat in shortened cake is distributed in the batter in emulsified form. Such batter is a mobile foam made rigid yet deformable by baking. Some of the ingredients in shortened cakes form true solutions and others are colloidally dispersed. Particles of flour are suspended in the liquid. The kind of ingredients, their proportions, and how they are manipulated are interrelated. How the cake is baked is the final contributing factor to the quality of the finished product.

A high-quality shortened cake has a flat or slightly rounded top. The crust should be fine grained and a uniform golden brown. The grain (cells) should be small and uniform, the cell walls thin, and the crumb resilient, soft, and velvety. The cake should be light, tender, and slightly moist. It should taste acceptably sweet and otherwise have a good flavor (21).

Emphasis on low-calorie and especially lowfat foods kindled interest in developing cakes with little or no fat and/or sugar. Regardless of how a cake formula is modified, the standard by which the finished product is judged is that of a high-quality shortened cake.

INGREDIENTS AND THEIR FUNCTIONS

Fat

One important function of fat in shortened cakes is to contribute tenderness. Shortened cakes were, until recently, made only from plastic fats such as butter and hydrogenated shortening. Plastic fats serve as a means of incorporating air bubbles into cake batter. Most hydrogenated shortenings are marketed containing from 10 to 12 percent gas by volume. This gas is distributed throughout the fat as bubbles from 2 to 10 micrometers in diameter (40). Additional air bubbles are incorporated in the fat by manipulating it with the blades of a beater. This technique is called creaming. Air bubbles are trapped in the liquid fat that surrounds the fat crystals.

All fats do not cream equally well. The form in which the crystals of a plastic fat exist influences how well that fat creams. Plastic fats whose crystals are stable in the beta prime form are superior for creaming. Such fats incorporate air bubbles one micrometer or less in diameter. The smaller and more numerous the crystals, the finer and more numerous are the bubbles of trapped air. Such fats when creamed have the consistency of whipped cream. Butter is not aerated so it needs more creaming than hydrogenated shortening. Regular lard does not cream as well as most plastic fats because of the presence of large crystals.

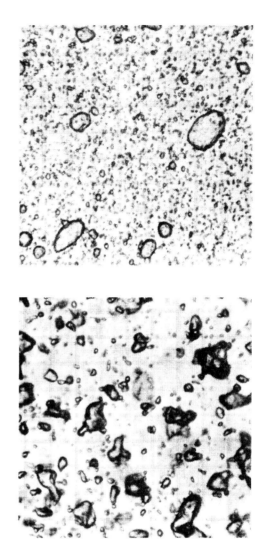

Figure 25-1. Rearranged lard with fine crystals (*top*) incorporates more and smaller air cells than does ordinary lard with coarse crystals (*bottom*). Original magnification × 194. (From C. W. Hoerr and D. F. Waugh, *Journal of the American Oil Chemists' Society* 32:38, 1955. Reprinted by permission.)

The illustrations in Figure 25-1 show the effects of the size of crystals of fat on the number, size, and distribution of air bubbles incorporated in the fat (23). The sample at the bottom is of ordinary lard, that on top, of rearranged lard, crystals of which are shown in Figure 15-4. Because of their small crystals, rearranged fats cream well. Size of the crystals and the creaming quality of a fat in turn affect the number, size, and distribution of gas cells in cake batter, as shown in Figure 25-2.

A fat with a wide plastic range is best for creaming. One disadvantage of using butter for shortened cakes is its narrow plastic range. A drop in temperature of a few degrees makes it too hard to cream and a rise of a few degrees makes it too soft. Hydrogenated vegetable shortenings maintain desirable plasticity over a wide range in temperature.

Aside from incorporating air, fat has another important function in shortened cakes. During baking, crystals in plastic fat melt, so fat makes cake batter more fluid and more

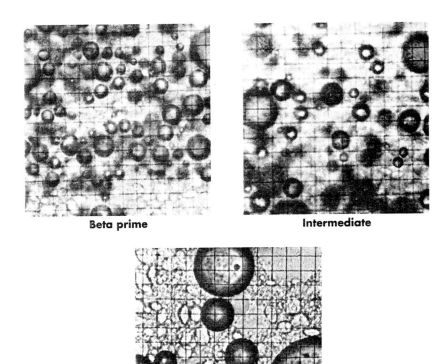

Beta prime   **Intermediate**

Beta

Figure 25-2. Photomicrographs of cake batter that show the effects of the type of crystals in a fat on the number, size, and distribution of air cells in a cake batter. Original magnification approximately × 200. Grid lines represent approximately 18 microns. (From C. W. Hoerr, *Journal of the American Oil Chemists' Society* 37:544, 1960. Reprinted by permission.)

mobile. With too little fat, the batter is not mobile enough to give with the expansion and oscillation of gas bubbles. An excess of fat makes the batter too fluid and too mobile. Optimum mobility is desired in cake batter because of its effect on the grain and on the textural qualities of the crumb (8). Fat helps determine whether the walls of dough in cake batter will explode or merely expand with the pressure of expanding gases. Fats help determine whether the crumb will be fragile or tough and thus act as tenderizing agents in cakes as they do in pastry.

Liquid fats cannot be creamed, so they do not aerate cake batter in this way. In fact, they act as antifoaming agents. Liquid fats and other ingredients are combined in one operation referred to as the single-stage method. Ingredients in packaged cake mixes are combined by this method. The use of liquid fat and the single-stage method of combining ingredients for shortened cake became possible only after a special type of surfactant became available. The single-stage method of combining cake batter is discussed in a subsequent section.

Emulsifiers

Hydrogenated shortenings on the market contain glyceryl monostearate plus some distearate. These mono- and diacylglycerols are lipophilic surfactants. Most hydrogenated shortening contain approximately three percent mono- and diacylglycerides. This level is adequate for making shortened cake but not so high that it lowers unduly the smoke point if the shortening is used for frying. Shortening with these surfactants should be creamed before it is incorporated with the other ingredients. An emulsifier is essential in those cakes made with a high ratio of sugar and liquid to flour.

The emulsifier in plastic shortening used for cake making results in a finer dispersion of fat throughout the batter. Batter that contains emulsifier is thinner, has a higher specific gravity, and has greater mobility. Somewhat less air is incorporated when the emulsifier is present, but the air is more finely dispersed. The smaller air cells that form in the presence of emulsifier make the grain of the cake finer. If gas cells are few, they become too large when carbon dioxide is released. The bubbles may migrate to the surface of the batter (20), especially during the early part of the baking. Losses of leaven and of cake volume result. Butter, once the preferred plastic fat for cake making, retains emulsifier from the cream but not enough to make the best cake. Addition of the optimum level of glyceryl monostearate to butter results in a superior cake (20,29). The photomicrographs in Figure 25-3 illustrate the effects of glyceryl monostearate on cake batter made with butter (29). Figure 25-3a shows a photomicrograph of batter that contains no emulsifier other than that which the butter contains normally. The fat is stained and appears in diffuse dark gray clumps. The round, dark-rimmed air bubbles appear to be associated with the fat. The batter shown in part *b* has added six percent glyceryl monostearate (based on the weight of the fat). In this batter the fat is so finely dispersed that it appears as a faint gray mist. The effect of the emulsifier on the quality of the cake is shown in Figure 25-4. Compare cakes 1 and 3 in each of the four series, *A* through *D*. Addition of emulsifier improved volume, grain, and texture of the cakes, as shown in the lower cake in each series. Cakes made with half butter for flavor and half hydrogenated shortening for superior creaming and emulsifying properties, a procedure that is feasible at home, yielded a cake more like one made from commercial shortening. Increasing the mixing time improved the all-butter cake made without emulsifier (19).

Monoacylglycerols are effective emulsifiers in cake batter when air bubbles are introduced by way of the fat. They do not work with more fluid batters, especially ones made with liquid fat and combined single stage, such as packaged cake mixes. Batters of this kind require a special type of emulsifier that is stable in the alpha crystalline form, referred to as alpha tending (7,47). One such surfactant that is used in packaged cake mixes is propylene glycol monostearate. A combination of an alpha-tending emulsifier with another fatty substance, such as propylene glycol monostearate and stearic acid, is even more effective. Alpha-tending emulsifiers not only promote better dispersion of the fat but also counteract its antifoaming action. When these emulsifiers collect at the interface between fat droplets and the rest of the batter, they form tough films that effectively seal off the fat from direct contact with the aqueous phase. Such a film is shown in Figure 25-5 (26,47). When this sealing occurs, the proteins in the batter (from eggs and milk) can foam and the batter can be aerated by beating rather than by creaming the air into the fat. Without these special surfactants, the fat would block foaming of the protein. These surfactants can be used with liquid as well as plastic fats, and they make possible packaged cake mixes that can be combined in one stage.

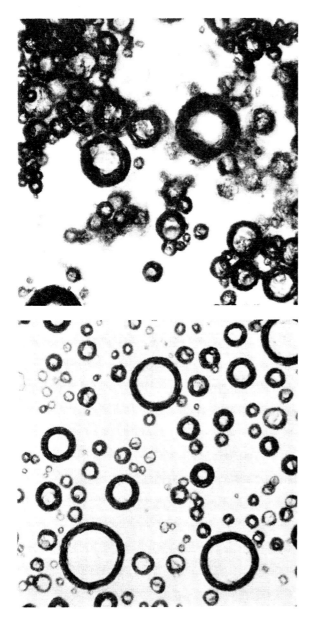

Figure 25-3. Effect of added emulsifier on the dispersion of gas cells in cake batter. (*top*) Batter made with butter without added emulsifier. The fat is stained and appears dark. The spheres with black outlines are gas bubbles. Other ingredients appear white. (*bottom*) Batter made with butter to which six percent glyceryl mono-stearate was added. Gas cells are evenly distributed. Fat is so well dispersed that little contrast exists between it and the other ingredients. Original magnification × 120. (From Martha Jooste and Andrea Mackey, *Food Research* 17:188. Copyright © 1952 by Institute of Food Technologists.)

Sugar

Sugar performs several functions in shortened cake besides the obvious one of making it sweet (2). Sugar contributes tenderness and facilitates the incorporation of air into plastic fats as they are creamed. As the sharp-edged sugar crystals are manipulated with the fat, air that adheres to faces of the crystals is introduced as small bubbles into the fat. Sugar must be in crystalline form to be effective for this purpose. The finer (and more numerous) the crystals, the greater is the number of air cells incorporated. Powdered sugar lacks the sharp crystal edges (present in granulated sugar) that are essential for pulling bubbles of air into

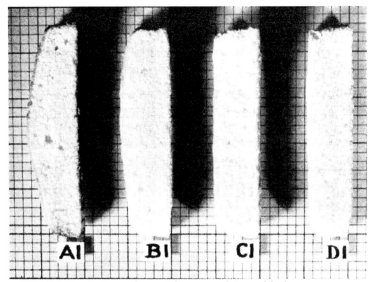

Butter cakes with no emulsier added.

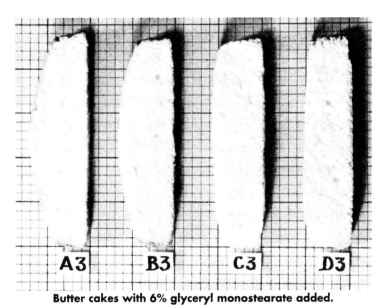

Butter cakes with 6% glyceryl monostearate added.

Figure 25-4. Effects of baking temperature and of emulsifier on the quality of shortened cakes. Oven temperature: A—218°C (425°F); B—190°C (375°F); C—163°C (325°F); D—143°C (300°F). (From Martha Jooste and Andrea Mackey, *Food Research* 17:192, 193. Copyright © 1952 by Institute of Food Technologists.)

fat during creaming. Sugar elevates the temperature at which the proteins of eggs coagulate and it raises the gelatinization temperature of starch (3,31). Sugars differ in this respect, with sucrose elevating it more than glucose and glucose more than fructose (4). When high-fructose corn syrup is substituted for sucrose in cake, the volume of the cake is less and browning is excessive (45). A lowered gelatinization temperature of the starch

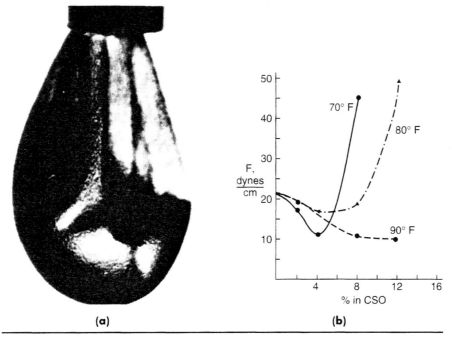

(a)   (b)

Figure 25-5. Function of an alpha-tending surfactant. (*a*) Formation of an interfacial film between a droplet of water and cottonseed oil (CSO). Withdrawal of part of the water resulted in partial collapse of the film of surfactant, which emphasized its integrity. (*b*) Effects of concentration and
temperature on the strength of the interfacial film formed by the surfactant. (From J. C. Wootton,
N. B. Howard, J. B. Martin, D. E. McOsker, and J. C. Holme, *Cereal Chemistry* 44:337, 1967.
Reprinted by permission.)

and early setting of the batter may account for the lower volume of the cake. The gelatinization temperature of starch in cake batter is considered a predictor of cake volume
(25). Inclusion of acidulants such as cream of tartar or glucono-delta-lactone in batter
made with high fructose corn syrup can reduce browning (28).

Eggs

The protein of eggs, in addition to aiding in the aeration of single-stage cake batter, also
serves as a means of incorporating air into cake batter made by conventional creaming, especially when the eggs are separated and the beaten whites are folded into the batter at the
end. Egg yolk, too, and especially the plasma with low density lipoprotein makes a major
contribution to the quality of shortened cakes. The higher the proportion of fat the greater
the need for the emulsifying action of egg and especially the yolk. Coagulation of the proteins of egg during baking contributes structure to the cake and balances the tenderizing
effect of sugar. The size of the eggs, unless eggs are measured or weighed, will make a difference in the cake.

Flour

Cake batter must contain ingredients that confer on it the ability to hold gas bubbles and that
make the baked cake rigid but still compressible. Flour is one such ingredient. One structural

material supplied by flour is a small amount of protein that is coagulated by heat. The main component, however, is starch, which, when it is pasted during baking, is essential for the structure of cake crumb (27,31). The material in the crumb of cake that once surrounded the gas cells in the batter is made in part of pasted starch granules. Size of the gas cells in shortened cake depends upon how much the batter expands during baking before the cells rupture. This in turn is influenced in part by the size of the particles of flour. Flour is pin-milled in the final step in the reduction of wheat endosperm to particles of a size optimum for making cakes. Conventionally milled flour particles are fragmented by high speed impact against pins or baffles. Pin-milling may improve baking performance by dislodging starch granules from the matrix of protein of the endosperm, thus making them available to water (14). Excessive damage to starch granules is avoided (32); otherwise, the granules absorb excess water, making the batter too viscous and reducing volume of the cake. Cake flour, because of the small size of the particles, yields a cake with small cells, which contributes to fine grain and velvety texture (37). Volume of the cake is greater, too (48).

Cake flour is treated with chlorine that bleaches its pigments, lowers its pH, and improves its baking performance. Higher levels of sugar and fat can be used with chlorine-treated flour. Batter made with untreated flour may rise, but it is unstable and likely to collapse near the end of the baking period. Both the lipids and especially the starch of flour appear to be involved in the beneficial effects of chlorination (33), but the mechanism is unclear.

Chlorine-treated cake flour gives a batter that is more viscous when it is heated to a temperature equivalent to that reached near the end of a baking period. The exudate of amylose from the starch of treated flour is greater than that from untreated flour (39), suggesting the importance of amylose in stabilizing the structure of the baked cake. Reasons for the effects of chlorine aside, treated flour yields cakes with larger volume, finer grain and better texture (43).

Leavening Agent

Air that is creamed into the fat clinging to the particles of sifted flour, and air that is introduced by means of the egg and by stirring the batter provide the gas cells in cake batter that eventually become the grain of the baked cake. These air cells provide focal points for the collection of steam that forms during baking and for the carbon dioxide liberated from the soda by the acid in the baking powder. A true pound cake is leavened by air and steam only; other shortened cakes are additionally leavened by carbon dioxide. The amount of baking powder required in a shortened cake depends upon how much air is creamed into the fat, on the number of eggs included, and on whether the egg is added whole or is separated and the beaten white folded in at the end of the mixing. Compared with a two-egg cake, a four-egg cake that also contains more fat, needs less additional leaven from baking powder.

If double-acting baking powder is used in a recipe originally formulated for single-acting powder, the cake may be overinflated. The cells tend to be coarse and the crumb fragmented. The double-acting baking powder releases more of its carbon dioxide as the batter is heated in the oven. A cake made with SAS-phosphate baking powder has a more alkaline crumb than does one made with soda and cream of tartar. The more acidic the cake batter, up to a point, the finer the grain, the more velvety the crumb, the whiter and sweeter is the cake (10). The emulsion is less stable in a batter that is neutral or slightly alkaline (1).

Heat penetration is slower in cake batter that contains an excess of soda as in devil's food cake. This fact, in addition to the effect of the excess soda on the batter, accounts in part at least for the coarse grain. The color of chocolate and devil's food cake is due to the pigments supplied by the cocoa or chocolate. These change color with a change in hydrogen-ion concentration. At a pH of 5.0 they are yellow. With increase in alkalinity the hue shifts to various shades of brown and finally to a mahogany red at pH 7.5 (18).

Liquid

Liquid in shortened cake batter performs a number of important functions (46). It dissolves the salt and sugar and makes possible the ionization of soda and acid in the baking powder so that they can react. Liquid disperses the fat and the flour and hydrates the protein and starch in the latter. The liquid also provides some steam to leaven the cake. Fluid milk is usually used, but water and milk solids may be substituted, the latter sifted with the dry ingredients. Fruit juices may serve as the liquid with or without the addition of soda to neutralize the acid. Liquid is needed to gelatinize the starch and so set the structure.

Salt

Salt is used for flavor. The proportion of salt to flour is somewhat less than for quick breads, possibly because of the high proportion of sugar or because cake recipes were first formulated for butter, which is usually salted.

PROPORTIONS OF INGREDIENTS

Balancing Ingredients in a Conventional Cake

Shortened cakes vary from a lean, one-egg cake to a rich pound cake. In all recipes regardless of the richness, the ingredients need to be in balance. Structural or toughening ingredients, eggs and flour, are balanced with tenderizing ingredients, fat and sugar. Liquid ingredients, milk, egg, and fat, are balanced with the dry ingredient, flour. An increase in one source of leaven necessitates a decrease in another.

A number of such balancings are illustrated in the conventional one-, two-, and four-egg cake formulas given in Table 25-1. Formulas for muffins and for a quick-mix cake are included. The quantity of flour is the same in all three conventional cakes. The proportion of sugar (approximately 100 percent of the weight of the flour) does not vary in this series. Each additional ¼ cup of fat is balanced in the formula by inclusion of one egg and by reduction of milk by ¼ cup. The weight of the egg approximates that of the fat. The egg supplies protein to counterbalance the fat, but of equal importance is the liquid which helps preserve the sugar/liquid ratio. If this is too high, gelatinization of starch is retarded and uptake of water by the starch does not occur at the critical point in baking when grain and texture of the cake crumb should be established (4, 31). In high-ratio cakes the sugar may equal 130 percent of the weight of the flour. An increase in sugar in a cake formula would necessitate a corresponding increase in liquid. Such a formula would in turn call for a higher level of emulsifier. An increase in egg is accompanied by a decrease in baking powder. In each of the conventional cake formulas, the volume of milk and fat approximates the volume of sugar.

Although ingredients in a cake recipe should be balanced, the balance need not be exact. For example, a three-egg cake recipe may be changed to a four-egg cake and the fat

TABLE 25-1
Formulas for Muffins, Three Conventional Cakes, and One Quick-Mix Cake

Ingredient	Muffins	CONVENTIONAL CAKES			Quick-Mix
		One Egg	Two Eggs	Four Eggs	
Flour[a]	3 cups	3 cups	3 cups	3 cups	2¼ cups
Salt	1 tsp	1 tsp	1 tsp	1 tsp	1 tsp
Baking powder	6 tsp	4½ tsp	3¾ tsp	3½ tsp	3 tsp
Sugar	3–6 Tbsp	1½ cups	1½ cups	1½ cups	1½ cups
Fat	3–6 Tbsp	¼ cup	½ cup	1 cup	½ cup
Egg	1½	1	2	4	2
Milk	2 cups	1¼ cups	1 cup	½ cup	1 cup

[a]Cake flour, except for muffins, for which all-purpose flour is used.

increased by somewhat more or somewhat less than ¼ cup without the cake being a failure. It is this tolerance for some variation that makes possible a very large number of combinations of proportions and innumerable new cake recipes. A balanced two-egg cake may have an ingredient either increased or decreased by up to 25 percent without making the cake a failure (13). Cake volume is likely to be increased with small increases of sugar, baking powder, or egg. When proportions of any of the three are decreased, volume is reduced. Increase in either the fat or the liquid reduces the cake volume. Any alteration in proportions that tends to make the volume greater tends to make the grain of the cake larger and the texture coarser. An increase in the proportions of either fat or sugar makes the crumb of cake more fragile and more tender, whereas a decrease in the proportions of either has a toughening effect. When the proportion of any one ingredient is altered by more than 25 percent without a compensating decrease or increase in another ingredient, the quality of the product is likely to be poor and the result a failure. Unbalanced proportions in a cake may be the result of a faulty recipe, errors in measuring, or deliberate alteration of proportions.

Single-Stage or Quick-Mix Formula

For cakes not made by the conventional method and for which most or all of the ingredients are combined in one or at most two steps, a special formula is used. A formula typical of a cake of this kind is like that for a balanced two-egg cake, except that the flour is reduced from 3 to 2¼ cups. Such high-sugar-ratio cake batters are thus richer and more fluid (36). The sugar in the quick-mix cake in Table 25-1 equals 139 percent of the weight of the flour. The proportion of liquid in the cake, which is high because of the sugar, is near the upper limit. Should the eggs be larger than average, the cup used to measure the milk larger than standard, or the flour have picked up moisture, the cake may be a failure. Shortening with alpha-tending emulsifier is needed for cakes combined single stage so the batter can be aerated. The fluid batter of a high-ratio cake makes it possible to disperse the ingredients more readily than in the case of a conventional formula. Packaged cake mixes can be combined so easily because they have a high ratio of liquid (and sugar) to flour, and the special emulsifier in the fat facilitates the incorporation of air in the aqueous phase of the batter (26,47). Such high-ratio cakes are moist and tender.

Lowfat and Low-Sugar Formulas

Conventional shortened cakes with their high levels of partially hydrogenated shortening and sugar are calorie-laden. Replacing hydrogenated shortening with vegetable oils (soybean and safflower) at reduced levels (24 and 66% reductions on a weight basis) has been reported to give satisfactory cakes (6). The availability of fat substitutes and of high potency sweeteners raises the possibility of more drastic alterations of cake formulas. No single ingredient duplicates the functional properties of fat. A combination of ingredients that mimics the lubricating effects of fat and replaces its bulk is required (30). Fat replacement is discussed in Chapter 15. One formula for a fat-free yellow cake contains guar and xanthan gums, modified starch, and polydextrose. A comparable formula for a fat-free yellow cake mix includes a proprietary blend of vegetable gum, emulsifier, modified starch, and skim milk powder (17). Another formula for a reduced calorie, fat-free cake contains xanthan gum, sucrose ester, acesulfame K, polydextrose, and sucrose at a reduced level. The cake was ranked for textural properties between a yellow layer cake made from a commercial mix and a commercial pound cake (16).

High potency sweeteners such as acesulfame K, sucralose (24), and aspartame, the latter encapsulated for release late in the baking period (38), have the potential for yielding cakes with reduced calories. A cake formula in which a small quantity of such a sweetener has replaced sugar should include one or more ingredients to supply bulk (Chapter 8) normally contributed by the sugar. In addition, provision is needed for duplicating the effects of sugar on delaying the gelatinization and pasting of the starch (25) and setting of the cake crumb.

A procedure similar to that used to predict appropriate proportions of ingredients for satisfactory cake made with canola oil (44) might be used to formulate low-calorie cakes. Data for cakes made from a limited number of combinations were used to construct surface contour maps from which suitable combinations of ingredients could be derived.

Adjustments for Altitude

To make cakes at high altitudes, the baking powder should be decreased because there is less air pressure to be overcome as the cake rises. A higher proportion of egg can be used at higher altitudes without making the cake tough. Also, because water vaporizes at a lower temperature at high altitudes, the liquid in the cake may need to be increased. A reduction in the proportion of sugar may be advisable. Alteration in the proportions of ingredients usually is not necessary below an elevation of 3,000 feet. At higher altitudes a cake may become overinflated and collapse during baking unless the recipe is modified. Recipes for cakes to be baked at different altitudes are available (15).

COMBINING INGREDIENTS FOR SHORTENED CAKES

Objectives

Regardless of the method used to combine ingredients for shortened cakes, one of the objectives is to distribute the salt and the baking powder evenly throughout the flour. This is accomplished by sifting together these dry ingredients or by adequate stirring in some cases. Good distribution of baking powder is essential if the cake is to have small cells and fine grain. A second objective is to disperse the fat. This is facilitated in conventional cakes by combining the egg with the creamed fat. The egg contributes emulsifier that, together with that in the fat, aids in dispersing the fat in the liquid. Aeration of the batter is accomplished in conventional cakes mainly by creaming the fat with sugar or in packaged mixes by stirring the batter. Folding beaten eggs into the batter near the end of the mixing is a third means of introducing air into cake batter. Finally, the batter is manipulated to dampen all ingredients and dissolve some without losing either too much of the liberated carbon dioxide or making the batter too viscous by overstirring.

Methods

A number of methods have evolved for combining ingredients for shortened cake. More than 600 routines are possible just by varying the order in which the main ingredients are combined. Commonly used methods include the muffin and muffin-meringue, conventional and conventional-sponge, pastry-blend, and the quick-mix.

Muffin Method

A simple and rapid way to combine ingredients for shortened cake is by the muffin method. Eggs and milk are blended, and together with the melted fat, stirred into the sifted dry ingredients. Batter for cake made in this way tends to be thin. It can be stirred more than muffin batter because of the higher proportions of fat and sugar. The volume of the cake tends to be smaller than that of cake made by the conventional method. Cells of cake tend to be large and the crumb coarse because of the poor dispersal of ingredients. The cake is likely to be less tender than it might be otherwise and the crust appears sugary. However, the quality of a lean, one-egg cake made by the muffin method may be nearly as good as one made by the conventional method, and less time and work are needed to combine ingredients. The cake may be quite acceptable if it is eaten while still warm. Such cakes stale more rapidly because of the poor dispersion of fat.

Cakes made with oil but combined by a method known as muffin-meringue compare favorably with cakes made from plastic fats combined by the conventional method (below). The muffin-meringue differs from the muffin method in that part of the sugar is beaten into the egg or the egg white. This meringue is then folded into the remainder of the ingredients, which have been combined by the muffin method.

Conventional Method

Creaming the sugar with the fat is the first step in combining cakes by the conventional method. Sugar crystals are manipulated with the shortening to produce an air-in-fat foam. Fats cream best at temperatures from 24° to 26°C (75° to 79°F). Below 20°C (68°F) the ratio of crystals to oil is too high for optimum creaming, that is, the fat is too firm. At temperatures above 30°C (86°F) the ratio of crystals to oil is too low to retain the air bubbles. Cake batter made at higher temperatures is not well aerated and tends to be thin.

Both sugar crystals and air bubbles are suspended in the liquid portion of the fat. The more the fat-sugar mixture is creamed, the more air is incorporated. When the creamed mass is light and fluffy, the eggs are added, usually one at a time, and blended with the creamed sugar and fat. At this point the mass should be well aerated, which is essential for optimum volume and grain. Under-creaming of the fat and sugar can be compensated for by additional manipulation of the creamed mass with the eggs.

After the eggs are incorporated into the fat-sugar foam, portions of both the liquid and the sifted dry ingredients (usually ½) are added and these are blended with the creamed mass. This is repeated with the second half of the liquid and dry ingredients. Blending should be slow but continuous to avoid lumps in the batter. The richer the batter (more fat or sugar) the more manipulation is required to give the batter optimum flow properties. At that stage, the fat is dispersed as lakes or even more diffusely in the aqueous phase of the batter. Air cells, once thought to move from the fat to the aqueous phase early in the baking period (8) were shown to be in the aqueous phase prior to baking (35).

The extent to which the batter is manipulated as well as how much the fat and sugar are creamed will influence grain, texture, and volume of the cake. If creaming of a conventional cake is skimped, cells are few and large, cell walls thick, and volume small because the batter is insufficiently aerated. If the batter is undermanipulated, ingredients are poorly dispersed and the batter is unable to withstand the pressure of expanding gases during baking. Such batter produces a cake of low volume with coarse, thick-walled cells, and a friable crumb. Batter overmanipulated at the final mixing stage will be too viscous and the gas cells unable to expand as they should during baking. Such batter gives a cake with a fine grain, but the cells have a tendency to form tunnels. The tight grain of the cake plus the loss of carbon dioxide during the excessive manipulation yield a cake of lowered volume. The appearance of the crust is one clue as to how much the batter was manipulated. If the crust has large pores, appears glazed, and browns excessively, the batter was probably undermanipulated. Cake with a dull crust that does not brown well or one with a peaked top due to tunnels may indicate overmanipulation.

Conventional-Sponge Method

A modification of the conventional method known as the conventional-sponge or conventional-meringue is similar to the conventional method. The difference is that the egg, or the egg white, is beaten with part of the sugar and this foam is folded into the batter at the end of the mixing period. This method of combining ingredients for shortened cake is especially recommended for those made from lard or other soft fats. If egg is added to creamed sugar and lard, the foam breaks and much of the air is lost from the creamed mass. This is attributed to a drop in temperature when the sugar dissolves in the liquid from the egg. This causes some of the liquid glycerides of the lard to crystallize and subsequent loss of much of the creamed air. Placing the container of creamed lard and sugar in a pan of warm water (not so warm as to melt the crystals in lard) before the eggs are added will minimize or prevent the drop in temperature. Adding the eggs after the flour is incorporated accomplishes the same thing, especially when part of the sugar is already dissolved in the egg.

Pastry-Blend Method

In the pastry-blend method, fat and flour are blended until they are fluffy. Sugar, salt, baking powder, and half the milk are combined with the fat-flour blend, followed by the egg and the remainder of the milk. This method gives a good dispersion of the fat and a cake with fine grain and texture.

Single-Stage or Quick-Mix Method

Cakes may be combined by a method known by such names as quick-mix, single-stage, dump, or one-bowl. Packaged cake mixes are combined by this method. A conventional cake formula combined by a quick-mix method will not yield a successful cake. A quick-mix method puts special demands on the proportions of ingredients (36) and on the emulsifier. A so-called high-ratio formula is required. Such a formula for a two-egg cake to be made by the single-stage method is given in Table 25-1. The ingredients, and especially the fat, should be at room temperature. To make a cake by the single-stage method, the fat and all or part of the liquid and the flavoring are added to the sifted dry ingredients. The mixture is stirred for a specified time or alternately for a specified number of strokes. Then the unbeaten egg, together with any liquid remaining, is added. Stirring is continued again for a specified time or number of strokes. The fluidity of the batter of a quick-mix cake accounts for the fact that the ingredients can be dispersed adequately by stirring without preliminary creaming of fat and sugar. Presence of an alpha-tending emulsifier in the fat in high-ratio cakes favors extensive dispersion of air cells in the batter in the absence of creaming.

BAKING

A stable, shortened cake batter, unlike that for meringue-type cake, can stand covered in the baking pan for some time without appreciable loss in quality. However, it is not advisable to allow the batter to stand in the bowl and transfer it later, because of loss of carbon dioxide. The baking pan should be approximately half full of batter.

Changes Effected by Baking

Baking is the last but a critical step in the production of a high quality shortened cake. The changes that take place in the batter as it is heated determine whether the finished cake's volume, grain, and texture measure up to the potential of the batter. Batter next to the sides and bottom of the baking pan heats first, that in the center last (34). This difference in temperature causes flow of the batter, an example of which is shown in Figure 25-6. Carbon dioxide and steam collect in the air cells. Heat enlarges these cells, most rapidly as the temperature approaches 80°C (176°F), thus causing the batter to rise. Buildup of pressure in the hot, fluid batter causes violent motion of the constituents (5). The ability of the batter to withstand this pressure is critical if it is to yield a cake of high quality. Emulsifier confers elasticity on the film of protein around gas bubbles. Polyvalent ions supplied by milk, eggs, flour, and leaven contribute to stability of the batter, too (26). The cake is likely to fall if the oven is opened and the temperature of the batter drops at this stage.

In the final phase of the baking period, films of batter surrounding enlarged gas cells rupture, due to coagulation of protein and absorption of water by pasting starch granules. The fluid, inflated, closed-celled batter is changed to an open-celled, deformable, sponge-

Figure 25-6. Partial cross section of a layer cake, showing the flow pattern of white and colored batters caused by convection currents during baking. (From H. B. Trimbo, S. Ma, and B. S. Miller, *Bakers Digest* 40(1):42, 1966. Reprinted by permission.)

like solid. Pasting of the starch grains may be incomplete because of insufficient water or because of the high level of sugar (14). Part of the fat appears at the air/cake crumb interface. Evaporation of moisture from the surface during the early part of the baking period keeps the surface cool, but eventually the crust gets hot enough to brown.

Heat Penetration during Baking

A baking temperature of 185°C (365°F) or even 190°C (375°F) gives cakes with greater volume and finer crumb than does a lower baking temperature. The effects of oven temperature on volume and grain of cakes are shown in Figure 25-4 (29). A preheated oven is recommended for cakes because of more rapid heat penetration. Baking temperature also affects the contour of the cake. Expansion in the interior after batter on the surface began to set accounts for the rounded top and the slightly humped top of cakes baked at 218° and 185°C (425° and 375°F), respectively.

Heat penetration in cake batter is influenced by factors in addition to the baking temperature (11). Heat transfer is discussed in Chapter 4. The emissivity of the baking pan, which depends upon the material and its finish, is one factor (9,12). Cakes baked in dark or dull pans will bake more quickly and the volume of the cake will be larger, the cells smaller, and the texture of the crumb fine and velvety. On the other hand, slower-baking pans, those that are bright and shiny, will give cakes with smaller volume and coarser grain. Two-thirds of the heating accomplished in an oven is effected by radiant energy. A bright, shiny surface deflects much of this radiant energy and so slows down the baking rate. Fast-baking pans, although they do produce a superior cake in most respects, do not give the best-looking ones. The top tends to be humped, and browning is less uniform. For appearance, choose a shiny pan at the expense of interior quality and volume. However, the combination of a reflective baking pan and a household oven as currently engineered represents an inefficient utilization of energy (34).

Tunnels are more likely to occur in shortened cake baked at a high temperature, in one baked in an eight-inch rather than a nine-inch pan, in cake with a low sugar/flour ratio (42) and in cake baked in a microwave oven (22).

REFERENCES

1. Ash, D. J., and J. C. Colmey. 1973. "The role of pH in cake baking." *Bakers Digest* 47(1):36–39, 42, 64. Factors influencing pH; effects on color, flavor, and stability of emulsion.

2. Baxter, A. J., and E. E. Hester. 1958. "The effect of sucrose on gluten development and the solubility of the proteins of soft wheat flour." *Cereal Chemistry* 35:366–74. An attempt to account for the effects of sucrose on baked products made with flour.

3. Bean, M. M., and W. T. Yamazaki. 1978. "Wheat starch gelatinization." 1. "Sucrose: Microscopy and viscosity effects." *Cereal Chemistry* 55:936–44. Effects of concentration on the initial stage and the extent of gelatinization of wheat starch grains.

4. Bean, M. M., W. T. Yamazaki, and D. H. Donelson. 1978. "Wheat-starch gelatinization in sugar solutions." 2. "Fructose, glucose, and sucrose: Cake performance." *Cereal Chemistry* 55:945–52. Effects of concentration as well as kind of sugar.

5. Bell, A. V., K. G. Berger, J. V. Russo, G. W. White, and T. L. Weathers. 1975. "A study of the micro-baking of sponges and cakes using cine and television microscopy." *Journal of Food Technology* 10:147–50. Temperature rise and gaseous diffusion and expansion.

6. Berglund, P. T., and D. M. Hertsgaard. 1986. "Use of vegetable oils at reduced levels in cake, pie crust, cookies and muffins." *Journal of Food Science* 51:640–44. Two oils at two levels in cake.

7. Birnbaum, H. 1978. "Surfactants and shortening in cake making." *Bakers Digest* 52(1):28, 30, 32, 34–35, 38. Surfactants for liquid and plastic shortenings.

8. Carlin, G. T. 1944. "A microscopic study of the behavior of fats in cake batters." *Cereal Chemistry* 21:189–99. Structure of shortened cake batters, effects of emulsifier, fate of air cells, and formation of crumb structure during baking.

9. Charley, H. 1950. "Effects of baking pan material on heat penetration during baking and on quality of cakes made with fat." *Food Research* 15:155–68. Volume and crumb characteristics of cakes baked in pans varying in emissivity.

10. Charley, H. 1951. "Heat penetration during baking and quality of shortened cakes varying in pH value." *Food Research* 16:181–86. Effects of two levels of cream of tartar and two levels of baking soda.

11. Charley, H. 1952. "Effects of size and shape of the baking pan on the quality of shortened cakes." *Journal of Home Economics* 44:115–18. Effects of pan depth; effects of the shape of pans with the same capacity.

12. Charley, H. 1956. "Characteristics of shortened cake baked in a fast- and in a slow-baking pan at different oven temperatures." *Food Research* 21:302–5. An attempt to compensate for the pan effect by alterations in baking temperature.

13. Davies, J. R. 1937. "The effect of formula and procedure variables upon cake quality." *Cereal Chemistry* 14:819–33. Liquid, fat, sugar, and baking powder varied; also mixing time, amount of batter in pan, and baking temperature.

14. Derby, R. I., B. S. Miller, B. F. Miller, and H. B. Trimbo. 1975. "Visual observation of wheat-starch gelatinization in limited water systems." *Cereal Chemistry* 52:702–13. Variations in water from 33 to 60 percent; effect of sugar on available water.

15. Dyar, E., and E. Cassel. 1948. "Mile-high cakes." *Colorado Agricultural Experiment Station Bulletin 404-A.* 27 pp. Recipes for different altitudes.

16. Frye, A. M., and C. S. Setser. 1992. "Optimizing texture in reduced calorie yellow layer cake." *Cereal Chemistry* 69:338–43. Successful formulation of shortening-free cake.

17. Glicksman, M. 1991. "Hydrocolloids and the search for the 'Oily Grail.'" *Food Technology* 45(10):94–103. Fat substitutes and formulas for lowfat and shortening-free cakes.

18. Grewe, E. 1930. "Effect of variation of ingredients on color of chocolate cake." *Cereal Chemistry* 7:59–66. Hydrogen-ion concentration and the color of chocolate cakes.

454

19. Guy, E. J., and H. E. Vettel. 1973. "Effects of mixing time and emulsifier on yellow cakes containing butter." *Bakers Digest* 47(1):43–46, 48. Character of the crumb with and without emulsifier.

20. Handelman, A. R., J. F. Conn, and J. W. Lyon. 1961. "Bubble mechanics in thick foams and their effects on cake quality." *Cereal Chemistry* 38:294–305. Technical treatment of the fate of gas bubbles in cake batter.

21. HEIB. "Finished foods—A first report." 1961. "Cake-mix cakes—shortening type." *Journal of Home Economics* 53:281–84. Factors contributing to success; defects and their causes.

22. Hill, M., and S. P. Reagen. 1982. "Effect of microwave and conventional baking on yellow cakes." *Journal of the American Dietetics Association* 80:52–55. Effect of turntable as well as type of oven.

23. Hoerr, C. W., and D. F. Waugh. 1955. "Some physical characteristics of rearranged lard." *Journal of the American Oil Chemists' Society* 32:37–41. Effects of rearrangement on creaming quality of lard and on aeration of cake batter.

24. Hood, I. L., and L. A. Campbell. 1990. "Developing reduced calorie baking products with sucralose." *Cereal Foods World* 35(12):1171–82. Its potential as a sugar substitute.

25. Horton, S. D., G. N. Lauer, and J. S. White. 1990. "Predicting gelatinization temperature of starch/sweetener systems for cake formulation by differential scanning calorimetry." *Cereal Foods World* 35:734–37, 739. Sweetener, water, and flour ratio and starch gelatinization temperature.

26. Howard, N. B. 1972. "The role of some essential ingredients in the formation of layer cake structure." *Bakers Digest* 46(5):28–30, 32, 34, 36–37, 64. Aeration, stability, and thermal setting of batter.

27. Howard, N. B., D. H. Hughes, and R. G. K. Strobel. 1968. "Function of starch granule in the formation of layer cake structure." *Cereal Chemistry* 45:329–38. Its role in thermal setting of the batter.

28. Johnson, J. M., and C. H. Harris. 1989. "Effects of acidulants in controlling browning in cakes prepared with 100% high-fructose corn syrup or sucrose." *Cereal Chemistry* 66:158–61. Cream of tartar and glucono-delta-lactone used.

29. Jooste, M. E., and A. O. Mackey. 1952. "Cake structure and palatability as affected by emulsifying agents and baking temperatures." *Food Research* 17:185–96. Effects of glyceryl monostearate on batters made with butter and with hydrogenated vegetable shortening; effects of baking temperature; photomicrographs of batter and photographs of cakes.

30. Kulp, K., K. Lorenz, and M. Stone. 1991. "Functionality of carbohydrate ingredients in bakery products." *Food Technology* 46(3):136–40, 146. Fat substitutes and bulking agents.

31. Miller, B. S., and H. B. Trimbo. 1965. "Gelatinization of starch and white layer cake quality." *Food Technology* 19:640–48. Interrelations of sugar, water, and gelatinization of starch as cake bakes.

32. Miller, B. S., H. B. Trimbo, and K. P. Powell. 1967. "Effects of flour granulation and starch damage on the cake making qualities of soft wheat flour." *Cereal Science Today* 12:245–47, 250–52. Effect of pin-milling.

33. Ngo, W., R. C. Hoseney, and W. R. Moore. 1985. "Dynamic rheological properties of cake batters made from chlorine-treated and untreated flours." *Journal of Food Science* 50:1338–41. Attempts to account for the action of chlorine reviewed.

34. Peart, V., S. T. Kern and D. P. DeWitt. 1980. "Optimizing oven radiant energy use." *Home Economics Research Journal* 8:242–51. Order in which areas of layer cake baked in a conventional and in a biradiant oven achieve doneness.

35. Pohl, P. H., A. C. Mackey, and B. L. Cornelia. 1968. "Freeze-drying cake batter for microscopic study." *Journal of Food Science* 33:318–20. Gas bubbles in the aqueous phase of batter.

36. Pyke, W. E., and G. Johnson. 1940. "Relation of mixing method and a balanced formula to quality and economy in high-sugar-ratio cakes." *Food Research* 5:335–59. Principles underlying balancing ingredients

in shortened cakes, with emphasis on cakes at high altitude.

37. Shellenberger, J. A., F. W. Wichser, and R. C. Lakamp. 1950. "Cake properties in relation to flour particle size." *Cereal Chemistry* 27:106–13. Effect of size of particles on cake quality; illustrated.

38. Staff. 1988. "Application of aspartame in baking." *Food Technology* 42(1):56, 58. Encapsulation for time/temperature release.

39. Telloke, G. W. 1985. "Chlorination of cake flour and its effect on starch gelatinization." *Stärke* 37:17–22. Effects on hot paste viscosity of batter and exudate of amylose.

40. Thompson, S. W., and J. E. Gannon. 1956. "Observations on the influence of texturation, occluded gas content, and emulsifier content on shortening performance in cake making." *Cereal Chemistry* 33:181–89. Cake quality affected by the interaction of occluded gas, emulsifier content, and manipulation.

41. Trimbo, H. B., S. Ma, and B. S. Miller. 1966. "Batter flow and ring formation in cake making." *Bakers Digest* 40(1):40–42, 44–45. A study of convection currents in the batter as it bakes.

42. Trimbo, H. B., and B. S. Miller. 1973. "The development of tunnels in cakes." *Bakers Digest* 47(5):24–27, 71. Contributing factors: mechanism of formation.

43. Tsen, C. C., K. Kulp, and C. J. Daly. 1971. "Effect of chlorine on flour proteins, dough properties, and cake quality." *Cereal Chemistry* 48:247–55. Advantages of chlorine treatment.

44. Vaisey-Genser, M., G. Ylimaki, and B. Johnston. 1987. "The selection of levels of canola oil, water and emulsifier system in cake formulation by response-surface methodology." *Cereal Chemistry* 64:50–54. Technique useful in arriving at optimum levels of ingredients.

45. Volpe, T. and C. Meres. 1976. "Use of high fructose syrups in white layer cake." *Bakers Digest* 50(2):38–41. Effects on cake quality.

46. Wilson, J. T. and D. H. Donelson. 1963. "Studies on the dynamics of cake-baking." I. "The role of water in the formation of layer cake structure." *Cereal Chemistry* 40:466–81. Influence of proportions of liquid on volume and contour of cake and on crumb quality.

47. Wootton, J. C., N. B. Howard, J. B. Martin, D. E. McOsker and J. Holme. 1967. "The role of emulsifiers in the incorporation of air in layer cake batter systems." *Cereal Chemistry* 44:333–43. Surfactants for aerating cake batter made by the single stage.

48. Yamazaki, W. T. and D. H. Donelson. 1972. "The relationship between flour particle size and cake volume potential among Eastern soft wheats." *Cereal Chemistry* 49:649–53. Importance of particle size.

Sponge, Angel Food, and Chiffon Cakes

26

Sponge and angel food cakes are sometimes referred to as foam cakes. Justification for so classifying these cakes is that a foam is formed first by beating egg whites and then adding the sugar, after which flour is incorporated into the watery film around the air cells. Such a designation may be misleading because almost all batters and doughs are foams. A more appropriate term for cakes of this type might be meringue cakes, because basically the batters are meringues into which cake flour has been incorporated.

DESIRABLE CHARACTERISTICS

A flat or slightly rounded top is desired in a cake of this type. The top crust should consist of numerous small pores and be an even, delicate brown. Crumb of angel cake should be snowy white, that of sponge cake a golden yellow, and chiffon cake a pale yellow. It should be slightly moist rather than either dry or sticky. Small, uniform cells with thin walls are desired. The crumb should be resilient yet tender. The cake should be light and have a delicate flavor (12).

INGREDIENTS AND THEIR FUNCTIONS

Sponge and angel food cake and, to a lesser extent, chiffon cake have high proportions of egg, sugar, and liquid to cake flour. Fat is used only in chiffon cake, which is made with salad oil (Table 26-1). Chiffon cake resembles sponge cake because of the proportion of eggs, but it also has some of the quality of a shortened cake due to the inclusion of salad oil and baking powder.

Eggs

Angel food cake is made from egg whites; sponge and chiffon cakes are made with yolks as well as whites. Eggs are important ingredients in cakes of this type both because of the quantity included and the functions they perform. The proteins of eggs make possible incorporation of air into the batter. Air provides approximately half the leavening in angel food cake (1). When egg yolk only is beaten as for sponge cake, the plasma and especially the low-density lipoproteins contribute to aeration. The high density granules that inhibit aeration do help to retain the incorporated air (18). Foam formation is discussed in Chapter 18 and the foaming of egg proteins in Chapter 21. Eggs supply water

TABLE 26-1
Formulas for Meringue-Type Cakes

Ingredients	Sponge	Angel Food	Chiffon
Cake flour	1 cup	1 cup	1⅛ cups
Sugar	1 cup	1¼ to 1½ cups	¾ cup
Egg yolk	½ cup	—	³⁄₁₆ cup
Egg white	¾ cup	1¼ to 1½ cups	½ cup
Salt	¼ tsp	¼ tsp	½ tsp
Cream of tartar	¾ tsp	1 to 1¼ tsp	¼ tsp
Vanilla	1 tsp	1 tsp	1 tsp
Water	3 Tbsp	—	⅜ cup
Salad oil	—	—	¼ cup
Baking powder	—	—	1½ tsp

that is essential if flour is to form a batter. Part of the water serves as a source of leavening agent when it is converted to steam. Water is essential for gelatinization and pasting of the starch that helps to set the cake crumb. Coagulation of egg proteins by heat during baking contributes markedly to the structure of cakes of this type. The proteins of eggs thus not only make possible the formation of a foam that becomes the grain of a cake but also contribute to the conversion of the foamy batter during baking to a moist, deformable sponge (6).

An early study (20) examined the role of the different proteins of egg white in the production of angel food cake. It established that the globulins are the chief foaming agent, that viscous ovomucin stabilizes the foam, and that heat-denaturable ovalbumin contributes to the structure of the baked cake. Egg whites with globulins and ovomucin removed require an extended beating time and give angel food cake with low volume. Globulins and ovomucin form an excellent batter that rises during baking, but the cake collapses. Failure can be attributed to lack of heat-denaturable protein. In a later study, individual proteins were separated from egg white and were tested individually and in different combinations for their ability to form foams and for their angel food cake-making potential (14). Globulins foam well and yield large cakes with excellent texture. Ovalbumin alone foams only after extended beating and yields cakes with large volumes but coarse texture. The other four proteins—conalbumin, lysozyme, ovomucin, and ovomucoid—have limited capacity for foam formation. Cakes made with globulins differ little in tenderness from those made with the recombined proteins. Cakes made with ovalbumin are only slightly less tender. The remaining proteins make less tender cakes. Interactions when two or more of the proteins are combined affect foam formation, volume, and tenderness of the cakes (15). Data from these interactions were used to determine that a combination of 0.2 to 1.0 percent ovomucin, 0.0 to 1.8 percent lysozyme, and 12.2 to 14.8 percent globulin is optimum for both foam formation and for volume of angel food cake. These values are in contrast to 1.5 percent ovomucin, 3.5 percent lysozyme, and 8 percent globulins in typical egg white. Although egg white as a foam- and cake-forming ingredient could be improved, the hen does a creditable job of formulating it without benefit of an in-house chemist.

Eggs of low quality give a cake of reduced volume (7). Commercial frozen and dried egg whites and egg yolks have been pasteurized or otherwise treated to eliminate viable salmonella. Inclusion of a whipping aid in the whites helps to counteract any deleterious effect of processing on foaming (26). Even so, dried whites in a packaged angel food cake mix not only can tolerate but, in fact, require far more beating than do fresh ones to produce a fine, stable foam. The freezing process itself does no damage to the foaming ability of frozen egg whites. Whites not exposed to heat prior to freezing whip to a foam more readily than do fresh whites and yield a cake of high quality (4, 21). The presence of fat is detrimental to foam formation (17). Traces of fat from a yolk that is broken when an egg is separated may retard foaming of the egg white and reduce the beaten volume. The deleterious effect of yolk on the volume and acceptability of angel food cake can be counteracted in part by supplementing the white with two percent of freeze-dried white (25).

Sugar

Sugar is a tenderizing ingredient used to counterbalance the eggs and flour. For a cake made near sea level, the weight of the sugar should not exceed the weight of the eggs by more than 25 percent. For higher altitudes (where the boiling point of water is low), the weight of sugar should be reduced or the flour increased (1). Otherwise, elevation of the coagulation temperature of egg proteins by the sugar and limited pasting of the starch will delay setting of the batter (8, 23). Tenderness increases as the ratio of sugar to flour increases to a maximum of 3:1 on a weight basis. Sugar dissolved in the aqueous film around the air bubbles retards or limits denaturation of the proteins thus keeping the films flexible. Sugar with a fine granulation that dissolves readily is preferred for meringue-type cakes. Sugar participates in the browning of the crust. Substituting high fructose corn syrup for ¼ of the sucrose has no marked effect on the quality of angel food cake, but higher levels of replacement affect volume, tenderness, and color or both crumb and crust adversely (5).

Acid

Meringue-type cakes are not really successful unless the batter contains acid (11) (Fig. 26-1). Although acid added to egg white decreases somewhat the yield of foam, cakes made from such foams are larger, have finer grain, and are more tender. This favorable effect of acid on cake is attributed to its stabilizing action on the protein that collects at the air–liquid interface in the foam (1). Presumably, acid enables the films of protein in the air cells of the foam, which serve as the basis for the cells of the cake, to last until the heat penetrates the cake enough to set the structure of the crumb. Acid changes the pale yellowish green flavonoid pigment in egg white to colorless form. Angel food cake made with acid is snowy white compared to the pale yellow of one without acid. Meringue-type cakes are made with either lemon juice or cream of tartar. Cream of tartar is superior to either citric or acetic acid, when the amount of acid added is sufficient to bring the pH of the batter to 6.0 or lower (1). The pH of angel food cake batter is near 5 compared to a pH of 8 to 9 for egg white.

Flour

Flour, like the proteins of egg, contributes structure to meringue-type cakes. Because of its composition and fine granulation, cake flour must be used for sponge and angel cakes if they are to be of top quality. For cakes of this type the proportion of flour should be less than half that of the eggs on a weight basis; otherwise, the cake will be tough.

Figure 26-1. Effects of increasing amounts of cream of tartar on grain and volume of angel cake. (*a*) 0.0 gram; (*b*) 0.4 gram; (*c*) 0.8 gram; and (*d*) 1.2 grams. (From Emily Grewe and A. M. Child, *Cereal Chemistry* 7:247, 1930. Reprinted by permission.)

Angel Food Cake Packaged Mix

The formula for angel food cake packaged mix includes sodium lauryl sulfate as a foam promoter in addition to the egg white, cream of tartar, sugar, and cake flour of traditional angel food cake. Baking soda and acid ingredients such as calcium acid phosphate and sodium aluminum phosphate are included as a source of carbon dioxide to supplement the air incorporated in the egg white foam. The mix may also contain one or more starches or starch derivatives such as modified cornstarch and maltodextrin or vegetable gums. These contribute viscosity to the batter and rigidity to the cake crumb.

MANIPULATION OF ANGEL FOOD CAKE BATTER

Angel food cake requires fewer ingredients than do other types of meringue cakes. Manipulation presents fewer problems, too. Even so, the technique used to manipulate ingredients for angel food cake may make the difference between success and failure.

Making the Meringue

For the conventional two-stage method, the egg whites, preferably at 21°C (70°F) (21), are beaten to the foamy stage. Salt and acid are added and beating is continued until the foam forms soft peaks but is still soft enough to flow in the bowl (Fig. 26-2). When the egg foam reaches this stage, a portion of the sugar should be added *promptly*. Beating (slow speed) each addition of sugar into the egg white dissolves the sugar and stabilizes the foam, which at this point consists of air cells surrounded by films of syrup containing egg pro-

Figure 26-2. Egg whites beaten to the soft peak stage. They are still glossy and moist-looking and will flow in the bowl if it is tipped. Prompt addition of sugar at this stage is essential to keep the foam from becoming stiff and inelastic. (Photograph by Wilbur Nelson.)

teins. If sugar is added too soon, the egg whites must be beaten longer, but there is less danger of overbeating the foam. If egg whites are overbeaten and the foam is made inelastic before the sugar is added, the cells break during subsequent manipulation. Leaven is lost and the gas cells are unable to expand as they should during baking. A cake compact and small in volume results.

After the last portion of sugar is added the foam should be beaten until it is fine grained. Cells in the baked cake are always somewhat coarser than they were in the meringue from which the cake was made. Heat expands air cells and generates steam that collects in and further inflates the cells. Movement of gases from smaller to larger bubbles also takes place until the batter sets (2). If the meringue is underbeaten, the cells of the cake will be large, the cell walls thick, the crumb gummy, and the volume of the cake small. If the meringue is overbeaten, the cells become very small, the foam inelastic, and the cake compact and lower in volume although fine grained. If the meringue is beaten to the optimum stage, the cells of the cake will be desirably small, the cell walls thin, the crumb tender, and the volume large. Up to a point, the more the meringue is beaten the larger will be the volume of the cake. However, a point is reached at which denaturation of protein in the film makes it inelastic and so offsets any increase in the amount of air incorporated. Overbeaten meringues lose additional air when flour is incorporated. The character of the meringue when incorporation of the flour begins is crucial in determining the quality of the cake.

Incorporation of Flour

The objective in folding the flour into meringue is to distribute the particles of flour uniformly in the syrupy film around the air cells. This requires deft handling. A flexible spatula or French whip may be used. Making a meringue of the egg white and part of the sugar strengthens the foam and minimizes loss of volume as flour is folded in. Too, flour can be distributed more readily if part of the sugar has been sifted with it. Sifting portions of the flour–sugar mixture over the surface of the foam and folding it into the foam *promptly* facilitates even distribution of the flour. Delay in folding may result in uneven distribution of the flour. Folding should be gentle and should be discontinued as soon as the flour is evenly distributed. The less the batter is folded after the flour is added, the less the flour is hydrated; the longer the batter is folded, the more water the injured starch granules absorb and the tighter the batter. Undermanipulation at this stage gives a tender cake but one with

(a)

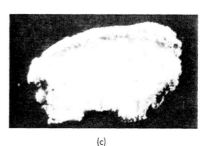

(b)

(c)

Figure 26-3. Extent of folding flour and sugar into angel food cake. (a) Under-manipulation gives uneven grain, coarse texture, and low volume. (b) Optimum and gentle folding gives moderately fine grain, light spongy texture, and good volume. (c) Overmanipulation and rough handling results in close texture and small volume. (From E. G. Halliday and I. T. Noble, *Hows and Whys of Cooking*, Chicago: University of Chicago Press, 1946. Reprinted by permission of Isabel Noble.)

coarse cells and uneven texture; overmanipulation makes for finer cells but a cake that is tougher, more compact, and smaller in volume. Figure 26-3 illustrates the effects of manipulation on cake quality.

MANIPULATION OF SPONGE CAKE BATTER

Making sponge cake involves more complicated procedures than making angel cake. Thus there are more opportunities for mistakes in technique. A number of different routines have been worked out for combining the ingredients of sponge cake. The one outlined below gives good results in the hands of the inexperienced. The yolks are beaten first because this foam does not set upon standing as does that from beaten egg white. The yolks should be beaten until they are *thick* and a light lemon color. A portion of the sugar may be beaten into this foam. The egg whites are beaten and made into a meringue with part of the sugar, as for angel food cake. The flour that has been sifted with the remainder of the sugar is folded into the beaten egg yolks. Excessive folding at this stage should be avoided. Otherwise the mixture will be so stiff that it is difficult to combine the yolk–flour mixture and the beaten egg white without loss of air. Finally, the yolk–flour mixture and the beaten whites are combined by folding until no streaks of white are visible. Folding should be continued no longer than is necessary to accomplish this. Otherwise the flour will absorb too much liquid and the foam will begin to collapse.

Alternate methods for combining the ingredients for sponge cakes include (1) combining the beaten egg yolk and beaten white before the flour is folded in; (2) making the sugar into a syrup (boiling point 118°C or 245°F) that is beaten into the beaten whites before the whites and beaten yolks are combined and the flour is folded in; and (3) beating the whole egg until it is very stiff and then beating in the sugar and finally folding in the flour. When the last method is used, the salt should be sifted with the flour rather than added to the eggs (3). Whipping reconstituted dried whole egg at 60°C (140°F) facilitates the formation of a foam (16). Inclusion of high HLB sucrose fatty acid esters yields sponge cake with improved tenderness, texture, and volume (22).

MANIPULATION OF CHIFFON CAKE BATTER

The proportion of ingredients for chiffon cake are the same as those for quick-mix cake (Chapter 25) except for the higher proportion of egg and the inclusion of cream of tartar in chiffon cake. Egg yolk, salad oil, water, and vanilla are added to the sifted dry ingredients (except the cream of tartar) and the batter is beaten until it is satiny smooth. The cream of tartar is added to the egg whites that have been beaten to the foamy stage and beating is continued until the foam forms stiff peaks. The egg foam is folded into the batter.

BAKING

These cake batters are unstable and they should be transferred to the baking pan and baked at once; otherwise, the batter tends to layer, with the largest air cells rising to the top.

Baking Pan

Angel or sponge cake batter may be baked in loaf pans as well as in the usual tubular angel food cake pan. The tube in the latter provides support for the cake as well as more surface for heating it. Sponge cake batter baked in a shallow pan is used for jelly rolls. Angel food cakes baked in aluminum or tinned pans have thinner, lighter brown crusts than do those baked in glass or enameled iron (24). It is essential to remove all trace of fat from the pan so that the cake batter can adhere as it rises and bakes. If the pan has been used for other purposes, it should be cleaned thoroughly. Hot water with some ammonia is particularly effective.

Baking Time and Temperature

Cakes of this type are baked in a preheated oven. Gas cells begin to expand when the temperature of the batter approaches 40°C (104°F), but the major expansion is due to steam that accumulates in the cells. The low baking temperature formerly recommended for meringue-type cakes was based on the reasoning that high temperatures should be avoided because these cakes contain a high proportion of eggs. The assumption was that a high oven temperature meant a high internal temperature in the cake. Actually, there is very little difference in internal temperature regardless of baking temperature (1). In addition, the effects of sugar on the coagulation temperature of the egg proteins and on the gelatinization of starch were not considered (9). In one study, cakes baked at 177°C (350°F) rather than 163°C (325°F), 149°C (300°F), or 138°C (280°F) were bigger and seemed more moist and more tender. The superior quality of the cakes baked at higher temperatures is attributed to more rapid setting of the batter and absorption of less water by the starch of

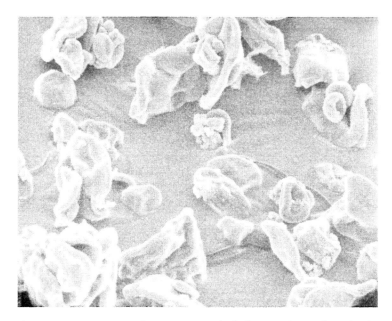

Figure 26-4. Scanning electron micrograph of wheat starch granules isolated from angel food cake. (From R. C. Hoseney, W. A. Atwell, and D. R. Lineback, *Cereal Foods World* 22(2):57, 1977. Reprinted by permission.)

the flour. The effects of even higher baking temperatures have been evaluated, resulting in the recommendation of a baking temperature of 204°C (400°F) or 218°C (425°F) (21). When the temperature of the coherent films that define the gas cells nears 88°C (190°F), the films lose their elasticity and expansion of the gas cells ceases (2). Breaks in the pasted starch-coagulated protein films allow passage of steam and air and establish the texture of the crumb. Explosive rupture of material around the gas cells occurs in cake batter made with chlorinated flour but not in batter made with nonchlorinated flour (2).

Approximate baking times are 30 and 25 minutes for the two higher baking temperatures compared to 40 minutes at 177°C (350°F). Cake baked at a higher temperature has larger volume and is more tender but tends to brown excessively. A few minutes overbaking does far more harm at a higher baking temperature. A piece of brown paper placed on a rack above the cake near the end of the baking period reduces excess browning of the top crust. More recently, angel cakes made from one-step packaged mix and baked at 177° or 191°C (350° and 375°F) were judged better in quality and had greater volume than cakes baked at 204° or 218°C (400° or 450°F) (10). Starch granules isolated from angel food cake show extensive folding and deformation, indicative of a fairly advanced stage of gelatinization (13) (Fig. 26-4).

Some shrinkage should be expected near the end of the baking period and as the cake cools. Because of the elastic character of baked meringue-type cakes, the pan should be upturned and the cake left to hang and stretch as it cools to room temperature before it is loosened and removed from the pan. Elasticity of the crumb makes the cake hard to cut. A sharp knife with a serrated edge and a sawing motion should be used. Dampening the blade facilitates cutting.

REFERENCES

1. Barmore, M. A. 1936. "The influence of various factors, including altitude, in the production of angel food cake." *Colorado Experiment Station Technical Bulletin 15.* 54 pp. Experimental data on the factors which contribute to success.

2. Bell, A. V., K. G. Berger, J. V. Russo, G. W. White, and T. L. Weathers. 1975. "A study of the micro-baking of sponges and cakes using cine and television microscopy." *Journal of Food Technology* 10:147–56. An inside view of sponge, pound, and high-ratio cakes as they bake.

3. Briant, A. M., and A. R. Willman. 1956. "Whole-egg sponge cake." *Journal of Home Economics* 48:420–21. Directions for making sponge cake from unseparated eggs.

4. Clinger, C., A. Young, I. Prudent, and A. R. Winter. 1951. "The influence of pasteurization, freezing, and storage on the functional properties of egg white." *Food Technology* 5:166–70. Angel food cake is the test material.

5. Coleman, P. E., and C. A. Z. Harbers. 1983. "High fructose corn syrup replacement for sucrose in angel food cake." *Journal of Food Science* 48:452–56. Four levels of replacement compared.

6. Davies, A. P. 1986. "Protein functionality in bakery products." In *Chemistry and Technology of Baking.* J. M. V. Blanshard, P. J. Frazier, and T. Galliard, eds. London: The Royal Society of Chemistry. Pp. 89–104. Emphasis on egg proteins in sponge cake.

7. Dawson, E. H., C. Miller, and R. A. Redstrom. 1956. "Cooking quality and flavor of eggs as related to candled quality, storage conditions and other factors." *U.S. Dept. Agr. Inf. Bull. No. 164.* 44 pp. Relationship between the candled characteristics of eggs and their functional properties in cooking; research at three experiment stations summarized graphically.

8. Derby, R. I., B. S. Miller, B. F. Miller and H. B. Trimbo. 1975. "Visual observation of wheat-starch gelatinization in limited water systems." *Cereal Chemistry* 52:702–13. Levels of water from 32 to 60 percent compared.

9. Donovan, J. W. 1977. "A study of the baking process by differential scanning calorimetry." *Journal of the Science of Food and Agriculture* 28:571–78. Effect of sugar on the temperature of gelatinization of starch and denaturization of protein.

10. Elgidaily, D. A., K. Funk, and M. E. Zabik. 1969. "Baking temperature and quality of angel cakes." *Journal of the American Dietetics Association* 54:401–6. Four temperatures compared, using a one-stage packaged mix.

11. Grewe, E., and A. M. Child. 1930. "The effect of potassium acid tartrate as an ingredient in angel cake." *Cereal Chemistry* 7:245–50. A neat experiment to assess the functions of cream of tartar in angel cake.

12. HEIB Finished foods—a second report. 1961. "Cake-mix cakes—foam type." *Journal of Home Economics* 53:759–62. Characteristics; factors for success; defects and their causes.

13. Hoseney, R. C., A. W. Atwell, and D. R. Lineback. 1977. "Scanning electron microscopy of starch isolated from baked products." *Cereal Foods World* 22(2):56–60. Extent of gelatinization of starch in starch–water and flour–water systems, in doughs, and starch isolated from baked products.

14. Johnson, T. M., and M. E. Zabik. 1981. "Egg albumin protein interactions in an angel food cake system" *Journal of Food Science* 46:1231–36. Contributions to foaming and to volume and tenderness of cake.

15. Johnson, T. M., and M. E. Zabik. 1981. "Response surface methodology for analysis of protein interactions in angel food cake." *Journal of Food Science* 46:1226–30. Optimum levels of ovomucin, lysozyme, and globulins for both foaming and cake volume.

16. Jordan, R., and M. S. Pettijohn. 1946. "Use of spray-dried whole-egg powder in sponge cakes." *Cereal Chemistry* 23:265–77. How to handle dried egg to obtain maximum foam volume.

17. Joslin, R. P., and B. E. Proctor. 1954. "Some factors affecting the whipping characteristics of dried whole egg powders."

Food Technology 8:150–54. Cause of the poor whipping ability and attempts to improve it.

18. Kamat, V. B., G. A. Lawrence, C. J. Hart, and R. Yoell. 1973. "Contribution of egg yolk lipoproteins to cake structure." *Journal of the Science of Food and Agriculture*. 24:77–88. The role of egg yolk protein fractions in foam formation.

19. Lineback, D. R., and E. Wongsrikasem. 1980. "Gelatinization of starch in baked products." *Journal of Food Science* 45:71–74. Cookies, angel food cake, and bread compared.

20. MacDonnell, L. R., R. E. Finney, H. L. Hanson, A. Campbell, and T. F. Sugihara. 1955. "The functional properties of egg white proteins." *Food Technology* 9:49–53. Early study of their roles in sponge cake making.

21. Miller, E. L., and G. E. Vail. 1943. "Angel food cake from fresh and frozen egg whites." *Cereal Chemistry* 20:528–35. Thick and thin frozen whites compared, beaten at four different temperatures; five baking temperatures compared.

22. Pierce, M. M., and C. E. Walker. 1987. "Addition of sucrose fatty acid ester emulsion to sponge cakes." *Cereal Chemistry* 64: 222–25. High HLB esters give cakes with improved texture, tenderness, and volume.

23. Pyke, W. E., and G. Johnson. 1940. "Preparing and baking yellow sponge cakes at different altitudes." *Colorado Experiment Station Technical Bulletin 27*. 22 pp. Problems involved in balancing recipes for different altitudes.

24. Reed, S. J., E. V. Floyd, and M. S. Pittman. 1937. "Effect of pan on temperature of baking and tenderness of angel food cake." *Journal of Home Economics* 29:188–92. Heat penetration in cakes, browning, and tenderness as affected by the baking pan.

25. Sauter, E. A., and J. E. Montoure. 1975. "Effects of adding 2% freeze-dried egg white to batters of angel food cakes made from whites containing egg yolk." *Journal of Food Science* 40:869–71. The beneficial effects of added white as related to the level of contamination.

26. Slosberg, H. M., H. L. Hanson, G. F. Stewart, and B. Lowe. 1948. "Factors influencing the effects of heat treatment on the leavening power of egg white." *Poultry Science* 27:294–301. Angel food cake is the test material.

PART VIII

Plant Foods

Fruits

27

Fruits are valued for their attractive color, for their pleasing aroma (due mainly to aldehydes, alcohols, and esters), for their sweet-tart taste, for their crisp, crunchy texture from water-inflated cells, and for the nutrients that they contribute to the diet. Fruits together with vegetables (Chapter 28) are emphasized in the Food Pyramid, designed as a guide to choose foods for a health-promoting diet. The per-capita consumption of fresh fruits was 58 kilograms (126.7 pounds) in 1994, up from 47.4 kilograms (104.8 pounds) in 1980 (42).

Most fruits consist of the pulpy, edible material that develops around and adheres to the seeds after a plant has flowered. The edible part may surround a core as in an apple (Fig. 27-1) or a hard stone as in apricots and peaches. A number of seeds may be enclosed in one ovary as in currants and gooseberries. The edible material may be surrounded by a hard rind as in muskmelon or by a leathery rind as in oranges and lemons. The fleshy fruit of the strawberry consists of the enlarged receptacle of the flower (Fig. 27-2). Both blackberries and raspberries are composed of the edible material around several ovaries from a single flower (Fig. 27-3). Pineapple, a multiple fruit, develops from several flowers, as do figs. Rhubarb, actually a stem, is considered a fruit.

Fruits are eaten raw, after freezing, or in dried form. In addition, fresh, frozen, or dried fruits may be cooked in a variety of ways. Elementary knowledge of the structure of plant material is basic to an understanding of the changes that take place in fruits before they are served. Much of the information that follows applies to vegetables as well as to fruits. In some cases the distinction between the two is a fine one. Tomatoes, served as juice for breakfast, do duty as a fruit, but for dinner they may be served as a vegetable. Used raw in salad, they are likely to be considered a vegetable. Botanically, cucumbers and squash are fruits, but in menu planning they are looked upon as vegetables.

STRUCTURE OF PLANT TISSUE

The basic structural unit of plant tissue is the cell. Fruits and vegetables, like cereals, are made of cells of different types. For example, the peel of an apple and the fleshy part underneath the skin are different because of differences in the structure of cells that make up the two types of tissue. Fruits and vegetables contain, in varying amounts, tissues of the following types: dermal, or protective; vascular, or food- and water-conducting; supporting; and parenchyma, or ground tissue. Parenchyma cells make up most of the edible parts of vegetables and fruits. (Fig. 27-4.) Typically polyhedral in shape, parenchyma

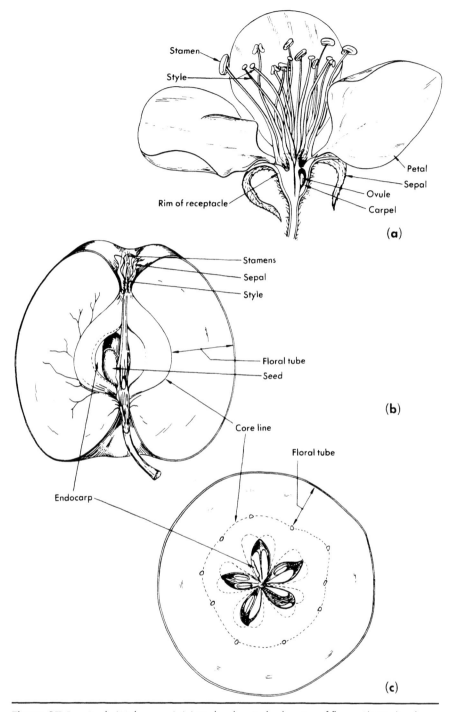

Figure 27-1. Apple (*Malus* genus). (*a*) Median longitudinal section of flower. (*b*) Median longitudinal section of mature apple. (*c*) Cross section of mature apple. (From *The Botany of Crop Plants* by W. W. Robbins. Copyright © 1917 by P. Blakiston's Son and Company. Used by permission of McGraw-Hill Book Company.)

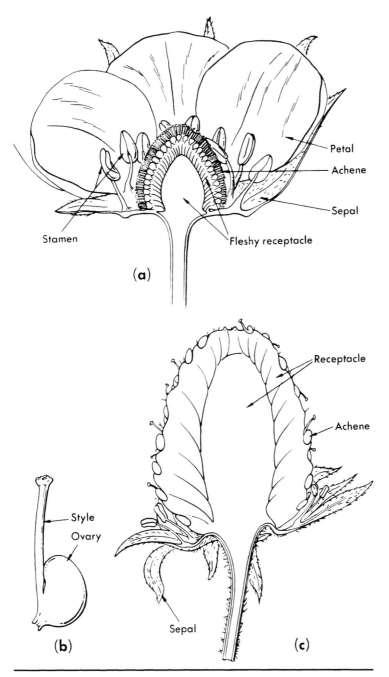

Figure 27-2. Strawberry (*Fragaria chiloensis*). (*a*) Median lengthwise section of flower. (*b*) Single achene. (*c*) Median lengthwise section of the aggregate fruit. (From *The Botany of Crop Plants* by W. W. Robbins. Copyright © 1917 by P. Blakiston's Son and Company. Used by permission of McGraw-Hill Book Company.)

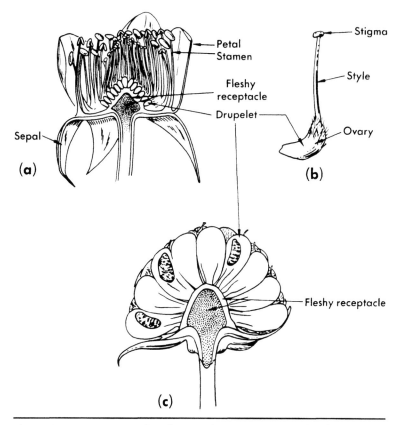

Figure 27-3. American red raspberry (*Rubus strigosus*). (*a*) Median lengthwise section of flower. (*b*) Single immature pistil. (*c*) Median lengthwise section of fruit. (From *The Botany of Crop Plants* by W. W. Robbins. Copyright © 1917 by P. Blakiston's Son and Company. Used by permission of McGraw-Hill Book Company.)

cells include those in which food is either synthesized or stored. Most of the cells of green leaves are examples of synthesizing cells, but the parenchyma cells that predominate in the edible part of an apple or potato store sugar and starch.

The Cell Wall

Plant cells are defined by a cell wall (Fig. 27-4) that surrounds and gives support to the cytoplasm of the cell (25, 47). Growing cells have a primary cell wall only, but in some tissues a secondary wall may be added to the primary wall once growth stops. Primary cell walls predominate in the edible parts of fruits. The walls are porous and permeable to water. They consist of roughly ¼ cellulose, ¼ hemicellulose, ⅓ pectic substances, and ⅙ protein (25).

Cellulose

Molecules of cellulose, β-1,4 linked glucose units (Chapter 9), are deposited in the cell wall in parallel array. These highly polymerized, linear molecules are joined in bundles of 60 to

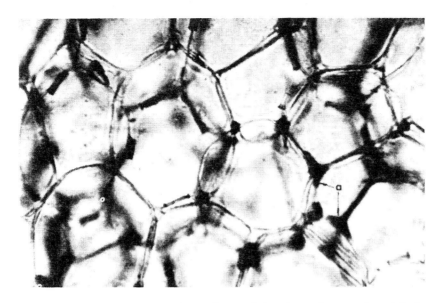

Figure 27-4. Microscopic view of parenchyma cells from living plant tissue (onion). Dark areas (*a*) are intercellular spaces filled with air. (Photograph by H. B. Currier, 1946. From T. E. Weier and R. Stocking, *Advances in Food Research* 2:299. Copyright © 1949 by Academic Press Inc.)

70 by intermolecular hydrogen bonds to form cellulose fibers that are highly crystalline in form (37). Extensive hydrogen bonding, both inter- and intramolecularly, account for the insolubility of cellulose fibers. The cellulose component provides flexibility and toughness to the cell wall.

Hemicellulose

Xyloglucans, polymers of the pentose (5-carbon), xylose, and glucose account for the major portion of hemicellulose in the cell wall. Glucuronoarabinoxylans, polymers of glucuronic acid, arabinose, and xylose, make up a minor fraction of the hemicelluloses of the cell wall (25). Hemicelluloses are not as highly polymerized as is cellulose and they are more vulnerable to degradation by alkali. When plant tissue is cooked in alkaline water (baking soda added), it becomes mushy due to the action of soda on the hemicelluloses of the cell wall.

The walls of parenchyma cells are relatively thin. In contrast, the walls of cells in outer or protective tissue that contain a higher proportion of celluloses and hemicelluloses are thick. The skin of apple, pear, tomato, and cucumber, and the rind of lemons and oranges are examples of such protective tissue. Cells that make up vascular tissue have thick cell walls high in cellulose, too. These are long slender cells united end to end to form hollow tubes whose function is to conduct either water or food throughout the plant. The walls of these cells and of those that form supporting tissue in plants may contain, in addition to cellulose, molecules of a group of substances known as lignin. Lignin, an aromatic substance derived from benzene, is the constituent that makes wood woody. It is deposited between crystallites of cellulose chiefly in secondary cell walls after growth ceases. The human digestive tract is unable to hydrolyze this material, and cooking has no effect on it. Edible parts of fruits do not usually contain heavily lignified tissue. However, the gritty deposits in pears, called sclereids, contain appreciable quantities of lignin.

Pectic Substances

Constituents of plant tissue known collectively as pectic substances are a part of the primary cell wall. They occupy the space, called middle lamella, between walls of adjacent cells. Pectic substances thus serve as the glue that converts groups of individual cells into tissue. Pectic substances are polymers of D-galacturonic acid united by the α-1,4-glycosidic linkage (11). The number of monomers varies from molecule to molecule. Occasional insertions of the sugar rhamnose via carbons 1,2 into the galacturonic acid chain results in a kink in the otherwise linear polymer. The sugars, arabinose and galactose, may be present, united to the polymer by glysosidic linkage via the rhamnose residues. These hairy regions, as they are called, contrast with the smooth regions of the polymer that contain no rhamnose but have xylose side chains (20). Carboxyl groups may be free or present as methyl esters. Formulas for galactose, galacturonic acid, and for a fragment of a pectin molecule are given below.

α-D-Galactose   α-D-Galacturonic Acid

Pectin

It is customary to classify pectic substances into one of three groups: pectic acids, pectinic acids (pectins), and protopectin. In pectic acids the carboxyl groups on the galacturonic acid residues in the polymer are not esterified. Pectic acids form salts, as do other acids and are assumed to be present in plant tissue as calcium or magnesium pectates. Pectinic acids have methyl ester groups esterified to some of the carboxyl groups along the galacturonic acid polymer as shown. If more than a negligible proportion of the carboxyl groups is esterified, the pectinic acid is designated as pectin. The nature of protopectin and the cause of its insolubility are still to be elucidated. Pectins and pectin gel formation are discussed in Chapter 31. Pectins are dispersible in water.

Glycoproteins

Proteins of the primary cell wall contain approximately 20 percent hydroxyproline (25). The sugar arabinose is joined to the protein via hydroxyl groups of the hydroxyproline residues and galactose by the hydroxyl groups of serine residues. Glycoproteins together with cellulose, hemicellulose, and pectic substances are deposited in the cell wall in such a way as to give structural integrity to plant tissue.

Cytoplasm

Inside the nonliving cell wall lies a protoplasmic membrane, also called plasmalemma, that encloses the protoplasm of the cell (Fig. 27-5). Just inside this membrane, in a narrow layer around the periphery of the cell, is the cytoplasm. The jellylike cytoplasm is colloidal in character and free to move about within the cell. Embedded in the cytoplasm are organized bodies called plastids. Fat droplets and pigments soluble in fat are contained within the plastids. In cells of certain plants the plastids serve as a storage place for starch, each starch-filled plastid constituting a starch granule. Cells of the potato as well as those of the endosperm of wheat and corn are packed full of such starch-filled plastids. (Fig. 10-2 and 28-3.) Also distributed throughout the protoplasm are the mitochondria in which enzymes are located. The nucleus of the cell is embedded in the cytoplasm.

Vacuole

A unique feature of most parenchyma cells is that up to 90 percent of the interior is occupied by one or more vacuoles or saclike spaces, shown schematically in Figure 27-5. Each is separated from the cytoplasm by a vacuolar membrane, also called a tonoplast.

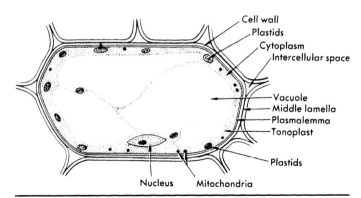

Figure 27-5. Diagram showing the main components of a parenchyma cell. (From V. A. Greulach and J. E. Adams. *Plants: An Introduction to Modern Botany*. Copyright © 1967 by John Wiley & Sons, Inc., New York, p. 114. Reprinted by permission.)

The vacuoles contain cell sap. Both the protoplasmic and the vacuolar membranes are semipermeable and osmotically active. They are made of a protein-lipid complex.

Intercellular Spaces

At the adjoining point of three or more cells, the fit may not be perfect. Instead, small spaces are left that become filled with intercellular gas. (Figs. 27-4, 27-5, and 27-6). These microscopic pockets of gas refract rays of light that hit them much as the pits in frosted glass make what was once clear glass appear milky white. These gas-filled spaces are mainly responsible for the opaqueness of uncooked plant tissue in contrast to the translucency of the cooked tissue. In some plant tissue the volume of intercellular gas is appreciable, in others negligible. Tissues from plums and potatoes contain relatively few intercellular spaces (38). In apples, however, gas-filled spaces between the cells may occupy 20 to 25 percent of the volume and account for the fact that apples float in water. Bobbing for apples in a tub of water on Halloween is possible because the fruit is buoyed up by this intercellular air. Otherwise, the fruit would sink.

COMPOSITION OF FRUITS

Water

Fruits tend to be juicy because of their high content of water, which varies from approximately 75 to 90 percent (Table 27-1). Dissolved in the water, the bulk of which is found in the vacuoles, are soluble substances like sugars, salts, organic acids, water-soluble pigments, and vitamins. Substances unable to dissolve in water are colloidally dispersed in it.

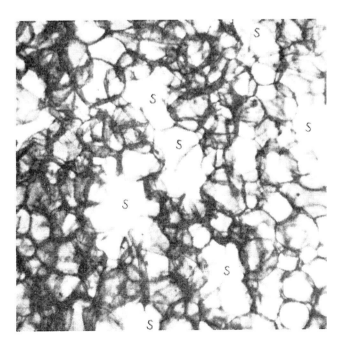

Figure 27-6.
Photomicrograph of the flesh of an apple (Gravenstein) showing parenchyma cells and large intercellular spaces (S). Tangential section. Original magnification × 40. (Courtesy of R. M. Reeve.)

TABLE 27-1
Composition of Raw Fruits (100-gram edible portion)

Fruit	Water (%)	Calories[a]	Protein (g)	Lipid (g)	Carbo-hydrate (g)	Calcium (mg)	Phos-phorus (mg)	Iron (mg)	Vitamin A Value (I.U.)	Thiamin (mg)	Ribo-flavin (mg)	Niacin (mg)	Ascorbic Acid (mg)	Fiber Crude (g)	Fiber Total Dietary (g)
Apple	83.9	59	0.2	0.3	15.3	7	7	0.2	53	0.02	0.01	0.08	5.7	0.8	2.2
Apricot	86.4	48	1.4	0.4	11.1	14	19	0.5	2,612	0.03	0.04	0.60	10.0	0.6	—[b]
Avocado	74.3	161	2.0	15.3	7.4	11	41	1.0	612	0.11	0.12	0.97	7.9	2.1	—
Banana	74.3	92	1.0	0.5	23.4	6	20	0.3	81	0.05	0.10	0.54	9.1	0.5	1.6
Cantaloupe	89.8	35	0.9	0.3	8.4	11	17	0.2	3,224	0.04	0.02	0.57	42.2	0.4	0.8
Grapefruit, white	86.8	32	0.6	0.1	8.2	15	7	0.1	10	0.04	0.02	0.27	37.0	0.2	0.6
Kiwi fruit	83.1	61	1.0	0.4	14.9	26	40	0.4	175	0.02	0.05	0.50	98.0	1.1	3.4
Lemon	89.0	29	1.1	0.3	9.3	26	16	0.6	29	0.04	0.02	0.10	53.0	0.4	—
Orange	86.8	47	0.9	0.1	11.8	40	14	0.1	205	0.09	0.04	0.28	53.2	0.4	2.4
Peach	87.7	43	0.7	0.1	11.1	5	12	0.1	535	0.02	0.04	0.99	6.6	0.6	1.6
Pear	83.8	59	0.4	0.4	15.1	11	11	0.3	20	0.02	0.04	0.10	4.0	1.4	2.6
Pineapple	86.5	49	0.4	0.4	12.4	7	7	0.3	23	0.09	0.04	0.42	15.4	0.5	1.2
Strawberry	91.6	30	0.6	0.4	7.0	14	19	0.4	27	0.02	0.07	0.23	56.7	0.5	2.6
Watermelon	91.5	32	0.6	0.4	7.2	8	9	0.2	366	0.08	0.02	0.20	9.6	0.3	0.4

[a] 1 kilocalorie = 4.185 kilojoules
[b] — = Data not available

Source: U.S.D.A., Agr. Handbook No. 8-9. Composition of Foods: Raw, Processed, Prepared. Revised 1982. Fruits and Fruit Juices.

Carbohydrates

Fruits contain appreciable amounts of carbohydrates. In fact, aside from water, carbohydrates are the main constituents in fruits. Included are sugars and starches, as well as celluloses, hemicelluloses, and pectic substances. An immature fruit such as an apple may contain a fair amount of starch. This disappears and sugar accumulates as the fruit ripens.

Celluloses, in addition to giving strength and support to plant cells and tissues, contribute to the textural qualities for which fruits and vegetables are prized. In addition, fruits and vegetables provide bulk in the diet because digestive juices lack enzymes capable of hydrolyzing the β-glucosidic linkage in cellulose (Chapter 9).

Protein, Fat, and Minerals

Fruits contain relatively small amounts of protein. One serving of most fruits contains one gram or less of protein. The amount of fat in most fruits is low, avocados and olives excepted. Fruits are low in calcium and phosphorus and most are not particularly good sources of iron.

Vitamins

Most fruits are low in the B vitamins. Citrus fruits, including oranges, lemons, and grapefruit, are excellent sources of ascorbic acid, as are two more seasonal fruits, cantaloupe and strawberries. Yellow fruits such as apricots, cantaloupe, and peaches are fairly good sources of beta carotene, a precursor of vitamin A. Among the fruits, oranges are one of the better sources of folic acid.

Organic Acids

Dissolved in the cell sap are a number of organic acids that, together with the sugars present, contribute to the taste of fruits. Common acids in fruits are citric, in high concentration in citrus fruits and the main acid in tomatoes; malic, the chief acid in apples and peaches; malic and tartaric in grapes; malic and oxalic in rhubarb; citric and malic in pineapple; and citric and benzoic in cranberries.

Limes and lemons have the lowest pH (are most acidic) with a pH of 2.0 to 2.2. Cranberries are a tart fruit, with a pH near 2.7. Within the range of pH 3.0 to 3.4 are red currants, gooseberries, prunes, apples, grapefruit, rhubarb, apricots, blackberries, and strawberries. The average pH for peaches, raspberries, blueberries, oranges, and pears falls within the range of 3.5 to 3.9. The pH of bananas (average 4.6) and figs is higher than that of most fruits (2), except watermelon, with a pH near 6.

RIPENING OF FRUIT

Fruits are living entities with a life span that includes growth to maturity, followed by ripening, and finally by senescence (25). Fruits such as apples, bananas, and pears may be harvested when they mature, after which they ripen. Other fruits such as berries and melons are usually harvested after they are partially or fully ripe. Ripening is a complex process genetically controlled. A series of biochemical reactions bring about changes in flavor, color, and texture of fruits that make them palatable. A decrease in acids and an increase in sugars alters the taste of fruits as they ripen. The sweetness of melons, peaches, and strawberries when they are fully ripe is due to their high levels of sugars. An increase in the sucrose content of ripening bananas from 0.3 to 11 percent when fully ripe has been reported. The starch content decreased from 25 to 1 percent (44). If an unripe banana is chilled or held in a cool place too long, hydrolysis of starch is retarded and the banana does not ripen normally (6, 24). On the other hand, bananas do not develop full yellow color if ripened at a high temperature (16).

The aroma of fruit, an important component of flavor, comes from substances synthesized during ripening. The aroma of a particular fruit is due to a complex mixture of volatile constituents. An odor is difficult to analyze because many of the components are unsaturated and highly unstable. These include esters, aldehydes, alcohols, ketones, and terpenes. Too, the amount of any one constituent is usually small. By means of gas chromatography coupled with other analytical techniques, constituents in the aroma of a number of fruits have been isolated and identified. Sensory evaluation of these compounds has been used to identify those that contribute to a general fruity odor and those that contribute to the specific character of the aroma. For example, three esters—amyl acetate, propionate, and butyrate—have been shown to possess bananalike aroma. Constituents that contribute to the fruity component of banana flavor are butyl and hexyl acetate and butyl and amyl butyrate (28). Information about the aroma of a number of fruits has been summarized (17).

A change in color accompanies a change in flavor when fruits ripen. Breakdown of chlorophyll and synthesis of carotenoid and anthocyanin pigments provide visual clues to the ripeness of a fruit.

The change in texture brought about by ripening improves markedly the palatability of a fruit. Ripening alters components of the cell wall and middle lamella, weakening resistance of fruit tissue to compression and fracture (25). The accepted explanation for the softening of fruits as they ripen is that a wall-bound and insoluble pectic substance (protopectin) is converted to water-dispersible pectin. A pectic enzyme, polygalacturonase, that hydrolyzes glycosidic bonds at random appears to be involved in the depolymerization of pectic substances in the cell wall. Pectin in the middle lamella is also subject to hydrolytic breakdown, resulting in less cell adhesion.

A number of workers have attempted to account for the marked difference in the texture of ripe, firm-fleshed cling peaches compared with soft-fleshed freestones. In an early study, no polygalacturonase was found in freestone peaches even though the intrinsic viscosity of the pectin decreased markedly as the fruit ripened (29). An increase in water-soluble pectin was reported in freestone peaches as they ripened, whereas the conversion of protopectin to soluble pectin was negligible in clings (23). Differences in pectinesterase activity failed to account for differences in texture between peaches of the two types (41). Later, the presence of polygalacturonase was reported in ripening peaches (36). Clings contain only exopolygalacturonase, which splits monomers from the reducing end of the chain, and this makes little difference in the size of the polymer or in its solubility. Freestones, on the other hand, contain both exo- and endopolygalacturonase. The latter hydrolyzes the chain at random, reducing the size of the molecule markedly and increasing its dispersibility.

Changes in the pectic substances that normally accompany ripening of juicy, soft-fleshed varieties may be altered if fruit picked before it is fully mature is held at 8°C (46°F) or lower for two weeks or more. A condition known as woolly breakdown occurs. A delay in the elaboration of pectinesterase and a deficiency of polygalacturonase result in insoluble pectic molecules that, by retaining water in the cell walls, may be responsible for the dry, woolly condition (15).

Cells of fruit require energy to stay alive and to bring about reactions involved in ripening. They obtain this energy from the oxidation of energy rich nutrients, mainly carbohydrates, stored in the cells. Oxygen is normally used, and carbon dioxide is given off as these stored constituents are utilized for energy, a process called respiration. A rapid rise in respiration occurs when fruits—including apples, avocados, bananas, pears, and tomatoes—begin to ripen (23). In contrast to these *climacteric* fruits, nonclimacteric fruits—grapes, pineapple, strawberries, and citrus fruit—ripen without an initial burst of respiration.

Ethylene (CH_2–CH_2) is a normal ripening hormone produced by fruit cells from the amino acid methionine (23). The conversion takes place in a series of steps, each of which is mediated by a specific enzyme, also formed in the cells as a fruit ripens. Without ethylene a fruit does not ripen; without the genetically directed ability to synthesize requisite protein no ethylene forms. In that case, a fruit grows to maturity but fails to ripen unless treated with exogenous ethylene. Such is FLAVR SAVR tomato, introduced in 1994. Genetic modification of the tomato plant conferred on it the ability to generate antisense RNA (33). This modified plant synthesizes a protein that blocks the penultimate step in the enzymatic conversion of methionine to ethylene. FLAVR SAVR tomatoes grow to maturity and remain in this state until exposure to ethylene triggers the ripening process.

Slowing Ripening and Postponing Senescence

Controlled Atmosphere Storage

Holding fruit at a low temperature (but above freezing) slows reactions involved in ripening and lengthens somewhat the time before the quality of a fruit begins to deteriorate. Exposure to an atmosphere with a low level of oxygen and an elevated level of carbon dioxide is even more effective in slowing respiration and delaying ripening and senescence. This procedure, called controlled atmosphere (CA) storage, first successfully applied to apples, is now used to prolong the storage life of other fruits and vegetables (26). Fruits differ in their tolerance for low levels of oxygen and for high levels of carbon dioxide. A variation of this procedure, modified atmosphere packaging, involves the use of plastic film with permeabilities that limit access of the food to oxygen and retain and build up the concentration of carbon dioxide.

Irradiation

This is another process that can be used to slow ripening and delay senescence in some fresh fruits and vegetables (39). A food is usually irradiated by exposing it to ionizing radiation from gamma rays emitted by the radioisotope cobalt-60. These very short electromagnetic rays readily penetrate food. They generate ions or free radicals from components in the food, including water, that inactivate enzymes in both the food and in microorganisms that contaminate the food. A food must absorb more gamma rays to sterilize it than to lengthen its shelf life. The amount of energy absorbed is controlled by how fast an item passes through a lead-lined chamber that contains the source of irradiation. Some irradiated foods, including strawberries, have been test-marketed. This fruit is susceptible to an organism that produces a white mold on the berries. This fungus can grow even at 0°C (32°F) so refrigeration alone does not prevent spoilage of this fruit.

PIGMENTS IN FRUITS AND VEGETABLES

Chlorophyll and Carotenoids

Meals would be drab and uninteresting were it not for the colorful pigments in fruits and vegetables. Both green chlorophyll and yellow carotenoids are found in the plastids of the cells dissolved in the fat. Few mature fruits contain chlorophyll in appreciable quantities except avocados, greengage plums, and gooseberries. When the last two are canned, they lose some of their color although they were never very green. Vegetables, especially green leafy ones, are richer sources of chlorophyll than are fruits. Discussion of chlorophyll and the retention of green color is deferred to Chapter 28.

Yellow apricots, muskmelon, oranges, peaches, and pineapple contain carotenoid pigments, as do red grapefruit, tomatoes, watermelon, and rose hips. Alteration of the color of fruits due to changes in the carotenoid pigments is slight and usually goes unnoticed. Carotenoid pigments are discussed in Chapter 28.

Flavonoid Pigments

Flavonoid pigments are phenolic compounds widely distributed in fruits and vegetables (9). They are water soluble and are found in the cell sap rather than in the plastids. Flavonoid pigments include the anthocyanins (literally, blue flower), the anthoxanthins (literally, yellow flower), and a third group that consists of a number of related phenolic compounds, many erroneously categorized as tannins. Structurally, pigments of both the anthocyanin and the anthoxanthin groups contain two 6-membered rings of carbon linked by a 3-carbon unit. The basic structure is illustrated with flavone, a representative of one subgroup of the anthoxanthins.

Flavone

The chief difference between anthocyanins and anthoxanthins lies in the central ring of the molecule. The basic structure of an anthocyanin pigment is shown here:

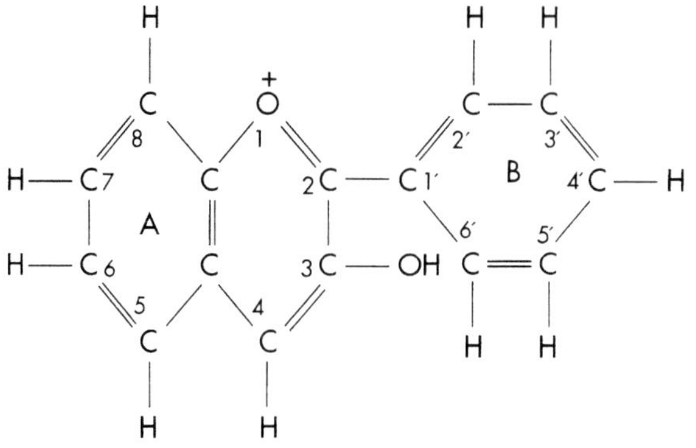

Basic Structure for Anthocyanin Pigments

The unit on the left is designated the A ring, that on the right the B ring. Atoms are identified by numbers, as shown.

Individual pigments within each of the two groups differ in accordance with the side groups attached and their position of attachment on the molecule. Pigments in both groups typically have hydroxyl (—OH) groups attached at positions 5 and 7 on the A-ring. In anthocyanins a sugar residue is attached at position 3 and frequently at position 5. Sugar is attached most frequently at position 7 and less commonly at positions 5 and 3 in the anthoxanthins. The sugar moiety contributes to the solubility of these pigments in water. A pigment from which the sugar residue has been hydrolyzed is known as an aglycone. An aglycone of an anthocyanin is called an anthocyanidin. Attached to the molecule at positions 3', 4', or 5' may be —OH groups or, in the case of anthocyanins, methoxyl (CH_3O—) groups.

Anthoxanthins

Anthoxanthins are more widely distributed in plants than are anthocyanins (9). Anthoxanthins found in fruits and vegetables include flavones, flavonols, and the flavanones. Differences in the central ring that contains the 3-carbon fragment (shown below with the A- and B-rings in skeleton) differentiate pigments of the three subgroups thus:

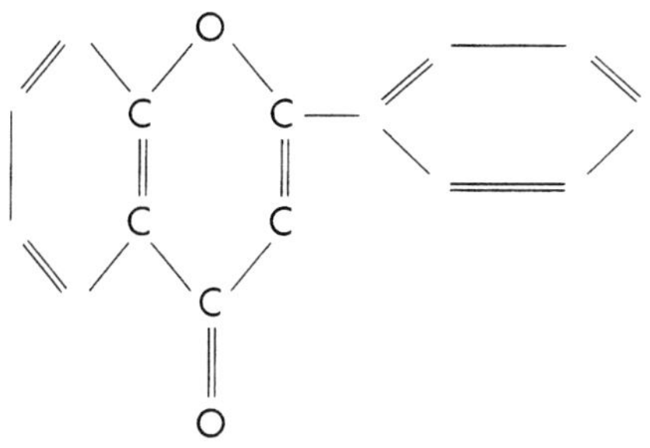

Flavone

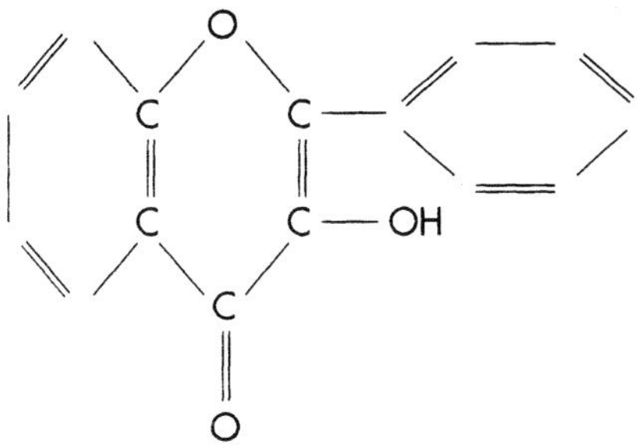

Flavonol

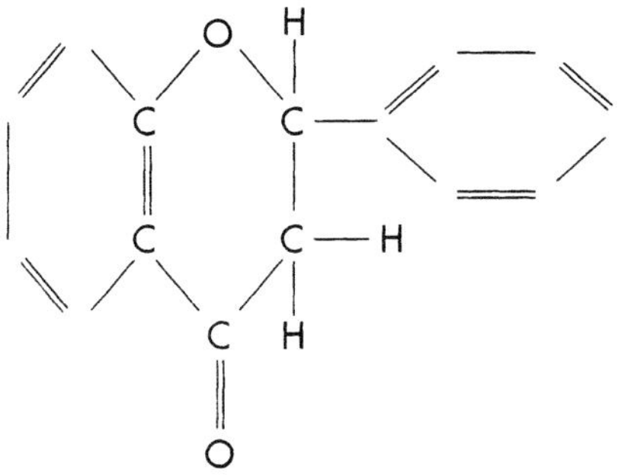

Flavanone

One of the most common anthoxanthins is the flavonol quercetin. Its formula is:

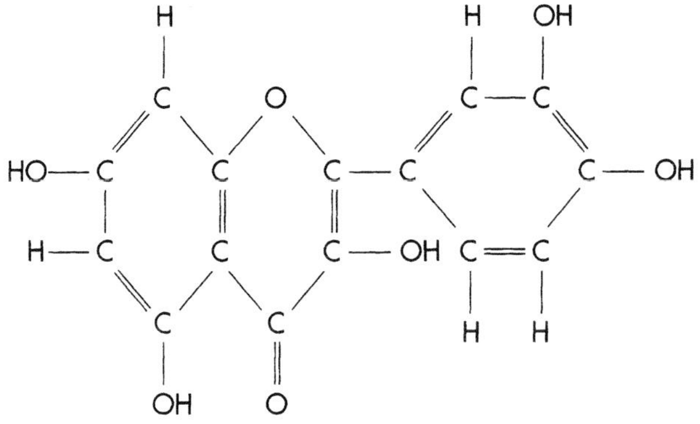

Quercetin

Most anthoxanthins occur as glycosides. One such glycoside is the flavanone naringin, the
7-rhamnoglucoside of naringenin, the bitter substance in grapefruit peel. Naringenin has
the formula shown below.

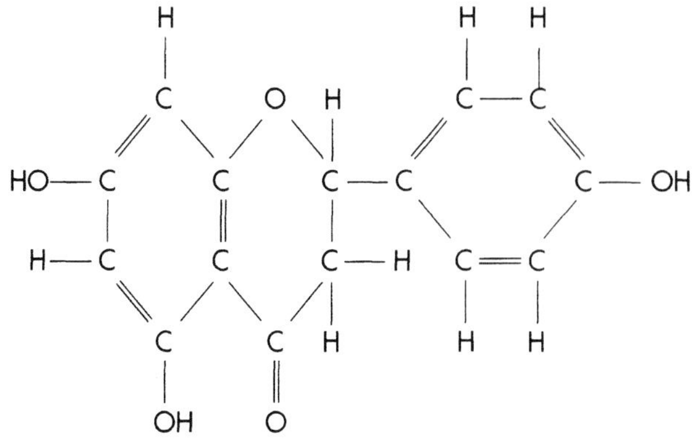

Naringenin

Anthocyanins

Pigments in this group have a greater impact on the color of fruits and vegetables than do the anthoxanthins. Anthocyanins may be red, purple, or blue of various shades (12). The potential color of any one anthocyanin depends on the groups of atoms attached to its basic structure and on the carbons to which they are attached. An increase in the number of hydroxyl groups in the B-ring shifts the hue of the pigment from red toward blue. Thus the aglycone pelargonidin with one hydroxyl group at carbon 4′ has a reddish hue, cyanidin with hydroxyl groups at 3′ and 4′ shows some shift towards the blue, and delphinidin with hydroxyl groups at positions 3′, 4′, and 5′ is definitely blue. The bright red color of strawberries is due mainly to a glucoside of pelargonidin. Substitution of methoxyl groups for hydroxyl groups in the B-ring shifts the color of the pigment toward the red but substituting a diglycoside for glucose at carbon 3 has the opposite effect.

Glycosides of cyanidin, the most common aglycone, are likely to be found in plants that are woody rather than herbaceous. The pigment is removed from plant tissue, usually by dilute hydrochloric acid, so the aglycone is obtained as the chloride. The formula for cyanidin chloride is:

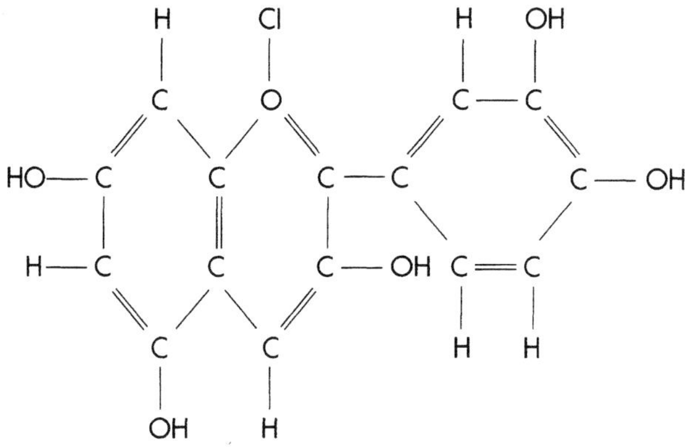

Cyanidin Chloride

Fruits containing cyanidin glycosides include blackberries, blueberries, boysenberries (a cross of blackberry, raspberry, and loganberry), sweet cherries (Windsor and Bing varieties), sour cherries, ripe gooseberries, pomegranates, and the skin of Jonathan and Stayman winesap apples and of Flame Tokay grapes. Most fruits analyzed contain more than one anthocyanin pigment. Cranberries contain a cyanidin glycoside but also one of peonidin, which is like cyanidin except the molecule contains a methoxyl group at position 3'. The presence of such a group shifts the hue of the pigment toward the red end of the spectrum. The pigments in concord grapes are derivatives of delphinidin, cyanidin, and malvidin (like delphinidin except that methoxyl groups have replaced the hydroxyls at positions 3' and 4'), giving a predominantly blue hue.

Anthocyanin and anthoxanthin pigments frequently occur in the same plant tissue. In some plant material the color of an anthocyanin pigment is intensified and also shifted to a bluer hue by the presence of an anthoxanthin, an effect referred to as copigmentation (4). Structures for copigments between anthocyanins and flavanols, such as quercetin and rutin, have been proposed (48).

Effects of Acidity on the Color of Flavonoids

Both anthocyanins and anthoxanthins are amphoteric compounds, with the ability to react with both acids and bases (9, 12). Anthoxanthins may change from a yellow color in alkaline medium to creamy white in neutral, to colorless in acid media, the condition that prevails in the cell sap. Anthocyanins undergo more pronounced changes in color with change in acidity, as shown on page 486. At low pH, 3.0 or less, an anthocyanin may be present as a red flavylium ion. An increase in pH to 4 or 5 favors the conversion of the flavylium ion by water to the colorless carbinol or pseudobase. At a pH of 6 to 7 the flavylium ion is converted to the purple quinoidal base (30). The red flavylium ion at low pH is stable, but in weakly acidic media the pigment exists either as a colored quinoidal base that is unstable and tends to fade or as a colorless carbinol base. This chameleonlike character (12) limits the usefulness of anthocyanins as coloring agents for food products. However, a new group of acylated anthocyanins appears to have potential as food colorants. The vulnerability of most anthocyanin molecules lies in the weak bond between carbon 2 and the oxygen in the central ring. An acylated pigment has a cinnamic acid such as caffeic, ferulic, or sinapic attached via a hydroxyl or a sugar on the B-ring. Such a substitution on the B-ring appears to stabilize the vulnerable link in the central ring so that the color is more stable. Grape skins contain acylated pigments and a generic product, enocyanin, has been approved by FDA as a coloring agent in beverages (22). Red cabbage is another food that contains acylated anthocyanins (32). A commercial product from this source has been produced but is not approved for use in foods in the United States. Ornamental plants such as *Tradescantia* and the Heavenly Blue cultivar of the morning glory appear to be more likely sources of acylated pigments than are food plants.

Shift in the hue of an anthocyanin from the purple of the quinoidal base to dark blue may occur under alkaline conditions. This may be observed in blueberry muffins and on the surface of dumplings made from baking powder biscuit dough cooked in blackberry juice. (A greenish hue sometimes observed is believed to be due to a mixture of yellow anthoxanthins and blue anthocyanins.) The same change may be observed when unrinsed utensils that contain juice from these fruits come in contact with alkaline dish water. Not all anthocyanin-containing fruit juices show this marked change in hue with change in pH.

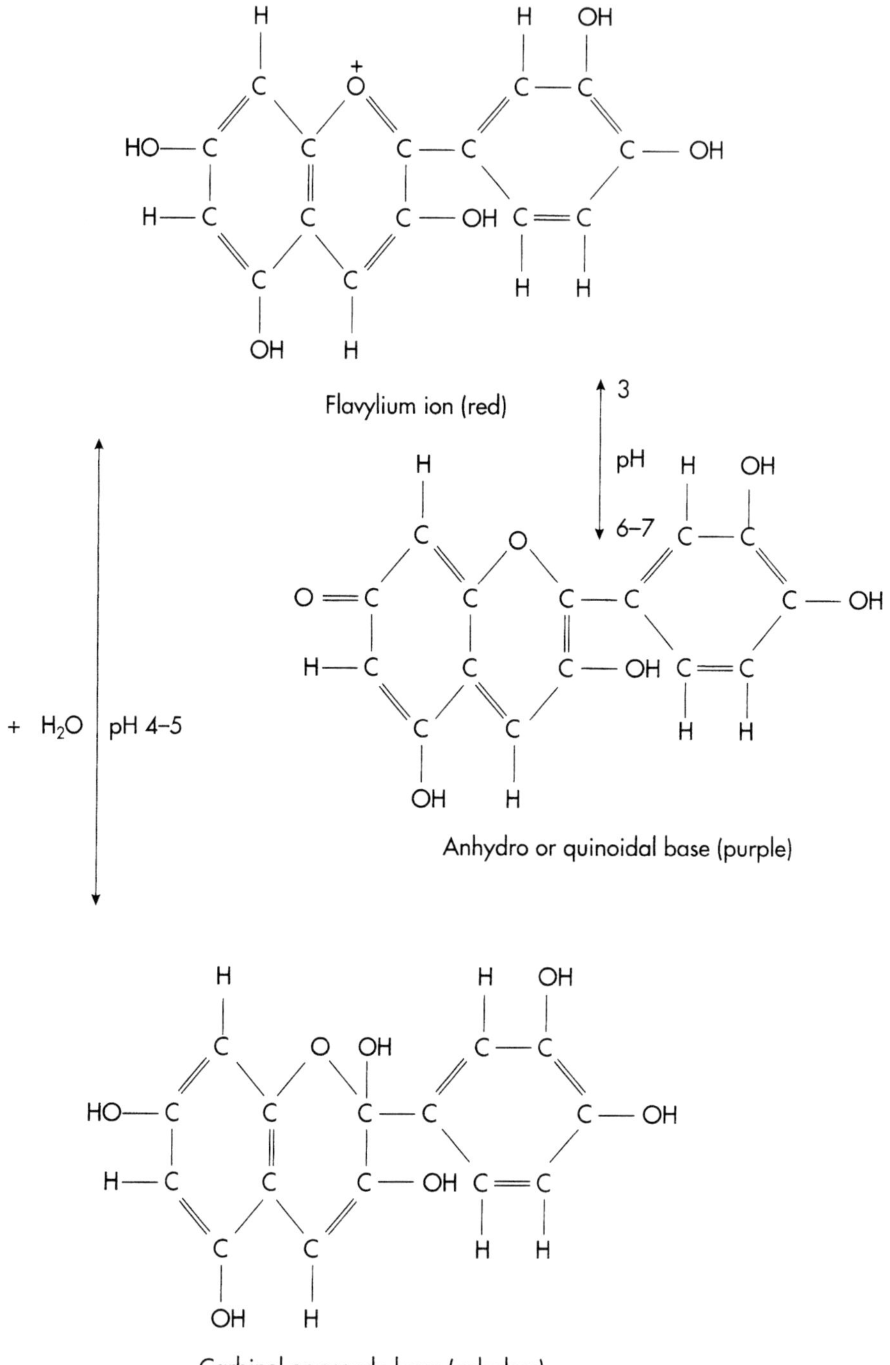

Flavylium ion (red)

3

pH

6–7

+ H₂O | pH 4–5

Anhydro or quinoidal base (purple)

Carbinol or pseudo base (colorless)

The groups attached to the basic structure and their position of attachment determine the response of the pigment to a change in environment. A free hydroxyl group at position 4′ and a minimum of four hydroxyl groups are essential for the formation of the salt of the color base and the blue color.

Effects of Metal Ions on the Color of Flavonoids

Both anthocyanin and anthoxanthin pigments react with metals. The products formed may bring about undesirable changes in the appearance of fruits and vegetables. An anthocyanin with two or three free hydroxyl groups on adjacent carbons may unite with aluminum, tin, or iron to form a blue, greenish blue, or slate-blue complex. For this reason contact of anthocyanin-containing fruits with utensils made of iron, tin, or, to a lesser extent, of aluminum should be avoided.

Corrosion of the tin can (actually iron coated with tin) and alteration of the color of an anthocyanin-containing food from red to purple to blue hue occur when such canned foods are stored (19). Because of this, cans coated with lacquer are used for such foods. Discoloration is reduced, but small openings in the lacquered lining permit localized corrosion of the can. The anthocyanin pigment combines with the metal ions as they are removed from the can by the acid present in the food. The pigment thus frees the acid for continued reaction with the can, but in restricted areas. Hydrogen gas is liberated, the can bulges, and in time the can is perforated. By the time the can begins to leak, the color of the food is altered. The less acidic the food, the more likely the can is to be perforated because it is the color base of the pigment that reacts with the metal.

Discoloration of an anthocyanin pigment by contact with metal is troublesome, but occasionally this characteristic may be used advantageously. For example, adding acid, usually in the form of lemon juice, to loganberry or blackberry juice shifts the color toward the red. If a bluish punch is desired, pineapple juice added with lemon juice prevents the shift in color. The small amount of iron dissolved in the pineapple juice from equipment used to prepare it for canning prevents the pigment from shifting to the red form. When either strawberry juice or cranberry juice is used as a base for punch, the punch is less likely to change in hue with addition of other ingredients because of the structure of the anthocyanin pigments involved.

Anthoxanthin pigments as well as anthocyanins react with or chelate metals. Sites where metal ions such as those of iron may unite with the pigment are at the two hydroxyl groups at positions 3′ and 4′, at the carbonyl ($—C = O$) group at position 4 and the hydroxyl group at position 3, or at the carbonyl group and the hydroxyl group at position 5. Products so formed may be bluish, greenish, or reddish. Anthoxanthins that have a hydroxyl group at either position 3 or 5 and a carbonyl at position 4 can unite with either tin or aluminum ions to form a bright yellow complex. Cooking water from yellow-skinned onions cooked in an aluminum pan may be bright yellow due to this complex (9).

Strawberry preserves undergo a change in color during storage. The bright red of the anthocyanin pigment in fresh preserves becomes duller and takes on a rusty brown tinge (44). The greater susceptibility to deterioration of color with certain varieties may be due to the higher content of phenolic compounds (1). Presence of oxygen and of reducing sugars and a high pH favor the breakdown of the pigment. Degradation of the anthocyanin is hastened by oxidation of the ascorbic acid present. Storage of the preserves in a warm place accelerates the loss of bright color. Some processors of strawberry preserves hold the berries as frozen stock and make preserves only when they are needed for the market. In this way they maintain a continuous supply of a product of good color.

Flavanols

Aside from the anthocyanins and the anthoxanthins, an assortment of phenolic compounds is present in fruits and vegetables. Browning of fruits, discussed in a subsequent section of this chapter, is attributed to the presence of one or more of these phenolic substrates. Catechin is one such, the formula of which is:

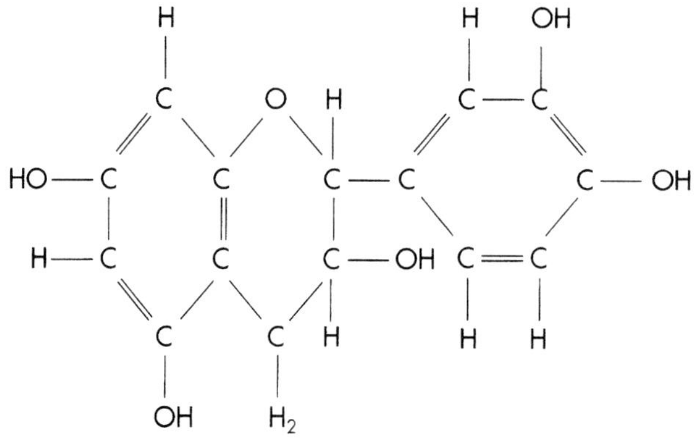

Catechin

Related to catechin is another group of compounds, the pro- or leucoanthocyanins. As the leuco prefix implies, compounds of this group are colorless.

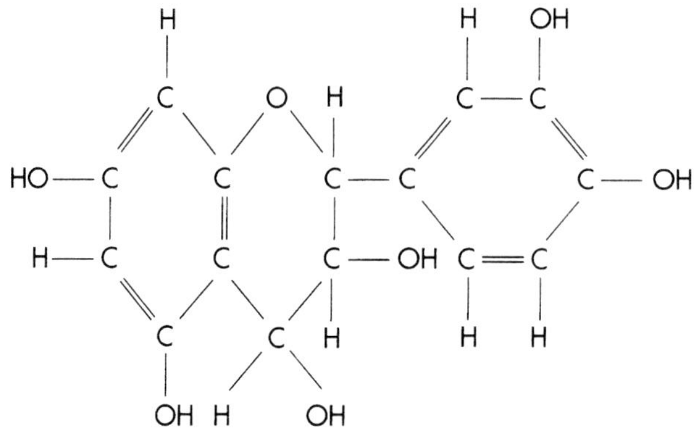

Pro- or Leucocyanidin

When a colorless proanthocyanin is heated in the presence of acid (and oxygen), the corresponding anthocyanidin is formed. This type of reaction is believed to be responsible for the pinkish hue of some canned pears (27). Leucocyanidin (above) is the most commonly occurring proanthocyanin. It is now thought that proanthocyanins in foods comprise the bulk of the compounds which in the past have been referred to as tannins. Astringency in foods (which, to a limited extent, is desirable) is attributed to compounds in this class (10).

Moisture Content and Texture

When a fruit or vegetable is a part of a growing plant, it gives off water in the form of vapor. This loss of water is compensated for by the uptake of water through the roots of the plant. Harvested fruits or vegetables stored in the open or in an uncovered container continue to lose moisture to the air and, cut off from a source of water, become dehydrated. The plant tissue assumes a limp and lifeless appearance. As long as cells of plant tissue remain alive the water content may increase or decrease rather markedly and rapidly without doing irreparable harm. Both vacuolar and protoplasmic membranes of living cells are semipermeable and osmotically active. Water may be drawn into cells when fruit or vegetable tissue is surrounded by water because of the solutes that are present. These solutes lower the vapor pressure of the water within the cell, permitting the entrance of water from around the tissue. The pressure required within the cell to prevent this entrance of water is known as osmotic pressure.

Actually, water molecules both enter and leave the cell, but the net flow is into the cell because of the concentration of solutes in the cell sap. Such vacuole-filled cells (Fig. 27-7) exert pressure on each other, and this gives to plant tissues their crispness. A lettuce leaf

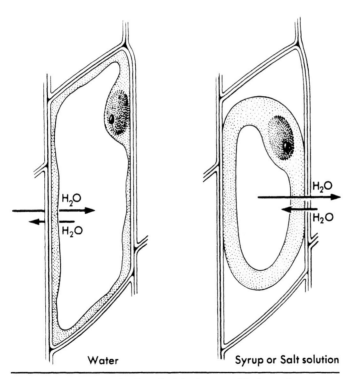

H_2O

H_2O

H_2O

H_2O

Water

Syrup or Salt solution

Figure 27-7. A turgid cell on the left. The water-filled vacuole exerts pressure on the cytoplasm, pressing it against the restraining cell wall. On the right, the loss of water from the vacuole allows the elastic cytoplasm to relax. Such a partially hydrated cell is limp instead of turgid. Loss of water (as vapor) to the air has a similar effect. (From V. A. Greulach and J. E. Adams. *Plants: An Introduction to Modern Botany.* Copyright © 1967 by John Wiley & Sons, Inc. Reprinted by permission.)

that is flabby due to loss of water from the vacuoles of the cell will rapidly refresh and become crisp when placed in cold water or even in air saturated with water vapor. Nutrients lost as a result of wilting are not regained, however.

Water may be drawn from cells by osmosis if plant tissue is placed in water that contains a solute in greater concentration outside the cell than inside (Figure 27-7). Sugar, acid, and salt especially cause withdrawal of water from cells with resulting loss in turgor. Salt sprinkled on the surface of a slice of cucumber draws moisture from the cells, which collects as beads of liquid, and the slice becomes flabby. Sugar sprinkled on sliced, raw fruit may cause the withdrawal of enough water from the cells to partly or completely cover the fruit with syrup.

The withdrawal or uptake of water affects the water activity of plant tissue. Changes in α_W are accompanied by complex changes in the texture profile of tissue (14). Loss of turgor and of fracturability of apple flesh accompanies a decrease in α_W from 0.99, essentially that of freshly harvested fruit, to an α_W of 0.85. Tissue becomes more deformable, too. Such aspects of texture as chewiness, springiness, and gumminess increase as the α_W decreases from 0.85 to 0.23. A decrease in deformation over this range is attributed to a decrease in the number of layers of water molecules associated with the solids of the tissue. Lowering the α_W from 0.23 to 0.12 results in a marked change in texture profile. This is attributed to a change from a multi- to a monolayers of adsorbed water molecules at hydrogen bonding sites on the tissue. Another sharp change in texture occurs when an α_W of 0.12 is reduced to 0.01. The texture profile at an α_W of 0.01 resembles that of fresh fruit except that the tissue is harder and more readily fractured. Thus the water content has a major impact on the textural properties of plant tissue. The effects of water are superimposed on the influence of the structural components of the tissue on texture.

Discoloration and Its Prevention

Under certain conditions a number of fruits, including apples, avocados, bananas, cherries, peaches, and pears, change from a creamy white to an unattractive brown or gray color. Bruising or other injury to the tissue disrupts the structural arrangement and disposition of constituents within the cells and allows the contents to make contact. This may lead to discoloration of uncooked fruit tissue as may cutting the fruit.

For browning to take place, a phenolic compound known as a substrate must be present in the raw tissue. There are a number of phenolic compounds that can serve as substrates for enzymatic browning of fruits (8). Besides catechin and its derivatives, these include tyrosine, caffeic acid, chlorogenic acid, procyanidin, dopamine, and the aglycones of certain flavonoids. Phenolic substances with ortho-dihydroxy or vicinal (on adjacent carbons) trihydroxy groups are susceptible to discoloration catalyzed by phenol oxidase enzymes. Oxygen, either from the air in contact with the cut surface or from intercellular spaces within the tissue, must come into contact with the substrate.

For discoloration to occur rapidly, an enzyme must be present in the tissue of raw fruit to catalyze the reaction. Enzymes that catalyze the oxidation (orthodiphenol: oxygen oxidoreductase) are known by a number of names—phenoloxidase, polyphenoloxidase, phenolase, or polyphenolase. The action of polyphenolase enzymes in the conversion of green to black tea is discussed in Chapter 6. Phenoloxidase enzymes, each of which may be specific for certain substrates, are present in many fruits and vegetables. If phenolic substrate and oxygen are in contact for several days, browning will take place even though phenoloxidase enzymes have been denatured by heating. Thus browning may be observed in canned fruits, such as pears and peaches, that stand above the surface of the liquid in inadequately vented jars.

The chemical changes that take place in the conversion of the colorless substrate in the intact fruit to the colored reaction products in injured tissue are complex. A shift from a quinol to a quinone form of the molecule (discussed under Antioxidants, Chapter 15), catalyzed by the enzyme, appears to be the first step. Then nonenzymatic oxidation and polymerization yield condensation products that are responsible for the discoloration.

Prevention of browning by elimination of the substrate is not practical. Apples, bananas, cherries, peaches, and pears contain one or more substrates for phenol oxidase enzymes. One variety of peach, Sunbeam, is an exception. It was developed and propagated because it is deficient in substrate. There is some indication that the stage of ripeness of a fruit may influence its susceptibility to discoloration. In one study, browning was less in bananas at the green-tip stage of ripeness than it was in riper fruit (46).

Different varieties of a fruit differ in susceptibility to browning. Of the seven apple cultivars in one study, the degree of browning was associated with higher polyphenoloxidase activity in three and with higher phenolic sustrate in four (18). The tentative conclusion of a study of 11 apple cultivars was that the amount of substrate, chiefly chlorogenic acid and proanthocyanin, had more effect on the degree of browning than did polyphenoloxidase activity (3).

Browning can be prevented by avoiding contact of oxygen with the substrate. Coating the fruit with sugar or covering it with syrup keeps atmospheric oxygen away from the surface. Sugar also reduces the concentration of oxygen dissolved in the syrup or water around the fruit. However, there is still the problem of intercellular oxygen.

A number of means are available to limit the activity of the phenol oxidase enzymes. The activity of the enzyme is temperature dependent, with the optimum near 43°C (109°F). If food is kept cold, browning is slowed, but, even in frozen storage, fruits brown unless they are treated to prevent it. Enzymes are proteins, easily denatured by heat as in blanching or cooking. The activity of phenol oxidase, like that of all enzymes, is pH dependent. Altering the hydrogen-ion concentration may effectively block its action. The cut surface of fruit may be coated with acid. Lemon or other citrus fruit juice may be used, as may a solution of cream of tartar. Lemon juice is effective for another reason. Its citric acid acts as a chelator of copper that phenolase enzymes require for activity. Concentrated sugar solution also depresses enzyme activity. Sugared sliced peaches do not brown as readily as unsugared.

Sodium chloride can inhibit the activity of phenol oxidase enzymes, but a concentration too high for palatability is needed. It is the chloride ion that is effective. A dilute salt solution will retard development of brown color for a limited time. Peaches prepared in quantity for canning may be placed in dilute salt solution as they are peeled and held until they are canned.

A solution of ascorbic acid is effective in preventing browning. It is possible that it acts as a reducing agent for the oxidized intermediate of a phenolic compound and thus prevents subsequent changes in the substrate, which would result in the formation of colored products. In addition, ascorbic acid is believed to act on some functional group in the enzyme (7). In work on bananas (45), fruit at the green-tip stage contained more of the substrate dopamine but also more ascorbic acid, which presumably blocked the initial step in the conversion of the substrate to dark melanin.

Treatment of fruits with sulfur dioxide effectively prevents browning. The sulfurous acid formed ($SO_2 + H_2O \rightarrow H_2SO_3$) is a strong reducing agent. It combines with quinones formed from phenolic compounds and so blocks further changes in the molecule. In addition, the sulfurous acid gradually reduces the effectiveness of the enzyme (21, 40). Instead of exposing fruit to sulfur dioxide fumes, it may be sulfured by dipping in a dilute solution of sodium bisulfite. If the sliced fruit is then immersed for a short time in a solution of dipotassium phosphate (K_2HPO_4), the odor of sulfur is less pronounced and the fruit remains crisp and does not brown subsequently (13). Calcium in the dip (0.1 percent from $CaCl_2$) acts synergistically with either SO_2 (0.3 percent) or ascorbic acid (1.0 percent). After a three-minute dip, slices of Golden Delicious apples did not brown for several weeks when held at 1°C (34). The use of sulfites to prevent discoloration of fresh fruits and vegetables, except potatoes, was banned by the FDA in 1986, its use on peeled potatoes banned in 1990. This action was taken when some fatalities occurred, especially among asthmatics, who had consumed sulfite-treated products. If packaged food contains 10 parts per million or more of sulfite, its label must indicate so. No single antibrowning substance is as effective as sulfite, with the possible exception of the amino acid cysteine (31). A sulfite alternative includes a blend of ascorbic acid, citric acid, and calcium chloride. A phosphate may also be included.

PREPARATION OF FRUIT FOR SERVING

Raw

Fruit should be washed thoroughly and drained before it is served. If a fruit such as an apple is to be served raw and with the skin on, washing with mild soap or detergent followed by thorough rinsing aids in removing from the waxy epidermis not only soil and microorganisms but traces of poison spray. It is probably good practice to discard the paring from the stem and blossom ends because these areas are hard to clean thoroughly.

A sharp knife with a thin blade should be used to cut the skin from an orange or grapefruit, to section grapefruit, and to slice an orange. A blade of four to five inches is a good length. A sawing motion both for paring and for slicing fruit permits the blade to move through the fruit without bruising it and with a minimum loss of juice.

Cooked

Fresh fruit may be cooked by stewing, making into sauce, or baking. Fruit may be cooked whole or in halves or quarters. Cooked, it may be served as stewed fruit or it may be sieved and served as sauce. In either case, the fruit should be put to cook in boiling water to shorten the cooking time. The amount of water depends upon the juiciness of the fruit, the ratio of fruit to the size of the container, and the amount of liquid that will evaporate from the container. Fruit is done when it is tender and translucent.

If apples are to be made into sauce, the core and skin may be left on. Only the stem and the parings in the depression at both stem and blossom ends need be removed. The skin may add color to the sauce. When the cooked apple is put through a sieve, inedible parts are removed. When apples are made into sauce in this way, waste averages somewhat less than when apples are pared and cored in advance. Apple sauce should be juicy but not runny, the texture should be fine grained rather than too smooth or too coarse, and it should have a mellow apple flavor. Some varieties of apples form sauce more readily than others. Ease of saucing appears more closely related to solubility of the pectic material in the middle lamella than to such structural features as cell size or amount of intercellular air spaces. However, tissue of apples that sauce readily appears to be blown apart by expanding bubbles of gas (38).

Both pears and apples may be baked. A hot oven and a covered baking dish for apples give a product with a clearer, brighter color and better flavor. A lid on the container shortens baking time although apples tend to lose their shape when they are baked in a covered utensil. Desirable texture and flavor in baked apples are associated with high acidity, but such fruit is more likely to lose its shape. The Red Delicious apple, which is low in acid, holds its shape exceedingly well when baked, but the cooked product is rather tasteless.

A number of fruits, including grapefruit, sliced bananas, apple rings, and pineapple slices, may be broiled, or fruit may be dipped in batter and deep-fat fried.

CHANGES IN FRUIT CAUSED BY COOKING

Crispness

When fruits and vegetables are heated, the cell membranes are denatured and lose their selective permeability. The passage of water and solutes across cell membranes is no longer governed by osmosis. Instead, both water molecules and solutes pass into and out of cells by diffusion. This process is slow, compared with the passage of molecules across a semipermeable membrane. Apple slices cooked in water lose some water to the surrounding liquid and solutes from the cell sap diffuse into the cooking water. The cells of cooked tissue are no longer taut with water and the tissues become limp. The flabbiness of cooked as well as wilted plant tissue is due to loss of water from the cell sap, but cells killed by heat can never again become turgid.

While fruit is still cooking it may float, buoyed up by steam generated within the tissue. Removed from the heat, it will sink. As its intercellular gas is replaced by water, cooking fruit becomes translucent.

Tenderness

When fruits and vegetables are cooked, they not only lose crispness but they also become tender. Conversion of insoluble pectic compounds in the middle lamella to water-dispersible form reduces adhesion between cells (43). As a result the tissue is more easily pierced with a fork or crushed by the teeth. Constituents in the cell wall are softened, except lignin, which is unaltered by cooking.

Sugar, especially in high concentration, slows down the tenderization by cooking because it interferes with the solubilizing of pectin. In fact, sugar is used in fruit jellies to aid in the conversion of a pectin sol to a gel (Chapter 31). Sugar in high concentration also dehydrates celluloses and hemicelluloses. The increased translucency of fruit cooked in syrup is due to alteration of the refractive index of cell wall constituents. Were prepared fruit put to cook in syrup instead of water, withdrawal of water from layers of cells on the surface would shrink and toughen the exterior of the pieces. It is for this reason that soft berries, which tend to disintegrate on cooking, are put to cook in concentrated sugar syrup. Preserved fruits are firm and hold their shape because of the heavy syrup in which they are cooked. If raw fruit is too firm, cooking in water to partially tenderize it before the sugar is added may be indicated. To obtain preserved fruit that is plump as well as firm and not shriveled, the concentration of syrup should be increased gradually during cooking.

In cooked fruit both cytoplasm and cell membranes are denatured. Sugar in the surrounding syrup passes from cell to cell to the interior of each piece, much as molecules of a copper sulfate crystal in the bottom of a beaker of water eventually diffuse and color the water uniformly. Diffusion continues until the concentration of sugar in the syrup and in the fruit reaches equilibrium. This requires some time, because diffusion is a much slower process than the passage of water in osmosis. Sugar diffuses more rapidly through the outer layers of cells of fruit cooked in water than in fruit, the outer layers of which have been toughened by cooking in concentrated syrup.

DRIED FRUIT

Cooking

Removal of water from fruit when it is dried makes the product tougher. Compare the tenderness of a fresh plum with that of a prune (a dried plum). When dried fruit is prepared for serving, the water removed from the cells by drying is returned by soaking and the tissues are softened by cooking. The cells in dried fruits are no longer alive. Hot water is used to soak the dried fruit to speed hydration of cell constituents. Usually, one hour is sufficient to allow water to diffuse into the interior of the fruit. The fruit is then simmered to soften the tissue. Sugar is added to dried fruit after the tissue is tenderized, because its presence in the cooking liquid only delays rehydration and tenderization. Cooked dried fruits improve if they are held at least overnight to allow sugar to diffuse into the fruit.

Tenderized dried fruits are an attempt by the producer to market a quicker cooking product to compete for the consumer's food dollar with other quick-cooking, time-saving products available. Such dried fruits have a high percentage of moisture so they need little if any soaking and a relatively short cooking period. The more moisture a dried product contains the less time it takes to "refresh" it.

Storing

Treating fruit such as apples, apricots, peaches, and pears with sulfur dioxide prior to drying yields a product that is bright and clear in color. Such fruits keep their bright colors if they are stored properly (5). Cool storage is recommended; otherwise the fruit will darken. Contact of the fruit with humid air should be prevented. The concentration of sugars in dried fruit is high. In a moist atmosphere, sugar from the fruit together with organic acids will dissolve in the moisture of the surface. If the fruit dries subsequently, this sugar will crystallize on or near the surface. This gives the dried fruit a dull, unappetizing appearance.

REFERENCES

1. Abers, J. E. and R. E. Wrolstad. 1979. "Causative factors of color deterioration in strawberry preserves during processing and storage." *Journal of Food Science* 44:75–78. Leucoanthocyanins, flavanols, and total phenols in two varieties.

2. AHEA 1993. *Handbook of Food Preparation.* pH of common fruits, p. 48. Alexandria, VA: American Home Economics Association.

3. Amiot, M. J., M. Tacchini, S. Aubert, and J. Nicolas. 1992. "Phenolic composition

and browning susceptibility of various apple cultivars at maturity." *Journal of Food Science* 57:958–62. Relative importance of different substrates and phenolase.

4. Asen, S., R. N. Stewart, and K. H. Norris. 1972. "Co-pigmentation of anthocyanins in plant tissue and its effect on color." *Phytochemistry* 11:1139–44. Copigmentation by the flavonol quercetin.

5. Barger, W. R., W. T. Pentzer, and C. K. Fisher. 1948. "Low temperature storage retains quality of dried fruit." *Food Industries* 20: F 1–4. (March). Effects of storage temperature and humidity on quality of dried fruit.

6. Barnell, H. R. 1943. "Studies in tropical fruit." XV. "Hemicellulose metabolism in banana fruit during ripening." *Annals of Botany, London* 7:297–323. Effects of storage temperature on ripening of bananas.

7. Baruah, P., and T. Swain. 1952. "The effect of I-ascorbic acid on the *in vitro* activity of polyphenoloxidase from potato." *Biochemical Journal* 55:392–399. Function of ascorbic acid in prevention of enzymatic browning.

8. Baruah, P., and T. Swain. 1959. "The action of potato phenolase on flavonoid compounds." *Journal of the Science of Food and Agriculture* 10:125–29. Substrates that participate in oxidative browning reactions.

9. Bate-Smith, E. C. 1954. "Flavonoid compounds in foods." *Advances in Food Research* 5:261–300. Classification, structure, properties, and distribution of flavonoid pigments; a review.

10. Bate-Smith, E. C. 1954. "Astringency in foods." *Food* 23:124–29. Nature of astringency, compounds responsible, and importance in certain foods.

11. BeMiller, J. N. 1986. "An introduction to pectins: Structure and properties." In *Chemistry and Function of Pectins*. M. L. Fishman and J. J. Jens, eds. Washington, D.C.: American Chemical Society. Pp. 2–12. A readable introduction.

12. Blank, F. 1947. "The anthocyanin pigments in plants." *Botanical Review* 13:241–47. Structures, reactions, colors; a review.

13. Bolin, H. R., F. S. Nury, and B. J. Finkle. 1964. "An improved process for preservation of fresh peeled apples." *Bakers Digest* 38:46–48. Use of dipotassium phosphate with sodium bisulfite as a browning inhibitor.

14. Bourne, M. C. 1986. "Effect of water activity on texture profile parameters of apple flesh." *Journal of Texture Studies* 17:331–40. Water activity from an a_w of 0.99 to 0.01 compared.

15. Buescher, R. W., and R. J. Furmanski. 1978. "Role of pectinesterase and polygalacturonase in the formation of woolliness in peaches." *Journal of Food Science* 43:264–66. One explanation for chilling injury.

16. Charles, R. J., and M. A. Tung. 1973. "Physical, rheological and chemical properties of banana during ripening." *Journal of Food Science* 38:456–59. Ripening at 16° and 25°C (60° and 75°F) compared.

17. Charley, H. 1972. "Fruits and vegetables." In *Food Theory and Applications*. P. C. Paul and H. H. Palmer, eds. New York: John Wiley & Sons. Pp. 306–8.

18. Coseting, M. Y., and C. Y. Lee. 1987. "Change in apple polyphenol oxidase and polyphenol concentrations in relation to degree of browning." *Journal of Food Science* 52:985–89. Ten cultivars compared.

19. Culpepper, C. W., and J. S. Caldwell. 1927. "The behavior of anthocyan pigments in canning." *Journal of Agricultural Research* 35:107–32. Effect of pigment on corrosion and pitting of the can.

20. De Vries, J. A., A. G. J. Voragen, F. M. Rombouts, and W. Plinik. 1986. "Structural studies of apple pectins with pectolytic enzymes." In *Chemistry and Function of Pectins*. M. L. Fishman and J. J. Jens, eds. Washington, D.C.: American Chemical Society. Pp. 38–48. Concept of smooth and hairy regions of pectin molecules.

21. Embs, R. J., and P. Markakis. 1965. "The mechanism of sulfite inhibition of browning caused by polyphenol oxidase." *Journal of Food Science* 30:753–58. Reaction with quinones and inhibition of the enzyme.

22. Francis, F. J. 1989. "Food colorants: Anthocyanins." *Critical Reviews in Food Science and Nutrition* 28:273–314. Interest in natural colorants; chemical structure and coloration; generic colorants from grapes and other plants.

23. Haard, N. F. 1984. "Postharvest physiology and biochemistry of fruits and vegetables." *Journal of Chemical Education* 61(4): 277–83. Ethylene, respiration, and climacteric and nonclimacteric fruit.

24. Haard, N. F., and D. Timbie. 1973. "Chilling injury in green banana fruit: Changes in peroxidase isoenzymes in soluble and particulate pools." *Journal of Food Science* 38:642–45. Failure to ripen and associated changes in the fruit.

25. John, M. A., and F. M. Dey. 1986. "Post harvest changes in fruit cell walls." *Advances in Food Research* 30:139–93. Constituents, their organization, ripening, and senescence.

26. Kader, A. A. 1986. "Biochemical and physiological basis for effects of controlled and modified atmospheres on fruits and vegetables." *Food Technology* 40(5):99–104. Explanation for some of the effects of such procedures.

27. Luh, B. S., S. J. Leonard, and D. S. Patel. 1960. "Pink discoloration of canned Bartlett pears." *Food Technology* 14:53–56. An attempt to link the pinkness of overheated canned pears to leucoanthocyanin content.

28. McCarthy, A. I., J. K. Palmer, C. P. Shaw, and E. E. Anderson. 1963. "Correlation of gas chromatographic data with flavor profiles of fresh banana fruit." *Journal of Food Science* 28:379–84. Components in banana flavor as analyzed by a flavor panel and by gas chromatography.

29. McCready, R. M., and E. A. McComb. 1954. "Pectic constituents in ripe and unripe fruit." *Food Research* 19:530–35. Changes in esterification and in polymerization of pectic substances in ripening peaches, pears, and avocado.

30. Mazza, G., and R. Brouillard. 1987. "Color stability and structural transformation of cyanidin 3,5-diglucoside and four 3-deoxy anthocyanins in aqueous solution." *Journal of Agricultural and Food Chemistry* 35:422–26. Effects of pH on tautomerization on color.

31. Molnar-Perl, I. and M. Friedman. 1990. "Inhibition of browning by sulfur amino acids." 3. "Apples and potatoes." *Journal of Agricultural and Food Chemistry* 38: 1652–56. Effectiveness of L-cysteine and reduced glutathione.

32. Murai, K. and D. Wilkins. 1990. "Natural red color derived from red cabbage." *Food Technology* 44(6):131. Effectiveness of the pigments as colorant.

33. Oeller, P. W., L. Min-Wing, L. P. Taylor, D. A. Pike, and A. Theologist. 1991. "Reversible inhibition of tomato fruit senescence by antisense RNA." *Science* 254:437–39. Genetic engineering.

34. Ponting, J., D. R. Jackson, and G. Waters. 1972. "Refrigerated apple slices: Preservative effects of ascorbic acid, calcium and sulfite." *Journal of Food Science* 37:434–36. Inhibition of enzymic browning.

35. Postlmayr, H. L., B. S. Luh, and S. J. Leonard. 1956. "Characterization of pectin changes in freestone and clingstone peaches during ripening and processing." *Food Technology* 10:618–25. Soluble and insoluble pectic substances; viscosity of syrup; and texture of canned fruit.

36. Pressey, R., and J. K. Avants. 1978. "Difference in polygalacturonase composition of clingstone and freestone peaches." *Journal of Food Science* 43:1415–17, 1423. Pectic enzymes and texture.

37. Preston, R. D. 1957. "Cellulose." *Scientific American* 197(3):157–62, 164–66, 168. Chemistry of cellulose and structure of cellulose fibers; illustrated.

38. Reeve, R. M., and L. R. Leinbach. 1953. "Histological investigation of texture in apples." I. "Composition and influence of heat on structure." *Food Research* 18:592–603. II. "Structure and intercellular spaces." *Food Research* 18:604–17. An attempt to account for differences in the textural quality of varieties of apples.

39. Rogan, A., and G. Glaros. 1988. "Food irradiation: The process and implications for dietitians." *Journal of the American Dietetics Association* 80:833–38. Source of the energy, chemical changes that result, and objectives.

40. Sayavedra-Soto, L. A., and M. W. Montgomery. 1986. "Inhibition of polyphenoloxidase by sulfite." *Journal of Food Science* 51:1531–36. Evidence for direct action on the enzyme.

41. Shewfelt, A. L. 1965. "Changes and variations in the pectic constitution of ripening peaches as related to product firmness."

Journal of Food Science 30:573–76. Three pectic fractions in freestones and clings at four stages of ripeness.

42. *Statistical Abstracts of the United States, 116 edition*, 1996. P. 148. Per-capita consumption of major food commodities: 1970–1994.

43. Sterling, C. 1963. "Texture and cell-wall polysaccharides in foods." In *Recent Advances in Food Science—3. Biochemistry and Biophysics in Food Research.* J. M. Leitch and D. N. Rhodes, eds. London: Butterworths. Pp. 259–76. A review article; comprehensive and technical.

44. Terra, N. N., E. Garcia and F. M. Lajolo. 1983. "Starch-sugar transformation during banana ripening: The behavior of UPD glucose phosphorylase, sucrose synthetase and invertase." *Journal of Food Science* 48:1097–2011. Transformation documented.

45. Tinsley, I. and A. H. Bockian. 1960. "Some effects of sugar on the breakdown of pelargonidin-3-glucoside model systems at 90°C." *Food Research* 25:161–73. Summary of factors that affect the destruction of anthocyanin in strawberry preserves; data on the effect of sugars on the pigment.

46. Weaver, C. and H. Charley. 1974. "Enzymatic browning of ripening bananas." *Journal of Food Science* 39:1200–2. Dopamine, ascorbic acid, polyphenol oxidase, and discoloration.

47. Whaley, W. G., H. H. Mallenhauer and J. H. Luch. 1960. "The ultra structure of the meristematic cell." *American Journal of Botany* 47:401–50. Structure of the developing plant cell; excellent electron micrographs; technical.

48. Williams, M. and G. Hrazdina. 1979. "Anthocyanins as food colorants: Effects of pH on the formation of anthocyanin-rutin complexes." *Journal of Food Science* 44:66–68. Proposed structures for copigment complexes.

Vegetables

28

Vegetables are valued in the diet for their texture, flavor, color, and nutritive value. Vegetables, with fruits (Chapter 27), rank in importance just above cereals in the Food Pyramid, the guide for choosing nutritious foods. Consumption of fresh vegetables, excluding potatoes, was 51.7 kilograms (113.9 pounds) per capita in 1994 compared to 41.9 kilograms (92.5 pounds) in 1980. Per capita consumption of potatoes was 64 kilograms (141 pounds) in 1994 compared to 51 kilograms (114.7 pounds) in 1980 (73). Potatoes are an important food crop, yielding more per acre than beans, wheat, and even corn (41). They rank second to corn for yield of food energy per unit of fuel energy expended (60). Soybeans and corn yield more protein per unit of land cultivated, but the quality of potato protein ranks second only to that of soybeans (41). In addition, the wide acceptance and mild flavor of potatoes that blends with other items in a menu help account for their high per capita consumption.

Vegetables are more varied in form than are fruits. Practically every part of a plant is represented by one or more vegetables. Spinach and cabbage are leaves; asparagus and celery are stems; carrots, parsnips, and sweet potatoes are roots; broccoli and cauliflower are flowers, although broccoli also includes leaves and stems; cucumber, pepper, squash, and tomato are fruits; beans, peas, and corn are seeds; onions are bulbs; white potatoes are tubers.

COMPOSITION

The composition of some of the more commonly used vegetables is given in Table 28-1. Vegetables are similar in composition to fruits. Like fruits, vegetables are characterized by a low concentration of fat and by a high moisture content. Except for beans and peas, most are low in protein.

Carbohydrates

Most vegetables are good sources of carbohydrates because of the sugars that are present. Beans, corn, peas, and potatoes, all of which store starch, are high in carbohydrates. Tubers of sunchokes (Jerusalem artichokes) accumulate the carbohydrate inulin, a polymer of fructose, instead of starch. Of the nonstarchy vegetables given in Table 28-1, beets, carrots, and onions are intermediate in carbohydrate content and the other vegetables contain approximately five percent. Vegetables are a somewhat better source of fiber than are fruits. Lignin, although not a carbohydrate, may be deposited along with cellulose in vascular tissue of mature vegetables.

TABLE 28-1
Composition of Commonly Used Vegetables (100-gram edible portion, raw)

Vegetable	Water (%)	Calories[a]	Protein (g)	Lipid (g)	Carbohydrate (g)	Calcium (mg)	Phosphorus (mg)	Iron (mg)	Vitamin A Value (I.U.)	Thiamin (mg)	Riboflavin (mg)	Niacin (mg)	Ascorbic Acid (mg)	Fiber Crude (g)	Fiber Total Dietary (g)
Beans lima	70.2	113	6.8	0.9	20.2	34	136	3.1	303	0.22	0.10	1.47	23.4	1.9	—[b]
snap	90.3	31	1.8	0.1	7.1	37	38	1.0	668	0.08	0.11	0.75	16.3	1.1	1.8
Beets	87.3	44	1.5	0.1	10.0	16	48	0.9	20	0.05	0.02	0.40	11.0	0.8	—
Broccoli	90.7	28	3.0	0.4	5.2	48	66	0.9	1,542	0.07	0.12	0.64	93.2	1.1	2.8
Cabbage	92.5	24	1.2	0.2	5.3	47	23	0.6	126	0.05	0.03	0.30	47.3	0.8	—
Carrots	87.8	43	1.0	0.2	10.1	27	44	0.5	28,129	0.10	0.06	0.93	9.3	1.0	3.2
Cauliflower	92.3	24	2.0	0.2	4.9	29	46	0.6	16	0.08	0.06	0.63	71.5	0.9	2.4
Corn, sweet	76.0	86	3.2	2.3	19.0	2	89	0.5	281	0.20	0.06	1.70	6.8	0.7	3.2
Lettuce, head	95.9	13	1.0	0.2	2.1	19	20	0.5	330	0.05	0.03	0.19	3.9	0.5	1.0
Onions	89.7	38	1.2	0.2	8.6	20	33	0.2	0	0.04	0.02	0.15	6.4	0.6	1.6
Peas	78.9	81	5.4	0.4	14.5	25	108	1.5	640	0.27	0.13	2.09	40.0	2.2	—
Potatoes, flesh	79.0	79	2.1	0.1	18.0	7	46	0.8	—	0.09	0.04	1.48	19.7	0.4	1.6
Soybeans, green	67.5	147	13.0	6.8	11.1	197	194	3.6	180	0.44	0.18	1.65	29.0	2.1	—
Spinach	91.6	22	2.9	4.4	3.5	99	49	2.7	6,715	0.08	0.19	0.72	28.1	0.9	2.6
Sweet potato	72.8	105	1.7	4.3	24.3	22	28	0.6	20,063	0.07	0.15	0.67	22.7	0.9	3.0
Tomatoes	93.8	21	0.9	0.3	4.6	5	24	0.5	623	0.06	0.05	0.63	19.1	0.7	1.3

[a] 1 kilocalorie = 4.185 kilojoules
[b] — = Data not available

Source: U.S.D.A. Agr. Handbook No. 8-11. Composition of Foods. Vegetables and Vegetable Products. Raw, Processed, Prepared. 1984, 1990 supplement.

Minerals and Vitamins

As a group, vegetables are richer in minerals and vitamins than are fruits. Thin, dark-green leafy vegetables are high in iron, riboflavin, ascorbic acid, and carotene (pro-vitamin A). Vegetables are a good source of thiamin. Thin green leaves other than those of the goosefoot family supply appreciable quantities of calcium. The oxalic acid present in spinach and other plants of this family binds the calcium in an insoluble form. Spinach, among the vegetables, is one of the better sources of folic acid.

Organic Acids

Vegetables contain a number of organic acids, metabolic products of the cells. Formulas for ten organic acids found in vegetables and fruits follow.

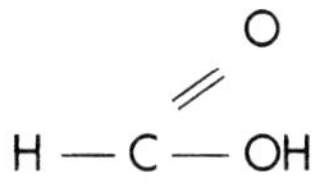

Formic

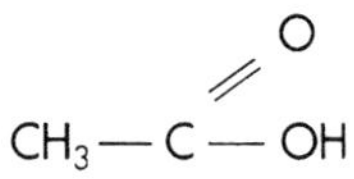

Acetic

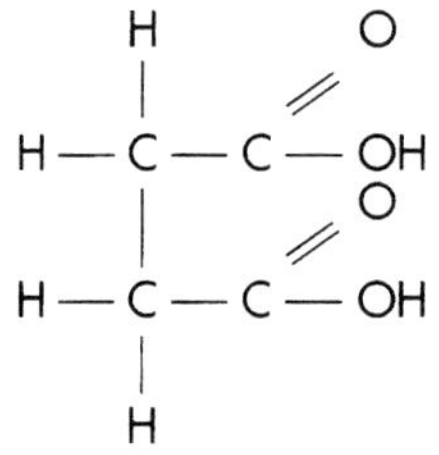

Succinic

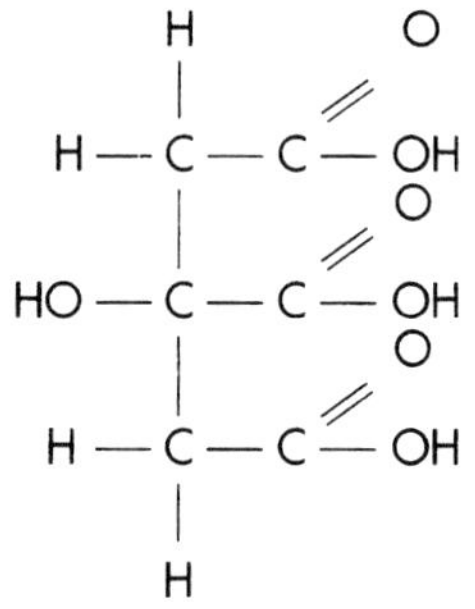

Citric

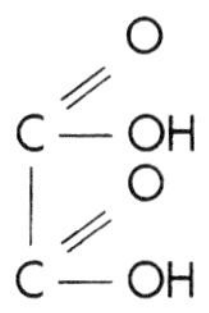

Oxalic

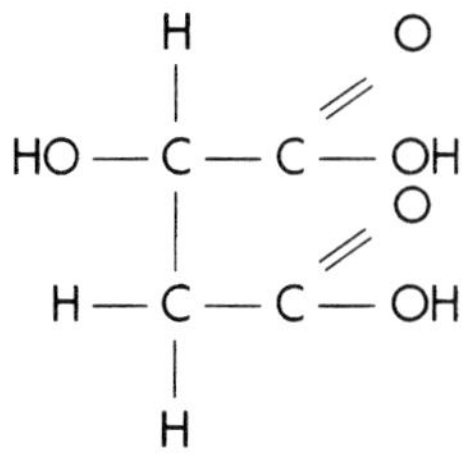

Malic

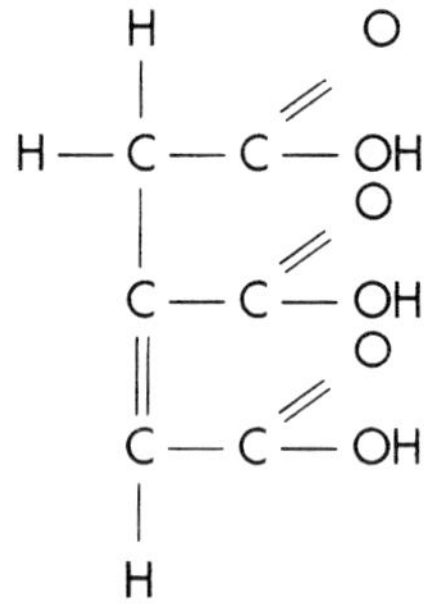

Aconitic

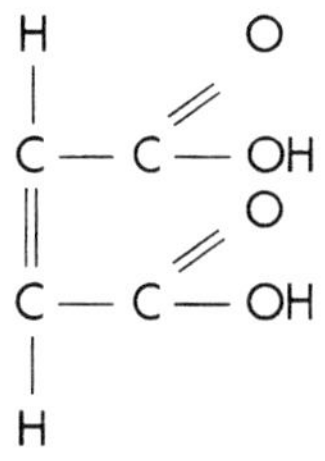

Fumaric

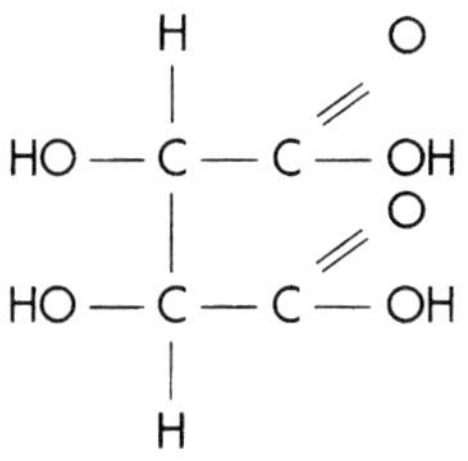

Tartaric

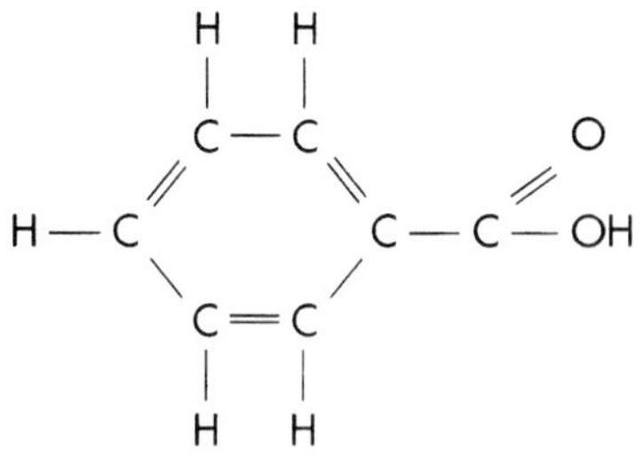

Benzoic

In acetic acid, a methyl group (CH_3—) has replaced the hydrogen in the formic acid. Oxalic acid consists of two carboxyl groups. Succinic acid has two carboxyl groups joined by a —CH_2—CH_2— fragment. Fumaric acid differs from succinic in that the two middle carbons are joined by a double bond. Malic acid is like succinic except that a hydroxyl (—OH) group has replaced a hydrogen on one of the two central carbon atoms; tartaric acid has an —OH group on each of the two middle carbons. Both citric and aconitic are tricarboxylic acids, the latter with a double bond between two of the carbons. Benzoic acid consists of a benzene ring to which is attached a carboxyl group. All of the organic acids above are soluble in water and two of them, formic and acetic, are volatile.

The concentration of acid is lower in vegetables than it is in fruits. Tomatoes, vegetables with the highest concentration of acid, have a pH that ranges from 4.0 to 4.6 or above. The pH of a number of vegetables falls within the range of pH 5.0 to 5.6. Potatoes, peas, and corn are higher (pH 6.1 to 6.3) (1).

TEXTURE OF VEGETABLES

Both structural components and turgor contribute to the texture of vegetables (81). The structural components of plant cell walls are arranged in accordance with basic mechanical engineering principles to provide support for the plant (75). Cellulose fibers embedded in amorphous hemicelluloses and pectic material give strength and some rigidity to cell walls. Continuation of this amorphous material between walls of adjacent cells causes them to adhere, so tissues of raw vegetables resist fracture.

The stage of maturity of a vegetable influences its texture. Ideally most vegetables are harvested while still immature and before accumulation of secondary cell wall material toughens them. This is in contrast to fruits, the structure of which is weakened by ripening after the fruit is mature (81). Parts of plants used as vegetables, from buds of broccoli to underground stems of potatoes and roots of carrots, differ markedly in their cellular makeup, unlike fruits that consist mainly of thin-walled parenchyma cells.

Water-conducting xylem and food-transporting phloem are important structural components of vegetables. These vascular tissues are segregated in some vegetables. Xylem is found in the central core that runs the length of the root of carrots and parsnips and the phloem surrounds the core. Vascular bundles are arranged in concentric circles in the edible part of beet root. Two other types of tissue, collenchyma and sclerenchyma, are prominent in some vegetable parts (81). The moderately thick-walled collenchyma gives strength to plant tissue and the thicker-walled sclerenchyma provide support. Each of these constituents influences the texture of plant parts in which it appears.

Sclerenchyma may become lignified in more mature vegetables. Lignified tissue may be present in the petioles of leaves of spinach, at the ends of broccoli stalks, and at the butt ends of asparagus spears. Asparagus is especially prone to toughening as it matures in the field and after it is cut for harvest. In stored spears, an increase in activity of an enzyme that can catalyze the first step in the conversion of phenylalanine to lignin, and an increase in the force required to shear the spears suggest involvement of the enzyme in lignification (61). However, demonstration of an increase in crude fiber, in shear force, and in deposition of lignin in stored spears, in both unblanched and those blanched to inactivate enzymes, points to nonenzymatic lignification (72).

QUALITY CHARACTERISTICS OF RAW VEGETABLES

A raw vegetable of high quality has a crisp texture, owing to the pressure that water-filled, turgid cells exert on one another. To maintain that crispness, vegetables should be handled to minimize loss of moisture. A vegetable with a high surface area such as leaves of chard or spinach loses moisture rapidly and soon wilts when exposed to air. A compact vegetable such as beet root held in air for several hours loses moisture and becomes flaccid. The cork-like surface of a potato slows but does not eliminate moisture loss.

Over time a potato becomes limp and pliable. Misting vegetables to retain their marketability is practiced by a number of retail establishments (5). Vegetables held under refrigeration will lose moisture until the air around the vegetable is saturated with water vapor. Storage should be in a covered container just large enough to accommodate the item. A small quantity of vegetable held in a vegetable crisper of a household refrigerator will become limp from loss of moisture in a few days.

Loss of moisture and wilting may do more harm than just to the texture of a vegetable. Losses of ascorbic acid and carotene are more rapid in vegetables that wilt rapidly (23). Retentions of chlorophyll and of reduced ascorbic acid is enhanced by misting, as with broccoli (5).

Indicators of quality that apply to all vegetables include a clear, bright appearance and firmness and freedom from cuts, bruises, and abrasions. Other attributes of quality vary with the vegetable. Spears of asparagus should be rounded instead of ridged and the tips should be compact. Snap beans should have thick, meaty walls rather than spongy ones and the pods should be straight. They should be crisp enough to break easily and with a snap. Heads of cabbage should be firm, with the outer leaves close together near the base. The leaves should look translucent rather than opaque and greenish rather than white. A white core rather than a yellowish one is another sign of quality. Stalks of celery should be thick, succulent, fine grained, and brittle. A large heart with the stalks fitting together compactly is an indication of high quality, as is the absence of deep ridges on the outside of the stalks. Broccoli stalks should be small, with translucent skin and small, dark-green leaves with short stems. The buds are closed and their surface covered with a satiny bloom. Cauliflower should be pearly white and compact with bright green leaves. Onions should have thin, dry skins and thin, firm necks. Green, brittle pods of peas that are well filled but not bulging are desired. Potatoes should be symmetrical and have shallow eyes. A russet skin is a characteristic of the variety, but a green color under the skin means that the potato was stored in light. Such green tissue may contain, in addition to chlorophyll, more than the trace normally present in potatoes of a group of glycoalkaloids frequently referred to as solanine (59). These glycoalkaloids, mainly α-solanine and α-chaconine, impart a bitter taste and a burning sensation. They are toxic as well (36). Sprouts are a potent source of these toxic compounds. Green areas should be cut away before the potato is cooked. Root vegetables should have clear, bright skins. They should be plump and free from whiskers. Spinach leaves should be dark green and glossy with succulent stems. Tomatoes should be a clear, bright red. The surface should be glossy and smoothly curved rather than angular. Of course, the variety of the vegetable influences to some extent the character of a particular sample. Danvers carrots differ from Chantenay; Blue Lake green beans differ from Kentucky Wonder.

Storage to Maintain Quality

Metabolic processes continue in plant tissue after harvest, utilizing sources of energy, especially sugars, that were synthesized by the growing plant. The flavor appeal of vegetables comes in part from the sweet taste of the sugars they contain. The sugar content of an immature vegetable may decrease rapidly once it is harvested. Decrease in sweetness is especially noticeable in peas, new potatoes, and sweet corn. Common sweet corn, believed to be a mutation of a Peruvian corn, has a *su* or sugary gene responsible for its sweetness (38). Plant breeders have modified this sweet corn to increase its sweetness. A cultivar with the *se* or sugary enhancer gene has twice as much sugar as does common sweet corn and one with the sh_2 (shrunken) gene, named for the appearance of the dried kernel, has almost three times as much sugar (90). Much of the sugar is sucrose, more than 90 percent in kernels with the sh_2 gene. Sweet corn accumulates phytoglycogen as it matures (38). Although the newer corns retain their sweetness better than common sweet corn, they still benefit from refrigerated storage as do all vegetables. Prompt cooling and refrigeration slow activity of enzymes involved in metabolic processes that would otherwise cause deterioration and lead to early senescence.

Mature, starchy potatoes held in cold storage accumulate sugar. Chips and fries made from such potatoes brown excessively and unevenly. Most cultivars must be brought to room temperature (21°C or 70°F) and held until the cells metabolize the accumulated sugar. One experimental potato can be used directly from cold storage. The starch in this tuber is higher in amylose, lower in amylopectin, more crystalline, and more resistant to α-amylase (4).

Sweet potatoes are not sweet when they are harvested. It is customary to hold the roots at 29° to 32°C (84° to 89°F) at 85 to 90 percent relative humidity for four to seven days. The curing temperature promotes the activity of α-amylase that converts the starch of the root to dextrins and sugar. A sweet potato that is moist rather than dry when cooked contains less residual starch and more dextrins of low molecular weight (86). Some cultivars are moister and sweeter than others when cooked. Sweet potatoes baked in a microwave oven resemble dry-meated rather than moist-meated ones, while the same cultivar baked in a conventional oven has more dextrins and sugar. Apparently, the slower heating in the conventional oven allows more time for the α-amylase to act (62).

Although many vegetables maintain high quality longer when stored at temperatures just above freezing, some vegetables of tropical or subtropical origin are damaged if stored at temperatures above freezing but below approximately 10°C (50°F) (44). Abnormal respiration may result in pitting, russetting, loss of color, or leatheriness. Vegetables that are susceptible to chilling injury and therefore should be stored in a cool but not a cold place, include peppers, cucumbers, eggplant, snap beans, sweet potatoes, tomatoes, and winter squash.

Several vegetables can benefit from controlled atmosphere (CA) storage, but safe levels of both oxygen and carbon dioxide must be determined for each vegetable (40). CA storage can be used to slow conversion of starch to sugar in potatoes, and the conversion of sugar to starch in peas and corn. Carbon dioxide can either inhibit or accelerate sprouting of potatoes, depending on concentration. An elevated level of carbon dioxide (10%) prevents toughening of asparagus spears and inhibits their elongation. Stems of broccoli are more tender following such storage. Yellowing of broccoli, which occurs within two or three days at room temperature, is best retarded by storage near 0°C (32°F) (47). For extended storage, a low level of oxygen (but not below 0.5 to 1.0 percent) or a high level of carbon dioxide (10%) retards yellowing. Controlled atmosphere storage must be tailored for each vegetable and for the specific effect desired.

PREPARATION FOR COOKING

Washing

Because the parts of plants used as vegetables grow in or near the soil, washing is even more important than it is for fruits. Vegetables need to be washed thoroughly to remove particles of soil and microorganisms that are in the soil. Vegetables may be contaminated with *Escherichia coli*. Their presence suggests that the food may have come into at least indirect contact with sewage, because these bacteria thrive in the human intestinal tract. Several changes of clean water do the job as well as running water, the use of which tends to be wasteful. Vegetables should be lifted from the water rather than the water drained off, in which case soil remains in the container with the vegetable. Lukewarm water cleanses better than cold. A vegetable brush aids in cleaning the surface of such vegetables as celery and potatoes.

Waste in Preparation

As with fruits, certain parts of vegetables that are considered unpalatable, if not inedible, are discarded. Vegetables usually need trimming, but unnecessary waste should be avoided. Table 28-2 gives the average percentage of waste from a few vegetables. Part of the waste is inherent in the vegetable. Percent of inedible material is low (9%) in onions and high (62%) in peas. The percentage of waste may be used to find the amount that should be subtracted from the weight as purchased (AP) to give the yield of edible portion (EP). The edible portion of peas costs somewhat more than twice as much as the same weight of vegetable as purchased. Figures given in Table 28-2 are averages for vegetables of typical quality. The percentage of waste for a particular sample of any one vegetable may vary from this average value, the amount depending on the quality of the vegetable. For example, the waste from trimmed broccoli on the market near growing areas is usually much less than the 39 percent given in the table.

The amount of waste varies not only with the vegetable but also with the tool and with the technique used to remove inedible parts. Potatoes serve as an example. The least waste probably occurs when the whole potato is boiled. Heating solubilizes the material that joins the periderm (Fig. 28-1) to the flesh, which permits a clean separation of the two and

TABLE 28-2
Waste from Representative Vegetables as Purchased

Vegetable	Waste (%)
Asparagus	47
Broccoli, untrimmed	39
Cabbage, untrimmed	20
Carrots, with tops	41
Carrots, without tops	18
Onions, mature	9
Peas (in pods)	62
Potatoes	19
Tomatoes, peeled	18

Source: U.S.D.A. Agr. Handbook No. 102. *Food Yields Summarized by Different Stages of Preparation.* Revised 1975.

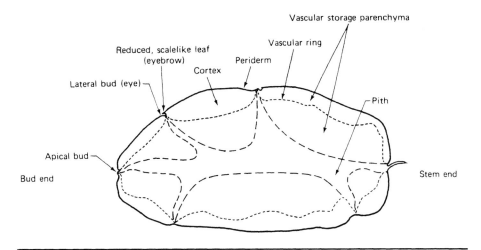

Figure 28-1. Longitudinal section of a potato tuber (*Solanum tuberosum*). (From D. L. Hsu and Marion Jacobson, *Home Economics Research Journal* 13:28. Copyright © 1974 by American Home Economics Association. Reprinted by permission of Sage Publications, Inc.)

a minimum of waste. However, this method of cooking may impart an undesirable flavor to the flesh. Removal of the periderm by abrasion or by scraping keeps waste low, as does a floating-blade peeler compared to a paring knife.

Discarding leaves of broccoli and cooking only stalks and buds represents another type of waste. The tender dark green leaves are, on a weight basis, more nutritious than the stalks. The green tender leaves at the base of a head of cauliflower that are sometimes discarded contain nutrients. The delicate green of these leaves gives a needed contrast to the whiteness of the flower. Leaves of celery can be chopped and used as seasoning in vegetable soup, stews, dressing or as part of the greens in a tossed salad. Vegetable parts that cannot be tenderized such as the ends of asparagus spears and broccoli stalks should be removed before the vegetable is put to cook.

COOKING METHODS

Vegetables are sometimes served raw; more frequently, they are cooked. Vegetables are heated to bring about desirable changes in texture and flavor. Heating also destroys a number of microorganisms that are present on the surface of vegetables.

A number of factors may influence the choice of cooking method for a vegetable. These include the presence in the vegetable of water-soluble nutrients, of pigments, of acids, and of certain flavor constituents. Of course the menu is a factor, too. Vegetables may be baked, boiled, steamed, or panned. Potatoes, either as chips or french fries, are cooked in deep fat as are onion rings dipped in batter. Deep-fat frying is discussed in Chapter 15. Most vegetables are low in calories. Added butter, bacon fat, sour cream, and sauces are not.

Baking

Vegetables may be baked in the skin as are potatoes or in the shucks as are roasting ears of corn, a method of cooking used by Native Americans. For the latter, the husks are opened enough to remove the silks and the entire ears are soaked in water. This keeps the husks from burning before the kernels are done. Or the shucks may be removed and the ear re-covered with aluminum foil. Most young, tender root vegetables may be baked in the skin, as may tomatoes. Onions may be so cooked or the skin may be removed and the onions wrapped in foil before they are baked. For scalloped potatoes, the skin of the potato is re-moved and the prepared vegetable is baked in a covered casserole that keeps the moisture in like a skin. The advantage of baking a vegetable is that no added water comes into con-tact with it to leach out water-soluble nutrients. The disadvantage is that heat penetration during baking is slow. Also, more fuel is required.

Boiling in the Skin

When a vegetable is boiled in the skin, enough water to cover and a lid on the container are used. The large amount of cooking water does not add unduly to the loss of nutrients during cooking because the skin on the vegetable is intact. Beets in their skins (with ap-proximately two inches of tops left on so that water-soluble nutrients and pigments do not leach out into the cooking water) may be cooked by this method. So may small Danish squash, for which the cooking time is a few minutes less than it is for baking the squash when it is cut in half. Baking time can be shortened by placing the squash with the cut sur-face down on the baking sheet or pan, rather than up. Corn may be cooked by boiling on the cob. Potatoes, both white and sweet, may be boiled in the skins.

Boiling Prepared Vegetables

Putting prepared vegetables in just enough boiling, salted water to prevent scorching and cooking with a lid on the container is a basic method of cooking vegetables. The water should be brought back to a boil as rapidly as possible and then the heat lowered to main-tain a slow boil. The aim is to have the vegetable just done when only a few drops of cook-ing water remain. This method minimizes losses of soluble nutrients to the cooking water. A container with a tight-fitting lid is needed, as is careful adjustment of the intensity of heat; otherwise, the vegetable may scorch.

Not all vegetables boiled in this way have the best color or flavor, however. Green veg-etables which need more than five to seven minutes to become tender may lose some of their bright green color when cooked by this method. Vegetables of the cabbage group (broccoli, Brussels sprouts, cabbage, rutabagas, and turnips) may have an unpleasant aroma (see discussion of sulfur compounds in vegetables, this chapter) when they are cooked by this method unless the vegetable is shredded or sliced so that it will be done within five to seven minutes. For the best color and aroma these vegetables may be put to cook in enough boiling, salted water to approximately cover the vegetable and without a lid. In this way the volatile acids escape along with steam and nonvolatile acids are diluted. This method of cooking minimizes undesirable changes in the color and flavor of these vegetables. Loss of water-soluble nutrients may be somewhat greater, but the more rapid warmup in excess boiling water may reduce destruction of ascorbic acid.

Steaming

When prepared vegetables are cooked by steaming, energy is transmitted by steam to the product suspended in a perforated container above vigorously boiling water. Most vegeta-bles can be steamed, but the cooking time is usually somewhat longer than for boiling. The advantage of steaming over boiling is that only that water from the steam that condenses comes in contact with the vegetable. Cooking in a pressure saucepan or cooker is actually steaming, although the temperature is elevated because of the steam pressure built up in the cooker. The equipment is usually operated at 15 pounds steam pressure, and the cooking temperature is 121°C (250°F) compared with approximately 100°C (212°F) in a steamer. This elevation of temperature under steam pressure causes a sharp reduction in cooking time.

Panning or Stir-Frying

This method may be used to cook leafy vegetables and succulent vegetables that can be shredded. Shredded beets, carrots, or cabbage may be cooked by panning, as may spinach. In panning, the vegetable is cooked to a large extent in steam from water that seeps out of the cut tissues. A heavy container with a tight-fitting lid is essential for panning. A small amount of fat in the container keeps the vegetable from sticking until enough of the cell sap can be drawn from the vegetable to start the cooking. The secret of success in panning is to have the pieces of vegetable thin so that heat will penetrate rapidly and the cooking time will be short. The heating unit should be set high enough to start cooking promptly and then lowered, not so much that cooking stops, but so that water will not evaporate from the utensil. The vegetable should be stirred for the first minute or two of the cooking period, but evaporation should be kept to a minimum. Panning as a method for cooking vegetables has all the advantages of cooking in a small amount of water plus a shorter cooking time because the vegetable is shredded or cut into thin slices.

EFFECTS OF COOKING ON TEXTURE OF VEGETABLES

Crispness

When pieces of crisp, raw vegetable are put to cook in boiling water, heat denatures the cytoplasm and the cell membranes. Cells no longer retain water; instead, they lose water by diffusion through the now permeable membranes. The limpness of cooked vegetables in contrast to the crispness of raw ones is due to this loss of water. Loss of water from cells killed by heat causes most vegetables (even though cooked in enough water to cover) to weigh less than they did raw. Starchy vegetables are an exception. A vegetable cooked by microwaves loses more water than does one boiled conventionally, even when the same volume of cooking water is used for each (66). This loss of water upon cooking is reflected in the somewhat diminished size of the cells from the phloem of carrot boiled on a conventional range and the greater shrinkage and pronounced folding of the cell walls of tissue cooked by microwaves (Fig. 28-2).

Tenderness

The crisp, coherent tissues of a raw vegetable provide a pleasing contrast to the soft texture of milk, cheese, eggs, meats, and starchy foods. In the interests of tenderness, somewhat less structural integrity may be desired in a cooked vegetable. However, vegetables should not be cooked until they lose completely those textural qualities for which they are valued. A soft, mushy product results when a vegetable is overcooked; an undercooked vegetable has lost crispness but lacks tenderness. A vegetable is at optimum doneness when it can be

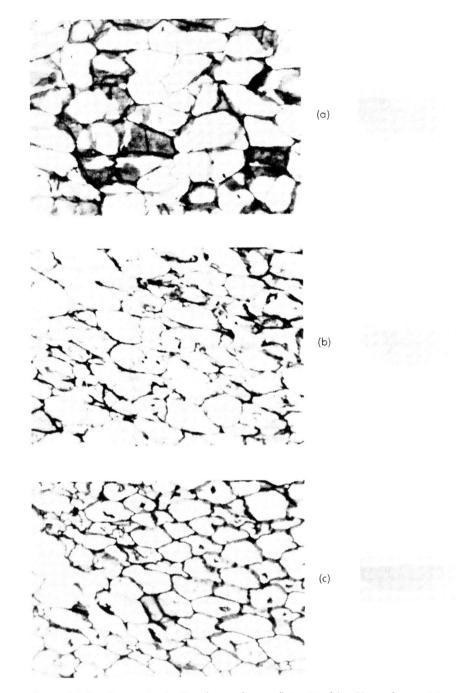

Figure 28-2. Cross section (× 2) and parenchyma cells (× 41) of the phloem of carrot: (a) raw; (b) boiled conventionally; (c) cooked by microwave energy. (Reprinted from Elaine Schrumpf and Helen Charley, *Journal of Food Science* 40:1025, 1975. Copyright © by Institute of Food Technologists. Reprinted by permission.)

pierced with a fork but not too readily. A number of factors influence the time required to accomplish this, so a range in recommended cooking times is usually given (1). Reducing the size of the pieces shortens cooking time required to tenderize a vegetable. Potatoes quartered or carrots sliced cook in less time than does a whole vegetable. A young, tender vegetable usually requires a shorter cooking time than does a mature one. A frozen vegetable cooks in less time than a corresponding raw one, due in part to the freezing process and to the fact that the vegetable was blanched before it was frozen. Most frozen vegetables should be put to cook without thawing because this minimizes loss of ascorbic acid.

Vegetables such as asparagus and broccoli present special problems. The lower half of the stem of both requires longer cooking time than the upper half. Buds of broccoli require even less cooking than the upper part of the stem. Getting all parts of the vegetable equally done is not easy. It is pointless to try to cook parts of a vegetable that contain appreciable quantities of lignin because they cannot be tenderized by cooking. Nonlignified parts will be overcooked and those that contain lignin will never become tender.

A vegetable cooks in much less time under steam pressure than it does by boiling at atmospheric pressure. In one study, diced carrots reached the just-done stage in 19 minutes by boiling (100°C or 212°F) but needed only 50 seconds in a pressure saucepan at 121°C (250°F) (12). Because vegetables cook so rapidly in a pressure saucepan, only a few seconds' difference in cooking time makes a marked difference in the doneness of the vegetable. In another study comparing two cooking methods, the outer layers of stems of broccoli cooked by microwaves were slightly tough when tissues in the center of the stem were so tender as to appear somewhat overcooked. Tissue in the core of carrots was slightly tough while that in the outer cylinder was spongy. Tissues in each vegetable were of more uniform doneness when cooked by boiling (66). Longer cooking times are needed to tenderize most vegetables at higher elevations, the actual increase depending upon the vegetable, on whether it is fresh or frozen, and on how the vegetable is cooked (microwave oven, conventional range, or pressure saucepan) (14).

An early study of the effects of heat on vegetables (carrots and parsnips cooked by steaming) established that pectin increased at the expense of protopectin, and that cell walls, viewed with a light microscope, were less dense (71). A scanning electron microscope was used in a later study to document in greater detail the effects of steaming, boiling, and cooking under steam pressure on the structure of carrot tissue (21). Separation of cells, evident in steamed phloem, is more pronounced in boiled tissue and even more extensive in that cooked under steam pressure. Cell walls, still rigid when the vegetable is steamed, show some disorganization when the vegetable is boiled, and much damage when cooked under steam pressure. The xylem cooked by steaming retains much of its cellular integrity. However, boiling results in extensive separation of cells and disruption of individual cells. Collapse of cells occurs in xylem cooked under steam pressure. The effects of heat on vegetables thus appears to vary with the tissue and with the method of application of heat.

Both experimental evidence and practical observations indicate that cooking alters the texture of vegetables. Identifying the mechanism(s) involved is another matter, although a number of papers related to the topic have been published. Depolymerization of pectin by β- or *trans*-elimination has been proposed to account for the partial disassembly of the cell walls of plant tissue when it is cooked (81). Under conditions of low acidity, as in vegetables, heat breaks glycosidic bonds that unite galacturonic acid units, and a double bond forms between carbon 4 that had participated in the glycosidic linkage and carbon 5 to which the —$COOCH_3$ group is attached. Lower molecular weight pectin fragments presumably are more soluble. One early study established that certain metal ions in the cooking water can influence the effects of cooking on tenderness of a vegetable. The presence of monovalent ions such as sodium or potassium give more tender carrot tissue and the presence of divalent ions such as calcium or magnesium yield firmer cooked tissue than cooking in water only (76). Acid in the cooking water firms the tissue, also.

A study using snap beans showed that the presence of sodium chloride in the water around the beans when they are heat processed as for canning results in softer tissue compared to beans processed as a water pack. The sodium chloride increases the amount of both pectin and calcium ions in the liquor around the beans. Sodium chloride added to beans processed in water increases the amount of calcium in the liquor but not the pectin. Heat is required for the latter (82). When processed snap beans from which salt has been leached are soaked in water containing sodium chloride, firmness of the tissue decreases, as does calcium in the pods. Calcium chloride in the soaking water increases firmness of the pods (80). Thus both monovalent and divalent ions influence the texture of a cooked vegetable.

It has been assumed that firmness of plant tissue is due to divalent calcium ions that cross-link ionized carboxyl groups of pectic molecules, as shown in Figure 31-1. This egg box model with calcium ions fitting in the pockets formed by adjacent pectic molecules is used to depict the formation of a gel from a dilute sol of low methoxyl pectin (Chapter 31). The validity of this model to account for the effects of calcium on the texture of vegetables has been questioned (51). A major reason is that the high methoxyl content of most pectic substances precludes sufficient ionic linkages from forming an insoluble pectic matrix in plant tissue. In a study of brined, acidified cucumbers it was shown that the effects of low levels of calcium ions on firmness of the tissue is due to interference with the softening effect of sodium chloride. Based on the relationship between the concentration of calcium ions and its effect on the tenderizing of plant tissue by sodium chloride, it was theorized that calcium ions may have saturated an unidentified binding site, preventing softening by sodium ions (51). That tissues were firmer regardless of the extent of methylation of the pectin suggests that calcium acts by a mechanism other than that of the egg box model. Factors responsible for the texture of raw vegetables and for the effects of heat on the texture of cooked vegetables are complex. Additional studies will no doubt clear up some of the uncertainties.

One practical application of the effect of acid on the texture of vegetables when heated can be cited. Thin slices of vegetable may be simmered for an hour in vegetable soup without the slices losing identity and shape when tomato juice is added along with the vegetables. Without the acid from the tomato, the slices would disintegrate into cells or groups of cells after an hour of cooking.

For a number of years, calcium chloride has been added to commercially canned tomatoes when they are processed (48). The firmness of tomatoes so treated is attributed to the formation of calcium pectate. The calcium in molasses added to parboiled dried beans for baked beans lengthens the cooking time needed to tenderize the beans.

Calcium ions affect the textural quality of peas. This vegetable contains phytic acid (inositol hexaphosphate) in the interior of the cell. Cooking disrupts the compartmentalization within the cell and cell contents come in contact with the cell wall and middle lamella. The phytic acid unites with calcium present in the tissue to form insoluble calcium phytate (phytin). This effectively ties up the calcium so that the peas can be tenderized by cooking. However, peas stored so that the enzyme phytase can hydrolyze phytic acid to inositol and phosphoric acid, neither of which binds calcium, remain firm or hard even with prolonged cooking (35).

Texture of Cooked Potatoes

Starch is a major component of the solids of a potato tuber. The amount of starch varies with the tubers and from one part of a tuber to another (Fig. 28-3). Starch granules in the storage parenchyma cells inside the vascular ring are largest, those in the pith or water-core are somewhat smaller, and those in parenchyma cells outside the vascular ring are smallest (65). Potatoes absorb water as they cook because of the pasting of the numerous starch granules (Fig. 9-8). This is in contrast to most vegetables that lose weight even when they are cooked in sufficient water to cover.

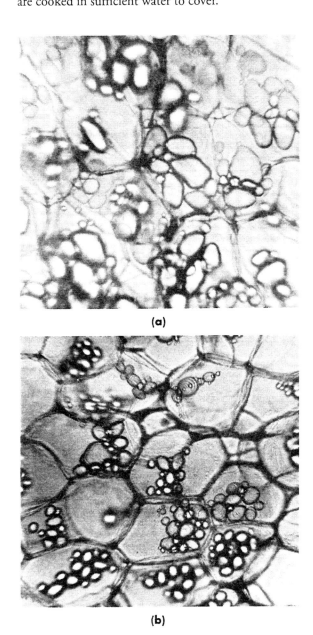

(a)

(b)

Figure 28-3. Starch granules in the parenchyma cells of potato. (*top*) Numerous, large granules in the larger cells of the storage parenchyma (Fig. 28-1). (*bottom*) Fewer granules in the pith or "water core" (Fig. 28-1). Original magnification × 150. (From R. M. Reeve, *American Potato Journal* 44:44, 1967; and *Economic Botany* 21:296, 1967. Used by permission of the *American Potato Journal* and the New York Botanical Garden.)

Texture of cooked tubers can vary from waxy to mealy (64). Waxy cooked potatoes appear translucent and feel pasty and wet on the tongue. Mealy potatoes appear glisteny and feel granular and dry. The cells of potatoes that are waxy when cooked continue to adhere while the cells of mealy potatoes tend to separate (Fig. 28-4) (75). Some mealy potatoes tend to slough excessively. The texture of cooked potatoes has been the subject of numerous studies, with early emphasis on both the starch and the pectic substances in the tuber. The results of one study show that while potatoes that are mealy when cooked tend to have a high starch content and a high specific gravity, a measure of solids in the tuber, starch content alone does not account for differences in texture (8), nor do differences in the pectic constituents (9). However, the calcium content of the tuber, the viscosity of the pectin solubilized when the tuber is treated with a calcium-sequestering agent, plus the starch content could account for much of the difference in texture. Obviously more than one factor influences cell adhesion. *Trans-* or β-elimination of pectin, favored by the pH of the tuber, has been proposed as a factor in loss of cell adhesion, as has the high content of potassium (34). Sloughing is more likely in tissue outside the vascular ring and in the bud rather the stem end of the tuber, both areas higher in potassium.

Why some potatoes are mealy and others soggy when cooked is still an unsettled question. However, measuring the specific gravity of a potato can give some indication of its texture when cooked (31). When potatoes are placed in a brine made from one cup of salt and 11 cups of water, some float and others sink (Fig. 28-5). A potato that floats in brine of this strength is less dense (has lower specific gravity) and the chances are good that the cells of this potato will adhere after it is cooked. This characteristic is desirable in a potato to be used for salad or scalloped potatoes. On the other hand, if the potato sinks, this means that the potato is dense and such potatoes tend to be mealy when cooked. For mashed potatoes this is a desirable characteristic, and many people consider it so for baked potatoes. Sinkers, with high specific gravity, have more starch than do floaters. This lends support to the theory that higher starch content and lower cell adhesion are related. Attempts have been made to market potatoes separated on the basis of specific gravity. The relation between specific gravity and texture of cooked potatoes is illustrated in Figure 28-6. Reservations have been expressed in regard to relying on specific gravity to predict cooking quality of potatoes (50). Two potatoes with the same specific gravity but representing different cultivars or grown under different conditions do not necessarily have the same texture when cooked.

Baked potatoes are a popular menu item. When foil-wrapped baked potatoes were compared with unwrapped ones, those in foil were judged comparable in mealiness, color, and flavor (19). A potato baked in a conventional oven (60 minutes at 205°C or 400°F) was ranked better than one baked in a microwave oven (five minutes) (53).

FLAVOR OF VEGETABLES AND THE EFFECTS OF COOKING

Information about the constituents responsible for the flavor and, especially, the aroma of a number of vegetables is available (37). Much work has been done with those vegetables that have a distinct aroma. Included are onions, garlic, and chives, of the genus *Allium,* and broccoli, cabbage, cauliflower, cress, kale, mustard, and turnip, of the genus *Brassica.* The latter belongs to the Cruciferae family. The distinctive aroma of these vegetables comes from sulfur-containing precursors.

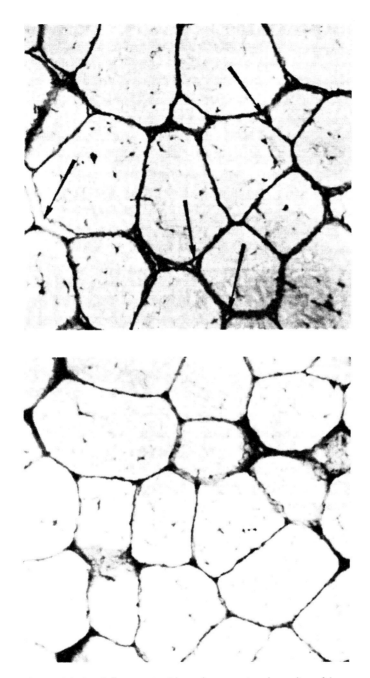

Figure 28-4. Cell separation (shown by arrows) and rounding of the cells characterize a mealy cooked potato (*top*). In a waxy or soggy potato (*bottom*) the cells adhere and remain angular. (From C. Sterling, "Texture of Cell-wall Polysaccharides in Foods" in *Recent Advances in Food Research-3—Biochemistry and Biophysics* in *Food Research,* J. M. Leitch and D. N. Rhodes, eds. Copyright © 1963 by Butterworths, London, p. 274. Reprinted by permission.)

Figure 28-5. Specific gravity of a potato is an index to its cooking quality. Floaters (in brine made of 1 cup of salt and 11 cups of water) are likely to be waxy when cooked, sinkers likely to be mealy. (Courtesy of Andrea Mackey and the Oregon Agricultural Experiment Station.)

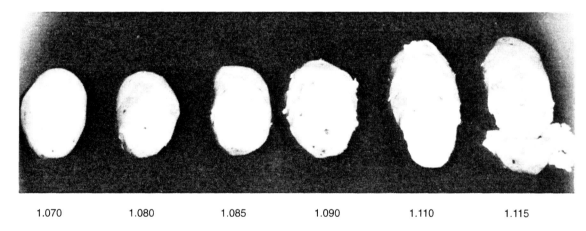

| 1.070 | 1.080 | 1.085 | 1.090 | 1.110 | 1.115 |

Figure 28-6. Texture of cooked potatoes that vary in specific gravity. Floaters with low specific gravity on the left to sinkers with high specific gravity on the right. (Courtesy of Andrea Mackey and the Oregon Agricultural Experiment Station.)

Mild Vegetables

Cooking should bring out or enhance the flavor of vegetables. Improper methods or overcooking may result in a loss of flavor or may develop an undesirable one (78). Loss of flavor in mild vegetables such as carrots and peas is primarily a decrease in sweetness, due to sugar dissolving in the cooking water. Contact of the vegetable with water should be kept to a minimum. Both a minimum of water and a short cooking time help maintain the sweet taste of vegetables.

Development of an undesirable flavor is to be guarded against as well as is loss of flavor. The flavor of even mild vegetables such as carrots and peas will become strong if the cooking time is prolonged. Even slight overcooking of a mild vegetable like peas does some damage to the flavor. Prolonged cooking produces an off flavor. Comparison of canned peas with fresh ones cooked until just tender illustrates the effect of longer time and higher temperature on the flavor of even a mild vegetable. The high input of heat is necessary if the canned product is to keep but the quality suffers. A high temperature short time process minimizes the damage.

Sulfur Compounds in Vegetables

Two groups of vegetables, one from the genus *Allium* of the lily family and the other mainly from the *Brassica* genus of the mustard family, the Crucifers, are noted for the sulfur compounds they contain. Two groups of sulfur-containing compounds, cysteine sulfoxides and glucosinolates, are found in these vegetables.

Cysteine Sulfoxides

Garlic, onions, chives, and leeks, members of the lily family, contain derivatives of the sulfur-containing amino acid cysteine (10). The main derivative in garlic, (+)-S-allyl-L-cysteine sulfoxide, known by the trivial name alliin, was identified first. Also present in raw garlic is an enzyme known as alliinase or cysteine sulfoxide lyase. Damage of the cells by slicing, mincing, or chewing brings the enzyme and substrate into contact. The enzyme converts the (+)-S-allyl-L-cysteine sulfoxide to ammonia, pyruvic acid, and diallyl thiosulfinate (allicin), the last a volatile compound that is responsible for the odor of garlic (10). The reaction is shown (7) as:

$$2CH_2 = CH - CH_2 - \overset{\overset{O}{\uparrow}}{S} - CH_2 - \underset{\underset{NH_2}{|}}{CH} - COOH + H_2O \xrightarrow{\text{Alliinase}}$$

(+) − S-Allyl − L − Cysteine Sulfoxide (Alliin)

$$\begin{matrix} CH_2 = CH - CH_2 - S = O \\ | \\ CH_2 = CH - CH_2 - S \end{matrix} + 2NH_3 + 2CH_3 - \overset{\overset{O}{\|}}{C} - COOH$$

Diallyl Thiosulfinate (Allicin)   Ammonia   Pyruvic Acid

The allicin is unstable and decomposes to give diallyl disulfide that makes some contribution to garlic odor.

Onions, chives, and leeks contain (+)-S-methyl- and (+)-S-propyl-L-cysteine sulfoxide, but little if any of the allyl compound. Present also is a sulfoxide lyase, which catalyzes the breakdown of these sulfoxides to dimethyl, dipropyl, and methylpropyl thiosulfinates. The dipropyl derivative is characterized as having a typical onionlike odor. The ratio of propyl to methyl derivatives decreases from the stronger onions to the mild chives, to the still-milder leeks (17). The thiosulfinates are unstable, and their decomposition products include aldehydes, alcohols, and dimethyl, dipropyl, and methylpropyl di- and trisulfides.

More abundant in onions than the methyl and propyl cysteine sulfoxides and possibly important as a flavor precursor (68) is (+)-S-propenyl-L-cysteine sulfoxide

$$CH_3 - CH = CH - \overset{\overset{\displaystyle O}{\uparrow}}{S} - CH_2 - \underset{\underset{\displaystyle NH_2}{|}}{CH} - COOH$$

This sulfoxide, a positional isomer of allyl sulfoxide, has been identified as the chief substrate for the cysteine sulfoxide lyase and the precursor of the lachrymator in onion (10, 69). When the tissue is cut, the enzyme catalyzes the breakdown of this sulfoxide to ammonia, pyruvic acid, and, instead of a thiosulfinate, thiopropanal sulfoxide (propanethial-S-oxide)

$$CH_3 - CH_2 - CH = S - O$$

The latter has been identified as the lachrymator in freshly cut onion tissue (16). The lachrymator is unstable and decomposes rapidly. Substances formed by the action of the lyase on the propenyl sulfoxide have been proposed as contributors to the biting sensation on the tongue, the bitterness, part of the odor of minced or chewed onion tissue, and the tear-eliciting effect (68).

The (+)-S-propenyl-L-cysteine sulfoxide has been proposed as the main, if not the only, precursor of compounds that have the characteristic odor of cooked onions (69), but both propyl and propenyl di- and trisulfides have been identified in the aroma of boiled onions and dimethyl thiophene in that of fried onions (11). Much of the odor of onions can be volatilized by cooking. It is a question of how much onion aroma one wants to retain. For little or none, the vegetable should be cooked in enough water to cover and without a lid. To retain as much as possible of the onion aroma, the vegetable should be cooked covered and in a minimum of water. The choice of cooking method might be influenced by whether the raw onions are mild or strong.

Onions increase in sweetness when they are cooked. The reason for this is still unclear, although it has been attributed to the production of *n*-propanethiol, a compound reputed to be many times sweeter than sucrose (89).

Vegetables that belong to the mustard family, the Cruciferae, constitute a second group high in sulfur-containing compounds. Included are broccoli, Brussels sprouts, cabbage, cauliflower, kale, kohlrabi, mustard, rutabaga, turnip, cress, radish, and horseradish, all except the last three members of the *Brassica* genus. Instead of propyl, propenyl, or allyl, however, only (+)-S-methyl-L-cysteine sulfoxide

$$CH_3 - \overset{\overset{\displaystyle O}{\uparrow}}{S} - CH_2 - \underset{\underset{\displaystyle NH_2}{|}}{CH} - COOH$$

is present. Two vegetables of the cabbage group, cauliflower and broccoli, contain high concentrations of this sulfoxide. Values of 2,380 micrograms per gram of vegetable have been reported for cauliflower, compared with 304 for cabbage. Buds of broccoli averaged 2,406 micrograms per gram, the leaves somewhat less and the stems least of all. Even so, the stems contained 850 micrograms per gram (55). Cysteine sulfoxide lyase, once considered absent from these vegetables, has been demonstrated in some, its inactivity attributed to its high-optimum pH.

Glucosinolates

The pungent flavor of raw Cruciferae vegetables comes not from the decomposition of cysteine sulfoxides but from another group of sulfur-containing compounds, the glucosinolates. Each member of the Cruciferae contains at least one glucosinolate (24). These compounds are glucosides, represented by the following type formula:

$$R - C \Big\langle \begin{array}{l} S - C_6H_{11}O_5 \\ N - O - SO_3X \end{array}$$

The X represents different bases attached to the sulfate ion. Phenylethyl, *p*-hydroxy benzyl, and allyl are among the 15 or so R groups that have been identified in glucosinolates of *Cruciferae*. A thioglucosidase, trivial name myrosinase, in tissues disrupted by cutting, shredding, or chewing brings about hydrolysis of the glucosinolate, freeing glucose and an unstable aglycone. Products formed from the latter depend on the R group and the pH of the product. Sinigrin, allyl glucosinolate, found in black mustard seed, horseradish, and cabbage, acted on by the enzyme yields glucose, potassium acid sulfate, and allyl isothiocyanate (a mustard oil) as follows (3):

$$CH_2 = CH - CH_2 - C \Big\langle \begin{array}{l} S - C_6H_{11}O_5 \\ N - O - SO_3K \end{array} \quad + \quad H_2O \quad \xrightarrow[\text{Ascorbic acid}]{\text{Thioglucosidase (myrosinase)}}$$

Sinigrin   Water

$$C_6H_{12}O_6 \quad + \quad KHSO_4 \quad + \quad CH_2 = CH - CH_2 - N = C = S$$

Glucose   Potassium   Allyl isothiocyanate (mustard oil)
             acid sulfate

The enzyme requires ascorbic acid for its action (88). Broccoli, cabbage, and cauliflower are good sources of ascorbic acid (Table 28-1) and they retain a high proportion of this vitamin when they are stored (2). Allyl isothiocyanate and other mustard oils give an agreeable pungent aroma to grated or shredded raw cabbage and to other *Crucifers*. The pungency of the mustard oil of radish is due to an R group found only in glucosinolates of plants in the genus *Raphanus* (24).

One glucosinolate, glucobrassicin, found in broccoli, cabbage, and cauliflower is of particular interest. The R group in glucobrassicin is indolylmethyl:

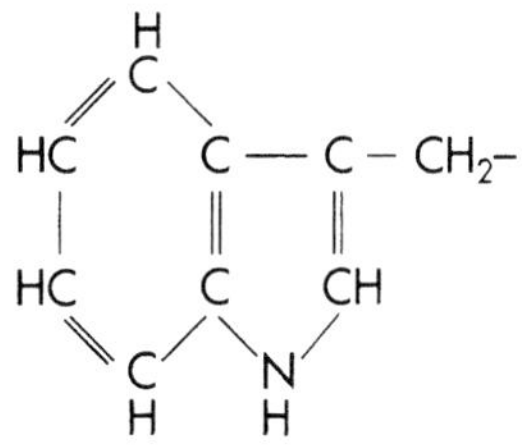

Indolylmethyl-radical

Action of the thioglucosidase on indolylmethyl glucosinolate results in the conversion of the radical to indole-3-carbinol, primarily:

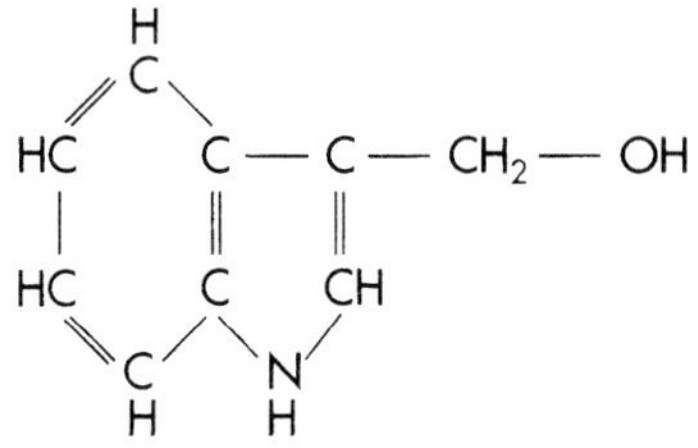

Indole-3-carbinol

This carbinol is effective in counteracting the effects of chemical carcinogens in experimental animals (15).

Cooking cabbage and other *Brassica* produces volatile and odorous compounds from sulfur-containing cysteine sulfoxides and glucosinolates. One-fourth of the total sulfur in the volatiles from cooked cabbage was reported to be in the form of H_2S, formed from the allyl isothiocyanate that resulted from the hydrolysis of sinigrin when the vegetable was cooked (70). Increasing the cooking time from five to seven minutes doubled the evolution of H_2S from cooked cabbage. Cauliflower yielded almost twice as much H_2S as cabbage, both cooked to the just-done stage. Dimethyl disulfide formed by hydrolysis of $(+)$-S-methyl-L-cysteine sulfoxide was identified in an early study as another important constituent in the aroma of cooked cabbage (20). In a later work little of the disulfide was found, but dimethyl sulfide constituted somewhat more than one-fourth of the total volatiles from cabbage that had been boiled for 10 minutes (52). Allyl isothiocyanate and allyl cyanide increased in the volatiles as the cooking time increased up to 20 minutes at which time breakdown of the sinigrin appeared to be complete. Two intensely unpleasant sulfur-containing compounds, one identified as dimethyl trisulfide, increased in the aroma of broccoli, Brussels sprouts, cabbage, and cauliflower as the cooking time was prolonged (54). Interaction of H_2S with an unstable intermediate in the decomposition of the sulfoxide was proposed as the source of the trisulfide.

Because of their higher content of cysteine sulfoxide, broccoli, Brussels sprouts, and cauliflower have the potential for becoming more malodorous than cabbage when overcooked. Cooking conditions for Brassica should minimize the production of volatile sulfur-containing compounds from the nonvolatile precursors. A short exposure of the vegetable to heat is recommended. The water should be boiling when the vegetable is put to cook; it should be returned to the boil as rapidly as possible. The vegetable should be cooked no longer than necessary to make it just tender. Enough water to almost cover the vegetable will dilute the acids from the vegetable and also permit it to be cooked uncovered. This allows the volatile acids to escape with the steam. Production of hydrogen sulfide and other sulfides is kept to a minimum when vegetables of the cabbage family are cooked in this way. An uncovered container also permits the escape of volatile sulfides that, if retained, would give the vegetable a disagreeable odor (27, 29).

Asparagus is another sulfur-containing vegetable of interest, not for its aroma when cooked, but because of the odorous compounds that appear in the urine of some individuals soon after they have eaten asparagus. Two S-methyl thioesters have been identified as the main contributors of the odor, but the precursor(s) in the asparagus that give rise to these compounds remain to be identified (87).

PIGMENTS IN VEGETABLES AND THE EFFECTS OF COOKING

The bright colors of vegetables contribute to the esthetic pleasure of eating. Too often these vivid hues are muted before the vegetables are served. Some knowledge of the structure and the basic reactions of plant pigments is essential for an understanding of the changes that take place in the color of vegetables and how these can be kept to a minimum. Flavonoid pigments which are found in vegetables as well as fruits are discussed in Chapter 27.

Chlorophyll

Green vegetables especially may undergo pronounced changes in color. The pigment involved is chlorophyll. A molecule of chlorophyll has four pyrrole groups, each a five-membered ring made of four carbon atoms and one of nitrogen (42). The four pyrrole groups are united to form a porphyrin ring as in myoglobin. Instead of the atom of iron in the molecule of myoglobin, chlorophyll contains magnesium. Phytol alcohol is attached by ester linkage to one of the pyrrole groups, methyl alcohol to a second. The phytyl residue with 20 carbon atoms in the chain is the part of the molecule which confers on chlorophyll its solubility in fat and fat solvents. Two forms of chlorophyll, chlorophyll *a*, which is an intense blue green, and chlorophyll *b*, which is a duller yellow green, are found in land plants. The two chlorophylls are present in an approximate ratio of three parts chlorophyll *a* to one part chlorophyll *b*. Chlorophyll *b* has a formyl group at the position marked with an asterisk instead of the methyl group in chlorophyll *a*, as shown on page 520.

Magnesium is rather easily displaced from the molecule of chlorophyll by organic acids. When hydrogens replace the magnesium, a pale greenish-gray compound known as pheophytin *a*, or an olive green pheophytin *b*, results.

Removal of the phytyl group from the molecule of chlorophyll is catalyzed by the enzyme chlorophyllase, found in some vegetables. Hydrolysis of the ester linkage yields a compound, known as a chlorophyllide, which is water soluble. A limited amount of chlorophyllide produced during storage of certain green vegetables prior to cooking possibly accounts for the light green tint of the cooking water from them. Under certain circumstances in the handling or processing of plant materials, both magnesium and the phytyl residue may be eliminated from the chlorophyll molecule. In this case the resulting compound, known as a pheophorbide, resembles pheophytin in color. This reaction takes place during brining of cucumber pickle stock (39).

Chlorophyll a^*

*From V. A. Greulach and J. E. Adams, *An Introduction to Modern Botany,* 2nd edition. Copyright
© by John Wiley & Sons, Inc. Used by permission of authors and publisher.
†Chlorophyll *b* has a —CHO group at the carbon marked instead of the —CH₃ group.

When a green vegetable first contacts boiling water, the green color becomes brighter. Greater translucency of plant tissue due to expulsion of intercellular air has been suggested as a possible cause (41). Exposure of a green vegetable to heat for a short time as in blanching or boiling for a few (five to seven) minutes at 100°C (212°F) induces epimerization (change in configuration) at carbon 10 and yields chlorophylls a' and b' (67). These epimers do not differ in color from chlorophylls a and b. Heating vegetable tissue also disrupts compartmentalization within the cells. Constituents, including organic acids, diffuse from the vacuoles throughout the cell and acids come in contact with chlorophyll. Cooking a green vegetable to the overdone stage results in displacement by acid of magnesium from the porphyrin ring, converting chlorophylls a' and b' to pheophytins a' and b'. Pheophytins, less colorful than chlorophylls, are unable to mask completely the yellow and orange pigments present in green plants. As a result, overcooked vegetables have a dull, olive-green color. Extended heating, especially at the temperature used to process canned vegetables, causes loss of $-COOCH_3$ at carbon 10, resulting in the formation of pyropheophytins a' and b' that are responsible for much of the color of canned green vegetables (67). If a canned vegetable is to keep, it must be processed so that it is effectively sterile. Microorganisms are degraded faster by heat than are the chlorophylls. A canned green vegetable processed at a high temperature for a short time (HTST) retains more of its chlorophyll and green color than does the same vegetable processed by the conventional lower temperature–longer time process (32). Changes in chlorophyll as affected by heating are summarized (67):

$$\text{Chlorophylls } a \text{ and } b \xrightarrow[-\text{Mg}]{+\text{H}^+} \text{Pheophytins } a' \text{ and } b' \xrightarrow[-\text{COOCH}_3]{\Delta} \text{Pyropheophytins } a' \text{ and } b'$$

Green vegetables that are lower in acid retain a higher percentage of chlorophyll and of their green color when they are cooked than do more acid vegetables. In one study frozen spinach and frozen peas, both with a pH of 6.7, retained two-thirds to three-fourths of their chlorophyll when the vegetables were cooked to optimum doneness, whereas green beans with a pH of 6.0 retained only one-fourth. As the pH of the cooking water for green beans was elevated from 6.2 to 7.0 by addition of buffer, the retention of chlorophyll increased (79).

Destruction of chlorophyll increases with cooking time. In the study referred to above, retention of chlorophyll in broccoli dropped from 82.5 percent when the cooking time was 5 minutes to 31.3 percent when the cooking time was 20 minutes. At the end of 5 minutes' cooking the retention of chlorophyll a was 78.7 percent, that of chlorophyll b 90.3 percent. After 20 minutes' cooking, retentions were 18.4 and 57.6 percent, respectively. Thus chlorophyll a is more readily converted to pheophytin than is chlorophyll b, to the greater detriment of color (79).

Because acids are present in plant tissue along with chlorophyll, the problem is how to minimize their effect during the cooking of vegetables. This may be accomplished by cooking the vegetable uncovered to eliminate volatile acids and by using enough water to cover the vegetable to dilute non-volatile acids (27, 28, 29). The major portion of the volatile acids is eliminated during the first few minutes the vegetable is in contact with the boiling water. Having the water boiling when the vegetable is put to cook and leaving the lid off at least for the first few minutes are recommended for better retention of color.

If a green vegetable is such that it will cook in a very short time, the color will be retained even when the vegetable is cooked in a small amount of water in a covered pan. In one study, broccoli cooked no longer than five minutes retained a good color regardless of the method used (26). The short time needed to cook panned cabbage accounts for its greenness. Shredded, panned green beans retain a good color for the same reason. Both broccoli and green beans cooked for the short time required in a microwave oven retain their color better than the same vegetables cooked in a small amount of water in a covered container; but those cooked by stir-frying retain even more color (22). Overcooking in a pressure saucepan, a matter of seconds, is detrimental to the color of the green vegetables. If the time required to cook a green vegetable is longer than five to seven minutes, enough chlorophyll will be converted to pheophytin to affect the color of the vegetable unless precautions are taken to minimize the effects of the acid. The better retention of color of frozen green vegetables during cooking is due to elimination of the major part of the plant acids as the vegetable was blanched prior to freezing.

Should a green vegetable be cooked in water that contains sodium bicarbonate, any soda not required to neutralize the acids in the cooking water will react with the chlorophyll. In this case the phytyl and methyl groups are displaced and bright-green, water-soluble chlorophyllin is formed. The sodium salt of chlorophyllin gives to cooked green vegetables an intense and artificial-appearing greenness. Vegetables cooked with soda tend to have a mushy texture, due to breakdown of hemicelluloses in the cell walls. Green vegetables cooked in just enough of a dilute solution (0.1 to 0.3%) of ammonium bicarbonate to prevent scorching keep their green color, and retention of ascorbic acid is unaffected by the bicarbonate. Calcium acetate added to the cooking water counteracts undue softening of the tissues (57).

Carotenoids

Carotenoids include the yellow, orange, and red-orange fat-soluble pigments (25). They are found in the chloroplasts of green leaves, where they are masked by the high concentration of chlorophyll and in such yellow vegetables as sweet potatoes, winter squash, and carrots. The red pigment in tomatoes is a carotenoid, lycopene. Carotenoid pigments are of two types, carotenes and xanthophylls. Carotenes, which include α- and β-carotene and lycopene, are hydrocarbons with 40 carbon atoms in the molecule. Xanthophylls contain, in addition to carbon and hydrogen, one or more atoms of oxygen.

Beta-carotene is the most common carotenoid. A molecule of β-carotene has a central chain of carbon atoms that unites the 6-membered ring structures at either end of the molecule, shown on page 523. The molecule is symmetrical, that is, the two halves are alike. In the human body a molecule of β-carotene can give rise to two molecules of colorless vitamin A. Alpha-carotene differs from β-carotene in that the position of the double bond in one of the rings is shifted to carbons 4′ and 5′. Alpha-carotene has only half the vitamin A value of β-carotene. In lycopene the rings at either end of the molecule are open and the molecule has two more double bonds than either α- or β-carotene, as also shown.

Lutein is one xanthophyll widely distributed in green leaves. It has the same structure as α-carotene except that an—OH group has replaced a hydrogen at carbon 3 and another —OH a hydrogen at carbon 3′. Another xanthophyll, cryptoxanthin, found in yellow corn, has the same structure as β-carotene except that one —OH group has replaced a hydrogen at carbon 3′. Zeaxanthin, more widely distributed than cryptoxanthin, is 3,3′-dihydroxy-β-carotene. A molecule of cryptoxanthin yields one molecule of vitamin A. Lutein and zeaxanthin have no vitamin A value.

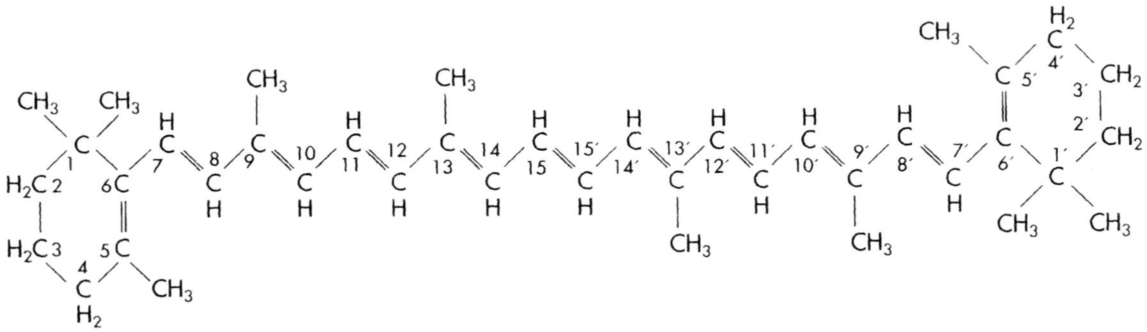

β-Carotene
(all-*trans*)

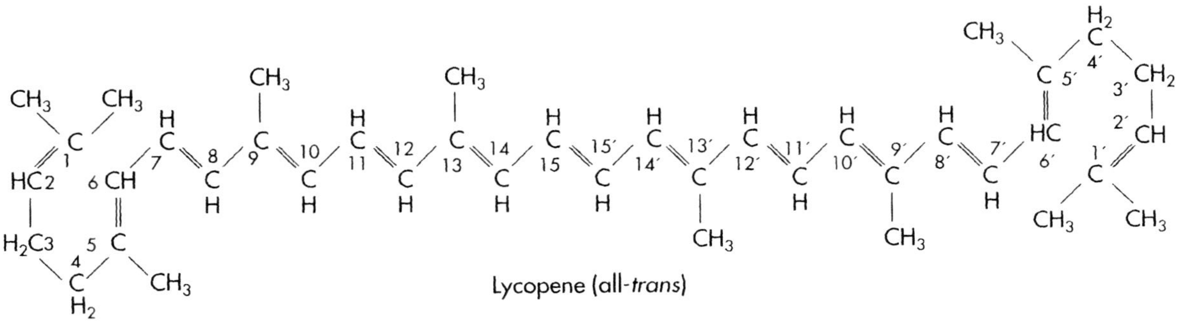

Lycopene (all-*trans*)

The red-orange color of β-carotene is due to the large number of conjugated double bonds (double bonds alternating with single bonds) in the molecule. Normally the central portion of the molecule is in the all-*trans* form as shown, which makes this part of the molecule linear. The double bonds are capable of resonance and are responsible for the hue of the carotenoid pigments. The more vivid hue of lycopene is due to the two additional double bonds in the molecule. Watermelon, pink grapefruit, and rose hips (the fruit of the rose), in addition to tomatoes, contain lycopene.

Isomerization of the molecule occurs when these unsaturated carotenoids are heated in the presence of acid. The all-*trans* form of the pigment changes over to a *cis* configuration. The bend occurs at a double bond, in which case the molecule is no longer linear. Such a *trans*→*cis* shift is discussed in Chapter 15, on fats. This change in shape reduces resonance in the molecule and so the intensity of the color. Beta-carotene in the *cis* form, for example, changes from the typical red-orange to a paler yellow-orange.

A change in the color of a vegetable that contains carotenoid pigments is not as noticeable as is that which often occurs in a green vegetable. Fat-soluble carotenoids are not lost to the cooking water, but appreciable amounts may dissolve in the table fat used to season a vegetable such as carrots. When slices of sweet potato or carrot have been in contact with boiling water for two or three minutes, the hue shifts slightly toward yellow. The β-carotene in the raw vegetable is localized in the chromoplasts and in carrots the highly concentrated pigment is deposited as crystals in a variety of shapes throughout the cytoplasm of the cells. These carotene bodies may be observed under the microscope in freehand sections of raw carrot. A brief exposure to boiling water causes the β-carotene to dissolve in the lipids which appear as droplets near the periphery of the cell. A change in physical state of the pigment thus accounts for the initial change in hue (63).

Longer heating, and especially overcooking, may result in a *trans*→*cis* shift and some loss in intensity of color (12). The longer the vegetable is cooked and the higher the temperature, the greater is the change in hue. Because of the quantity of carotene present, cooked carrots are still bright and attractive. In the case of rutabagas, cooking intensifies the color. This is attributed to the presence of *cis*-lycopene in the raw vegetable. During cooking some of the molecules isomerize to the more colorful *trans* form (33).

Anthocyanins

These water-soluble cell sap pigments can be leached from a vegetable by the cooking water. Cooking in a steamer or in a pressure saucepan or by panning, all of which limit the contact of the vegetable with water, are better methods than boiling in water to prevent loss of anthocyanins from vegetables due to solution. If the vegetable is boiled, a small amount of cooking water reduces solution of the pigments of this group. Red cabbage is one anthocyanin-containing vegetable which is cooked, especially in certain regions of the United States. The pigment in red cabbage is actually purple in the raw tissue. It is confined to the outer layers of cells of the cabbage leaf. Unless the cooking water is acidified, the pigment will change to a dull and unappetizing blue. It is to prevent this that slices of sour apple are sometimes included with red cabbage when it is cooked. Certain minerals react with anthocyanin pigments to give a blue-colored complex. Red cabbage shredded with a nonstainless-steel blade, such as a floating-blade peeler, turns blue very rapidly from the reaction between the iron of the peeler and the pigment of the cabbage. Addition of acid shifts the pigment to the flavylium ion and a red color. Anthocyanins are discussed more fully in Chapter 27.

Betalains

The betalains consist of two groups of pigments, the violet-red betacyanins and the yellow betaxanthins, so named for their supposed relationship to anthocyanins and anthoxanthins, respectively. Betalains contain nitrogen and are unrelated chemically to the flavonoid pigments. Betanin is one pigment of the betacyanin group and vulgaxanthin one of the betaxanthin group (49). Betanin is a glycoside which upon hydrolysis yields glucose and betanidin, the aglycone found in most betacyanins.

Betanidin, R = H
Betanin, R = glucose

Betanin is responsible for the purplish red color of beet roots. The pigment is water-soluble, so this vegetable should be cooked to minimize contact of water with the tissues. Beets cooked with the skin intact and with one to two inches of stem attached may be boiled in sufficient water to cover the vegetable without unacceptable loss of pigment and color. Pared and sliced or cubed beets should be cooked in a small amount of water. Cooking in a steamer or in a pressure saucepan or shredding and panning minimize leaching of betanin. Acid does not have a marked effect on the color of betacyanins (83).

The pigment of beets is not stable at the high temperature required to process the canned product. The ratio of betanin to isobetanin, its epimer, is 25:1 in raw beets and 2.5:1 in the sterilized vegetable. Thermal breakup of betanin, presumably at carbon 11, gives cyclodopa, the portion that contains the nitrogen, and betalamic acid, an aldehyde that includes the remainder. Once processed beets cool, some regeneration of betanin occurs (84).

The pigment from beets, in addition to that of red cabbage, has been considered as a possible natural food colorant (58).

Anthoxanthins

Normally, these water-soluble pigments are colorless in plant tissue and so go unnoticed in vegetables as well as in fruits. In alkaline medium they turn creamy white to yellow. Onions, cauliflower, turnips, and white cabbage all contain flavonols. If the last three vegetables are cooked for an extended period, hydrogen sulfide will be liberated from the sulfur-containing compounds in these vegetables. The flavonols are closely related chemically to anthocyanins except that the former are in a higher state of oxidation. Hydrogen sulfide is a reducing agent, and this compound presumably reduces the molecules of the flavonols present in the vegetable to anthocyanins. The pinkish tint in overcooked cabbage, cauliflower, and turnips is attributed to the conversion of a small amount of colorless and more highly oxidized pigment to a colored, less oxidized anthocyanin.

Discoloration of Potatoes

Enzymic Discoloration of the Raw Vegetable

The combination of a potato's constituents predisposes it to discoloration. The tuber contains a hydroxyphenolic substrate, mainly tyrosine, and phenolic oxidase enzymes (56). Sufficient copper is present for the enzyme to act and the pH of the tuber is favorable. These constituents are compartmentalized in the intact tuber. Disruption of the fine organization of the cells, as when tissue is bruised, brings these constituents into contact, and the limited amount of oxygen permits slow discoloration. When the cut surface of a tuber is exposed to the oxygen of the air, discoloration is rapid and extensive. It appears first as a pinkish hue, which changes to brown and finally to a dark gray.

Covering the cut surface of a potato with water or with a dilute sodium chloride solution excludes oxygen and prevents action of the enzymes temporarily. Any slight discoloration that develops disappears when the potato is cooked. However, more than a temporary blockage of enzyme action is needed for potatoes prepared in bulk for chips and fries. A combination of substances is required to replace treatment with bisulfite, an effective antibrowning agent, use of which was banned in 1990 because of its possible adverse effects on health. Ascorbic acid is included in the mix. It functions by reducing the oxidized phenolic substrate, thus blocking the first step in its conversion to products that discolor the potato. Citric acid included in the treatment limits activity of the enzymes by chelating trace metals, especially copper, and by lowering the pH so that it is unfavorable for activity of the enzymes. Inclusion of potassium sorbate in the treatment controls activity of yeast and molds on the potatoes. Tubers thus treated can be held under refrigeration for up to two weeks without discoloration (46).

Stem-End Blackening of Cooked Potato

This defect observed in some potatoes is another example of discoloration due to phenolic compounds. Diffuse gray-blue-black areas appear, usually in the stem rather than the bud end of the potato, and in the cooked rather than the raw (85). This discoloration that appears after the potato cools is believed to be due to a complex between the iron from the potato and *ortho*-dihydroxy phenols, probably chlorogenic acid. The colorless substrate in the potato unites with ferric iron to form the colored complex (6). Enzymes in the raw potato maintain reducing conditions that keep the iron in the ferrous state. These are inactivated during cooking.

Some lots of potatoes are more susceptible to stem-end blackening than are others. Soil and climate appear to influence the susceptibility of potatoes to this type of discoloration. An appreciable amount of citrate in the potato ties the iron and so helps prevent stem-end blackening (6). If the pH of the cooking water is 5 or less, stem-end blackening can be minimized in potatoes that are susceptible. Adding 1.5 grams (½ teaspoon) of cream of tartar per half liter (pint) of cooking water when the potatoes are half-done or 1.5 grams

(½ teaspoon) per half kilogram (pound) to mashed potatoes are procedures recommended for potatoes that are susceptible to stem end blackening (13).

NUTRITIVE VALUE AND PALATABILITY OF COOKED VEGETABLES

Vegetables lose nutrients when they are cooked, mainly by solution to the cooking water, but destruction of certain nutrients may occur, also. Sugars, water-soluble vitamins, and minerals may dissolve in the cooking water that is often discarded. Minerals are not destroyed during cooking, nor are starches and sugars, unless the vegetable is scorched, but both thiamin and ascorbic acid may be altered when a vegetable is cooked. Heat changes thiamin to a form that can no longer function as a vitamin in the body. Losses of 5 to 18 percent have been reported. Ascorbic acid not only dissolves in the cooking water but it is also susceptible to oxidation during cooking. The molecule so altered can no longer participate in the reactions in the body where it is needed. Oxidizing enzymes in plant tissue catalyze the oxidation of ascorbic acid when oxygen is present. The greatest destruction occurs during the first two or three minutes of the cooking period (30) while the cooking water is returned to boiling. To minimize destruction, water should be boiling when a vegetable is put in to cook, not only to inactivate the ascorbic acid oxidase but also to expel oxygen from the tissues and to eliminate dissolved oxygen from the cooking water. Water should be returned to the boil promptly. Once the vegetable is heated, little oxidation occurs, but loss due to solution continues as long as the vegetable is in contact with the cooking water.

Contact of the vegetable with the cooking water should be kept to a minimum to reduce loss of nutrients due to solution (29, 78). Using a small amount of cooking water when a vegetable is boiled is recommended for this reason. Alternately, a vegetable may be boiled in the skin where feasible. The vegetable should be cooked only until it is barely done. Steaming either in a steamer or in a pressure saucepan reduces contact of the vegetable with water. Overcooking in the latter is measured in seconds rather than minutes.

A number of studies have been concerned with the effects of the method of cooking on the retention of nutrients in vegetables. Because it is doubly vulnerable, retention of ascorbic acid has been used frequently as an index to the effects of the method of cooking on other nutrients. In one study, no marked difference was found in the retention of ascorbic acid in vegetables cooked in a steamer, in a pressure saucepan, or in a small volume of water, but retention was much less when cooking was done in enough water to cover the vegetable. Broccoli retains only 33 percent of its ascorbic acid when cooked in excess water, whereas retentions range from 67 to 82 percent for the other three methods (28). Retention of thiamin and of riboflavin in cabbage and in peas cooked in water to cover is less than when these vegetables are cooked in a small amount of water in a covered pan, in a steamer, or in a pressure saucepan (68). Whether frozen peas are cooked by microwaves or by conventional boiling makes little difference in retention of ascorbic acid, of thiamin, or of riboflavin (77). Retention of folacin is essentially the same whether frozen vegetables are cooked in a microwave oven or on a conventional range. Retentions vary from 78 to 105 percent for frozen green beans, peas, and spinach, but only 51 to 59 percent for frozen broccoli (43). Retention of ascorbic acid is greater when broccoli, cabbage, and cauliflower are cooked by microwaves rather than in a pressure saucepan (27). Another study, however, found little difference in retention when beans, broccoli, cabbage, cauliflower, peas, and spinach were cooked by these two methods (45).

The method of cooking that gives the greatest retention of nutrients may not yield the most acceptable cooked vegetable from the standpoint of appearance or flavor. This is true especially of sulfur-containing and of green vegetables that need more than five to seven minutes of cooking to make them tender. A small amount of water in a covered utensil favors the retention of nutrients but confines acids that favor decomposition of chlorophyll and of sulfur-containing compounds. Broccoli, cabbage, and cauliflower, in one study, were mildest when boiled in water to cover in an uncovered container, strongest cooked in a pressure saucepan, and intermediate when cooked by microwaves (27). The color of broccoli and cabbage was greenest when these vegetables were cooked uncovered in water to cover. But in another study (18) the flavor of broccoli was judged equally good whether the vegetable was cooked by microwave or in a small amount of water, but the color was greener when the vegetable was cooked by microwaves. In yet another study, broccoli cooked by stir-frying was greenest and that cooked by microwaves greener than that cooked in a small amount of water in a covered pan (22). Peas cooked in a pressure saucepan were more palatable than those boiled in a covered or an uncovered pan or those cooked in a steamer (78). Frozen peas cooked by microwaves had somewhat better color than did those cooked in a small amount of water in a covered pan, but the skins were not so tender, and if overcooked for only 30 seconds, the peas were hard and shriveled (77). Thus it is obvious that there is no one method that is best for all vegetables for both palatability and retention of nutrients. A sensible approach is to emphasize conservation of nutrients but not to the point that the vegetable is so unpalatable that it will not be eaten.

Basic rules for cooking vegetables are summarized:

1. Start the vegetable to cook in boiling, salted water.
2. Return water to a boil as fast as possible.
3. Cook in barely enough water to prevent scorching and with a lid on the pan (unless color or flavor will be damaged).
4. Cook the vegetable only until barely done.
5. Serve promptly.

REFERENCES

1. AHEA 1993. *Handbook of Food Preparation.* Yields of vegetables per market unit, p. 180; timetable for cooking, p. 140; pH of foods, p. 48.
2. Albrecht, J. A., H. W. Schafer, and E. A. Zottola. 1990. "Relationship of total sulfur to initial and retained ascorbic acid in selected cruciferous and noncruciferous vegetables." *Journal of Food Science* 55:181–83. High retention in most crucifers.
3. Bailey, S. D., M. L. Bazenet, J. L. Driscoll, and A. I. McCarthy. 1961. "The volatile sulfur components of cabbage." *Journal of Food Science* 26:163–70. Constituents in the odor of fresh cabbage.
4. Barchello, V., R. Y. Yada, R. H. Coffin, and D. W. Stanley. 1990. "Low temperature sweetening in susceptible and resistant potatoes: Starch structure and composition." *Journal of Food Science* 55:1054–59. Starch granules may be involved in chill-resistance.
5. Barth, M. M., A. K. Perry, S. J. Schmidt, and B. P. Klein. 1992. "Misting affects market quality and enzyme activity of broccoli

during retail storage." *Journal of Food Science* 57:954–57. Retention of color and chlorophyll enhanced.

6. Bate-Smith, E. C., J. C. Hughes, and T. Swain. 1958. "After-cooking darkening of potatoes." *Chemistry & Industry.* Pp. 627–28. Interaction of factors that influence darkening.

7. Bernhard, R. A. 1964. "Sweet smell of success." *Food Technology* 18:999. Odorous substances in onions.

8. Bettelheim, F. A., and C. Sterling. 1955. "Factors associated with potato texture." I. "Specific gravity and starch content." *Food Research* 20:71–80. Eight varieties compared.

9. Bettelheim, F. A., and C. Sterling. 1955. "Factors associated with potato texture." II. "Pectic substances." *Food Research* 20:118–29. Neither pectic fractions nor starch alone can account for differences in texture.

10. Block, E. 1985. "The chemistry of garlic and onions." *Scientific American* 252:114–19. Details of chemical reactions.

11. Boelens, M., P. J. de Valois, H. J. Wobben, and A. van der Gen. 1971. "Volatile flavor compounds from onion." *Journal of Agricultural and Food Chemistry* 19:984–91. Freshly cut, boiled, and fried onions analyzed.

12. Borchgrevink, N. C., and H. Charley. 1966. "Color of cooked carrots related to carotene content." *Journal of the American Dietetics Association* 49:116–21. Comparison of carrots cooked in a saucepan and in a pressure saucepan and overcooked in a pressure saucepan.

13. Bowman, F., and F. Hanning. 1949. "Procedures that reduce darkening of cooked potatoes." *Journal of Agricultural Research* 78:627–36. Effect of acid on the texture, flavor, and color of potatoes that tend to darken after cooking.

14. Bowman, F., E. Page, E. E. Remmenga, and D. Trump. 1971. "Microwaves *vs.* conventional cooking of vegetables at high altitude." *Journal of the American Dietetics Association* 68:427–33. Thirteen fresh and nine frozen vegetables in saucepan, pressure saucepan, and by microwaves.

15. Bradfield, C. A., and L. F. Bjeldanes. 1987. "High performance liquid chromatographic analysis of anticarcinogenic indoles in *Brassica oleracea.*" *Journal of Agricultural and Food Chemistry* 35:46–49. Substrate and autolytic products.

16. Brodnitz, M. H., and J. V. Pascale. 1971. "Thiopropanal S-oxide: A lachrymatory factor in onions." *Journal of Agricultural and Food Chemistry* 19:269–72. Identification of the lachrymator.

17. Carson, J. F., and F. J. Wong. 1961. "The volatile flavor component of onions." *Journal of Agricultural and Food Chemistry* 9:140–43. An attempt to identify the constituents in the aroma of onions.

18. Chapman, V. J., J. O. Putz, G. L. Gilpin, J. R. Sweeney, and J. N. Eisen. 1960. "Electronic cooking of fresh and frozen broccoli." *Journal of Home Economics* 52:161–65. Effects on texture, color, and ascorbic acid content; cooking times varied.

19. Cunningham, H. H., and M. V. Zaehringer. 1972. "Quality of baked potatoes as influenced by baking and holding methods." *American Potato Journal* 49:271–79. Effects of wrapping in foil.

20. Dateo, G. P., R. C. Clapp, D. A. M. MacKay, E. J. Hewitt, and T. Hasselstrom. 1957. "Identification of the volatile sulfur components of cooked cabbage and the nature of the precursors in fresh vegetable." *Food Research* 22:440–47. Source of cooked cabbage aroma.

21. Davis, E. A., J. Gordon, and T. E. Hutchinson. 1976. "Scanning electron microscope studies on carrots: Effects of cooking on the phloem and xylem." *Home Economics Research Journal* 4:214–24. Microstructure of carrot tissue steamed, boiled, and pressure cooked.

22. Eheart, M. S., and C. Gott. 1965. "Chlorophyll, ascorbic acid, and pH changes in green vegetables cooked by stir-fry, microwave, and conventional methods and a comparison of chlorophyll methods." *Food Technology* 19:867–70. Green beans and broccoli were the vegetables tested.

23. Ezell, B. D., and M. S. Wilcox. 1962. "Loss of carotene in fresh vegetable as related to wilting and temperature." *Journal of Agricultural and Food Chemistry* 10:124–26. Wilted and crisp vegetables compared at

temperatures of 0°, 10°, and 21°C (32°, 50°, and 70°F).

24. Fenwick, R. G., R. K. Heaney, and W. J. Mullin. 1983. "Glucosinolates and their breakdown products in food and food plants." *CRC Critical Reviews in Food Science* 18:123–201. A review.

25. Frank, S. 1956. "Carotenoids." *Scientific American* 194(1):80–84. Relation of carotene to chlorophyll and possible role in photosynthesis.

26. Gilpin, G. L., J. P. Sweeney, V. J. Chapman, and J. N. Eisen. 1959. "Effects of cooking methods on broccoli." II. "Palatability." *Journal of the American Dietetics Association* 35:359–63. Color, texture, flavor, and chlorophyll content.

27. Gordon, J., and I. Noble. 1959. "Comparison of electronic *vs.* conventional cooking of vegetables." *Journal of the American Dietetics Association* 35:241–44. Color, flavor, and ascorbic acid content of vegetables of the cabbage family cooked by conventional boiling, in a pressure saucepan and in an electronic range.

28. Gordon, J., and I. Noble. 1959. "Effect of cooking method on vegetables: Ascorbic acid retention and color difference." *Journal of the American Dietetics Association* 35:578–81. Eleven vegetables cooked by four different methods.

29. Gordon, J., and I. Noble. 1964. " 'Waterless' vs. boiling water cooking of vegetables." *Journal of the American Dietetics Association* 44:378–82. Flavor, color, and ascorbic acid content of five vegetables of the cabbage family.

30. Gould, S., D. K. Tressler, and C. G. King. 1936. "Vitamin C content of vegetables." V. "Cabbage." *Food Research* 1:427–34. Concentration in the raw vegetable and changes during cooking.

31. Greenwood, M. L., M. H. McKendrick, and A. Hawkins. 1952. "The relationship of the specific gravity of six varieties of potatoes to their mealiness as assessed by sensory methods." *American Potato Journal* 29:192–96. Six varieties varying in mealiness compared.

32. Gupta, S. M., H. M. El-Bisi, and F. J. Frances. 1964. "Kinetics of thermal degradation of chlorophyll in spinach purées." *Journal of Food Science* 29:379–82. Less damage to chlorophyll with HTST processing.

33. Hanson, S. W. 1954. "The effect of heat treatment on some plant carotenoids." In *Color in Foods*. K. T. Farrell, J. R. Wagner, M. S. Peterson, and G. MacKinney, eds. Quartermaster Food and Container Institute. Surveys Progr. Military Subsistence Problems, Series I, No. 5. Pp. 136–59.

34. Hughes, J. C., A. Grant, and R. M. Faulks. 1975. "Texture of cooked potatoes: The effect of ions and pH on the compressive strength of cooked potatoes." *Journal of the Science of Food and Agriculture* 26:739–48. Factors contributing to loss in cellular adhesion.

35. Isherwood, F. A. 1955. "Texture in fruits and vegetables." *Food Manufacturing* 30:206–16. Effects of starch, of enzymes, and of cell wall constituents on texture.

36. Jadhav, S. J., D. K. Salunke, R. E. Wyse, and R. R. Dalvi. 1973. "Solanum alkaloids: Biosynthesis and inhibition by chemicals." *Journal of Food Science* 38:453–55. Formulas for the alkaloids and effect of ultraviolet light on their synthesis.

37. Johnson, A. E., H. E. Nursten, and A. A. Williams. 1971. "Vegetable volatiles: A survey of components identified." *Chemistry & Industry*. Part 1. 556–65. Part 2. 1212–24. Data for 20 vegetables.

38. Johnson, L. 1991. "Corn: Production, processing and utilization." In *Handbook of Cereal Science and Technology*. K. J. Lorenz and K. Kulp, eds. New York: Marcel Dekker, Inc. Pp. 50–131. Sweet corn included.

39. Jones, I. D., R. C. White, and E. Gibbs. 1963. "Influence of blanching or brining treatments on the formation of chlorophyllides, pheophytins, and pheophorbides in green plant tissue." *Journal of Food Science* 28:437–39. Changes in chlorophyll in snap beans, okra, turnip greens, and pickling cucumbers.

40. Kader, A. A. 1986. "Biochemical and physiological basis for effects of controlled and modified atmospheres on fruits and vegetables." *Food Technology* 40(5):99–104. How and when such treatments are effective.

41. Kaldy, M. S. 1972. "Protein yield of various food crops as related to protein value."

Economic Botany 26:142–44. Potatoes, corn, and legumes compared.

42. Kamen, M. D. 1958. "A universal molecule of living matter." *Scientific American* 199(2):77–78, 80, 82. Relation of chlorophyll, hemoglobin, and cytochromes.

43. Klein, B. P., H. C. Lee, P. A. Reynolds, and N. C. Wangles. 1979. "Folacin content of microwave and conventionally cooked frozen vegetables." *Journal of Food Science* 44:286–88. Broccoli, green beans, peas, and spinach studied.

44. Kozukue, N. B., and K. Agata. 1972. "Physiological and chemical studies of chilling injury in pepper fruit." *Journal of Food Science* 37:708–11. Metabolic changes responsible for the symptoms.

45. Kylen, A. M., V. R. Charles, B. H. McGroth, J. M. Schleter, L. C. West, and F. O. Van Duyne. 1961. "Microwave cooking of vegetables." *Journal of the American Dietetics Association* 39:321–26. Ascorbic acid and palatability of seven fresh and three frozen vegetables.

46. Langdon, T. T. 1987. "Prevention of browning in fresh potatoes without the use of sulfiting agent." *Food Technology* 41(5): 64, 66–67. Components of the substitute and their functions.

47. Lipton, W. J., and C. M. Harris. 1974. "Controlled atmosphere effects on the market quality of stored broccoli (*Brassica oleraceae* L. Italica group)." *Journal of the American Society of Horticultural Science* 99:200–5. Effects of temperature and levels of O_2 and CO_2 on yellowing of broccoli.

48. Loconti, J. D., and Z. I. Kertesz. 1941. "Identification of calcium pectate as the tissue firming compound formed by treatment of tomatoes with calcium chloride." *Food Research* 6:490–508. Effectiveness of calcium chloride treatment of canned tomatoes.

49. Mabry, T. J., and A. S. Dreiding. 1968. "The betalains." In *Recent Advances in Phytochemistry.* T. J. Mabry, R. E. Alston, and V. C. Runeckles, eds. Pp. 145–60. A review.

50. McComber, D. R., E. M. Osman, and R. A. Lohnes. 1988. "Factors related to mealiness of potatoes." *Journal of Food Science* 53:1423–26. Specific gravity of four cultivars failed to predict mealiness.

51. McFeeters, R. F., M. M. Senter, and H. P. Fleming. 1989. "Softening effects of monovalent cations in acidified cucumber mesocarp tissue." *Journal of Food Science* 54:366–70. Adequacy of egg box model to account for effects of ions on texture questioned.

52. MacLeod, A. J., and G. M. MacLeod. 1970. "Effects of variations in cooking methods on the flavor volatiles of cabbage." *Journal of Food Science* 35:744–50. Conventional boiling and microwave-cooking with and without added water.

53. Maga, J. A., and J. A. Twomey. 1977. "Sensory comparison of four potato varieties baked conventionally and by microwaves." *Journal of Food Science* 42:541–42. Appearance and flavor compared.

54. Maruyama, F. T. 1970. "Identification of trimethyl sulfide as a major aroma component of cooked brassicaceous vegetables." *Journal of Food Science* 35:540–43. Broccoli, Brussels sprouts, cabbage, and cauliflower studied.

55. Morris, C. J., and J. F. Thompson. 1956. "The identification of (+)-S-methyl-L-cysteine sulfoxide in plants." *Journal of the American Chemical Society* 78:1605–8. Concentration in cabbage and other crucifers.

56. Muneta, P. 1977. "Enzymatic blackening of potatoes: Influence of pH on dopachrome oxidation." *American Potato Journal* 54:387–93. Conversion of tyrosine to melanin reviewed.

57. Odland, D., and M. S. Eheart. 1974. "Ascorbic acid retention and organoleptic quality of green vegetables cooked by several techniques using ammonium carbonate." *Home Economics Research Journal* 2:241–50. Color and texture of broccoli, Brussels sprouts, cabbage, kale, and green beans.

58. Pasch, J. H., and J. H. von Elbe. 1978. "Sensory evaluation of betanine and concentrated beet juice." *Journal of Food Science* 43:1624–25. Possible replacement for Red No. 2 and No. 4 food dyes.

59. Patil, B. C., D. K. Salunke, and B. Singh. 1971. "Metabolism of solanine and chlorophyll in potato tubers as affected by light and specific chemicals." *Journal of Food*

Science 36:474–76. Conditions for accumulation of pigment and alkaloids.

60. Pimentel, D. W., J. K. Dritschilo, J. Krummel, and J. Kutzman. 1975. "Energy and land constraints in food protein production." *Science* 190:754–61. Options for use of resources to meet the world's food needs.

61. Powers, J. R., and S. R. Drake. 1980. "Effect of cut and field-holding conditions on activity of phenylalanine ammonia-lyase and texture in fresh asparagus spears." *Journal of Food Science* 45:509–10, 513. Effects of cutting and exposure to light.

62. Purcell, A. E., and W. M. Walter, Jr. 1988. "Comparison of carbohydrate components in sweet potatoes baked by convection heating and by microwave heating." *Journal of Agricultural and Food Chemistry* 36:360–62. Action of α-amylase favored by slower heating.

63. Purcell, A. E., W. M. Walter, and W. T. Thompkins. 1969. "Relationship of vegetable color to physical state of the carotenes." *Journal of Agricultural and Food Chemistry* 17:41–42. Cause of the change in hue of carrots and sweet potatoes early in the cooking period.

64. Reeve, R. M. 1954. "Histological survey of conditions influencing texture in potatoes." I. "Effects of heat treatment on structure." *Food Research* 19:323–32. Potatoes from a mealy and from a non-mealy variety compared.

65. Reeve, R. M. 1967. "Suggested improvements for microscopic measurement of cells and starch granules in fresh potatoes." *American Potato Journal* 44:41–50. Distribution of starch granules of different sizes.

66. Schrumpf, E., and H. Charley. 1975. "Texture of broccoli and carrots cooked by microwave energy." *Journal of Food Science* 40:1025–29. An attempt to account for the effects on texture.

67. Schwartz, S. J., and T. V. Lorenzo. 1990. "Chlorophylls in foods." *CRC Critical Reviews in Food Science and Nutrition* 29:1–17. Chlorophyll derivatives in processed foods.

68. Schwimmer, S. 1968. "Enzymic conversion of *trans*-(+)-S-1-propenyl-L-cysteine sulf-

oxide to the bitter and odor-bearing components of onion." *Phytochemistry* 7:401–4. Flavor and tear-eliciting components.

69. Schwimmer, S. 1969. "Characterization of the S-propenyl-L-cysteine sulfoxide as the principal endogenous substrate of L-cysteine sulfoxide lyase of onion." *Archives of Biochemistry and Biophysics* 130:312–20. An important source of the odor of cooked onions.

70. Simpson, J. I., and E. G. Halliday. 1928. "The behavior of sulphur compounds in cooking vegetables." *Journal of Home Economics* 20:121–26. Effects of cooking time on the evolution of H_2S from cabbage and cauliflower.

71. Simpson, J. I., and E. G. Halliday. 1941. "Chemical and histological studies of the disintegration of cell-membrane materials in vegetables during cooking." *Food Research* 6:189–206. Effects of steaming on the pectic substances in carrots and parsnips; a chemical and microscopic study.

72. Smith, J. L., D. W. Stanley, and K. W. Baker. 1987. "Nonenzymatic lignification of asparagus." *Journal of Texture Studies* 18:339–58. Lignification in blanched as well as unblanched spears.

73. *Statistical Abstracts of the United States, 116 edition.* 1996. "Per capita utilization of selected commercially produced fresh fruits and vegetables: 1970 to 1993." Washington D.C.: Bureau of the Census. P. 148.

74. Sterling, C. 1955. "Effect of moisture and high temperature on cell walls in plant tissues." *Food Research* 20:474–79. Effect of cooking on plant tissue.

75. Sterling, C. 1963. "Texture and cell-wall polysaccharides in foods." In *Recent Advances in Food Science—3. Biochemistry and Biophysics in Food Research.* J. M. Leitch and D. N. Rhodes, eds. London: Butterworth. 259–76. A review.

76. Sterling, C. 1968. "Effects of solute and pH on the structure and firmness of cooked carrots." *Journal of Food Technology* 3:367–71. Effects of pH 3 to 8 and of mono-, di-, and polyvalent ions compared.

77. Stevens, H. B., and F. Fenton. 1951. "Dielectric vs. stewpan cookery: Comparison

of palatability and vitamin retention in frozen peas." *Journal of the American Dietetics Association* 27:32–35. Palatability and retention of nutrients.

78. Sutherland, C. K., E. G. Halliday, and W. F. Hinman. 1947. "Vitamin retention and acceptability of fresh vegetables cooked by four household methods and by an institutional method." *Food Research* 12:496–509. Ascorbic acid, thiamin, and riboflavin in cabbage, spinach, and peas cooked in water to cover, in a minimum of water, in a steamer, and in a pressure saucepan.

79. Sweeney, J. P., and M. E. Martin. 1961. "Stability of chlorophyll in vegetables as affected by pH." *Food Technology* 15:263–66. Six vegetables varying in pH value compared; effects of cooking time on chlorophylls *a* and *b*.

80. Van Buren, J. P. 1984. "Effects of salts added after cooking on the texture of canned snap beans." *Journal of Food Science* 49:910–12. An attempt to learn possible mechanisms of softening of tissue.

81. Van Buren, J. P. 1979. "The chemistry of texture in fruits and vegetables." *Journal of Texture Studies* 10:1–23. Structural components and effects of heat processing on texture.

82. Van Buren, J. P. 1983. "Two effects of sodium chloride softening of the texture of canned snap beans." *Journal of Food Science* 48:1362–63. Softening due to displacement of calcium or to degradation of pectin.

83. Von Elbe, J. H., I. Maing, and C. H. Amundson. 1974. "Color stability of betanin." *Journal of Food Science* 39:334–37. Effects of pH, heat, oxygen, and light.

84. Von Elbe, J. H., S. J. Schwartz, and B. E. Hildenbrand. 1981. "Loss and regeneration of betacyanin pigments during processing of red beets." *Journal of Food Science* 46:1713–15. Lability of the pigment to heat.

85. Wager, H. G. 1955. "Why cooked potatoes blacken." *Food Manufacturing* 30:499–501. Review article on the nature of and possible contributing factors to stem-end blackening in cooked potatoes.

86. Walter, W. M., Jr., A. E. Purcell, and A. M. Nelson. 1975. "Effects of amolytic enzymes on 'moistness' and carbohydrate changes in baked sweet potato cultivars." *Journal of Food Science* 40:793–96. Cause of moist and dry textured sweet potatoes.

87. White, R. R. 1975. "Occurrence of S-methyl thioesters in urines of humans after they have eaten asparagus." *Science* 189:810–11. Identification of the odorous compounds.

88. Wilkinson, A. F., M. J. C. Rhodes, and G. R. Fenwick. 1984. "Myrosenase activity of *Cruciferae* vegetables." *Journal of the Science of Food and Agriculture* 35:543–52. Products formed; role of ascorbic acid.

89. Yamanishi, T., and K. Oriaka. 1955. "Chemical studies on the change in flavor and taste of onions by boiling." *Journal of Home Economics* (Japan). 6:45. Cited in *Journal of Food Science* 33:298 (1968). Possible cause of the increase in sweetness when onions are cooked.

90. Zhu, S., J. R. Mount, and J. L. Collins. 1992. "Sugar and soluble solids in refrigerated sweet corn (*Zea mays* L.)." *Journal of Food Science* 57:454–57. One cultivar each of three genotypes analyzed.

Legumes

29

Legumes (beans, peas, and lentils) are the dried seeds from plants that belong to the Leguminosae family, hence the name given to foods of this group (10). Legumes supply 20 percent of the dietary protein worldwide (33). Soybeans, one kind of legume, yield a high return of protein, based on the arable land and the fossil energy used to produce them. Although legumes are not used as extensively here as in many parts of the world, a number of varieties of common beans (*Phaseolus vulgaris*) are used in this country. In 1993, the per-capita consumption of beans in the U.S. averaged 6.5 pounds compared to the world average of approximately 9 pounds (27). Safflower, sesame, and sunflower seeds, grown mainly for their oils, yield meals high in protein, with lysine as a limiting amino acid (4).

VARIETIES OF LEGUMES USED FOR FOOD

There are several varieties of legumes used for food for which grade standards have been established (45), including the following beans: small white (called "navy" in the Great Lakes region), medium white (Great Lakes region), light and dark red, and white kidney, marrow, yelloweye, great northern, butternut, pinto, small and large white (Pacific coast), western red kidney, pink (California small pink), small red (red Mexican, California red, Idaho red), bayo, cranberry, and blackeye. The last, referred to as cowpeas, actually belong to the bean family but of the genus *Vigna*. The others belong to the *Phaseolus* genus. Included in the standards are those for limas and baby limas (*Phaseolus lunatus*). Two varieties of peas (*Pisum sativum*) are commonly used. The smooth-coated pea, when mature, yields the split pea of commerce. The wrinkled or sweet garden pea is harvested when immature and is considered a green vegetable in menu planning. Other legumes include chick peas (*Cicer arientinum*), also known as garbanzos, lentils (*Lens culinaris*), peanuts (*Arachis hypogaea*), and soybeans (*Glycine max*). Principal types of dry beans are shown in Figure 29-1.

COMPOSITION AND NUTRITIVE VALUE

Beans are valued for their contributions to a healthful diet. They are low in fat, cholesterol, and sodium, and rich in complex carbohydrates and fiber. The composition of representative legumes is given in Table 29-1. Included for comparative purposes are rolled oats, rice, nuts, and round steak. Both raw and cooked values are given for legumes and cereal. The yield by weight of the cooked legumes compared to the raw ranges from 2.1 to 3.2. When cooked, the 100 grams of dried legumes will measure approximately 1¼ cups, and the cereals will yield somewhat less than 3 cups. The approximate measures for 100 grams of nuts are 1 cup for English walnuts (halves), just under 1 cup for pecan halves, a generous ¾ cup for black walnuts (broken kernels), and a skimpy ¾ cup for whole kernel almonds.

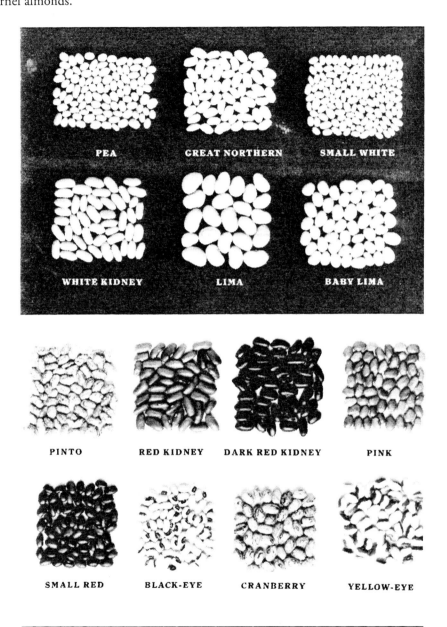

Figure 29-1. Principal types of dry beans: (*top*) white, (*bottom*) colored. (Courtesy of the United States Department of Agriculture.)

TABLE 29-1
Composition of Legumes and Representative Cereals, Nuts, and Lean Meat (100-gram edible portion)

Food	Water (%)	Calories[a]	Protein (g)	Lipid (g)	Carbohydrates (g)	Calcium (mg)	Phosphorus (mg)	Iron (mg)	Vitamin A Value (I.U.)	Vitamin A Value (R.E.)	Thiamin (mg)	Riboflavin (mg)	Niacin (mg)	Ascorbic Acid (mg)	Crude Fiber (g)	Total Dietary Fiber (g)
Legume																
Baked beans, canned, plain	72.7	93	4.8	0.5	20.5	50	104	0.3	17	17	0.15	0.06	0.43	—[c]	1.1	7.7
Beans, common white (great northern)																
Raw	10.7	339	21.9	1.1	62.4	175	447	5.5	3	0	0.65	0.24	2.0	5.3	6.7	40.0
Cooked	69	118	8.3	0.5	21.1	68	165	2.1	1	0	0.16	0.06	0.68	1.3	3.0	5.4
Beans, kidney																
Raw	11.8	333	23.6	0.8	60.0	143	407	8.2	8	1	0.53	0.22	2.1	4.5	6.2	—[c]
Cooked	66.9	127	8.7	0.5	22.8	28	142	2.9	0	0	0.16	0.06	0.58	1.2	2.8	—[c]
Beans, pinto																
Raw	11.0	340	20.9	1.1	63.4	121	418	5.9	5	1	0.56	0.24	1.4	7.3	6.0	—[c]
Cooked	64.3	137	8.2	0.5	25.7	48	160	2.6	2	0	0.19	0.09	0.40	2.1	3.0	—[c]
Beans, large lima																
Raw	10.2	338	21.5	0.7	3.4	81	385	7.5	0	0	0.51	0.20	1.5	0	6.3	19.0
Cooked	69.8	115	7.8	0.4	20.9	17	111	2.4	0	0	0.16	0.06	0.4	0	3.1	7.2
Cowpeas, black-eyed																
Raw	12.0	336	23.5	1.3	60.0	110	424	8.3	50	5	0.85	0.23	2.1	1.5	4.6	27.0
Cooked	70.0	116	7.7	0.5	20.8	24	156	2.5	15	2	0.20	0.06	0.50	0.4	2.3	9.6
Lentils																
Raw	11.2	338	28.1	0.96	57.1	51	454	9.0	39	4	0.48	0.25	2.6	6.2	5.2	—[c]
Cooked	69.6	116	9.0	0.38	20.1	19	180	3.3	8	1	0.17	0.07	1.1	1.5	2.8	—[c]
Peanuts, oil roasted	2.0	581	26.4	49.3	18.9	88	517	1.8	0	0	0.25	0.11	14.3	0	5.3	8.8

Peanut butter, smooth	1.4	588	24.6	50.0	20.7	34	323	1.7	0	0	0.14	0.10	13.1	0	2.4	6.0
Peas, split																
Raw	11.3	341	24.6	1.2	60.4	55	366	4.4	149	15	0.73	0.22	2.9	1.8	3.7	—c
Cooked	69.5	118	8.3	0.4	21.1	11	99	1.3	7	1	0.19	0.06	0.9	0.4	2.0	—c
Soybeans																
Raw	8.5	416	36.5	19.9	30.2	277	704	15.7	24	2	0.87	0.87	1.6	6.0	5.0	—c
Cooked	62.6	173	16.6	9.0	9.9	102	245	5.1	9	1	0.16	0.29	0.4	1.7	2.0	—c
Tofu, regular	84.6	76	8.1	4.8	1.9	105	97	5.4	85	9	0.08	0.05	0.2	0.1	0.1	1.2
Nuts																
Almonds, oil roasted	4.4	598	20.0	52.2	20.4	266	520	3.7	0	0	0.21	0.78	3.4	0.6	2.7b	11.2
Pecans	4.8	667	7.8	67.6	18.2	36	291	2.1	128	13	0.85	0.13	0.9	2	1.6b	6.5
Walnuts, black	4.4	607	24.4	56.6	12.1	58	464	3.1	296	30	0.22	0.11	0.7	—c	6.5b	5.0
Walnuts, English	3.7	642	14.3	61.9	18.3	94	317	3.8	124	12	0.39	0.15	1.0	3.2	4.6b	4.8
Cereal																
Rice, long-grain white																
Raw	11.6	365	7.1	0.7	80.0	28	115	4.3	—c	—c	0.58	0.05	4.2	0	0.30	1.0
Cooked	68.7	129	2.7	0.3	27.9	11	47	1.1	—c	—c	0.16	0.01	1.5	0	0.1	0.5
Rolled oats																
Raw	8.8	384	16.0	6.3	67.0	52	474	4.2	101	—c	0.73	0.14	0.78	—c	1.1	10.3
Cooked	85.3	62	2.6	1.0	10.8	8	24	0.7	16	—c	0.11	0.02	0.13	—c	0.2	—c
Beef, round, choice, raw	62.2	241	19.4	17.5	0	5	186	1.9	—c	—c	0.10	0.17	3.5	0	0	0

a1 kilocalorie = 4.185 kilojoules

bInsoluble dietary fiber

c— = Data not available

Source: U.S. Dept. Agr. Handbook No. 8-12 Composition of Foods: Nut and Seed Products: Raw, Processed, Prepared. Revised 1984; No. 8-13 Composition of Foods: Beef Products: Raw, Processed, Prepared. Revised 1986; No. 8-16 Composition of Foods: Legumes and Legume Products: Raw, Processed, Prepared. Revised 1986; No. 8-20 Composition of Foods: Cereal Grains and Pasta: Raw, Processed, Prepared. Revised 1989.

The major portion of the legume protein is present in organized structures called protein bodies (33) that are interspersed among the starch grains within the cells. These proteins, which are globulins, are stored by the seed as a reserve nutrient for a new plant. As a group, legumes contain approximately twice as much protein as cereals and, on a per-serving basis, about half as much protein as lean meat. Mature soybeans are higher in protein than most legumes. The quality of the protein is as important as the quantity. Legumes are better than cereals as a source of the essential amino acids isoleucine, leucine, phenylalanine, threonine, and valine. In particular, their especially high content of lysine, an essential amino acid in which cereals are low, makes legumes good supplements for cereals. The sulfur-containing amino acids of dried legumes, methionine and cystine, appear to be poorly utilized (12). Cereals complement legumes for these two amino acids, so beans and rice and beans and corn are nutritious combinations. Other complementary combinations are navy beans and Brazil nuts (1), or navy beans and sesame seed protein (6). Soybeans are not only higher in protein than other legumes, but also richer in essential amino acids. Adequately processed soy products provide protein of equivalent value to animal proteins, although formulas for newborns should be supplemented with methionine (47). Soy flours and grits and soy protein concentrates and isolates are widely used. Soy protein concentrates can be made into textured protein fibers by thermoplastic extrusion and isolated soy protein can be spun into protein fibers. Both textured vegetable protein and spun protein fibers are used as meat extenders or to fabricate meat analogs (41).

Beans and peas are low in fat (less than 2%) and high in carbohydrates (approximately 60%) and dietary fiber. Peanuts and soybeans are exceptions. Peanuts, because of their high fat content, resemble nuts, and soybeans are high in protein as well as fat. Beans are better sources of calcium than cereals are. Soybeans contain more calcium than other legumes. Calcium from common beans is absorbed about half as well as that from milk (46), whereas calcium absorption from soybeans is better than that from other legumes (17). The phosphorus content of legumes is high. Much of the phosphorus in mature beans, in contrast to the immature, is present as phytic acid or inositol hexaphosphoric acid (28). Legumes are somewhat better sources of iron and equal or better sources of thiamin than are whole grain cereals. Legumes compare favorably with lean meat as a source of iron and are a better source of thiamin. Most legumes contain somewhat more riboflavin than rolled oats or whole wheat but less niacin than whole wheat. Lean meat is superior to both whole grain cereals and legumes as a source of riboflavin or niacin. Legumes supply B_6, folacin, pantothenic acid, and biotin—other vitamins of the B-complex (31, 38). Ascorbic acid and vitamin A values in legumes are negligible. The starch content of most legumes is high.

Legumes, especially chick peas, soybeans, navy beans, and kidney beans, contain appreciable amounts of saponins (13). These triterpenoid glycosides cause the liquid to foam (35) and sometimes overflow the container when certain legumes are cooked.

Increased consumption of beans has been advocated for their high dietary fiber content and for their hypocholesterolemic and hypoglycemic effects by the National Cancer Institute, the National Heart Association, and the National Diabetes Association.

Immature beans can be eaten as vegetables, but most legumes are harvested in the mature dry stage. The entire bean is usually consumed but milled fractions are used to make precooked products or ones that cook rapidly. Figure 29-2 outlines processing schemes for converting dry beans into edible products. The intact bean may be roasted, puffed, sprouted, canned in brine or sauce, boiled in water, or cooked at an elevated temperature under steam pressure (44). Soybeans can be made into a variety of unique products in-

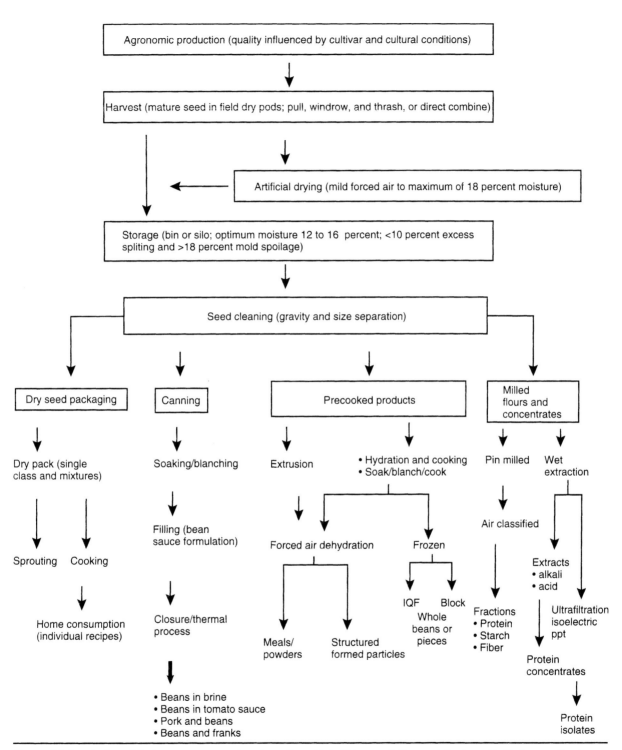

Figure 29-2. Outline of dry bean processes and products. (From M. A. Uebersax, S. Ruengsakulrach, and L. G. Occeña, *Food Technology*, 45:104, 1991.)

cluding soy beverages and tofu. Those foods form the basic part of the daily diet for people in East Asia, but are not as popular in the West. Tofu is the curd prepared from soy milk by coagulating the protein with salt. Magnesium or calcium salts are typically the coagulants used in processing soybeans into tofu. When calcium salts are used, tofu provides a good source of well absorbed calcium (34) as well as high quality protein.

COOKING LEGUMES

Cooking gelatinizes the starch, alters the texture, and improves the flavor of legumes, thus making them palatable. Moderate heating increases the availability of the proteins of most legumes (3) and eliminates toxic substances from some (25, 26). Dried beans contain lectins (hemaglutinins), which are toxic, and several other antinutritional factors including goitrogenic factors and tannins. However, lentils are low in antinutritional factors (5). Raw soybeans and most other beans contain a trypsin inhibitor that prevents the digestive enzyme trypsin from hydrolyzing proteins into amino acids. Soybeans are usually steam heated to 100°C (212°F) for 15 minutes to optimize nutritional factors. Boiling for 40 minutes inactivates trypsin inhibitor in red kidney beans (11). Microwave heating for nine minutes inactivates the antinutritional constituents of soybeans (15). Lectins are more easily inactivated by heat than are trypsin inhibitors because 10 minutes at 100°C (212°F) is sufficient to completely inactivate lectins (11). Commercial extrusion reduced trypsin inhibitor activity of blended navy and pinto beans and corn meal by 70 to 85 percent (14).

Soaking

Dried beans, because of their low moisture content, cook faster if they are given a preliminary soaking. A bean consists of two cotyledons encased in a seed coat known to botanists as the testa (Fig. 29-3). The seed coat is quite impermeable to water, as demonstrated in the following way (42). The hilum, or scar where the bean was attached to the pod, was coated with beeswax. The weight gain of beans so treated and soaked in cold water was compared to that for untreated beans. In 24 hours beans with the hilum waterproofed gained in weight 0.28 percent, while untreated beans gained 79 percent. This effectively demonstrates that water enters the bean at the hilum. From there it seeps around the periphery of the bean and causes the seed coat to wrinkle. These wrinkles are eliminated when the cotyledons swell subsequently and fill the seed coat. The higher the moisture content after soaking, the shorter the cooking time (21). How fast dried beans take up water depends on its temperature. The weight of dried beans soaked in water at room temperature (20°C or 68°F) becomes stationary after 16 hours compared to 5 hours at 40°C (104°F), 4 hours at 50°C (122°F), 1.5 hours at 60°C (140°F), and 0.8 hour at 90°C (194°F) (23). Soaking at temperatures of 60°C (140°F) and above increases the amounts of calcium, magnesium, thiamin, riboflavin, and niacin leached from the beans. Roughly half the oligosaccharides are removed, too. Heating dried beans in boiling water for two minutes and then allowing them to soak for one hour prior to cooking renders a product as good as that from an overnight soak in cold water (9). When a short soak in hot water is used, the beans should be cooked in the soaking water to conserve both water-soluble vitamins and minerals. Lentils and split peas cook satisfactorily without prior soaking. For

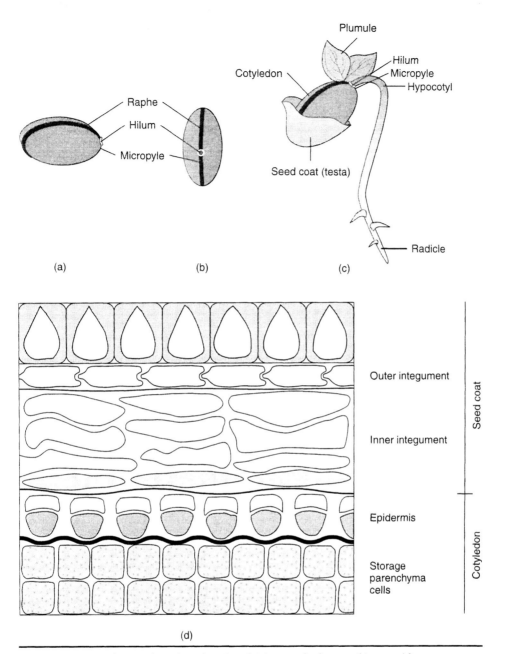

Figure 29-3. Dry beans (*Phaseolus vulgaris*) seed: (*a*) external side view; (*b*) external face view; (*c*) cross section; (*d*) detailed cross section across seed coat and cotyledon. (From S. K. Sathe, and S. S. Deshpande, *Encyclopedia of Food Science: Food Technology and Nutrition.*)

soaking (and cooking) dried legumes, two to three cups (500 to 750 milliliters) of water per cup (250 milliliters) of dried material are used.

Alternatives to traditional soaking for accelerating hydration and cooking of dried legumes include vacuum infiltration, treatment with ultrasonic sound, and exposure to gamma irradiation (44). One attempt to make beans quick cooking involves soaking the dried beans after preliminary vacuum infiltration with a solution made of sodium chloride, sodium tripolyphosphate, sodium bicarbonate, and sodium carbonate (37). However, the high sodium content and cost have made this method unattractive commercially.

Cooking Time and Doneness

Cooking legumes weakens intercellular bonding material so that pressure of a fork or the teeth causes the intact, starch-filled cells to separate. Most dried legumes require gentle boiling for approximately 1½ hours. Lentils, split peas, and blackeye peas cook in less than an hour, however. Soybeans when thoroughly cooked never have the mealy texture of other dried beans. Separation of the cells of cooked beans contrasts with raw beans, where pressure causes fracture across cell walls, exposing the starch-filled interior (Fig. 29-4) (36). As legumes are cooked, phytic acid unites with calcium in the pectic substances that bond adjacent cells, making the material soluble (20).

The temperature of the water in which the beans are soaked influences the cooking time. For example, dried small white beans cook in the least time after they have been soaked in water at 90°C (194°F) rather than at lower temperatures (to 20°C or 68°F) (23). The high temperature inactivates the enzyme phytase present in the bean that would otherwise eliminate the calcium-sequestering ability of phytic acid by catalyzing its hydrolysis to inositol and inorganic phosphate. Beans soaked in water at 60°, 70°, or 80°C (140°F, 158°F, or 136°F) take longest to cook, presumably because the phytic acid is hydrolyzed by phytase and can no longer bind divalent ions. The shorter cooking time (10 minutes) needed to bring about complete separation of the cells of quick-cooking lima beans compared with the 45 minutes for water-soaked beans can be attributed to chelation of divalent ions in the pectic substances between cells by the salts used to make the beans quick

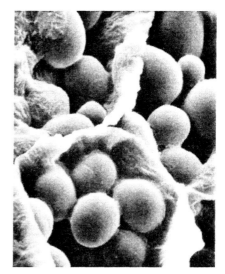

Figure 29-4. Scanning electron micrograph of a section through a raw, hydrated lima bean cotyledon, showing starch granules in parts of three cells. (Reprinted from L. B. Rockland and F. T. Jones, *Journal of Food Science* 39: 343. 1974. Copyright © by Institute of Food Technologists.)

cooking (36). Although soaking dried beans in water at 90°C (194°F) shortens the cooking time needed to tenderize them, the starch granules remain birefringent longer (19), as do those in beans soaked in salt solution used to make them quick cooking (16). Hard water prolongs the cooking time for dried beans (42). It is possible that both calcium and magnesium ions in hard water cause some interference with the tenderizing of dried beans during cooking because of their reaction with pectic constituents. If the water is extremely hard, the beans may be made uncookable. Addition of soda to the soaking and cooking water will shorten the time appreciably. The amount recommended is ⅛ teaspoon per cup of beans (9). Apparently this small amount of soda has no effect on the loss of thiamin during cooking and the quality of the cooked bean is almost as good as without soda. An excess of soda should be avoided because this makes the beans dark and mushy and because of the possibility of greater loss of thiamin. Cooking time for dried legumes may be shortened by the use of steam under pressure. Actual cooking times for soaked legumes range from 3 to 10 minutes under 15 pounds (103.4 kPa) pressure (9).

Two ingredients commonly added to beans when they are baked are molasses and tomato juice. Both prolong the time required to make the beans tender (42). This effect is attributed to the calcium in the former and to the acid in the latter. Partially cooking the beans before adding either ingredient is recommended to keep the cooking time reasonably short.

Storage

Beans deteriorate in both flavor and texture in six months at room temperature (25°C or 77°F) if the moisture content is above 13 percent, but will keep up to two years if the moisture content is 10 percent or below (40).

The conditions under which dried beans are stored influence the cooking time. Extended storage at high temperature (approximately 29°C or 84°F) and high relative humidity (approximately 65%) prolongs cooking time, and makes beans hard-to-cook. This hard-to-cook defect may be the result of several reactions that are accelerated under these storage conditions (19). Phytase hydrolyzes phytic acid, which releases calcium and magnesium. Increased membrane degradation allows these cations to diffuse to the middle lamella where they form unsoluble salts with pectic substances. The concentration of insoluble pectic salts increases under these storage conditions. Insolubilization of the pectic substances alone could increase cooking time but decreased solubility of starch and protein may also play a role. Such adverse storage conditions lower the digestibility of the protein and the availability of the sulfur-containing amino acids, too (2). The hard-to-cook defect is reversible when seeds are stored subsequently at low temperatures (6.5°C or 44°F) (18).

Seasoning

Addition of salt to dried legumes (approximately one teaspoon per cup) is essential to make them palatable. It is more effective if added early in the cooking period. Palatability of cooked legumes may be enhanced by the judicious addition of onion, celery, parsley, carrots, or tomato along with herbs or spices to season.

Yield of Cooked Legumes

The volume of a pound of dried legumes ranges from 2 to 2½ cups. Legumes increase two to three times in volume when cooked (29). This means that a pound of dried legumes will yield from four to seven cups cooked.

Preparing entrees of legumes is more time-consuming than is cooking meat, but legumes are a nutritious and relatively inexpensive meat substitute. Legumes give variety to the diet and could well occupy a more prominent place.

Canning

Dry beans to be canned commercially are generally soaked at room temperatures for eight to twelve hours or at 82° to 100°C (180° to 212°F) for 20 to 40 minutes. Hydrated beans are blanched for three to eight minutes after which they are packed in tins and covered with brine prior to thermal processing. Equilibration of processed beans with the brine takes two to four weeks.

FLATUS AFTER INGESTING LEGUMES

The flatus experienced by many individuals from five to seven hours after ingesting beans contains elevated levels of hydrogen and especially of carbon dioxide. Hydrogen is elevated in the breath, too (8). The increase in hydrogen comes from two oligosaccharides—raffinose and stachyose—which, because of a lack of α-galactosidase in the upper intestinal tract, are attacked by microorganisms in the lower intestines. Because these sugars are water soluble, discarding the soak-and-cook waters will remove most of these sugars. However, substantial amounts of total solids, vitamins, and minerals will also be removed (43). Extrusion reduces raffinose and stachyose contents of pinto bean flour by 47 and 60 percent, respectively (7) without leaching nutrients. Sprouts of beans reduce flatulence potential (30). Germination of legumes has other positive effects. Lectins are decreased and part of the phytic acid is hydrolyzed (40). The saponin content of legumes is lowered when they sprout (22).

REFERENCES

1. Antunes, A. J., and P. Markakis. 1977. "Protein supplementation of navy beans with Brazil nuts." *Journal of Agricultural and Food Chemistry* 25:1096–98. Effectiveness of methionine rich nuts.

2. Antunes, P. L., and V. Sqarbieri. 1979. "Influence of time and conditions of storage on technological and nutritional properties of a dry bean (*Phaseolus vulgaris* L.) variety Rosinha G_2." *Journal of Food Science* 44:1703–6. Temperatures of 12°, 25°, and 37°C (54°, 77°, 98°F) and relative humidities of 52 percent, 65 to 70 percent, and 76 percent compared.

3. Bates, R. P., F. W. Knapp, and P. E. Araujo. 1977. "Protein quality of green mature, dry mature, and sprouted soybeans." *Journal of Food Science* 42:271–72. Protein efficiency ratio of the three forms, raw and heated.

4. Betschart, A. A., C. K. Lyon, and G. O. Kohler. 1975. "Sunflower, safflower, sesame, and castor protein." In *Food Protein Sources*, N. W. Pirie, ed. Cambridge University Press. Pp. 79–104. A review.

5. Bhatty, R. 1990. "Cooking quality of lentils: Role of structure and composition of cell walls." *Journal of Agricultural and Food Chemistry* 38:376–83. Antinutritional factors in lentils.

6. Boloorforooshan, M., and P. Markakis. 1977. "Protein supplementation of navy beans with sesame seed." *Journal of Food Science* 44:390–97. Effect on protein efficiency ratio.

7. Borejszo, Z., and K. Khan. 1992. "Reduction of flatulence-causing sugars by high temperature extrusion of pinto bean high starch fractions." *Journal of Food Science*

57(3):771–72, 777. Extrusion reduces oligosaccharide content of pinto bean.

8. Calloway, D. H., C. A. Hickey, and E. L. Murphy. 1971. "Reduction of intestinal gas-forming properties of legumes by traditional and experimental food processing methods." *Journal of Food Science* 36:251–55. Flatus-forming legumes.

9. Dawson, E. H., J. C. Lamb, E. W. Toepfer, and H. W. Warren. 1952. "Development of rapid methods of soaking and cooking dried beans." *U.S. Department of Agriculture Bulletin No. 1051*. 53 pp. Methods of soaking, type of water, addition of soda, and cooking temperature studied.

10. Deschamps, I. 1958. "Peas and beans." In *Plant Protein Foodstuffs*. A. M. Altschul, ed. New York: Academic Press. Pp. 717–35. Types of legumes, botanical information, and use.

11. Dhurandhar, N. V., and K. C. Chang. 1990. "Effect of cooking on firmness, trypsin inhibitors, lectins, and cystine/cysteine content of navy and red kidney beans (*Phaseolus vulgaris*)." *Journal of Food Science* 55:470–74. Effect of cooking on antinutritional factors.

12. Evans, R. G., D. H. Bauer, K. A. Sisak, and P. A. Ryan. 1974. "The availability for the rat of methionine and cystine contained in dry bean seed (*Phaseolus vulgaris*)." *Journal of Agricultural and Food Chemistry* 22:130–33. Evidence of poor utilization.

13. Fenwick, D. E., and D. Oakenfull. 1983. "Saponin content of food plants and some prepared foods." *Journal of the Science of Food and Agriculture* 34:186–91. Legumes as a source of saponins.

14. Gujska, E., and K. Khan. 1991. "Functional properties of extrudates from high starch fractions of navy and pinto beans and corn meal blended with legume high protein fractions." *Journal of Food Science* 56:431–35. Extrusion effects of antinutritional factor.

15. Hafez, Y. S., A. I. Mohamed, F. M. Hewedy, and G. Singh. 1985. "Effects of microwave heating on solubility, digestibility and metabolism of soy protein." *Journal of Food Science* 50:415–17, 423.

16. Hahn, D. M., F. T. Jones, I. Akhavan, and L. B. Rockland. 1977. "Light and scanning electron microscope studies on dry beans: Intracellular gelatinization of starch in cotyledons of large lima beans (*Phaseolus lunatus*)." *Journal of Food Science* 42:1208–12. Quick-cooking and conventional dried beans compared.

17. Heaney, R. P., C. M. Weaver, and M. L. Fitzsimmons. 1991. "Soybeans phytate content: Effect on calcium absorption." *American Journal of Clinical Nutrition* 53:745–47. Calcium absorption in humans from soybeans high and low in phytate.

18. Hentges, D. L., C. M. Weaver, and S. S. Nielsen. 1990. "Reversibility of the hard-to-cook defect in dry beans (*Phaseolus vulgaris*) and cowpeas (*Vigna unguiculata*)." *Journal of Food Science* 55:1474, 1476. Storage at 6.5°C, 71 percent RH progressively reversed the hard-to-cook defect with time.

19. Hentges, D. L., C. M. Weaver and S. S. Nielsen. 1991. "Changes of selected physical and chemical components in the development of the hard-to-cook bean defect." *Journal of Food Science* 56:436–42. Mechanism of the hard-to-cook bean defect in two cultivars of cowpeas and five cultivars of dry beans under four storage conditions.

20. Isherwood, F. A. 1955. "Texture in fruits and vegetables." *Food Manufacturing* 30:399–402, 420. Textural changes in plant material including the role of phytin.

21. Jackson, G. M., and E. Varriano-Marston. 1981. "Hard-to-cook phenomenon in beans: Effects of accelerated storage on water absorption and cooking time." *Journal of Food Science* 46:799. Effects of moisture content on cooking times.

22. Joad, S., B. M. Chauhan, and A. C. Kapoor. 1986. "Saponin content of chick peas and black gram: Varietal differences and effects of processing and cooking methods." *Journal of the Science of Food and Agriculture* 37:1121–24. Effects of sprouting, soaking, and cooking.

23. Kon, S. 1979. "Effect of soaking temperature on cooking and nutritional quality of beans." *Journal of Food Science* 44:1329–34. Temperatures from 20°C to 90°C (68° to 194°F) compared.

24. Kon, S., A. C. Olson, D. F. Frederick, S. B. Eggling, and J. R. Wagner. 1973. "Effects of different treatments on phytate and soluble sugars in California small white beans (*Phaseolus vulgaris*)." *Journal of Food Science* 38:215–17. Enzymes activated at 55°C (131°F).

25. Liener, I. 1979. "Significance for humans of biologically active factors in soybeans and other food legumes." *Journal of the American Oil Chemists Society* 56:121–29. Toxic substances present.

26. Liener, I. E. 1976. "Legume toxins in relation to protein digestibility: A review." *Journal of Food Science* 41:1076–81. Trypsin inhibitor and lectins in legumes.

27. Lucier, G. 1994. "Economic trends in world and U.S. dry edible beans." *Michigan Dry Bean Digest* 18:18–21. Production and consumption trends for dry beans.

28. Makower, R. U. 1969. "Changes in phytic acid and acid-soluble phosphorus in maturing pinto beans." *Journal of the Science of Food and Agriculture* 20:82–84. Immature and mature beans compared.

29. Meiners, C. R., N. L. Derise, H. C. Lau, M. G. Crews, S. J. Ritchey, and E. W. Murphy. 1976. "The content of nine mineral elements in raw and cooked mature dry legumes." *Journal of Agricultural and Food Chemistry* 1126–30. Ten legumes analyzed.

30. Nnanna, I. A., and R. D. Phillips. 1990. "Protein and starch digestibility and flatulence potential of germinated cowpeas." *Journal of Food Science* 55:1(151–53, 183). Effects of sprouting potential on flatulence factors.

31. Ogunmodide, B. K., and V. A. Oyenuga. 1970. "Vitamin B content of cowpeas (*Vigna unguiculata* Walp)." II. "Pyridoxine, pantothenic acid, biotin and folic acid." *Journal of the Science of Food and Agriculture* 21:87–91. Three varieties of cowpeas tested.

32. Pernollet, J. -C. 1978. "Protein bodies of seeds: Ultrastructure, biochemistry, biosynthesis and degradation." *Phytochemistry* 17:1473–80. Storage depot for proteins and phytic acid in cotyledons of legumes.

33. Pimentel, D., W. Dritschilo, J. Krummel, and J. Kutzman. 1975. "Energy and land constraints in food protein production." *Science* 190:754–61. Options for use of resources to meet the world's food needs.

34. Poneros, G. A., and J. W. Erdman, Jr. 1988. "Bioavailability of calcium from tofu, tortillas, nonfat dry milk and mozzarella cheese in rats: Effect of supplemental ascorbic acid." *Journal of Food Science* 53: 208–10, 230. Bioavailability of calcium from tofu in rats.

35. Price, K. R., I. T. Johnson, and G. R. Fenwich. 1987. "The chemistry and biological significance of saponins in foods and feeding stuffs." *CRC Critical Reviews in Food Science* 26:27–135. A review.

36. Rockland, L. B., and F. T. Jones. 1974. "Scanning electron microscope studies on dry beans: Effects of cooking on the cellular structure of cotyledons of rehydrated large lima beans." *Journal of Food Science* 39: 342–46. Water-soaked and salt-soaked beans compared.

37. Rockland, L. B., and E. A. Metzler. 1967. "Quick cooking lima and other dry beans." *Food Technology* 21:344–48. Salts used in the treatment.

38. Rockland, L. B., C. F. Miller, and D. M. Hahn. 1977. "Thiamine, pyridoxine, niacin and folacin in quick-cooking beans." *Journal of Food Science* 42:25–28. Quick-cooking versus conventional dried beans.

39. Sathe, S. K., and S. S. Deshpande. 1993. "Beans (Phaseolus spp.): The Crops and their importance." In *Encyclopedia of Food Science: Food Technology and Nutrition* Vol. 1. London. pp. 317–22. A review.

40. Sathe, S. K., S. S. Deshpande, and D. K. Salunke. 1984. "Dry beans of phaseolus: A review," part 3. *CRC Critical Reviews in Food Science and Technology* 21:137–95. Effects of processing.

41. Shaner, K. M., and R. E. Baldwin. 1979. "Sensory properties, proximate analysis and cooking losses of meat loaves extended with chickpea meal or textured plant protein." *Journal of Food Science* 44:1191–93. Effects on flavor and juiciness.

42. Snyder, E. B. 1936. "Some factors affecting the cooking quality of the pea and Great Northern type of dry beans." *Nebraska Agriculture Experiment Station Research Bulletin* 85. 31 pp. Early and fundamental

work on the problems involved in the cooking of dry beans.

43. Uebersax, M. A., and S. Ruengsakulrach. 1989. "Structural and compositional changes during processing of dry beans (*Phaseolus vulgaris*)." In *Quality Factors of Fruits and Vegetables.* J. J. Jen, ed., American Chemical Society, Washington, D.C., ACS Symp. Series 405, p. 111. A review.

44. Uebersax, M. A., S. Ruengsakulrach, and L. G. Occeña. 1991. "Strategies and procedures for processing dry beans." *Food Technology* 45(11):104–11. A review.

45. United States Department of Agriculture. Bureau of Agricultural Economics. *Handbook of Official U.S. Standards for Beans.* 34 pp. Varieties and grades.

46. Weaver, C. M., R. P. Heaney, W. R. Proulx, S. M. Hinders, and P. T. Packard. 1993. "Absorbability of calcium from common beans." *Journal of Food Science* 58:1401–3. Calcium absorption in humans from three common beans.

47. Young, V. R. 1991. "Soy protein in relation to human protein and amino acid nutrition." *Journal of the American Dietetics Association* 91:828–35. Review of soy protein quality.

PART IX

Gels

Gelatin Gels

30

Gelatin has a long history of use as a gelling agent. Although vegetable gums have replaced gelatin in many instances, such products do not duplicate the melt-in-the-mouth sensation of gelatin. Gelatin is utilized as a gelling agent in such food products as molded desserts (either plain or with fruit), molded vegetable salads, aspics, whips, sponges, and creams. Gelatin is a most effective gelling agent. As little as one part gelatin can set or immobilize 99 parts of water by weight.

MANUFACTURE OF GELATIN

Gelatin is produced whenever tough cuts of meat are tenderized by cooking. Commercial gelatin is derived from pig skin, demineralized bone (ossein), and cowhide (5, 9). Pig skins, which come from young animals, are given a preliminary treatment with mild acid. Cowhides and bones are treated with alkali, either caustic soda for a few days or lime in which they are soaked for as long as 20 weeks. Treatment with alkali removes amide groups from the amino acids asparagine and glutamine of collagen, yielding a product with an isoelectric point near pH 5 compared to values of 6 to 9 for an acid-treated product. Pretreatment also removes impurities and disrupts any covalent bonds that cross link collagen monomers. The pretreated collagen is extracted with portions of water at increasingly higher temperatures. Hot water breaks hydrogen bonds that link the three gelatins in the collagen triple helix (3, 4), converting insoluble collagen to soluble gelatin. The gelatin sol is filtered, clarified, and concentrated. The concentrate is allowed to gel in thin layers, after which it is dried. Gelatin is marketed in the form of coarse particles or fine powder, the former unflavored and the latter fruit-flavored and sweetened.

GELATIN GEL FORMATION

Dried gelatin exists as a partially crystalline glassy polymer (8). In this respect, gelatin is analogous to native (ungelatinized) starch. Dry gelatin contains approximately 10 percent moisture; because of its low content of plasticizing water, its glass transition temperature is in the range of 80° to 90°C (176° to 194°F). Melting point of the crystallites is approximately 110° to 115°C (230° to 239°F).

Dispersing Dried Gelatin

Dispersing gelatin in hot liquid is preliminary to the formation of a gel. Boiling liquid is used because of the high transition temperature of gelatin in the glassy state. As molecules of plasticizing water diffuse into the amorphous regions of gelatin, its glass transition temperature drops rapidly. When the water content reaches 35 percent, the glass transition temperature is lowered to near $-12°C$ (10°F), and the crystallites then melt near 37°C (98.6°F). Once the crystallites melt, water then acts as a solvent for the molecules of gelatin that, in solution, are considered to exist as random coils (8). Gelatin can be made so that it disperses in cold liquid. This is accomplished by maintaining the extracted gelatin above the melting temperature so no crystallites form before it dries (8). Cold water-soluble gelatin is a sol, not a gel, that has been concentrated by drying. To disperse it requires dilution by water not the break-up of crystallites. The long thin molecules of gelatin impart viscosity to the liquid in which they are dispersed.

Gelation of a Gelatin Sol

As a sol of gelatin cools, it becomes more viscous. However, more than thickening is involved in conversion of a sol to a gel (5, 9, 11). Gelation of gelatin involves a change in state, from a viscous liquid to a viscoelastic solid, which is considered a prototype gel (5). The accepted model for a gelatin gel is a network of molecules stabilized at intervals by so-called junction zones. Evidence suggests that segments of three gelatin molecules unite in a partial reformation of the collagen triple helix to form the crystallites of the junction zones (Fig. 30-1) (7). An individual molecule can participate in more than one junction zone. The remainder of the molecule exists as a random coil that bridges the gap between crystallites and is part of the amorphous area of a gel. Two conditions are required for a gelatin molecule to participate in the formation of a helix. A sequence of glycine–proline–proline (or hydroxyproline) residues in the chain is essential, as is a shift in the relevant peptide bonds from *cis* to *trans* isomers (11, 5).

A gelatin gel has a liquid phase as well as a network of protein. The two phases of a gel appear to be mutually supportive—the liquid keeping the network from collapsing and the network keeping the liquid from flowing (10). Stability of a gel requires a delicate osmotic balance. Polymer–solvent attraction must be balanced against polymer–polymer attraction. There is evidence that water molecules in a gel are less mobile than are those in bulk

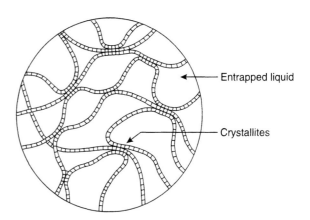

Entrapped liquid

Crystallites

Figure 30-1. Network of gelatin molecules in a gel, shown schematically.

water (6). Even so, that molecules can diffuse from one part of a gel to another can be demonstrated by penetrating a gelatin gel with a toothpick previously dipped in food coloring. Held for a day or two under refrigeration, the gel will be uniformly colored throughout. If polymer–polymer attraction is excessive, the network of the gel shrinks and liquid is expelled. Manipulation of a gel, such as cutting or spooning, will also result in synerisis.

The conversion of a gelatin sol to a gel is temperature-dependent, and the gel that forms is thermo-reversible. Gelation takes place only in a supercooled sol. How the sol is cooled affects the melting point of the gel and its rigidity. A rapid drop in temperature results in the formation of numerous crystal nuclei, but the gel melts at a lower temperature than does one cooled slowly. Slow cooling of a sol permits the formation of more heat-stable junction zones. Once a gel forms and then liquefies, the gel reforms faster subsequently. This suggests that gelation may occur in two stages, a period of preliminary orientation of the molecules in the sol and the final establishment of the network. The first is a relatively slow process and the latter takes place rapidly once it starts. Acid prolongs the setting time of a gelatin sol and lowers the liquefying temperature of a gel.

The rigidity of a gelatin gel, once it is formed, increases with time. The most rapid increase in firmness takes place during the first day. A gelatin sol will attain maximum rigidity in the shortest time if it is temperature cycled. A sol held for a time near 0°C (32°F) to permit many nuclei to form and then maintained at 15°C (59°F) to complete gelation developed maximum rigidity sooner than did a gel cooled from 37° to 15°C (98.6° to 59°F) (2).

USE OF GELATIN IN FOODS

The pulverized form of gelatin used in flavored packaged mixes can be dispersed by adding boiling water and stirring because the pieces of gelatin are so fine. Pieces of granular gelatin are too large for directly applied hot water to disperse them readily. Instead, the granules are soaked for a short time in three to four volumes of cold liquid. This preliminary hydration of the granules facilitates the dispersion of the gelatin molecules as a sol by hot water. To effect the dispersion, hot water may be added to the hydrated gelatin. The water should be hot enough so that the final temperature is at least 35°C (95°F). Alternately, the hydrated granules may be converted to a concentrated sol by heating over hot water. It is difficult to disperse this concentrated sol of gelatin in the cold liquid specified in some recipes. Cold liquid in small portions should be added to the concentrated gelatin sol (not warm sol to cold liquid!). Each portion should be stirred in thoroughly before the next one is added. Otherwise the gelatin will solidify in rubbery strands and lumps instead of forming a uniform sol.

Proportions of Gelatin

The amount of gelatin needed to gel a liquid varies from one to two percent. With one tablespoon (15 milliliters) or seven grams of gelatin per pint (500 milliliters), proportions frequently used, the percentage is 1½. Enough gelatin should be used so that the gels resist melting at normal serving temperatures. The proportion may be increased if the gel is to be served on a warm day. Too much gelatin makes a stiff, rubbery gel. Ideally, the gel should be just firm enough to hold its shape, yet tender and quivery. The amount of gelatin may need to be increased slightly in a tart jelly because acid lowers the temperature at which a gel liquefies as well as the temperature required for the gel to form. Acid also affects the clarity of a gelatin dispersion. The isoelectric point of alkaline-processed gelatin is near 4.7 to 5.0. When such gelatin is dispersed in water, the sol is cloudy. Increments of acid added to the water increases the clarity of the sol.

Fruit and Vegetable Jellies

If fruits or vegetables are to be combined with gelatin, the sol should be cooled and allowed to stand until it is the thickness of thick egg white and until the gel is just ready to form. At this stage the gelatin sol is thick enough to keep the vegetable or fruit from floating. Uncooked fruit is especially likely to float because it is buoyed up by the pockets of intercellular gas in the fresh tissue. Raw figs, kiwi, and pineapple cannot be used because a gel will not form. These fruits contain proteolytic enzymes that not only bring about the conversion of collagen to gelatin (Chapter 22) but also catalyze the hydrolysis of peptide bonds in gelatin. Because heat inactivates these enzymes, a canned (but not frozen) form of these fruits may be used.

Whips, Sponges, and Creams

Before a sol is beaten for whips, sponges, and creams, it should cool to 10°C (50°F) and stand until it has reached the consistency of thick egg white. Whipping a gelatin sol at this stage will yield a foam of at least double the volume the original sol. After it is whipped, gelatin molecules in the fluid of the foam will set the liquid. A whip or a sponge is thus a combination of a foam and a gel. A sponge differs from a whip in that beaten egg whites are incorporated in the former. For creams, whipped cream is folded into the gelatin foam. Gelatin is used to set the custard for Spanish cream.

Unmolding Gelatin Gels

The container in which the gelatin sol is to set may be oiled *lightly* with salad oil for ease in unmolding. When the container with the gel is dipped momentarily in lukewarm water, the oil becomes more fluid. Hot water should not be used, because this will melt the gel. Even after the container is dipped in warm water the gel will not leave it readily as air pressure of 15 pounds per square inch is holding the gel to the mold. Loosening the gel at one side of the container will allow air to come between the gel and the container; and the gel will then slide free.

REFERENCES

1. Engel, J. 1987. "Folding and unfolding of collagen triple helices." In *Advances in Meat Research*. Vol. 4. *Collagen as a Food*. A. M. Pearson, T. R. Dutson, and A. J. Bailey, eds. New York: Van Nostrand Reinhold. Pp. 145–81. Cis ⇌ trans isomerization of peptide bonds and gelation.

2. Ferry, J. D. 1948. "Mechanical properties of substances of high molecular weight." IV. "Rigidity of gelatin gels: Dependence on temperature and molecular weight." *Journal of the American Chemical Society* 70:2244–49. Temperature cycling and strength of gelatin gels.

3. Gross, J. 1961. "Collagen." *Scientific American* 204(5):121–30. Chemistry and structure of collagen: illustrated.

4. Harrington, W., and P. von Hippel. 1961. "The structure of collagen and gelatin." *Advances in Protein Chemistry* 16:122–27. Properties of gelatin gels.

5. Ledward. D. A. 1986. "Gelation of gelatin." In *Functional Properties of Food Macromolecules*. J. R. Mitchell and D. A. Ledward, eds. London and New York: Elsevier Applied Science Publishing Company. Pp. 171–201. Conversion of collagen to gelatin; mechanism of gelation.

6. Naryshkina, E. P., V. Yakolkov, A. I. Dolinnyi and V. N. Izmailova. 1982. "Study of gelatin gel formation by high resolution nuclear magnetic resonance." *Kolloidn ZK* 44:356. *Chemical Abstracts* Vol. 97 # 2442x (1982). Decreased mobility of water molecules in gelatin gels.

7. Oakenfull, D. 1984. "A method for using measurements of shear modulus to estimate the size and thermodynamic stability of junction zones in noncovalently cross-linked gels." *Journal of Food Science* 49:1103–4, 1110. Junction zones in gelatin gels.

8. Slade, L., and H. Levine. 1987. "Polymer-chemical properties of gelatin in foods." In *Advances in Meat Research*, Vol. 4. *Collagen as a Food*. A. M. Pearson, T. R. Dutson, and A. J. Bailey, eds. New York: Van Nostrand Reinhold. Pp. 251–66. Gelatin—a partially crystalline, amorphous polymer.

9. Stainsby, G. 1987. "Gelatin gels." In *Advances in Meat Research*, Vol. 4. *Collagen as a Food*. A. M. Pearson, T. R. Dutson, and A. J. Bailey, eds. New York: Van Nostrand Reinhold. Pp. 209–22. Source and production of gelatin; renaturation and gelation.

10. Tanaka, T. 1981. "Gels." *Scientific American* 244:124–36, 138. Gelation, a balancing of opposing forces.

11. Ziegler, G. R., and E. A. Foegeding. 1990. "The gelation of proteins." *Advances in Food and Nutrition Research* 34:203–98. Gelatin, a prototype gel, included.

Fruit Pectin Gels

31

A fruit pectin jelly is a deformable solid that results when a pectin sol is transformed into a gel. Association of portions of adjacent pectin molecules to form junction zones gives a three-dimensional structure to a gel. Those sections of pectin molecules between junction zones form voids that retain the liquid. Reports of early studies of some of the parameters of fruit pectin jelly formation (8, 9) included this characterization of that "elusive substance, a good fruit jelly:

> Ideal fruit jelly is a beautifully colored, transparent, palatable product obtained by so treating fruit juice that the resulting mass will quiver, not flow, when removed from its mold: a product with texture so tender that it cuts easily with a spoon, yet so firm that the angles so produced retain their shape; a clear product that is neither syrupy, gummy, sticky nor tough; neither is it brittle and yet it will break, and does so with a distinct, beautiful cleavage which leaves sparkling characteristic faces. This is that delicious, appetizing substance, a good fruit jelly.

A fruit pectin jelly with all of these qualities is not always achieved. A balance among the main constituents—pectin, sugar, acid, salts, and water, each with a specific function—is required. Pectin is the unique component in this type of product.

PECTIN CHEMISTRY

Pectins are polymers of α-D-galacturonic acid in the C_1 configuration.

Anion	Methylester

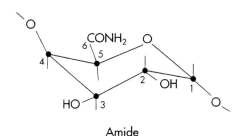

Amide

Galacturonic acids are joined by 1, 4-glycosidic linkage to form polymers of a few hundred to a thousand monomers (5). Variable percentages of the carboxyl groups of pectin molecules exist as methyl esters, the presence of which differentiates pectin (pectinic acid) molecules from those of pectic acid (Chapter 27). Those pectins with more than 50 percent and up to 80 percent of their carboxyl groups present as methyl esters are designated high methoxyl pectins, or simply pectins. Those with fewer than 50 percent of the carboxyl groups esterified are designated low methoxyl pectins (5). The galacturonic acid sequence in pectins is interrupted by a $(1{\rightarrow}2)$ insert of the sugar rhamnose. This $(1{\rightarrow}2)$ linkage results in a kink in an otherwise linear pectin molecule (4). A rhamnose insert has been reported after every 25 or so galacturonic acid residues in apple, citrus, and sunflower pectin (15), as well as blocks of rhamnose inserts at longer and irregular intervals (7). Two other sugars, galactose and arabinose, are present in citrus pectin (11). Pectins of apple, apricot, peach, and pear contain the sugar xylose, in addition. These three sugars, united to the main chain as side chains, form the hairy regions of a pectin molecule (7).

Pectins are thus a heterogeneous assortment of polymers that vary in degree of polymerization, in methoxyl content, in kind, and in distribution of sugars. In addition, the stage of ripeness of a fruit and the way the pectin is extracted from cell walls and middle lamella contribute to the heterogeneity.

SOURCES OF PECTIN

Pectins are obtained in quantities from two agricultural waste products, citrus albedo and apple pomace. Waste from the processing of sugar beets contains pectin with a low methoxyl content, but the presence of acetyl side chains limits its gel-forming capacity (13). Sunflower head waste has been analyzed as a potential source of usable pectin (6). Pectin is extracted from albedo and pomace with hot water that contains acid. This pectin (with the grade specified) is available in dried form for commercial use in jellies, marmalade, and confections. The grade, determined by the USA-SAG method, indicates the weight of sucrose that when combined with a unit weight of the pectin will yield jelly of a specified rigidity as measured by its sag when turned from a mold. A grade of 150, for example, indicates that 150 grams of sucrose combined with 1 gram of the pectin can form a jelly of a specified rigidity (5). The grade of a pectin thus indicates its sugar-carrying capacity.

Packages of dehydrated pectin, with the requisite amount of acid, are available in retail quantities as is pectin in sol form. Directions that accompany the pectin specify the amount of sugar to be combined with it. The quantity is based on the sugar-carrying capacity of the pectin.

Certain fruits when heated in a limited volume of water yield extracts of pectin of high quality and of sufficient concentration for making jelly. Such fruits include apples (tart), blackberries, crabapples, cranberries, currants, gooseberries, grapes (Concord and wild), guavas, lemons, loganberries, plums (sour), and raspberries (black and red). These fruits contain, in addition to the pectin, sufficient acid to make jelly. Other fruits that are good sources of pectin are sweet apples, prune plums, oranges, and quinces, but the first two are deficient in acid, as are some samples of the last two fruits. Apricots, pomegranate, rhubarb, and strawberries are sufficiently tart, but their pectin contents are low or of poor quality. Peaches and pears are deficient both in pectin and in hydrogen-ion concentration. Not only do fruits differ in pectin content, but different tissues of an individual fruit do as well. The skin and core area of an apple and the albedo of an orange are richer in pectin than are the pulpy areas of these fruits.

The type of pectic substance in a fruit varies with its maturity. Insoluble protopectin predominates in immature fruit. Protopectin yields water-dispersible pectin when fruit tissue is extracted with hot water. As fruits approach maturity, the protopectin content decreases and water-dispersible pectin predominates. As fruits go from just ripe to overripe, two types of enzymes may degrade pectic substances. One enzyme, polygalacturonase, catalyzes the hydrolysis of the glycosidic bonds in the galacturonic acid polymer. A marked drop in viscosity of a pectin sol occurs when only a fraction of the glycosidic bonds in the polymer are hydrolyzed. In addition, pectin methylesterase may cause demethylation of the pectin. This alters conditions under which the pectin can form a gel. Complete demethylation yields pectic acid.

COMPONENTS OF PECTIN GELS

Water

Water dissolves acids, sucrose (or other polyols), and salts of divalent ions. In addition, water disperses pectin as a colloidal sol because of the numerous polar groups on the molecule. Ionized carboxyl groups stabilize the dispersion (10).

Acid

The main function of acid in pectin gel formation is to depress ionization of carboxyl groups (10). This permits the close approach of pectin molecules, essential if junction zones are to form. Acids utilized to lower the pH of a pectin sol include citric, malic, tartaric, and fumaric.

Pectin

Asymmetric molecules of pectin form the three-dimensional network that gives structure to a gel. Segments of pairs of pectin molecules participate in interchain associations called junction zones, while nonlinear segments of the molecules caused by rhamnose inserts provide spaces that hold liquid (4). The length of a pectin polymer and its methyl ester content influence the conditions under which a gel network forms.

Calcium Ions

The junction zones of a low methoxyl pectin gel differ from those of a high methoxyl pectin gel. Divalent ions such as calcium must be present for a low methoxyl pectin sol to become a gel. The association of segments of pectin molecules via calcium ions is considered intermolecular chelate binding rather than electrostatic interaction (11). From 7 to 14 uninterrupted galacturonic acid units are minimum for formation of junction zones (5, 15). An eggbox model of a portion of a junction zone with calcium ions in pockets formed by pairs of low methoxyl pectin molecules is shown in Figure 31-1.

Sucrose

A sol of high methoxyl pectin is transformed into a gel only when a cosolute such as sucrose or other polyol is present in sufficient concentration. The following has been proposed to account for the role of sucrose in pectin gel formation (17). Numerous hydroxyl groups on a pectin molecule facilitate its dispersion in water, but methyl groups are nonpolar. Presence of these hydrophobic groups interferes with the normal hydrogen bond interchange among water molecules in the vicinity of a methyl group. These water molecules form a highly structured, hydrogen-bonded cage around each methyl group. Sucrose molecules disrupt the cage of water molecules, freeing methyl groups for hydrophobic interaction with each other. Thus sucrose contributes to the gelation of a high methoxyl pectin indirectly by its effect on the water in which the pectin is dispersed. Given sufficient acid to depress ionization of carboxyl groups, pairs of adjacent pectin molecules can approach closely enough for both hydrogen bonding between polar groups and interaction between methyl groups. Based on the above scenario, a portion of a junction zone of a high methoxyl pectin gel is shown in Figure 31-2 (13). Although hydrogen bonds (indicated by dotted lines) contribute a high proportion of the energy involved in stabilizing junction zones, hydrophobic interaction of methyl groups (shown as dark circles) is required, too.

   Other polyols such as glucose, fructose, and glycerol may be used instead of sucrose, but the conditions for gelation and the character of the gel differ with each polyol. The geometry of the polyol, that is, the distribution and orientation of (—OH) groups, appears to be the issue, not its effect on the colligative properties of water (12). The stabilizing effect of sucrose on hydrophobic interactions in pectin gels is analogous to the effect of sucrose in protecting globular proteins against denaturation by heat (Chaper 18).

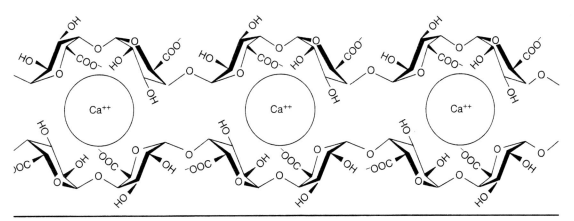

Figure 31-1. Junction zones in a low-ester pectin gel shown as an egg-box model. (From S. H. Christensen, *Food Hydrocolloids*, Vol. III, 1986, M. Glicksman, ed. P. 223. Reprinted by permission of CRC Press, Inc., Boca Raton, FL.)

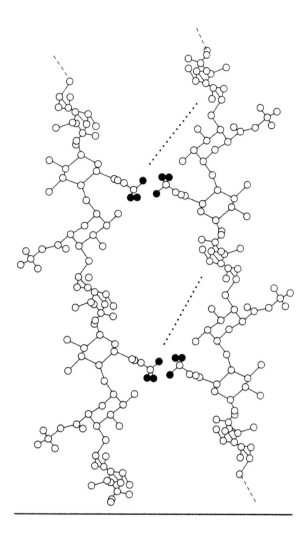

Figure 31-2. Portion of a junction zone in a high methoxyl pectin gel, with hydrophobic interaction between pairs of methyl groups (filled circles) and hydrogen bonds (indicated by dotted lines). (From D. Oakenfull and A. Scott, *Journal of Food Science* 49:1093, 1984. Reprinted by permission.)

To summarize, pectins form gels of two types, depending on the proportion of carboxyl groups present as methyl esters. High methoxyl pectins, those with 55 to 80 percent of carboxyl groups present as methyl esters, form gels if the pH is 3.4 or less and if a cosolute such as sucrose or other polyol is present in sufficient concentration. Divalent ions make limited contribution to gelation of high methoxyl pectins. Low methoxyl pectins, those with fewer than 50 percent of carboxyl groups as methyl esters, form gels with the aid of divalent ions such as calcium and with a cosolute that decreases in concentration as the methyl ester content of the pectin decreases. If the methyl ester content of the pectin is low enough, only divalent ions are required for gel formation.

CONTROLLING THE VARIABLES IN A PECTIN GEL

Production of a pectin gel with the characteristics enumerated at the beginning of this chapter requires that the concentration of constituents be balanced in the finished product. The proportions of hydrogen ions, sugar, salts, and pectin determine whether a gel will form and, if so, the temperature at which it begins to set and the quality of the gel. The concentration of each can vary, but within restricted limits. A slight excess of one variable may compensate for a slight deficiency of another. Except for this, failure in jelly making would be far more common.

Hydrogen-Ion Concentration

Most fruit pectins will form a gel at a hydrogen-ion concentration that falls within the pH range of 2.8 to 3.4. Unless the pH is below 3.5, a gel is unlikely to form. The hydrogen-ion concentration that is optimum for gel formation varies with the quality of the pectin, especially with its methoxyl content (4), with the salts present in the fruit extract, and with the concentration of sugar in the finished jelly. A pH meter is required to measure the hydrogen-ion concentration of a pectin sol. A rough estimate of the acidity of a pectin extract may be made by comparing its tartness with that of one volume of lemon juice diluted with eight volumes of water. Lemon juice (pH 2.2 to 2.4) is usually used to supplement the acidity of fruits that are lacking in tartness, although tartaric acid is more effective (8) than citric acid in promoting gel formation because it is more highly ionized. Although acid is required for pectin gel formation, in excess it gives a brittle gel that is subject to syneresis.

Sucrose Concentration

The higher the methoxyl content of the pectin, the higher the ratio of sucrose required to effect gelation. The concentration of sucrose required to form a gel may be as low as 40 percent or as high as 70 percent, but it usually falls within the range of 60 to 65 percent. A 60-percent sucrose solution boils at 103°C (217°F); a 65-percent sucrose solution boils near 104°C (219°F); one that boils near 105°C (221°F) has a sugar concentration near 68 percent. This means that most pectin gels form when the sugar concentration is sufficient to raise the boiling point of the mixture to 103° to 105°C (217° to 221°F) (9). The precise concentration that is optimum depends upon the particular pectin molecules involved, the hydrogen-ion concentration of the pectin sol, and the salts present. For cranberries to gel the concentration of sugar must be kept below 60 percent (2). This is due in part to the low pH of cranberries. Unripe gooseberries, which are equally tart, require less than a 60-percent sugar concentration for gel formation, also. A 67-percent sucrose solution is saturated at room temperature (20°C or 68°F) (Chapter 8). Inversion of part of the sucrose by acid as the jelly boils plus the presence of pectin prevent the precipitation of sucrose crystals in jelly that has been boiled to 105°C (221°F) or higher. Sucrose crystals may form in jellies made with a commercial pectin concentrate that requires a boiling time too short (one minute) for sufficient inversion of sucrose to take place.

Two ways are available to control the concentration of sugar in finished jelly. The mixture may be boiled to a predetermined weight, which is calculated on the basis of the weight of sugar combined with the fruit pectin extract. Alternately, the boiling point of the jelly may be used as an index to the sugar concentration (and doneness) of the jelly, as is the practice for candies and frostings (Chapter 8).

Pectin Concentration

The concentration of pectin in finished jelly usually varies between 0.5 and 1 percent. A cranberry jelly with a pectin content of 0.18 percent is atypical (2). Cranberries contain pectin of unusually high quality and low pH (2.7 to 2.9).

When pectin is extracted from fruit with hot water, the quantity and sugar-carrying capacity of the pectin is unknown. If more sucrose is combined with this extract than the pectin it contains requires, and the mixture is then boiled until the sucrose is sufficiently concentrated (103° to 105°C or 217° to 221°F), the pectin will be insufficiently concentrated and either a weak gel or no gel forms. If, instead, this mixture is boiled until enough water has evaporated so that the pectin is sufficiently concentrated, a jelly can form but it will be sticky and sucrose may crystallize from the supersaturated solution. If the volume of sugar that is combined with the extract is insufficient for the sugar-carrying capacity of the pectin, the pectin will become too concentrated by the time sufficient water is evaporated to concentrate the sucrose. A stiff jelly is the result. Even when sucrose is combined with the extract in proportion to the gel-forming potential of its pectin, no gel or a weak one results if insufficient water is evaporated (boiling point of the mixture too low) or a stiff gel results if too much water is evaporated (boiling point of the mixture too high). The effects of the variables discussed above on the quality of fruit pectin jellies are summarized in Table 31-1.

Despite the hurdles, it is possible to make high quality pectin jelly with a fruit pectin extract. Determining the sugar-carrying potential of the pectin extract is essential. One sure way to do this is to make a series of test jellies, varying the proportions of sugar and possibly the amount of acid. Of course, this is impractical when jelly is made in small quantities. An estimate of the jelly-forming capacity of the pectin in an extract can be obtained by precipitating the pectin. To do this, two volumes of ethanol are added to one volume of the extract in a test tube or graduated cylinder that is slowly inverted and then uprighted. The size and coherence of the precipitated pectin gives some indication of the sugar-carrying and gel-forming potential of the pectin extract.

The viscosity of a fruit pectin extract is a better index of its sugar-carrying capacity; the more concentrated the pectin, the more viscous is the extract. In addition, the higher the molecular weight of the pectin and the higher the proportion of methyl groups with their water cages, the more viscous is the dispersion and the higher the proportion of sucrose necessary to effect gel formation (4, 5).

A Jelmeter may be used to measure the viscosity of a pectin sol (Fig. 31-3). This device is an adaptation of a viscometer (1). It consists of a small test tube to the lower end of which is attached a fine capillary tube. When liquid is confined and allowed to flow through a narrow space like the bore of the capillary, the flow pattern is described as laminar. As mol-

Figure 31-3. A Jelmeter used to measure the viscosity of a pectin extract, which indicates its sugar-carrying capacity. The Jelmeter is calibrated to read in cups of sugar required for each cup of extract.

TABLE 31-1
Effects of Variables on Fruit Pectin Jellies

Ratio of Sugar to Pectin	Test for Doneness	Effect(s) on Jelly
In excess	Jelly boiled to 103°–105°C	No gel or weak one
	Jelly boiled to give sheet test	Sticky jelly; sucrose may crystallize
Too low	Jelly boiled to 103°–105°C	Jelly firm and rubber-like
	Jelly boiled to give sheet test	
Optimum	Jelly boiled above 105°C	Firm gel; slightly sticky
	Jelly boiled to less than 103°C	No gel or a weak one

ecules of water flow through the capillary, they move in columns that slide past each other in telescopic fashion. The symmetrical shape of water molecules (essentially spherical) favors this laminar flow. The long, asymmetrical molecules of pectin interspersed among the molecules of water disrupt this flow. As a result, the molecules of dispersing liquid are delayed in their passage through the capillary. A liquid with a slower rate of flow is more viscous. The greater the concentration of pectin molecules and, even more important, the greater the length of the pectin molecules, the more viscous is the pectin sol (15) and the higher its sugar-combining capacity. If the extract needs acid, it should be added before the viscosity is measured. The extract should be at room temperature when the test is made. If the extract is too warm, the flow is speeded; if at refrigerator temperature, it is retarded. In either case, a false reading results.

To make the test, the Jelmeter is filled with the pectin sol. The sol is allowed to flow from the Jelmeter for exactly one minute. The upper tube of the Jelmeter is calibrated to read in cups of sugar per cup of fruit pectin extract. The first mark below the top of the Jelmeter, which reads 1¼ cups, is for the most viscous sol. One that is more viscous, that is, flows less than this distance in the time specified should be diluted with water or a juice free of pectin. Otherwise the fruit pectin extract cannot dissolve enough sugar for the jelly-forming potential of the pectin present. A pectin sol that flows so fast that it goes below the lowest mark, which indicates ½ cup of sugar per cup of pectin sol, is too low in jellying power to make satisfactory jelly without the addition of pectin concentrate.

SETTING TIME AND TEMPERATURE

All pectin gels do not begin to set at the same temperature. High methoxyl pectins with 70 to 80 percent of carboxyl groups esterified are rapid setting (i.e., have a high setting temperature). Slow setting pectins with 65 to 75 percent of the carboxyl groups as methyl esters must be cooled to a lower temperature before a gel begins to form (3, 5). As a jelly mixture cools, a temperature is reached first that favors hydrophobic interaction between methyl groups. With additional cooling, a temperature is arrived at that favors hydrogen bonding between polar groups (14). Factors in addition to the pectin influence the setting time of a gel. The higher the concentration of hydrogen ions (the lower the pH) and the higher the concentration of cosolute the higher the setting temperature. If the setting temperature is too near the boiling point of the mixture, a gel may begin to form as the mixture is poured. Disruption of a gel, once it starts to form, weakens the final product. Manufacturers circumvent this problem by adding the hot mixture to the acid in the jelly glass. To prevent premature gelation of cranberry pectin gel, the sucrose concentration should be kept below 60 percent.

JELLY MADE WITH PECTIN CONCENTRATE OR POWDER

Use of either commercial product provides more control over the variables in jelly. Both forms of pectin contain sufficient acid. The volumes of sugar and of fruit juice specified in the directions that accompany each product are such that pectin, sugar, and hydrogen ions are in balance when the ingredients are combined. Low methoxyl pectins, including amidated pectin in which an (—NH$_2$) group replaces an (—OCH$_3$) group are available that will form jelly with reduced sugar content (5). The short boiling period of these products serves only to dissolve the sugar and disperse the pectin. Sugar is dissolved in the fruit juice before liquid pectin is added, but powdered pectin is first dispersed in the fruit juice and then the sugar is added. The boiling period is too short to hydrolyze the sugar, but it does maintain fruit flavor.

JELLY MADE WITH FRUIT PECTIN EXTRACT

Extraction of Pectin

Fruits that are just ripe or slightly underripe should be used. However, unripe apples should not be used because the starch that is present makes the jelly cloudy. Some fully ripe fruit may be included for color, aroma, and taste. Soft fruits should be crushed and firm fruits sliced thinly or chopped to facilitate extraction of pectin. If the fruit lacks sufficient tartness to make jelly, acid is added at this point because it aids in the extraction of pectin with high jellying power. Thin slices of lemon, minus the *yellow* part of the rind, may be cooked along with the fruit. The pulp supplies acid, and the albedo supplies pectin. Water is essential for the extraction of pectin but soft, juicy fruits may need little if any additional water. Firm fruits need only enough water to cover (approximately one cup per pound or 250 milliliters per ½ kilogram). An excess should be avoided because it dilutes the pectin and must be boiled away when the jelly is made.

A simmering temperature is sufficient to extract the pectin from fruit pulp. The cooking time varies with the fruit and with its firmness. Soft fruits require 5 to 10 minutes. Firm fruits like apples may need to be cooked 15 to 20 minutes. Long cooking should be avoided because heating the pectin after it has been removed from the tissues hydrolyzes (depolymerizes) it and lowers its jelly-making capacity. For fruits rich in pectin a second extraction may be made. The first should be drained from the pulp, a small amount of water added, and the pulp simmered a second time. Most of the color, the acids, and the salts are removed by the first extraction. The second extraction may yield almost as much pectin as the first, however. The yield of extract averages 1 to 1⅓ cups per pound of fruit.

Clarification

The cooked fruit is first strained to separate pulp from extract. The latter is then clarified by allowing it to drip through a jelly bag made of closely woven cloth or several thicknesses of cheesecloth. Squeezing the pulp increases yield but tends to make the extract cloudy.

Testing for Pectin

The sugar-carrying capacity of the extract should be tested, preferably with a Jelmeter. Otherwise, ¾ cup sugar per cup of extract should be used. The yield of jelly will be greater, the higher the proportion of sugar to fruit extract.

Boiling the Jelly

The extract should be combined with an amount of sugar appropriate for the jellying power of the pectin before boiling begins. Sugar retards depolymerization of the pectin as the mixture boils. Cooking lots should be kept small (two to four cups) and the heating unit should be large enough and hot enough to maintain a full, rolling boil. Long, slow evaporation hydrolyzes pectin and brings about extensive inversion of sucrose (Chapter 8).

The capacity of the container should be four times the volume of the fruit extract to allow for foaming of the jelly as it boils. The clarity of jelly compared to the fruit extract from which it is made is due to material collecting in the foam.

Assessing Doneness

When jelly is made by the hot evaporation method, the boiling point of the mixture may be used as one index to doneness. All fruit pectin extracts do not form the best gels at the same sucrose concentration, however. Although most are done at a sugar concentration represented by a boiling point range of 3° to 5°C (5° to 9°F) above the boiling point of water (103° to 105°C or 217° to 221°F at sea level and with barometric pressure at 760 mm of mercury), some should be boiled somewhat short of this concentration and others may require a slightly higher concentration. The exact concentration of sugar will depend upon the quantity and quality of the pectin and upon the hydrogen-ion concentration of the mixture.

The following test may be used to determine whether the concentrations of pectin and hydrogen ions are high enough to form a gel. The mixture should be removed from the hot unit momentarily to avoid overcooking it while the test is being made.

A small amount of the hot syrup is rolled in the bowl of a metal spoon to cool it slightly. The mixture is then allowed to drip off the edge of the spoon. Incipient gelation thickens the mixture and causes heavy drops of liquid to coalesce and break or cut away sharply as they leave the spoon in what is known as the sheet test (Fig. 31-4). A sheet test is an indication that all the variables that influence gel formation are at least sufficiently concentrated. It is not a guarantee that the jelly has not been cooked beyond the optimum stage, however. The ability to recognize the sheet test when it first appears takes some experience; it is complicated by the fact that all fruit pectins do not sheet in the same fashion. If a jelly fails to give a sheet test when it is boiled to 105°C (221°F), addition of lemon juice is a way to rule out a deficiency of hydrogen ions as the cause. If a mixture that is sufficiently tart still fails to gel when the boiling point reaches 106.9°C (224°F), equivalent to a 70-percent sucrose solution, this indicates that too much sugar was combined with the original extract for the jellying power of the pectin. Adding one teaspoon of liquid pectin per cup of original fruit extract and boiling the mixture for 30 seconds to a minute may give a gel.

KEEPING QUALITY OF PECTIN JELLY

The concentration of sugar in jelly boiled to 103° to 105°C (217° to 221°F) lowers the vapor pressure of the water and the water activity, a_W, sufficiently that the growth of most

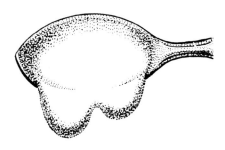

Figure 31-4. The sheet test for the doneness of jelly. (From Helen Charley, *Food Study Manual*. Copyright © 1971 by the Ronald Press Company, New York, p. 253. Reprinted by permission.)

microorganisms is limited (Fig. 5-9). However, molds can grow on the surface of jelly that is exposed to air. Traditionally, paraffin or a wax seal has been used to exclude air from the surface of jelly and so inhibit mold growth. A break in the seal or a pocket of air trapped underneath with mold spores may result in mold growth. Because of this and because certain molds produce mycotoxins, processing jelly in ½-pint or 1-pint canning jars with self-sealing lids in a boiling water bath is recommended. A processing time of five minutes is recommended for altitudes up to 1,000 feet and an additional processing time of one minute for each additional 1,000 feet of altitude (17).

Crystals in Jelly

Sucrose crystals may form in jellies boiled to a high temperature and especially in those that lack tartness. Crystals are likely to form in jellies made with pectin concentrate and a short boil, which gives little opportunity for inversion of sucrose. Glasslike crystals of potassium acid tartrate are likely to form in grape jelly. Chilling the grape pectin extract for 24 to 48 hours and decanting the liquid above the sediment is recommended. Grape jelly made in small lots and used promptly will be free of crystals, because they form slowly. Reducing the concentration of cream of tartar by diluting grape pectin extract with that from other fruit, such as apple, is also recommended to prevent crystal formation.

REFERENCES

1. Baker, G. L. 1934. "A new method for determining the jellying power of fruit-juice extractions." *Food Industries* 6:305, 315. Relation of viscosity to jellying power; use of the pipette from which the Jelmeter evolved.

2. Baker, G. L., and R. F. Kneeland. 1936. "Cranberry pectin properties." *Industrial and Engineering Chemistry* 28:372–75. The uniqueness of cranberries as jelly forming fruit.

3. Barford, N. M., and K. S. Pedersen. 1990. "Determining the setting temperature of high-methoxyl pectin gels." *Food Technology* 44(4):139–41, 148. Factors affecting setting temperature.

4. BeMiller, J. N. 1986. "An introduction to pectins; structure and properties." In *Chemistry and Functions of Pectins*. M. L. Fishbein and J. J. Jen, eds. Washington D.C.: American Chemical Society. ACS Symposium Series 310. Pp. 2–12. Composition and gel-forming potential.

5. Christensen, S. H. 1986. "Pectins." In *Food Hydrocolloids*, Vol. III. M. Glicksman, ed. Boca Raton, FL.: CRC Press. Pp. 205–30. Models of junction zones in high and low ester pectins.

6. Chang, K. C., and A. Miyamoto. 1992. "Gelling characteristics of pectin from sunflower head residues." *Journal of Food Science.* Potential use as a low-methoxyl pectin.

7. DeVries, J. A., F. M. Rambouts, A. G. J. Veragen, and W. Pilnik. 1982. "Enzymatic degradation of apple pectins." *Carbohydrate Polymers* 2:25–33. Distribution of the components.

8. Goldthwaite, N. E. 1909. "Contributions on the chemistry and physics of jelly-making." *Industrial Engineering Chemistry* 1:333–40. An early attempt to put jelly making on a scientific basis; importance of acid.

9. Goldthwaite, N. E. 1910. "Contributions to jelly-making." *Industrial and Engineering Chemistry* 2:457–62. Relation of boiling point to doneness.

10. Hinton, C. L. 1940. "The quantitative basis of pectin jelly formation in relation to pH conditions." *Biochemical Journal* 34: 1211–33. An attempt to account for the effect of pH on the gel formation by pectin; technical.

11. McCready, R. M., and M. Gee. 1960. "Determination of pectic substances by

paper chromatography." *Journal of Agriculture and Food Chemistry* 8:510–13. The nongalacturonide constituents in pectins from different sources.

12. Oakenfull, D., and A. Scott. 1984. "Hydrophobic interaction in the gelation of high methoxyl pectins." *Journal of Food Science* 49:1093–98. Contributions of hydrogen bonding and hydrophobic interaction to pectin gel formation; geometry of a sugar and its action as a cosolute.

13. Phatak, L., K. C. Chang, and G. Brown. 1988. "Isolation and characterization of pectin in sugar beet pulp." *Journal of Food Science* 53:830–33. Acetyl and ferulic acid groups inhibit gelation.

14. Pippen, E. L., T. H. Schultz, and H. S. Owens. 1953. "Effect of degree of esterification on viscosity and gelation behavior of pectin." *Journal of Colloid Science* 8:97–104. Association of ester groups and hydrogen bond formation as influenced by temperature.

15. Powell, D. A., E. R. Morris, M. J. Gridley, and D. A. Reese. 1982. "Conformation and interactions of pectins." II. "Influence of residue sequence on chain association in calcium pectate gels." *Journal of Molecular Biology* 155:517–31. Distribution of rhamnose residues and interchain association.

16. USDA. 1994. "Preparing butters, jams, jellies and marmalades." In *Complete Guide to Home Canning: Guide 1: Principles of Home Canning*. Pp. 30–32. Processing jellies.

17. Wilkinshaw, M. D., and S. Arnott. 1981. "Conformations and interactions of pectins." II. "Models for junction zones in pectinic acid and calcium pectate gels." *Journal of Molecular Biology* 153:1075–85. Mechanisms of gel formation.

Index

A

A-band, 371, 373, 374, 397
Acacia, 111, 157
Acesulfame K, 35, 37, 449
Acetic acid, 36, 93, 223, 278, 501
Acetin (acetylated) fats, 256
Acetylmethyl carbinol, 93
Acid(s)
    in angel food cake, 459
    of baking powders, 199–202
    in candy syrup, 129–130
    effects on chlorophyll, 519–522
    in coffee, 92, 93
    effects on color of tea, 103
    effects on egg foam, 360
    effects on flavonoid pigments,
        485–487
    effects on casein, 316, 321, 327, 334
    effects on pasting of starch, 155
    effects on yeast, 205, 223
    fatty, 244–246
    formulas for, 500
    in fruits, 478
    ionization in water, 80
    in pectin gels, 558, 561
    reactions with sodium bicarbonate,
        197–198, 199–201
    salt, taste effects on, 36
    and sourness, 31
    sweetness, taste effects on, 36
    in vegetables, 500–501
    See also specific acids
Aconitic acid, 198, 500
Acrolein, 265
Actin, 371, 395, 419
α-actinin, 386, 395
Actomyosin, 374, 385, 427, 431
Affective testing, 8, 11–12
Agar, 111, 157
Aging (conditioning) of meat, 385–386

Aglycone, 482, 484
AH-B-X theory, sweetness, 32–33
Air, as leavening agent, 196, 198, 208
Air, bubbles in angel food cake, 457
    in crystalline candies, 132–133
    in egg foams, 82, 357, 359–361
    in frozen desserts, 110, 113
    in plant tissue, 473, 475, 476
    in shortened cakes, 198, 439–441,
        442, 443–444, 446, 452
    in whipped cream, 318–319
    in yeast dough, 184, 229
Alanine, 296, 297
Albumen of eggs, 341–342
Alcohols, sweet, 34, 120–121
Aldehydes, 32, 93, 102, 125, 140, 479
Al dente, 190
Alginate, 111, 156
Alitame, 35
Alkalinity
    and color of chocolate cake, 447
    and water in making fondant, 129
Alkaloids, bitter, 35
Allicin, 515
Alliin, 515
Alliinase, 515
All-purpose flour, 178, 179, 223, 280
Alpha-carotene, 522
Alpha-casein, 310, 917
Alpha helix, 300
Alpha-lactalbumin, 310, 317
Alternative sweeteners, 34–35,
    119–120
Altitude
    and boiling point of water, 78
    and proportions of ingredients in
        cakes, 449, 459
Amaranth, 166
Amino acids, 295–299
    deficiencies in cereals, 163, 165
    in flour proteins, 180–181

and nonenzymatic browning, 304
structure of, 295, 297–299
sulfhydryl groups in, 296, 299
type formula for, 295
R groups, 296, 299
    hydrophilic, 301, 305
    hydrophobic, 305
Ammonium bicarbonate, 197
Amylase(s), 503
    in egg yolk, 356
    in flour, 224
Amylomaize, 143
Amylopectin, 143, 149, 151, 152, 168
Amylose, 141–143, 147, 151
Androstenone, 37, 398, 400
Angel food cake, 457–462
    baking time/temperature, 463–464
    folding in flour, 461–462
    ingredients in, 457–459
    leavening gases in, 196, 198,
        457–458
    meringue for, 459, 460–461
    packaged mix, 460
Anhydrous monocalcium phosphate,
    201
Anthocyanins
    acylated, as food colorants, 485
    in fruits, 482, 484–485, 486, 487
    in vegetables, 524
Anthoxanthins
    in fruits, 481, 482–483, 485, 487
    in vegetables, 525–526
Antioxidants, 262–264
Apples
    anatomy of, 470
    browning of, 491, 494
    effects of cooking on texture,
        492–493
    parenchy cells of, 476
Arabinose, 157, 474, 475
Arachidonic acid, 246

Arginine, 296
Aroma
    of coffee, 93
    of fruit, 479
    of rancid fat, 260–262
    of sulfur-containing vegetables,
        415–419
    of tea, 102
    of yeast breads, 235
Arrowroot, 153
Ascorbic acid, 478
    cooking loss in vegetables, 527
    as flour improver, 189
    in fruits, 478
    inhibitor of enzymatic browning,
        491, 526
Asparagine, 296, 375
Asparagus
    lignin in, 501
    odor in urine from, 519
Aspartame, 35, 109, 119, 120, 449
Aspartic acid, 35, 296, 297, 311
Astaxanthin, 434
Astringency
    of proanthocyanins, 488
    sensation of, 38–39
    of tea, 99–100, 101
Avidin, 343
A_W, water activity, 83–84, 490, 565
Azodicarbonamide, 189

B

Baking chocolate, 104
Baking powder, 198–202
    acids of, 199–202
    carbon dioxide from, 198–201
    double-acting, 199, 201, 446
    in quick breads, 208
    in shortened cakes, 446
    sodium bicarbonate in, 198
Baking soda. See Sodium bicarbonate
    combined with sour milk, 202
Baking utensils
    and energy transfer, 55, 56
    for microwave cooking, 58
Bananas, 478, 479, 493
Barley, 168
Barometric pressure, and boiling point
    of water, 78
Bases, ionization in water, 80
Beans
    processed products, 539
    side view and cross section, 541
    See Legumes
Beef. See Meat

Beets, betanin in, 525
Behenic acid, 246
Bel Paese, 327, 330, 337
Benzoic acid, 478, 500, 501
Beta-amylase, 224
Beta-carotene, 522–524
Beta-casein, 310, 317
Beta crystals in fat, 248, 250
Beta-glucans, 168, 170
Beta-lactoglobulin, 310, 322
Betalains, 525
Betanin, 525
Beta-pleated sheet, 300, 352
Beta prime crystals in fat, 248, 250
Beta spiral, 300
Biscuits, 202, 219–220
Bitter compounds, 35, 91, 483–484,
    502
Bitterness, taste perception of, 35
Black tea, 99, 101–102, 103
Bleaching agents, flour improvers, 189
Bloom on chocolate, 252
Blue cheese, 333
Bostwick consistometer, 13
Braising, meat, 401, 404–405
Bread flour, 178, 179, 223
Breads
    quick, 207–221
    sour dough, 205
    staling, 152, 235–236
    yeast, 223–237
    See also specific quick breads
Brick cheese, 327, 330
Brie, 327, 329, 337
Brine, and freezing of frozen desserts,
    111–113
British thermal unit (Btu), 53
Brittles, 126, 130, 131
Broccoli
    sulfur compounds in, 512, 516,
        517, 518
    palatability and nutrients of cooked,
        518–519, 527–528
Broiling
    meat, 401, 402–403
    poultry, 419
Bromelain, 386, 554
Browning
    baked products, 208, 225, 234
    non-enzymatic, 304
Brown rice, 167
Brown sugar, 122
Brussels sprouts, sulfur compounds in,
    516, 518
Bulgur, 168
Bulking, agents, 120

Butter, 252, 266, 277, 316
    fatty acid content, 254, 255
    water-in-oil emulsion, 277–278
Buttermilk, 316
Butylated hydroxyanisole (BHA), 262,
    263, 264
Butylated hydroxytoluene (BHT), 262
Butyric acid, 245, 246, 251, 260

C

Cabbage
    sulfur compounds in, 512, 516,
        517, 518
    palatability and nutrients in cooked,
        527–528, 518–519
Caciocavallo cheese, 331
Caffeic acid, 92
Caffeine, 91
    bitterness of, 35, 36
    in chocolate/cocoa, 104
    in coffee, 91
    in tea, 99
Cake flour, 178, 446
    chlorine-treated, 446
Cakes
    angel food cake, 457–462
    chiffon cake, 457–459, 463–464
    shortened cakes, 439–453
    sponge cake, 457–459, 462–463
    See individual cakes
Calcium, in hard water, 86
Calcium ions, and texture of vegeta-
        bles, 510
    in low methoxy pectin gels,
        558–559
Calcium peroxide, 189
Calcium phosphocaseinate, 311
Calorie, 53
Camembert, 327, 329, 337
Campylobacter jejuni, 61, 64–65
Candies, 126–134
    agitation and crystal formation,
        131–134
    amorphous (noncrystalline), 126,
        130–131, 134
    cold water test for, 128
    compared to frozen desserts,
        134–135
    crystallization in, 118, 126,
        128–129, 131–134
    divinity, 133–134
    doneness of, 126, 128
    fudge and fondant, 131–133
    interfering substances in, 128–131
Candling, eggs, 347

Canola oil, 253, 254
Caprenin, 258
Caramelization, 125
Caramels, 126, 127, 130, 131
Carbohydrates
   in cereals, 165, 166
   in fruits, 478
   starches as, 139–142
   sugars as, 122
   in vegetables, 498
Carbon dioxide
   from baking powder, 198–201
   from baking soda, 196–198
   in controlled atmosphere storage, 480
   in coffee, 91, 94
   in flatus, 544
   as leavening agent, 196–198
   in water, 88
   from yeast, 196, 202–204, 225
Carob, 14
Carotenoids
   in fruits, 481
   in vegetables, 522–524
Carrageenans, 111, 157, 315
Carrots
   hue of cooked, 524
   texture of cooked, 507–509
Casein micelles, 310–311, 312, 321
Caseins, 82, 320, 321, 334–335
Catechins, 488
   in tea, 100–101
Category scaling, 6–9
Cathepsins, 385
Cauliflower
   sulfur compounds in, 512, 516,
      517, 518
   palatability and nutrients in cooked,
      518–519, 527–528
Cellulose
   in cereals, 165
   chemical structure, 142
   in plant cell walls, 472–473, 478,
      501
Celsius scale, 51, 52
Cephalins, 273
Cereals, 162–172
   amino acid deficiencies of, 163, 165
   composition and nutritive value,
      163, 164–166
   consumption, 163
   cooking, 169–171
   economy of, 162–163
   enriched/fortified, 167
   fiber in, 165, 167
   flour, 174–175
   grain, structure of, 163–164, 165

instant cereals, 168
popcorn, 169–170
ready-to-eat, 168–169
requiring cooking, 167–168
rice, 166, 167–168
α-chaconine, 502
Chalazae, 342
Chapati, 195
Cheese, 325–339
   analogs, 325
   blending with liquid, 339
   cheddar, 327, 330, 334–336
   composition and nutritive value of,
      337, 338
   cottage, 325, 327, 334
   low fat, 325, 335–336
   melting of, 337
   milks used for, 325
   mold-ripened, 327, 333
   process cheese, 336–337
   ripened by bacteria, 327
   ripening, 325–326
   types of, 325, 327, 329–332
   tyrosine crystals in, 336
   from unpasteurized milk, 336
   unripened, 325, 327, 328–329
   varieties of, 328–333
Cheese fondue, 363
Cheese soufflé, 363
Chemometrus, 19
Chemosensory properties of
   foods, 23–36
   odor, 24–28
   taste, 29–36
   sensory testing, 5–12
Chicken. *See* Poultry
Chiffon cake, 453, 457, 463
   baking time/temperature, 463–464
   combining ingredients, 463
Chilling injury, 503
Chives, sulfur compounds in, 512,
   515
Chlorogenic acid, 92, 95, 491
Chlorophyll(s), 481, 519–520
Chlorophyllase, 519
Chlorophyllide, 519
Chocolate/cocoa, 103–104
   baking, 104
   beverage from, 104
   cocoa butter (fat), 104, 252
   conversion from cacao bean,
      103–104
   methylxanthines in, 104
Chymopapain, 386
Chymosin, 110, 334–335
Ciguatera fish poisoning, 429

Citric acid, 36, 263, 478, 500, 501,
   526
cis-trans isomers, 245, 254, 524
Clostridium botulinum, 61, 62, 64
   and nitrites, 391
Clostridium perfringes, 61, 65
   on poultry, 421
Cocoa butter, 104
Coconut oil, 252, 253, 254
Coffee, 90–98
   aroma of, 93
   beverage, characteristics, 90
   brewing, 94–97
      coffee/water proportions, 94
      methods, 95–98
      time/temperature, 94–95
      water for, 95
   constituents in, 90–93
      caffeine, 91, 95
      carbon dioxide, 91
      chlorogenic acid, 92
      trigonelline, 92
   grinds, 94
   holding brewed, 98
   market forms of, 93
   roasting of beans, 90
   staling, prevention of, 98
Colby cheese, 331
Collagen, 375–376, 393–394, 431,
   434
Collenchyma, 501
Colligative properties, of solution,
   81–82, 113
Colloidal dispersions (SOLS), 82
   in milk, 310–311
   pectin, 556, 559
   proteins as, 302–303
Color of foods
   of fruits, 481, 484–487
   measurement of, 14–15
   meat, 376–377, 388–391, 391–393
   of vegetables, 519–526
   visual aspects, 23
Colorimeter, 14
Conalbumin, 343, 351
Conching, 104
Condensed milk, 315
Conduction of heat, 53
Conjugated double bonds, 236–237,
   524
Conjugated proteins, 302
Connective tissue, 374–376, 384,
   393–394, 398, 431
Consistency
   of fats, 252
   of frozen desserts, 115

Consistency (*continued*)
of candies, 126, 130
as textural component, 40
Consistometer, 13, 17
Controlled atmosphere storage, 480, 503
Convection currents, heat transfer
by, 54
in liquid, 56
in an oven, 55–56
in a refrigerator, 60
Cooked salad dressings, 277
Corn, cereal, 168
high lysine, 165
Corn, vegetable, 503, 505–506
Cornflakes, 168
Cornmeal, 49, 168
Corn oil, 253, 254
Corn starch, 82, 150–151, 152
waxy, 150–151, 152
Corn syrups, 119, 129
high fructose, 34, 119, 444, 445,
459
as interfering sugar in candies, 129
Cottonseed oil, 253, 254
Cranberries, 485, 558, 561
Cream, 315
whipping of, 318–320
Cream cheese, 325, 327, 328
Cream horns, 290
Creaming
of fat and sugar, 210, 439, 440
of milk, 312, 313
Cream puffs, 195, 214, 216
Cream of tartar, 199, 208, 263
Crêpes, 213
Crispness, 40
component of texture, 40
of fruits, 489–490
of pastry, 287, 289
of vegetables, 507
Cruciferous vegetables, sulfur
compounds in, 506, 512, 515–519
Cryptoxanthin, 522
Crystallites
of amylopectin in starch granules,
147, 149
of amylopectin in stale bread, 152,
235–236
of amylose in pasted starch gels, 152
Crystallization
in candies, 118, 126, 128, 131–134
in frozen desserts, 107–109, 111, 113
inhibition of, 128, 129
Crystals
fats, 248–249, 250, 252
sucrose, 121, 123, 132

water, 74, 75
Curdling of milk, 321
Cured meats, 390–391
warmed-over flavor in, 400
Custards, 354–355
baked, 355, 356
stirred (soft), 355
Cyanidin chloride, 484–485
Cyclamates, 34
Cysteine, 297, 492
Cysteine sulfoxide(s), 515–517
Cystine, 296, 297, 538
Cytoplasm, plant tissue, 475

D

Decaffeinated coffee, 91
d-Decalactone, 322
Deep-fat frying, 264–266
Denatured globin hemichrome, 392
Descriptive testing, 6, 9–10
Desmin, 374, 386, 419
Dextran, 158
Dextrin, 224
Dextrose, 120
equivalent, 129
Diacetyl, 93
Diacetyl tartaric acid, 189
Diacylglycerides, 247
Diallylthiosulfinate, 515
Dietary fiber, 166, 167, 477, 499, 538
Difference testing, 5–6
Dilatency, 156
Dimethyl disulfide, 93
Disaccharides, 122, 140
Discrimination testing, 5–6
Disulfide bond, 189, 228, 296, 299
Divinity, 127, 133–134
Doneness of foods
candies, 126–128
fish, 434
poultry, 421–422
testing for, 60
yeast breads, 234–235
Double-boiler, heat transfer in, 56–57
Dough, yeast, 223–233
air bubbles in, 229
baking, 233–235
combining ingredients, 227–228
conditioners, 186, 189, 223–224
fermentation of, 231–232
schedule, 226
gluten in, 179–181, 184–186, 187,
188, 189
inflation of, 231–232
ingredients in, 186, 223–226

kneading, 179, 184–186, 210,
228–231
lipids in, 181–183
proofing dough, 232–233
proportions of ingredients, 226–227
punching dough, 232
water in, 183–184, 224
Doughnuts, fat absorption in,
265–266
Dried milk solids, 315–316
foams from, 318
Drip coffee, 96, 98
Duo-trio test, 6
Durum wheat, 174, 179, 189, 190

E

Edam cheese, 327, 331
EDTA, 263
Egg(s)
albumen, 341–342
as binding/thickening/gelling agent,
351–352
candling, 347
composition, 344
in custards, 354–355
deterioration of, 345–346
discoloration of hard cooked, 353
dried, 350
fried, 353–354
frozen, 350
grades of, 347, 348
hard cooked in shell, 352–353
pathogens in, 64, 352, 354
in popovers, poached, 353
in quick breads, 208–209
resistance to spoilage, 347, 350
scrambled, 354
in shortened cakes, 445
size of, 350–351
in sponge-type cakes, 459
storage of, 346
structure of, 341–342
substitutes, 363–364
Egg foams in
fondue, 363
meringues, 361–362
puffy omelet, 362
soufflé, 363
Egg white
in angel food cake, 457–459,
460–461
coagulation by heat, 351–352
composition of, 343, 344
foams from, 356–357, 359, 361
effects of heat on, 351–352

pH, 345–346
proteins of, 343, 458
stages of beating, 357, 359
Egg yolk, 342, 343–345
amylase in, 356
composition of, 343, 344
as emulsifier, 214, 273, 274
foam from, 361
granules, 343
low-density lipoproteins, 274, 343, 345, 445, 457
in mayonnaise, 275–276
phospholipids of, 273, 274
plasma, 343
proteins of, 343
in shortened cake, 445
in soft pie filling, 356
structure of, 342
vitelline membrane, 342
Elaidic acid, 251
Electromagnetic waves, 21–22, 57–58
Emulsifiers (surfactants), 274, 442, 445
alpha-tending, 442, 445, 448
fatty acid derivatives as, 272
functions of, 269–272
hydrophilic/lipophilic balance, 272
lecithin as, 273, 274
phospholipids as, 273
proteins as, 272
Emulsion(s), 269–279
cream puff as an, 214
French dressing as an, 275
emulsifiers, 271–274
mayonnaise, 275–277
milk as an, 311–312, 320
phases of, 269
shortened cake as an, 442
stability of, 278
types of, 271, 272, 277
Endomysium, 374
Endosperm, 164, 174, 176
Energy, units of measure, 53
Energy transfer, 53–56
baking utensils and, 55, 56
by air, 56
by conduction, 53–54, 56
by convection currents, 54, 55, 56
by fats, 264
by radiation, 53, 55
by water, 56, 79
See also Heat
Enzymes, 303, 304
and discoloration of fruits, 490–491
and discoloration of potato, 526

and production of corn syrup, 119, 129
meat tenderizers, 386
proteins as, 303–304
Epigallocatechin gallate, 101
Equal, 35
Escherichia coli, 61, 62, 65, 334, 504
Essential oils, tea, 102
Esters, 479
chlorophyll as, 519
in fruit aroma, 479
glycerides as, 246–247
pectin as, 557
Ethylene, 480
Evaluation of food
consumer testing, 11–12
descriptive testing, 6, 9–10
difference/discrimination testing, 5–6
instrumental tests, 12–19
judges, training for, 10–11
sensory analysis, 3–5
Evaporated milk, 315
carra geenan in, 157, 315
foam from, 318

F

Fahrenheit scale, 51, 52
Farina, 166, 168
Fats
acetin (acetylated), 256, 258
antioxidants for, 262–264
of chocolate/cocoa, 104, 252
consistency of, factors affecting, 252
crystalline forms, 248–250, 252
van der Waals forces in, 248
effects on gluten, 186
eggs, 344
and energy transfer, 264
fatty acids in, 253, 254, 255
in frozen desserts, 109–110
functions in foods, 243, 258
galaetolipids, 183, 243
as glycerides, 246–248
interesterification, 256
in meat, 253, 254, 370, 376, 377
in milk, 309
odor, absorption by, 260
oils, 252, 253–256
in pastry, 281, 282
plastic fats, 252, 256
phospholipids, 183, 243, 273, 311, 343, 400, 423
polymorphism, 248–249
in poultry, 420

in quick breads, 208
rancidity, 260–262
free radicals, 260–262
lipase, 260, 314
lipoxidase, 262
prooxidants, 262
in shortened cakes, 439–441
specific heat of, 76–77
storage conditions, 262
structured, 256
sources of, 243
substitutes for, 258–259
in yeast dough, 181–183, 225
See also specific types of fats and Frying
Fatty acids, 244–246
chemical formulas for, 246
cis-trans isomers of, 245, 251, 254, 256
inedible fats, 253, 254, 255
melting points of, 249, 251
hydrogenation of, 253, 254, 256
saturated, 244–245, 247, 251, 253
unsaturated, 244–245, 251, 253
Filled milk, 317
Fish oils, 253
Fish, 426–434
bacterial and viral hazards, 430
composition of, 427, 428
consumption, 426
cooking of, 431–434
frozen, 431
freshness of, 427, 429
marine toxins, 429–430
market forms of, 427
muscle, structure of vertebrates, 431, 433
parasites in, 430
types of, 426–427
Flaked cereals, 168, 170
Flatulence, from legumes, 544
Flavonoid pigments, 481–488
effects of acids on, 485–487
effects of metal ions on, 487–488
in fruits, 481–488
Flavanols, 488
as antioxidants, 262
in tea, 100–101
Flavor
instrumental measures of, 15–16
perception of, 23–24
potentiators, 37
relationship to texture, 40–41
warmed-over, 401, 423
Flavor profile analysis, 9–10
FLAVR SAVR tomato, 480
Flavyliumion, 485, 486

Flour, 174–179
    based on hardness of wheat,
        174–175, 179
    chlorinated, 446
    classed by use, 178–179
        all-purpose, 178, 179, 223
        bread, 178, 179, 223
        cake, 178
        cakes, chlorine-treated, 446
        cookie, 178
        pastry, 178
    density of, 189
    in dough formation, 179–186
    enrichment of, 167, 187
    enzymes in, 224
    gluten of, 179, 181
    improvers, 186, 189
    instantized, 176, 178
    lipids of, 181–183
    measuring of, 48–49
    milling of, 176–178
    pin-milled, 446
    proteins of, 176, 180–181
    self-rising, 199, 201
    as thickener, 154, 155, 178
    use in
        sponge type cakes, 459
        pastry, 280
        quick breads, 207, 213, 214,
            216, 219
        in shortened cakes, 445–446
        in yeast breads, 223–224, 226, 228
Flour milling, 176–178
Foams
    colloidal dispersion as, 82
    egg foams, 356–363, 359, 361
    meringues, 361–362
    of milk proteins, 317–318
    of proteins, 305
    whipped cream, 318–320
Fondant, 40, 131–133
Fondue, baked, 196, 363
    swiss, 339
Food Additive Amendment, 119
Food and Drug Administration
    (FDA), 34–35, 37
Food, Drug, and Cosmetic Act, 119
Forced convection-microwave oven, 56
Forced convection oven, 56
Formic acid, 500, 501
Free radicals, 260–262
Freeze-drying, 74
Freezing mixture, for frozen desserts,
    112–113
Freezing point of water, 52, 74
    effects of salt, 113

effects of sugar on, 18
French dressing, 275
Fried eggs, 353–354
Frozen desserts, 107–115
    agitation of mix, 113–114
    characteristics of, 115
    emulsifiers in, 110–111
    fat in, 109–110
    freezing mixture, components of,
        112–113
    freezing process, 111–114
    hardening, 114
    ice crystal formation, affecting
        factors, 107–111
    low-fat, 110
    milk solids in, 108, 110
    stabilizers in, 111
    standards (Federal), 108
    still-frozen, 115
    sugar in, 107, 108–109
Fructose, 34, 118, 129
Fruits, 469–494
    acids in, 478
    anatomy of, 470–472
    aroma of, 479
    CA storage of, 480
    climacteric, 480
    composition, 476–478
    consumption, 469
    discoloration of, 490–492
    dried, 494
    irradiation of, 480–481
    pectin from, 558, 564
    pigments in, 481–488
    postharvest changes in, 489–492
    ripening of, 478–480
    structural components, 469, 472–476
    texture
        of raw, 489
        of cooked, 493–494
Frying, 264–266
    and absorption of fat, 265
    deterioration of oil, 265
    hazards of, 266
    heat transfer involved, 264
    smoke point, 265
    temperature of oil, 264
Fudge, 40, 127, 128, 130, 131–133
Fumaric acid, 500, 501
Furans, 172
Furfural, 93, 125

G

Galactolipids, 183
Galactose, 34, 157, 474

Galacturonic acid, 474, 556
Gallic acid, 100
Gallocatechin, 100
Garlic, diallyl thiosulfinate from,
    515
Gelatin, 302, 406
    cold water soluble, 552
    in frozen desserts, 111
    a glassy polymer, 551
    production of, 551
Gelatin gels, 551–554
    effects of temperature on, 553
    formation, 552–553
    proportion to liquid, 553–554
    unmolding, 554
    whips/sponges/creams, 554
Gelatinization of starch granules,
    149–150
    effects of acid on, 155
    effects of sugar on, 154–155
Gelation of pasted starches, 152,
    153–154
Gellan gum, 158
Gels, 82, 304
    of casein, 334–335
    as colloidal dispersion, 82
    of gelatin, 552–553
    of pasted starch granules, 152
    of pectin, 558–560
    syneresis of, 553, 561
Gjetost, 328, 337
Glass transition temperature (T_g),
    85–86, 147, 148, 149, 179,
    183, 224, 228, 551
Glassy/rubbery polymers, 85–86
    gelatin, 552
    gluten, 179, 183, 224, 228
    starch granules, 147, 149
Gliadin, 181, 183
Globulins, 458
Glucobrassicin, 518
Gluconic acid, 198, 201
Glucono-delta-lactone, 201, 445
Glucose, 34, 118, 120, 139–140
Glucosinolates, 517–518
Glutamic acid, 180, 296, 297, 311
Glutamine, 296, 375
Glutathione, 204, 228
Gluten, 179–181, 184–186, 187, 188,
    189
Glutenin, 181, 182, 183
Glycerides, 246–248
Glycerol, 32, 271, 272
Glyceryl monostearate, 251, 271
Glycine, 180, 296, 297, 375
Glycoalkaloids, 502

Glycolipids, 225
Glycoproteins, 475
Glycyrrhizin, 119
Gorgonzola cheese, 327, 333
Gouda, 327, 331
Grades of
    eggs, 347, 348
    meat, 387–388
    milk, 314
    pectin, 557
    poultry, 417
Graininess, as texture, 39–40
Granular cereals, 168
Grape Nuts, 168
GRAS list, 120
Green tea, 99, 100, 101
Griddle cakes, 220–221
Gruyère, 327
Guaiacol, 93
5'-guanylate (GMP), 35, 37
Guar gum, 111, 158, 449
Gum arabic, 157
Gum drops, 154
Gum tragacanth, 157

H

Hazard Analysis and Critical Control
    Point (HACCP) system, 61
Heat
    and control of microorganisms, 61,
        64–65
    temperature scales for intensity of,
        51–52
    verbal descriptions of common tem-
        peratures, 52
    See also Energy transfer
Hedonic rating scale, 8, 11
Hemicellulose, 155, 163, 472, 473,
    522
High-fructose corn syrup (HFCS), 34,
    119, 459
Histidine, 296
Hominy, 168
Homogenized, milk, 313
Honey, 118, 129, 197–198
Horseradish, sulfur-containing com-
    pounds in, 516, 517
Hydrocolloids, 82, 155, 259
Hydrogenation, 253, 254, 256
    and trans fatty acids, 254, 256
Hydrogen bond, 73, 74, 77, 80–81,
    142, 228, 300, 301, 303, 559
Hydrogen ions, 32
Hydrogen sulfide, 525–526
Hydrometer, 12

Hydrophilic/lipohilic balance (HLB),
    272
Hydroxylysine, 375
5-hydroxymethyl furfural, 125

I

I-band, 371, 373, 374, 397
Ice, crystalline state of water, 74
Ice cream, 107, 108
    See also Frozen desserts
Indole-3-carbinol, 518
5'-inosinate (IMP), 35, 37
Inositol hexaphosphate, 262
Instant yeast, 203, 204
Instrumental food testing, 12–19
    color measurement, 14–15
    flavor measurement, 15–16
    for textural properties, 16–19
Intercellular spaces, plant tissue, 473,
    475, 476
Interesterification, fats, 256
Inulin, 498
Invertase, 118, 204
Ionization, 79–80
Irradiation, fruits, 480–481
Isoelectric point, 223, 296, 327
Isoleucine, 296, 297, 538
Isomalt, 35, 120

J

Jelly
    gelatin in, 554
    See also Pectin gels
Jelmeter, 16, 562–563
Joule, 53

K

Kaempferol, 100
Kappa-casein, 310–311
Karaya, 111
Kelvin scale, 52
Ketones, 93, 125, 479
Kilocalorie, 53
Kilojoule, 53
Kiwi, 554

L

Lachrymator in onions, 516
Lactalbumin, 300
Lactase, 109
Lactic acid, 197, 223, 316, 327
Lactobacillus bulgaricus, 316
Lactobacillus sanfrancisco, 205

Lactose, 34, 109, 124, 316, 327
Lamb. See Meat
Lard, 243, 249, 281
Latent heat, 76, 77
Lauric acid, 246
Leavening agents, 195–205, 208
    air, 196, 457
    carbon dioxide, 196–198
        from baking powder, 198–202
        from baking soda and acid, 202
        from yeast, 202–205
    in quick breads, 208
    in shortened cakes, 446–447
    in sponge-type cakes, 457
    steam, 195, 208
Lecithin, 272, 273, 274
Lectins, 540
Leeks, 515
Lefse, 195
Legumes, 534–544
    anatomy of Phaseolus vulgaris, 541
    antinutritional factors in, 540
    composition and nutritive value,
        534–538
    consumption, 534
    canning, 544
    cooking, 540, 542–543
    dietary fiber in, 538
    flatus from, 544
    processing of dried beans, 539
    saponins in, 538
    storage of, 543
    tofu, 540
    varieties of, 534, 535
Leucine, 180, 296, 297, 311, 538
Leucocyanidin, 488
Lignin, 473, 498, 501
Limburger, 327, 329
Limes, 478
Lignin, 498
Linoleic acid, 246, 251, 253,
    336–337
Linolenic acid, 246, 251, 253
Lipase, 260, 314
Lipoxygenase, 262
Lipids. See Fats; Fatty acids
Listeria monocytogenes, 61, 62, 65
Livetins, 343
Locust bean gum, 111, 157–158
Lollipops, 127
Low-fat foods
    cheese, 325, 335–336
    frozen desserts, 110
    shortened cakes, 449
Lukewarm, temperature for, 52
Lycopene, 523, 524

Lysine, 296, 297
  in cereals, 163, 165
  in collagen, 375
  in legumes, 538
Lysozyme, 343, 347

M

Macaroni, 179, 189
Magnesium salts, 35, 87
Magness-Taylor fruit tester, 18
Magnetron, 57
Magnitude estimation, 6, 8, 9
Maillard reaction, 104
Malic acid, 36, 478, 500, 501
Maltitol, 120
Maltodextrins, 109, 120, 259
Maltose, 34, 120, 204
  chemical structure, 140–141
Mannitol, 34, 120
Mannose, 34
Marbling of meat, 387, 388
Margarine, 252, 253–254, 256
  water-in-oil emulsion, 277–278
Marshmallows, 127, 134
Mayonnaise, 156, 275–277
Measurement
  capacities and tolerances of utensils
    for, 45–47
  of ingredients, techniques for,
    47–49
  metric (SI) and traditional systems
    of, 44–45
  weights of equal volumes of com-
    mon ingredients, 49–50
Meat, 368–406
  A-band, 371, 373, 374, 397
  actin, 371, 395
  α-actinin, 386, 395
  actomyosin, 374, 385
  androstenone, 37, 398, 400
  calcium-activated proteases, 385
  cathepsins, 385
  collagenin, 375–376, 393–394
  color of, 376, 388–391
  composition of, 368, 370
  conditioning, 385–386
  connective tissue, 374–376, 384,
    393–394, 398
  consumption, 368
  cured meats, 390–391, 400
  cuts of, 377–381
  denatured globin hemichrome, 392
  desmin, 374, 386
  fats in, 253, 254, 370, 376, 377
  grades, 387–388

I-band, 371, 374, 397
  inspection of, 386–387
  marbling, 376, 383–384, 388
  metmyoglobin, 389–390
  muscle fibers, 370–374, 375,
    384–385, 394–395
  myofibrils, 370, 371, 384
  myofilaments, 370, 371–374
  myoglobin, 376, 388–390
  myosin, 371, 395
  pathogens of, 64–65, 391, 402
  nebulin, 374, 376, 386
  nitric oxide myoglobin, 390
  nitrosamines, 391
  nitrosyl myoglobin, 390
  oxy myoglobin, 389–390
  perphyrin ring, 388
  rigor, 384
  sarcomere, 371, 374, 385, 397
  storage of cooked, 406
  storage of uncooked, 391
  structure of, 369, 371–376
  tenderizers, 386
  titin, 374, 386
  toughness of, 383–385
  tropomyosin, 374, 395
  troponin, 374, 386, 395
  types of, 368, 376–377
  warmed-over flavor, 400
  z-line, 371, 374, 386, 396, 397
Meat, cooking, 391–406
  effects on connective tissue,
    393–394, 398
  effects of fat content of raw,
    400–401
  effects on flavor, 398
  left-over meat, 400
  effects on muscle fibers, 394–397
  effects on nutritional value, 401
  effects on pigments, 391–393
  effects on tenderness, 393, 398
  frozen meat, 406
  methods of, 401–406
    dry media, 401, 402–404
    moist media, 401, 404–405
    microwaving, 405–406
Medium chain triglycerides, 256
Mellorine, 107, 108
Menhaden oil, 254
Meringues, 157, 361–362
  for angel food cake, 459, 460–461
  beading of, 362
Metal, effects on color of fruits,
  487–488
Methionine, 296, 297, 538
Methylxanthines, 37

  in chocolate products, 104
  in coffee, 91
  in tea, 99
Metmyoglobin, 389–390
Microwave oven, 57–60
  cooking fish, 433
  meat, 405–406
  vegetables, 509, 527–528
  generation of microwaves, 57–58
  heating by microwaves, 59
    advantages, 58
    disadvantages, 59–60
  utensils for, 58
Milk, 308–322
  casein(s) of, 310, 311, 317, 320
    in cheese-making, 325, 334–335
  casein micelles, 310–311, 312,
    321
  colloidal dispersion, 310–311
  composition, 308–309
  condensed, 315
  cream, 312, 315
  curdling of, 321
  dried solids, 315–316
  effects of acid on casein of, 321
  effects of heat on proteins of,
    321–322
  emulsified fat in, 311–312, 320
  evaporated, 315
  fat content, 308, 309, 311–312,
    314–315
  fat globule membrane, 311–313
  flavor of heated, 322
  fortified, 314
  grades of, 314
  holding temperature, safe, 322
  homogenization of, 313, 314
  lactose in, 310, 316, 327
  lipase in, 311, 314
  light, exposure to, 322
  pasteurization of, 313–314
  proteins of, 310
    as emulsifiers, 320
  types of products, 314–317
  whey (serum) proteins, 310, 316,
    317, 320, 322
  whipped cream, 318, 320
    aerosol packed, 320
Milk foams, 317–320
Minerals
  in cereal, 165, 166
  in eggs, 344
  in fruit, 477, 478, 500
  in meat, 370
  in milk, 309
  in poultry, 420

in seafood/fish, 427, 428
in vegetables, 499
Moisture analyzer, 12
Molasses, 122, 198
Molds
growth and water activity, 84
on pectin gels, 566
in ripened cheese, 327, 333
on yeast breads, 237
Mollusks, 427
Monellin, 35, 119
Monoacylglyceride, 246–247, 442
Monocalcium phosphate, 201
Monosaccharides, 122, 139
Monosodium glutamate (MSG), 35
flavor potentiation mechanism, 37
Mouthfeel, sensory aspects, 38–39
Mozzarella, 329
Muenster cheese, 327, 330
Muffins, 216–219
Muscle fiber
effects of cooking on, 394–398
of fish, 431
of meat, 40, 370–374, 375,
384–385, 394–395
of poultry, 419
and toughness, 384–385
Mustard, 275, 516
Myocommata, 431
Myofibrils, 370, 384–385, 431
Myofilaments, 370, 371–374
Myoglobin, 376, 388–390
Myosin, 371, 395, 419, 431
Myotomes, 431
Myricetin, 100
Myristic acid, 246
Myrosinase, 517
Mysost, 329

N

Naringenin, 483–484
Naringin, 35, 483
Nebulin, 374, 376, 386, 419
Neufchâtel cheese, 325, 328, 337
Neurotoxic shellfish poisoning, 429
Niacin, 92, 369, 370, 417, 420, 477
N-FLATE, 259
Nitrites, in cured meat, 390–391, 400
Nitrosamines, 391
Nitrosyl myoglobin, 390
Nonfat dried milk, 315
Noodles, dough of, 189
5′-nucleotides, as flavor potentiators,
35, 37
NutraSweet, 35

O

Oat bran, 168
Oats, cereal, 168
Odor, sensory perception of, 24–28
Oil-in-water emulsions, 271, 272
Oils. *See* Fats
Oleic acid, 246, 247, 251, 253
Olestra, 259
Olfaction, 24–28
and age, 38
genetic factors, 37
Olive oil, 253, 254
Omega-3 fatty acids, 253, 427
Omega-6-fatty acids, 246, 253, 427
Omelet, French, 354
Omelet, puffy, 196, 361, 362
Onions
cysteine sulfoxide in, 515–516
lachrymator in, 516
On-line sensing, 19
Oolong tea, 99, 102
Orange pekoe tea, 102
Osmotic pressure, 489
Ovalbumin, 343, 351, 458
Oven, conventional
baking utensils, 55
heat transfer in, 54, 55–56
Ovomucoid, 343
Oxalic acid, 478, 500, 501
Oxidizing agents, flour improvers,
186, 189
Oxymyoglobin, 389–390

P

Paired comparison test, 6, 7
Palmitic acid, 245, 246, 247
Palm oil, 254
Panbroiling, meat, 401, 403–404
Panfrying, meat, 404
Panning, vegetables, 507
Papain, 386
Papaya enzymes, 386
Para-kappa casein, 335
Paralytic shellfish poisoning, 429
Parasites
in fish/shellfish, 430
in pork, 59, 402
Parenchyma cells, 164, 469, 472–476
constituents, 472–475
cellulose, 472–473
glycoproteins, 474–475
hemicellulose, 473–474
pectic substances, 474–475
structural parts, 472–476

cell wall, 472–475
cytoplasm, 475
intercellular space, 476
vacuole, 475
Parmesan cheese, 332
Pasta, 187, 189
flour for, 179
Pasteurization, of milk, 313–314
Pasting, starch granules, 150–152
Pastry, conventional, 280–290
baking of, 286
characteristics of, 280, 287–289
ingredients and functions, 280–282
manipulation of ingredients, 282–285
shaping/rolling dough, 285
Pastry, puff, 289–290
Pathogens, 61–65
cold-tolerant (psychrophilic), 62, 65
in eggs, 64, 352, 354
on meat, 64–65
on poultry, 417, 421
in shellfish, 65
in soil, 64, 65
temperature and control of, 61–62,
64–65
in vegetables, 504
water activity and growth of, 84
Patty shells, 290
Peaches, texture of, 479–480
Peanut oil, 254
Pectin, 474, 556–557
commercial sources of, 557
in fruit, 475, 479, 493, 558, 564
grades of, 557
a hydrocolloid, 82, 155
molecular structure, 556–557
market forms of, 563–564
methoxyl content, 560
Pectinesterase, 479–480, 555
trans-elimination, 509
Pectin gels, 556–566
characteristics of, 556
components of, 558–560
control of variables in, 360–363
crystals in, 566
from dried and liquid concentrates,
131, 557, 563–564
from fruit pectin extract, 564–565
tests for pectin, 562–563
tests for acidity, 561
fruits suitable for, 558
junction zones in, 558–560
low sugar, 560, 563
mold growth on, 565–566
setting time/temperature, 563
tests for doneness, 565

Penetrometer, 18
Peptide bond, 299
Percolated coffee, 96
Phenolic substances
    as antioxidants, 262–263
    bitterness of, 35, 92
    and browning of fruit, 490–491
    in coffee, 92
    in tea, 99–102
Phenoloxidase, 490
Phenylalanine, 35, 296, 538
Phenylketonuria (PKU), 35
Phenylthiocarbamide (PTC), 37
Phloem, 501
Phosphatase, 114
Phosphatidyl choline, 273
Phosphatidyl ethanolamine, 273
Phospholipids, 183, 225, 243, 273,
    311, 343, 400, 423
    as emulsifiers, 273–274
Phosvitin, 343
pH, of water, 88
pH meter, 12, 561
Phytase, 528
Phytic acid, 262
Phytin, 223
Phytol alcohol, 519
Pie filling, soft, 356
Pineapple, raw and gelatin, 554
Planimeter, 13
Plant tissue, 469–476. *See also*
    Parenchyma cells
Plastic fats, 252, 256, 287, 439, 440
Plastids, 475
Poaching eggs, 353
Poaching, fish, 434
Polenta, 171
Polydextrose, 109, 110, 120, 449
Polygalacturonase, 479–480, 558
Polyhydric alcohols, 118, 120
Poly-L-proline helix, 300, 302
Polymorphism, fats, 248–249
Polyoxyethylene sorbitanesters
    (TWEENS), 272
Polysaccharides, 122
Polysorbate 60, 189
Popcorn, 171–172
Popovers, 195, 213–214
Pork
    parasite in, 59, 402
    See also Meat
Porphyrin ring, 388
Port du Salut, 330, 337
Potassium bromate, 189
Potatoes, 498, 504
    anatomy, 505

discoloration of raw, 526
glycoalkaloids in, 502
specific gravity of, 512, 514
stem-end blackening of cooked,
    526–527
texture of cooked, 511–512, 513,
    514
Potato starch, 149–151, 152
Poultry, 415–423
    annual per-capita consumption, 415
    composition and nutritive value of,
        417, 420
    cooking, 419–422
    frozen, 422
    grades of, 417, 418
    inspection of, 416
    leftovers, storage/reheating, 423
    market classes of, 415
    pathogens on, 417, 421
    pink color in refrigerated cooked,
        423
    raw, handling of, 417
    warmed-over flavor, 423
Preserves, interfering sugars in, 131
Pressure saucepan
    boiling point of water, 78–79
    cooking vegetables, 507
Primal cuts, of meat, 377–379
Proanthocyanin(s), 488, 491
Process cheese, 336–337
    anticarcinogen in, 336–337
Proline, 180, 296, 298, 375
Proofing yeast dough, 232–233
Propylene glycol monostearate, 442
Propyl gallate (PG), 262, 263
Proteases, 224, 225, 385
Proteins, 299–306
    alpha helix of, 300–301
    amino acids in, 295–299
    beta pleated sheet of, 300, 304
    beta spiral, 300
    in cereals, 163, 164, 165
    as colloidal sols, 302
    conjugated, 302
    denaturation of, 303, 304,
        321–322, 357, 433
    disulfide bonds in, 296, 299, 301
    in eggs, 343, 344, 458
    as emulsifiers, 272–273, 305–306
    as enzymes, 303–304
    in fish, 428
    in flour, 176, 180–181
    as foaming agents, 305, 317,
        356–357
    as gelling agents, 304–305
    hydrogen bonding in, 300

isoelectric point, 296
    in legumes, 538
    in meat, 368, 370
    in milk, 308, 310, 317, 334
    peptide bonds in, 299, 334
    poly-L-proline helix in, 300
    in poultry, 420
    properties of, 302–303
    sources of essential amino acids, 303
    structure, levels of, 299–302
    sulfhydryl groups in, 296, 299
Provolone, 331
Pseudoplastic, 156
Psychrophilic organisms, 62, 65
Pyrazines, 172

Q

Quality assurance testing, 13
Quantitative description analysis, 10
Quercetin, 483
Quiche Lorraine, 355
Quick breads, 201–221
    baking, 212–213
    balancing ingredients in, 209
    ingredients in, 207–209
    manipulation of ingredients
        purposes, 212
        techniques, 210
    utensils for making, 210–211
    See also individual quick breads
Quinoa, 166

R

Radiation, heat transfer by, 53
Radish, sulfur compounds in, 516,
    517
Raffinose, 544
Rancidity, anatomy of, 260–262, 400,
    423
Raspberries, anatomy of, 472
Rating difference test, 6, 7
Ratio scaling, 6, 8, 9
Recommended Dietary Allowance
    (RDA), 167
Reference Daily Intake (RDI), 167
Refractometer, 12
Refrigeration, perishables, 52, 60–61,
    62, 64
Rennet, 334
Resonance of conjugated double
    bonds, 389, 524
Retail cuts, of meat, 379–381
Rhamnose, 157